1,000 DAYS *in* AMERICA

Designed during the patriotic fervor of the Revolutionary War, the American flag represented the original 13 colonies as stars.

1,000 DAYS in AMERICA

AN ILLUSTRATED HISTORY OF THE MOMENTS THAT DEFINED A NATION

Foreword and Interviews by

DAVID M. RUBENSTEIN

Prologue by

DAVID TREUER

NATIONAL GEOGRAPHIC

WASHINGTON, D.C.

N CAN FILLED W
MASSIVE LOCKS.

CONTENTS

OPPOSITE (FROM L TO R): John Hancock's signature on the engrossed copy of the Declaration of Independence; "George Washington" by Gilbert Stuart, ca 1821; a vintage poster of celebrated magician Harry Houdini's "death-defying mystery"; pouring metal at Chicago's South Works

FOREWORD BY DAVID M. RUBENSTEIN

EVERYWHERE IN THE WORLD, people like to celebrate their birthdays. Countries are no different. They like to note their creation and to celebrate what they have achieved, and do so in a way that offers hope for the future.

And that is what is happening in the United States in 2026: The country is celebrating what it has achieved since the Second Continental Congress agreed to the Declaration of Independence on July 4, 1776, and actually signed it—in an act of treason—in early August 1776.

But with its semiquincentennial celebration, the country is also looking to the future, with the hope that the next 250 years can be as impactful for America's citizens and the world as the prior 250 years.

By the end of its initial 250 years, the United States had developed into the world's most dominant economic, financial, military, geopolitical, scientific, technological, intellectual, and cultural country in the world.

To be sure, none of the signers of the declaration would have predicted that a three-million-person group in 13 colonies (later states) could have ever risen to such heights. After all, in 1776, the 13 colonies had not yet won the war for independence against the British; had a weak government structure (under the Articles of Confederation); occupied only a relatively narrow strip of land along the eastern seaboard; had a ragtag, underfed, underclothed, and underarmed militia; and seemed completely dependent on financial and military support from various European rivals of the British. Surviving the war was of more immediate concern to the Founding Fathers than dominating the world.

Indeed, it seems hard to believe that any Founding Father would have dared to imagine in his wildest dreams what the United States was able to do in the ensuing 250 years.

A U.S. Shipping Board Emergency Fleet Corporation poster, ca 1941–45 ***OPPOSITE:*** An estimated 40 percent of current U.S. citizens can trace their ancestry to immigrants who arrived at Ellis Island.

Congress of the United States

begun and held at the City of New-York, on
Wednesday the fourth of March, one thousand seven hundred and eighty nine

THE Conventions of a number of the States, having at the time of their adopting the Constitution, expressed a desire, in order to prevent misconstruction or abuse of its powers, that further declaratory and restrictive clauses should be added: And as extending the ground of public confidence in the Government, will best ensure the beneficent ends of its institution.

RESOLVED by the Senate and House of Representatives of the United States of America, in Congress assembled, two thirds of both Houses concurring, that the following Articles be proposed to the Legislatures of the several States, as amendments to the Constitution of the United States, all, or any of which Articles, when ratified by three fourths of the said Legislatures, to be valid to all intents and purposes, as part of the said Constitution; viz.

ARTICLES in addition to, and Amendment of the Constitution of the United States of America, proposed by Congress, and ratified by the Legislatures of the several States, pursuant to the fifth Article of the original Constitution.

Article the first.... After the first enumeration required by the first Article of the Constitution, there shall be one Representative for every thirty thousand, until the number shall amount to one hundred, after which the proportion shall be so regulated by Congress, that there shall be not less than one hundred Representatives, nor less than one Representative for every forty thousand persons, until the number of Representatives shall amount to two hundred, after which the proportion shall be so regulated by Congress, that there shall not be less than two hundred Representatives, nor more than one Representative for every fifty thousand persons.

Article the second.... No law, varying the compensation for the services of the Senators and Representatives, shall take effect, until an election of Representatives shall have intervened.

Article the third.... Congress shall make no law respecting an establishment of religion, or prohibiting the free exercise thereof; or abridging the freedom of speech, or of the press, or the right of the people peaceably to assemble, and to petition the Government for a redress of grievances.

Article the fourth.... A well regulated militia, being necessary to the security of a free State, the right of the people to keep and bear arms, shall not be infringed.

Article the fifth.... No Soldier shall, in time of peace be quartered in any house, without the consent of the owner, nor in time of war, but in a manner to be prescribed by law.

Article the sixth.... The right of the people to be secure in their persons, houses, papers, and effects, against unreasonable searches and seizures, shall not be violated, and no Warrants shall issue, but upon probable cause, supported by oath or affirmation, and particularly describing the place to be searched, and the persons or things to be seized.

Article the seventh.... No person shall be held to answer for a capital, or otherwise infamous crime, unless on a presentment or indictment of a Grand Jury, except in cases arising in the land or naval forces, or in the Militia, when in actual service in time of War or public danger; nor shall any person be subject for the same offence to be twice put in jeopardy of life or limb, nor shall be compelled in any criminal case to be a witness against himself, nor be deprived of life, liberty, or property, without due process of law; nor shall private property be taken for public use without just compensation.

Article the eighth.... In all criminal prosecutions, the accused shall enjoy the right to a speedy and public trial, by an impartial jury of the State and district wherein the crime shall have been committed, which district shall have been previously ascertained by law, and to be informed of the nature and cause of the accusation; to be confronted with the witnesses against him; to have compulsory process for obtaining witnesses in his favor, and to have the assistance of Counsel for his defence.

Article the ninth.... In suits at common law, where the value in controversy shall exceed twenty dollars, the right of trial by jury shall be preserved, and no fact tried by a jury shall be otherwise re-examined in any Court of the United States, than according to the rules of the common law.

Article the tenth.... Excessive bail shall not be required, nor excessive fines imposed, nor cruel and unusual punishments inflicted.

Article the eleventh.... The enumeration in the Constitution, of certain rights, shall not be construed to deny or disparage others retained by the people.

Article the twelfth.... The powers not delegated to the United States by the Constitution, nor prohibited by it to the States, are reserved to the States respectively, or to the people.

ATTEST,

Frederick Augustus Muhlenberg Speaker of the House of Representatives.
John Adams, Vice-President of the United States, and President of the Senate.

John Beckley, Clerk of the House of Representatives.
Sam. A. Otis Secretary of the Senate.

IT SEEMS HARD TO BELIEVE THAT ANY FOUNDING FATHER WOULD HAVE DARED TO IMAGINE IN HIS WILDEST DREAMS WHAT THE UNITED STATES WAS ABLE TO DO IN THE ENSUING 250 YEARS.

How did the United States become such a global colossus in so many areas? Who were the people who made this possible? What events made these relatively weak 13 colonies the unimaginably strong 50 states?

Of course, there is no one answer. There are many answers—unforeseen in 1776, 1876, or even 1976.

In these pages, National Geographic has conjured up the singular events that shaped the sweeping American story. Over the course of the book's journey, readers will witness the crackling interactions between American politics, culture, and innovation: a series of transformations that transpired sometimes over decades, sometimes in an instant. By presenting the arc of the nation through these snapshot moments, this book captures the power of individuals to create change and the determination of the American people's will to continue defining themselves. To provide perspective and context, National Geographic has invited four distinguished scholars—Annette Gordon-Reed, Douglas Brinkley, Michael Beschloss, and Walter Isaacson—to explain how this 250-year transformation occurred, and in the process changed the world.

Can this kind of American leadership continue another 250 years? Of course, we have learned already that predictions 250 years down the road are not likely to be accurate. However, the country's commitment to the rule of law, equal opportunities, civil rights and liberties, free enterprise, capitalism, entrepreneurship, the American dream, and human dignity and freedom are certainly the types of commitments that are likely to make the next 250 years as impactful as the first 250 years.

None of us reading this book will be here in 250 years. But our progeny will be, and our obligation as Americans is to provide for them the building blocks to make the next quarter millennium even better than the prior one. A high bar, and one America can no doubt meet.

As Warren Buffett, perhaps America's greatest investor, has frequently noted, "Never bet against America."

The Bill of Rights proposed 12 amendments to the Constitution during the First Congress in September 1789. Ten of those amendments would be ratified by 1791.

PROLOGUE BY DAVID TREUER

SOMETIME AFTER 5:42 P.M. on March 5, 1770, a group of boys—among them a wigmaker's apprentice named Edward Garrick, bound to John Piemont's wig shop on King Street in Boston—started throwing snowballs and debris near Boston Common in the Massachusetts Bay Colony. Their target was Captain-Lieutenant John Goldfinch and other soldiers in the English 29th Regiment of Foot. Garrick was 13 years old and, by most accounts, drunk. Evidently, he believed that Captain-Lieutenant Goldfinch had skipped on his wig bill (though Garrick seems to have been wrong: Goldfinch *had* paid his debt to Piemont).

The boys threw things, Goldfinch's soldiers intervened, and things escalated. (In the two years leading up to the snowball fight, both colonists and English soldiers had incited increasing incidents of assault in the wake of the Stamp Act and the Townshend Acts, both new taxes the British Parliament had imposed on the American colonies to raise revenue.)

Hugh White, a British soldier on guard at the Boston Custom House, overheard the altercation between the boys and the soldiers. He yelled at Garrick and told him to have more respect for Goldfinch. Garrick insulted White and poked or pushed him. White hit Garrick in the head with the butt of his musket.

Garrick, his head bleeding, fled to a British barracks. His friends and fellow apprentice Bartholomew Broaders continued to tangle with the soldiers. While nursing his wound, Garrick told a crowd of colonists gathered out front about what had happened. Inflamed by the boy's treatment at the hands of the British, they walked back to Boston Common, where the taunting, arguing, and assault continued to escalate.

Eventually, the colonists were joined by a group of men—mostly sailors—carrying clubs and sticks. Most likely scared and overwhelmed, the nine soldiers of the 29th Regiment of Foot opened fire. Five colonists were killed and six were wounded.

The first to die was Crispus Attucks. The mixed-race sailor of Narragansett and African descent was shot twice in the chest. One bullet gored "the right lobe of the lungs, and a

The figures of Liberty and Justice sit atop the signatures to the Declaration of Independence, with the nation's symbol, an eagle, in the center. ***OPPOSITE:*** A 19th-century hand-colored engraving depicts the moment in 1770 when British soldiers opened fire on demonstrators in what would become known as the Boston Massacre.

great part of the liver most horribly" according to *An Impartial History of the War in America, Between Great Britain and the United States* (1781).

It was the first death in what Samuel Adams would eventually deem the "Boston Massacre" and the first death in what we would all come to call the American Revolution. After he was killed, Attucks's body lay in state in Faneuil Hall (later referred to as the "Cradle of Liberty"). It was there still on the morning of March 6, when colonists met to discuss next steps, but was later buried in a mass grave with the other victims of the massacre.

It shouldn't be surprising that the first stops on the map of the American Revolution began with a debt and a drunken snowball fight resulting in the death of a formerly enslaved mixed-race man. Or that it happened on Boston Common and the so-called Cradle of Liberty. But then again, Boston Common and Faneuil Hall had been exercising and taking liberties long before that cold day in 1770.

IN 1620, WHEN ENGLISH COLONISTS disembarked at Plymouth, Massachusetts, they stepped onto troubled land. Land that was troubled in two directions: east and west. They found Native nations that had been associating—sometimes productively and at others destructively—with various European powers (Nordic, English, French, Dutch, Spanish) for more than 200 years.

Not that the preceding millennia had been a period of untrammeled growth (or, conversely, of decay). For at least 50,000 years and perhaps much longer, Native nations in North America had been living, growing, moving, fighting, shrinking, moving again, growing again, disappearing, and reappearing. In new places, with new languages and new agendas.

Historically, Native nations had existed as agricultural and sedentary empires (like the Maya, Aztec, and the mysterious Mississippian megaculture at Cahokia, sited at the confluence of the Mississippi and Missouri Rivers). Armed with food technology—mostly corn that spread from Central America—Cahokia at its height in A.D. 1200 spanned more than 4,000 acres and was home to roughly 40,000 citizens within the walls of the city (with many more likely scattered among farms and satellite settlements across the region). It wouldn't be until 1740—roughly 500 years later—that Philadelphia would surpass it as the largest American city.

Smaller nations—for example, the peoples who would become the Lakota, Cheyenne, Blackfeet, and other Plains tribes—adapted to their respective climates and cultural concerns and were more nomadic. Others—the Tongva, Miwok, Pomo, and hundreds more in what is now California—were sedentary and small: Each cleaved to its own valley. And still others (including my own tribe, the Ojibwe, and our neighbors across the country, including the Haudenosaunee, Huron, Ho-Chunk, Illini, Choctaw, Cherokee, Shawnee) existed somewhere in between. Not unlike the Europeans who came to these shores starting in 1492, they lived relatively stable lives in mostly sedentary communities, surviving through a combination of trade, agriculture, hunting, and conquest. By 1620, however, our nations and lands were troubled (to say the least) by the newly arrived Europeans—though not necessarily for the reasons put forth by earlier historians.

The most commonly held and promoted assumption is that Native people—starting from the margins of the North American continent and working in—suffered not only conquistadorial violence but also diseases of European origin. And that's true: Many of us died at the hands of English, Spanish, Dutch, and French, felled by their guns, swords, hands, and (in the case of the Spanish) their dogs. But these direct deaths (between 100,000 and 200,000 over hundreds of years) pale in comparison to deaths by disease, which account for the loss of millions. Some estimates suggest that by 1900, 95 percent of the Indigenous population—numbering around 50 million in 1492—had died from the ravages of smallpox and other Old World pathogens: so-called "virgin soil epidemics" against which Indigenous people had no natural immunity. That's the most oft told story. But it's not the whole story.

Europe had, in the past, been confronted by virgin soil epidemics of her own: the bubonic plague, for starters. Also known as the black plague, the infection has been traced back to the Tian Shan range between China and Kyrgyzstan more than 2,500 years ago. It followed trade routes and populations until it erupted at a Crimean fort in 1347. Between 1347 and 1351, some 75 million to 200 million (a third to half) of the populations of Europe, the Levant, and North Africa died horribly, since people had no immunity. But by the 16th century—exactly when European colonizers came to *our* shores in force—European population levels rebounded and exceeded pre-plague levels rather than dying out. Why?

During those roughly 200 years, Europeans got married and had children. They had steady and reliable access to food, clothing, shelter. They began—often because of their overseas exploits in Africa and North America and Asia—to enjoy a better standard of living. The marriages lasted, the children survived. Infant mortality went down, and the immune systems of the population (thanks to better housing, food, and clothing) improved.

This is the natural course of epidemics (even of the "virgin soil" variety). The disease runs its course, the survivors develop immunity, and the population rebounds. But this was not the case in North America. Instead of enduring a pandemic and then recovering, the Indigenous people of North America were forced to endure another few rounds of cruelty that prevented us from having the *chance* to recover. We were enslaved and trafficked.

Indigenous citizens in the Caribbean were crowded into camps and forced to comb the islands in search of gold; Indigenous citizens in what is now Mexico were similarly confined to camps, where they were undernourished and overworked mining for silver. They carried the metal on their backs up rickety ladders from down below and smelted it with lead, handling it with their bare hands and crushing it with their unshod feet. For most of them, life expectancy was two to three years after enslavement. Tribes along the Atlantic littoral from Florida to Maine were taken and sent to the Caribbean to replace those who had succumbed to disease and starvation.

NATIVE NATIONS IN NORTH AMERICA HAD BEEN LIVING, GROWING, MOVING, FIGHTING, SHRINKING, MOVING AGAIN, GROWING AGAIN, DISAPPEARING, AND REAPPEARING.

Located on 2,200 acres in what is now Illinois, the Cahokia Mounds are all that remain of the most sophisticated prehistoric Indigenous civilization north of Mexico.

In 1614, John Smith was sailing north along the New England coast on a two-ship trading mission, looking mostly for fish and furs. Smith returned to England, but left his colleague Thomas Hunt in New England, where he was to fill the second ship with cod and sail for Málaga, Spain. Not content with fish or the profits they were going to realize from the sale, Hunt hatched other plans. After sailing into Plymouth Harbor to trade with a village of Patuxet, he coaxed 20 of them on board to trade "shipside." Once they arrived, they were confined to the ship; Hunt weighed anchor and sailed across Cape Cod Bay, where he captured seven more Natives from a Nauset community. And *then* he sailed for Spain.

Hunt stopped at Gibraltar, where he tried to sell some of his captive cargo. But he was deterred from selling all of them by Catholic friars, who kept a few to "be instructed in the Christian faith," according to politician James Phinney Baxter. Among the captives was a young Patuxet man named Tisquantum, shortened by his captors to Squanto. He likely spent four years enslaved in Spain and as much time in England the same way before returning, somehow, to New England around 1619.

Tricked into boarding Hunt's ship, separated from his family and language, kept prisoner belowdecks, sold into slavery twice: Squanto was bereft of everything that makes a human being. And when he returned to Plymouth Harbor—to his homelands and to his native village and family—they were all gone. Between 1616 and 1619, villages up and down the Atlantic coast had been struck by a plague, which was exacerbated by the theft of Native bodies, the enslavement of Native human beings, and the disruption of war. The village was gone; the lodges were nothing more than rotting lattices of sticks. Bones littered the ground. Squanto had no one to turn to—and indeed, nowhere to return.

By 1620, when the Pilgrims arrived at Plymouth, all they found was a mound in the dunes near the shore. They dug it up to expose a grave, followed by more mounds and more graves. Some contained seed corn, which they took. Then they came to an abandoned village, where they stole acorns, corn, and beans. And so, the first act of the English and Spanish immigrants in the nation that would become America was to capture and enslave the bodies of its Native denizens. Once ashore, they took—or tried to take—our food and means to survive.

During the Pequot War (1636–37), Native Americans were enslaved in greater numbers and used locally, as well as shipped to the Caribbean. We were traded for enslaved Africans and vice versa in a disgusting form of human arbitrage: Enslaved Africans from Provincetown Island in the Spanish Caribbean were shipped north in exchange for Pequots.

But it wasn't until King Philip's War (1675–76) that we were enslaved en masse. Captured combatants among the allied tribes fighting the English were sold into slavery; those who surrendered or refused to fight alongside the English were sold in equal numbers.

Fifty-five years later, King Philip—the Wampanoag leader who tried to hold the English back and deter them from taking even more Native lands and possessions—was assassinated in Plymouth on August 12, 1676. His body was drawn by four horses until it was ripped into four parts; for decades, his head was displayed as a warning on a stick outside Plymouth.

That same year, on Boston Common—where Crispus Attucks (of the Narragansett tribe) would be killed almost a century later—50 Indians were tortured, executed, and displayed in rituals of violence. Among them was a Nipmuc war leader named Matoonas who was tied to a tree, shot to death, and then beheaded. Afterward, his head was stuck on the end of a pike—just as his son's had been five years earlier.

The colonists even assassinated an Indian man named Old Tom who was a "praying Indian" (meaning he had converted to Christianity) and was *not* a soldier: He had been one of King Philip's prisoners. But it didn't matter. The spectacle did.

Meanwhile, a 10-minute walk from Boston Common on the site of what is now Faneuil Hall, other rituals of theft were taking place, for this was where Boston's slave market once stood, where our ancestors and those of African American cousins and family were enslaved. Peter Faneuil built Faneuil Hall (which has been called, unironically, the "Cradle of Liberty") to sell enslaved people.

After King Philip's War, the taking of our land and our bodies expanded as the frontier moved from ships to the Atlantic coast and offshore islands. Virginia's slave codes, published in 1705, stated that "all servants imported and brought into the Country, by sea or land, who were not christians in their native country … shall be accounted and be slaves … All negro, mulatto, and Indian slaves … within this dominion, shall be held … to be real estate … And if any slave resist his master, or owner, … correcting such slave, and shall happen to be killed in such correction … the master … shall be free and acquit of all punishment … as if such accident had never happened."

Eventually, roughly 347,000 of us in North America became the property of the British, Spanish, and Dutch. Along our rivers and up and down the East Coast and around Florida and through the Caribbean we were taken—sometimes by force, other times by trickery—and brought to Hispaniola, Spain, Italy, England, Barbados. Gaspar, a 13-year-old boy who was "tricked" by a Spanish merchant in Hispaniola, was taken to Spain, where he lived and spent the rest of his life. A Taíno man discovered that his children and wife were captured by Columbus; he paddled in a canoe out to the ship holding them and begged to be enslaved, too, so as not to be separated from his family.

This process—this movement of the frontier from the ship to our bodies, and the conditions in which we were forced to live—accounts for the loss of ourselves, our kin, our nations, and ultimately our land. Just as much happened in our homelands and to us in the 284 years between 1492 and 1776 as what occurred during the smaller sum of the years after the birth of the nation. By the time 1776 rolled around, there had already been a 284-year-long process of violent taking.

Which leads me to this: Many may believe that the American Revolution and the resulting nation were born out of the heads and ideals of "our" founders as they faced east toward Britain. But in truth, it was born out of a habit of conquest as the colonizers faced west toward the frontier. Toward us.

IN 1672, GEORGE WASHINGTON'S great-grandfather John Washington was 39 years old when he proposed to meet with Doeg and Susquehannock leaders incensed at the dispossession of their lands in what is now Maryland. At the meeting—under a flag of truce—John Washington murdered five of the unarmed Indigenous men. Afterward, the survivors referred to him as Conotocarious, or "Devourer of Villages."

Eighty years later, Washington's great-grandson George came to Seneca homelands during the French and Indian War. He and his men burned villages, destroyed crops, and murdered many citizens of the Haudenosaunee (Iroquois) Confederacy. In 1753, Seneca leader Tanacharison bestowed George with the same nickname as his great-grandfather.

In 1779, during the Revolutionary War, under orders from General Washington, Gen. John Sullivan led an expedition that burned and razed more than 40 villages, took corn, and burned fields. When Washington had empowered the Sullivan campaign a year earlier, he earmarked $932,743 to be spent destroying Indian nations; this represented 85 percent of the total budget for the American government that year. His instructions to Sullivan on May 31, 1779, were just as clear: "The immediate objects are the total destruction and devastation of their settlements and the capture of as many prisoners of every age and sex as possible. It will be essential to ruin their crops now in the ground and prevent their planting more." But just in case his genocidal intent wasn't clear enough, he added: "The country may not be merely overrun but destroyed."

On July 5, 1779, Gen. Enoch Poor delivered an "Independence Day" speech to the troops involved in the Sullivan expedition. In it, he demonstrated that brevity isn't just the soul of wit but also of cruelty: "Civilization or death to all American savages."

Unsurprisingly, the expedition did not choose "civilization" for my ancestors. Instead, on April 19, 1780, American troops crossed Oneida Lake and burned more than 50 houses, killed nearly 20 Onondaga, and captured 33 more. Later, when Sullivan himself arrived at Chenussio—a large Seneca village in what is now Geneseo, New York—the expedition destroyed everything. Sullivan reported that he put his men "to work in the surrounding two hundred acres of vegetable gardens and cornfields, gathering the tall corn and piling it on torn-down houses to fuel huge fires. They demolished the entire town, with an estimated fifteen thousand bushels of corn."

Cayuga relatives weren't safe either. Sullivan's forces "ravaged the southwestern shore of Cayuga Lake, burning, pillaging, and killing as much as they could, with [Col. John] Butler destroying three towns and associated fields, while Dearborn mangled six." By the time the campaign was over, American troops had burned down more than 500 houses, obliterated entire villages, destroyed more than 50,000 bushels of corn and—in a heartbreak that would be repeated against the Diné at Canyon de Chelly in New Mexico a century later—demolished acres and acres of carefully cultivated fruit trees. Not listed are the many more Native people who—having lost their homes (including their plates and silverware and pots and blankets), their orchards, their corn, and their vegetable gardens—died of starvation and exposure in the coming winters.

When Seneca leader Cornplanter met Washington in 1790, he observed: "When your army entered the country of the Six Nations, we called you Town Destroyer. And to this day when your name is heard, our women look behind them and turn pale, and our children cling close to the necks of their mothers."

WHO ULTIMATELY WOULD (AND *SHOULD*) PROFIT FROM WESTWARD EXPANSION OF THE ORIGINAL 13 COLONIES?

THE REVOLUTIONARY WAR—and the American republic that emerged from it—was less about Great Britain and more about Native people and our land than is commonly taught. It was fought, for the most part, *because* of us and our land. The Stamp Act of 1765 and the Tea Act of 1773 were public eruptions of a long-simmering subterranean question: Who ultimately would (and *should*) profit from westward expansion of the original 13 colonies? Who should profit from the theft of our land? The colonists or the crown?

It's no accident (nor poorly staged harborfront drama) that the colonists dressed as Mohawk Indians to dump tea in Boston Harbor in 1773. It was never about the tea. More to the point, it was symbolic theater that begged a very specific question: Who will get to colonize the land beyond the frontier? Who will get to profit from it?

In fact, in the wake of the Seven Years' War, which nearly bankrupted the crown, and after widespread famine in India crashed *those* markets, the Tea Act was meant to boost British profits by reducing taxes on tea imported to America. The colonists (and the merchant class in particular) had been smuggling tea into America and undercutting British tariffs; the crown was trying to even the playing field.

Marilyn Berry Morrison, chief of the Roanoke-Hatteras Tribe and chairperson of the Algonquian Indians of North Carolina, 2017

And so it follows that the "Americans" weren't on a quest for freedom. Not exactly. They were fighting for the freedom to smuggle. For the freedom to steal. After that brave action, British Parliament passed a handful of laws meant to punish the colonists that would become known as the Intolerable Acts: the Boston Port Act, the Massachusetts Government Act, the Administration of Justice Act, and the Quartering Act.

All of this culminated in the most "intolerable" act of the bunch: the Quebec Act, which extended Britain's newly acquired land in Canada south across the Great Lakes, bounded by the Allegheny, Ohio, and Mississippi Rivers and including most of present-day Ohio, Indiana, Michigan, and Wisconsin. Relying on their charters, several colonies (notably Virginia) claimed portions of this territory. But they did not exercise effective control over trade with the Native people, check the trespassing of squatters, restrain the aggression of land companies, or prevent the inroads of land-hungry colonists, who for the most part defrauded the Native Americans in trade and land purchases. Actually, there was no civil government, no legal acts, no order.

This situation could not be tolerated. Civil government and the control and legalizing of trade and land transfers were imperative. In light of the increasing hostility of Native Americans against the actions of white transgressors, and determined to instill law and order, the British government deemed the area in salutary neglect—or incompetence—in order to exert increasing control.

And that's what was really at the heart of the Revolutionary War: who got to take what and how much, and by what means, from Native nations west of the 13 colonies. This nation—which, without a trace of irony, would declare itself the "land of the free and the home of the brave"—was not separating from England solely over the issue of "taxation without representation." The conflict was also based in who would profit from westward expansion and control. And inherent in that expansion was the stealing of land and freedoms.

The two original sins of the republic—theft and slavery—were personified in the figure of Crispus Attucks, the mixed-race sailor who was the first to die in the Boston Massacre. Native and Black. Both sides dispossessed—one side of its land, the other of its freedom. And murdered in a place that was almost a shrine to both evils.

But Attucks wasn't the only person to die on Boston Common on that cold night in March 1770. Nor was he the only person to lie in state at Faneuil Hall. James Caldwell, a sailor, was shot and killed shortly after Attucks fell. Caldwell was 17 years old, and the ship he was assigned to, the *Hawk,* typically sailed a route between the West Indies and Boston. It was part of what was known as the triangular trade, in which enslaved humans in the West Indies were forced to grow sugarcane and distill it into molasses. This was shipped to and sold in New England, where it was distilled into rum, then shipped to and sold in England, where it was used to enslave and traffic more people to the West Indies.

Why these two boys came to Boston Common and joined in on what, at some point, must have been fun—or perhaps a revolutionary example of "boys being boys"—is lost to time. Attucks and Caldwell were both sailors who regularly sailed between North America and the West Indies. I wonder if that's where their similarities—not to mention their identities—ended.

But to know such a thing, we have to know how they saw themselves. Did they exist easily or uneasily in their respective categories? Did Attucks see himself as mixed? Or Black? Or Native? Or even white? Did Caldwell think of himself as Irish? Or British? Or landless? Or white?

But the one identity that remains just out of reach is that most elusive and troubled one of all: American. That would have had to wait—though of course the boys were murdered too soon to have realized it. Caldwell could have claimed citizenship in a few short years; Attucks would have had to wait until 1868 and the ratification of the 14th Amendment to claim his (that is, if he understood himself as Black). If he understood himself as predominantly Native, he would have to wait a full 150 years to become an American—till 1924 with the enactment of the Indian Citizenship Act.

Regardless, what happened to both these boys is a weight around the neck of the country that the republic has yet to shake off. Not a curse exactly. Or a false start. But it was, and remains, a complicated start. And its echoes continue to reverberate in the chambers of America's beating heart.

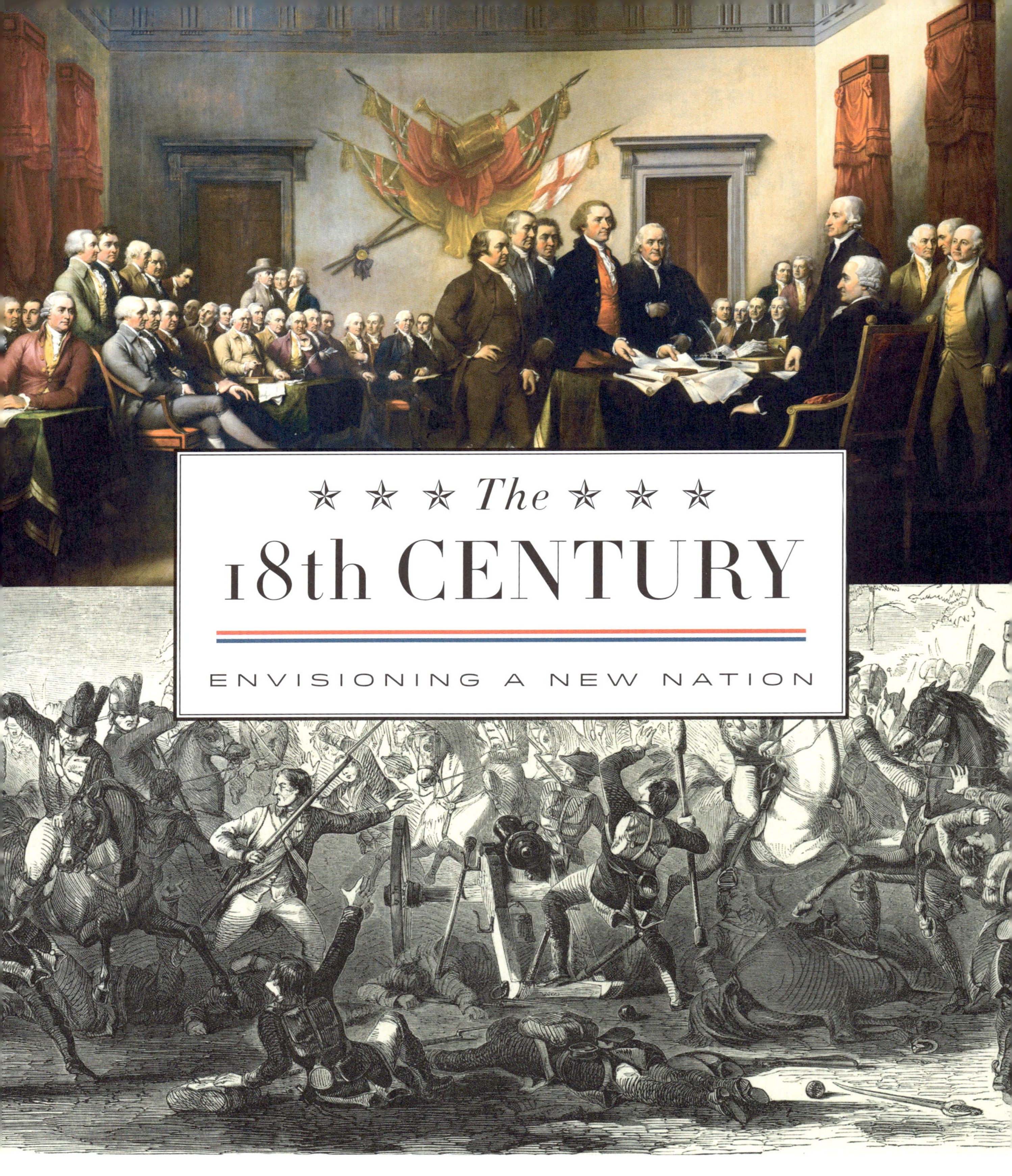

★ ★ ★ *The* ★ ★ ★
18th CENTURY

ENVISIONING A NEW NATION

A LITTLE REBELLION NOW AND THEN IS A GOOD THING.

Thomas Jefferson, *in a letter to James Madison (1787)*

ANY SINGLE DAY can inflect history, especially in a brand-new nation. Consider John Trumbull's 1818 painting "Declaration of Independence," seen by millions each year where it hangs in the U.S. Capitol Rotunda. It has the grand look and famous faces of an important event, but the scene the artist intended to depict—the declaration's presentation to the Continental Congress on July 4, 1776—never occurred. There was no formal ceremony to accept Thomas Jefferson's declaration; after it was adopted, a clerk needed time to boldly ink the text onto parchment, and "the signing began on August 2, and continued through the year as absent delegates returned to Philadelphia," historian David McCullough has noted (the final man didn't add his signature until 1777). Trumbull would explain in his autobiography that "the great object of his life" was completing portraits of America's founding and its actors; for the setting, he took liberties creating a composite scene.

Compare Trumbull's setting to where Congress would have actually met and "the room is wrong, the doors are in the wrong place. The chairs are wrong," McCullough says. "Yet none of this really matters." What does matter, he says, is the scene's powerful symbolism. It shows dozens of patriots who risked treason charges to endorse, what McCullough calls, "a declaration of political faith and brave intent freely arrived at by an American congress. And that was something entirely new under the sun."

A vintage Fourth of July greeting card features the opening lines from "Yankee Doodle," a popular song of the colonial era. ***OPPOSITE TOP:*** When painter John Trumbull reimagined the presentation of the draft Declaration of Independence to the Second Continental Congress, he managed to fit 42 of the declaration's 56 signers into the scene. ***OPPOSITE BOTTOM:*** "Buford's Massacre," a battle at the border of North and South Carolina, turned public sentiment against the British after their troops pursued fleeing American infantrymen and killed even those trying to surrender.

JUNE 29, 1767

Parliament passes the Townshend Acts

The four acts levied taxes on glass, lead, and other essentials of colonial life.

DECEMBER 16, 1773

Boston throws a tea party

To protest the crown's tax on tea, colonists dumped chests of it from British ships into Boston Harbor.

JUNE 19, 1775

George Washington is appointed commander in chief of the Continental Army

The Second Continental Congress chose the Virginian war veteran to lead troops fighting for what he called "the American cause."

JULY 2, 1776

Second Continental Congress votes for independence

Delegates declared the colonies' political ties to the British crown "totally dissolved."

JULY 4, 1776

Declaration of Independence is adopted

After delegates discussed and revised it, a declaration draft was approved; it would be inscribed on parchment for signing later.

DECEMBER 26, 1776

George Washington crosses the Delaware

General Washington and 2,400 troops braved treacherous ice to surprise British forces, energizing the Revolution.

OCTOBER 19, 1781

The British surrender at Yorktown

Unable to escape U.S. troops' siege, British general Charles Cornwallis's forces laid down their arms, effectively ending the Revolutionary War.

SEPTEMBER 3, 1783

Treaty of Paris is adopted

Officially ending the Revolutionary War, it declared the United States an independent nation.

MAY 23, 1785

Benjamin Franklin invents bifocals

The "double glasses" he invented eliminated switching between close and distant vision spectacles.

America's first treasury secretary, Alexander Hamilton was not yet 50 when he was fatally shot in a duel with political foe Aaron Burr.

TIMELINE

1763-1799

WHEN BRITAIN SENT SUPPLIES BUT WEIGHED THEM DOWN WITH TAXES, AMERICANS REBELLED. SOME IN PARLIAMENT CALLED THEM INGRATES; OTHERS CALLED THEM "SONS OF LIBERTY."

DUBLIN NATIVE ISAAC BARRÉ joined the army of Great Britain as it and other European powers pursued the Seven Years' War on several continents. Serving in North America (where the conflict was called the French and Indian War), Barré fought alongside the American colonists who helped Britain secure victory in 1763. A musket ball strike left Colonel Barré with a blind eye and half his face disfigured; he was elected to Parliament as a war hero. There, Barré squared off against soon-to-be Chancellor of the Exchequer Charles Townshend, who insisted that the American colonies paid too little toward their own support. Townshend endorsed taxing many necessities the colonies imported from Britain—paper, glass, paint, lead, tea—and during a parliamentary debate in February 1765, Townshend depicted the colonists as ingrates. "Children planted by our care, nourished by our indulgence until they are grown to a degree of strength and opulence" he called them—yet unwilling to "contribute their mite" to the crown's coffers. Known as an orator, Barré aimed a scathing rebuttal at Townshend: "They planted by your care? No! Your oppression planted them in America. They fled from your tyranny," he thundered. "They protected by your arms? They have nobly taken up arms in your defense." That day, Barré coined a name worn proudly as Americans launched their revolution: "Sons of Liberty."

MAY 25, 1787
Constitutional Convention convenes
Delegates from seven of the 13 states gathered and chose George Washington to preside.

APRIL 30, 1789
George Washington takes the presidential oath
After unanimously winning the electoral vote, Washington was sworn in as president and John Adams as vice president.

SEPTEMBER 24, 1789
Supreme Court is established
One of Congress's first acts created a high court to hear lower courts' appeals.

MARCH 1, 1790
U.S. Census is established
A requirement to tally everyone in U.S. households by categories noting age, gender, race, and free or enslaved status was passed.

MARCH 28, 1791
Pierre L'Enfant creates the federal city
His plan had a grid of streets, intersecting diagonal avenues, and the Capitol on a hill as a focal point.

DECEMBER 15, 1791
Bill of Rights is ratified
The first 10 amendments to the Constitution were ratified by the required three-fourths majority.

DECEMBER 9, 1793
Noah Webster publishes New York's first daily newspaper
Though a Federalist, editor Webster promised his publication's coverage would be "impartial."

MARCH 14, 1794
Eli Whitney's cotton gin revolutionizes the economy
The machine efficiently separated cotton fibers from seeds, fueling the growth of cotton farming—and slavery in the South.

DECEMBER 14, 1799
George Washington dies at Mount Vernon
In retirement, he died with acute throat inflammation developed after cold days on his land.

Named for surveyors who set a colonial land boundary, the Mason-Dixon Line became known as the dividing line between North and South.

1. FEBRUARY 10, 1763

TREATY OF PARIS IS SIGNED

The momentous agreement ended what Europeans called the Seven Years' War. (In North America, it was referred to as the French and Indian War because the French and their Indian allies had fought British forces over North American territory, mostly in the Ohio River Valley.) With its adoption, Britain, the victor, now controlled all of France's previous territory east of the Mississippi as well as Spanish Florida. But British coffers were drained by the war, and Parliament resisted funding a large military presence in America to protect colonists in the new territories. Instead of signaling prosperous times ahead, the treaty began unraveling trust—and loyalty—between the crown and its American colonies.

2. NOVEMBER 15, 1763

MASON AND DIXON COME TO AMERICA

English astronomer Charles Mason and respected surveyor Jeremiah Dixon arrived in Philadelphia on this day, charged with establishing an official boundary between Pennsylvania and Maryland. Both colonies had been given as royal charters to wealthy families, but the Penns of Pennsylvania and the Calverts of Maryland had argued for decades over which colony owned the land between the 39th and 40th parallels. After five years of surveying, Mason and Dixon established an initial boundary, but the final line wouldn't be settled until 1779. In the century to come, the "Mason-Dixon Line" would become the unofficial demarcation between North and South.

3. MARCH 22, 1765

PARLIAMENT PASSES THE STAMP ACT

This famously unpopular act of the British Parliament taxed the colonists for paper goods and legal documents. The Quartering Act, which required colonists to provide housing and food for British troops, followed. Both acts created such dissent that delegates from nine colonies—Massachusetts, Rhode Island, Connecticut, New York, New Jersey, Pennsylvania, Delaware, Maryland, and South Carolina—convened in New York seven months later as "the Stamp Act Congress" and issued a series of resolutions to the king, respectfully protesting the circumstances and conditions of the new taxes.

4. MAY 30, 1765

PATRICK HENRY TAKES A STAND

On this day, the fiery young Virginia orator and future statesman stood in the colony's House of Burgesses to rail against George III, using such threatening language that the Speaker of the House objected. Though Henry's exact words are lost to history, legend attributes him with this menacing warning: "Caesar had his Brutus, Charles the First his Cromwell, and George the Third ..." Though Henry never finished the threat, he is said to have ended his speech with, "If this be treason, make the most of it."

5. AUGUST 14, 1765

LIBERTY TREE IS BORN

Early this August morning, Bostonians discovered an effigy of a local merchant who had been complying with the hated Stamp Act hanging from a 120-year-old elm near Boston Common. A painted sign read, "What Greater Joy did ever New England see / Than a Stampman hanging on a Tree!" Soon, hundreds of townsfolk gathered under the elm's canopy, establishing the "Liberty Tree" as a rallying point and emblem of protest. Ten years later, the occupying British Army chopped down the elm, an act that failed to erase the potency of its symbolism.

GREAT BRITAIN HATH NO MORE RIGHT TO PUT THEIR HANDS INTO MY POCKET, WITHOUT MY CONSENT, THAN I HAVE TO PUT MY HANDS INTO YOURS.

George Washington, *letter to a friend (1774)*

In Boston, independence-minded colonists rallied at the site of the Liberty Tree—even after the British Army felled the towering elm.

Britain's tax on tea was characterized as hurting colonists "worse than a bayonet" in this political cartoon published in 1767 in Boston.

6. APRIL 7, 1766

BOSTON WOMEN HOLD A PATRIOTIC SPINNING BEE

On this day, the *Boston Gazette* reported, 18 women "exhibited a fine example of industry by spinning from sunrise until dark and displayed a spirit for saving their sinking country." This new form of patriotism was a way for colonists to wean themselves from British fabrics as war approached. As the years progressed, women continued to come together in groups to spin, and young girls were taught the old craft. Homespun clothes would become the fashion: a sign of protest against the British and their taxes. Three years later, a "Homespun Ball" was held in Williamsburg, Virginia.

7. APRIL 24, 1767

CURTAIN RISES ON THE NEW WORLD'S FIRST PLAY

On this evening, the first ever American production of a play by an American playwright was performed at Philadelphia's Southwark Theatre. *The Prince of Parthia* was penned by young playwright and poet Thomas Godfrey, Jr., son of a prominent Philadelphia family. The play was performed by the American Company, whose leader, David Douglass, had founded the Southwark the year before and would go on to open other permanent theaters in Newport, Rhode Island; New York City; Annapolis, Maryland; Williamsburg, Virginia; and Charleston, South Carolina.

8. JUNE 29, 1767

PARLIAMENT PASSES THE TOWNSHEND ACTS

The new laws, adopted on this day, heaped yet more taxes on the beleaguered colonists—this time on glass, lead, paper, and tea. The acts were named for their originator, British financial minister Charles Townshend, who a few years earlier had described the American colonists as "Children planted by our care, nourished by our indulgence." "No taxation without representation," already a patriotic rallying cry, underpinned further protest. By August the following year, Boston merchants agreed to stop trading with Britain.

9. JULY 7, 1768

"SONG FOR AMERICAN FREEDOM" FANS PATRIOTIC FERVOR

After the galvanizing tune appeared on this day in *The Pennsylvania,* other journals published the lyrics, and it became known as the "Liberty Song." Set to the Royal Navy's "Heart of Oak," the rousing lyrics began: "COME, join hand in hand, brave AMERICANS all, And rouse your bold hearts at fair LIBERTY's call; No *tyrannous acts* shall suppress your *just claim*, Or stain with *dishonor* AMERICA's name." Two years later John Adams observed that the tune cultivated "the Sensations of Freedom." He was apparently right, as it would soon become the unofficial anthem of the revolution to come.

Hannah Winthrop was among the Bostonians who supported the rebellion with acts such as spinning at home instead of importing English fabric.

10. SEPTEMBER 29, 1768

"YANKEE DOODLE" RAISES A RUCKUS

As British troops arrived in Boston Harbor to occupy the city, they played "the Yankee Doodle Song," featuring lyrics that poked fun at the uncouth colonists. In fact, the well-known and well-worn "Yankee Doodle" ditty had vague New England origins before the British adopted it and changed the lyrics. In the first winter of their occupation, British officers disrupted a dance when they called for the band to "play the Yankee Doodle tune … and not being gratified, they grew noisy and clamorous."

A statue at Solvang, California's Mission Santa Inés honors Father Junipero Serra.

11. JULY 1, 1769

FATHER JUNIPERO SERRA LANDS IN CALIFORNIA

On this day, Serra—a Spanish priest and Franciscan friar—arrived in present-day San Diego and founded a mission there. Over the next 13 years, he would establish eight more outposts in Upper California (then a Spanish possession), stretching as far north as present-day San Francisco. The mission system was critical to Spain's colonization of California and its avowed aim of converting Indigenous peoples to Catholicism. In exchange for their (seldom voluntary) conversion, Indigenous peoples were required to live and work within the confines of a mission, creating a system of tax-paying Spanish colonial citizens. The system would devastate the Native American population, and in 2015, Father Serra's canonization rekindled controversy about his legacy.

12. JANUARY 16, 1770

HANDEL'S *MESSIAH* DEBUTS STATESIDE

Held on this day at Burns' Coffee House—also known as Mr. Burns's Rooms, a popular gathering place in Lower Manhattan—the performance was actually a benefit concert to aid, well, the performer. The bankrupt William Tuckey, an Englishman, had been a "vicar choral" in Bristol before coming to New York and taking a job at Trinity Church. He lost that job for "refusing to officiate in time of Divine Service." How well he performed Handel's sweeping 1741 oratorio was not reported.

13. FEBRUARY 1, 1770

THOMAS JEFFERSON'S FAMILY HOME BURNS DOWN

Jefferson was born in a farmhouse outside Charlottesville, Virginia. It sat on an estate known as Shadwell—the largest in the area. He rarely lived there, as he was educated in the Virginia Tidewater, but his mother and siblings did. As eldest son, Jefferson inherited the estate when his father died in 1757. Hearing of the fire, Jefferson grieved the loss "of every paper I had in the world, and almost every book." By then, however, he had begun building his beloved home, Monticello, on a nearby mountaintop on estate property.

ON THAT NIGHT THE FOUNDATION OF AMERICAN INDEPENDENCE WAS LAID.

John Adams, *speaking of the Boston Massacre (1786)*

14. MARCH 5, 1770

BOSTON MASSACRE TAKES ITS TOLL

Tensions between Bostonians and occupying British troops reached a boiling point on this cold March night. According to John Adams, "a motley rabble of saucy boys" had gathered outside the customhouse, and when a British contingent appeared to protect it, the "rabble" hurled icy snowballs, oysters in shells, rocks, and clubs. Upon being hit in the head, a soldier accidentally discharged his musket, causing his fellows to open fire; five Bostonian men were killed in the ensuing "massacre." Adams took the unpopular role of defense attorney for the British officer in charge of the contingent and won an acquittal. He later wrote that the trial "procured me Anxiety ... enough," but was "one of the most gallant ... Actions of my whole Life."

15. MARCH 26, 1772

A FEMALE PATRIOT MAKES THE PLAY THE THING

On this day, the Boston newspaper *Massachusetts Spy* published scenes from a new play, *The Adulateur.* Written by Mercy Otis Warren, now considered America's first female playwright, the political satire criticized how the Massachusetts royal governor had handled the Boston Massacre. Since it was not acceptable for women to write plays, the scenes were published anonymously. But Warren soon became an influential voice in the patriotic movement—and in the founding of the country.

16. OCTOBER 3, 1772

ALEXANDER HAMILTON FILES A STORY

Then a merchant's clerk on St. Croix, the parentless teenager gave his account of a recent hurricane to a local paper, which published his arresting story anonymously. So taken were local businessmen and the island's governor with the writer's general acumen and vivid prose—he described "roaring of the sea and wind, fiery meteors flying about ... the ear-piercing shrieks of the distressed"—that they sought out his identity and established a fund to send him to North America for an education. By the following year, Hamilton was enrolled at King's College in New York, now Columbia University.

17. NOVEMBER 4, 1772

SAMUEL ADAMS GETS FED UP

A patriot and a founder of Boston's Sons of Liberty, Adams wrote a letter on this day to fellow patriot James Warren, imploring him to establish a Committee of Correspondence in Plymouth and further the effort to unite the colonies against the British. "I have not at present time or Inclination to take up your thots in complaining of Tyrants and Tyranny. It is more than Time that this Country was rid of both," he wrote. Considered a firebrand by many, including his cousin John, Adams was a harbinger of the revolutionary spirit that would soon sweep the colonies.

Revolution was brewing, literally, when colonists dumped 342 chests of British tea from ships into Boston Harbor to protest tea taxes.

18. JUNE 19, 1773

THE WASHINGTONS LOSE A DAUGHTER

One of two surviving children from Martha Washington's first marriage, 17-year-old Patsy Custis was raised at Mount Vernon, where she suffered terribly from epilepsy. Both Martha and George tried to help the girl, consulting various doctors and holding her during seizures. When Patsy succumbed on this day, family accounts say George knelt beside her with tears streaming down his face, praying for her recovery. In his journal, he wrote simply, "About five oclock poor Patcy Custis Died Suddenly."

19. NOVEMBER 25, 1773

ICE CREAM MAKES ITS PRINT DEBUT

The New World's first advertisement for the cold delight appeared in *Rivington's New-York Gazetteer* on this day. Confectioner Philip Lenzi, who had just arrived from London, placed the ad and is attributed with opening the first ice cream parlor in New York in 1774. Flavors of the era included fruits like raspberry, strawberry, apricot, and lemon as well as pistachio, Parmesan, and tea—though the latter would become controversial in the colonies.

20. DECEMBER 16, 1773

BOSTON THROWS A TEA PARTY

On this day, several dozen men disguised as Native Americans boarded three British ships in Boston and dumped their cargo—342 chests of tea—into the harbor. The previous spring, Parliament had passed the hated Tea Act, taxing colonists and forcing them to buy surplus tea from British merchants. In response, many boycotted the beloved brew. New

York and Philadelphia banned British tea ships, but the royal governor in occupied Boston wouldn't allow that. Instead, the ships anchored there became the legendary hosts of the Boston Tea Party. An outraged Parliament reacted by closing Boston Harbor and passing other so-called Coercive Acts, which Americans referred to as the Intolerable Acts.

21. JANUARY 29, 1774

BENJAMIN FRANKLIN IS DRESSED DOWN

For some years, Franklin had lived in London, representing Pennsylvania's interests against the powerful Penn family. A loyal subject of the king, he often counseled his powerful British friends on ways to deal with the increasingly restless colonists. But after the Boston Tea Party, ministers lost all patience with America, and apparently with the sage Franklin. His comeuppance took place on this day before Britain's Privy Council, with the solicitor

Benjamin Franklin had long worked amicably with British officials until, in a public meeting, one accused him of fomenting rebellion.

Called "Shaking Quakers" for their worship movements, members of the utopian sect came to the colonies fleeing persecution in Britain.

general calling him a "true incendiary ... [who] has forfeited all the respect of societies and of men." Their loss. The following year, when his allegiance to the opposition party increased Parliament's ill will toward him, Franklin returned to Philadelphia—and his destiny as a leading patriot.

22. AUGUST 6, 1774

SHAKERS ARRIVE IN NEW YORK

Fleeing persecution in Britain for spreading a blasphemous new religion centered on celibacy, a belief in gender and racial equity, and the concept of a father-mother God (as opposed to a solely father-figure God), Ann Lee and eight of her followers arrived in the New World on this day. By 1776, they had established their first community outside Albany. Despite more persecution in America, 19 prosperous Shaker communities eventually stretched from Maine to Kentucky. Shaker furniture and music continue to enjoy a following to this day, and the Sabbathday Lake Shaker community in Maine is still active.

23. SEPTEMBER 5, 1774

FIRST CONTINENTAL CONGRESS CONVENES

Hoping to find a mutual path forward against unjust treatment by the British, prominent colonists gathered in Philadelphia's Carpenters' Hall on this day, with delegates from every colony except Georgia attending. But their own interests hampered progress. Not until October 20 did they adopt Articles of Association, stipulating that if the Intolerable Acts were not repealed by December 1, the colonies would boycott British goods. The Virginia delegates, which included Patrick Henry, Richard Henry Lee, and George Washington, left a particularly strong impression; John Adams called them "the most spirited and consistent," and a Maryland merchant described them as "haughty Sultans of the South" who "juggled the whole conclave."

24. FEBRUARY 26, 1775

SARAH TARRANT FACES DOWN THE REDCOATS

As tensions between the colonists and Britain ramped up, soldiers marched on to Salem, Massachusetts, to capture the colonial guns and cannons located there. Upon arrival, they found the northern entry to the city, a small drawbridge, partially raised and a rowdy crowd of armed locals waiting to stop them. According to an eyewitness account, once night had fallen and after several tense hours of peaceful standoff, the soldiers were permitted to cross "in a peaceful manner" 275 yards into the town on the British colonel's word of honor. As the soldiers retreated from Salem, nurse Sarah Tarrant yelled down, "Go home and tell your master he has sent you on a fool's errand and has broken the peace of our Sabbath. What! do you think we were born in the woods, to be frightened by owls?" When a British soldier aimed his musket at her, she shouted defiantly, "Fire if you have the courage, but I doubt it!" The man was ordered back into line and the retreat continued.

A future Virginia governor, fiery orator Patrick Henry is perhaps best known for a single line: "Give me liberty or give me death!"

25. MARCH 23, 1775

PATRICK HENRY PREACHES LIBERTY OR DEATH

In what would become a turning point toward revolution, brilliant orator and future Virginia governor Patrick Henry passionately addressed delegates at the Second Virginia Convention, a gathering of influential leaders from the colony. The convention had rejected British rule, and to avoid interference from the royal governor in Williamsburg, it convened at St. John's Church in Richmond. There, the outspoken Henry warned that negotiation with Britain was futile, and that a militia should be raised to defend American liberties. "Is life so dear, or peace so sweet, as to be purchased at the price of chains and slavery? Forbid it, Almighty God!" he thundered. "I know not what course others may take; but as for me, give me liberty or give me death!"

26. APRIL 14, 1775

ABOLITION FINDS A VOICE

The first abolitionist society in America was founded by Philadelphia Quakers, who met in a local tavern on this day to adopt a constitution for "The Society for the Relief of Free Negroes Unlawfully Held in Bondage." The coming revolution hampered the society's activities in the years immediately following, but by the late 1780s, the reorganized Pennsylvania Abolition Society had become a strong antislavery voice in the state, with Benjamin Franklin as its president. Today, the society continues to work to combat racism and improve the lives of African Americans in Pennsylvania.

27. APRIL 18, 1775

"THE BRITISH ARE COMING!" PROVIDES A RALLYING CALL

Joseph Warren, president of the Massachusetts Provincial Congress, received news that British troops, known as regulars, were readying for a march in Boston on this day—probably to Lexington to capture celebrated New England patriots Samuel Adams and John Hancock and on to Concord to capture the colonists' munition stores. Four rode forth that night, including one Paul Revere, to warn the patriots in Lexington and nearby

The French built this New York fort, the British captured it and named it Ticonderoga—and colonial forces overran it in a 1775 attack.

villages. Revere delivered his warning, "The regulars are coming out," around midnight, thus inspiring Longfellow's 1860 epic—but not always factual—poem *Paul Revere's Ride.*

28. APRIL 19, 1775

"THE SHOT HEARD ROUND THE WORLD" IGNITES THE REVOLUTION

Warned by Paul Revere on his night ride that the British were marching on Lexington, local militiamen began converging on the village through the cold early hours before dawn. They were waiting, arms at the ready, with the command not to shoot first. As the British advanced, the local force was ordered by their captain to disperse when a shot suddenly rang out, though who fired it remains unknown to this day. In an instant, the American Revolution became a reality, as redcoat and patriot began the mortal combat that would last for years to come.

LISTEN, MY CHILDREN, AND YOU SHALL HEAR / OF THE MIDNIGHT RIDE OF PAUL REVERE.

Henry Wadsworth Longfellow, *"Paul Revere's Ride" (1860)*

29. APRIL 21, 1775

"GUNPOWDER INCIDENT" BACKFIRES

On this day, Virginia's royal governor, Lord Dunmore, ordered his troops to remove the gunpowder stored in the Williamsburg Magazine, a type of storehouse, and transport it to a waiting British ship. When colonials learned it was gone, they mobilized an armed response. In explanation, the governor said he'd removed it to protect it from a rumored slave rebellion. Few believed him, and one of the disbelievers—the revolutionary firebrand Patrick Henry—called up his local militia, marched on Williamsburg, and encamped there for several months. Dunmore and his family fled the Governor's Palace, never to return. But he was not done with the patriots. Dunmore and his forces soon ignited the Revolution in Virginia.

30. MAY 10, 1775

COLONIALS WIN THEIR FIRST VICTORY

Farmer and military veteran Ethan Allen and his Green Mountain Boys, of what is present-day Vermont, made plans to take the strategic British Fort Ticonderoga on Lake Champlain and its much needed armaments. But when they reached the lakeshore, they found another patriot with the same idea—Connecticut-born Benedict Arnold, who had planned to go it alone against the British. After some tussling for command, Arnold and Allen joined forces. Before dawn on this day, the patriots took the British garrison by surprise, with Arnold demanding that the captain "deliver me the fort instantly … In the name of the great Jehovah and the Continental Congress." The captain complied, and in Philadelphia the Second Continental Congress convened that very day.

31. JUNE 10, 1775

JOHN ADAMS CREATES AN ARMY

Standing before the Second Continental Congress, Adams proposed the establishment of a continental army to officially bring together militiamen who had already taken up arms against the British. Four days later, Adams rose again and put forward Virginian George Washington for commander in chief. This proposal sat poorly with then president of the Continental Congress, John Hancock, who wanted the role for himself. Both of Adams's proposals were eventually accepted, with a unanimous vote for Washington, who assumed the leadership role he would rarely leave again.

32. JUNE 17, 1775

RAGTAG AMERICANS HOLD BUNKER AND BREED'S HILLS

On the evening of June 16, American militiamen began digging and erecting fortifications on Breed's Hill overlooking Boston from the Charlestown Peninsula. The following morning, British troops spotted them and cannonaded the colonial posts for two hours from the water. They then swarmed the peninsula in full British splendor and, as legend has it, the Americans were commanded not to fire "until you see the whites of their eyes." They did as they were ordered and "sustained the Enemy's Attacks with great Bravery and Resolution," as described by 21-year-old militia member Amos Farnsworth. At day's end, the redcoats controlled both Breed's and Bunker Hills—but had suffered casualties of more than a thousand men to the Continentals' 450. The damage to their imperial prestige and expansion of the colonial fighting spirit was incalculable.

33. JUNE 19, 1775

GEORGE WASHINGTON TAKES COMMAND OF THE CONTINENTAL ARMY

On the day before the official documents were signed naming George Washington the general and commander in chief of the newly formed army, he penned a poignant letter to his wife, Martha, saying: "I am now set down to write to you on a subject, which fills me with inexpressible concern … It has been determined in Congress, that the whole Army raised for the defence of the American Cause shall be put under my care, and that it is necessary for me to proceed immediately to Boston to take upon me the command of it." The generalship would prove to require all his fortitude. He would not return to his beloved Mount Vernon home for six years, leaving Martha and his cousin, Lund, to run the estate and plantation.

34. JULY 5, 1775

OLIVE BRANCH PETITION IS ADOPTED

Hoping to explain its position to King George III, the Continental Congress appointed a committee to draft a letter to His Majesty. John Dickinson, a respected delegate and writer, composed most of it, assuring King George that they did not want independence but were loyal subjects who were seeking a peaceful settlement with the crown. They also wrote that, as British citizens, they had the right to self-govern and believed their contributions to the success of the "mother country" should be rewarded with "fair treatment." As Dickinson predicted, the petition went nowhere, with the king refusing even to read it. His

rejection convinced many colonists that the British were not willing to reconcile with them or consider their concerns—and that independence was the only path forward.

John Trumbull's 1786 rendering of the Battle of Bunker Hill depicts the moment that American general Joseph Warren was mortally wounded.

35. JULY 29, 1775

A UNITED CURRENCY DEBUTS

To help pay expenses as they fought the British, the Continental Congress passed a series of resolutions to create a new currency for the United Colonies. On this day, Congress authorized the printing of the first batch of "Continental dollars" and appointed joint treasurers to oversee the currency. Some colonies already had their own paper money, based on different exchange rates. The Continental bills became the first to share a unified exchange and to be used across all 13 colonies. Because Congress lacked the authority to levy taxes to back the currency, it depreciated quickly. The British also circulated counterfeit versions to undermine the Continentals' worth. The expression "not worth a Continental" soon became ubiquitous.

SPOTLIGHT

THE LIBERTY BELL

O

ONE OF THE UNITED STATES' most recognizable symbols of freedom, this iconic bell resounds with lore and legend. Purchased in 1751 to mark the 50th anniversary of Pennsylvania's founding charter, it echoes the founders' principles with this inscription: "Proclaim Liberty throughout all the land unto all the inhabitants thereof" (Leviticus 25:10).

A London foundry cast the bell—made mostly of copper and weighing just over a ton. According to Pennsylvania assemblyman Isaac Norris, the bell had no sooner been installed in the State House steeple on March 10, 1753, when "it was cracked by a stroke of the clapper … as it was hung up to try the sound." The State House bell was melted down and recast by local metalworkers in Philadelphia to improve its durability and tone.

Undocumented legend says the bell was rung in 1776 on July 4—the first Independence Day—and July 8, to herald the first public reading of the Declaration of Independence. From the 1830s, when it became an emblem of the antislavery movement, it was best known as the Liberty Bell. After repairing a crack that appeared in 1843, the bell rang on special occasions and for the final time on February 22, 1846, sounding the anniversary of George Washington's birth. This national symbol of freedom and unity now sits silent at Independence National Historical Park, across the road from Independence Hall in the nation's first capitol, where it once hung. Two other bells are also on view at the historical park: the Bicentennial and Centennial.

The Liberty Bell was last rung ceremonially on February 22, 1846—the anniversary of George Washington's birthday—when it cracked irreparably.

☆ ☆ ☆

IT IS THE VOICE NOT SIMPLY OF A BELL BUT OF A PEOPLE WITH THE ASPIRATIONS AND IDEALS OF HUMAN LIBERTY IN THEIR HEARTS.

Leigh Mitchell Hodges, New York Times Magazine *(1941)*

36. OCTOBER 13, 1775

U.S. NAVY IS BORN

On this day, the Continental Congress appointed an advisory committee to work on protecting American waters from the British—the first step in the long process of creating a real navy. The committee quickly approved plans to supply George Washington, in Boston, with an armed schooner and sloop to capture British supplies. That fall, it passed resolutions to purchase ships and take other actions in naval preparedness: small steps in the face of an enemy with the most formidable navy the world had ever known. Not until the late 1790s did the United States truly begin to build a naval force.

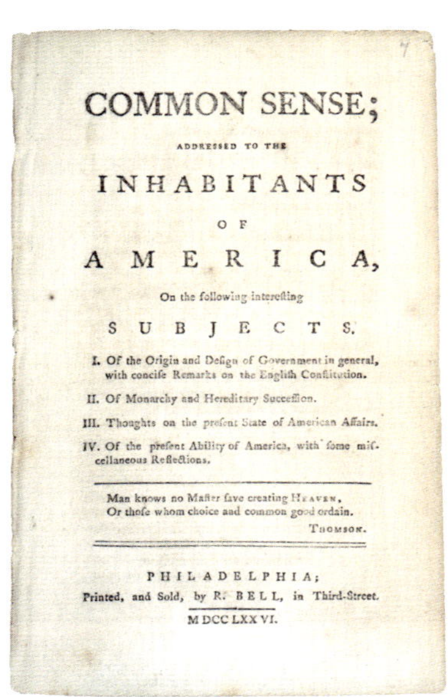

COMMON SENSE;

ADDRESSED TO THE

INHABITANTS

OF

AMERICA,

On the following interesting

SUBJECTS.

I. Of the Origin and Design of Government in general, with concise Remarks on the English Constitution.

II. Of Monarchy and Hereditary Succession.

III. Thoughts on the present State of American Affairs.

IV. Of the present Ability of America, with some miscellaneous Reflections.

Man knows no Master save creating HEAVEN,
Or those whom choice and common good ordain.
THOMSON.

PHILADELPHIA;
Printed, and Sold, by R. BELL, in Third-Street.
MDCCLXXVI.

Thomas Paine wrote such a compelling treatise on American independence that his celebrated manifesto *Common Sense* sold some 120,000 copies within three months.

37. NOVEMBER 7, 1775

LORD DUNMORE BUILDS THE BRITISH ARMY

Hoping to build his forces fighting the patriots in Virginia, the royal governor issued what became known as Lord Dunmore's Proclamation. It declared "all *indented Servants, Negroes,* or others … *free* that are able and willing to bear Arms" for the crown. He eventually created a regiment of 800 formerly enslaved Black individuals. But despite his will to fight, Dunmore realized by the following August that his efforts were futile. He sailed with his troops for Staten Island, where they were absorbed into the British ranks. Throughout the colonies, the chaos caused by conflict allowed many thousands of enslaved people to escape behind British lines to what they hoped would be freedom.

38. DECEMBER 9, 1775

HENRY KNOX PROVIDES REINFORCEMENT TO THE CONTINENTAL ARMY

Dispatched by Gen. George Washington, the 25-year-old Knox, a former bookseller, and his small detachment began loading artillery from Fort Ticonderoga, located in upstate New York, onto boats bound for Boston, where a siege by the British was underway. For the next eight weeks, Knox's sled teams hauled nearly 60 tons of ordnance across 300 miles of frozen lakes, mountains, and marshes, crossing the Hudson River four times and providing the means to break the stalemate with the British. His "noble train of artillery" included dozens of cannons (one weighing 5,000 pounds), heavy mortars, and an immense store of shot and gunpowder—all critical to the Continental Army's success. The British would evacuate Boston three months later.

39. DECEMBER 31, 1775

BATTLE OF QUÉBEC ENDS IN DISASTER

In mid-September 1775, General Washington issued orders to invade Canada, hoping to push out the British and coax French Canadians to the side of the patriots. By mid-November, Continental forces under Gen. Richard Montgomery had taken Montréal from the redcoats. Moving north, they were joined by forces under the command of

Benedict Arnold, who had battled the Maine wilderness to get there. Montgomery found the young Arnold "active, intelligent, and enterprising." On this New Year's Eve, as a blizzard raged, the combined Continental troops attacked well-fortified Québec City. Montgomery died early in the attempt, and Arnold—later infamous for his defection to the British—was wounded. Far from garnering sympathy, the battle further entrenched the British in Canada and turned locals against the American cause.

40. JANUARY 10, 1776

COMMON SENSE MAKES A SPLASH

The fiery manifesto by Founding Father, political thinker, and Englishman Thomas Paine, published in Philadelphia on this day, proclaimed that "the cause of America is, in great measure, the cause of all mankind." The pamphlet, written in plainspoken style, spread quickly through the colonies, igniting patriotic fervor. Paine had arrived in Philadelphia the previous year, a 37-year-old who had left behind both a failed marriage and failed

Fatally shot during Continental forces' failed assault on Québec, Richard Montgomery was the first American general killed in the Revolutionary War.

The Declaration of Independence draft committee was (from left) Robert Livingston, Roger Sherman, John Adams, Thomas Jefferson, and Benjamin Franklin.

business endeavors. One acquaintance found him "coarse and uncouth ... and a disgusting egotist." But prominent Philadelphians Benjamin Rush and Benjamin Franklin saw his potential as a writer and ensured the people of the colonies read his words. Paine quickly became one of the great writers of the Revolution, going on to author *The American Crisis* series.

41. MARCH 31, 1776

ABIGAIL ADAMS TAKES A STAND

As she was struggling to raise their children and keep their farm going while her husband, John, was in Philadelphia on business, Abigail Adams wrote him a passionate letter on this day. "In the new Code of Laws … I desire you would Remember the Ladies, and be more generous and favourable to them than your ancestors," she began. "If perticuliar care and attention is not paid to the Laidies we are determined to foment a Rebelion, and will not hold ourselves bound by any Laws in which we have no voice, or Representation." While her words evoked the circumstances of many in her cohort, her plea went largely unheeded, and she and her peers continued to be denied the power to vote, own property, or manage legal affairs. American women would not gain a full measure of the rights men possessed for almost 200 years.

42. JUNE 7, 1776

LEE RESOLUTION—A PRECURSOR TO INDEPENDENCE—IS INTRODUCED

On this day, the respected Virginia delegate Richard Henry Lee submitted a proclamation to the Second Continental Congress: "These United Colonies are, and of right ought to be, free and independent States" and should form "a plan for confederation" as well as "foreign Alliances." In response, Congress formed three committees, one for each of the three issues that Lee introduced. Anxious to have their constituents weigh in on the Lee Resolution, congressional delegates deferred the vote of approval for weeks as the committees worked toward consensus.

I AM WELL AWARE OF THE TOIL AND BLOOD AND TREASURE, THAT IT WILL COST US TO MAINTAIN THIS DECLARATION.

John Adams, *letter to Abigail Adams (1776)*

43. JUNE 11, 1776

THOMAS JEFFERSON HUNKERS DOWN TO WRITE THE DECLARATION OF INDEPENDENCE

The five-man committee appointed by the Continental Congress to draft the independence declaration called for in the Lee Resolution included John Adams, Benjamin Franklin, and a recently arrived young Virginian named Thomas Jefferson. Jefferson was chosen to do the drafting and, as Adams said, he "brought with him a reputation for literature, science, and a happy talent for composition." Sitting in a rented room at a portable desk of his own design, Jefferson began composing on this day, incorporating Lee's language and other Enlightenment ideas of liberty and equality. Before the month's end, he sent drafts to Adams, then Franklin, both of whom made minor changes before submitting it to Congress for approval.

44. JULY 1, 1776

CAESAR RODNEY RIDES FOR LIBERTY

Caesar Rodney, a Delaware delegate to the Continental Congress, was frail and ill, with much of his face eaten away by cancer. As a result, he was in his Delaware home on this day when he got word that the other two members of his delegation had split their votes on independence. When Rodney, a patriot, learned the next vote on the resolution would take place the following day, he rode 80 miles through the night in a thunderstorm to reach Philadelphia. He arrived just in time to cast his ballot for the cause.

The American smallpox epidemic lasted from 1775 to 1782. Though many people received inoculations, it claimed an estimated 130,000 lives.

45. JULY 2, 1776

SECOND CONTINENTAL CONGRESS VOTES FOR INDEPENDENCE

When Congress adopted part of the Lee Resolution on this day, the United Colonies asserted that they had become free and independent states "absolved from all allegiance to the British Crown, and that all political connection between them … is totally dissolved." As John Adams wrote, "The Second Day of July 1776 will be the most memorable Epocha, in the History of America … It ought to be solemnized with Pomp and Parade, with Shews, Games, Sports, Guns, Bells, Bonfires, and Illuminations from one End of this Continent to the other from this Time forward forever more." Public reaction was mixed, with some favoring independence while others feared chaos.

46. JULY 4, 1776

DECLARATION OF INDEPENDENCE IS ADOPTED

After two days of debating, changing, and removing parts of Thomas Jefferson's initial draft, Congress adopted a final version of the Declaration of Independence on this day (though they had no idea of its true significance at the time). Broadsides were printed and sent out through the colonies, causing public jubilation and emboldening further resistance against British rule. On August 2, delegates began signing a copy engrossed on parchment with the heading "The unanimous Declaration of the thirteen United States of America." John Hancock, president of the Second Continental Congress, boldly signed first. On reading it, Virginian John Page wrote to his friend Jefferson in postscript, "I am highly pleased with your Declaration. God preserve the united States."

47. JULY 8, 1776

ARTICLES OF CONFEDERATION ARE PRESENTED TO CONGRESS

Drafted mostly by Founding Father John Dickinson, who would go on to be known as the "president" of both Delaware and Pennsylvania and "penman of the Revolution," the articles laid out the ways the former colonies could be joined in a very loose confederation. Essentially, the country's first formally adopted rules of governance weren't ratified by the states for another five years. But the name for the new nation used in the document—"the United States of America"—was formally adopted two months later on September 9, 1776.

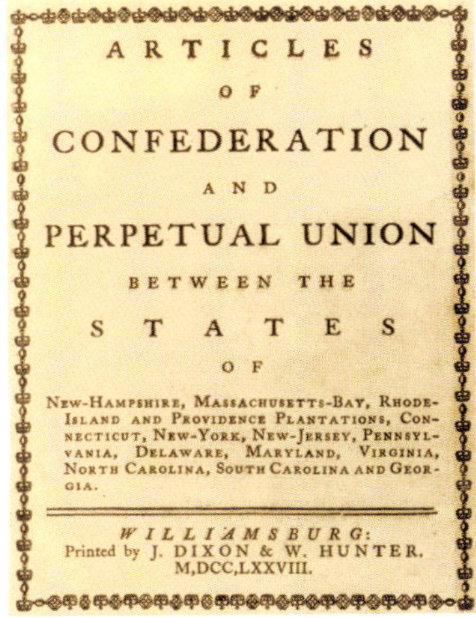

ARTICLES
OF
CONFEDERATION
AND
PERPETUAL UNION
BETWEEN THE
STATES
OF
NEW-HAMPSHIRE, MASSACHUSETTS-BAY, RHODE-ISLAND AND PROVIDENCE PLANTATIONS, CONNECTICUT, NEW-YORK, NEW-JERSEY, PENNSYLVANIA, DELAWARE, MARYLAND, VIRGINIA, NORTH CAROLINA, SOUTH CAROLINA AND GEORGIA.

WILLIAMSBURG:
Printed by J. DIXON & W. HUNTER.
M,DCC,LXXVIII.

The Articles of Confederation laid out basic rules of governance and was the first document to use a new name for the nation: the United States of America.

48. JULY 13, 1776

SMALLPOX BECOMES A DREADED ENEMY

With a smallpox epidemic raging, Abigail Adams wrote to her husband, John, then serving in the Continental Congress in Philadelphia. She had taken their four children to Boston to be inoculated. "Our Little ones stood the opperation Manfully," she wrote. "Such a Spirit of innoculation never before took place; the Town and every House in it, are as full as they can hold." The following February, General Washington ordered that his troops be inoculated, observing that "we should have more to dread [of smallpox] than from the Sword of the Enemy." The epidemic raged on until 1782, killing at least 130,000 and leaving many more scarred from the "pox."

49. AUGUST 30, 1776

HEAVY FOG SAFEGUARDS WASHINGTON'S ARMY

Having lost the days-long Battle of Long Island, the Continental Army found themselves surrounded in Brooklyn by the British. General Washington remained resolute: Under cover of night, he ordered his men ferried across the East River. But most had not yet crossed as the sun rose. Suddenly, a thick fog descended, obscuring the river, allowing all 9,000 Continentals to cross to safety in Manhattan. "Less than an hour after," one captain recalled, "the fog having dispersed, the enemy was visible on the shore we had left." Weather would not always be on the Americans' side, but in this instance, it saved the Revolution.

Known for flouting George Washington's orders, Gen. Charles Lee was belatedly following one when the British took him prisoner.

50. SEPTEMBER 9, 1776

JOHN ADAMS AND BENJAMIN FRANKLIN TAKE A ROAD TRIP

Dispatched by the Continental Congress to meet with Royal Navy admiral Richard Howe, who wanted to negotiate an end to the war, the two patriotic leaders embarked on a dangerous trip to Staten Island. On the way, they shared a bed in a New Jersey inn. Despite the critical assignment, the men argued over whether to keep the single window in their room open, with Franklin in favor and Adams against. Franklin then began to harangue Adams "upon Air and cold and Respiration and Perspiration." Adams recounted that he was "so much amused that I soon fell asleep, and left him and his Philosophy together."

51. SEPTEMBER 22, 1776

NATHAN HALE IS HANGED

The 21-year-old captain in the Continental Army had volunteered to go behind enemy lines in occupied New York to report on British troop movements. When a mysterious fire engulfed much of the tip of Manhattan the night of September 20, Hale and a hundred other Americans suspected of spying were rounded up. Recognized as a patriot by a British officer, Hale was executed for being a spy. It is said that as he was about to be hanged, Hale quoted lines from *Cato,* a popular play about a Roman statesman who resisted Julius Caesar and killed himself rather than submit to tyranny. History remembers Hale's words as his own: "I regret that I have but one life to lose for my country."

52. NOVEMBER 18, 1776

FIRST NATIONAL LOTTERY IS ESTABLISHED

The colonies—now states—had run successful lotteries for decades, and Congress hoped to generate funds the same way to support the cost of war. On this day, it designated four classes within the lottery, each with 100,000 tickets, and expected to generate some $1,500,000. But slow ticket sales and the fluctuation in the value of the Continental dollar led to woeful results, with less than $100,000 landing in federal coffers.

THE TIME IS NOW NEAR AT HAND WHICH MUST PROBABLY DETERMINE WHETHER AMERICANS ARE TO BE, FREEMEN, OR SLAVES ... THE FATE OF UNBORN MILLIONS WILL NOW DEPEND, UNDER GOD, ON THE COURAGE AND CONDUCT OF THIS ARMY.

George Washington, *general orders (1776)*

53. NOVEMBER 20, 1776

GEORGE WASHINGTON FEARS DEFEAT

On November 16, the British had launched 8,000 men at strategic Fort Washington overlooking the Hudson. By that afternoon, they had taken the fort, its armaments, and 2,800 remaining Continental soldiers—irreplaceable losses. On this day, the Americans also abandoned Fort Lee, across the Hudson from Fort Washington. New York was now under British control, and General Washington's depleted army was on the run into New Jersey. Even his own senior officers were beginning to doubt Washington's ability to command. His close aide, Joseph Reed, worried about the general's "indecisive mind … how often I have lamented it in this campaign."

54. DECEMBER 7, 1776

VIRGINIA CLAIMS KENTUCKY TERRITORY

In 1775, a group of land speculators formed the Transylvania Company to sell tracts of wilderness land rights that they had recently purchased from the Cherokee. The 20 million acres spanned the area north of the Cumberland River and southeast of the Ohio River. The legislature of the territory's Virginian neighbors to the east had other ideas for this rich region. On this day, it created Kentucky County, ignoring the company's claims to the land. Kentucky remained a part of Virginia until June 1, 1792, when it became the 15th state.

55. DECEMBER 13, 1776

GEN. CHARLES LEE IS CAPTURED

Once a respected British officer, Lee was General Washington's second-in-command in the Continental Army. Yet through the perilous fall of 1776, the obstreperous general refused to bring his New York forces to Washington's aid in New Jersey. Finally, he marched forth, straying from the safety of his army to enjoy the company of a lady overnight at

Widow White's Tavern in Basking Ridge. On the morning of this day, British dragoons surrounded the inn and took Lee prisoner, carrying him off "in high triumph, and with every Mark of Indignity—not even suffering him to get his Hat." Released in a prisoner exchange in the spring of 1778, Lee was reinstated as a Continental commander. He disgraced himself for a final time by his lackadaisical performance at the Battle of Monmouth two months after his release.

56. DECEMBER 26, 1776

WASHINGTON CROSSES THE DELAWARE

In a move on Christmas night that would either end the Revolution or keep it alive, General Washington led 2,400 men, dozens of horses, and 18 cannons across the Delaware River by boat as a nor'easter churned the ice-chunked waters and a snowstorm whipped at the men's faces and, as one soldier put it, "blew a perfect hurricane." By 3 a.m. on this day, they had all made it across. By 9 a.m., they had overcome the Hessian mercenaries, German soldiers employed by the British, in Trenton, New Jersey. Washington's password for the night's march was "victory or death." Without success at Trenton, the artillery and supplies acquired and confidence they inspired, the momentum the Revolution needed to succeed would have been lost.

57. MAY 20, 1777

TREATY OF DEWITT'S CORNER IS ADOPTED

On this day, delegates from the Lower Cherokee Nation and white officials signed a treaty at this South Carolina trading post. The peace agreement allotted almost all Cherokee lands in the state to the Americans. For the past year, the British had been inciting Indigenous peoples along the western frontier to attack white settlers as a way to punish the colonists for the Revolution. These attacks led to bloody conflict and, in the end, the Indigenous peoples suffered the most, with the wide destruction of towns and fields, loss of land, and displacement of Native communities through bloodshed and exploitative contracts such as this.

58. JUNE 13, 1777

MARQUIS DE LAFAYETTE ARRIVES IN AMERICA

On this day, the 19-year-old nobleman and a handful of other French volunteers landed in South Carolina, then trekked hundreds of miles north to Philadelphia, "often sleeping in the woods, starving, prostrated by the heat," according to one member of the traveling party. Already a major general in France, Lafayette had become captivated by the American Revolution and had actually bought the ship that transported him and his volunteers across the Atlantic. But when he finally met George Washington, the general was initially unimpressed with the arrogant French volunteer, as many of them were clamoring to join the Revolution. Lafayette persisted and soon became one of Washington's most trusted officers.

59. JULY 4, 1777

FIREWORKS AND BONFIRES LIGHT UP THE FOURTH

One year after the Declaration of Independence was adopted, Philadelphia and Boston became the first cities to officially celebrate the anniversary of the country's birth. The *Pennsylvania Evening Post* described "demonstrations of joy and festivity … The evening was closed with the ringing of bells and … a grand exhibition of fireworks … the city was beautifully illuminated." The Fourth of July would not become an official federal holiday until 1938.

60. JULY 24, 1777

COLONIAL WOMEN TAKE ON INFLATION

Angered by merchants hoarding and overcharging for sugar, coffee, and flour, people across New England began staging food riots. Abigail Adams described how, on this day, as many as a hundred women in Boston "assembled with a cart and trucks, marched down

Depicted in a 19th-century print, Gen. George Washington's family bids adieu to the Marquis de Lafayette after his visit to his friend and ally at Mount Vernon.

to the warehouse [of a coffee and sugar merchant] and demanded the keys." When the merchant refused, one woman "seized him by his neck and tossed him into the cart. Upon his finding no quarter, he delivered the keys." The women loaded up the goods. But before carting them away, rumor had it, they spanked the merchant, as a "large concourse of Men stood amazd."

61. SEPTEMBER 19, 1777

BATTLE OF SARATOGA BEGINS

All summer, a huge British Army under Gen. "Gentleman Johnny" Burgoyne had been marching south from Canada, determined to end the Revolution once and for all. When they at last faced off on this day against a major Continental force south of Saratoga, New York, the conflict was fierce but inconclusive. Having lost a significant number of men, the British dug in, licked their wounds, and waited for reinforcements, even as they ran short of supplies. Finally, they struck again on October 7—and, as in the first skirmish, the hero of the day was American general Benedict Arnold. Defeated, Burgoyne surrendered on October 17, turning the tide of war—and the opinions of the European powers, which now took America's fighting ability seriously.

In a letter to her husband, John, Abigail Adams recounted the looting of a Boston store that sold overpriced goods, one of many food riots aimed at greedy colonial merchants.

62. SEPTEMBER 26, 1777

THE BRITISH MARCH INTO PHILADELPHIA

General Washington had tried to stop the enemy's advance before the redcoats reached the Continental capital—but on September 11, he lost to the British at the Battle of Brandywine, southwest of the city. After sustaining significant losses, Washington and his troops retreated east. Soon after, Washington dispatched his aide, Alexander Hamilton, to warn Congress and Philadelphians that Richard Howe's army was on the way. The mission was a success; all members of Congress had evacuated by the time the redcoats took control of the United States capital on this day. The occupation proved to be short-lived and inconsequential to the Revolutionary cause.

63. DECEMBER 19, 1777

CONTINENTAL ARMY ENCAMPS AT VALLEY FORGE

On this day, General Washington's army, made up of disparate colonial militias and their camp followers, limped into a hilly, wooded area nearly 20 miles northwest of British-occupied Philadelphia to set up winter quarters. The troops—hungry, exhausted, and many wounded—cobbled together small log huts, cramming perhaps a dozen men into each. Starvation, cold, and disease plagued them through that historic winter. Martha Washington joined her husband there in February, and as one camp dweller observed, "Every fair day she might be seen, with basket in hand ... going among the keenest and most needy sufferers and giving all the comforts to them in her power."

Through a frigid winter at Valley Forge, Pennsylvania, George Washington's troops held on despite constant hunger and lingering injuries.

64. JANUARY 20, 1778

JAMES COOK ENCOUNTERS THE HAWAIIAN ISLANDS

Captain Cook, a renowned explorer, had set sail from England in July 1776 on his third Pacific voyage. His crew spotted the island of Oahu on January 18, 1778, but sailed on. Forty-eight hours later, Kauai came into view, and Cook's H.M.S. *Resolution* and H.M.S. *Discovery* anchored offshore on this day. His ships were probably the first European ones Native Hawaiians saw, and the crewmen the first Europeans they encountered. Cook and his men established friendly relations with the local villagers and leaders, but when they returned a year later, those relations soured. On February 14, 1779, after nearly a month of hospitality on the Big Island, Cook attempted to kidnap a ruling chief, referred to locally as a king. Thousands confronted Cook and his men, igniting a skirmish that ended in Cook's death and dismemberment. Hawaii would become the country's 50th state in 1959.

Prussian Baron Friedrich Wilhelm von Steuben helped turn the Continental Army from a ragtag band of fighters into a disciplined force.

65. FEBRUARY 6, 1778

AMERICA'S FIRST MILITARY TREATY IS ADOPTED

Thanks to the diplomatic finesse of Benjamin Franklin, the French government and its new young king Louis XVI finally agreed to sign a formal alliance with the United States on this day. What would become known as the Treaty of Alliance proved decisive, bringing France and its might into the war on the side of the Revolution. Congress approved the treaty three months later, and French troops joined the patriotic forces in midsummer.

66. FEBRUARY 17, 1778

JOHN ADAMS AND JOHN QUINCY ADAMS SET SAIL FOR PARIS

The newly appointed American minister to France and his 10-year-old son had never been on a large ship when they set sail aboard the frigate *Boston*. The nearly seven-week voyage was an odyssey, filled with stormy seas, intense illness, and battles with the British and privateers. When they finally arrived in France, Adams discovered that his mission—to enlist the French as allies against the British—was moot, thanks to the recent Treaty of Alliance signed the month prior. Nevertheless, John and John Quincy—both later American presidents—were deeply affected by their time in Europe—that "great Theater of Arts, Sciences, Commerce and War."

67. FEBRUARY 23, 1778

FRIEDRICH WILHELM VON STEUBEN ARRIVES AT VALLEY FORGE

A Prussian baron and high-placed officer in its army during the Seven Years' War, Steuben soon captivated George Washington and his starving troops with his imposing size and military bearing. Using salty language, he taught Washington's men the art of military drill and discipline. His training and philosophy spread through the camp, transforming the Continental Army into a true fighting force. Steuben continued as a trusted officer in Washington's army until war's end. Though he disliked what he saw as American arrogance and lamented undertaking "the defense of a country where every farmer is a general," he was responsible for the "Blue Book" of regulations the U.S. Army used until 1814. Steuben eventually bought a farm in New York's Mohawk Valley and ended his days there.

WE ARE ALL IN FINE SPIRITS AND HAVE GOOD CROPS GROWING. WE INTEND TO FIGHT HARD IN ORDER TO SECURE THEM.

Daniel Boone *(1778)*

68. MAY 15, 1778

ONEIDA AND TUSCARORA OFFER AID TO THE CONTINENTAL ARMY

On this day, at the invitation of George Washington, some 50 warriors from the two great tribes arrived at Valley Forge. Washington hoped they could help stop supplies and intelligence from getting into the hands of British in the area, enabling the Continentals to counter the increasing number of enemy raids. The Native delegation brought along dozens of baskets filled with dried white corn, and Polly Cooper, an Oneida woman, taught the starving Americans how to prepare it. Legend has it that in gratitude for her work, Martha Washington presented her with a black shawl.

69. JUNE 20, 1778

DANIEL BOONE PROTECTS FORT BOONESBOROUGH

Indigenous attacks against white settlers living along the Kentucky River had been on the rise since 1777. Many settlers fled to Fort Boonesborough, named for its leader, Daniel Boone. Beginning in April of that year, Shawnee chief Blackfish led a series of failed attacks on the fort. In February 1778, the Shawnee took Boone captive while he was out hunting. Overhearing plans for a new attack on Boonesborough in June, Boone managed to sneak away and reach the fort on this day, giving advance warning. Three months later, the British-backed Shawnee tried again, but their 10-day siege of the fort also ended in failure.

SPOTLIGHT

GRAND OL' FLAG

PHILADELPHIA SEAMSTRESS BETSY ROSS had a few ideas when the statesmen arrived with a sketch of a flag, so the legend goes. She noted the 13 stripes, alternating red and white, and the 13 white stars on a blue background. But in the drawing that Gen. George Washington brought, the stars were six-pointed; perhaps five-pointed instead, Ross suggested, and arranged in a circle?

So goes the creation story, passed down by Ross' descendants, of the national flag that the Continental Congress approved in 1777 on June 14 (now commemorated as Flag Day). The number 13 represented the young Union's states—so after Kentucky and Vermont were admitted in 1794, the flag was redesigned with 15 stripes and 15 stars.

That's the version that the commander of Baltimore's Fort McHenry wanted visible for miles during the War of 1812, so he ordered one 30 feet by 42 feet—so large that the only place seamstresses could piece it together was a brewery floor. After U.S. forces held the fort through a 25-hour bombardment, the British fleet withdrew; a lawyer named Francis Scott Key saw the flag still waving and described the scene in verse.

What remains of the flag Key christened "the star-spangled banner" is now meticulously preserved at the Smithsonian's National Museum of American History. By law last revised in 1959, U.S. flags have 13 stripes honoring the original colonies, with the option to add "as many stars … as there are States."

'TIS THE STAR-SPANGLED BANNER—O LONG MAY IT WAVE / O'ER THE LAND OF THE FREE AND THE HOME OF THE BRAVE!

Francis Scott Key, *original lyrics of "The Star-Spangled Banner" (1814)*

Makers of the first U.S. flags placed the 13 stars in a design they chose. By 1912, when federal law set a pattern, there were 48 stars and states.

70. JUNE 28, 1778

MOLLY PITCHER CHARGES INTO THE BREACH

On this fiercely hot day, the longest battle of the Revolution raged around Monmouth, New Jersey. The Continentals and George Washington emerged victorious, restoring the general's reputation after a number of defeats. But the encounter also forged a new reputation. Mary Ludwig Hays had followed her husband, William, into war, laundering and cooking for his unit. Described by fellow soldiers as a pregnant 22-year-old with incredible courage who could curse as well as any of the men, she became known as "Molly Pitcher" for the pitchers of water she hauled to wounded men. When William collapsed from heatstroke, she took his place at the cannon, firing on the enemy with great skill and establishing herself as a heroine of the Revolution.

71. AUGUST 8, 1778

AN ALLIED ATTACK MISFIRES

America's first joint military operation with their French allies was focused on the British garrison at Newport, Rhode Island. Finally in American waters, the French fleet, commanded by Adm. Charles-Hector, comte d'Estaing, would attack from the sea, while Gen. John Sullivan would lead the Continentals in a land attack. But on this day, Sullivan advanced 24 hours early—and worse still, a large British fleet suddenly appeared. Two days later, a fierce storm blew up, forcing an end to naval operations. D'Estaing sailed to Boston for repairs, but American generals sent letters accusing him of betrayal. In early November, d'Estaing sailed away, preferring to fight the British in the Caribbean.

72. OCTOBER 12, 1778

CONTINENTAL CONGRESS PROHIBITS FUN

Colonists had long enjoyed gambling, sports, theater, and various card games. But Congress wanted to curtail such frivolities during wartime, believing they would prevent the unity of purpose that was required. "Whereas true religion and good morals are the only solid foundations of public liberty and happiness," it proclaimed on this day, states should suppress "theatrical entertainments, horse racing, gaming, and such other diversions as are productive of idleness, dissipation, and a general depravity of principles and manners." A second injunction was passed days later, deeming anyone who acted, promoted, encouraged, or attended such plays "accordingly dismissed."

73. DECEMBER 29, 1778

THE WAR MOVES SOUTH

On this day, the British quickly took the poorly defended city of Savannah. The small Georgia river town was no great prize at the time, but it offered the British a foothold in the South with the larger city of Charleston, South Carolina, an easy march away. Since the first shots fired at Lexington in 1775, the Revolution had been fought mostly in New

England and the mid-Atlantic. With the battle in the North effectively stalemated, some 3,000 redcoats sailed from New York in late November and were established off the coast of Georgia within a month. Britain's Southern Strategy relied heavily on enlisting the many loyalists in the South, offering freedom to any enslaved peoples who fought for them.

74. FEBRUARY 18, 1779

INTRIGUE REIGNS AT THE GRAND ALLIANCE BALL

Hosted by Gen. Henry Knox and his wife, Lucy, on the first anniversary of the Treaty of Alliance with France, this grand event was held on a New Jersey estate and attended by some 400 people. It opened with George Washington dancing with Lucy Knox, a woman known for her good humor, judgment, and extravagant, Marie Antoinette-style hairdos. General Washington famously loved dancing, but his wife, Martha, did not. Knox later reported in a letter that Washington danced that night with the beautiful young Caty Greene, wife of Gen. Nathanael Greene, for three hours without pause.

Molly Pitcher earned the respect of all those around her during the Battle of Monmouth, when she helmed a cannon during combat.

Benedict Arnold's second wife, Margaret "Peggy" Shippen, and their daughter Sophia, 1787

75. APRIL 8, 1779

BENEDICT ARNOLD GETS MARRIED

Arnold's union with the beguiling Philadelphia loyalist Margaret "Peggy" Shippen marked the beginning of a major shift in allegiance for one of America's prominent generals. Admired as a fighter but distrusted for his ethics, Arnold had been appointed military governor of Philadelphia: both the seat of independence and a hotbed of loyalists. The arrogant Arnold had become disillusioned with the Revolution and by what he perceived as a lack of respect by Continental leaders for his accomplishments. Still part of George Washington's inner circle (even as he questioned the American experiment), plagued by a politically motivated investigation into his character, and deeply in debt, Arnold was an easy target for Peggy's close friend, the British spymaster John André. The fallout from this encounter made Benedict Arnold's name synonymous with betrayal to this day.

76. AUGUST 29, 1779

BATTLE OF NEWTOWN WREAKS HAVOC

Under orders from George Washington to achieve "total destruction and devastation" of the Haudenosaunee (Iroquois) settlements, Gen. John Sullivan and his troops attacked this village near present-day Elmira, New York. The consequences of this minor Continental victory for the deflated redcoats and Haudenosaunee allies of the British (the Mohawk, Onondaga, Cayuga, and Seneca) were significant. As ordered, Sullivan burned the more than 40 Haudenosaunee villages, destroying their crops and stores of grain. This campaign earned Washington the title of "Town-destroyer" among the Seneca Nation. Many refugees fled to Canada; they continued to launch retaliatory, if ineffective, raids against the American frontier throughout the remainder of the war.

77. SEPTEMBER 6, 1779

PAUL REVERE IS ARRESTED

When a disastrous failed attack on the British in Castine, then part of Massachusetts (now Maine), ended in a rout, Revere, a lieutenant colonel in the Massachusetts militia, was one of the officers accused of creating the debacle. Placed under house arrest for insubordination, he suffered "every disgrace that the malice of my enemies can invent"—though in fact he had a reputation of being high-handed with both his troops and other officers. Hoping to clear his name, Revere pressed for a court-martial hearing; that wouldn't happen until 1782, when the former silversmith was acquitted of all charges of disobeying orders.

YANKEES DO NOT HAUL DOWN THEIR COLORS TILL THEY ARE FAIRLY BEATEN.

John Paul Jones, *Continental Navy captain (1779)*

78. SEPTEMBER 23, 1779

A NAVAL BATTLE FOR THE AGES PROVES AMERICAN METTLE

In one of the finest moments in U.S. naval history, the much outgunned *Bonhomme Richard* captured the British man-of-war *Serapis* off the British coast in a feat that defied all odds. The *Richard,* "an old Indiaman, clumsy and crank, smelling strongly of the savor of tea, cloves, and arrack," was captained by John Paul Jones, an officer in the Continental Navy; he had already proved himself a wily strategist in raids along the British coast. During the nearly four-hour battle with the formidable, 44-gun *Serapis,* Jones's badly damaged ship managed to stay afloat—in part because he lashed together the two entangled ships, declaring famously, if perhaps apocryphally, "I have not yet begun to fight!"

79. FEBRUARY 11, 1780

BRITISH ATTEMPT TO KIDNAP GEORGE WASHINGTON

From their position in New York, a contingent of some 300 British troops crossed the frozen Hudson River on this day and stealthily headed for General Washington's winter headquarters in Morristown, New Jersey. But the deep snows of that brutal winter thwarted their progress. Though the kidnap plot failed, a fellow general warned Washington that "there is not a sufficient body of troops near enough to render you secure." Washington ordered some increased patrols, but his focus remained mostly on his freezing, starving army—and in fact no further kidnapping attempts were forthcoming.

Approaching by land at Charleston, South Carolina, instead of its seaward side, the British captured the city from the Continental Army.

80. MARCH 1, 1780

PENNSYLVANIA PASSES GRADUAL ABOLITION ACT

Though the act, ratified on this day, did not free enslaved people by default, it went further than previous laws in other states and is seen as the first extensive abolition legislation in the Americas. It stated that people born to an enslaved mother after the act's passage would become free when they reached 28 years of age. Those already enslaved would remain so unless their enslavers failed to register them annually. It also banned the importation of more enslaved people and created other obstacles to slavery. The bill passed 34 to 21 and inspired other northern states to pass similar bills in the years to come.

81. MAY 4, 1780

AMERICAN ACADEMY OF ARTS AND SCIENCES IS FOUNDED

The goal of this prestigious academic organization, chartered by the Massachusetts legislature, was "to cultivate every art and science which may tend to advance the interest, honor, dignity, and happiness of a free, independent, and virtuous people." The brainchild of John Adams, the academy held its first meeting in Harvard's Philosophy Chamber on May 30; charter members included Adams, Benjamin Franklin, George

Washington, and John Hancock. To this day, it continues to "address critical challenges facing our global society."

82. MAY 12, 1780

CHARLESTON SURRENDERS TO THE BRITISH

The richest city in America finally fell to the British on this day after a siege that had begun weeks before. Gen. George Washington had urged his commander there, Maj. Gen. Benjamin Lincoln, to abandon the city, but the citizenry convinced Lincoln to keep his forces in place. On May 11, the British began firing heated shells that set fire to parts of the town, and the Continentals saw no other option but surrender. Some 2,500 much needed American soldiers were captured, and the victory brought many South Carolinians to the loyalist side.

83. MAY 19, 1780

A "DARK DAY" IN NEW ENGLAND DAWNS

Morning skies turned black, and darkness fell over the land from Canada to New Jersey. Birds grew quiet, and people prayed. Was this the end of the world? A Connecticut councilman wasn't hedging his bets. He opposed adjourning the council meeting on this day, noting, "The day of judgment is either approaching, or it is not. If it is not, there is no cause for an adjournment; if it is, I choose to be found doing my duty." Scientists now believe the day-long darkness was the result of thick smoke from Canadian wildfires.

John Adams conceived the idea of the American Academy of Arts and Sciences, whose charter members included other Founding Fathers.

84. JULY 11, 1780

A FRENCH SQUADRON ARRIVES IN AMERICA

The promised French forces, long awaited by the Americans, finally arrived at Narragansett Bay off Newport, Rhode Island, on this day, led by the battle-seasoned Comte de Rochambeau. "I have, sir, the greatest desire to present my respects to your Excellency," Rochambeau wrote to Gen. George Washington, "and to give you Verbally fresh assurances of the Veneration that I have for your Excellency." After meeting the count, Washington was "confirmed by what I have seen myself, in the high opinion of his abilities and personal qualities." Despite their mutual regard, Rochambeau fortunately did not succumb to Washington's pressure to launch a joint attack on the British in New York. A bigger allied victory was to come.

85. SEPTEMBER 25, 1780

BENEDICT ARNOLD COMMITS TREASON

Gen. George Washington had appointed Benedict Arnold, at Arnold's urging, commander of the strategic West Point garrison on the Hudson River. On this day, Washington, accompanied by the Marquis de Lafayette and Alexander Hamilton, stopped at the nearby

Arnold mansion for a visit with the respected commander. But one of Arnold's aides explained that he had been called to the garrison. In fact, he had fled to the British, knowing that his treason was about to be exposed. That afternoon, Washington learned that Arnold had given British spymaster John André a map of West Point's fortifications, a travel pass behind American lines, and notes from a war council meeting. "Arnold has betrayed us!" Washington told Hamilton, "Whom can we trust now?"

86. JANUARY 5, 1781

RICHMOND FALLS TO THE BRITISH

Distraught, Governor Thomas Jefferson had virtually no soldiers to defend the new Virginia capital when Benedict Arnold, now a British commander after his betrayal of the Continental cause, sailed up the James River to take his shot. Arnold's 1,600 troops, mostly loyalists, landed at nearby Westover Plantation on January 4; in response, Jefferson ordered all military supplies removed from Richmond to keep them out of British hands. Then, he fled. On this day, Arnold marched into the undefended city and soon wrote to Jefferson, demanding the military supplies and stores of tobacco in exchange for sparing the capital. When Jefferson refused, Arnold put Richmond to the torch.

When British forces surrendered to the Americans and French at Yorktown, Virginia, the major fighting of the Revolutionary War was concluded.

87. MARCH 1, 1781

ARTICLES OF CONFEDERATION ARE RATIFIED

Sometimes called the first constitution, this "league of friendship" among the newly minted states was adopted on November 15, 1777, by the Second Continental Congress, then sent to the states for ratification. But disputes over territorial boundaries, voting, and representation would delay the process for years. The final state to hold out, Maryland, ratified on this day. But the articles resulted in a weak and ineffective alliance in which states were more competitors than allies in growing and governing the new nation.

88. JUNE 3, 1781

JACK JOUETT TAKES A RIDE

As the British continued to threaten Richmond, Virginia, Governor Thomas Jefferson and state legislators relocated to Charlottesville, Virginia. But British commander Banastre Tarleton and his dragoons went after them. When they stopped at Cuckoo Tavern, about 40 miles from Charlottesville, 26-year-old militiaman Jack Jouett spotted them. Mounting up, he rode all through this night to reach Monticello the next morning. Warned by Jouett of Tarleton's approach, most legislators fled to Staunton—Jefferson was just riding away from Monticello as Tarleton pounded onto the grounds. Legislator Daniel Boone was not so lucky and was briefly taken captive. In Virginia, Jouett's ride is now legendary as an act of courage.

WE ARE AT THE END OF OUR TETHER, & THAT NOW OR NEVER OUR DELIVERANCE MUST COME.

George Washington *(1781)*

89. AUGUST 22, 1781

"MUM BETT" WINS HER FREEDOM

After only a day of deliberations, a jury in western Massachusetts ruled that an enslaved woman owned by a prominent Berkshire family should be freed. Known as "Mum Bett" by her often cruel owners, she had overheard the observation "that all people were born free and equal." Believing this could apply to her, she sought out a local lawyer, who took her case. After winning her freedom, she changed her name to Elizabeth Freeman. Two years later, Massachusetts outlawed slavery. Freeman's gravestone reads: "She could neither read nor write, yet in her own sphere she had no superior or equal."

90. OCTOBER 19, 1781

THE BRITISH SURRENDER AT YORKTOWN

After a relentless American siege that began on October 9, British general Charles Cornwallis tried and failed to evacuate his troops across the York River. On October 17, the British flew a white flag to signal a request for negotiations. On this day, a line of redcoats, flanked by American and French soldiers, marched to a field outside the small port town and laid down their arms as the American band played "Yankee Doodle." Cornwallis did not attend, "obeying sensations which his great character ought to have stifled,"

Gen. Henry Lee declared. The American victory at Yorktown marked the beginning of the end of the War of Independence.

91. NOVEMBER 5, 1781

MARTHA WASHINGTON LOSES HER LAST CHILD

Twenty-six-year-old John Parke Custis was the only surviving child of Martha Washington's first marriage (she and George never had children of their own). Raised at Mount Vernon, "Jacky" had four surviving children of his own when he finally convinced General Washington to allow him to serve as a civilian aide-de-camp during the final push at Yorktown. Disease was rife among the troops there, and just weeks after the British surrender, Custis died of "camp fever"—probably typhoid. Two of his children, Nelly and George, came to live at Mount Vernon after their father's death.

92. MAY 20, 1782

THOMAS JEFFERSON IS "CURED" OF POLITICS

Feeling that his governorship of Virginia had ended badly, Thomas Jefferson wrote to his friend James Monroe, declaring "his determination to retire from public employment" as he is "thoroughly cured of every principle of political ambition … I am persuaded that having hitherto dedicated to [the public] the whole of the active and useful part of my life, I shall be permitted to pass the rest in mental quiet." His beloved wife, Martha, was dangerously ill, and a few months later she died, leaving Jefferson—a devoted but exacting father—to raise their two young daughters alone.

DEBORAH SAMPSON.
Published by H. Mann 1797

After about a year and a half serving as a man in the Continental Army, Deborah Sampson was unmasked. She was honorably discharged.

93. MAY 23, 1782

DEBORAH SAMPSON ENLISTS IN THE CONTINENTAL ARMY

On this day, a 21-year-old former indentured servant named Deborah Sampson enlisted in the Continental Army, using the alias Robert Shurtliff. Nearly a year and a half later, a doctor discovered her gender when she fell ill with fever. Because she had served well and been wounded in a skirmish with loyalists, Sampson was honorably discharged. In 1805, after gaining support from patriot Paul Revere, she was granted a pension from the government: the first woman to gain this privilege. She was also the first woman to launch a lecture tour, which she conducted through several northern states in 1802–03.

94. JUNE 20, 1782

CONGRESS APPROVES DESIGN FOR THE GREAT SEAL OF THE UNITED STATES

The plan to produce an official seal for the nation was a long time coming. The Continental Congress had appointed a commission to create one on July 4, 1776, but submissions from three different commissions were rejected. But on this day, a heraldic design featuring an eagle holding a banner reading E PLURIBUS UNUM—OUT OF MANY, ONE—was adopted. The obverse image of the seal is used to stamp official documents and acts as a kind of national coat of arms, adorning passports, military buttons, and doorways of embassies and other government buildings.

95. MAY 13, 1783

SOCIETY OF THE CINCINNATI IS FOUNDED

One of the nation's oldest hereditary organizations, the society was established by Continental Army officers encamped at Newburgh, New York, "to perpetuate … the remembrance of this vast event [the Revolutionary War]" and "the mutual friendships which have been formed under the pressure of common danger." Named for wartime Roman leader Lucius Quinctius Cincinnatus, who gave up his power to return to his farm and embody civic virtue, the group was nonetheless accused by some of encouraging elitism and acting as a shadow government. Elected as its first president, George Washington attempted to quell criticism by making reforms to the exclusive society—most importantly by objecting to hereditary membership and national meetings.

96. SEPTEMBER 3, 1783

TREATY OF PARIS IS ADOPTED

After more than a year of talks among British, U.S., Spanish, and French emissaries, this crucial treaty between the United States and Britain was signed at the residence of the

U.S. officials rejected several Great Seal designs before choosing one bearing the Latin phrase *E pluribus unum*—Out of many, one.

Thomas Paine said he was a "farmer of thoughts," not land—but in thanks for his patriotic writing, he was deeded 277 acres in New York.

British negotiator. It began with the sanguine promise "to forget all past Misunderstandings and Differences that have unhappily interrupted [our] good Correspondence and Friendship," and included generous boundaries for the United States, which would allow for western expansion. Yet the American ministers—John Adams, John Jay, and an ailing Benjamin Franklin—knew Britain hoped to control U.S. trade relations and its importance as an independent country. They would be proved right.

97. NOVEMBER 25, 1783

NEW YORK CITY IS FREE AT LAST

After occupying New York for seven years, the British finally set sail on this chilly afternoon, which would later become known as Evacuation Day. George Washington, with Governor George Clinton beside him and American troops marching behind, rode triumphantly into the city as crowds cheered or joined the procession. On December 4, Continental officers gathered downtown at Fraunces Tavern. With tears in his eyes, Washington addressed them with these words: "With a heart full of love and gratitude, I now take leave of you. I most devoutly wish that your latter days may be as prosperous and happy as your former ones have been glorious and honorable."

98. FEBRUARY 22, 1784

EMPRESS OF CHINA SETS SAIL

Chartered by the Continental Congress and funded by American financiers, the three-masted schooner broke free of ice in the Hudson and set sail on this day for Canton (Guangzhou), China, carrying some 30 tons of ginseng root—much prized for its medicinal value by the Chinese—along with cotton, lead, and furs. By late August, the *Empress* was offshore of Canton, where it stayed for more than four months. It returned to New York in May 1785 with Chinese porcelain, tea, and other coveted goods. The voyage boosted national pride and opened the China trade.

99. JUNE 16, 1784

THOMAS PAINE RECEIVES A GIFT OF LAND

New York State, grateful for Paine's inspiring writings during the Revolution, presented him with a 277-acre farm outside New Rochelle that a fleeing loyalist had abandoned. An urbanite by nature, Paine had declared himself not a farmer but a "farmer of thoughts." He spent the coming decade in England and France, writing *Rights of Man* and *The Age of Reason.* While in Paris, Paine objected to the execution of King Louis XVI and was thrown in jail for 11 months. Upon returning to America in 1802, Paine found himself unpopular for his criticisms of George Washington and was shunned by his neighbors in New Rochelle. He died in New York City on June 8, 1809.

EVERY AGE AND GENERATION MUST BE AS FREE TO ACT FOR ITSELF IN ALL CASES AS THE AGE AND GENERATIONS WHICH PRECEDED IT.

Thomas Paine, The Rights of Man *(1791-92)*

100. AUGUST 3, 1784

THOMAS JEFFERSON ARRIVES IN PARIS AS MINISTER TO FRANCE

Jefferson arrived in France on this day to take up his new role as foreign minister, relieving Benjamin Franklin of his long service the following year. For the next five years, Jefferson would revel in his new Parisian life and in France generally. "Were I to proceed to tell you how much I enjoy their architecture, sculpture, painting, music, I should want for words," he wrote a friend. France's neoclassical architecture influenced Jefferson's later improvements to Monticello and other major landmarks. His time in Paris coincided with growing unrest against Louis XVI, and he worked with his friend, the Marquis de Lafayette, to mediate tensions among the king, the aristocracy, and the populace.

101. AUGUST 16, 1784

BENJAMIN FRANKLIN BURNS A BRIDGE

Franklin's extramarital but acknowledged son, William, was the last royal governor of New Jersey. Imprisoned by the patriots in 1776 for conveying plans to the British, he and his father did not communicate again until 1784. Franklin, still in Paris that August, received a letter from William, who wrote back from London on this day: "I received your Letter … and am glad to find that you desire to revive the affectionate Intercourse that formerly existed between us." The two never reconciled, although history disagrees about who is to blame. Franklin wrote William again years later, accusing his son of "taking up arms against me."

102. AUGUST 23, 1784

THE STATE OF FRANKLIN IS BORN

Delegates from three counties in what was then North Carolina voted on this day to become an independent state, at first called Frankland and then Franklin (in the hopes of gaining support from Benjamin Franklin). Its governor was "Nolichucky Jack" Sevier. For four years, the tentative state of Franklin existed independently on land seized from local Native Americans, before being returned to the Union and eventually becoming part of Tennessee. (The celebrated frontiersman, politician, and military officer Davy Crockett was born a Franklinite.)

103. JANUARY 6, 1785

POTOMAC COMPANY IS CHARTERED

Spearheaded by George Washington, the company was established to make the Potomac River more navigable from its headwaters to the tidewater and to link it to the James and

This wood engraving from 1787 depicts the moment a militia fired upon the Shaysites.

Ohio Rivers by a system of roads, canals, and locks. Washington was ever interested in commerce and what is now called infrastructure; he wanted to connect the coast to the rich resources and settlements of the interior. Though the Potomac Company initially struggled with mounting debt, labor shortages, and weather, it survived and thrived into the next century.

104. MAY 23, 1785

BENJAMIN FRANKLIN TAKES PRIDE IN HIS NEW INVENTION

In a letter to a friend, Franklin said he was "happy in the invention of double spectacles, which serve for distant objects as well as near ones." He explained that he "had formerly two Pair of Spectacles, which I shifted occasionally ... Finding this Change troublesome, and not always sufficiently ready, I had the Glasses cut, and half of each kind associated in the same Circle." Some evidence indicates that Franklin may have invented bifocals years before. Among his other creations were the Franklin stove (a metal-lined fireplace), swim fins, and the lightning rod.

105. SEPTEMBER 11, 1786

ANNAPOLIS CONVENTION ASSEMBLES

To help mitigate rising tensions among the states, delegates convened as "Commissioners to Remedy the Defects of the Federal Government." Only a dozen men from five states (Pennsylvania, Delaware, New York, New Jersey, and Virginia) gathered in what had briefly been the capital city of the United States. Though they accomplished little, two Founding Fathers—Virginian James Madison and New Yorker Alexander Hamilton—met and formed a strong bond. The delegates determined that a future convention to "render the constitution ... adequate to the exigencies of the Union" was needed because the existing Articles of Confederation were clearly toothless and inadequate to create an overall federal structure binding the states together.

106. JANUARY 25, 1787

SHAYS'S REBELLION IS QUASHED

On a frigid snowbound day in Springfield, Massachusetts, an armed militia force led by former Army colonel William Shepard fired into a group of 1,500 men known as Shaysites, killing four and dispersing the rest. Led by Daniel Shays, former captain of the 5th Massachusetts Regiment of the Continental Army, the group was made up of farmers in western Massachusetts who had served in the Revolution and now faced unreasonable taxes and debt collection. In protest, they disrupted courts across the state and aimed to seized the federal armory in Springfield on this fateful day. Their "rebellion" shocked many prominent leaders, including George Washington, who feared that if the federal authority "shrinks, or is unable to enforce its laws ... anarchy & confusion must prevail."

ANNETTE GORDON-REED

ANNETTE GORDON-REED IS THE CARL M. LOEB UNIVERSITY PROFESSOR AT HARVARD UNIVERSITY. SHE HAS WON 16 BOOK PRIZES, INCLUDING THE PULITZER PRIZE FOR HISTORY AND THE NATIONAL BOOK AWARD.

DAVID M. RUBENSTEIN: Considering the growing size and wealth of the colonies—and the way Britain treated them—was the split with England inevitable?
ANNETTE GORDON-REED: Historians don't like to talk about inevitability—nothing *had* to happen the way it did. I don't think the split with England was inevitable at that particular moment in time. But it would've happened later, as Americans came into their own.

DMR: Could the war have been avoided if Britain had responded more favorably to American protests?
AGR: Americans didn't want to be independent; they just wanted Great Britain to live up to what they considered to be the rights of British America. But Britain was stubborn about keeping American colonists in check. If they had been more conciliatory, it's possible we could have ended up like the commonwealths of Canada or Australia.

DMR: The Americans appealed to King George, thinking he was the ultimate decision-maker and not Parliament. Who was actually making the decisions?
AGR: That would be Parliament and the prime minister, who advised the king. But it was not the king making this decision.

DMR: Washington lost more battles than he won. How did the Americans manage to win the war with so few resources and battlefield victories?
AGR: The French helped us. They were our first allies, and without the French, we might not have won the war.

DMR: Could George Washington be considered a military genius, or was he simply lucky to lead at a time when the British made so many strategic and tactical mistakes?
AGR: The British did make some mistakes. But Washington was a great leader in the sense that he brought the 13 colonies together; he was probably the only person who could have done that at the time. It's hard for us to imagine how different the colonies were from each other. They were thought of as separate countries. There was some dissatisfaction with Washington, but he stuck with it, and Americans stuck with him.

DMR: The Americans created an explanation for the war, now called the Declaration of Independence, that was largely drafted by Thomas Jefferson. Why did they feel a need for such a statement, and why was Jefferson asked to draft it?
AGR: They wanted to join the community of nations. It wasn't enough to break off and go out on their own; they had to have alliances and support. The declaration was as much a foreign policy document as a domestic one. It spoke to the world to say, "We're going to join these 'civ-

ilized' nations"—we would say "western" now—"because we have declared our rights." Jefferson was asked to write the declaration because he had written *A Summary View of the Rights of British America* [a 1774 tract outlining Jefferson's argument that Britain had no right to exert authority over the colonies]. His talent as a writer helped him become the principal drafter of the declaration.

DMR: Why was the preamble to the Declaration of Independence not seen as significant at the time, but is now viewed as the essence of our democracy?
AGR: The first statement of the preamble provided a way for a country that was not supposed to have a national race, religion, or anything like it, to knit itself together. This was supposed to be a country based upon ideals and ideas. In that preamble, Jefferson explained why they, as a people, had the right to strike out on their own: because their rights had been trampled upon by the British.

DMR: What were the main reasons given by Jefferson in his draft declaration to break from England? Was his draft changed by the Second Continental Congress?
AGR: There were a lot of changes made to the draft. The passage most cited criticized King George III for not allowing Virginia and other states to stop the slave trade. It would have been important language to keep, because Jefferson referred to Africans as people and asserted that they had a sacred right to life and liberty. That was taken out because members of the southern delegations objected.

DMR: Were those who signed the Declaration of Independence committing treason?
AGR: It would've been considered treason for them to declare their independence from the king. So they were all facing the possibility of a death sentence if they lost the war.

DMR: What percentage of the colonial population supported the break from England, and what percentage were loyalists to Britain? What percentage didn't want to get involved?
AGR: While we don't have precise numbers, John Adams famously divided [this estimate] into thirds, and he was probably right. The patriots would have been in the minority; people who were neutral and loyalists would group together. It's amazing to think about people saying, "We're going to have a new country." Think about it today. What percentage of people would join with that now versus those who might stay loyal?

DMR: After the Treaty of Paris, the war was resolved. Why did the Articles of Confederation not work?
AGR: It was too loose a confederation. There had to be unanimous consent, and they couldn't agree on taxes, on a common defense: A nation has to be able to defend itself. And if they couldn't raise money for a military or navy, they'd have all kinds of problems. So they felt they had to do something different. They were, in essence, 13 separate countries. It wasn't until they experienced the difficulty of this that they decided to scrap the Articles of Confederation and do something different.

DMR: Who led the effort to get rid of the Articles of Confederation?
AGR: James Madison thought there should be a strong constitution. He was the person who talked about the weaknesses of the articles. It was a daring thing to do—to think of making that kind of change and devising a stronger national government. There were people in Madison's native Virginia, like Patrick Henry, who were very concerned that a national government would trample upon their rights, as the British had done.

DMR: How many people attended the Constitutional Convention, and who were the prominent figures?
AGR: The prominent gentlemen of the colonies participated: Madison, Alexander Hamilton, and John Jay ended up writing the Federalist papers and arguing for ratification.

DMR: How many women and African Americans were at the Constitutional Convention?
AGR: None.

DMR: What was the major issue that arose at the convention?
AGR: The question of how to count the population for

purposes of a House of Representatives and electoral college. The southern delegates—particularly from South Carolina—were concerned about any measures that might be construed as a mechanism to weaken slavery. The big difference was not between big states and little states; it was between states that enslaved people and states that didn't.

DMR: Is the word "slavery" ever mentioned in the Constitution?
AGR: No. They were very reticent about using that phrase in a supposed charter of freedom.

DMR: Why was separation of power such an important concept?
AGR: The founders studied ancient republics and basically re-created what they thought of as the classical model for a republic: You would check the power of each branch. They started out wary of an executive branch, because they had the example of the king. With three branches that would check power, no one would be able to predominate over the other. And that would be a way of preserving liberty.

DMR: Why was there initially no Bill of Rights?
AGR: Hamilton believed the language of the Constitution as it stood would provide all that was needed. Jefferson and others thought there should be a Bill of Rights.

DMR: Why did some of the signers of the Constitution feel they needed to advocate for the Constitution's adoption? Did they foresee ratification being difficult to achieve?
AGR: The anti-Federalists were a prominent group of people who had concerns about what a national government could do; there was powerful opposition and very eloquent writings against it. Jay, Madison, and Hamilton decided they needed to push back. They wrote the Federalist papers under the collective pseudonym Publius to defend the Constitution and explain why it should be ratified. In some ways, it was the existence of a strong opposition that prompted them to action. Powerful entities could scuttle everything, and all they had worked for would be for naught.

DMR: Was there opposition to George Washington as president? Did he want the job?
AGR: There was no opposition. Washington was the one person everyone thought could be the leader of a new nation. There was a norm at the time to express reticence about being a leader; you didn't want to appear too ambitious, so you'd say, "The people have put me in this place. I'm doing this reluctantly." But I believe he wanted to be president. Just not forever.

DMR: Why was Adams selected as vice president, Jefferson as secretary of state, and Hamilton as secretary of treasury? Did they get along?
AGR: Adams was, while not single-handedly responsible for the American Revolution, very much a catalyst for all this. He was from Massachusetts. With Washington, this put Virginia and Massachusetts together: symbolically important for two different regions to come together.

Hamilton was Washington's aide-de-camp during the war. He and Jefferson were both learned, intelligent people. So Washington thought about their talents, intelligence, and connections when making these decisions.

Eventually, it became a case of people who think they're the smartest person in the room. There was a great rivalry between Hamilton and Jefferson. Hamilton had been close to Washington as a fellow service member; Jefferson and Washington were Virginians, so Jefferson thought Washington would take his side on everything. It turned out that Washington was more of a nationalist than Jefferson. Hamilton essentially won Washington's favor, and Jefferson resigned and went back to Monticello in 1794.

DMR: What did Washington accomplish as president? What were his biggest challenges?
AGR: The big thing Washington established was leaving office. That's probably his greatest gift. People assumed a person who had that kind of power would stay; nobody thought he would leave after two terms. So I think establishing the voluntary [resignation] of presidential power is his most important legacy.

A map of North America at the time of the Declaration of Independence shows the borders of some states looking quite different than they do now.

DMR: Why was the capital moved from New York to Philadelphia to Washington, D.C.?

AGR: The common story is that it was part of a deal. New York and Philadelphia were somewhat of an anathema to the South, which could lend credence to the idea that the national government was northern and would be antithetical to southern interests. So the southerners—Jefferson, Madison—and Hamilton met. In exchange for supporting legislative initiatives, Hamilton agreed they could move the capital closer to the South. Washington himself selected the site in D.C.

DMR: Washington was succeeded by John Adams. Was there opposition to Adams, or was it an easy election?

AGR: It wasn't easy. There were people who didn't like Adams—he had a very irascible personality. But he became president and, as the person who came in second under the rules of that time, Jefferson became vice president.

DMR: What events in the 1700s do you think were most important to America becoming the country it has become today?

AGR: The Declaration of Independence and the break from Great Britain. I think starting out the way we did as a country created part of our understanding of the American spirit as a people who guard their liberty very, very closely. This would become an important part of the Constitution. It connects the two documents that guide us today: the Constitution and Declaration of Independence.

Every day, someone—whether it's a police officer or judge—has to make a determination about whether an action is constitutional. The document itself has been changed over the years, but the fact is that we're still connected to it. We don't cite the declaration as law, but it guides us alongside the Constitution every single day.

107. APRIL 16, 1787

FIRST AMERICAN COMEDY MAKES ITS DEBUT

Performed in Manhattan by the Old American Company, as David Douglass' group was known then, *The Contrast* parodied the ongoing postwar debate in America about the pursuit of luxury versus virtue (considered a European sensibility). Its author, Royall Tyler, was a well-connected New England lawyer and war veteran who wanted to remain anonymous for having written the comedy. The small John Street Theatre, in what is now the Financial District, was modeled on the American Company's Southwark Theatre in Philadelphia. It was the only theater in New York to survive the war.

108. MAY 25, 1787

CONSTITUTIONAL CONVENTION CONVENES

Delegates from seven of the 13 states gathered one rainy spring day in Philadelphia. George Washington, who had reluctantly left his life as a farmer to attend, was quickly nominated and unanimously elected president of the convention. Ben Franklin had planned to make the nomination, but the weather and his health confined him to his nearby home. In the

State delegates spent nearly four months in convention sessions before they signed an agreed-upon draft of the U.S. Constitution.

long summer days to come, windows were shuttered in the Assembly Room to keep the proceedings private. Every day, Virginian James Madison sat near the front and took copious notes that would become the de facto historical record of the proceedings.

109. JULY 13, 1787

NORTHWEST ORDINANCE IS ADOPTED

Even as the Constitutional Convention met, the Confederation Congress created a method for admitting new states to the Union from the "Territory of the United States North-West of the River Ohio" (now Ohio, Michigan, Indiana, Illinois, Wisconsin, and part of Minnesota). "Not less than three nor more than five States" were to be carved from the territory, and territorial inhabitants were guaranteed a bill of rights. The 1787 ordinance replaced but included many of the provisions of a 1784 version drafted by Thomas Jefferson.

110. JULY 15, 1787

SALLY HEMINGS ARRIVES IN PARIS

The 14-year-old girl, enslaved by Thomas Jefferson, came to France as a companion to his daughter Polly. Hemings also shared a father with Jefferson's deceased wife, Martha, making them half sisters. During Hemings's Paris stay, Jefferson is believed to have become sexually involved with her. Able to live as a free woman if she remained in France, Hemings only agreed to return to America, and to slavery, if Jefferson ensured her future children's freedom. Their relationship continued in Virginia, where Hemings gave birth to at least six children by Jefferson. Despite documentary evidence and oral histories, Jeffersonian experts initially denied the relationship between the two. But in 1998, a DNA study confirmed it.

111. JULY 16, 1787

CONNECTICUT COMPROMISE IS PASSED

Adopted at the Constitutional Convention on this day by a vote of five states to four, the agreement finally broke the impasse between large and small states. Introduced by Connecticut judge Roger Sherman, it called for a bicameral legislature, with representation in the House based on a state's population and equal representation for each state in the Senate. Sherman's approach also provided a solution to another thorny issue: The president and vice president would be elected by state electors, and the number of electors assigned to a state would be equal to its senators and House members. Sherman is the only Founding Father to have signed all four of the nation's principal founding documents.

112. SEPTEMBER 17, 1787

CONSTITUTION DAY DAWNS

On this day, an agreed-upon draft of the Constitution was finally signed. George Washington wrote to the Marquis de Lafayette that the charter was "now a child of fortune, to be fostered by some and buffeted by others." It included seven sweeping articles, and opened with the

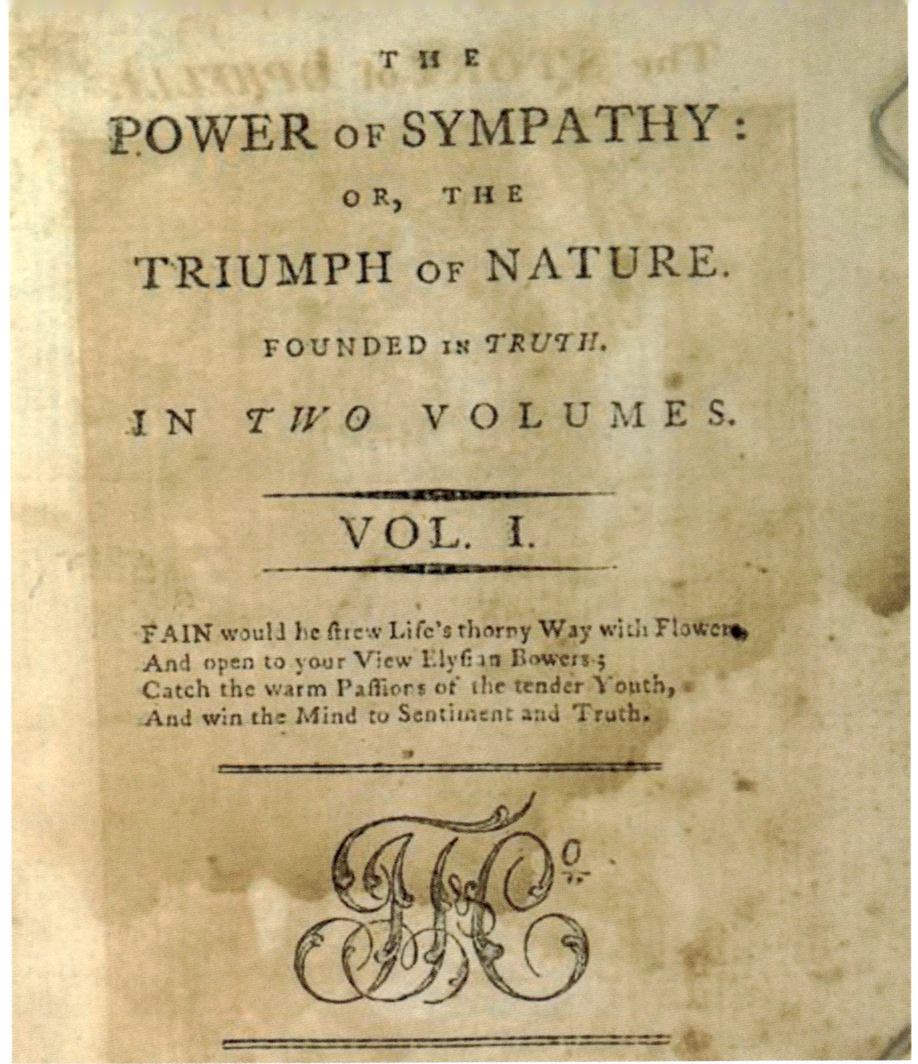
THE

POWER OF SYMPATHY:

OR, THE

TRIUMPH OF NATURE.

FOUNDED IN *TRUTH*.

IN *TWO* VOLUMES.

VOL. I.

FAIN would he ſtrew Life's thorny Way with Flowers,
And open to your View Elyſian Bowers;
Catch the warm Paſſions of the tender Youth,
And win the Mind to Sentiment and Truth.

Published anonymously by a Boston author, the first American novel was written in a cloying style and included a steamy plot line.

now famous preamble, "We the People of the United States, in Order to form a more perfect Union ..." Pennsylvania delegate Gouverneur Morris did most of the drafting, but changes were made to his original. Three delegates refused to sign—two because the Constitution did not include a bill of rights. Nine states were needed to ratify and make it law.

113. OCTOBER 27, 1787

FIRST FEDERALIST PAPER IS PUBLISHED

Debuting in New York's *Independent Journal,* these crucial essays arguing for New York to ratify the Constitution were the brainchild of Alexander Hamilton, then a New York City lawyer and delegate to the Constitutional Convention. "After an unequivocal experience of the inefficiency of the subsisting federal government, you are called upon to deliberate on a new Constitution for the United States of America," it began. According to his wife, Eliza, Hamilton was aboard a sloop on the Hudson River when he conceived the idea for these foundational essays. He recruited James Madison and John Jay as collaborators; in all, 85 articles appeared, written under the pseudonym Publius. Ultimately, they were compiled in two volumes and distributed across the new nation.

114. APRIL 13, 1788

NEW YORKERS RIOT AGAINST GRAVE ROBBING

What became known as the "Doctors' Riot" turned into a bloody affair on this day when 2,000 to 5,000 people formed a mob marching down Broadway, angry at the theft of corpses secretly exhumed from local graves (most from the potter's field or the African Burial Ground in Lower Manhattan). The culprits? "Physic" (or medical) students, who learned their trade through dissection and took what they needed from cemeteries. The riot lasted several days; at its end, as many as 20 people were dead. The following January, the state legislature passed a statute prohibiting "the odious practice of digging up and removing for the purpose of dissection, dead bodies."

115. JUNE 21, 1788

THE CONSTITUTION BECOMES LAW

The momentous bill became official on this day when New Hampshire—the ninth state required for ratification—signed on. Delaware had been the first to ratify, on December 7, 1787, soon followed by Pennsylvania, New Jersey, Georgia, and Connecticut. But other states were concerned that the new law did not protect such freedoms as speech and religion, and that it concentrated power in the hands of the federal government. In February 1788, delegates John Hancock and Samuel Adams put forth the Massachusetts Compromise, guaranteeing that amendments protecting individual freedoms would be immediately proposed. Its passage cleared the way for ratification.

THE ACCUMULATION OF ALL POWERS, LEGISLATIVE, EXECUTIVE, AND JUDICIARY, IN THE SAME HANDS ... MAY JUSTLY BE PRONOUNCED THE VERY DEFINITION OF TYRANNY.

James Madison, *Federalist papers, no. 47 (1787-88)*

116. JANUARY 21, 1789

FIRST AMERICAN NOVEL IS PUBLISHED

Released on this day, William Hill Brown's *The Power of Sympathy: or, The Triumph of Nature Founded in Truth* was both sentimental and titillating. The epistolary novel featured unknowingly incestuous lovers and offered no happy endings. Published anonymously, it did not sell well. Brown, the son of the Boston clockmaker who made the clock in the city's famous Old South Church, continued to write poems and essays before his early death, probably from malaria, at age 27.

117. MARCH 4, 1789

FIRST MEETING OF CONGRESS CONVENES

The session—the first under the Constitution—took place in New York City on this day. But with only 22 of 81 members present, it fell short of a quorum. Not until April did enough members appear to attain the attendance necessary for voting. The former Continental Congress had designated New York as the temporary seat of government until a permanent capital city could be chosen; to meet the moment, city hall received a facelift, overseen by French designer Pierre L'Enfant. It was renamed Federal Hall.

118. APRIL 6, 1789

GEORGE WASHINGTON IS ELECTED FIRST PRESIDENT

The first presidential election got off to a rocky start. Under the Constitution, state electors, chosen in whatever way each state determined, would be the only Americans voting—each elector could cast one vote each for president and vice president. New York did not pass an act to choose electors in the time required, so it fielded none; neither did North Carolina or Rhode Island, as they had not yet ratified the Constitution. But the 69 electors from 10 states who did vote unanimously elected George Washington. John Adams received the second highest number of votes to become the country's vice president.

119. APRIL 30, 1789

GEORGE WASHINGTON IS SWORN IN AS FIRST PRESIDENT

On his way to New York from Mount Vernon for the inauguration, Washington had been feted in almost every town he passed through and cheered on by admiring citizens. For the inaugural ceremony itself, Congress chose an outside balcony of Federal Hall overlooking Wall Street, so that "the greatest number of people of the United States, and without distinction, may witness the solemnity." After his swearing in, Washington addressed Congress: "I behold the surest pledges, that … no local prejudices, or attachments; no separate views, nor party animosities, will misdirect … this great assemblage … That the foundations of our National policy will be … exemplified by all the attributes which can win the affections of its Citizens, and command the respect of the world." To celebrate the historic event, church bells rang out throughout the city and fireworks illuminated the skies.

120. JUNE 8, 1789

JAMES MADISON INTRODUCES THE BILL OF RIGHTS

Presented to the House of Representatives on this day, the bill proposed amendments to the Constitution, an issue the new legislators did not see as a priority. But Madison "hounded his colleagues relentlessly" to get it done. His official proposal began, "A number of States, having at the time of their adopting the Constitution, expressed a Desire … that further … restrictive Clauses should be added." After some tinkering, Congress enumerated 12 rights of individuals and sent them to the president as amendments to the Constitution in the fall. George Washington in turn forwarded them to the states for ratification; 10 were formally adopted a few months later.

121. AUGUST 25, 1789

THOMAS JEFFERSON LENDS A HAND

Soon after Bastille Day, as royalist resentment festered in the French capital, the Marquis de Lafayette asked his friend, Thomas Jefferson, to host a private dinner at his Paris home—with an ulterior motive: "We shall Be some Members of the National Assembly—eight of us whom I want to Coalize as Being the only Means to prevent a total dissolution and a civil war," he wrote. "These gentlemen wish to Consult You and me." As Louis XVI's reign began to unravel, Lafayette—and Jefferson—hoped to move France away from chaos and toward democracy. Six weeks later, Louis XVI would ratify the Declaration of the Rights of Man and of the Citizen—a foundational document of the French Revolution.

122. SEPTEMBER 11, 1789

ALEXANDER HAMILTON BECOMES FIRST SECRETARY OF THE TREASURY

One of President George Washington's close confidants and his former aide-de-camp, Hamilton was a leading voice for federalism, a system that divides power between multiple

For his presidential inauguration in 1789, George Washington traveled from Mount Vernon to New York by carriage, by barge, and atop his horse, Prescott.

James Madison was influential in adding several "safeguards" to the Constitution–amendments collectively known as the Bill of Rights.

levels of government (though with a strong central component). During his vigorous reign at the Department of the Treasury, he created a national monetary system with a federal budget and taxes; a central bank to regularize currency; and a funded debt to help states pay off the enormous financial obligations they had incurred during the Revolution. He also created the U.S. Coast Guard and the customs service. Although many historians see Hamilton's contributions as vital to the new nation, he faced strong headwinds at the time—particularly from his archrivals, Thomas Jefferson and James Madison.

123. SEPTEMBER 24, 1789

SUPREME COURT IS ESTABLISHED

On this day, President George Washington signed the Judiciary Act—one of the first laws of the new Congress—which mandated a federal court system regulated by Congress and separate from state courts. To be known as the Supreme Court, the body would take appeals from cases heard in the federal courts and some heard in state courts. The federal appellate system, which now operates as a layer between the federal district courts and the Supreme Court, would not be created until 1891—in part so that the Supreme Court justices wouldn't have to ride circuit to hear cases in various regions. The president also submitted his first nominees—six in total—to Congress.

124. SEPTEMBER 25, 1789

CONGRESS ACCEPTS THE BILL OF RIGHTS

After some adjusting to James Madison's initial proposal, Congress enumerated 12 rights of individuals to be included as amendments to the Constitution. They forwarded these to President George Washington, who in turn sent them to the states for ratification. Today, those amendments are known as the Bill of Rights and are invoked more often than the original articles of the Constitution. They guarantee such individual freedoms as speech, religion, the press, and the right to bear arms and receive fair treatment in judicial proceedings.

125. NOVEMBER 23, 1789

THOMAS JEFFERSON RETURNS HOME

Landing in Norfolk, Virginia, after more than five years as minister to France, the eminent diplomat learned from local officials that he had been appointed to George Washington's Cabinet as the first secretary of state, in charge of all foreign (and many domestic) affairs. Jefferson had planned to leave public service to focus on his plantation, Monticello, and personal life, but he told the Norfolk officials, "That my country should be served is the first wish of my heart." He served from March 22, 1790, to December 31, 1793, when once again he planned to return to private life. "It will be no loss to the public, and a great relief to me," he wrote to a friend.

"I am as happy no where else ... I hope my days will end, at Monticello," Thomas Jefferson said of his Virginia home.

126. MARCH 1, 1790

U.S. CENSUS IS ESTABLISHED

During its second session, Congress passed the Census Act of 1790 on this day. It required that U.S. marshals assigned to judicial districts visit every household to establish the number of people in five categories: free white males 16 and older; free white males under 16; free white females; other free persons; and enslaved peoples. Though the marshals had expected some resistance, households generally complied. Still, George Washington and Thomas Jefferson both believed the final total for the first census—3.9 million—was probably lower than the actual number of people then living in the 13 states and the districts of Kentucky, Maine, and Vermont, and the Southwest Territory (Tennessee).

127. JUNE 20, 1790

A "DINNER TABLE BARGAIN" BUILDS AMERICA

On this evening, Thomas Jefferson hosted a dinner for Alexander Hamilton and James Madison to attempt a compromise between them on two issues that had ground government to a halt: what to do about the war debts many states still owed, and where to establish the permanent national capital. The compromise reached that night made Philadelphia the temporary capital for 10 years, until a permanent capital on the Potomac River could be established. In exchange, Madison agreed to support Hamilton's plan to have the federal government cover existing state war debts—a plan Madison had opposed because his state, Virginia, had already paid off most of its debt. Their bargain went a long way to establish a path forward for a stronger United States.

128. AUGUST 17, 1790

PRESIDENT WASHINGTON AFFIRMS SUPPORT FOR RELIGIOUS EQUALITY

On this day, Newport, Rhode Island's Hebrew Congregation wrote the president with an impassioned view: "Deprived as we heretofore have been of the invaluable rights of free Citizens, we now … behold a Government … which to bigotry gives no sanction,

President George Washington tapped Pierre L'Enfant to create a plan for a new capital city bounded on two sides by the Potomac River.

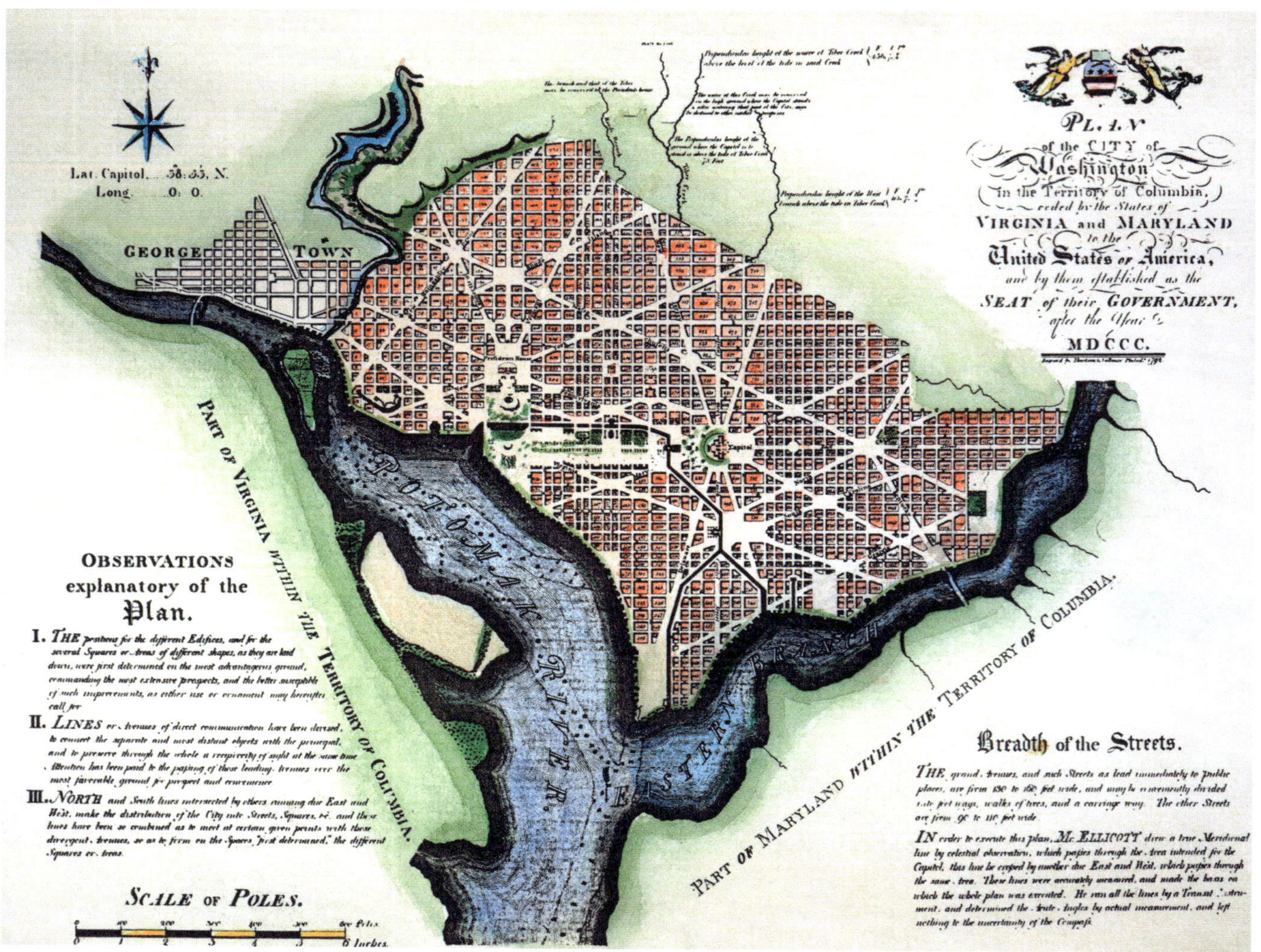

to persecution no assistance—but generously affording to All liberty of conscience." In a letter Washington wrote the following day, he reflected what he felt was America's governing creed: that people of all religions would be treated equally. His letter concluded, "May the father of all mercies scatter light and not darkness in our paths, and make us all in our several vocations useful here, and in his own due time and way everlastingly happy."

129. DECEMBER 20, 1790

AMERICA'S FIRST COTTON MILL OPENS

On this day, Slater Mill began operating in Pawtucket, Rhode Island, using falls on the Blackstone River for power. Samuel Slater, a recent English immigrant who had worked in English mills, taught local mechanics to make the mill's machines, which could brush and spin cotton into yarn. The mill ushered in the American industrial age, luring some people off the farm and into "mill villages," where workers—many children from eight to 14 years old—labored long hours.

NO NATION PERHAPS HAD EVER BEFORE THE OPPORTUNITY OFFERD THEM OF DELIBERATELY DECIDING ON THE SPOT WHERE THIER CAPITAL CITY SHOULD BE FIXUD.

Pierre L'Enfant, *writing to George Washington (1789)*

130. MARCH 28, 1791

PIERRE L'ENFANT CREATES THE FEDERAL CITY

Trained at France's Royal Academy of Painting and Sculpture, Pierre L'Enfant came to America to volunteer in the Continental Army. After the war, he gained a reputation as a civic designer, and President George Washington asked him to visit the new capital site on the Potomac. On this day, L'Enfant presented Washington with a sketch of his plan. Though never fully realized, the plan's basics still define the U.S. capital, with diagonal streets interrupted by parklike squares and the placement of the Capitol Building on a hilltop as the seat of government, a natural "pedestal waiting for a monument," wrote L'Enfant.

131. MAY 19, 1791

FRENCH ÉMIGRÉS FLEEING REVOLUTION ARRIVE IN PHILADELPHIA

On this day, the *Charming Sally* docked in the temporary U.S. capital with 15 refugees on board from the French colony of Saint-Domingue (in present-day Haiti), where divisions among French plantation owners gave way to a bloody revolt by enslaved people. Over the next 30 months, 3,000 more French colonists and enslaved peoples of African descent would arrive in the city, bringing their Francophone, Caribbean culture with them. An additional 25,000 refugees fleeing the French Revolution also arrived in Philadelphia during this period, fomenting a lively cultural imprint on the city through craftsmanship and architecture alongside cafés, shops, and culinary purveyors. When political conditions in France improved in the coming years, many returned home.

132. AUGUST 1, 1791

ROBERT CARTER EXECUTES A DEED OF EMANCIPATION

Seventy years before the Civil War, the scion of one of Virginia's wealthiest families decided on this day to take steps toward liberating the more than 450 enslaved people on his estates, despite strong opposition from family members, neighbors, and fellow Virginians. As the inheritor of hundreds of enslaved people, Carter turned against slavery over the course of the American Revolution, influenced by the discussions of the time in conjunction with a religious conversion. While his 1791 action took decades to be fully realized, it constituted the largest individual manumission until 1860. When completed, 500 to 600 people were freed from bondage.

133. AUGUST 19, 1791

THOMAS JEFFERSON ELUCIDATES HIS VIEW ON RACE

African American mathematician and surveyor Benjamin Banneker wrote to Thomas Jefferson on this day regarding the secretary's views on racial inequity, saying, "I apprehend you will embrace every opportunity, to eradicate that train of absurd and false ideas and opinions which so generally prevails with respect to us, and that your Sentiments are concurrent with mine ... [W]e are all of the Same Family, and Stand in the Same relation to [God]." Jefferson responded in a way uncharacteristic of the times and of other racist observations he'd previously made, assuring Banneker that "nature has given to our black brethren, talents equal to those of the other colours of men, & that the appearance of a want of them is owing merely to the degraded condition of their existence." Jefferson went on to recommend Banneker to assist in surveying the new federal capital on the Potomac.

134. DECEMBER 15, 1791

BILL OF RIGHTS IS RATIFIED

After more than two years, the necessary three-fourths majority required for official ratification was finally achieved on this day when Virginia's legislature became the 11th state to sign on. The legislature accepted only 10 of the 12 proposed amendments to the Constitution; the two not approved concerned compensation for senators and representatives and the number of constituents necessary for each member of the House. Virginia lawmaker George Mason had been the strongest voice for a bill of individual rights, and his Virginia Declaration of Rights, written in 1776, is echoed in the Constitution's first 10 amendments.

135. MAY 17, 1792

BUTTONWOOD AGREEMENT IS ADOPTED

For two months, the nation had been in the throes of the first financial panic brought on by speculation in securities, a run on banks, and tightening credit at the First Bank of the United States. In response, 24 New York stockbrokers met under a buttonwood tree (located, according to legend, near what is now 68 Wall Street) and agreed on this day to set rules for trading as a means of bolstering public faith in markets and ensuring that deals were conducted between a select group of trusted parties. In that era, most trading was informal and conducted in coffeehouses, and the pact was not a law. But it was a first step in the long process that eventually led to the creation of the New York Stock Exchange.

136. MAY 29, 1792

GEORGE VANCOUVER NAMES PUGET SOUND

British general Vancouver had been dispatched to settle a territorial dispute with Spain in the Pacific Northwest and to search for the elusive Northwest Passage linking the Atlantic and Pacific. Vancouver sailed the H.M.S. *Discovery* around the Cape of Good Hope, stopping in Australia, New Zealand, and Hawaii before heading east across the Pacific to America. His lieutenant Peter Puget spent a week exploring what he called the Southeast Inlet and meeting its Native peoples. Vancouver named the inlet Puget's

An expedition led by British general George Vancouver mapped and named dozens of sites in the Pacific Northwest, including Mount Rainier.

Sound on this day, later shortened to Puget Sound. Over the course of nearly five years, Vancouver mapped dozens of geographical features in the Pacific Northwest and named landmarks such as Mounts Baker, Rainier, and St. Helens after prominent Englishmen. Washington would become the 42nd state in 1889.

137. OCTOBER 1, 1792

A DOMESTIC SCANDAL MAKES NEWS

Teenager Ann Cary Randolph, nicknamed Nancy, a member of Virginia's powerful Randolph family, had been living on her sister's plantation, known as Bizarre. On this day, Nancy traveled to the neighboring Glentivar estate with her sister and brother-in-law, Richard. During the night, she was heard screaming, and Richard went to tend to

A decade after hot-air balloon flight debuted over Paris, a French inventor launched America's first piloted balloon from Philadelphia.

her. Rumors went on to claim that Nancy and Richard had killed Nancy's baby, believed to be fathered by Richard. In 1793, they were put on trial for murder. The case pulled in respected jurist and future Supreme Court Justice John Marshall and former Virginia governor Patrick Henry. Nancy and Richard were eventually acquitted; today it is believed that she had a miscarriage.

138. DECEMBER 5, 1792

BOSTON POLICE RAID THEATER PERFORMANCE

In 1750, the rather puritanical Massachusetts General Court had outlawed public "stage plays" because they increased "immorality, impiety, and a contempt for religion." Nevertheless, clandestine theaters used creative language and exploited loopholes to stage productions and provide entertainment to the public. On this day, police raided one such theater in Boston, the Board Alley Exhibition Room, interrupting a "moral lecture" of Richard Brinsley Sheridan's *School for Scandal.* The raid ignited another round of public backlash against the restrictive laws, compelling Governor John Hancock to consider repealing the act. Though he never did, a bill passed by the state legislature in 1793 permitted Boston "to have a Theater erected, and Stage Plays performed" under certain regulations. The city's first legal theater opened on Federal Street the following year, and performances resumed without police intervention.

WHAT A SIGHT! HOW DELICIOUS FOR ME TO ENJOY IT.

Jean-Pierre Blanchard, *pilot of America's first balloon flight (1793)*

139. JANUARY 9, 1793

FIRST PILOTED BALLOON LIFTS OFF IN AMERICA

In 1783, the first hot-air balloon, created by the Montgolfier Brothers, floated animal, and then human, passengers above Paris. Ten years later, French inventor Jean-Pierre Blanchard launched his own revolutionary flight from a prison yard in Philadelphia, America's temporary capital, while President George Washington watched. It stayed aloft for 46 minutes, landing in Gloucester County, New Jersey. Two years later, Blanchard and physician John Jeffries made the first flight across the English Channel, from Dover to Calais.

140. FEBRUARY 13, 1793

PRESIDENT WASHINGTON IS UNANIMOUSLY ELECTED TO A SECOND TERM

George Washington had planned to serve only one term, but pressure to keep him in office was fierce—in part because he was a moderate force offsetting the growing tensions between Alexander Hamilton's Federalists and Thomas Jefferson's small-government Republicans. Revered by a public who trusted only him to lead the country, he nonetheless felt "deficient in many of the essential qualifications" and believed that others "would be better able to execute the trust." Though tired, plagued by health problems, and anxious to return to his Virginia plantation, Washington once again answered the call of duty, with John Adams as his vice president.

SPOTLIGHT

EARLY TECHNOLOGIES

I

IN THE YEARS SURROUNDING THE American Revolution, the nascent republic's inventors produced a wide array of tools and technologies. Among the best known of the innovators is Benjamin Franklin. By the mid-1700s, Franklin had pioneered a system of mail-order cataloging—with purchases delivered by the postal system he had helped establish—and had invented the Franklin stove, a metal baffle–lined fireplace that yielded more heat and less smoke than open hearths.

Contemporaries doubted Franklin's theory that lightning was electricity, and his attempt to prove that produced the caricature of the statesman flying a kite as a lightning bolt strikes it. Though accounts differ, Franklin likely positioned a metal key outside during a thunderstorm and, via a wire attached to it, detected ambient electricity. What he learned allowed him to invent a valuable safety device in the 1750s: the lightning rod, a pointed iron shaft placed on a building's apex and wired to harmlessly conduct electrical charges to the ground.

Other ingenious inventions followed, including the cotton gin, a machine Eli Whitney built in 1793 that deseeded and combed cotton boll fibers, revolutionizing how southern states handled what became their key cash crop; the flatboat, devised in 1782 by Jacob Yoder, for commercial use carrying freight and passengers on river routes; and the swivel chair, which Thomas Jefferson had adapted from a stationary chair. In this seat, he's believed to have drafted the Declaration of Independence.

This undated painting depicts the supposed moment lightning struck Benjamin Franklin's kite, racing down the string.

I BEGIN TO BE ALMOST SORRY I WAS BORN SO SOON, SINCE I CANNOT HAVE THE HAPPINESS OF KNOWING WHAT WILL BE KNOWN 100 YEARS HENCE.

Benjamin Franklin *(1783)*

141. JULY 25, 1793

PRESIDENT WASHINGTON APPROVES A PLAN FOR THE NEW CAPITOL BUILDING

Despite 17 entries, an earlier design competition had produced no plans deemed acceptable for the official seat of American government. But belatedly, a physician living in the British West Indies named William Thornton submitted a winning design for a building in three sections, with a domed middle. Thornton had no architectural training, but Thomas Jefferson, a connoisseur of architecture, called his design "simple, noble, beautiful, excellently distributed and moderate in size." On September 18, President George Washington laid the cornerstone with Masonic ceremony. Among those who labored on the construction of the vast marble seat of government were many enslaved African Americans "hired out" by their owners in Maryland and Virginia, who pocketed the wages.

142. AUGUST 5, 1793

BENJAMIN RUSH IDENTIFIES YELLOW FEVER EPIDEMIC

On this day, Benjamin Rush, a Founding Father of the nation and leading doctor in Philadelphia, began to diagnose yellow fever in the city during the first epidemic of the disease that would plague America. Rush tried to treat it by bleeding patients aggressively and administering heavy doses of mercury: both deadly regimens in their own right. He also believed African Americans were immune to the illness and asked them to deal with the sick or dead. Yellow fever ultimately killed 5,000 people, nearly 10 percent of the city's population.

While working as a tutor on a Georgia plantation, Eli Whitney paused his law studies to hone a groundbreaking device: the cotton gin.

143. DECEMBER 9, 1793

NOAH WEBSTER PUBLISHES NEW YORK'S FIRST DAILY NEWSPAPER

A respected writer, editor, and staunch Federalist associate of Alexander Hamilton, Noah Webster launched his newspaper—*The American Minerva, Patroness of Peace, Commerce, and the Liberal Arts*—on this day with the pledge that it would be "chaste and impartial ... Personalities, if possible, will be avoided." Part of a wave of newspapers that sprang up in the 1790s, *The American Minerva* was renamed the *Commercial Advertiser* in 1797 and *The Globe and Commercial Advertiser* in 1904. After publishing continuously for 130 years, the daily was ultimately absorbed by another paper in 1923.

144. MARCH 14, 1794

ELI WHITNEY'S COTTON GIN REVOLUTIONIZES THE ECONOMY

Yale-educated Whitney had reluctantly left his native Massachusetts to become a private tutor on a Georgia plantation. Supported by the plantation owner, Whitney worked in secret on an engine ("gin") that had the means of separating cotton fibers from the sticky seeds of short-staple cotton. "One man and a horse will do more than fifty men with the

A physician with no architectural training created the design chosen for the U.S. Capitol Building, with side wings framing a domed middle.

old machines," Whitney claimed. His cotton gin was patented on this day, but its success had unfortunate results: Its efficiency led to the growth of vast cotton plantations fueled by enslaved families.

145. AUGUST 7, 1794

THE PRESIDENT RAISES A MILITIA AGAINST THE WHISKEY REBELLION

On this day, President George Washington reluctantly called up a militia against farmers in western Pennsylvania who had been protesting the 1791 tax on spirits distilled in America. The tariff affected them directly, since they distilled the corn and rye they grew into popular liquors when they were unable to ship them east—and, like other Americans, they resented the new taxes the federal government levied. Their protests, collectively known as the Whiskey Rebellion, had been growing increasingly violent, and Washington believed they threatened the rule of law. He took command of the troops marching on the protesters—the only president to do so in a combat situation—and the rebel protesters dispersed. Washington's actions were criticized by proponents of states' rights.

146. AUGUST 3, 1795

TREATY OF GREENVILLE IS ADOPTED

Under duress, Indian nations ceded their lands in present-day Ohio, Indiana, Illinois, and Michigan to the United States on this day. In the previous two decades, American forces had violently and repeatedly attacked Great Lakes tribes, destroying their villages and

Great Lakes-area Indian tribes signed over land to U.S. troops in exchange for a promise that "hostilities shall cease." They didn't.

lives. Maj. Gen. Anthony Wayne negotiated the 1795 treaty with tribal leaders; it began: "Henceforth all hostilities shall cease; peace is hereby established, and shall be perpetual; and a friendly intercourse shall take place between the said United States and Indian tribes." The peace was short-lived, as white settlers pushed onto the newly established Indian territories.

147. FEBRUARY 5, 1796

JAMES HEMINGS IS GRANTED HIS FREEDOM

As Thomas Jefferson's Paris-trained chef de cuisine, James Hemings—an older brother of Sally Hemings—had prepared food for some of the greatest figures of the day. In a 1793 agreement, Jefferson promised that if Hemings would "go with me to Monticello" and train someone there to cook, he would be "made free." Upon training his younger brother Peter Hemings, James was made free on this day. When elected president, Jefferson assumed James would want to work for him at his Washington, D.C., residence. Several times, Jefferson reached out to him through an intermediary, but James wanted direct communication from Jefferson and never received it. After briefly returning to work at Monticello in 1801, James Hemings, then 36, died—perhaps by suicide.

148. APRIL 12, 1796

PRESIDENT WASHINGTON SITS FOR GILBERT STUART

As president, George Washington was often asked to sit for portraits, as were other leading figures of the day. Though he despised the days-long process, he collaborated with leading portraitists, including Gilbert Stuart. Born in Rhode Island, Stuart established himself as a portraitist in England but slid into debt and fled. Back in America, he planned to paint famous men—"I expect to make a fortune by Washington alone," he wrote. Now known as the father of American portraiture, Stuart would paint the first six presidents. Washington's sittings for him resulted in the haunting Athenaeum portrait (the image on the dollar bill) and the well-known Lansdowne portrait of a standing Washington clad in black. Despite entreaties from Martha after her husband's death, Stuart never gave her a version of the Lansdowne. Of the three copies he painted, one hangs in the East Room of the White House.

149. APRIL 28, 1796

FIRST COOKBOOK BY AN AMERICAN IS PUBLISHED

Amelia Simmons wrote *American Cookery,* published on this day, to inspire her fellow New Englanders to celebrate the bounty of the land. Her recipes included cranberry sauce, johnnycakes, a custardy pumpkin pie, stuffed goose, and other distinctly American delights. The title page reads "By Amelia Simmons, An American Orphan"; the 47-page opus also included advice to young female orphans. For 30 years, the book inspired cooks from New England and New York to the Midwest. The Library of Congress has listed *American Cookery* among its "Books That Shaped America."

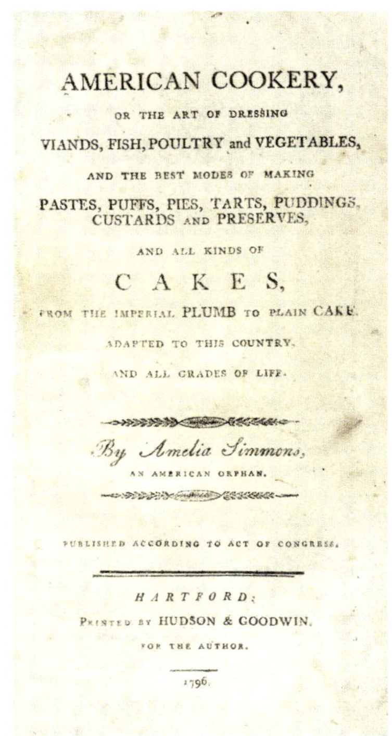

AMERICAN COOKERY,
OR THE ART OF DRESSING
VIANDS, FISH, POULTRY and VEGETABLES,
AND THE BEST MODES OF MAKING
PASTES, PUFFS, PIES, TARTS, PUDDINGS, CUSTARDS AND PRESERVES,
AND ALL KINDS OF
CAKES,
FROM THE IMPERIAL PLUMB TO PLAIN CAKE.
ADAPTED TO THIS COUNTRY,
AND ALL GRADES OF LIFE.

By Amelia Simmons,
AN AMERICAN ORPHAN.

PUBLISHED ACCORDING TO ACT OF CONGRESS.

HARTFORD:
PRINTED BY HUDSON & GOODWIN.
FOR THE AUTHOR.
1796.

The first cookbook written by an American, *American Cookery* by Amelia Simmons, is now on the Library of Congress's list of "Books That Shaped America."

150. JUNE 23, 1796

SENECA LEADER RED JACKET SPEAKS OUT

Meeting on this day in Buffalo, New York, with land developer Moses Cleaveland (who would lend his name to one of Ohio's great cities), Red Jacket and other members of the Haudenosaunee (Iroquois) Confederacy protested white encroachment on their lands in what is now northeastern Ohio. In a contemporary report, Red Jacket, a leader of the Seneca Nation, reportedly told Cleaveland: "You white people make a great parade about religion, you say you have a book of laws ... given you by the Great Spirit, but is this true?" No, he told his Haudenosaunee brethren. All the whites "want is money."

151. SEPTEMBER 19, 1796

GEORGE WASHINGTON ISSUES A FAREWELL ADDRESS

The president's historic remarks, directed to his "Friends and Fellow-Citizens," were published on this day in Philadelphia's *American Daily Advertiser.* Largely written by Alexander Hamilton but edited by Washington, the statement announced his decision not to seek a third term. He wrote that he would carry "to my grave" the hope that "Heaven may continue to you the choicest tokens of its beneficence; that your Union and brotherly affection may be perpetual;

that the free constitution ... may be sacredly maintained; that its Administration ... may be stamped with wisdom and virtue; that, in fine, the happiness of the people of these States, under the auspices of liberty, may be made complete." His words are quoted to this day.

152. NOVEMBER 4, 1796

JOHN ADAMS IS ELECTED PRESIDENT

John Adams, a Federalist, prevailed by three electoral votes over his friend turned rival, Democratic-Republican Thomas Jefferson, who would become vice president. Though the candidates did not go out on the stump themselves, their operatives were relentless. A Federalist paper had accused Jefferson of an affair with an enslaved woman (which was true), while Republican tacticians referred to Adams as "His Rotundity," one even claiming he was a hermaphrodite. In his farewell address, George Washington had warned that political parties could take "the place of the delegated will of the Nation" and be run by an "artful and enterprising minority." The vitriol and partisanship of this first election after his departure would prove him right.

John Adams, the country's second president, as depicted by Gilbert Stuart, 1823

153. FEBRUARY 21, 1797

RIGHT TO VOTE IS EXTENDED TO INCLUDE ALL NEW JERSEY WOMEN

New Jersey was the only state to enfranchise 18th-century women. Its 1790 Election Law gave "all free Inhabitants of this State of full Age, and who are worth Fifty Pounds" the right to vote—but only in seven of the state's 13 counties. An amended law passed on this day extended the privilege to all counties. This action, along with a push by the new political parties to spur participation, resulted in far more women voting that year. Nearly 11 years later, an 1807 law took the right away, limiting the vote to "free, white, male citizens" at least 21 years of age.

154. SEPTEMBER 14, 1798

CHARLES BROCKDEN BROWN PUBLISHES A GOTHIC NOVEL

Sometimes called the "father of the American novel," Brown gave up an apprenticeship with a prominent Philadelphia lawyer and became part of a New York literary circle that espoused the progressive ideas of British writers of the time. His first published novel—*Wieland or, The Transformation: An American Tale,* released on this day—was based on true events and includes spontaneous combustion, along with madness and murder caused by "inner voices." Brown followed it with three more novels that, like *Wieland,* foreshadowed the works of 19th-century American masters Nathaniel Hawthorne and Edgar Allan Poe.

155. DECEMBER 14, 1799

GEORGE WASHINGTON DIES SUDDENLY

At last able to oversee the farm work at Mount Vernon again, the 67-year-old Washington did not let weather deter him. On December 13, after two wet and frigid days on the land, he had a sore throat but told his secretary, "You know I never take anything for a cold." By the following evening, Washington was dying with acute throat inflammation. "I die hard," he said, "but I am not afraid to go." At his funeral, Gen. Henry Lee famously proclaimed him "First in war, first in peace, and first in the hearts of his countrymen." Washington's will stipulated that his slaves be freed at Martha's death. In the end, fewer than half of those in bondage at Mount Vernon were emancipated. The others were bound to the estate of Martha's first husband.

ALL IS NOW OVER, I SHALL SOON FOLLOW HIM! I HAVE NO MORE TRIALS TO PASS THROUGH!

Martha Washington, *on the passing of her husband (1799)*

After a cold quickly worsened into acute throat inflammation, George Washington died in his bedroom at his Mount Vernon, Virginia, home.

★ ★ ★ The ★ ★ ★
19th CENTURY

AGE OF UPHEAVAL

GOVERNMENT OF THE PEOPLE, BY THE PEOPLE, FOR THE PEOPLE, SHALL NOT PERISH FROM THE EARTH.

Abraham Lincoln, *Gettysburg Address (1863)*

THE YOUNG COUNTRY started the century with 16 states and ended it with 45. With growth came growing pains; with expansion, upheaval—but also progress and invention. Throughout the century, Americans were at war: the War of 1812 against Britain, the Mexican-American War (1846–48), the Spanish-American War (1898), and the continuation of the American Indian Wars, with more than a dozen major conflicts with Indigenous peoples over land and rights. The defining struggle of the nation, Union against Confederacy (1861–65), tested whether a citizenry torn apart over principles could be knit together again. The nation's most deadly conflict (estimates range from 618,000 to 750,000 killed) and its rancor proved hard to overcome. Restoration-era reforms sought equal treatment for four million formerly enslaved people but were blocked by Jim Crow laws and groups like the Ku Klux Klan. Despite the society's divisions, American ingenuity and industrialization thrived in the 1800s. The steamboat and the transcontinental railroad advanced commerce and transportation; the telegraph, telephone, and typewriter streamlined communication. America's population exploded—from some 5.3 million people in 1800 to some 76.2 million by 1900, including tens of millions of immigrants borne on successive waves, mostly from Europe. In an 1893 poem that became lyrics for an anthem, Katharine Lee Bates described an America stretching "from sea to shining sea!"

The U.S. flag adorns sheet music of "The Star-Spangled Banner." Amateur poet Francis Scott Key wrote its lyrics after watching Baltimore's Fort McHenry withstand a British assault in September 1814; while the song was popular throughout the 1800s, it would not become the U.S. national anthem until 1931. **OPPOSITE TOP:** "The President's House," painted around 1837 by an unknown artist, depicts the White House as viewed from the Potomac River. **OPPOSITE BOTTOM:** Ellis Island in New York Harbor was once America's busiest immigration inspection station; some 12 million immigrants were processed at its facilities between 1892 and 1954.

NOVEMBER 17, 1800
Congress relocates to the new federal city
Government entities moved from Philadelphia to a capital still under construction.

MAY 2, 1803
Louisiana Purchase is signed in Paris
France sold 828,000 acres west of the Mississippi to the United States, doubling its size.

JUNE 18, 1812
James Madison signs a declaration of war with Great Britain
Weary of Britain's sea and land attacks, U.S. forces tried but failed to rout the British from Canada.

APRIL 14, 1828
Webster's *American Dictionary of the English Language* is published
Already the author of an English dictionary, Noah Webster created this one to reflect America's distinct "identity of language."

FEBRUARY 23, 1836
The Alamo is besieged
Texas settlers seeking independence held the San Antonio fortress for 13 days before Mexican forces overran it.

AUGUST 10, 1846
Smithsonian Institution is born
Scientist James Smithson's bequest created an institute "for the increase and diffusion of knowledge."

MARCH 6, 1857
Supreme Court issues Dred Scott decision
The ruling determined that the Constitution considered enslaved people "property," effectively denying them most civil protections.

DECEMBER 20, 1860
South Carolina secedes from the Union
Certain that Abraham Lincoln's election would mean slavery's end, this state was the first to secede.

SEPTEMBER 22, 1862
Emancipation Proclamation is issued
It decreed that on January 1, 1863, all enslaved people in Confederate states "shall be then, thenceforward, and forever free."

Bicycle racer Major Taylor was the first African American to reach the world champion level in a sport. By the age of 20, he held seven world records.

TIMELINE

1800-1899

WORDS LED TO BLOODSHED AMONG CONGRESS MEMBERS, OFTEN WHEN DEBATING SLAVERY. "I HAVE SEEN PISTOLS LAID ON DESKS LIKE INKSTANDS," A WORRIED CLERK REPORTED.

HISTORIAN JOANNE FREEMAN counted more than 70 violent incidents among Congress members from 1830 to 1860. As a U.S. House clerk in the mid-1800s, New Hampshire native Benjamin Brown French documented the proceedings of Congress—including, as it turned out, bloody fights between Southerners and Northerners. French spent more than 35 years in the congressional orbit and kept detailed diaries, from those and other sources.

Some of these disputes arose from an honor code that made any insult a pretext for a duel: Representative William Graves from Kentucky challenged Representative Jonathan Cilley from Maine after Cilley refused a letter Graves tried to hand him. French wrote of the February 1838 duel, "At the third fire, the ball from Graves' rifle passed through Cilley's body, severing the artery of the thigh. He fell and died almost instantly."

In session, Southerners often cut off antislavery speech by accosting the speaker; indeed, French's diary describes "men grappling and cursing like brutes" during an 1840s House floor brawl. In 1856, after Senator Charles Sumner from Massachusetts gave a speech denouncing enslavers—including his colleague, Senator Andrew Butler from South Carolina—Representative Preston Brooks from South Carolina came to Sumner's Senate desk and beat him over the head with a cane until it broke. "The deed was monstrous," French wrote. "I fear for the Republic."

Six weeks after Abraham Lincoln was elected president in November 1860, South Carolina became the first state to secede from the Union.

NOVEMBER 19, 1863

Lincoln delivers the Gettysburg Address

In a watershed speech at the Pennsylvania battle site, Abraham Lincoln rededicated the Union to "the unfinished work" of the fallen.

APRIL 9, 1865

Robert E. Lee surrenders to Ulysses S. Grant

With the Confederate capital captured and his troops depleted, the Confederate general admitted defeat at Appomattox Court House, Virginia.

APRIL 14, 1865

Abraham Lincoln is assassinated

As Lincoln watched a play, Confederate sympathizer John Wilkes Booth shot the president in the head. By morning, Lincoln was dead.

MARCH 1, 1872

Yellowstone is established as the world's first national park

The preserved area included scenic wonders in 3,400 square miles of Wyoming, Montana, and Idaho.

SEPTEMBER 20, 1873

For first time, New York Stock Exchange closes

After an investment bank collapsed and Wall Street suspended trading, panic and a depression followed.

MARCH 10, 1876

Alexander Graham Bell's telephone is inaugurated

The inventor spoke into a speech transmitter he invented; his assistant, in another room, heard him.

JANUARY 27, 1880

Thomas Edison patents incandescent light

The inventor's bulb and socket improvements paved the way for widespread use of electric light.

MAY 21, 1881

Clara Barton founds American Red Cross

Tending wounded during the Civil War inspired the celebrated nurse to found the aid group.

FEBRUARY 15, 1898

U.S.S. *Maine* explodes in Havana's harbor

The ship's destruction turned public opinion against Spain; 10 weeks later, the Spanish-American War began.

156. APRIL 24, 1800

AMERICA'S NATIONAL LIBRARY IS ESTABLISHED

As the young nation prepared to move its seat of government from Philadelphia to Washington, D.C., President John Adams approved funds for a federal library in the new capital on this day. The Library of Congress, established with 3,000 books, would be housed in the Capitol; when that building was burned in August 1814 during the War of 1812, the whole collection was lost. It would be rebuilt the next year with more than 6,400 books: the personal library of former president Thomas Jefferson, which Congress had purchased. Today, the Library of Congress is the largest library in the world and adds an estimated two million items to its collection each year.

157. NOVEMBER 1, 1800

THE WHITE HOUSE BECOMES A HOME

On this day, John Adams became the first president to spend a night in the still unfinished President's House—eventually known as the White House. Writing to his wife, Abigail, the following day, Adams ended with, "I pray Heaven to bestow the best of Blessings on this House … May none but honest and wise Men ever rule under this roof." Adams's words were later carved into the mantel in the State Dining Room. Abigail reluctantly joined him, as she had wanted to spend time at last with family and friends in Quincy, Massachusetts, and tend the Adams farm there. As first lady, she continued her no-nonsense ways and famously hung laundry to dry in the East Room.

158. NOVEMBER 17, 1800

CONGRESS RELOCATES TO THE NEW FEDERAL CITY

On this day, the governing bodies of the United States moved from Philadelphia to the city of Washington, the federal capital and officially part of the territory of Columbia. (Territories were an intermediate step toward statehood, though Washington was never granted that status.) The 1800 census recorded the city's population as 10,066 white people, 793 free Black people, and 3,244 enslaved people. Few federal buildings had been constructed, but the north wing of the Capitol topped Jenkins Hill. The lower land along the Potomac River was marshy but slated for federal development. Some government agencies temporarily moved into one of the so-called Six Buildings—adjacent, privately owned brick row houses on Pennsylvania Avenue.

159. FEBRUARY 4, 1801

JOHN MARSHALL BECOMES CHIEF JUSTICE OF THE SUPREME COURT

A distant cousin of Thomas Jefferson, Marshall had been a Virginia lawyer, diplomat, and politician for decades when President John Adams appointed him secretary of state in 1800. The following year, Adams nominated him as chief justice, and the Senate confirmed the nomination. Marshall filled both roles through Adams's presidency. He served 34 years

As chief justice, John Marshall instituted the practice of issuing consensus majority opinions instead of the judgments of individual justices.

as chief justice—the longest-serving ever—and transformed the Supreme Court into a powerful governmental force coequal with the executive and legislative branches. Today, he is known as the Great Chief Justice.

160. FEBRUARY 17, 1801

THOMAS JEFFERSON IS ELECTED PRESIDENT

At the time, electors were charged with voting for two men, without specifying president or vice president. Thomas Jefferson and his running mate, Aaron Burr, both received 73 votes initially, with Jefferson's rival, John Adams, receiving 65. The tie was sent to the House for a runoff, where representatives voted repeatedly and inconclusively for six days. Then, after backroom maneuvering by Alexander Hamilton against Burr, Jefferson won on the 36th ballot. On March 4, he walked from his boardinghouse to the Senate chamber and delivered his inaugural address, extolling "a wise and frugal Government, which shall restrain men from injuring one another, shall leave them otherwise free to regulate their own pursuits."

161. NOVEMBER 16, 1801

FIRST ISSUE OF *NEW-YORK EVENING POST* APPEARS

No longer a force in federal politics and living again in New York, Alexander Hamilton had remained devoted to his Federalist ideals and wanted a vehicle to give them voice. He raised the money and hired the staff for the Federalist-leaning *New-York Evening Post*—today the oldest continuously active newspaper in America. Its second week of publication, the *Post* reported on a duel waged over politics between George Eacker, a young New York lawyer, and Hamilton's son Philip, who was mortally wounded in the duel. Today, the newspaper, now called the *New York Post,* has a circulation of approximately 500,000.

162. MARCH 16, 1802

U.S. MILITARY ACADEMY IS ESTABLISHED

On this day, President Thomas Jefferson signed legislation authorizing a corps of engineers to be "stationed at West Point in the state of New York," and to "constitute a Military

Although Napoleon wasn't present at the signing of the Louisiana Purchase, artist Victor Adams added him to this depiction of the treaty ceremony.

Academy." Jefferson had initially opposed an "officer class" in the United States, and as president he worked to reduce the size of the army. But he also wanted to educate officers for this smaller army and cooperated with Congress to create the academy. In its first decades, West Point was devoted largely to civil and military engineering, as well as military discipline. It is the oldest continuously occupied regular army post in the U.S. Today, it has an undergraduate enrollment of approximately 4,000 students.

163. FEBRUARY 24, 1803

MARBURY V. _JAMES MADISON_ DECISION ESTABLISHES JUDICIAL REVIEW

In the final hours before leaving the presidency, John Adams appointed William Marbury to the judiciary. The appointment had not gone through when his successor, Thomas Jefferson, was sworn in, and Jefferson refused to honor it. Marbury appealed his case to the Supreme Court, citing a clause in the Judiciary Act of 1789. In a turning point moment, the Court ruled unanimously that the clause itself was unconstitutional, reaffirming its power of judicial review and establishing an important addition to the country's core system of checks and balances. In his opinion, Chief Justice John Marshall proclaimed, "It is emphatically the province and duty of the Judicial Department to say what the law is."

YOUR OBSERVATIONS ARE TO BE TAKEN WITH GREAT PAINS & ACCURACY TO BE ENTERED DISTINCTLY, & INTELLIGIBLY.

Thomas Jefferson, *instructions to Meriwether Lewis (1803)*

164. MAY 2, 1803

LOUISIANA PURCHASE IS SIGNED IN PARIS

Dispatched to France to offer Napoleon $10 million for the Port of New Orleans and the Florida territories, which France had colonized, U.S. ministers Robert Livingston and James Monroe received a counteroffer of $15 million for all of France's lands west of the Mississippi—essentially, a rate of four cents an acre. President Thomas Jefferson approved the sale (the treaty was antedated to April 30), with congressional approval following in October. The Louisiana Purchase added 828,000 acres to the United States, doubling its size. "Let the Land rejoice, for you have bought Louisiana for a Song," Gen. Horatio Gates crowed to Jefferson.

165. JUNE 19, 1803

MERIWETHER LEWIS PLANS A TRIP

On this day, the now renowned soldier and politician wrote to his former commander, William Clark, asking him to join an expedition west. President Thomas Jefferson had hired Lewis to be his personal secretary and, after mentoring him, chose him to lead an exploratory expedition through the new Louisiana Purchase lands. Lewis's seven-page letter described the expedition to Clark, a respected leader and frontiersman, and offered to make him co-commander. "If therefore there is anything ... which would induce you to participate with me in it's fatiegues, it's dangers and it's honors, believe me there is no man on earth with whom I should feel equal pleasure in sharing them." They would set off 11 months later.

166. JULY 17, 1803

NOTORIOUS JOURNALIST JAMES CALLENDER DROWNS

Over the course of his notorious career, the muckraking journalist had earned many enemies, including his former friend Thomas Jefferson. An early and ardent supporter of Jefferson and the Republicans, Callender had expected President Jefferson to appoint him Richmond, Virginia, postmaster, a sought-after and lucrative position. But the president felt Callender had become too unstable. Rebuffed, Callender turned his pen on Jefferson, writing that Jefferson had fathered children by Sally Hemings. (Callender had also previously exposed the affair between Alexander Hamilton and Maria Reynolds.) Observed in a drunken stupor in Richmond on this day, Callender was later found drowned in the James River.

167. FEBRUARY 16, 1804

AMERICANS RAID TRIPOLI HARBOR

The frigate U.S.S. *Philadelphia* was taken captive outside the harbor in Libya and towed inside, but Lt. Stephen Decatur carried out a plan to keep it from enemy use. He and his crew, disguised as Maltese, sailed a ship flying British colors into the harbor and, on this night, set fire to the *Philadelphia*. British Adm. Lord Horatio Nelson declared the feat "the most bold and daring act of the Age." Pope Pius VII observed that the Americans "had done more to humble and humiliate the anti-Christian barbarians on the African coast in one night than all the European states had done." (The Marines' storming of the fortress of Derna the following year—"The shores of Tripoli"—is cited in the "Marines' Hymn.")

168. JULY 11, 1804

AARON BURR DUELS ALEXANDER HAMILTON

Alexander Hamilton, the former treasury secretary, and Aaron Burr, the sitting vice president under Thomas Jefferson, had known each other for decades, initially as lawyers in New York. But politics had turned them into enemies, and Hamilton intrigued against Burr in his election bids for both the presidency and the governorship of New York. When a newspaper quoted Hamilton as calling Burr "a dangerous man ... who ought not to be trusted," Burr became determined to call him out. On a muggy July morning on bluffs above the Hudson in Weehawken, New Jersey, the two enemies faced off. Burr delivered a mortal shot, while Hamilton's shot was so far off that it was probably an intentional miss. The following day, surrounded by family and friends, Alexander Hamilton died, and New York mourned.

169. SEPTEMBER 25, 1804

TWELFTH AMENDMENT IS RATIFIED

Congress proposed this law to avoid ties like the one that had occurred in the recent 1800 presidential election. The new amendment stipulated that electors meeting in their states would cast two votes—one for president and the other for vice president—and that one

of those candidates must not be from the electors' home state. If no one candidate received a majority of the total votes, the House of Representatives would vote for president among the top contenders. Delaware, Connecticut, and Massachusetts did not ratify the amendment, and Massachusetts only did so in 1961.

Sacagawea, a Shoshone woman well-versed in tribal languages and lands, helped Meriwether Lewis and William Clark explore property acquired in the Louisiana Purchase.

170. NOVEMBER 15, 1805

MERIWETHER LEWIS AND WILLIAM CLARK REACH THE PACIFIC

The Corps of Discovery, tasked with exploring the newly acquired Louisiana Territory and finding a water route to the Pacific, set off down the Missouri River on May 14, 1804. It crossed the plains and the Bitterroots, a treacherous range in the Rockies, then paddled downriver on the Columbia for weeks. On November 7, Clark observed in his journal, "Great joy in camp we are in View of the Ocian," but it was actually only the Columbia River Estuary, still more than 20 miles from the ocean. It would take eight more days of wind and rain to reach the end point of the Corps' long pilgrimage: the Pacific. The group built the simple Fort Clatsop as a winter headquarters, then headed east, toward home, a few months later.

171. MARCH 29, 1806

PRESIDENT JEFFERSON SIGNS LEGISLATION FOR THE NATIONAL ROAD

The law created an east-west interstate extending from the Potomac River at Cumberland, Maryland, to the Ohio River at Wheeling, Virginia (now West Virginia). At the time, most travel and commerce happened via waterways, but Jefferson hoped that an overland route would promote trade and create a "union of sentiment." The three states it traversed had to grant permission to the federal government to build it; construction did not begin until 1811. Almost three decades later, the highway had grown to cover 620 miles. Today, the eastern leg of U.S. 40 bears the title Historic National Road.

172. MARCH 2, 1807

CONGRESS PROHIBITS THE IMPORTATION OF ENSLAVED PEOPLE

Under Article I of the Constitution, the "importation" of people could not be outlawed before 1808. With the deadline looming, Congress passed legislation "to prohibit the importation of slaves in any port or place within the jurisdiction of the United States, from and after the first day of January [1808]." Though the act didn't put an end to the domestic sale of already enslaved people or the practice of slavery, it did assess penalties on international traders. In practice, though, passengers aboard ships caught illegally trading were often brought into the United States—instead of being returned to their home countries—and sold into slavery.

As renowned a hostess as her husband, President James Madison, was a politician, Dolley Madison regularly invited guests of all stations to the White House.

173. SEPTEMBER 6, 1810

JOHN JACOB ASTOR'S *TONQUIN* JOINS THE FUR TRADE

On this day, the *Tonquin* sailed from New York, dispatched by John Jacob Astor. The son of a German butcher, Astor had arrived in New York around 1784 and became involved in the fur business, ultimately establishing a network of fur trading posts in the Pacific Northwest. In March 1811, after sailing around Cape Horn, the *Tonquin* reached the mouth of the Columbia River and a coastline "studded with gigantic trees ... many of them measuring fifty feet in girth." The *Tonquin* men built Fort Astoria, which became the main trading post for Astor's Pacific Fur Company and the first permanent U.S. settlement on the Pacific coast.

174. JANUARY 13, 1811

DOLLEY MADISON THROWS A PARTY

In the winter of 1811, Dolley Madison hosted one of her celebrated "Wednesday night squeezes." Hosted weekly at the White House by the vivacious and politically astute first lady, these soirees of up to 300 guests crammed into a reception room were open to any citizen who had called on the first lady or her husband, President James Madison, during the week prior. In a January 13 letter, aspiring writer Washington Irving (who would later find fame as the author of the short stories "Rip Van Winkle" and "The Legend of Sleepy Hollow") described how he left behind the "dirt & darkness" of Washington, D.C., and entered the "blazing splendour of Mrs. Madison's Drawing room. Here I was most graciously received—found a crowded collection of great and little men, of ugly old women, and beautiful young ones … Mrs. Madison is a fine, portly, buxom dame—who has a smile & pleasant word for every body."

175. NOVEMBER 7, 1811

BATTLE OF TIPPECANOE IS WAGED

On this day, militia forces under Indiana territorial governor William Henry Harrison beat back an attack by warriors of a new Native American confederacy formed by Shawnee chief Tecumseh and his brother, Tenskwatawa (known as "the Prophet"). The brothers were intent on fighting white incursions into their treaty lands in western Indiana, but Tecumseh was away recruiting men from southern tribes to join the cause when the Shawnee took on Harrison's forces. The Shawnee village of Prophetstown was torched, and the Prophet lost his following. In 1840, Harrison won the U.S. presidency on the slogan "Tippecanoe and Tyler too" (John Tyler became his vice president).

IT IS DEEPLY LAMENTED THAT SO MANY VALUABLE LIVES HAVE BEEN LOST IN THE ACTION WHICH TOOK PLACE ON THE 7TH.

James Madison, *speaking to Congress regarding Tippecanoe (1811)*

176. FEBRUARY 7, 1812

MASSIVE EARTHQUAKE STRIKES MISSOURI

The final and most severe of three huge earthquakes that took place from December 1811 through February 1812, this seismic event had a magnitude estimated to range anywhere from 7.0 to 8.8 at its epicenter near the town of New Madrid, Missouri. It spawned

Though Congress outlawed the "importation of slaves," effective January 1, 1808, the practices of selling and enslaving people continued.

Reelfoot Lake in northwestern Tennessee and created temporary waterfalls on the Mississippi, as well as causing the river to run backward. With aftershocks felt throughout the central and eastern U.S., it still ranks as the largest earthquake ever recorded east of the Rocky Mountains.

177. JUNE 18, 1812

JAMES MADISON SIGNS A DECLARATION OF WAR WITH GREAT BRITAIN

For years, the Royal Navy had violated American maritime rights and trade, often "impressing" or seizing U.S. seamen it claimed were British deserters and forcing them to work on British ships. The British had also allied themselves with Native American tribes to thwart the westward expansion of American settlers. Finally, Congress and the president had enough. But because America had only 16 warships to Britain's 500, they decided against taking on the British at sea, instead aiming their sights on British-controlled Canada. But the three 1812 campaigns to conquer the northern neighbor would all fail.

178. AUGUST 23, 1814

STEPHEN PLEASONTON SAVES THE DECLARATION OF INDEPENDENCE

As British troops approached the capital city, clerks in the nascent federal bureaucracy were told to pack up critical documents. State Department clerk Stephen Pleasonton and his colleagues packed the original Declaration of Independence, Constitution, Articles of Confederation, Bill of Rights, and other papers into linen bags and hauled them by cart to a nearby gristmill. Fearing the British would find them there, they reloaded the documents onto farm wagons and took them 35 miles northwest to a deserted mansion in Leesburg, Virginia, where they were safe from the marauding enemy.

179. AUGUST 24, 1814

THE CAPITOL AND WHITE HOUSE BURN

After sailing up the Chesapeake Bay and Patuxent River, the British landed at Benedict, Maryland, and marched overland to Washington, D.C. On this day, they torched the uncompleted Capitol Building, the White House, and nearly all the other public buildings in the new city. A rainstorm doused the fires, but not before they inflicted great damage. Despite that, on September 19, the Senate convened in the only building able to accommodate them: Blodgett's Hotel, located at 7th and E Streets NW. It would be four years before the gutted Capitol was able to house Congress again.

180. SEPTEMBER 14, 1814

"THE STAR-SPANGLED BANNER" MAKES WAVES

On September 13, lawyer Francis Scott Key was on an American frigate on the Patapsco River near Baltimore, Maryland. He had come the previous week to negotiate the release of a friend being held by the British on their flagship. The British agreed to the terms but insisted that Key and his friend stay nearby, as they had learned of plans to bombard Baltimore. On this night, Key watched as enemy shells cannonaded Fort McHenry, lighting the sky. Yet at dawn, the U.S. flag was still flying above the fort. In the morning, Key wrote his famous poem, which ends: "O say does that star-spangled banner yet wave / O'er the land of the free and the home of the brave?" Set to music, it became popular and was declared the official national anthem in 1931.

181. JANUARY 8, 1815

ANDREW JACKSON GAINS A NAME FOR HIMSELF

Recently promoted to major general of the U.S. Army, Jackson learned that the British had their eyes on New Orleans. Through the month of December, he assembled a motley force of militia, frontiersmen, pirates, Choctaw Indians, and Free Men of Color.

On August 24, 1814, British forces marched on Washington, D.C., setting fire to the White House, the Capitol, and other public buildings—key moments in the War of 1812.

As postwar confidence and harmony swept the nation, President James Monroe's two terms became known as the "era of good feelings."

They dug fortifications along the east bank of the Mississippi, five miles south of the city. Despite being outnumbered nearly two to one, Jackson's forces repulsed the attacking British, winning what would become known as the Battle of New Orleans. Hero of the last major combat in the War of 1812, Jackson gained national attention as "Old Hickory," a man of strength and courage.

182. MARCH 4, 1817

JAMES MONROE IS INAUGURATED AS THE FIFTH PRESIDENT

The last of the "Virginia dynasty"—four of the five earliest presidents were Virginians—Monroe was a protégé of Thomas Jefferson and a lawyer by profession. He had served as U.S. senator, minister to Paris, governor, secretary of war, and, for six years, secretary of state. In his inaugural address, Monroe praised the U.S., but warned that "when the people become ignorant and corrupt ... they degenerate into a populace ... incapable of exercising the sovereignty ... Let us ... promote intelligence among the people as the best means of preserving our liberties." His two terms become known as the "era of good feelings."

183. APRIL 15, 1817

AMERICAN SCHOOL FOR THE DEAF IS FOUNDED

At the behest of his neighbor, whose daughter was deaf, Rev. Thomas Hopkins Gallaudet had traveled to Paris to visit a pioneering school where sign language was being taught. Returning home with a teacher from the school, Gallaudet raised funds to open an American counterpart in Hartford, Connecticut. The first school for the deaf in the Western Hemisphere, it continues to operate to this day. Almost 50 years later, Gallaudet's son, Edward Miner Gallaudet, would serve as the first president of Gallaudet University in Washington, D.C., established by an act of Congress in 1864.

AS THE ANIMAL WAS SEEN SO IMPERFECTLY AND IN SWIFT MOTION, GREAT ALLOWANCE MUST BE MADE.

John Davis, *resident of Massachusetts, on the sighting of a sea serpent (1817)*

184. AUGUST 18, 1817

SEA SERPENTS ARE SIGHTED IN GLOUCESTER, MASSACHUSETTS

Reports of the fabled creatures appeared on this day in the *Boston Daily Advertiser.* Tales of the Gloucester sea serpent dated back to the 1600s, but in August 1817, "hundreds of people" reported seeing a "prodigious snake" over the course of several days; some claimed the beast was 100 feet long with a girth as big as a barrel. The newly formed Linnaean Society of New England investigated and declared it had found a new genus. But other experts disagreed, and the Linnaean Society eventually backed down.

185. OCTOBER 20, 1818

TREATY OF 1818 IS SIGNED, CREATING THE LONGEST UNDEFENDED BORDER IN THE WORLD

Also known as the Convention of 1818 between the United States and the United Kingdom, the agreement, signed in London, established the 49th parallel—stretching from the Lake of the Woods (on what is now the Ontario-Manitoba border) to the Rocky Mountains—as the boundary between the U.S. and Britain's Canadian territories. It also gave American fishermen access to the rich waters around Newfoundland and Labrador, and allowed for a decade of joint occupation of Oregon Country (the area west of the Rocky Mountains) by Britain and the U.S.

186. SEPTEMBER 29, 1819

FIRST AMERICAN WHALING SHIPS ARRIVE IN HAWAII

The *Balena* and *Equator,* both Massachusetts whalers, anchored in the Big Island's Kealakekua Bay. Just three years later, some 60 whaleships were making port in the Sandwich Islands (as the Hawaiian Islands were then called), and more soon filled the waters off Honolulu, Oahu, and Lahaina on Maui. After an 8,000-mile journey from New England, they reprovisioned in the Sandwiches and replaced ill crewmen with Native seamen before heading to the rich sperm whaling waters in the Sea of Japan. Having access to these ports greatly bolstered America's prosperous and growing whaling industry.

187. MARCH 3, 1820

MISSOURI COMPROMISE IS ADOPTED

This bill marked a turning point in American history. Championed by Speaker of the House Henry Clay, it was precipitated by the Missouri Territory's application for statehood—the first territory west of the Mississippi to do so. Factionalism ran high in Congress between pro- and antislavery representatives, and on other regional issues between North and South. Hoping to quell the growing disunion, Kentuckian Clay proposed admitting Missouri as a slave state and Maine as free. Accepted by Congress, his compromise bill established a line in the Louisiana Purchase lands that ran east to west along the 36th parallel, with slavery allowed in the lower half and prohibited in the upper half.

To Europe's headless horseman tales—Ireland's Dullahan, Germany's hunting devil—Washington Irving contributed his notorious short story "The Legend of Sleepy Hollow."

188. MARCH 15, 1820

"THE LEGEND OF SLEEPY HOLLOW" IS PUBLISHED

Washington Irving's spooky tale of a headless horseman appeared in the serial collection known as *The Sketch Book of Geoffrey Crayon, Gent.* Irving wrote the story while on a tour of Europe, where tales of headless horsemen abounded. He set his tale in his native Hudson Valley, near Tarrytown, New York, where a headless horseman (who may have been the ghost of a Hessian horseman still seeking revenge after losing his head in the Revolutionary War) strikes fear in the heart of villagers. The tale, along with Irving's "Rip Van Winkle," quickly became distinctly American classics.

189. MAY 8, 1823

"HOME, SWEET HOME" DEBUTS AND IS A HIT

The beloved song was performed during the premiere of the opera *Clari, the Maid of Milan* in London's Covent Garden theater district. Later adapted, it became immensely popular with American audiences, particularly during the Civil War; the Library of Congress called it "America's first bona fide hit song." Despite that, New Yorker John Howard Payne, who wrote the lyrics, received very little compensation for his memorable verses, as was often the case for songwriters at that time. "'Mid pleasures and Palaces though we may roam / Be it ever so humble, there's no place like home!"

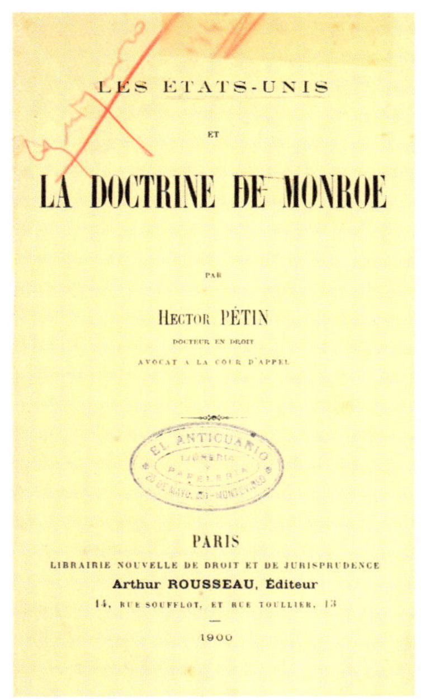

LES ETATS-UNIS

ET

LA DOCTRINE DE MONROE

PAR

HECTOR PÉTIN

DOCTEUR EN DROIT

AVOCAT A LA COUR D'APPEL

PARIS

LIBRAIRIE NOUVELLE DE DROIT ET DE JURISPRUDENCE

Arthur ROUSSEAU, Éditeur

14, RUE SOUFFLOT, ET RUE TOULLIER, 13

1900

President James Monroe's foreign relations doctrine—here, in French—formalized the Americas' resistance to colonization from abroad.

190. DECEMBER 2, 1823

PRESIDENT UNVEILS HIS MONROE DOCTRINE

In his annual address to Congress, President James Monroe outlined his doctrine for foreign relations on this day. Though largely ignored outside the U.S. at the time, the doctrine established two centuries of U.S. foreign policy by asserting that "the American continents, by the free and independent condition which they have assumed and maintain, are henceforth not to be considered as subjects for future colonization by any European powers." In the lead-up to the 1962 Cuban missile crisis, President John F. Kennedy declared the Monroe Doctrine to be the reason "why we oppose what is happening in Cuba today."

191. JUNE 25, 1824

ANDREW JOHNSON RUNS AWAY

On this day, tailor James Selby placed an ad in a Raleigh, North Carolina paper, offering a $10 reward for the return of two apprentices: "RAN AWAY from the Subscriber … WILLIAM and ANDREW JOHNSON … I will pay the above reward to any person who will deliver said apprentices to me in Raleigh, or I will give the above Reward for Andrew Johnson alone." The brothers had apprenticed under their mother and step-father, but after two years on the run, Andrew, then 17, returned to his family in Raleigh. Thirty-nine years later, he became the controversial 17th president of the United States.

192. OCTOBER 18, 1824

MARQUIS DE LAFAYETTE MARKS THE 43RD ANNIVERSARY OF YORKTOWN VICTORY

President James Monroe invited the much beloved Revolutionary ally to the United States, where Lafayette embarked on a 13-month Farewell Tour, visiting all 24 states and receiving a hero's welcome. During his visit, the Marquis de Lafayette was reunited with James Armistead Lafayette. Enslaved during the Revolution, James had served as a double agent, reporting to the marquis on Benedict Arnold; James took the name Fayette after he was freed. The marquis also spent time at the homes of former presidents Thomas Jefferson and James Madison and paid his respects at Mount Vernon.

193. FEBRUARY 9, 1825

HOUSE OF REPRESENTATIVES ELECTS JOHN QUINCY ADAMS

Adams became the sixth president of the United States after the electoral college failed to produce a winner. The general election had four candidates: William Crawford; House Speaker Henry Clay; Andrew Jackson, the hero of the Indian Wars and Battle of New Orleans; and Secretary of State Adams. In the end, Adams won after a single round of voting in the House, though Jackson had received more votes in both the electoral college and popular count. Clay, meanwhile, had lobbied House members to support Adams; after the election, Adams later made Clay his secretary of state. Jackson accused the two of making a "corrupt bargain."

After electoral votes failed to decide a four-way presidential race, a U.S. House vote sent John Quincy Adams to the White House.

194. OCTOBER 26, 1825

ERIE CANAL OPENS

On this day, New York Governor DeWitt Clinton boarded the *Seneca Chief* in Buffalo to travel from Lake Erie to New York City on the new, 363-mile-long, four-foot-deep canal. He emptied two casks of water from the lake into the Atlantic, celebrating the "Wedding of the Waters." Critics called the Erie Canal "Clinton's Folly," expecting it to have little long-term use. But the waterway was a success and incorporated into the much larger New York State Barge Canal in the early 1900s. It remained vital until the 1970s, when trucking and railroads increasingly overtook moving freight.

195. FEBRUARY 4, 1826

JAMES FENIMORE COOPER PUBLISHES *THE LAST OF THE MOHICANS*

Cooper's beloved novel was the second in his series of five wildly popular fictional stories known collectively as the Leatherstocking Tales. They featured the adventures of frontiersman Natty Bumppo (Leatherstocking) and recounted the world of settlers and Native Americans in the 18th-century American frontier. *The Last of the Mohicans* takes place during the French and Indian War and is set near Lake George, New York, at the base of the Adirondack Mountains.

196. JULY 4, 1826

THOMAS JEFFERSON AND JOHN ADAMS PASS AWAY

Initially close compatriots in Paris, Jefferson and Adams became bitter political foes. But in 1812, the two great founders reconciled and began an epic correspondence. On the 50th anniversary of their Declaration of Independence, the two died within hours of each other: Jefferson, 83, at Monticello, and Adams, 90, in his Quincy, Massachusetts, home. According to John Quincy Adams, his father's last words were, "Thomas Jefferson survives"—but Jefferson had died five hours earlier. Five years later, President James Monroe also died on July 4.

197. FEBRUARY 28, 1827

BALTIMORE AND OHIO RAILROAD IS CHARTERED

For decades, canals had been seen as the most modern form of transport, but after Britain's invention of the steam locomotive in 1825, Americans began to consider rail. The line became the country's first regular carrier of passengers and freight, opening its first route

ALWAYS VOTE FOR PRINCIPLE, THOUGH YOU MAY VOTE ALONE, AND YOU MAY CHERISH THE SWEETEST REFLECTION THAT YOUR VOTE IS NEVER LOST.

John Quincy Adams

Passengers pose with a locomotive of the Baltimore and Ohio Railroad, America's first regular rail carrier of freight and passengers.

Noah Webster created his *American Dictionary* to distinguish the "identity of language" he perceived between Old World and American English.

with 14 miles of track in 1830. Twenty years later, 9,000 miles of track laced the country. John Stevens, a New Jersey inventor and rival to Robert Fulton (credited with developing the first steamboat), was a great champion of the new form of transport. Today, he is considered the American "father of railroads."

198. MARCH 16, 1827

FREEDOM'S JOURNAL IS FOUNDED IN NEW YORK CITY

The first newspaper owned and operated by African Americans, the four-page weekly was established the same year slavery was abolished in New York State. It championed the rights of Black Americans and argued against slavery, but also ran articles intended to entertain or educate. After six months, editor John Russwurm began to promote the American Colonization Society, which supported shipping African Americans to the new African colony of Liberia. His views cost the paper readers, and he ultimately emigrated to Liberia himself. In 1829, Samuel Cornish, the paper's co-founder, attempted to revitalize it, but it ceased publication later that year.

199. DECEMBER 13, 1827

ORIGINAL DELMONICO'S OPENS

The famed restaurant began as a small café and pastry shop run by Italian-Swiss brothers Giovanni and Pietro Delmonico in Lower Manhattan; within a decade, they introduced fine dining, wines, and an à la carte menu to the American public. Relocated to an imposing triangle building, Delmonico's—or the Citadel, as New Yorkers called it—became the standard bearer for haute cuisine, known for such signature dishes as the Delmonico steak, introduced in 1850, and lobster Newburg. Revived several times under new ownership, it remains a New York City icon.

200. FEBRUARY 21, 1828

***CHEROKEE PHOENIX* IS PUBLISHED**

The first issue of the newspaper, printed in both English and Cherokee, was published in New Echota, Georgia, the capital of the Cherokee Nation. It was the first newspaper founded by Native Americans and the first in a Native American language, allowing its editors to go on to write in Cherokee about the Indian Removal Act in 1830. Only seven years before the paper first published, the Cherokee had no written language. But polymath Sequoyah created a Cherokee syllabary, with 86 written symbols to signify different sounds, after he saw that whites could communicate through "talking leaves," or written pages.

201. APRIL 14, 1828

WEBSTER'S *AMERICAN DICTIONARY OF THE ENGLISH LANGUAGE* DOCUMENTS THE COUNTRY'S LANGUAGE

In 1806, Noah Webster had published *A Compendious Dictionary of the English Language*. But as a proud American, he wanted to create a truly American lexicon. In the preface of his *American Dictionary,* he explained that in the U.S., "although the body of the language is the same as in England … yet some differences must exist. Language is an expression of ideas; and if the people of one country cannot preserve an identity of ideas, they cannot retain an identity of language." In 1841, the Merriam brothers bought the rights to publish revised versions of Webster's dictionary and released it as the enduring Merriam-Webster's dictionary.

202. MARCH 4, 1829

ANDREW JACKSON IS INAUGURATED AS PRESIDENT

"Old Hickory" swept into office as the seventh president on a landslide victory of populism. After the swearing in at the Capitol, the White House was open to the public, and hordes of well-wishers descended, packed so tightly and rambunctiously that they spilled bowls

continued on page 120

SPOTLIGHT

THE VISUAL ARTS

IN THE 19TH CENTURY, the visual arts—like the United States itself—emerged as a vibrant realm of talented innovations and expanding landscapes. Historical tableaux remained popular, as did stately likenesses by portraitists such as John Singer Sargent and Gilbert Stuart (whose portrait of George Washington was the model for the image on the $1 bill).

But U.S. artists also were pioneering new styles and forms, depicting routines of everyday life and scenery of the nation, especially its new territories. Massachusetts-born Winslow Homer became known for powerfully evoking maritime and seaside scenes, as well as life in rural America and during the Civil War. George Caleb Bingham, who was also a politician, came to be called "the Missouri Artist" for his renderings of the new frontier and those exploring it, especially along the Missouri and Mississippi Rivers.

New aesthetics and specialties also developed. Painting panoramic scenes full of realistic detail, Frederic Edwin Church pioneered what became the Hudson River school of landscape art from his impressive home overlooking the New York river. Thomas Moran was the first painter to capture the wonders of Yellowstone, after joining an 1871 government surveying expedition to the region; he visited Yosemite in 1872 and the Grand Canyon the following year. And although women artists of this era often were dismissed, painter Mary Cassatt persevered in her native Pennsylvania, then in Paris; she became the first American to exhibit with the French Impressionists and helped introduce the movement in her homeland.

Largely self-taught, vaunted American painter Winslow Homer created "Artists Sketching in the White Mountains" in 1868, after summer visits to that area of New Hampshire.

CAN YOU OFFER ME ANYTHING TO COMPARE TO THAT JOY TO AN ARTIST?

Mary Cassatt

This 1863 engraving depicts Nat Turner meeting with co-conspirators in Southampton County, Virginia, in what would become America's deadliest slave revolt.

continued from page 117

of punch, stood on furniture in work boots, and created general mayhem. According to a South Carolina senator and supporter of Jackson, it was a "regular Saturnalia"; even the "Servant [61-year-old Jackson] in the presence of his Sovereign, the People" seemed overwhelmed at his inauguration. His harsh policies relating to Native American and enslaved people would make his presidency divisive; he was censured by the Senate in 1834, accused of assuming "authority and power not conferred by the Constitution and laws, but in derogation of both."

203. MAY 28, 1830

PRESIDENT ANDREW JACKSON SIGNS INDIAN REMOVAL ACT INTO LAW

The new decree provided for "an exchange of lands with the Indians residing in any of the states or territories, and for their removal west of the river Mississippi." As a federal treaty commissioner, Jackson, a veteran and hero of the Indian Wars, was authorized to negotiate with the tribes and "solemnly to assure" them "that the United States will forever secure and guaranty to them, and their heirs or successors, the country so exchanged with them." Almost 70 Indian removal treaties were negotiated during Jackson's tenure as president, with 50,000 humans displaced to new territories, where their land claims were often unprotected and they were subjected to prejudice and abuse.

204. JANUARY 28, 1831

EDGAR ALLAN POE IS COURT-MARTIALED

A cadet at the U.S. Military Academy, Poe was dismissed after only months at West Point, found guilty of gross neglect of duty and disobedience of orders. Yet before his arrival, he had served two very successful years in the Army. Had he remained in the military, he may have foregone his penchant for writing poetry and failed to explore a new genre: horror. In the two decades left to him after West Point, Poe would write such classics as "The Raven," "The Pit and the Pendulum," "The Tell-Tale Heart," "Annabel Lee," and "Eldorado."

I DEMANDED NOTHING THAT WAS NOT CLEARLY IN ACCORDANCE WITH JUSTICE AND HUMANITY.

William Lloyd Garrison, *abolitionist and co-founder of* The Liberator *(1868)*

205. MAY 9, 1831

ALEXIS DE TOCQUEVILLE ARRIVES IN AMERICA

Two minor French court officials, Tocqueville and Gustave de Beaumont, had been sent to the United States to study experimental prisons in America. But the two young men decided to spend most of their time watching American democracy at work, because most Europeans did not understand the concept of a democratic system. In nine months, the two traveled thousands of miles along the East Coast and west to the Mississippi. Returning to France, Tocqueville spent the next eight years writing *Democracy in America.* "The people reign over the American political world," he wrote, "as God rules over the universe."

206. AUGUST 21, 1831

NAT TURNER REBELS

Declaring that he was called upon by God to do so, Turner, an enslaved Virginia preacher, orchestrated the country's most deadly slave revolt. Beginning at 2 a.m., Turner and his followers attacked and killed his master's family in their home, then continued their rampage through southeastern Virginia's Southampton County the following day. Fifty-five white men, women, and children were killed before the rebels were crushed. Turner himself avoided arrest for two months before being caught, tried, and hanged in Jerusalem, Virginia.

207. JANUARY 6, 1832

ABOLITIONIST FOUNDS NEW ENGLAND ANTI-SLAVERY SOCIETY

William Lloyd Garrison, an outspoken Massachusetts abolitionist and co-founder of the antislavery newspaper *The Liberator,* spearheaded the society, which held its first meeting at the African Meeting House in Boston. Officially calling for an immediate end to slavery, it sent lecturers throughout the North and petitioned Congress to promulgate the antislavery message. It also encouraged the formation of other antislavery societies. In 1834, the organization became part of Garrison's American Anti-Slavery Society, founded the year before.

208. APRIL 5, 1832

SAUK CHIEF BLACK HAWK LEADS HIS PEOPLE HOME

Though an 1804 treaty deemed that the Sauk could remain on their northern Illinois land as long as it was in U.S. government possession, by 1832 white settlers had purchased the land in such numbers that Black Hawk and his people were in effect removed from the region. After being barred from the land, Black Hawk led some 1,200 men, women, and children back to their homeland on the Illinois side of the Mississippi. The situation quickly escalated into the Black Hawk War. A 23-year-old Abraham Lincoln served briefly in the Illinois militia, who made up part of the force opposing Black Hawk. The effects of the war on the Sauk were brutal: Only 150 of Black Hawk's people survived it.

When some 1,200 Sauk men, women, and children and their chief, Black Hawk, tried to reclaim Illinois land taken by white settlers, all but 150 were killed in what became known as the Black Hawk War.

209. NOVEMBER 12, 1832

"JUMP JIM CROW" MAKES ITS DEBUT

On this night, Manhattan's Bowery Theatre erupted in applause for a song-and-dance routine performed by New York comedian Thomas Rice. In blackface and wearing ragged clothes, Rice would become famous for his performance, which was possibly based on an enslaved man with physical disabilities or a boy who worked in the stables behind the theater. In the act, Rice belted out, "O, Jim Crow's come to town, as you all must know. / An' he wheel about, he turn about, he do jis so." The piece furthered the popularity of minstrel shows and originated the demeaning slur "Jim Crow." It lived on as a descriptor of the unfair laws of the coming era of discrimination in the South.

210. JANUARY 1, 1835

NATIONAL DEBT HITS ZERO FOR THE FIRST—AND LAST (AS OF NOW)—TIME

President Andrew Jackson came into office with big plans for fiscal change, including eliminating the national debt. He had achieved that, in part, by selling off federal lands, which led to a real estate bubble and, eventually, surplus federal money. But Jackson had already eliminated the National Bank. So he gave the surplus to state banks, which in turn led to overspending, borrowing, and an even bigger financial bubble, which burst with the financial Panic of 1837. The depression it caused lasted six years, the longest in U.S. history.

211. OCTOBER 21, 1835

WILLIAM LLOYD GARRISON HOLDS TO HIS PRINCIPLES

The celebrated abolitionist was attending a meeting of the Boston Female Anti-Slavery Society, held in the offices of his own *Liberator* newspaper. It was rumored that his friend,

British abolitionist George Thompson, would be speaking there; this infuriated a group of local businessmen, who were invested in textiles and needed slave labor to harvest cotton. The men descended on the *Liberator* offices, grabbed Garrison, tied a rope around his waist, and marched him through the streets. They also threatened to tar and feather him, but the mayor intervened.

212. DECEMBER 29, 1835

U.S. AND CHEROKEE NATION ADOPT THE TREATY OF NEW ECHOTA

In the Georgia town of New Echota, a Cherokee delegation met with U.S. officials and ceded seven million acres of traditional homeland east of the Mississippi to the U.S. in exchange for five million dollars and land in the new Indian Territory (now Oklahoma). Cherokee leader John Ross, who had not been part of the delegation, and the majority

In an 1832 New York City minstrel show, a demeaning performance by a character in blackface turned his name, Jim Crow, into a racial slur.

For 13 days in 1838, Texas colonists seeking independence from Mexico defended the Alamo. All were killed when Mexican forces overran it.

of the 16,000 citizens of the Cherokee Nation opposed the bargain. With this in mind, President Martin Van Buren offered to extend removal by two years—but that did little to encourage the Cherokee to leave their ancestral lands.

213. FEBRUARY 23, 1836

THE ALAMO IS BESIEGED

Since the previous October, fighting had been ongoing in the Texas Revolution against Mexico. White colonists who had migrated to Texas at the invitation of Mexico now wanted independence. Expecting attack, the Americans had fortified San Antonio's historic fortress/mission, known as the Alamo. On this day—one of the most legendary in the Texas Revolution—Mexican Gen. Antonio López de Santa Anna laid siege to the fortress, where some 150 defenders were holed up (among them, fabled frontiersmen

Davy Crockett and Jim Bowie.) On March 6, Santa Anna attacked and the Alamo fell. The occasion would live on vividly in Texas memory.

214. APRIL 21, 1836

TEXAS GAINS INDEPENDENCE FROM MEXICO

Near the mouth of the San Jacinto River, Gen. Sam Houston and some 900 Texan troops faced off against Mexican Gen. Antonio López de Santa Anna's 1,200-man force in the crucial Battle of San Jacinto. On this afternoon they took the Mexicans by surprise, roaring into battle with the cry of "Remember the Alamo!" In a mere 18 minutes, they subdued the Mexicans, killed half their force, and ensured independence for Texas. For the next 10 years, the Republic of Texas would exist as an independent country, with Sam Houston as its president for five of those years.

I AM DETERMINED TO SUSTAIN MYSELF AS LONG AS POSSIBLE ... VICTORY OR DEATH.

William B. Travis, *commander of the Texas forces at the Battle of the Alamo (1836)*

215. JUNE 29, 1837

HORACE MANN PLANTS A SEED

A lawyer by training and former state senator, Mann—later known as "the Father of American Education"—became secretary of the Massachusetts Board of Education on this day. His ideas for tax-supported "common schools" open to all children eventually led to a system of public education in America. Mann also encouraged the development of teachers' colleges and nonsectarian school curricula—a precursor to the idea of separation of church and state in public schools. Education was imperative for a democracy, Mann believed, touting that citizens need to "understand something of the true nature and functions of the government under which they live."

216. OCTOBER 21, 1837

OSCEOLA IS BETRAYED AND CAPTURED

Probably born in Alabama to a Creek mother and Scottish father, Billy Powell, as he was known, escaped to Spanish Florida during the Creek War of 1813–14. He took the name Osceola and became a respected leader among the Seminoles, an aggregate of displaced Native Americans and people who had escaped slavery. The Second Seminole War proved to be America's most costly conflict against the Indians, as Osceola frequently outmaneuvered U.S. forces. On this day, Osceola met to negotiate with U.S. Gen. Thomas Jesup under a white flag of truce. But he was taken captive instead and spent the remaining few months of his life in prison.

217. MAY 10, 1838

U.S. MILITARY FORCEFULLY RELOCATES A NATION—AND CREATES A TRAIL OF TEARS

On this day, Maj. Gen. Winfield Scott issued a proclamation to the Cherokee Nation: "The President ... has sent me with a powerful army, to cause you ... to join that part of

The 1,000-plus-mile march that forced 17,000 Cherokee from their homeland in 1838 earned the name Trail of Tears because thousands died during the relocation.

your people who have already established in prosperity on the other side of the Mississippi." Between 1838 and '39, 16,000 Cherokee were forced from their homes onto what would become known as the Trail of Tears. During the thousand-mile-long march to Indian Territory, more than 4,000 died, a fifth of the Cherokee population. The Chickasaw, Choctaw, Muscogee Creek, and Seminole tribes were also subject to forced relocations, sometimes walking the vast journey in chains.

218. AUGUST 18, 1838

WILKES EXPEDITION SETS SAIL

Officially known as the U.S. South Seas Exploring Expedition, the voyage was led by 40-year-old Charles Wilkes, head of the federal Depot of Charts and Instruments. Charged with exploring and charting the Pacific Ocean, Antarctic, and Pacific Northwest, its six sailing ships carried some 300 crew members, a linguist, geologist, botanist, naturalist, other scientists, and two artists. The group was also asked to "collect, preserve, and arrange every thing valuable in the whole range of natural history." The general findings of the four-year expedition put America on the map as a new leader in scientific research, and the 40 tons of specimens it procured would become the core of the Smithsonian Institution's collection.

219. JULY 1, 1839

ULYSSES GRANT GETS A NEW NAME

As a young man, Grant disliked working in his family's Ohio tannery, so his father worked to get him appointed as a cadet at the U.S. Military Academy at West Point. He was nominated by Congressman Thomas L. Hamer, who got his name wrong on the application form. Born Hiram Ulysses Grant, the young man often went by Ulysses. But the congressman had instead nominated Ulysses S. Grant, erroneously using his mother's maiden name, Simpson, as a middle initial. While Grant tried to correct the mistake, he had no luck. The name stuck, and he eventually entered history as U. S. Grant.

220. MARCH 4, 1841

"LOG CABIN & HARD CIDER CANDIDATE" BECOMES THE NINTH U.S. PRESIDENT

When war hero and former territorial governor William Henry Harrison ran against incumbent President Martin Van Buren in 1840, the 67-year-old was criticized as too old: A *Baltimore Republican* newspaper editorial sneered that Harrison should retire to his log cabin with "a barrel of hard cider." But Harrison's campaign capitalized on the insult to humanize him as the "Log Cabin & Hard Cider Candidate," and he won, becoming the oldest president (at the time) to take office. On April 4, Harrison added the grim distinction of being the first president to die in office: After a cold he caught on inauguration day turned to pneumonia, he passed away, just one month after taking office.

221. APRIL 10, 1841

FIRST ISSUE OF *NEW-YORK TRIBUNE* APPEARS

The newspaper's editor, the obstreperous 31-year-old Horace Greeley, would rule the publication for the next 30 years. Unlike other "penny papers" of the day, Greeley's *Tribune* did not focus on the crime reporting, scandal, and human-interest stories that garnered readers; instead, it ran book reviews, covered politics from a Whig (or anti-Jackson) perspective, and pursued other, more lofty topics. "I cherish the hope that the stone which covers my ashes may bear to future eyes the still intelligent inscription, 'Founder of the New York Tribune,'" Greeley later wrote in his memoir.

222. JULY 28, 1841

MYSTERIOUS DEATH OF A SHOPGIRL SPARKS SPURIOUS NEWSPAPER COVERAGE

Writers who frequented John Anderson's tobacco store—from "penny press" newspaper reporters to literary figures such as James Fenimore Cooper and Washington Irving—went there not just to buy, but also to admire comely Mary Cecilia Rogers, the 20-year-old clerk they nicknamed "the Beautiful Cigar Girl." Rogers's body was found on this day—

three days after she didn't return home for dinner—floating in the Hudson River. Newspapers competed breathlessly on the true crime story, speculating about clues and suspects from Rogers's fiancé to gang members. The case never was solved, but Edgar Allan Poe fictionalized Rogers's murder in his story "The Mystery of Marie Rogêt."

223. AUGUST 11, 1841

FREDERICK DOUGLASS DELIVERS HIS FIRST ADDRESS FOR A WHITE AUDIENCE

The great social reformer spoke before a mostly white audience at an antislavery meeting in the athenaeum on Massachusetts's Nantucket Island. Abolitionists William Lloyd Garrison and William Coffin had urged Douglass to make the speech, though, at the time, Douglass was technically a fugitive (he had escaped bondage only a few years before). Over the next two years, he lectured twice more at the Nantucket Atheneum; his time there among the abolitionists set him on the path to becoming one of America's great antislavery orators.

Frederick Douglass gave his first antislavery speech in 1841 to a mostly white audience in Massachusetts.

224. SEPTEMBER 29, 1841

AMERICA'S FIRST STATE FAIR OPENS

In the fair's rainy, two-day run, 10,000 to 15,000 people flocked to Syracuse, New York, a central point on the Erie Canal and a hub of farming in the state, to see exhibits of farm animals and hear speeches by various public figures. The concept of an event celebrating the skills and culture of farm life soon spread to other states, and today, usually near summer's end, all states hold state fairs.

225. JANUARY 1, 1842

P. T. BARNUM OPENS HIS AMERICAN MUSEUM

As a 12-year-old, the circus impresario P. T. Barnum was hired to participate in a cattle drive to Brooklyn; that visit convinced him to leave his family's Connecticut farm life behind. At 31, he opened his museum on lower Broadway in Manhattan with exhibits on the arts, history, literature, technology, and the "natural curiosities" that would ultimately define his legacy. One of the most famous of Barnum's performers was "Gen. Tom Thumb," who stood less than three feet tall. Barnum's museum eventually occupied four buildings and was the hub of New York attractions for 23 years.

226. JANUARY 22, 1842

CHARLES DICKENS ARRIVES IN BOSTON

The wildly popular British author of *Oliver Twist* was given an enormous welcome when he arrived to learn about American democracy and institutions and to visit schools such as the Perkins School for the Blind. At first, he enjoyed his celebrity, but soon became annoyed by it—"If I turn into the street, I am followed by a multitude," he observed. The adulation waned as Dickens pressed the United States to adopt an international copyright, which would protect his work (and wouldn't happen until 1891). His tour resulted in his often critical travelogue, *American Notes.* "It would be well," he wrote, "for the American people as a whole, if they loved the Real less, and the Ideal somewhat more … if there were greater encouragement to lightness of heart and gaiety, and a wider cultivation of what is beautiful, without being … useful."

227. MAY 22, 1843

GREAT MIGRATION TO OREGON BEGINS

On this day, aspiring pioneers set out from the town of Elm Grove, near Independence, Missouri, and headed west in search of adventure and land. Led by missionary Marcus Whitman, who had made the trip the previous year, the group—at least 120 wagons, close to a thousand people, and several thousand head of oxen and cattle—set off in stages, the mule trains in the lead and the slower ox-drawn wagons behind. After 2,000 miles and arduous months crossing the plains and mountains of the West, some 700 people arrived in Oregon Territory that fall. By 1845, several thousand men, women, and children were making the migration to Oregon each year.

In 1843, pioneers covered 2,000 miles across modern-day Kansas, Nebraska, Wyoming, Washington, and Idaho before reaching the Oregon Trail's end in that state.

In 1847, the Battle of Buena Vista proved a strategic U.S. victory during the Mexican-American War when Gen. Zachary Taylor's troops defeated a much larger Mexican contingent led by Antonio López de Santa Anna.

228. SEPTEMBER 9, 1843

HOMEMADE ICE-CREAM MAKER IS PATENTED

Philadelphian Nancy M. Johnson received patent no. 3,254 from the U.S. Patent Office for her invention of an "artificial freezer": a cylinder sitting in a larger cylinder of salt and ice that allowed consumers to create ice cream at home. The ingredients were poured into the smaller cylinder, and a hand-powered shaft with beaters churned the mixture into smooth ice cream. Mrs. Johnson broke ground in listing herself rather than her husband (then the norm) as the inventor of the new machine.

229. MAY 24, 1844

FIRST AMERICAN TELEGRAPH MAKES ITS DEBUT

On this day, Samuel Morse, inventor of the dots-and-dashes system known as Morse code, transmitted a message over copper wire from the U.S. Capitol to Baltimore. Its contents? The biblical quote, "What hath God wrought?" The telegraph had been developed decades earlier in France, but Morse, an arts professor at New York University, received funding from Congress for his version of telegraphic communication. Slowly, the initial telegraph line extended north to New York; gradually, other companies opened other networks. In 1861, Western Union built the first transcontinental telegraph line.

230. MARCH 22, 1845

AMERICA'S "JOHNNY APPLESEED" DIES

On this day, the obituary for John Chapman appeared in the *Fort Wayne Sentinel.* The pioneer and nursery man introduced trees grown with seeds (as opposed to grafting) across the Midwest. Known for his kindness and generosity, Chapman was also unconventional; the obituary described his "eccentricity and the strange garb he usually wore." In the decades to come, the strange man who wandered the wilderness of Ohio and Indiana would be resurrected in legend as the iconic Johnny Appleseed.

231. JULY 4, 1845

HENRY DAVID THOREAU MOVES TO WALDEN POND

The celebrated poet, essayist, and naturalist would live at the bucolic site near Concord, Massachusetts, for just over two years in a cabin he built by hand. Nearly 28 years old, he had been working in his father's pencil-making factory in town, where he was also part of Ralph Waldo Emerson's circle of intellectuals. As he explained in his masterpiece, *Walden,* "I went to the woods because I wished to live deliberately, to front only the essential facts of life, and see if I could not learn what it had to teach, and not, when I came to die, discover that I had not lived."

SIR, I GIVE IN, IT IS AN ASTONISHING INVENTION.

Cave Johnson, *American politician, on the telegraph (1844)*

232. MAY 13, 1846

CONGRESS DECLARES WAR ON MEXICO

President James Polk had been pressing for war, claiming that Mexicans had attacked Americans north of the Rio Grande (though Mexico, too, had claimed that territory). Initially, Polk was met with opposition from the antislavery northern Whigs, which included soon-to-be-congressman Abraham Lincoln. Ironically, like the powerful southern senator John Calhoun, they feared that if the U.S. acquired new territory in the Southwest, the issue of slavery there would rekindle regional tensions. Despite that concern, the House voted overwhelmingly for war with Mexico, and the Senate did, too, by a margin of 40 to 2.

233. MAY 22, 1846

ASSOCIATED PRESS IS BORN

As war with Mexico began, the publisher of the *New York Sun,* Moses Beach, convinced four other newspapers to join him in funding a system of communication that would allow them to break war news quickly to their readers: Couriers on horseback would ferry reporting north from the front lines to Montgomery, Alabama. From there, stagecoaches would transport the reporting to Richmond, Virginia, where the southernmost U.S. telegraph office was located; then it would be telegraphed to New York. Today, the Associated Press (AP) encompasses a global network of reporting whose mission is "to advance the power of facts."

British scientist James Smithson's sizable bequest enabled the creation of the Smithsonian Institution, now the world's largest museum complex.

234. AUGUST 10, 1846

LAW CREATES THE SMITHSONIAN INSTITUTION

British scientist James Smithson had bequeathed his considerable estate to create "at Washington, under the name of the Smithsonian Institution, an establishment for the increase and diffusion of knowledge." Though Congress had authorized acceptance of his gift in 1836, its members then debated what exactly the institution should be. Finally, in 1846 an Act of Organization passed the Senate and, on this day, President James Polk signed it into law. Today, the Smithsonian ranks as the largest museum complex in the world, with 21 museums, a zoo, and several research facilities.

235. OCTOBER 16, 1846

ETHER IS USED TO ALLAY PAIN

On this day, physicians gathered at Boston's Massachusetts General Hospital watched a tumor being removed from the neck of a patient anesthetized using ether by

William T. G. Morton, a dentist of questionable ethics who claimed he had discovered the chemical's pain-relieving properties. Soon thereafter, Morton patented etherization in both the United States and England so that he would have exclusive use of it. But Morton's instructor, chemist and geologist Charles Thomas Jackson, maintained that he had discovered the process and told Morton about it. The controversy has never been fully resolved.

236. FEBRUARY 19, 1847

RESCUERS REACH SURVIVORS OF THE DONNER-REED PARTY

Led by 65-year-old farmer George Donner and his neighbor, James Reed, the group of 87 men, women, and children left Illinois on April 14, 1846, headed for California. Near Utah, they were persuaded by guide Lansford Hastings to take his new cutoff, which he promised would save them time. It did not, and in October, low on provisions and exhausted, they were trapped by snows in the Sierra Nevada and remained there for four months. Forty died, and the survivors resorted to cannibalism. About 15 men and women had left the party in December to go for help, and on this day the first of three rescue parties made it to the camp.

The Donner-Reed party's quest to reach California was doomed by wintry conditions like those in this depiction of pioneers snowbound in the Sierra Nevada.

237. JULY 24, 1847

MORMONS ARRIVE IN THE GREAT SALT LAKE VALLEY

The Latter-day Saints, who combined Christian beliefs with the teachings of their founder and prophet, Joseph Smith, had been driven from Nauvoo, Illinois, by persecution, culminating in the murder of Smith. With Brigham Young as their new leader, several thousand members of the Latter-day Saints pushed west, looking for isolated land where they could worship freely. When Young saw the Great Salt Lake Valley, he declared, "God has shown me that this is the spot to locate this people, and here is where they will prosper … Thousands of Saints will gather in from the nations of the earth." Mormons now celebrate July 24 as Pioneer Day.

238. SEPTEMBER 11, 1847

"OH! SUSANNA" MAKES ITS DEBUT

First performed at Andrews' Eagle Ice Cream Saloon in Pittsburgh, Pennsylvania, the song became the unofficial anthem of the California gold rush; its composer, Stephen Foster, went on to write many popular tunes, forging a complicated musical legacy: Some songs, including "Oh! Susanna," were created in the blackface minstrel tradition, but more sensitivity to the plight of enslaved Americans is reflected in his later tunes. Abolitionist Frederick Douglass felt that songs like Foster's "My Old Kentucky Home" (Kentucky's state song, still performed, with some controversy, before the start of the Kentucky Derby) could help awaken "the sympathies for the slave, in which anti-slavery principles take root and flourish." Today, Foster is considered the "father of American music."

239. NOVEMBER 1, 1847

HENRY WADSWORTH LONGFELLOW PUBLISHES *EVANGELINE*

Longfellow's first epic poem is the story of a girl expelled from Canada's Acadia region and her search for her lost love; published to popular acclaim, it became the most recognized work of his lifetime. He would go on to set more epic moments in American history to poetry, but also wrote shorter verse. Considered America's most preeminent 19th-century poet, Longfellow believed that a poem should "have power to quiet / The restless pulse of care, / And come like the benediction / That follows after prayer." His Cambridge, Massachusetts, home, Craigie House, had been George Washington's headquarters in the early days of the Revolution; Longfellow would make it the headquarters of the New England intelligentsia.

Hailed as 19th-century America's leading poet, Henry Wadsworth Longfellow was known for poems that immortalized moments in history, folklore, and myth.

240. DECEMBER 3, 1847

FIRST ISSUE OF THE *NORTH STAR* APPEARS IN ROCHESTER, NEW YORK

The antislavery newspaper was founded and edited by the prominent Black abolitionist Frederick Douglass, who chose the name because many people escaping enslavement followed the North Star to freedom. He chose Rochester as the city of publication because it was one of the final stops on the Underground Railroad, leading to Canada. In 1851, the *North Star* merged with another paper to become *Frederick Douglass' Paper,* which increasingly gave voice to the idea that slavery is in violation of the Constitution.

241. JANUARY 20, 1848

GARRICK ARRIVES IN NEW YORK CITY

One of multiple ships that brought starving Irish immigrants to the United States during the harshest winter of Ireland's potato famine, the *Garrick* set sail from Liverpool on December 11, 1847. During its 40-day Atlantic crossing, 33 babies were born on board. But over the course of the voyage, so many died aboard the *Garrick*—and other passenger ships carrying Irish immigrants across the sea—that the vessels became known as "coffin ships." About a quarter of Ireland's population at the time—1.5 to 2 million—emigrated to the United States between 1845 and 1855, the years during and immediately following the harrowing Great Famine.

242. JANUARY 24, 1848

GOLD IS DISCOVERED AT SUTTER'S MILL

Banking that Mexico's Alta California would soon be in U.S. hands, white settlers began moving in during the Mexican-American War. Among them were entrepreneurs John Sutter and James Marshall, who hired workers to build a sawmill on the American River near Coloma. When Marshall went to inspect the millrace, his "eye was caught by something shining in the bottom of the ditch ... I reached my hand down and picked it up; it made my heart thump, for I was certain it was gold ... Then I saw another." By May, news of the discovery had reached San Francisco, and the California gold rush was on, as thousands flocked to the territory, hoping to strike it rich.

243. JANUARY 31, 1848

KITE CONTEST SPURS CREATION OF NIAGARA FALLS BRIDGE

Builders had been hired to construct a suspension bridge at the narrowest point on the Niagara River's Whirlpool Gorge, near the famous falls. To start, they needed to string a wire from the American bank to the Canadian—and so they sponsored a kite-flying contest in the dead of winter. American teenager Homan Walsh tried his hand but initially failed, leaving him stranded in Canada for eight days after icy waters stopped the ferry home from departing. He tried again and succeeded, flying a kite line across the river with a cable in tow. Bridgebuilding could then begin.

LOOK, THEN, INTO THINE HEART, AND WRITE!

Henry Wadsworth Longfellow, *"Prelude" (1839)*

Fortune hunters who joined the California gold rush (1848-1855) used wooden sluice boxes and flowing water to filter gold from dirt and gravel.

244. FEBRUARY 1, 1848

JOHN HUMPHREY NOYES IS NAMED THE LEADER OF ONEIDA UTOPIA

On this day, John Humphrey Noyes established the Oneida Community in New York, one of the perfectionist communal societies sprouting up across the United States. The Noyesians, as they came to be called, believed Jesus had made his second coming in A.D. 70, enabling humans to create a heaven on Earth. In Oneida, they occupied a 93,000-square-foot mansion and shared mutual property and children as the community practiced a form of free love and open criticism among members. In June 1879, harassed by local leaders, Noyes fled to Canada; some remaining members formed what became Oneida Limited, one of the world's largest producers of tableware.

245. FEBRUARY 2, 1848

INSUBORDINATE DIPLOMAT SIGNS THE TREATY OF GUADALUPE HIDALGO

The U.S. Army had prevailed in the Mexican-American War, but President James Polk recalled diplomat Nicholas Trist from treaty negotiations in Mexico City because he wanted them to take place in Washington. Trist ignored the recall: "Knowing it to be the very last chance and impressed with the dreadful consequences to our country which cannot fail to attend the loss of that chance, I decided … to attempt to make a treaty; the decision is altogether my own." Trist's treaty officially ended the war and brought territory, including present-day California, Utah, Nevada, most of Arizona, and parts of New Mexico, Colorado, and Wyoming into the Union.

246. MAY 31, 1848

CONGRESS PURCHASES THE WRITINGS OF THE LATE JAMES MADISON

The fourth president had not wanted his private papers to be released during his lifetime and bequeathed them to his wife, Dolley. Still a political and social force in Washington, she lobbied hard to have the government acquire them. In 1837, Congress had bought Madison's copious notes from the Constitutional Convention—the most complete record of those historic proceedings. Now, it purchased the rest of what Dolley believed were her husband's unpublished papers. But unbeknownst to her, some had been removed by her son, John, to pay off his debts. Many have since been recovered and are now housed in the Library of Congress.

247. JULY 19, 1848

FIRST WOMEN'S RIGHTS CONVENTION ASSEMBLES

On this day, some 300 people convened in the Wesleyan Chapel in Seneca Falls, New York, to champion women's rights. One of the female abolitionists who organized the convention, Elizabeth Cady Stanton, emerged as a leader, proclaiming: "We are assembled … to declare our right to be free as man is free, to be represented in the government which we are taxed to support." In the decades to follow, Stanton would

Conventions to promote women's rights drew suffragists, including Elizabeth Cady Stanton—and some public criticism, as in this 1859 *Harper's Weekly* cartoon mocking featured speakers.

become one of the strongest voices in the women's rights movement, speaking and writing in favor of female suffrage, property and child-rearing rights, and abolition.

248. JANUARY 23, 1849

ELIZABETH BLACKWELL GRADUATES FROM NEW YORK'S GENEVA MEDICAL COLLEGE

Blackwell's matriculation made her the first female physician in America. She had completed a summer internship between terms at Philadelphia's Blockley Almshouse, where "the medical head of the hospital, Dr. Benedict, was most kind … But the young resident physicians … were not friendly. When I walked into the wards they walked out." Yet when she completed her exams at Geneva, the "students received me with applause—they all seem to like me and I believe I shall receive my degree with their united approval; a generous and chivalric feeling having conquered any little feelings of jealousy." Throughout her long career, Blackwell promoted the role of women physicians and became a prominent member of the medical community. English by birth, she finished her career at the newly established London School of Medicine for Women.

SPOTLIGHT

FOOD ADVANCEMENTS

WHAT 19TH-CENTURY AMERICANS put on their tables depended largely on their wealth and station, the seasonal availability of foods, and regional tastes flavored by the local recipes of Native Americans and dishes immigrants imported. As the century began, most meals took place at home and food provisioning was mostly on a small scale; households dined on plants and animals they could harvest, forage, hunt, or breed, and shopped at markets where farmers, fishers, and hunters offered their wares. Though most families lacked such means of refrigeration, by 1803 an icehouse built at Thomas Jefferson's Monticello cooled with ice cut from a river; they ate fresh foods in season and foods preserved by salting, smoking, pickling, or drying for the nongrowing season.

People of lesser means seldom had fresh dairy, eggs, and meat; they leaned more on cheaper ingredients, with stews and corn bread as staples. More affluent citizens ate greater varieties of fresh foods and often multicourse meals, including pastries, roasts, and sweets. Meanwhile, "American cuisine" continued to evolve, stemming from regional differences in ingredients and preparations, producing a rich variety of options: New England brown bread, seafood, and fish; mid-Atlantic boiled dinners, dumplings, and puddings; southern fried and simmered dishes seasoned with African, French, and Spanish influences; and western frontier wild game, corn, and dried fruits.

By the century's end, as cities grew, food supply systems were centralized and industrializing and restaurants proliferated, enriched by the influx of immigrants' culinary specialties.

Over the course of the 19th century, raising and slaughtering livestock changed from a farm-based endeavor to a meatpacking industry centered on Chicago's Union Stock Yard.

THERE IS NO REASON WHY THE POOR MAN SHOULD NOT HAVE AS WELL PREPARED AND PALATABLE FOOD AS THE WEALTHY.

Marion Cabell Tyree, Housekeeping in Old Virginia *(1878)*

Soprano Jenny Lind, aka "the Swedish Nightingale," began a 150-concert U.S. tour in 1850 with a performance at New York City's Castle Garden.

249. APRIL 10, 1849

INVENTOR WALTER HUNT PATENTS THE SAFETY PIN

Hunt had invented a number of items before the safety pin, including the first workable sewing machine, which he didn't patent, and mill machinery. He sold most of the rights to his inventions to pay back debts, and this also applied to the safety pin. Owing $15 to the draftsman who made drawings for his patent applications, Hunt sold the patent—no. 6,281—to W. R. Grace and Company for a reported $400. In the decades to come, his simple innovation would make millions.

250. JANUARY 29, 1850

SENATOR HENRY CLAY PRESENTS HIS COMPROMISE RESOLUTIONS

Actually a set of proposed laws, Clay's eight bills, presented to the U.S. Senate, addressed the regional tensions that resulted from the new territory acquired from Mexico. In his introduction, Clay observed that it is "desirable, for the peace, concord, and harmony of the Union of these States, to settle and adjust amicably all existing questions of controversy between them arising out of the institution of slavery." His resolutions allowed California's admission to the Union as a free state, set up territorial governments for Utah and New Mexico, and created a more aggressive version of the 1793 Fugitive Slave Act, which required the return of escaped people to their enslavers.

251. MARCH 16, 1850

NATHANIEL HAWTHORNE'S *THE SCARLET LETTER* IS PUBLISHED

One of the first mass-produced books in America, Hawthorne's indelible novel had an original print run of 2,500 copies and sold out in 10 days; two weeks later, 2,500 more copies were released. The story focuses on Hester Prynne, an unmarried Puritan woman who gives birth to a daughter and must subsequently wear a scarlet *A*, signifying her adultery. Some 20 years had passed since Hawthorne published his first novel anonymously, but he followed *The Scarlet Letter* a year later with another unsettling New England tale, *The House of the Seven Gables*. Both are considered literary classics.

252. SEPTEMBER 1, 1850

"SWEDISH NIGHTINGALE" LANDS IN NEW YORK CITY

Wildly popular in Europe, soprano Jenny Lind was greeted by 30,000 fans as she disembarked from the ship *Atlantic;* what became known as "Lindmania" ensued. P. T. Barnum convinced her to do an American concert tour, but financing that arrangement required him to risk almost everything he owned. His bargain paid off—Lind performed 93 concerts to large crowds and then continued to tour on her own, earning in total some $350,000 (more than $14 million in today's dollars). She donated most of the money to Swedish charities, particularly to the endowment of free schools.

By the time she addressed a convention promoting women's rights in 1851, Sojourner Truth was already known as a preacher and antislavery activist.

253. SEPTEMBER 18, 1850

FUGITIVE SLAVE ACT OF 1850 BECOMES LAW

The broad outline of what would become the Fugitive Slave Act, a far more aggressive version of a 1793 law regarding enslaved people who had escaped, was first offered as a salve to legislators and owners in slave states by Henry Clay in his compromise resolutions in January 1850. For African Americans, the act spelled doom: Even if enslaved people managed to escape to a free state or territory, they could be taken captive there and returned to their owners. Anyone helping them could be fined $1,000. The act would have far-reaching political, legal, and human repercussions.

254. MAY 29, 1851

SOJOURNER TRUTH GIVES HER MOST FAMOUS SPEECH

Formerly enslaved, Truth observed at the Woman's Rights Convention in Akron, Ohio, that she "can do as much work as any man." She championed women's rights and concluded, "Man is in a tight place, the poor slave is on him, woman is coming on him, and he is surely between a hawk and a buzzard." What she did not say, according to most

Entering New York City's competitive publishing market in 1851, the *New York Times* promoted itself as a source of unbiased coverage.

historians, are the famous words, "Ain't I a woman," for which the speech would become known. Truth was born in New York and spoke only Dutch until she was nine, rather than the southern dialect the line would indicate.

255. JUNE 5, 1851

HARRIET BEECHER STOWE PUBLISHES *UNCLE TOM'S CABIN*

Stowe's now renowned depiction of slavery began to appear in serial form in the *National Era,* an antislavery magazine, in 41 weekly installments. Readers avidly followed the travails of two enslaved people: Eliza, who escapes to Canada, and Tom, who is sold by his original enslaver; both encounter various cruelties by white overlords on their journeys. On March 18, 1852, Stowe's story was published as a two-volume book, with some significant differences from the serialized version. Her novel sold 10,000 copies domestically in the first week and 300,000 in the first year. In that same year, enthusiasts in Great Britain bought 1.5 million copies.

256. AUGUST 12, 1851

ISAAC SINGER PATENTS A COMMERCIAL SEWING MACHINE

The son of German immigrants, Singer took jobs in small factories, always with an eye on improving machinery. In Boston, he worked in the shop of machinist Orson Phelps, who was building a sewing machine with a curved needle that sewed in circles. Singer replaced the curved needle and patented his model with a straight needle that moved up and down. Singer and Phelps built the first machines in the Boston shop, but in 1853 Singer Manufacturing Co. opened in New York City. Constant improvements in the design popularized Singer sewing machines, eventually creating a global phenomenon. They are still sold today.

257. SEPTEMBER 17, 1851

FIRST OF NUMEROUS TREATIES FAILS TO SECURE PEACE BETWEEN TRIBES AND SETTLERS

After years of skirmishes between the Native Americans of the Plains and white settlers who wanted to cross their lands, terms for the first Fort Laramie treaty were set on this day. Among other points, tribes were promised payments and protection from the U.S. government for allowing settlers safe passage—but the government failed to pay, the promised protection failed, and the agreement crumbled. By 1868, a second Treaty of Fort Laramie was drawn up. Tribes agreed to relinquish thousands of acres and not attack settlers in return for exclusive use of a reservation in the Dakota Territory and hunting and fishing rights in the Black Hills. That pact, too, was broken. In 1877, the U.S. government would seize the Black Hills after gold was found. Though the Supreme Court in 1980 declared the seizure illegal and ordered compensation paid to the Sioux Nation, the tribe refused payment and demanded the land's return.

258. SEPTEMBER 18, 1851

FIRST ISSUE OF THE *NEW YORK TIMES* APPEARS

Initially published as the *New-York Daily Times,* the landmark newspaper was founded by Henry Jarvis Raymond and George Jones, who had been with Horace Greeley's *New-York Tribune*. At the *Times,* Raymond became editor in chief, intent on serving up unbiased, unsensationalized coverage of the news. In its first decade, the paper attracted a Republican antislavery audience and supported Abraham Lincoln in his first presidential campaign. Once civil war engulfed the country, it sent reporters south to cover the fighting firsthand. In the 1870s, the *New-York Times* grew to national prominence with its coverage of the Tammany Hall scandal. Today, it is often considered America's paper of record.

259. OCTOBER 29, 1851

"WASHINGTON CROSSING THE DELAWARE" IS EXHIBITED

The dramatic painting by German-born artist Emanuel Leutze appeared in the United States for the first time at the Stuyvesant Institute in New York. Living in Düsseldorf, Germany,

Artist Emanuel Leutze painted "Washington Crossing the Delaware" at epic size: roughly 12.5 feet high by 21.25 feet wide.

when he painted the commanding image of George Washington facing weather and ice, Leutze had used the frozen Rhine as a model for the Delaware. His rendition immediately became an iconic American image, with 50,000 people paying to see it at the Stuyvesant. Prominent business baron Marshall O. Roberts bought the painting from Leutze for what was then a breathtaking sum of $10,000. The Metropolitan Museum of Art owns it today.

260. NOVEMBER 14, 1851

MOBY-DICK IS PUBLISHED IN THE UNITED STATES

Herman Melville's great classic of whaling and the human spirit did not achieve critical or commercial success; to try to support his family, Melville continued farming in western Massachusetts. He later served as a customs inspector in New York City, and when he

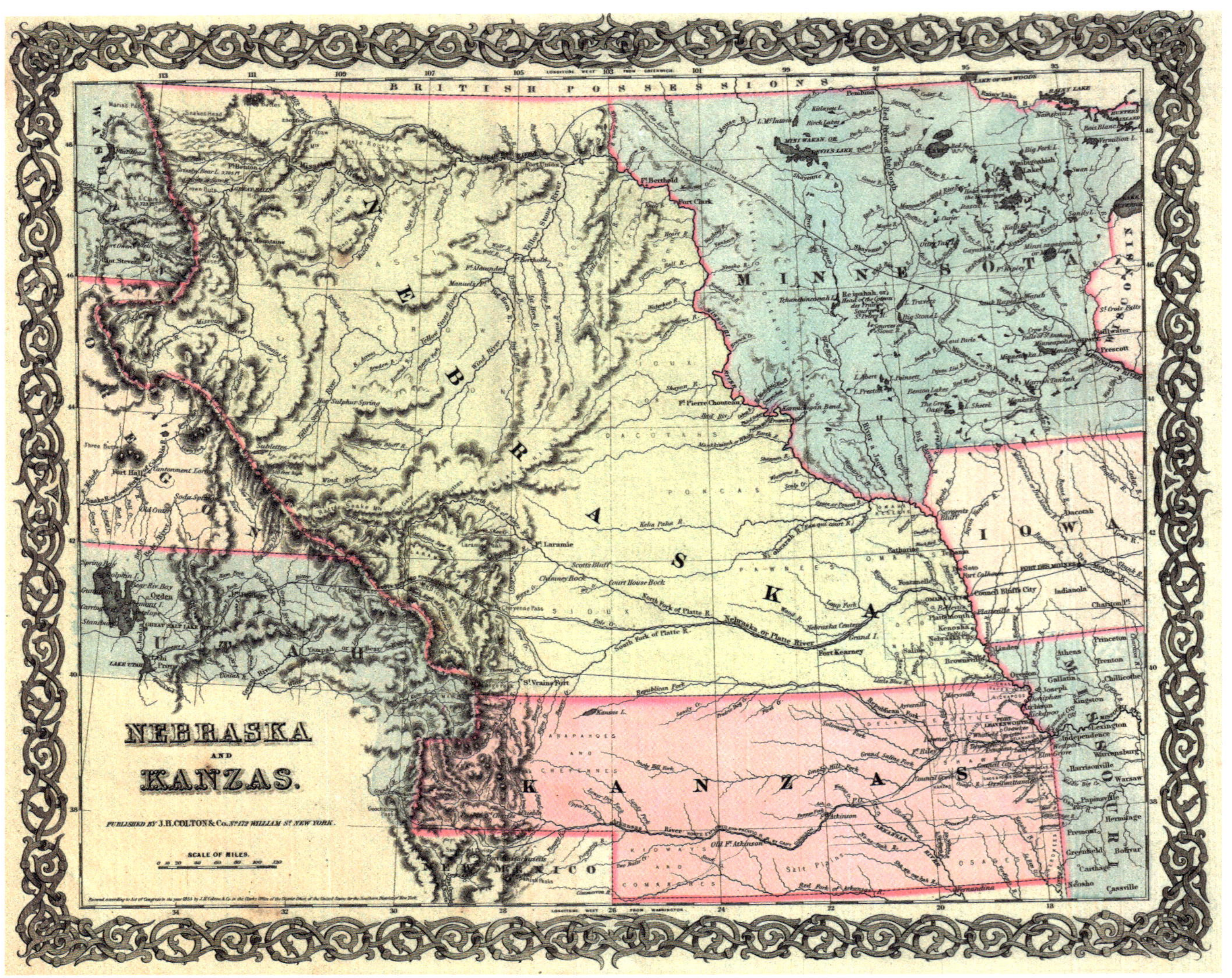

By passing the Kansas-Nebraska Act in 1854, Congress redivided the territory and overturned a ban on slavery north of the 36th parallel.

died in 1891, the *Times* observed, "There has died and been buried in this city ... a man who is so little known, even by name ... that only one newspaper contained an obituary account of him." Not until the 1920s did the literary public embrace Melville as one of America's greatest writers.

261. JULY 14, 1853

COMMODORE MATTHEW PERRY DELIVERS A LETTER TO JAPAN

On this day, the naval officer presented emissaries of the Japanese emperor with a letter from President Millard Fillmore "propos[ing] to Your Imperial Majesty that the United States and Japan should live in friendship and have commercial intercourse with each other." Perry had sailed a small fleet of four black warships to Edo (Tokyo) Bay with orders to negotiate a treaty with the isolationist kingdom. Not until March 31 of the following year did the Japanese agree to open two ports to the U.S. and to allow American whaling ships to buy coal and water from them.

Published in 1851, Herman Melville's *Moby-Dick*—which famously begins "Call me Ishmael"—wasn't instantly popular, but it is now considered a literary classic.

262. MARCH 20, 1854

REPUBLICAN PARTY IS BORN

A group of concerned citizens in Ripon, Wisconsin, met in the town's Little White Schoolhouse to protest a proposed bill known then as "the Nebraska bill," which had recently passed the Senate; if passed by the House, the bill would have allowed for the spread of slavery. At the meeting, Alvan Bovay proposed the name for a new political party: the Republican Party. "We went into the little meeting ... Whigs, Free Soilers, and Democrats. We came out of it Republicans," he later said. A native New Yorker, Bovay had moved to Ripon and later served in the Wisconsin legislature. The Little White Schoolhouse is now considered the birthplace of the Republican Party.

263. MAY 30, 1854

KANSAS-NEBRASKA ACT BECOMES LAW

In early January, Illinois senator Stephen Douglas proposed what was known as "the Nebraska bill," which would divide the Nebraska Territory (which included all or part of current-day Nebraska, Kansas, Wyoming, Colorado, Montana, and the Dakotas) into two territories—Kansas and Nebraska—and allow the citizens of each "popular sovereignty" to decide whether to allow or prohibit slavery. The bill would overturn the 1820 Missouri Compromise, which had outlawed slavery north of the 36th parallel. The House passed it on May 22, and on this day, it was signed into law.

264. JULY 8, 1854

RIOTS AGAINST IRISH IMMIGRANTS BREAK OUT IN MASSACHUSETTS

Essex County, Massachusetts, was home to many Irish workers who came to work in mills and on construction projects. But the county also saw the rise of the Know-Nothings, a

By running four miles in a blistering seven minutes 19.75 seconds, the racehorse Lexington set a world record in 1855 that stood for 20 years.

nativist, anti-Catholic political movement. As an economic depression descended and jobs become scarce, the movement became more belligerent. On a hot July afternoon and into the night, nativists marched on an Irish community in Lawrence with brickbats. Gunshots were heard, and the mayor called on the military to disperse the mob. Days earlier, similar acts had happened against the Irish in nearby Manchester, New Hampshire. The Know-Nothing Party would win some significant local and state elections in the coming years, but it had largely collapsed by the end of the decade.

265. JULY 16, 1854

ELIZABETH JENNINGS GRAHAM FIGHTS STREETCAR SEGREGATION

On her way to play the organ at her church, the 24-year-old African American schoolteacher boarded a horse-drawn streetcar in Manhattan that did not have the required "Colored Persons Allowed" sign. The conductor forcibly removed her, and the next day a large group supporting her gathered to protest at her church. Graham took legal action against the streetcar company. Represented by a young Chester Arthur (later to become president of the United States), she won her case and was rewarded damages, spurring more actions toward racial equality.

266. OCTOBER 5, 1854

NATIONAL BABY SHOW OF OHIO GIVES BIRTH TO BEAUTY CONTESTS

On this day, 127 infants were put on display at the Clark County Fair in a contest to choose the "finest." (The winner was Alfretta Ronemus, a 10-month-old from South Vienna, Ohio.) A Cleveland newspaper predicted that such contests would be "a new feature in Agriculture shows," but other magazines and newspapers loudly protested the idea. The Chicago-based magazine *Prairie Farmer* admonished readers that "children are not mere animals," and a Georgia newspaper called the show "indescribably sacrilegious and vulgar." To no avail. Baby beauty contests became popular in the second half of the century, pitting hundreds of babies—and parents—against one another.

267. DECEMBER 24, 1854

HARRIET TUBMAN RETURNS TO MARYLAND

On hearing that her three enslaved brothers were about to be sold away from their families on the Eastern Shore, Tubman returned to the state she had escaped in 1849. She sent her siblings a coded message "to be always watching unto prayer, and when the good old ship of Zion comes along, to be ready to step on board." They were, and by December 29, Tubman had led them and several others to the Pennsylvania Anti-Slavery Society office of African American freedom fighter William Still in Philadelphia. "Moses," as Tubman became known, was the most famous conductor on the Underground Railroad.

LEXINGTON, OF BOSTON STOCK, HAS GAINED THE PRIZE, A PURSE OF $20,000.

New-York Daily Times, *on the Great Horse Race at New Orleans (1854)*

268. APRIL 2, 1855

AMERICAN THOROUGHBRED WINS A "RACE AGAINST TIME"

On this day, famed Thoroughbred racehorse Lexington broke the four-mile record in what was dubbed a "race against time." Running against a stopwatch rather than other horses, he clocked in at seven minutes 19.75 seconds, a world record that would stand for 20 years. His endurance was even more remarkable, considering that today's Triple Crown races are less than two miles. Lexington also became the leading sire of the 19th century, as well as the inspiration for the first mass-produced stopwatch. Geraldine Brooks's novel *Horse,* based on his story, was a *New York Times* bestseller in 2022.

269. SEPTEMBER 26, 1855

JOHN D. ROCKEFELLER FINDS A JOB

The 16-year-old Rockefeller had spent six weeks searching for work in Cleveland, but on this day, Isaac Hewitt, a local shipper and merchant, interviewed him and declared, "We'll give you a chance." Rockefeller became a bookkeeping clerk in the small firm. But he also bought a notebook and scrupulously accounted his own meager income and expenditures (which, even then, included charity). Rockefeller went on to become an aggressive titan of industry and founder of Standard Oil, but celebrated "Job Day" throughout his life.

270. MAY 21, 1856

SLAVERY SUPPORTERS SACK LAWRENCE, KANSAS

On this day, a band of some 700 proslavery men, led by a county sheriff, sealed off the town, blew up the Free State Hotel, and robbed the homes of abolitionist leaders. Established by antislavery New Englanders two years before, Lawrence had become a mecca for other folks looking to settle in Free-State Kansas. The "sack," as the Republican papers called it, sparked months of violence in "Bleeding Kansas," some perpetuated by the violently antislavery John Brown. In Congress, too, tensions ran high. "Everybody here feels as if we are on a volcano," South Carolina congressman Laurence Keitt wrote. The event was a turning point in the run-up to the Civil War.

271. MAY 22, 1856

ANTISLAVERY SENATOR CANED IN CONGRESS

On May 19, Massachusetts's outspoken antislavery senator Charles Sumner had taken to the floor to deliver a fiery speech condemning those who sought to turn Kansas into a slave state, which included a vicious personal attack against proslavery senator Andrew Butler of South Carolina. Three days later, Butler's kinsman, Congressman Preston Brooks, entered the Senate chamber where Sumner was still working, though the body had adjourned. Wielding a metal-topped cane, he approached the unsuspecting Sumner and hit him repeatedly on the head until he was unconscious. No one detained Brooks as he strolled from the chamber, and he was enthusiastically reelected. Sumner recovered and resumed his seat in the Senate for another 18 years.

Two years after its founding by politicians opposed to the expansion of slavery, the new Republican Party held its first convention in 1856.

272. JUNE 17, 1856

FIRST NATIONAL CONVENTION OF THE REPUBLICAN PARTY ASSEMBLES

The two-year-old party—with its mélange of former Whigs and antislavery advocates, including former Democrats—kicked off its first convention in Philadelphia with almost 600 delegates in attendance. They easily nominated 43-year-old John C. Frémont, "the pathfinder of the West" and briefly a California senator, for president. The vice presidential choice was more difficult; among the names put forward was a former one-term congressman from Illinois named Abraham Lincoln. William L. Dayton, a former senator from New Jersey, eventually won the slot, and the convention closed with enthusiastic support for its campaign slogan, "Free Soil. Free Speech. Free Men. Frémont."

273. AUGUST 18, 1856

GUANO ISLANDS ACT ALLOWS AMERICANS TO SEIZE LAND

Seabird and bat poop was such a valuable component of fertilizer in the 19th century that Congress passed a law that stipulated, "Whenever any citizen of the United States discovers a deposit of guano on any island, rock, or key, not within the lawful jurisdiction of any other government, and not occupied by the citizens of any other government," he could take possession of the territory, though all of its guano must be used by American citizens only. The U.S. claimed about 100 islands this way, but most claims were later abandoned; the law is still on the books.

274. AUGUST 23, 1856

EUNICE NEWTON FOOTE DEFINES A FACTOR OF CLIMATE CHANGE

In a series of simple experiments conducted that year, scientist and women's rights advocate Eunice Newton Foote filled 30-inch-long cylinders with various gases and mixtures: air (both moist and dry), oxygen, carbon dioxide, and hydrogen. The cylinder containing carbon dioxide heated the most when placed in direct sunlight. In a paper presented on this day to the American Association for the Advancement of Science (AAAS), she wrote that "an atmosphere of that gas would give to our earth a high temperature."

Scientist Eunice Newton Foote's experiments with sunlight's effects on various gases foresaw carbon dioxide's role in global warming.

Paddle wheel steamboats—here, racing on the Mississippi River—transported passengers, freight, and touring "showboat" entertainers.

275. FEBRUARY 16, 1857

MARK TWAIN EXPLORES THE MISSISSIPPI RIVER

In Cincinnati, a 21-year-old Samuel Clemens—later, the acclaimed author of *The Adventures of Tom Sawyer* and *Adventures of Huckleberry Finn (Tom Sawyer's Comrade)*—boarded the steamboat *Paul Jones* and headed downriver to New Orleans. On the trip, he befriended the pilot, Horace Bixby, and became so enamored of riverboat travel that he abandoned his earlier idea of continuing on from New Orleans to the Amazon. Instead, he apprenticed under Bixby. Clemens's piloting career ended in 1861, as the Civil War curtailed river travel, but his experience led him to take the pen name Mark Twain—the two-fathom mark, a safe depth for riverboats on a line measuring river depth.

276. MARCH 6, 1857

SUPREME COURT ISSUES DRED SCOTT DECISION

Enslaved man Dred Scott and his wife, Harriet, had lived with their enslaver for years in Illinois and Wisconsin, a free state and free territory, before they all moved to Missouri, a slave state. The Scotts sued for their freedom based on Missouri's "once free, always free" doctrine. The case ground through the courts for 11 years before the Supreme Court finally ruled that a "free negro of the African race, whose ancestors were brought to this country and sold as slaves, is not a 'citizen' … The Constitution … recognises slaves as property, and pledges the Federal Government to protect it. And Congress cannot exercise any more authority over [that] property." The decision effectively meant that African Americans, whether enslaved or free, had no protection in the federal courts and that Congress could not ban slavery in the territories. Considered one of the worst edicts in history, it moved the country closer to civil war.

277. MARCH 23, 1857

FIRST AMERICAN PASSENGER ELEVATOR BEGINS OPERATION

The cutting-edge invention was inaugurated in the newly completed, five-story E. V. Haughwout Building in Manhattan. Elisha Graves Otis, founder of Otis Elevator, incorporated a safety device that stopped the elevator from falling if the cable snapped. Haughwout had commissioned the elevator, which traveled at a speed of 40 feet a minute and was powered by a steam engine in the basement, to attract clients to his high-end emporium, which sold fine china, cut glass, and silver. (Today's elevators, by comparison, travel at a speed of 40 feet a second.) Now a designated city landmark, the building still stands on lower Broadway.

WHAT CAN BE THE END OF ALL THIS BUT ANOTHER GENERAL COLLAPSE LIKE THAT OF 1837, ONLY UPON A MUCH GRANDER SCALE?

***New York Herald**, on the Panic of 1857 (1857)*

278. MAY 5, 1857

***THE ATLANTIC* IS FOUNDED**

While dining together at Boston's Parker House hotel, a group of prominent Massachusetts intellectuals that included Henry Wadsworth Longfellow, Oliver Wendell Holmes, Ralph Waldo Emerson, and James Russell Lowell decided to create a new nonpartisan magazine focusing on politics, literature, and the arts. (Harriet Beecher Stowe, author of *Uncle Tom's Cabin,* had been invited to join them, but she declined when she learned that alcohol would be served.) Holmes proposed the name *The Atlantic* to suggest that the new publication was an ocean away from Old World publications. The first issue of the magazine appeared the following November, and it is still published today.

279. AUGUST 24, 1857

PANIC OF 1857 HITS

When the New York branch of the Ohio Life Insurance and Trust Company failed on this day, panic threatened. In response, bankers restricted even simple transactions, but those very actions were taken as a sign that financial collapse was imminent. Stockholders and others sold at a loss. Then in mid-September, a steamship transporting millions of dollars in gold from the San Francisco Mint to create a reserve for eastern banks sank in a hurricane. On October 14, all banking in New York and throughout New England was

This circa 1873 print of New York City shows 843-acre Central Park, now one of the world's best known urban preserves.

suspended. For 18 months, the nation suffered through an economic downturn that reverberated worldwide.

280. APRIL 28, 1858

CENTRAL PARK IS BORN

Five years prior, New York State had designated funds to purchase a wide swath of Upper Manhattan as a natural haven in the increasingly cramped city. On this day, the "Greensward Plan," submitted by Frederick Law Olmsted and Calvert Vaux, won the competition to design what would become known as Central Park. The tract, rocky and swampy, included small farms and settlements, among them Seneca Village, a vibrant African American community. All were bought through eminent domain, and park commissioners stipulated that the new park include a parade ground, ball fields, a winter skating area, a grand fountain, an observatory, a flower garden, and a music hall. The Greensward Plan offered all that within a naturalistic landscape.

281. AUGUST 16, 1858

FIRST TRANSATLANTIC CABLE MESSAGE IS SUCCESSFULLY TRANSMITTED

The message—102 words in all and celebrating the "link between the nations, whose friendship is founded upon their common interest"—was sent by Queen Victoria to President James Buchanan. It took 16.5 hours to reach the White House and was received via a galvanometer, which detects and measures electric current. Two ships—one British-backed and one American-backed—had laid the cable. Meeting mid-Atlantic, the former steamed east to Ireland and the latter west to Newfoundland. In London, the *Times* enthusiastically declared that, with the cable, "The Atlantic is dried up, and we become in reality as well as in wish one country."

282. AUGUST 27, 1858

SECOND LINCOLN-DOUGLAS DEBATE CHANGES HISTORY

Some 15,000 people converged on Freeport, Illinois, to see tall, awkward Abraham Lincoln take on the short, dapper Stephen Douglas. Both men were running for the Illinois Senate seat, and their seven debates would "set the prairies on fire." On this cloudy day, Lincoln cornered Douglas by asking how a territory could prevent slavery; Douglas responded that it could simply not pass legislation protecting those who enslaved people. Douglas's Freeport Doctrine helped him win the Illinois Senate seat, but in his 1860 presidential bid, it cost him the South. In that race, Lincoln prevailed.

A hunter's discovery of gold while sifting sand with his drinking cup set off the spring 1859 rush of gold prospectors to Colorado.

283. JANUARY 7, 1859

GEORGE JACKSON STRIKES GOLD IN COLORADO

For decades, rumors of gold in the Colorado Rockies had tempted men to search for it, and George Jackson was no exception. On a winter hunting trip, he ventured far into the mountains, leaving his companions behind. He camped on a sandbar in Chicago Creek near current-day Idaho Springs and made a bonfire to melt the frozen sand. Panning a small portion of the wet sand in his drinking cup, he quickly found some gold. He marked the location, and in the spring returned with a team of wagons and men. The Colorado gold rush was on.

284. FEBRUARY 27, 1859

CONGRESSMAN KILLS RIVAL IN LAFAYETTE SQUARE

As New York congressman Daniel Sickles approached his friend Philip Barton Key II (Francis Scott Key's son and a U.S. attorney), Key greeted him with grace. But Sickles yelled, "You villain, you have dishonored my house and you must die!" He then shot Key several times, killing him. While both men were known womanizers, Sickles's rage stemmed from an affair Key was having with his wife. At his trial, Sickles's lawyer used a new defense: temporary insanity. The jury deliberated less than an hour before returning a not-guilty verdict. High society's verdict was harsher; both Sickles and his wife were banished.

In this circa 1860 photo, Harriet Lane, niece of President James Buchanan, sports the day's leading fashion accessory: a cage of hoops shaping the skirt.

285. AUGUST 27, 1859

PENNSYLVANIA STRIKES BLACK GOLD

On this Sunday in the lumber town of Titusville, William "Uncle Billy" Smith saw what he and the rest of the crew had dreamed of: a dark liquid floating on top of the water in a shallow, 69.5-foot well they had drilled. For a year the team, led by E. L. Drake, had been hell-bent on a "lunatic" scheme: to strike oil in the northwestern corner of the state. Now they had, ushering in the petroleum age in America. Pennsylvania would remain at the center of the oil boom for the next 40 years.

286. OCTOBER 16, 1859

JOHN BROWN LEADS A RAID

At 8 p.m. the ardent Kansas abolitionist and 18 of his men embarked upon their plan to take the federal arsenal and armory at Harpers Ferry, Virginia (now West Virginia). By 10 p.m., they had done so, and Brown declared, "I want to free all the negroes in this state ... and if the citizens interfere with me, I must only burn the town and have blood." The local militia and townsfolk attacked Brown's force, and U.S. Marines arrived to join them. By October 18, 17 people were dead, the raid was over, and Brown was soon to be jailed. Convicted of murder and treason, he was hanged six weeks later.

287. FEBRUARY 27, 1860

ABRAHAM LINCOLN SPEAKS AT THE COOPER INSTITUTE

In Lower Manhattan, Lincoln, then a prominent Republican politician, delivered a powerful speech that changed history. Invoking the founders and the Constitution often, he argued, "Wrong as we think slavery is, we can yet afford to let it alone where it is," but not "allow it to spread." "Let us have faith," he concluded, "that right makes might, and ... dare to do our duty." Before the speech, he had visited Mathew Brady's studio, where the photographer made a compelling image of the tall, imposing Lincoln that is widely known today. Both speech and portrait propelled Lincoln into the national spotlight; he would win the presidency later that year.

AS TO THE WHISKERS, HAVING NEVER WORN ANY, DO YOU NOT THINK PEOPLE WOULD CALL IT A PIECE OF SILLY AFFECTATION IF I WERE TO BEGIN IT NOW?

Abraham Lincoln, *in a response to Grace Bedell (1860)*

288. MARCH 15, 1860

HOOP SKIRTS CUT A WIDE SWATH

Circled by hoops of whalebone, cane, or steel wire, women of every class sported these strange "cage crinoline" concoctions. Hoop skirts gave their wearers the appearance of a small waist against a domed bottom that fashion had long dictated, but without wearing the layers of petticoats previously required for the desired look. The capacious, yet inexpensive, skirts made quite a statement, taking up considerable space on sidewalks, hallways, and benches; some boasted a circumference of 12 to 15 feet.

289. OCTOBER 15, 1860

LITTLE GIRL INSPIRES ABRAHAM LINCOLN'S BEARD

During Lincoln's heated presidential campaign of 1860, he received a letter from 11-year-old Grace Bedell: "[I] want you should be President of the United States very much so I hope you wont think me very bold to write to such a great man ... I have got 4 brother's and part of them will vote for you any way and if you will let your whiskers grow I will try and get the rest of them to vote for you you [sic] would look a great deal better for your face is so thin." Lincoln heeded Bedell's advice and soon began to grow a beard.

290. NOVEMBER 6, 1860

ABRAHAM LINCOLN IS ELECTED PRESIDENT

Four candidates faced off in this election fraught by sectionalism and the issue of slavery. Stephen Douglas ran as a Northern Democrat; Abraham Lincoln as a Republican; incumbent vice president John Breckinridge as a Southern Democrat; and John Bell as the candidate for the Constitutional Union Party. Lincoln and his running mate, Senator Hannibal Hamlin from Maine, emerged victorious with almost 40 percent of the popular vote, while Douglas, the next closest contender, took 29 percent. When Lincoln heard the results of the election, he reportedly rushed to tell his wife, an astute political thinker in her own right: "Mary, Mary, we are elected."

291. DECEMBER 20, 1860

SOUTH CAROLINA SECEDES FROM THE UNION

Certain that the election of Abraham Lincoln would lead to the end of slavery, the state's secession declaration averred that "the People of South Carolina … have solemnly declared that the Union heretofore existing between this State and the other States … is dissolved, and that the State of South Carolina has resumed her position among the nations of the world." In the next six months, 10 other southern states would follow: Mississippi on January 9, Florida on January 10, Alabama on January 11, Georgia on January 19, Louisiana on January 26, Texas on February 1, Virginia on April 17, Arkansas on May 6, North Carolina on May 20, and Tennessee on June 8.

292. FEBRUARY 4, 1861

APACHE CHIEF AND ARMY LIEUTENANT BEGIN A DEADLY MISADVENTURE

In Apache Pass, a Chiricahua stronghold in southern Arizona, Chief Cochise met with a U.S. Army detachment led by Lt. George Bascom. Bascom accused him of leading a raiding party that attacked a white family's ranch and kidnapped their son. Cochise denied it, but over the next weeks, relations between the U.S. and the Chiricahua deteriorated, with misconduct on both sides. The "Bascom Affair" set off 11 years of attacks by Cochise and his followers—part of the 24-year-long conflict known as the Apache Wars.

293. FEBRUARY 23, 1861

BALTIMORE PLOT AGAINST ABRAHAM LINCOLN IS THWARTED

At 3:30 a.m., President-elect Lincoln deboarded his inaugural train in a nearly empty station in Baltimore; he had been warned repeatedly that if he stuck to the original schedule, he would be assassinated there. Reluctantly, he agreed to enter Washington in secret. With railroad detective Allan Pinkerton guarding him, he made his way by carriage to another Baltimore station and arrived early—and safely—in Washington. Ever eager, the press had a field day lampooning the president-elect for sneaking into the capital.

294. MARCH 11, 1861

CONSTITUTION OF THE CONFEDERATE STATES OF AMERICA IS ADOPTED

One week after Lincoln's inauguration, a Congress of Delegates from the seceded southern states met in Montgomery, Alabama, and unanimously adopted a constitution for the Confederacy. Drafted weeks earlier, much of the document mirrored the governmental guidelines outlined in the U.S. Constitution. But the Confederate version included the provision that "the institution of negro slavery, as it now exists in the Confederate States, shall be recognized and protected by Congress and by the Territorial government."

295. MARCH 16, 1861

SAM HOUSTON IS DRIVEN FROM OFFICE

As both governor of Texas and the hero of Texas independence from Mexico, Houston had argued fervently against the state's secession from the Union. But the people disagreed. On this day, officials at the Texas Secession Convention voted to remove him when he refused to take an oath of loyalty to the Confederate States of America. Houston agreed to abide by their vote. "I love Texas too well to bring civil strife and bloodshed

continued on page 160

After Chiricahua Apache denied U.S. Army claims that they had attacked white ranchers, simmering hostilities grew into the Apache Wars, which lasted 24 years.

SPOTLIGHT

RELIGION

AS THE NATION'S territory and population grew, new religious traditions arose. Thanks to the Bill of Rights, observance couldn't be mandated or denied to U.S. citizens. Yet throughout the 1800s, religious movements and beliefs had significant impact on society and culture.

With the dawn of the 19th century, evangelists from Protestant denominations joined forces for a "Second Great Awakening" of the faithful: Traveling preachers held revivals and camp meetings, fervent religious services that emphasized personal salvation over doctrine. The phenomenon drew more membership, notably to Methodist and Baptist churches; it also encouraged believers to work for social reforms, including the temperance and abolition movements.

In 1830 in western New York, the Mormon Church (later renamed the Church of Jesus Christ of Latter-day Saints) was founded by Joseph Smith, combining mainstream Christian precepts with Smith's teachings. Ostracized for their beliefs, church members fled west; after Smith was killed in 1844, his followers settled in Utah, where the church still is based.

The nation's religious dynamics were also changed by major waves of immigration from Europe. The first stemmed mostly from the continent's western and northern nations; the second was drawn mostly from eastern and southern nations. The newcomers—from Roman Catholic and Eastern Orthodox Christian churches, branches of Judaism, and new Protestant denominations—created religious and cultural diversity that went on to earn the United States the label "melting pot."

Religious revival meetings on the frontier attracted hundreds of people who camped for days to listen to preachers and share communal religious experiences with their neighbors.

RELIGION IS A MATTER WHICH LIES SOLELY BETWEEN MAN & HIS GOD, THAT HE OWES ACCOUNT TO NONE OTHER FOR HIS FAITH OR HIS WORSHIP.

Thomas Jefferson *(1802)*

continued from page 157

upon her," he said. Loyal to the end, he hoped his epitaph would read: "He loved his country, he was a patriot; he was devoted to the Union."

296. APRIL 12, 1861

CONFEDERATES BEGIN CIVIL WAR WITH ATTACK ON FORT SUMTER

After Abraham Lincoln's election, local militia seized U.S. forts and property throughout the seceded southern states. A Confederate delegation from South Carolina approached lame-duck President James Buchanan and demanded that such installations and properties in their state be relinquished to them. He refused. Federal forces guarding Charleston Harbor, the Confederacy's largest seaport, took up positions at Fort Sumter, and before dawn on this day, a Confederate battery fired the first mortar at the fort. On April 14, the outgunned Federal garrison was forced to abandon the fort but did so "with colors flying and drums beating." The Civil War had begun.

Unwilling to invade seceding southern states, Robert E. Lee declined the Lincoln administration's request that he command the Federal Army.

297. APRIL 18, 1861

UNION OFFERS ROBERT E. LEE COMMAND OF FEDERAL ARMY

Francis Preston Blair made the offer at the behest of President Abraham Lincoln and Secretary of War Simon Cameron, who, according to Blair's notes, "expressed themselves as anxious to give the command of our army to Robert E. Lee." A 31-year veteran of the U.S. Army, General Lee declined, "stating, as candidly and courteously as [he] could, that, though opposed to secession and deprecating war, [he] could take no part in an invasion of the Southern States." He submitted his resignation from the Army on April 20 and two days later accepted command of state forces in Virginia, which had just voted for secession from the Union.

298. APRIL 19, 1861

PRESIDENT LINCOLN DECLARES A BLOCKADE OF SOUTHERN PORTS

The command extended across seven Confederate states. Lincoln's secretary of state, William Seward, had pushed for the blockade to hobble the South's export of cotton and its import of vital goods. On April 27, Lincoln extended the blockade to include Virginia and North Carolina. By July, the Union Navy had blockaded all major southern ports, but some blockade runners carrying foreign imports and war matériel managed to evade northern detection for much of the conflict.

299. MAY 20, 1861

CONFEDERATE CONGRESS VOTES TO RELOCATE TO VIRGINIA

Previously located in Montgomery, Alabama, the legislative body voted to move itself to Richmond, the capital city of newly seceded Virginia and the second largest city in the

In the opening act of the Civil War in 1861, Confederates fired on Federal forces at Fort Sumter, located in South Carolina's Charleston Harbor.

Confederacy. Home to a number of factories—in short supply in the largely nonindustrialized South—the city was also the base of Tredegar Iron Works, where munitions, railroad tracks, and other war matériel were manufactured. Richmond's population soon tripled, and in the war years to come, it housed the seat of government, factories, hospitals for the wounded, and prisons for the enemy. It was also the prime target of Union forces.

300. JULY 4, 1861

THE 37TH CONGRESS CONVENES

Despite wartime conditions, in its short lifetime (July 4, 1861–March 3, 1863) this assembly passed legislation that would effect great change across the country. Among its major accomplishments: the Homestead Act and the Department of Agriculture Act in May 1862, the Morrill Land Grant College Act in July, the first of a set of antipolygamy

In Virginia, Confederate soldiers posed for a photograph before fighting at Bull Run, where the Union lost the war's first major battle in 1861.

laws, and the Union Pacific Railroad Charter. Before it expired in March 1863, the 37th Congress established the National Academy of Sciences, but also passed more controversial acts, allowing President Abraham Lincoln to suspend habeas corpus and requiring military conscription for all males aged 20 to 45.

301. JULY 21, 1861

FIRST BATTLE OF BULL RUN RAGES IN VIRGINIA

On July 16, some 35,000 Federal troops began their march from Washington to a creek in Manassas, Virginia, to take on Confederates positioned there. Civilians followed with picnic baskets, excited to watch. On July 18, skirmishes gave the South time to reinforce. The true battle began on July 21, with the North initially having the upper hand. Then, Brig. Gen.

Thomas J. Jackson and his men took a hill and held firm. Confederate forces rallied, with one general proclaiming, "There stands Jackson like a stone wall." By day's end, the Union had lost the first major battle of the war, and Stonewall Jackson became a legend.

302. AUGUST 5, 1861

CONGRESS ADOPTS THE FIRST NATIONAL INCOME TAX

To help finance the war effort, Congress levied taxes on individuals and corporations via the Revenue Act of 1861: 3 percent on earnings more than $800. While this act was largely ineffective, an expanded, more successful 1862 act soon passed, taxing incomes between $600 and $10,000 at 3 percent, and 5 percent for those higher. In 1864, as the war continued to drain public coffers, a third bill raised tax rates considerably: 5 percent on incomes from $600 to $5,000, 7.5 percent on incomes $5,000 to $10,000, and 10 percent on anything higher.

I SAW IT COMING, AND FOR 12 YEARS I WORKED, NIGHT AND DAY, TO PREVENT IT, BUT I COULD NOT.

Jefferson Davis, *regarding the Civil War (1864)*

303. NOVEMBER 6, 1861

CONFEDERATE VOTERS ELECT JEFFERSON DAVIS AS THEIR PRESIDENT

Davis's credentials were impressive: a West Point graduate and a hero of the Mexican-American War, former secretary of war and U.S. senator from Mississippi. (He was also the former son-in-law of President Zachary Taylor.) Though he was a wealthy planter who owned enslaved people, Davis had argued against secession—that is, until Mississippi seceded in January 1861. The next month, he was named provisional president of the Confederacy, and on this day, southern voters officially elected him to that office.

304. NOVEMBER 19, 1861

POET JULIA WARD HOWE WRITES "BATTLE HYMN OF THE REPUBLIC"

On November 18, social activist and poet Julia Ward Howe and her husband visited Union troops in the Washington, D.C., area. At one point, soldiers serenaded them with the marching song "John Brown's Body." Howe was encouraged to write new lyrics to the tune, and before dawn the next day, she woke to find the "wished-for lines … arranging themselves in my brain. I lay quite still until the last verse had completed itself … [then] began to scrawl the lines almost without looking." Her "Battle Hymn of the Republic" carried the Union through the war.

305. DECEMBER 11, 1861

GREAT FIRE OF CHARLESTON SPARKS HISTORIC FLAMES

On a mild winter night, a fire broke out in a factory building, and the wind soon spread it to other buildings in the area. As the blaze moved southwest, it destroyed homes, businesses, and churches. Cutting a 540-acre path of ruin across the city to the Ashley River, it remains the worst fire in the city's history. What started it is still unclear, but in his diary, the fire chief blamed the destruction on bad equipment and inadequate water sources.

306. JANUARY 10, 1862

CALIFORNIA IS DELUGED

On Governor Leland Stanford's inaugural day, torrential rains from an ongoing atmospheric river inundated the state, melting mountain snows and causing its biggest recorded flood; the rain and snowmelt also impacted other western states. "From the Sierra Nevada to the Coast Range is apparently one sheet of yellow rippling water," a California newspaper reported. Some 4,000 people in the state died from the flood, and farms and ranches were destroyed. Starvation and economic depression were close behind.

307. FEBRUARY 20, 1862

ABRAHAM LINCOLN'S SON DIES IN THE WHITE HOUSE

The celebrated poet Emily Dickinson was around 17 in this circa 1847 portrait.

Eleven-year-old William Wallace Lincoln, known as Willie, and his younger brother, Tad, had contracted what was then called "bilious fever"—probably typhoid derived from bad drinking water sourced from the nearby canal or Potomac River. Both parents were overwhelmed with grief. "He was too good for this earth! ... But we loved him so!" his father said. Willie was Mary Todd Lincoln's favorite, and after his death, the first lady did not leave her bed for three weeks; thereafter, she held séances, hoping to contact him. She would never fully recover from the loss.

308. FEBRUARY 25, 1862

LEGAL TENDER ACT PASSES

Much debated by Congress, the Legal Tender Act was finally enacted as a means to help finance the Civil War. The bill authorized the Treasury Department to print $150 million in paper money—"greenbacks"—that were not backed by gold and silver. The paper currency could be used for all transactions except to pay interest on public debt or import duties. Considered by many to be an overreach of federal power, the act was overturned in 1870 by the Supreme Court, which at that time had two vacant seats. But the next year, with two new justices in place, the ruling was quickly reversed. Meant to be a temporary measure, the act has held, making paper money the currency of the nation.

309. MARCH 1, 1862

EMILY DICKINSON PUBLISHES A POEM

On this day, Dickinson's now famous poem "Safe in their Alabaster Chambers" was published anonymously in the *Springfield Daily Republican* under the title "The Sleeping." Several other poems by the 31-year-old Massachusetts woman had been published in that respected newspaper, probably without her knowledge. While she continued to write prolifically in the next few years, she became more reclusive and averse to publishing her work; only a handful of other pieces were printed in her lifetime. At her death, 40 small hand-stitched books of some 1,800 handwritten poems were found in a locked chest in her room. Today, Dickinson is considered one of America's greatest poets.

310. MARCH 9, 1862

IRONCLAD WARSHIPS FACE OFF IN THE BATTLE OF HAMPTON ROADS

This morning, the C.S.S. *Virginia* and the U.S.S. *Monitor* met and fired on each other, to no avail. Their armor plates deflected enemy cannonballs and issued in a new age of naval warfare. After four hours, the *Virginia* turned back to port in Norfolk. Two months later, as President Abraham Lincoln and many others watched from Union-controlled Fort Monroe in Confederate Virginia, the retreating Confederates set their ironclad juggernaut on fire and destroyed it, fearing the invading North would capture it. By year's end, the *Monitor,* too, was gone, felled by a storm off the North Carolina coast.

311. APRIL 16, 1862

DISTRICT OF COLUMBIA ADOPTS THE EMANCIPATION ACT

This act was the first federal law to free people of African descent from bondage in the U.S. and allowed for compensation—up to $300 for each enslaved person who was emancipated—to their enslavers (if they were loyal to the Union). The new act also provided for voluntary

When his son Willie died in 1862 at age 11, likely of typhoid, a grieving President Abraham Lincoln declared him "too good for this earth!"

The first combat encounter of ironclad warships, the Civil War's Battle of Hampton Roads in 1862 was a standoff between the U.S.S. *Monitor* and C.S.S. *Virginia*.

colonization, and any formerly enslaved person who chose to emigrate would be given $100. In the nine months that followed, almost 3,000 people held in bondage in Washington were emancipated, thus alleviating the capital city of the "national shame" of slavery.

312. MAY 20, 1862

CONGRESS PASSES THE HOMESTEAD ACT

A boon to aspiring landowners, the new law stated that any adult head of household or person over 21 who had never taken up arms against the U.S. government could, for a minimal fee, claim 160 acres of surveyed public land. Even those who filed to become naturalized citizens could make a claim. Claimants were required to live on and farm the land, and if they did so for five years, the land became theirs. Despite Congress's good intentions, the act opened the way to land grabs by speculators, loggers, ranchers, and railroads. But it did help settle the western territories.

313. SEPTEMBER 17, 1862

BATTLE OF ANTIETAM IS FOUGHT IN MARYLAND

On America's bloodiest day, the farmland along the banks of Antietam Creek in northern Maryland became a killing field as Robert E. Lee's forces faced George McClellan's. Some 132,000 men (87,000 Union troops and 45,000 Confederates) fought through the long hours; by evening, 22,700 had become casualties of the inconclusive bloodbath. "The slain lay in rows precisely as they had stood in their ranks a few moments before," Union Gen. Joseph Hooker lamented. Alexander Gardner, an employee of well-known photographer Mathew Brady, took what are now historic images of the battle's grim aftermath.

IT IS MY GREATEST AND MOST ENDURING CONTRIBUTION TO THE HISTORY OF THE WAR ... AND THE GREAT EVENT OF THE 19TH CENTURY.

Abraham Lincoln, *on the Emancipation Proclamation (1865)*

314. SEPTEMBER 22, 1862

PRESIDENT LINCOLN ANNOUNCES THE EMANCIPATION PROCLAMATION

In July, Abraham Lincoln "had about come to the conclusion ... that we must free the slaves or be ourselves subdued," as he told Gideon Welles, his secretary of the Navy. His Cabinet insisted that he make no such move until the Union Army had scored a victory. Lincoln claimed Antietam as such and issued a historic decree to go into effect on January 1, 1863: "all persons held as slaves within any State ... in rebellion against the United States, shall be then, thenceforward, and forever free." Though the order did not free enslaved people in the states that had remained in the Union, Lincoln saw it as a first step. "I never, in my life, felt more certain that I was doing right, than I do in signing this paper," he asserted.

315. JANUARY 6, 1863

JAMES PLIMPTON PATENTS FOUR-WHEELED ROLLER SKATES

Public skating had become a popular pastime when Plimpton, who went on to own rinks in New York City and Newport, Rhode Island, developed a new and improved roller skate. He had been inspired two years earlier when, he explained, "being in bad health, I was advised to practise ice skating, and I derived much benefit from it." When ice was unavailable, he tried roller skating and liked that as well. This led to his improved design, which allowed users—both children and adults—to turn and steer more easily and safely. The invention led to a national boom in roller skating.

316. MAY 1, 1863

BATTLE OF CHANCELLORSVILLE HERALDS STONEWALL JACKSON'S END

The new head of the Army of the Potomac, Hooker marched 97,000 troops through northern Virginia to dislodge Robert E. Lee's army, encamped south of the Rappahannock River. Hooker declared, "May God have mercy on General Lee, for I will have none." On

May 2, outnumbered two to one, Lee and Stonewall Jackson divided their forces, and Jackson swept around the enemy. His surprise attack pushed the Union back, but just hours later Jackson was mortally wounded, mistakenly shot by one of his own men. By May 6, Hooker was in retreat. The battle claimed 30,700 casualties and cost the South one of its greatest generals.

317. MAY 18, 1863

CORNELIUS VANDERBILT ACQUIRES THE NEW YORK & HARLEM RAILROAD

At almost 70 years old, the legendary steamship magnate "Commodore" Vanderbilt shifted his focus to railroads and began taking control of existing regional lines in the Northeast, Midwest, and Canada. He had grown up a poor Staten Island boy, but at the age of 16 had started a ferry service to Manhattan. Thirty years later, he owned 100 steamboats. At his death in 1877, he was the richest man in the U.S.

318. JULY 1, 1863

BATTLE OF GETTYSBURG BEGINS

Robert E. Lee's army and the Union army under Gen. George Meade converged at the small crossroads of Gettysburg in southern Pennsylvania. For three days, in oppressive summer heat and across rocky terrain, they pounded each other. On day three, Lee ordered George Pickett to charge the Union position atop Cemetery Ridge. More than half the 13,000 men who made "Pickett's Charge" became casualties or were wounded, missing, or taken prisoner. When Lee retreated on July 4, total casualties numbered 28,000 Confederates and 23,000 Union men. "All this has been my fault," Lee observed. "It is I that have lost this fight."

319. JULY 4, 1863

SIEGE OF VICKSBURG ENDS

On this Independence Day, Confederate forces surrendered to Ulysses S. Grant after a 47-day Union siege. Civilians and Confederate troops in the strategic Mississippi River town suffered: "Dogs howled through the streets at night; cats screamed . . .; an army of rats, seeking food, would scamper around your very feet." Desperate for food themselves, people ate all three. Abraham Lincoln and Jefferson Davis both knew Vicksburg was a critical holding; Davis called it the "nailhead that holds the South's two halves together." With that nailhead gone and the Union victory at Gettysburg, the war turned a corner.

320. SEPTEMBER 26, 1863

"WHEN JOHNNY COMES MARCHING HOME" TAKES ITS PLACE IN THE LIBRARY OF CONGRESS

Renowned Boston bandleader Patrick Gilmore and his ensemble had enlisted early in the war to play on the Union troops. In the early years of the war, they witnessed some of the worst battles. By 1863, Gilmore was based in New Orleans as grand master of the Union Army. There, he composed the words and music to "When Johnny Comes Marching Home," said to have been inspired by an African American spiritual. The song captured the public's heart, with its promise that "We'll all feel gay / when Johnny comes marching home." Embraced by families on both sides of the Civil War, it would also provide comfort for Americans in later conflicts.

321. OCTOBER 3, 1863

ABRAHAM LINCOLN IMPLORES THE NATION TO OBSERVE THANKSGIVING

The president invited his fellow citizens "to set apart and observe the last Thursday of November next as a Day of Thanksgiving and Prayer to our beneficent Father" and to "fervently implore the interposition of the Almighty hand to heal the wounds of the nation." He made his proclamation at the urging of Sarah Josepha Hale, the influential 74-year-old

In 1863, three grueling days of assaults at Gettysburg, Pennsylvania, resulted in more than 50,000 casualties before the Confederates retreated.

"editress" of the popular *Lady's Book* magazine. Hale had lobbied for Thanksgiving for decades and was also a champion of women's education, equality, and independence.

322. NOVEMBER 19, 1863

PRESIDENT LINCOLN DELIVERS THE GETTYSBURG ADDRESS

At the dedication of a cemetery for those who died in the ferocious Pennsylvania battle, the great orator Edward Everett was the keynote speaker. His address, lasting two hours, moved some in the crowd of 15,000 to tears. Abraham Lincoln had been asked to follow with "a few appropriate remarks." His two-minute, 272-word speech begins, "Four score and seven years ago our fathers brought forth on this continent, a new nation, conceived in Liberty, and dedicated to the proposition that all men are created equal." Lincoln finished so quickly that the audience was slow to offer polite applause. He believed the speech to be "a flat failure." Yet Lincoln's short speech has echoed through the decades as the ultimate promise of America.

Abraham Lincoln's two-minute speech at the dedication of the Gettysburg cemetery in 1863—immortalized as the Gettysburg Address—has become one of the defining events in U.S. history.

323. DECEMBER 2, 1863

STATUE OF FREEDOM CROWNS THE CAPITOL DOME

When the Civil War began, the Capitol Building was in the midst of expansive construction, its dome half built. President Abraham Lincoln ordered the dome completed: "If people see the Capitol is going on, it is a sign we intend this Union shall go on." On this day, the final, fifth piece of the 19.5-foot Statue of Freedom was hoisted into place atop the dome. The 12 forts surrounding Washington honored the event with cannons booming; artillery nearby fired a 35-gun salute, one volley for each state of the Union, including those that had seceded.

324. DECEMBER 8, 1863

PRESIDENT LINCOLN ISSUES PROCLAMATION OF AMNESTY AND RECONSTRUCTION

Using his constitutional power to pardon, Lincoln declared: "Whereas, it is now desired by some persons heretofore engaged in … rebellion to resume their allegiance to the United States, and to reinaugurate loyal state governments within and for their respective states: Therefore … all persons who have, directly or by implication, participated in the existing rebellion … a full pardon is hereby granted to them … with restoration of all rights of property, except as to slaves." The proclamation was a first step in Lincoln's plans for Reconstruction, but those plans were ended by an assassin's bullet.

325. MARCH 9, 1864

ULYSSES S. GRANT TAKES COMMAND OF THE UNION ARMY

At President Lincoln's urging, Congress allowed Grant the rank previously held, among active officers, only by George Washington: lieutenant general of the Army. After success at Vicksburg, Lincoln had declared, "Grant is my man, and I am his, the rest of the war."

Grant had fought and won victories in the western theater, while Union generals in the east failed time and again. Now Lincoln brought Grant east, and the new commander laid plans for "total war": Gen. William Tecumseh Sherman was to attack Atlanta; Gen. George Meade, along with Grant himself, would pursue Robert E. Lee's army; and Benjamin Butler, at Fort Monroe, Virginia, would march on to Richmond. The 1864 campaign was one of the costliest of the war, but it succeeded in bringing the South to its knees. By 1865, the destruction was nearing its end.

326. AUGUST 19, 1864

ABRAHAM LINCOLN AND FREDERICK DOUGLASS HATCH A PLAN

Lincoln and Douglass met three times, and at their second encounter, Lincoln explained that he did not expect to win the upcoming presidential election. Because a new president might well reverse his decisions regarding the South and slavery, he had a proposal: Would the widely respected abolitionist Douglass help create a clandestine network in the Confederate states that would allow as many enslaved people as possible to escape north? Lincoln had expected the Emancipation Proclamation to trigger a mass exodus of enslaved people north, but that had not happened. Douglass agreed to help make the plan a reality.

Despite the ongoing Civil War, construction of the U.S. Capitol was completed, and the Statue of Freedom was installed atop the dome in 1863.

After marching across Georgia (and pillaging along the way, as in this depiction), Gen. William Tecumseh Sherman's 60,000 Union troops took the city of Savannah in 1864.

327. NOVEMBER 8, 1864

NATION REELECTS ABRAHAM LINCOLN

In the race against the Democratic candidate (and his own former general), George McClellan, Lincoln handily won the electoral vote, 212 to 21. In the popular vote, the Lincoln–Andrew Johnson ticket took 55.1 percent to McClellan–George Pendleton's 44.9 percent. Going into the fall election, Lincoln had expected to lose, but Union victories in Atlanta and Virginia's Shenandoah Valley had given him electoral momentum. And to Lincoln's great comfort, the Federal soldiers fighting the brutal war had voted overwhelmingly for their commander in chief. Many greeted the news with jubilation, and two nights later a huge crowd gathered on the White House lawn as "martial music, the cheers of the people, and the roar of cannon, shook the sky."

328. DECEMBER 21, 1864

SAVANNAH FALLS

Union Gen. William Tecumseh Sherman had completed his planned "March to the Sea" across Georgia from Atlanta to the port of Savannah. He felt the march would demonstrate "to the World, foreign and domestic, that we have a power which Davis cannot resist. This may not be war, but rather Statesmanship." Sherman's army of 60,000 lived off local harvests during the five-week march and left a swath of destruction in its wake. On December 22, the general sent Abraham Lincoln a telegram: "I beg to present you, as a Christmas gift, the city of Savannah."

329. JANUARY 16, 1865

GENERAL SHERMAN ISSUES SPECIAL FIELD ORDER NO. 15

The general was pressed by Congress, Secretary of War Edwin Stanton, and Black community leaders to issue this order (now colloquially known as "40 acres and a mule"), because William Tecumseh Sherman himself was not an abolitionist. Per the order, coastal land from Charleston, South Carolina, to Jacksonville, Florida, would be redistributed to Black families in 40-acre plots: "No white person whatever ... will be permitted to reside [there]; and the sole and exclusive management of affairs will be left to the freed people themselves," it declared. In six months, 40,000 freedmen claimed 400,000 acres, but the victory of ownership would be short-lived. Less than a year later, after Andrew Johnson became president, he ordered the land returned to its previous white owners.

The "cracked plate" image of Abraham Lincoln: Only one print was made from the damaged negative.

330. FEBRUARY 5, 1865

PHOTOGRAPHER CAPTURES LINCOLN'S "CRACKED PLATE" IMAGE

On this winter day, Abraham Lincoln sat for war and portrait photographer Alexander Gardner in his Washington, D.C., studio. Using the mammoth glass plates then available, Gardner captured the kind but haggard face of the man who had fought four years to reunite the Union. The glass negative cracked, leaving a line across Lincoln's skull, but Gardner was still able to make one print. It would become the final and most haunting image of Father Abraham.

331. MARCH 4, 1865

PRESIDENT LINCOLN GIVES HIS SECOND INAUGURAL ADDRESS

On a windy wet day, Abraham Lincoln faced an enthusiastic crowd gathered below the east front of the Capitol. In his high-pitched but clear voice, he delivered one of the most famous—and shortest—inaugural speeches in history. It concluded: "With malice toward none; with charity for all; with firmness in the right, as God gives us to see the right, let us strive on to finish the work we are in; to bind up the nation's wounds; to care for him who shall have borne the battle, and for his widow, and his orphan—to do all which may achieve and cherish a just and lasting peace among ourselves, and with all nations."

332. APRIL 9, 1865

ROBERT E. LEE SURRENDERS TO ULYSSES S. GRANT

After a year of vicious battles and a 292-day siege of Lee's army in Petersburg, Virginia, Lee had retreated west, hoping to resupply his dwindling forces at the village of Appomattox. When he found Union forces there already, he knew he must "go and see General Grant—and I would rather die a thousand deaths." The surrender took place at the home of Wilbur McLean, and Ulysses S. Grant was magnanimous in victory: Lee's men, he said, could return to their homes and take their horses, as Lee had requested. "The war is over," Grant declared. "The Rebels are our countrymen again."

333. APRIL 14, 1865

CONFEDERATE SUPPORTERS ATTACK ABRAHAM LINCOLN AND WILLIAM SEWARD

On this afternoon, the president and first lady took a carriage ride around Washington, D.C.; Mary Todd Lincoln said later that she had never seen her husband "so supremely cheerful." That night, they attended a performance at Ford's Theatre, something the president always enjoyed. At 10:15, one of the actors, John Wilkes Booth, quietly entered their box and shot President Lincoln in the head. Leaping onto the stage, Booth shouted "Sic Semper Tyrannis"—"Thus Always to Tyrants." At about the same time, a Booth accomplice attacked Secretary of State William Seward in his home, stabbing him in the neck and face. Seward survived, but by the next morning, Lincoln was dead and Andrew Johnson was president.

334. APRIL 26, 1865

JOHN WILKES BOOTH DIES

The Confederate diehard and another member of his conspiracy, David Herold, fled through southern Maryland, crossing the Potomac and then to Port Royal, Virginia. They were holed up in a local barn when a posse of detectives and soldiers, tipped off about the fugitives, surrounded them and demanded their surrender. Herold came out, but Booth did not. The barn was set fire to force his hand, but one of the posse shot through a chink in the wall, mortally wounding Booth. As he lay dying, Booth said, "I die for my country."

335. MAY 4, 1865

NATION BURIES ABRAHAM LINCOLN

The great man's final resting place was Springfield, Illinois, where he had spent much of his life as a lawyer, father, and husband. On this hot spring day, his body was placed in a receiving vault, with his son Willie's beside it. Lincoln's funeral train had stopped in Baltimore, Philadelphia, and New York, where his body was put on public view. Along the route, mourners lined the tracks, and the train made more stops in the Midwest before finally bringing Father Abraham home. An estimated one million people paid their respects to the man who had saved the Union.

336. MAY 5, 1865

CONFEDERATE GOVERNMENT DISSOLVES

Jefferson Davis and his small Cabinet held their final meeting at the Georgia State Bank in Washington, Georgia. They'd fled Richmond, Virginia, after Robert E. Lee's surrender, but Davis had hoped that southern forces in the west would keep fighting. That was not to be. On May 7, Davis's entourage was joined by family and the group kept moving south, aware that Union pursuers could be closing in. On May 9, they camped near a creek in Irwin County; the next morning Union cavalry surrounded them and captured Davis. He would spend the next two years imprisoned at Fort Monroe, Virginia.

337. JUNE 19, 1865

TEXAS COMMUNITIES REJOICE WITH EMANCIPATION DAY

Even with the Confederacy dissolved, Texas held out as a slave state. Federal forces took Galveston on June 18, and on the 19th, Maj. Gen. Gordon Granger appeared on the

Henry Ward Beecher's memorial sermon in 1865 declared Abraham Lincoln had "come near to the promised land of peace, into which he might not pass over."

Walt Whitman's moving 1865 poem about Abraham Lincoln's death, "O Captain! My Captain!" was one of his best known and most popular published works.

balcony of a home that had served as a regional headquarters for the Confederate Army. He read General Order No. 3, which began: "The people of Texas are informed that, in accordance with a proclamation from the Executive of the United States, all slaves are free." The following year, Black communities in Texas celebrated the day as Emancipation Day, and the tradition spread to other states. In 2021, Juneteenth became a federal holiday.

338. AUGUST 7, 1865

JOURDON ANDERSON PUTS HIS FOOT DOWN

Some former enslavers believed their now freed captives would return to work for them. When Anderson, an African American freedman, received such a letter from his former enslaver, Col. P. H. Anderson, he wrote back: "If you fail to pay us for faithful labors in the past, we can have little faith in your promises in the future. We trust the good Maker has opened your eyes to the wrongs which you and your fathers have done to me and my fathers, in making us toil for you for generations without recompense." He ended with, "Say howdy to George Carter, and thank him for taking the pistol from you when you were shooting at me."

339. NOVEMBER 4, 1865

WALT WHITMAN LAMENTS ABRAHAM LINCOLN'S DEATH IN POETRY

The great poet's tribute to the fallen president, "O Captain! My Captain!," first appeared in the *Saturday Press,* a literary weekly based in New York. The poem, now much recited, began: "O captain! my captain! our fearful trip is done; / The ship has weathered every rack, the prize we sought is won." Whitman was in Washington, D.C., for much of the Civil War, serving as a volunteer nurse who cared for the wounded. He often saw Lincoln in passing and came to greatly admire the man and his resolve to save the nation. Whitman also wrote a longer, elegiac poem to his hero: "When Lilacs Last in the Dooryard Bloom'd."

TRUTH IS STRANGER THAN FICTION, BUT IT IS BECAUSE FICTION IS OBLIGED TO STICK TO POSSIBILITIES; TRUTH ISN'T.

Mark Twain *(1897)*

340. NOVEMBER 18, 1865

TALL TALE OF A FROG LAUNCHES THE CAREER OF MARK TWAIN

He had been a printer's apprentice, a Mississippi riverboat pilot, and a silver prospector—but what Samuel Clemens truly wanted to be was an author. His writing career took off on this day when the *New York Saturday Press* newspaper published his short story "Jim Smiley and His Jumping Frog." A tall tale about a compulsive gambler who bet on a trick frog he'd trained, the popular story was the first big splash for Mark Twain, Clemens's pen name. After that story (later renamed "The Celebrated Jumping Frog of Calaveras County"), Twain would produce an abundance of fiction and nonfiction, including some of American literature's landmark works, including *The Adventures of Tom Sawyer* and *Adventures of Huckleberry Finn.*

341. NOVEMBER 24, 1865

BLACK CODES ENACTED IN MISSISSIPPI

After the January 1865 passage of the 13th Amendment outlawing slavery, Mississippi became the first state to pass laws limiting the rights of freedmen. These codes restricted formerly enslaved people from serving as witnesses in cases between white litigants; seeking a better-paying job; marrying a spouse of another race; and owning property outside cities, which prevented them from becoming self-sufficient farmers. Other southern states soon passed similar acts. But the 1868 passage of the 14th Amendment, which guaranteed equal protection under the law, and the 15th Amendment, which passed in 1870 and guaranteed voting rights, helped counter such decrees—though not the inclination to enact them. In the decades to come, southern legislatures passed other discriminatory Jim Crow laws.

DOUGLAS BRINKLEY

DOUGLAS BRINKLEY IS THE KATHERINE TSANOFF BROWN PROFESSOR IN HUMANITIES AND PROFESSOR OF HISTORY AT RICE UNIVERSITY, CNN'S PRESIDENTIAL HISTORIAN, AND A CONTRIBUTING EDITOR AT *VANITY FAIR*.

DAVID M. RUBENSTEIN: The 19th century began with John Adams following George Washington as president. Was he popular?

DOUGLAS BRINKLEY: He was. He was our top legal scholar during that period. He was also our first vice president, and nobody knew what a VP was supposed to do yet. He came into office popular, well liked, with a lot of integrity.

DMR: Adams wanted to serve two terms, but lost the election to his own vice president, Thomas Jefferson. How could he run against his own president with whom he was serving?

DB: During his presidency, Adams became entangled in the Alien and Sedition Acts. He tried to deport French people on American soil back to France. Jefferson was connected to that as his VP, but Jefferson was a Francophile. He and Jefferson had totally different views on what American democracy would be, and it became, I think, the most important election in American history. It gave birth to the political party system of today.

DMR: Before the 12th Amendment, a vice president could run against a president, because of the way the Constitution originally worked. Whomever got the most votes became president, and the second most became vice president.

DB: Exactly. Your VP was always ready to not only jump into being president, but to be the leader of an opposition party. The year 1800 defines where we're at today—where you have two parties that go at each other.

DMR: How did Jefferson justify the Louisiana Purchase? He thought the government shouldn't overreach, but buying that much land wasn't approved.

DB: Jefferson wanted one thing—control of the city of New Orleans. It was assumed that the Mississippi River would be the end of the United States. He dispatched James Monroe, a future president, and Robert Livingston, an entrepreneur, to negotiate with Napoleon Bonaparte to buy New Orleans. Napoleon offered the entire Louisiana Territory for a song, as they say: $16 million and you double the size of America. Jefferson was elated. The problem was that Congress and the Senate were *not* enthused, and Jefferson had to sell it to Capitol Hill as a national security matter.

DMR: James Madison succeeded Jefferson as president and served two terms. He got into a fight with the British, resulting in the War of 1812. What was that war? Why did the British burn the White House and the Capitol Building?

DB: The War of 1812 is really a second American Revolution. There would be no United States without going through that grand ordeal. The British had designs on Canada, while we were fumbling around as a new nation.

In a skirmish, we burned some buildings, which gave the British the excuse to burn Washington, D.C.—what a symbolic act that would be. So they burned the White House and the Capitol Building down. And then, fate: a big storm poured rain and blew off all the rooftops. Everything turned to mud. So even though the British burned Washington, they left in disarray. Madison went down in history as winning the War of 1812. But it was close.

DMR: Madison was succeeded by James Monroe. What was his famous Monroe Doctrine, and why did he issue it?
DB: From 1817 to 1825, Monroe tried to heal the nation after the War of 1812. On the surface, the Monroe Doctrine was about America not allowing the militarization of this hemisphere. Most of the world laughed at or ignored it; you can give a declaration, but if you don't have a way to protect a hemisphere, it's foolhardy. But that turns out to be a foundational document of principle that the United States has clung to. It gave the justification of a military doctrine for the Navy: We built the Panama Canal, and therefore, we can protect this entire hemisphere. Some see it as American arrogance. Others see it as an American sphere of influence.

DMR: Why did John Quincy Adams become a member of the House of Representatives for more than two decades after serving as president?
DB: John Quincy Adams wasn't considered a very successful president. But when he left the White House, he impacted what the next president could do. He ran against slavery and won a seat in Congress. Imagine a former president just grabbing a desk, fighting against slavery for 16 years, being a leading abolitionist. His ability to pinpoint slavery as *the* issue that we had to rectify in order to be a union was exemplary.

DMR: The first president from the South was Andrew Jackson. What did he try to do as president? How has his image changed?
DB: Jackson was a military man. Coming from Tennessee, he represented "frontier democracy" and became a symbol of the nonintellectual side of America. His stock is sinking because we now consider his treatment of Native Americans—particularly the Trail of Tears—as a genocide. You can argue what that word means, but Jackson was different than other presidents on Native American issues. He wanted an extermination.

DMR: What was the Alamo?
DB: The Alamo is shorthand now for 1836, when the independence movement of Anglo and German Europeans who had moved to Texas launched and symbolized their desire to break from Mexico. [Mexican president Antonio López de] Santa Anna's troops defended the mission in large numbers, while a small group was determined to give their lives for independence. At the Battle of the Alamo, these men were besieged, but they held their own, knowing they'd probably die. They lost, but it created time for Texans to regroup and beat Mexico at the Battle of San Jacinto. So, for Texans, the Alamo is a place of manifest destiny.

DMR: In the 1840s and '50s, southern states increasingly enslaved people. Some in the northern states felt slavery was immoral and should be abolished. How did the government deal with this tension?
DB: That's the crucial question in American history. One answer begins with transportation. Economically, the Midwest began connecting to the East, isolating the South. That meant you could ship goods from the Midwest to New York, Philadelphia, Baltimore, or Europe. Before this, you had to go down the Mississippi River to sell your produce. You'd get paid, then you'd work back via the Natchez Trace.

Now imagine Abraham Lincoln as a young man going down the Mississippi from Illinois. When he saw the slave markets in New Orleans, his jaw dropped, because he couldn't believe the inhumanity of it all. It was one thing to think people had slaves. It's another to witness the horror of the slave markets. Brave voices—from John Quincy Adams to William Lloyd Garrison to Frederick Douglass—started demanding abolition. It created "the great divide."

DMR: Why were southern states so interested in having new states admitted to the Union as states where slavery was permitted?

DB: The balance in this period was trying to have an equal number of slave states and free states. So with the Missouri Compromise in 1850, you let Maine in as a free state, but you let Missouri in as a slave state. This, in hindsight, is a false errand. Once Britain did away with slavery, once the North industrialized, people started gathering to the abolitionist crusade, and the writing was on the wall.

DMR: How did Lincoln first come to public attention? What was his position on slavery?
DB: Lincoln lived in Springfield, Illinois. It allowed him to go all over the state because it's centrally located, so he could travel around as a lawyer. His thoughts on slavery were an evolution, but I think his trip to New Orleans turned him toward finding slavery more morally repugnant. The question was, How does one politically eradicate this without just being a revolutionary?

DMR: Several southern states seceded from the Union upon Lincoln's election in 1860. What were his feelings on this?
DB: Lincoln was first and foremost a Unionist. He wasn't rabidly antislavery, but it was clear by his first inaugural address that this was the defining issue of his time. For him, it wasn't abolitionists versus slave owners; it was Unionists versus Confederates. How could he pull himself—and the nation—out of this jam? One of the great reasons we honor Lincoln is because of how he handled this issue.

DMR: Why were the Battle of Gettysburg and the Gettysburg Address so significant?
DB: The address wasn't considered significant at the time, but what we're awed by is Lincoln's ability to write deeply, thoughtfully, and eloquently. You can marry the Gettysburg Address with the Emancipation Proclamation. All start to show a philosophy of Lincoln's, which is that our nation had to rid itself of slavery. We had to stay together as a union, never separate. And that our Republic—our virtues, our liberty—were meant to succeed. No matter how bad another president thinks they had it, Lincoln had it worse.

DMR: How did Ulysses S. Grant emerge as the one Union general able to consistently win battles?
DB: In those days, you wanted to be good on a horse to be in the military. Grant was remarkable, but his other gift was his ability to write clearheaded battlefield reports. He wasn't seen as a dandy; he was in the mud with the troops. And he'd lived in St. Louis, Galena, and Memphis, and that was the topography we needed to win.

DMR: Why did John Wilkes Booth assassinate Lincoln? Did he expect to become a hero?
DB: Booth was angry at Lincoln. I don't think he wanted to be captured or was doing it just for headlines. He thought the war would continue if Lincoln was killed—that it might get another round.

DMR: Andrew Johnson succeeded Lincoln as president. Why was he impeached?
DB: It was a mistake, in retrospect, for Lincoln to pick Johnson for VP. But you can understand asking somebody from the South, if you're trying to unite the country. But just because Appomattox happened didn't mean all the sentiments healed overnight. Once Johnson came in, his Confederate sympathies started coming up. He started abusing power. He was impeached, and it deeply scarred his reputation. Johnson never purged himself of the Lost Cause of the Confederacy, and that's what he needed to have become a successful president.

DMR: What were the impacts of the civil rights amendments to the Constitution?
DB: After the Civil War, you started seeing a great boon of Black participation in democracy. It brought Black America to a kind of equal footing, but of course it quickly would get squashed; the South wouldn't tolerate it. They found ways to circumvent the law and do voting rights restrictions and keep Black Americans from having power. There was a very short-lived period of almost quasi-equality that was gone by the 1890s.

DMR: How did Ulysses S. Grant fare as president?
DB: Grant never ranked highly because there was a feeling that he either drank or played cards, or he wasn't meant to deal with the bureaucratic inertia of being president, or he

Ulysses S. Grant, commander of the Union Army, poses with his generals in this 1865 painting.

didn't have a legal mind. But we now understand Grant's attempt to heal the nation through Reconstruction as epic. He was trying to live by the spirit of Lincoln's inaugural addresses, the Emancipation Proclamation, and the founding documents. But corruption started tainting him a little bit.

DMR: How did James Garfield get elected president, and what led to his assassination?

DB: Garfield was a first-rate soldier in the Civil War, brilliant and charismatic. There are indicators he would've been a great president, but he was shot early on. The assassination of Lincoln, followed by the assassination of Garfield, then the assassination of [William] McKinley, all make this a period of political violence—this killing of three presidents in a row. All Republicans.

DMR: How important was the transcontinental railroad?

DB: The transcontinental railroad, I think, is the epic moment during the Civil War that's not about the war, per se, but Lincoln's ability to win. It connected East to West, and that was game-changing. That railroad made the steamboat and horse and buggy seem antiquated. By the 1870s, America had become an industrial revolution giant.

DMR: What do you regard as the most significant occurrences of the 19th century?

DB: Our mindset of western expansion and this notion that we can defend the Atlantic *and* the Pacific. The culmination of the 19th century comes with the idea that we are willing to be a global power. There is isolationism there, but in the end, commerce and trade in a global fashion prevailed.

DMR: What person or people had the most impact on the 19th century, and why?

DB: Lincoln is in a category of his own. To inherit such a debacle, where the entire country was crumbling and whole states were saying goodbye—to persevere through that took a special kind of intellect, cunning, morality, humanity, and decency. We are very blessed to have had a figure like that at that time.

Founding members dubbed the Ku Klux Klan a "social club," but they wore identity-concealing hoods when they attacked and terrorized Black people.

342. DECEMBER 24, 1865

CONFEDERATES IN TENNESSEE FORM KU KLUX KLAN

On this day in Pulaski, Tennessee, a half dozen veterans of the defeated Confederate Army convened a group they called the Ku Klux Klan, from the Greek *kyklos* for "circle." What they considered a "social club" was in fact a hate group composed of white supremacists and segregationists bent on stopping Reconstruction. Wearing white robes and sheets to frighten their targets and disguise their identities, Klan members conducted nighttime raids, assaulting and killing Black Americans and anyone who defended them. By the time the U.S. Congress condemned the group with the 1871 Ku Klux Klan Act, its members had become politically powerful throughout the South.

343. DECEMBER 25, 1865

UNION STOCK YARD TRANSFORMS CHICAGO INTO A MEAT-PROCESSING HUB

"Hog Butcher for the World"—that was poet Carl Sandburg's description of Chicago, a city whose livestock slaughter and processing business centered on the Union Stock Yard. Opened on this day, "The Yard" eventually would cover more than a square mile on the city's South Side; within five years of its founding, some two million animals a year were processed there. The Union Stock Yard became ground zero for issues of labor relations, meat industry standards, and workplace safety—or lack thereof, as described by investigative journalist Upton Sinclair in his meatpacking-plant exposé and novel *The Jungle.*

344. APRIL 9, 1866

CONGRESS PASSES FIRST CIVIL RIGHTS ACT

On this day, the U.S. House overrode President Andrew Johnson's veto to pass the nation's first civil rights legislation, a bill stating that "all persons born in the United States," other than nontaxed Native Americans, were "hereby declared to be citizens of the United States" and, as such, guaranteed "full and equal benefit of all laws." With slavery recently abolished by ratification of the Constitution's 13th Amendment, congressional Republicans hastened to enact more laws to protect Black people's rights in the postwar South. But Johnson differed with many legislators in his approach to Reconstruction. Though Johnson had given amnesty to thousands of former Confederates who went home to build new lives, many others wanted to keep emancipated Black families from doing the same.

345. JUNE 6, 1866

"LONG DRIVE" ESTABLISHES THE GOODNIGHT-LOVING TRAIL

Two ranchers wanted to drive 2,000 head of longhorn cattle from north-central Texas to Fort Sumner, New Mexico—but the most direct route would take them through country that the Comanche controlled. So on this day, Texans Charles Goodnight and Oliver Loving set off on a longer, safer route that would eventually take on their names. With

Covering more than one square mile on Chicago's South Side, the Union Stock Yard, inaugurated in 1865, was hailed as the largest livestock mart in the world.

portions once used by a stagecoach line, the route started out southwest before following the Pecos River northwest through Texas, then north into New Mexico, and later into Colorado. It became a popular route for cattle drivers. Goodnight and Loving ran drives on it until Loving died from gangrene after being mortally wounded in a Comanche attack in New Mexico in 1867.

346. MARCH 30, 1867

U.S. ACQUIRES THE LAND THAT WILL BECOME ALASKA

Russian and U.S. officials agreed on this day to the U.S. purchase of "Russian America": about 375,000,000 acres of land on the northwest tip of North America. It would soon be known as Alaska, a name drawn from an Aleut word meaning "great land." The price: $7.2 million, or about two cents an acre. Critics of the purchase called it "Seward's Folly," for the deal's U.S. negotiator, Secretary of State William Seward. But criticism died back as the territory became known for its natural resources, including rich gold strikes. In 1959, Alaska was proclaimed the nation's 49th state.

Originally published in two volumes beginning in 1868, Louisa May Alcott's *Little Women* was a hit with readers and was later turned into a single book.

347. OCTOBER 14, 1867

PRESIDENT LINCOLN'S WIDOW SULLIES HER REPUTATION

During Abraham Lincoln's presidency and the widespread suffering caused by the Civil War, the president's wife, Mary Todd Lincoln, was criticized for spending freely and sporting fine clothes. After her husband's assassination, Mary wore only mourning clothes and feared she'd end up penniless. So, with her dressmaker, Elizabeth Keckley, she hatched a plan to go to New York City and discreetly sell her wardrobe and jewelry. She was persuaded she'd get higher prices if she confirmed the items were hers—but when the public found out what she was attempting, the plan failed and Mary Todd Lincoln was ridiculed.

348. MAY 26, 1868

CONGRESS ATTEMPTS TO IMPEACH PRESIDENT ANDREW JOHNSON

With the Civil War over, the U.S. government's priority became Reconstruction. Republicans who controlled Congress passed measures to protect the rights of newly freed Black people, and when President Andrew Johnson vetoed them (and tested the bounds of another law he felt curtailed his presidential authority), the House voted to impeach him. The impeachment trial went forward in the Senate, where Republicans had a sufficient majority to remove Johnson. But on this day, the trial ended with the president's acquittal by one vote on each article of impeachment—"not because a majority of senators supported his policies, but because a sufficient minority wished to protect the office of the president and preserve the constitutional balance of powers," according to a modern analysis.

349. JULY 9, 1868

RATIFICATION OF 14TH AMENDMENT ASSURES CITIZENSHIP FOR FORMERLY ENSLAVED PEOPLE

As congressional Republicans fought to ensure equal legal and civil rights for Black people freed from enslavement, the 14th Amendment to the Constitution was a controversial but critical step. In June 1866, Congress sent the states the proposed amendment. It granted citizenship to all people born or naturalized in the U.S.—including formerly enslaved people—and stated that governments couldn't deprive "any person of life, liberty, or property without due process of law," nor deny them "the equal protection of the laws." On this day—nearly two years after Congress proposed the amendment—it was ratified by the necessary 28 out of 37 states and became U.S. law.

I WANT TO DO SOMETHING SPLENDID ... SOMETHING HEROIC OR WONDERFUL, THAT WON'T BE FORGOTTEN AFTER I'M DEAD.

Louisa May Alcott, *Jo March in* Little Women *(1868)*

350. SEPTEMBER 30, 1868

FIRST VOLUME OF *LITTLE WOMEN* IS PUBLISHED

Thirty-five-year-old Louisa May Alcott's story of the March family, based loosely on her own family's life in a Massachusetts village, immediately became successful, selling out its initial print run of 2,000 copies in the first two weeks of publication. She began the second volume on November 1. "I can do a chapter a day, and in a month I mean to be done," she wrote in her journal. (She finished it in two.) Known in the U.S. as *Little Women, Book Two* and in Britain as *Good Wives,* it, too, enjoyed commercial and critical success, selling 1,000 copies a month. The two volumes were eventually published as one book, still in print today.

351. OCTOBER 12, 1868

MARSHALL FIELD OPENS A STORE AND LAUNCHES A MERCANTILE EMPIRE

When he went to work in a Chicago dry goods store at age 21, could Marshall Field have imagined his name would adorn a world-famous retail enterprise? Perhaps not, but on this day, Field and his business partner, Levi Leiter, opened what would become a landmark in department store history. Though their opulent building was destroyed in the Great Chicago Fire of 1871, and again six years later, the partners reopened. After Leiter retired, the store name became Marshall Field's, and the founder continued to pioneer what the Chicago History Museum calls "a new style of urban retailing ... featuring a vast array of goods elegantly displayed in separate departments."

352. MARCH 4, 1869

PRESIDENT ULYSSES S. GRANT URGES BLACK VOTING RIGHTS IN HIS INAUGURAL ADDRESS

Republican Ulysses S. Grant, the highest-ranking Union general at the end of the Civil War, was elected president in 1868; he succeeded Andrew Johnson, a Democrat, who was Abraham Lincoln's vice president and assumed the presidency after his assassination. The two men had sharply different views on Reconstruction and were so at odds that Johnson didn't attend Grant's swearing-in ceremony on this day. In his inaugural address, Grant advocated "proper treatment" and citizenship for Native Americans, urged passage of the 15th Amendment giving Black men the vote, and called on every citizen "to do his share toward cementing a happy union."

In 1869, dignitaries drove a golden spike into a railroad tie to connect tracks laid from the east and west into one transcontinental rail line across the United States.

353. MAY 4, 1869

FIRST PROFESSIONAL BASEBALL GAME IS PLAYED, SPURRING "AMERICA'S PASTIME"

Early versions of the game had been played for more than a century when, in 1857, the National Association of Base Ball Players (NABBP) was founded. A few years later, Civil War soldiers taught each other "base ball" during the war and brought the game home at its end. On this day, the first professional team, the Cincinnati Red Stockings, played the first game against another Cincinnati NABBP team, the Great Western Base Ball Club. The Red Stockings won 45 to 9, and went on to a 57–0 record in NABBP play. There was no budget for a team in 1871, so Red Stockings players dispersed; some went to Boston, taking their nickname with them and notching four league championships by 1875. From its roots in European folk games, baseball was becoming America's pastime.

Played in Cincinnati in 1869, the first professional baseball game pitted the Great Western Base Ball Club against the Cincinnati Red Stockings. The Red Stockings won 45 to 9.

354. MAY 10, 1869

A GOLDEN SPIKE SECURES THE FINAL STRETCH OF RAILROAD SPANNING THE U.S.

The railroad track had been laid from two directions, to meet at a spot called Promontory Summit in the Utah Territory: 690 miles laid by the Central Pacific Railroad starting at Sacramento, California, and 1,086 miles laid by the Union Pacific Railroad starting near Council Bluffs, Iowa. On this day, as eastbound and westbound locomotives faced each other on the nearly touching tracks, the transcontinental railroad was officially joined when railroad officials using a silver hammer tapped a 17.6-karat gold spike into a tie made of California laurelwood. (To prevent theft, it was immediately removed.)

355. JULY 4, 1869

COWBOYS COMPETE AT THE WORLD'S FIRST RODEO

Like anything won in spirited competition, the title "World's First Rodeo" may always be contested. But the *Guinness Book of World Records* awarded that designation to events on this day in Deer Trail, Colorado, where area ranches' hardiest cowboys and least-broken "outlaw" horses came together for a "bronco bustin' contest." The objective: Stay atop a horse without getting bucked off. As reported by the newspaper *Denver Field and Farm,* the winner was cowboy Emilnie Gardenshire of Mill Iron ranch. His tenacious 15-minute ride on bronco Montana Blizzard won him the title Champion Bronco Buster of the Plains, along with a suit of clothes from a Denver dry goods store.

356. AUGUST 24, 1869

CORNELIUS SWARTWOUT OF TROY, NEW YORK, PATENTS A STOVETOP WAFFLE IRON

Waffle irons of various sorts had been around for centuries. But Swartwout's version had a handle and a clasp so that the waffle could be easily flipped, thus avoiding burns to the

Seated despite Southern Democrats' opposition, educator and preacher Hiram Rhodes Revels became the first African American senator in 1870.

maker or to the waffle (and messy spills of the setting batter). Most stoves at the time were either fueled by wood or coal. In honor of Swartwout's patent, fans of the culinary delight now celebrate August 24 as National Waffle Day.

357. SEPTEMBER 24, 1869

GOLD MARKET SCHEMERS TRIGGER BLACK FRIDAY

As President Ulysses S. Grant and U.S. Treasury Secretary George Boutwell strategically managed sales of Treasury gold to stabilize the postwar economy, two conspirators schemed to influence gold policy and corner the gold market. The schemers—investors Jay Gould and James Fisk, with help from Abel Corbin, the husband of Grant's sister—aimed to use insider information to manipulate prices as they bought up the precious metal. But Grant learned of the plot and on this day ordered a sale that dropped gold's price and sank the schemers' plans. This so-called Black Friday shocked Wall Street and triggered months of economic turmoil. Fortunately, the nation avoided a depression.

358. NOVEMBER 6, 1869

WITH FIRST U.S. INTERCOLLEGIATE FOOTBALL GAME, GRIDIRON ERA DAWNS

The game was new, the rules newly agreed upon, and the Rutgers College student newspaper's coverage unconventional when the Rutgers Queensmen played the visiting Princeton Tigers on this day in intercollegiate football's first game. The *Targum's* article reported that "Princeton had the most muscle, but didn't kick very well"; that the Rutgers team, "though comparatively weak, ran well, and kicked well"—except when one player, "in his ardor, forgot which way he was kicking." Still, Rutgers won. But Princeton won a rematch a week later and a third game was never played, so both New Jersey schools ended the 1869 college football season with a 1–1 record.

359. FEBRUARY 3, 1870

CONGRESS RATIFIES THE 15TH AMENDMENT

Drafted to prevent states from discriminating against African American men, the bill stated that "the right of citizens of the United States to vote shall not be denied or abridged by the United States or by any State on account of race, color, or previous condition of servitude." But under its edicts, women of all races were still excluded from voting. And many states—particularly those in the former Confederacy—came up with new ways to discriminate against Black men by instituting poll taxes and literacy tests. The guarantee of universal suffrage was still decades away.

[IT'S] THE ONLY PUBLIC BUILDING OF RECENT YEARS WHICH APPROACHES IN DIGNITY AND GRANDEUR THE MUSEUMS OF THE OLD WORLD.

New-York Evening Post, *on the Metropolitan Museum of Art and its additions (1902)*

360. FEBRUARY 25, 1870

U.S. SENATE SEATS ITS FIRST BLACK MEMBER

To fill an open seat for a partial term, Mississippi lawmakers chose Hiram Rhodes Revels to represent the state in the U.S. Senate. Southern Democrats in the Senate opposed Revels, while the Republican majority supported him—and after a party-line vote of 48 to 8, Revels became the Senate's first African American member on this day. Born in 1827 in North Carolina to free parents of Black, European, and Native American ancestry, Revels was an ordained minister who had preached around the country and organized Black schools and churches. In the Senate, he promoted civil rights; after his term, he became president of Alcorn University, the first U.S. land-grant school for Black students.

361. APRIL 13, 1870

NEW YORK CITY'S METROPOLITAN MUSEUM OF ART IS CREATED

Over a Paris dinner four years earlier, American art patrons, including celebrated lawyer John Jay II, had discussed their vision: a "national institution and gallery of art" with an extensive, inspiring collection. On this day, that vision took form when the Metropolitan Museum of Art was incorporated. Over time, its main building, on the east edge of Manhattan's Central Park, would be surrounded by additions, making it the largest art museum in the Americas. Popularly known as The Met, it's renowned for distinguished collections of classical antiquities, American artworks, and the largest collection of Egyptian art outside of Cairo.

362. MAY 31, 1870

CONGRESS PASSES ENFORCEMENT ACT TO COMBAT KLAN ACTIVITY

Despite the constitutional amendments declaring Blacks' rights as citizens, the Ku Klux Klan continued to terrorize many who tried to register, vote, or run for office, serve on juries, or testify in court. President Ulysses S. Grant urged Congress to intervene, and on this day lawmakers did just that, passing the first of three Enforcement Acts. This act made it illegal for groups to "go in disguise" to try to keep citizens from exercising their rights. Two more measures, passed in early 1871 and known as the Ku Klux Klan Acts, would empower the federal government to supervise elections to stop interference and dispatch armed forces to prevent intimidation and violence.

363. MARCH 3, 1871

CONGRESS PROHIBITS NEGOTIATION WITH NATIVE AMERICAN TRIBES

Since President George Washington's time, the U.S. government had regarded Native American tribes as independent nations when it came to negotiating treaties. But that policy fell from favor after the Civil War, as zealous lawmakers focused on rebuilding a single, unified nation. Congress adopted a resolution prohibiting the negotiation of any further treaties with tribes and attached it to an appropriations bill, which President Ulysses S. Grant signed on this day. Though existing treaties remained on paper, the Indian Appropriations Act laid the groundwork for nullifying them by ending recognition of Native American tribes as sovereign nations.

364. OCTOBER 6, 1871

CHORAL GROUPS POPULARIZE AFRICAN AMERICAN SPIRITUALS

Founded in Nashville, Tennessee, as a college for formerly enslaved people, Fisk University was sinking in debt. So faculty member George White put together a choral ensemble and took it on a national fundraising tour that launched on this day. The Fisk Jubilee Singers—named for the Old Testament "year of jubilee," when the enslaved would be freed—became known for their superb voices, as well as the music they introduced to racially diverse audiences: the African American spirituals once known as "slave songs." Various incarnations of the group would tour the United States and the world into the 21st century.

365. OCTOBER 8, 1871

GREAT CHICAGO FIRE BURNS A THIRD OF THE CITY; WISCONSIN AND MICHIGAN ALSO ABLAZE

After a drought-ridden summer, Chicago was tinder dry on this day when a fire in a West Side barn surged through neighborhoods on driving winds. The blazes incinerated

even "fireproof" structures and were not quenched until October 10. The disaster—300 deaths, a third of the city destroyed, $200 million in damages—would go down in history as the Great Chicago Fire. Also on this day, flames engulfed huge tracts of northeastern Wisconsin and Michigan's Upper Peninsula, while superheated updrafts produced fire tornadoes. The resulting Peshtigo Fire (named after the Wisconsin town it consumed) was the deadliest wildfire in American history, burning about 1.2 million acres and claiming up to 2,500 lives.

Touring the world performing African American spirituals helped the Fisk Jubilee Singers, depicted here in the 1870s, raise funds for their school, Fisk University.

366. NOVEMBER 18, 1871

HARPER'S WEEKLY CARTOONIST HELPS BRING DOWN NOTORIOUS "BOSS" TWEED

The literary magazine often featured cartoons by the day's leading illustrator, Thomas Nast. On this day, its pages portrayed the arrest of infamous New York City politician

Known to Indigenous people as "land of the burning ground" for its geothermal features, Yellowstone was declared the first national park in 1872.

William "Boss" Tweed, whose reign was replete with graft, bribes, and political corruption. Tweed had been convicted in 1873 but escaped custody in December 1875 while on an allowed family visit. He fled to Cuba, then Spain, where officials recognized him from Nast's cartoons. They detained him and returned him to the U.S. in November 1876. He died in prison.

367. MARCH 1, 1872

YELLOWSTONE BECOMES THE COUNTRY'S FIRST NATIONAL PARK

For more than 10,000 years, Indigenous peoples called the western United States near the Yellowstone River headwaters "home"—an area the Crow named "land of the burning ground" for its geothermal and volcanic features. Starting in the late 1860s, government-backed teams of surveyors and scientists began exploring the region. Among them was geologist Ferdinand Vandeveer Hayden, whose expedition revealed extraordinary natural wonders. Both houses of Congress passed a bill preserving "as a great national park" some 3,400 square miles of land in Wyoming, Montana, and Idaho. On this day, President Ulysses S. Grant signed the act establishing Yellowstone as the first national park.

368. MAY 10, 1872

FIRST WOMAN CANDIDATE FOR PRESIDENT IS NOMINATED

Although U.S. women couldn't vote, the Constitution didn't bar them from running for office. So on this day, the pro-suffrage Equal Rights Party nominated Victoria Woodhull as its presidential candidate. With her sister, Woodhull had founded the first female-run Wall Street financial firm and published a newspaper espousing progressive political reforms. Critics questioned the party's substance; it nominated Woodhull to be president, even though she hadn't reached the minimum age (35), and named abolitionist Frederick Douglass as its vice presidential candidate, although he had not signed on. Ultimately, suffrage leaders would distance themselves from Woodhull, whose support of communism, a woman's right to control her own sexuality ("free love"), and spiritualism cost the party support.

IT SHOULD BE THE DUTY OF GOVERNMENT ... TO MAINTAIN EQUALITY AMONG THE PEOPLE.

Victoria Woodhull *(1872)*

369. JUNE 2, 1872

MOTHER'S DAY FOR PEACE JOINS A GROWING EFFORT THAT LEADS TO A NATIONAL HOLIDAY

On this day, "Battle Hymn of the Republic" author Julia Ward Howe organized an event in Boston called Mother's Day for Peace. The day was part of Howe's appeal to the women of the world to prevent future conflicts like the Civil War and Europe's Franco-Prussian War. In West Virginia, public health advocate Ann Jarvis had a kindred goal: In 1868, she had convened a "Mother's Friendship Day" to bring together formerly warring American families. Her daughter, Anna Jarvis, extended that legacy by establishing a day to honor and provide care and support for mothers on the second Sunday of May. The U.S. holiday—formalized by a presidential proclamation in 1914—continues today.

370. NOVEMBER 5, 1872

PRESIDENT GRANT WINS A SECOND WHITE HOUSE TERM

As Ulysses S. Grant ran for a second White House term, he faced a revolt by party mates calling themselves Liberal Republicans and objecting to his Reconstruction and civil rights policies, as well as cronyism in appointments. After the Liberals nominated prominent *New York Tribune* newspaper editor Horace Greeley to run against Grant, the Democratic Party also made Greeley its candidate. On this election day, Grant prevailed, receiving 56 percent of the popular vote and 82 percent of the electoral vote. Though women couldn't legally vote, Susan B. Anthony cast a vote for Grant; she was later arrested. Suffering from "nervous prostration" after the bruising campaign, Greeley soon entered a sanatorium. He died there on November 29.

371. MARCH 3, 1873

COMSTOCK ACT, FORBIDDING "INDECENT" MAIL, IS PASSED

Passage of the Comstock Act by the U.S. Congress on this day outlawed using what was then known as the Post Office Department to send any "obscene, lewd, lascivious, indecent, filthy or vile article, matter, thing, device, or substance." Named for Anthony Comstock, a zealous foe of anything he considered pornographic, the federal statute also outlawed sending items or information that could facilitate contraception or abortion. Congress didn't remove the Comstock Act's provisions governing contraception until 1971. In 1973, the act essentially became inactive after the Supreme Court's *Roe* v. *Wade* ruling confirmed a constitutional right to abortion, but the issue was revived again in 2022 after *Roe* was overturned by the Supreme Court.

372. MAY 20, 1873

"WAIST OVERALLS" PATENT IS GRANTED TO LEVI STRAUSS

Reno, Nevada, tailor Jacob Davis had the idea to reinforce the most tear-prone parts of work trousers with metal rivets—to better handle the rough wear of laborers and gold miners. On this day, the patent for the riveted pants design was issued to Davis and his business partner, Levi Strauss, the dry goods merchant who had sold Davis the denim fabric for the garments. Though the sturdy pants would be called "waist overalls" (or just overalls) for most of the next century, by the 1960s they were popularly known as blue jeans.

373. SEPTEMBER 20, 1873

BANK FAILURE SETS OFF PANIC OF 1873

This was a day of catastrophic firsts. The bankruptcy of the nation's first investment bank, Jay Cooke & Company, set off an economic depression—and for the first time in its history, the New York Stock Exchange suspended trading, staying closed for 10 days to try to quell the financial panic. Cooke & Company's collapse, due to its investments in the Northern Pacific Railway, wiped out the bank's depositors and Northern Pacific bond- and stockholders. The Panic of 1873 triggered a depression that lasted more than five years, bankrupted 121 railroads and 18,000 other companies, drove U.S. unemployment to 14 percent, and crushed investors' confidence in the stock market.

374. NOVEMBER 20, 1874

TEMPERANCE UNION IS FOUNDED TO PROMOTE PROHIBITION, SOCIAL REFORMS

In Cleveland on this day, a convention of several hundred women established the Woman's Christian Temperance Union with a constitution that called for "the entire prohibition of the manufacture and sale of intoxicating liquors as a beverage." The group decried alcohol as contributing to many social ills, from impoverishment of households to abuse of women and children. It was soon expanded into an international organization that advocated for other issues affecting women and families, including international peace, public health, workplace wages and conditions, a ban on prostitution, and women's voting rights.

375. NOVEMBER 24, 1874

ILLINOIS FARMER PATENTS BARBED WIRE

In the American Great Plains, settlers lacked the plentiful trees and rocks used elsewhere for fencing. They tried stringing wire, which snapped when cattle leaned on it—that is, until Michael Kelly threaded metal spikes onto a double-wire "thorny fence" that kept animals away. Inventors tried hundreds of variations of the fencing. But on this day, a patent for the barbed wire design most common today was issued to Illinois farmer Joseph Glidden, who also developed the machinery to inexpensively mass-produce it. The advent of barbed wire allowed homesteaders to secure land, changing forever the lives of Indigenous people and open-range cattle ranchers.

Durable work trousers reinforced with metal rivets were the trademark product of Levi Strauss & Co., founded in San Francisco in 1853.

The Horticultural Hall was among more than 200 buildings erected in Philadelphia to house the first world's fair in the United States in 1876.

376. MARCH 1, 1875

CIVIL RIGHTS ACT OF 1875, GUARANTEEING EQUAL ACCESS, BECOMES LAW

Charles Sumner, a Republican senator from Massachusetts, introduced a bill in 1870 to guarantee that U.S. citizens, regardless of color, would have equal access to accommodations, public transportation, churches, cemeteries, theaters, and public schools. Sumner considered it the crowning achievement of Reconstruction—but it had yet to pass when he died in 1874. Sumner begged Frederick Douglass and others gathered at his deathbed: "Don't let the bill fail." Though it differed in parts from Sumner's intended bill, the Civil Rights Act of 1875 finally became law on this day.

377. MAY 17, 1875

KENTUCKY DERBY—AND A RACING TRADITION—IS BORN

Now considered the most prestigious horse race in the United States, the inaugural Kentucky Derby took place on this day. Run at what is now known as Churchill Downs in Louisville, the race was won by a horse named Aristides, ridden by African American jockey Oliver Lewis. In the years since, some aspects of the race have changed—today it's 1.25 miles instead of 1.5 miles and is run annually on the first Saturday in May—but others endure. It's a millinery wonder, with spectators wearing elaborate hats. And it draws faithful audiences: 150,000 onlookers at the track and as many as 20 million television viewers.

378. MAY 19, 1875

COURT RULES MARY TODD LINCOLN INSANE

The former first lady's eldest son, Robert, had become increasingly worried about his mother's paranoia, compulsive shopping, and health complaints. He reluctantly took her to court for a sanity hearing in Chicago, where she had been living in a hotel. After a three-hour trial, the jury declared her to have mental illness, and she was escorted to a sanatorium in Batavia, Illinois. In September, she was released to her sister's custody in Springfield, Illinois; the following year, she was ruled competent. She spent the next four years in Europe, then returned to Springfield, dying there in 1882 at age 63.

THE DAY WILL COME WHEN THE MAN AT THE TELEPHONE WILL BE ABLE TO SEE THE DISTANT PERSON TO WHOM HE IS SPEAKING.

Alexander Graham Bell *(1906)*

379. MARCH 10, 1876

FIRST WORDS ARE TRANSMITTED OVER THE FIRST TELEPHONE

Born in Edinburgh, Scotland, Alexander Graham Bell became a speech coach like his father. At 24 he moved to Boston, where he taught speech for the deaf, conducting sound experiments in his spare time. Bell worked with mechanic Thomas Watson on an invention he believed could transmit speech and was granted a patent for "the method of, and apparatus for, transmitting vocal or other sounds telegraphically." On this day, Bell tested the device by speaking into the transmitter, "Mr. Watson, come here, I want to see you," words Watson confirmed he heard on the receiver in another room.

380. MAY 10, 1876

AMERICA'S FIRST WORLD'S FAIR IS STAGED

To celebrate the 100th anniversary of the Declaration of Independence, the Centennial Exposition of 1876 opened on this day in Philadelphia. It was the first world's fair in the United States, and more than 200 buildings were built to stage it, including a 21.5-acre main exhibition hall, Earth's largest building at the time. The event showed off technological wonders, from a steam-powered monorail to sewing machines and typewriters; new foodstuffs such as popcorn, ketchup, and root beer; and historic objects including Alexander Graham Bell's first telephone and the right hand and torch of the Statue of Liberty. During the fair's six months, almost 10 million people visited.

381. JUNE 25, 1876

GEORGE CUSTER IS SLAIN AT BATTLE OF THE LITTLE BIGHORN

After gold was discovered on Black Hills land reserved for the Sioux by a U.S. government treaty, prospectors and soldiers poured in. In response, many Sioux and Cheyenne tribe members fled to Montana, joining Chiefs Crazy Horse and Sitting Bull in a camp by the Little Bighorn River. When the Sioux and Cheyenne didn't return to the reservation, Lt. Col. George Armstrong Custer and his Seventh Cavalry tried to force them to return. Misinformed about the tribes' strength, on this day Custer and commanders Marcus Reno and Frederick Benteen attacked. Reno and Benteen's forces were driven back, while Custer and his troops were killed at what became known as the Battle of the Little Bighorn.

382. DECEMBER 6, 1876

A DISPUTED PRESIDENTIAL ELECTION COMES DOWN TO A SINGLE ELECTORAL VOTE

After an inconclusive presidential contest between Republican candidate Rutherford B. Hayes and Democratic candidate Samuel Tilden, states' electors gathered on this day to tally the popular vote. But in South Carolina, Florida, Louisiana, and Oregon, conflicting panels of electors sent two different sets of electoral votes to the Senate president, who was constitutionally required to certify them (an event that returned to the news 144 years later, when the 2020 vote count was disputed). After months of maneuvering and filibuster threats, on March 2, 1877, Hayes was awarded the presidency with 185 electoral votes to Tilden's 184.

383. MAY 6, 1877

CRAZY HORSE SURRENDERS IN GREAT SIOUX WAR

A warrior and respected leader of the Oglala band of the Lakota Sioux, Crazy Horse never signed treaties, rejecting reservation life and the white man's ways. He led his tribe in the 1876–77 conflicts known as the Great Sioux War, including the Battle of the Little Bighorn, and joined with the Cheyenne to resist U.S. government efforts to invalidate a treaty granting the tribes Black Hills land. On this day, convinced that the government would pursue his people as long as they ran, Crazy Horse and 1,100 followers surrendered at Fort Robinson in Nebraska; he would die on September 5 after being stabbed in a scuffle with a soldier.

384. MAY 10, 1877

PRESIDENT HAYES INSTALLS FIRST TELEPHONE IN THE WHITE HOUSE

As the 19th president of the United States, Rutherford B. Hayes would need to talk to—and hear from—large numbers of people. Why not tap technology to expedite that task? On this day in Washington, D.C., Hayes—call him the first early-adopter president—had a telephone device installed in the telegraph room of the presidential residence. Because Alexander Graham Bell had proved the invention workable a little over a year before, Hayes got a choice phone number: the single digit "1." And initially, the telephone could be called from only one place: the Treasury Department next door.

385. JULY 16, 1877

GREAT RAILROAD STRIKE YIELDS LITTLE FOR WORKERS

Four years into an economic depression, railroad companies had repeatedly used the downturn to weaken the industry's fledgling unions and reduce pay. In spring 1877, the Pennsylvania Railroad (America's largest) cut wages by 10 percent twice in two months. After the Baltimore & Ohio (B&O) Railroad announced another 10 percent wage cut to take effect on this day, a wave of strikes spread from Maryland and West Virginia to Pennsylvania, New York, and several midwestern states. Workers walked off the job, blocked trains, damaged cars and tracks, set fires, and exchanged gunfire with strikebreakers. Federal troops were sent in to restore order, and the strikes were over in a few weeks. The outcome: 1,000 people injured, 100 killed, and no major gains for workers.

Chief Crazy Horse surrendered to the U.S. government in 1877, a few months after a U.S. Army attack on a Lakota and Cheyenne village, depicted here by Frederic Remington.

SPOTLIGHT

THE INDUSTRIAL REVOLUTION

WITH ITS NATIONHOOD SECURED, the United States was plunged into another transition: the industrial revolution. The nations of Europe had already experienced the phenomenon, as their rural, agrarian societies transformed into urban, mechanized societies. In America's industrial shift, technology advanced at a remarkable pace, yielding a variety of made-in-America inventions: the mechanical grain reaper and gramophone, the typewriter and transcontinental railroad, the sewing machine and steamboat.

On New York's Hudson River in 1807, Robert Fulton debuted the steam-powered vessel, which significantly enhanced shipping and travel. In Massachusetts in the 1830s, Samuel Morse and collaborators developed an electric telegraph and Morse code to carry its messages. In New York in 1844, Charles Goodyear received a patent for the chemical process he called vulcanization, which improved rubber's durability and flexibility. And in Wisconsin in 1866, Christopher Latham Sholes co-invented the typewriter (with the QWERTY key arrangement still in use today).

The innovations kept on coming. In Utah, the first transcontinental rail line was completed in 1869. In New Jersey in 1879, Thomas Edison perfected the incandescent light bulb, two years after he had patented the phonograph. In the 1880s, Nikola Tesla patented innovations in alternating current for electricity generation, transmission, and motors.

But behind the appearance of prosperity, Mark Twain observed deep corruption and income inequality. So he dubbed the era "the Gilded Age"—a golden veneer concealing the instability beneath.

The 19th-century process of cotton manufacture included separating and spacing threads on a loom, as shown in this 1840 book illustration.

THE RESULT IS A BRIGHT, BEAUTIFUL LIGHT, LIKE THE MELLOW SUNSET OF AN ITALIAN AUTUMN.

New York Herald, *on the electric bulb (1879)*

386. DECEMBER 1, 1877

PALEONTOLOGY'S "BONE WARS" LEADS TO DISCOVERY OF *STEGOSAURUS*

It was known as the Great Dinosaur Rush, or simply the Bone Wars: the feverish one-upmanship between paleontologists Othniel Charles Marsh and Edward Drinker Cope to extract and identify dinosaur bones from fossil beds in the American West. In an article published on this day in the *American Journal of Science,* Marsh described "one of the most remarkable animals yet discovered"—a new reptile that he dubbed *Stegosaurus armatus* and dated to the Upper Jurassic (163.5 million to 145 million years ago). At first, Marsh mistakenly thought its triangular bone plates formed a turtle-like shell (thus the name *Stegosaurus,* which means "roof lizard"). But further study and new specimens situated the plates along the dinosaur's spine.

387. DECEMBER 24, 1877

THOMAS EDISON FILES PATENT FOR THE PHONOGRAPH

Thomas Edison's work on the telegraph and telephone sparked a related idea: a machine that would be able to reproduce those devices' audible messages. Edison began with a thin membrane that vibrated when sound entered a mouthpiece and attached to it a needle that turned the sound vibrations into grooves on a tinfoil-wrapped metal cylinder. The needle unit could then replay the sounds by tracing the cylinder's grooves. On this day, Edison filed for a patent for his new invention: the phonograph. Over the years he and

Eadweard Muybridge's system of mechanized camera shutters confirmed that a horse's four feet simultaneously left the ground as it galloped, as depicted in this 1887 image.

other inventors, including Alexander Graham Bell, developed improved versions using wax cylinders—and what was first imagined as a business tool became a musical entertainment hit.

388. JUNE 15, 1878

EADWEARD MUYBRIDGE DEVELOPS MOTION PHOTOGRAPHY

At a time when horses were essential transportation, Leland Stanford aimed to solve the mystery of their locomotion: As they ran, did all four feet leave the ground at once? To find the answer, the wealthy businessman and racehorse owner hired photographer Eadweard Muybridge; while prevailing photography methods used long exposure times, Muybridge had mechanized camera shutters to take exposures of one-thousandth of a second. On this day at a California racetrack, Stanford's prize horse, pulling a cart, ran across a dozen trip wires that triggered Muybridge's cameras—and resulting photos captured the animal in motion, at times with all four hooves in the air. Muybridge would go on to produce motion studies of other subjects.

389. JULY 29, 1878

GREAT ECLIPSE OF 1878 DRAWS CROWDS TO ROCKY MOUNTAIN STATES

In a century already notable for discoveries in space science, the opportunity to study a total solar eclipse loomed large. On this day, the choicest U.S. viewing area in the path of totality were the Rocky Mountains. Known as the Great Eclipse of 1878, it drew multiple expeditions to the mountaintops of Colorado and Wyoming, populated by the era's top astronomers and other science luminaries, plus plenty of tourists. Observers did not find a new planet between Mercury and the sun—an initial report that they did was soon disproved—but did discover streamers, giant solar rays extending out millions of miles from the sun.

More than 3,000 Indigenous students died at white-run boarding schools between 1828 and 1970, a 2024 *Washington Post* investigation found. This image was taken on New Year's Day in 1900.

390. NOVEMBER 1, 1879

BOARDING SCHOOLS TRY TO FORCE NATIVE AMERICAN ASSIMILATION

Aiming to make westward expansion easier and less costly than outright war, U.S. officials began enrolling Indigenous children in white-run Christian day schools in an attempt to assimilate tribal peoples into western culture. When that didn't break children's bonds to their family and culture, they were forcibly moved to boarding schools and seldom allowed to go home. Most drastically, students were shipped cross-country to institutions like Pennsylvania's Carlisle Indian Industrial School, which opened on this day. Deemed a model for such institutions, Carlisle deprived children of their language, clothes, and customs, used harsh discipline, and subjected students to starvation and physical abuse; its founder's philosophy was "Kill the Indian, and Save the Man." Many boarding schools were closed in the 1930s. But not until 1975 did U.S. law give tribes control of their own schools.

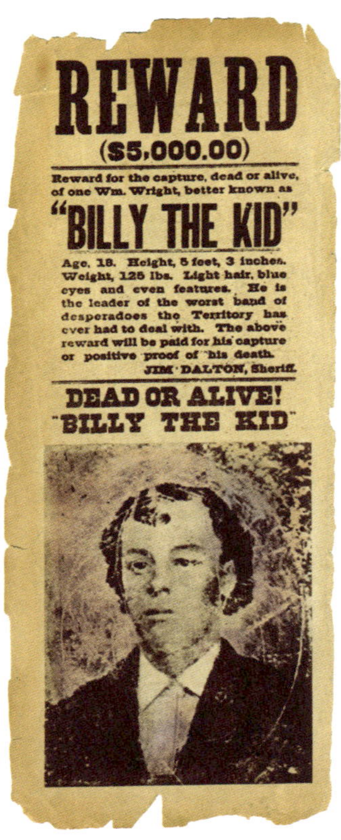

He was born Henry McCarty and used the aliases Kid Antrim and William Bonney, but he was best known as Billy the Kid when he died in July 1881.

391. JANUARY 27, 1880

PATENT ISSUED TO THOMAS EDISON MOVES AMERICA "INTO THE ELECTRIC AGE"

The patent issued to Thomas Edison on this day used the term "electric lamp." But what it actually confirmed was Edison's light bulb improvements—a stronger filament inside an airless bulb—that paved the way for widespread use of electric light. According to the National Archives, "Edison propelled the United States out of the gaslight era and into the electric age." Within a few years, an Edison Illuminating Company power station in Lower Manhattan was furnishing electricity to power homes' incandescent lamps at roughly the same cost as gas lighting.

392. APRIL 13, 1880

GEORGE EASTMAN PATENTS A PROCESS TO MAKE PHOTOGRAPHY SIMPLER

At 24, George Eastman enjoyed taking photographs—but not the messy, multistep process required to prepare the necessary glass plates: coating them with egg white, then chemicals, then light-sensitive silver nitrate. Eastman developed a manual way to precoat the plates but found the results inconsistent. So he designed and built an apparatus that could handle and more uniformly coat larger amounts of glass. On this day, he was granted a patent for his invention; by early 1881, he'd founded his own business. Into the 20th century, the name Eastman Kodak Company would be synonymous with consumer photography.

393. MAY 21, 1881

CLARA BARTON FOUNDS AMERICAN RED CROSS

A former schoolteacher, Clarissa Harlowe Barton—known as Clara—was living in Washington, D.C., working for the government when the Civil War broke out. She quit her job and began carrying supplies to Union soldiers. Present at major battles in South Carolina, Virginia, and Maryland, she learned to tend the wounded and became known as "the angel of the battlefield." Visiting Europe after the war, Barton learned of the Red Cross, a neutral humanitarian aid movement founded there in 1863. On this day, she established the American Red Cross; she would serve as its president for 23 years.

394. JULY 2, 1881

PRESIDENT JAMES GARFIELD SHOT AT A RAILROAD STATION IN WASHINGTON, D.C.

Four months after he took office, James Garfield was about to board a train in a Washington, D.C., railroad station when he was shot twice by Charles Guiteau, a disgruntled political office seeker who said "the Deity" wanted him to remove the president. One bullet only grazed Garfield, but the other entered his back to the right of his spine—and at a time when antiseptic measures weren't widespread, his wound likely was examined with unwashed hands. Though the nation's top physicians were summoned and kept Garfield alive for 80 days, he died on September 19 of sepsis. Convicted of murder, Guiteau was hanged on June 30, 1882.

395. JULY 14, 1881

BILLY THE KID MEETS HIS END

At trial, the 21-year-old said his name was William H. Bonney, Jr., though as a child he was known as Henry McCarty. He claimed to have killed 21 men, but the truth may be closer to 10. What's not in dispute: Billy the Kid was a notorious outlaw in the West with a hefty bounty on his head, and his legend only grew after his short life ended. Most histories say that happened on this day in Fort Sumner, New Mexico, when Sheriff Pat Garrett shot him a couple months after the convicted murderer had broken out of jail. Today, tourists visit Fort Sumner to see the Kid's purported burial site, where his gravestone has been stolen and replaced more than once.

A STRUGGLE OR TWO, A LITTLE STRANGLING SOUND AS HE GASPED FOR BREATH, AND THE KID WAS WITH HIS MANY VICTIMS.

Pat Garrett, *Lincoln County sheriff, on Billy the Kid's death (1882)*

Clara Barton's Civil War volunteer work and exposure to Europe's Red Cross movement influencec her to found the American Red Cross in 1881.

Tombstone, in Arizona Territory, hired the Earp brothers and Doc Holliday to roust outlaws. The result: three gunslingers dead and three lawmen wounded in the 1881 Gunfight at the O.K. Corral.

396. OCTOBER 26, 1881

GUNFIGHT AT O.K. CORRAL UNFOLDS

Tombstone was a silver-mining boomtown, 30 miles from the Mexican border in the Arizona Territory. The town's business owners hired Marshal Virgil Earp, his brothers Morgan and Wyatt, and their friend Doc Holliday to protect it from outlaws and rustlers. On this day, the Earps and Holliday set out to disarm five outlaws: Ike Clanton and his brother Billy, Frank McLaury and his brother Tom, and Billy Claiborne. After 30 shots were fired in 30 seconds, Virgil and Morgan Earp, as well as Holliday, were wounded, and three outlaws—Tom, Frank, and Billy Clanton—were dead. The shoot-out went down in history as the Gunfight at O.K. Corral and has been immortalized in numerous films and books.

397. NOVEMBER 16, 1881

***THE PORTRAIT OF A LADY* IS PUBLISHED**

Henry James described *The Portrait of a Lady* as a story about "a certain young woman affronting her destiny." The young woman is Isabel Archer, a naive American with a free-spirited nature and a new inheritance; *The Portrait of a Lady*, published as a book on this day, is widely hailed as James's masterpiece. He was already an established writer, known for deftly contrasting American and European societies. With *Portrait*—serialized in the *Atlantic Monthly* before it was published in book form—James broke new literary ground, moving away from Victorian sentimentality to the subtleties of the modern novel.

398. MAY 6, 1882

CONGRESS PASSES BAN ON CHINESE IMMIGRANTS

On this day, for the first time in U.S. history, workers of an ethnic group were denied entry to the country for fear they would threaten "the good order of certain localities." Congress's passage of the Chinese Exclusion Act was driven by prejudice and U.S. laborers' fear of losing jobs to Chinese laborers, especially on the West Coast. It imposed a 10-year ban on Chinese immigrants and required certification if U.S. residents from China wanted to leave and return to the country. In 1892, when the act expired, Congress extended it 10 more years; some form of exclusion was in force through the mid-1900s. Congress condemned the act in 2012.

399. MAY 30, 1883

BROOKLYN BRIDGE STAMPEDE SPARKS APPREHENSION

Spanning New York City's East River to connect the boroughs of Brooklyn and Manhattan, the new Brooklyn Bridge was a monumental engineering feat: the world's longest suspension bridge at 1,595 feet. Visitors flocked to its pedestrian walkway—but on this day, six days after the bridge opened, a woman's fall on the access stairs triggered a panic in the crowd of thousands, setting off a stampede in which 12 died. To quiet lingering public concern about the bridge's safety, the next year showman P. T. Barnum would walk the span himself while leading 21 elephants and 17 camels from his circus.

400. OCTOBER 15, 1883

SUPREME COURT INVALIDATES A LAW GUARANTEEING EQUAL ACCOMMODATIONS

By an 8-1 decision, the Supreme Court overturned the Civil Rights Act of 1875, which aimed to protect African Americans' rights. The high court declared unconstitutional parts of the act guaranteeing equal accommodations, ruling that the Constitution doesn't empower the federal government to prohibit racial discrimination by nongovernment organizations and individuals. Overturning the act only codified the weak enforcement that already existed. Historian John Hope Franklin would later write: "Long before the act was struck down by the Court it had become a casualty in the war waged by white supremacists who were determined" to deny people of color the rights emancipation promised.

On an Arctic research expedition that started with 25 crewmen, starvation and disease left only seven alive when the stranded group was rescued in 1884.

401. NOVEMBER 2, 1883

EMMA LAZARUS GIVES THE STATUE OF LIBERTY ITS VOICE

At a fundraiser on this day for the pedestal of the Statue of Liberty, the only entry read was "The New Colossus," a sonnet composed by the poet and Jewish American activist Emma Lazarus. Lazarus wrote the poem for auction in tribute to immigrants she'd met doing charitable work. It described the statue, soon to be shipped from France, as the "Mother of Exiles" that would welcome the world's refugees: "Give me your tired, your poor, / Your huddled masses yearning to breathe free, / The wretched refuse of your teeming shore. / Send these, the homeless, tempest-tost to me, / I lift my lamp beside the golden door!" Lazarus died in 1887; her poem, long forgotten, was posted at the statue in 1903.

402. NOVEMBER 18, 1883

NORTH AMERICAN CLOCKS ARE SYNCHRONIZED

At noon, clocks across North America were synchronized—the debut of a new system that standardized time on the continent by geographic region. Though a few official time arbiters had existed (such as London's Royal Observatory setting Greenwich Mean Time by the globe's 0° meridian), each U.S. and Canadian railroad kept the time for its operations, and each town set its watches by a prominent local clock. To eliminate the discrepancies caused by that approach, the new system drew up boundaries for eastern, central, mountain, and Pacific time zones, each with a standard time an hour earlier than the preceding. The plan wasn't immediately popular but would become U.S. law in 1918.

403. JUNE 22, 1884

MAROONED IN THE ARCTIC, LADY FRANKLIN BAY EXPEDITION IS RESCUED

The U.S. Army's Arctic weather expedition, led by Lt. Adolphus Greely to Ellesmere Island off Greenland in 1881, was supposed to be resupplied in 1882 and relieved in 1883. But weather kept those missions from reaching Greely's 25-person crew. Several struck out across the ice in search of help or food, but without success. Demoralized by the failed efforts and drastically low on rations, men began dying of starvation and disease. On this day, a Navy rescue vessel found what remained of the expedition: Greely and six survivors. (Rescuers reported that seven of the dead showed signs of cannibalism, but Greely denied it.)

WE HAVE BEEN LURED HERE TO OUR DESTRUCTION ... TO DIE IS EASY; VERY EASY; IT IS ONLY HARD TO STRIVE, TO ENDURE, TO LIVE.

Adolphus Greely, *on the doomed Lady Franklin Bay expedition (1884)*

404. JULY 21, 1884

GROVER CLEVELAND'S BID FOR PRESIDENCY IS EMBROILED IN A PATERNITY SCANDAL

A few months before Americans went to the polls to elect a new president, the Buffalo *Evening Telegraph* newspaper published the news that Democratic presidential candidate Grover Cleveland was the father of a son outside his marriage. Supporters of Cleveland's opponent, Republican congressman James Blaine of Maine, taunted Cleveland with the chant, "Ma, Ma, where's my pa?" Blaine's candidacy was shadowed by charges he had used his political position for personal gain, and Cleveland won the election. After, Cleveland's supporters retaliated with their own chant: To "Where's my Pa?" they responded, "Gone to the White House, ha ha ha!"

405. MAY 4, 1886

HAYMARKET SQUARE BOMBING DERAILS LABOR UNIONS' PROGRESS

Chicago's growing industries drew unions that urged laborers to seek better conditions, such as workdays of eight hours instead of the 10 to 12 most toiled. On May 1, 35,000

After seven Chicago policemen were killed in 1886 during a union rally in Haymarket Square, pro-union anarchists were convicted and unionism's reputation suffered.

Chicago workers went on strike and were soon followed by tens of thousands more. At one plant on May 3, police shot at strikers, killing as many as six, though reports vary. A mass meeting was called for on this day at Haymarket Square, and when police tried to end it, a bomb was thrown at them, killing seven officers and several civilians. The incident sparked a general condemnation of unions; though there was no evidence they'd been involved in the bombing, eight pro-union anarchists were convicted and seven were sentenced to death. In 1889, socialists and unionists would declare May 1 a holiday to honor workers in memory of Haymarket Square.

406. MAY 8, 1886

JOHN PEMBERTON SERVES UP THE FIRST COCA-COLA

The Atlanta, Georgia, pharmacist took a jug of his syrup to Jacobs' Pharmacy on Peachtree Street, combining the syrup with soda water before offering it to patrons for a nickel a glass. Pemberton touted his medicinal Coca-Cola as a tonic to "cure all nervous afflictions—Sick Headache, Neuralgia, Hysteria, Melancholy." Other pharmacies soon served it as well. Pemberton died two years later, before Coca-Cola became America's most iconic drink. Today, 1.9 billion servings are imbibed each day across 193 countries around the world.

407. JUNE 26, 1886

BUFFALO BILL'S WILD WEST SHOW TAKES NEW YORK

Like many a showman, William Cody may have embellished his image—as a teen, did he really ride for the Pony Express?—but one origin story holds up: The expert shot became "Buffalo Bill" by bagging thousands of bison to feed railroad work crews. He'd later spin his frontier adventures into "Buffalo Bill's Wild West," a stunt show performed on this day at a Staten Island, New York, amusement ground. With riding and shooting displays, animal acts, dramatic reenactments, and stars including Annie Oakley and Chief Sitting Bull, versions of Cody's show would tour America and Europe until the early 1900s, burnishing a popular mythology of the Old West.

Audiences in America and Europe flocked to the entertaining Wild West exploits that William "Buffalo Bill" Cody presented in his touring shows.

408. OCTOBER 28, 1886

STATUE OF LIBERTY IS DEDICATED

Presented on this day in New York Harbor: a towering figure named Liberty Enlightening the World. Some 151 feet tall from her sandals to the top of her torch, she was a goodwill gift from France's people to Americans; the statue's sculptor Frédéric-Auguste Bartholdi introduced her as "the symbol of unity and friendship between two nations." When he released the French *tricolore* flag that veiled her 17-feet-tall-by-10-feet-wide copper face, crowds topping a million welcomed her with celebrations throughout the city. Familiarly known as Lady Liberty, she would retain her bright-penny color for several decades before oxidizing to today's green patina.

409. DECEMBER 8, 1886

AMERICAN FEDERATION OF LABOR LAUNCHES

"Pure and simple" unionism—that's what labor leader Samuel Gompers advocated at the founding of the new American Federation of Labor (AFL) on this day in Columbus, Ohio. Gompers believed a narrow focus on securing the right to bargain collectively for working conditions, wages, and benefits would succeed where other strategies had failed. The AFL steered away from the labor reformist approach of trying to effect political change to benefit workers. It also resisted representing unskilled workers, so those workers' unions formed the Congress of Industrial Organizations—with which the AFL ultimately would merge in 1955.

410. JANUARY 11, 1887

DUKE FAMILY BLAZES PATH TO TOBACCO INDUSTRY DOMINANCE

On this day, W. Duke, Sons & Company registered the trademark for its Duke's Mixture brand smoking tobacco, packaged for sale with cigarette rolling papers. It was another milestone for a family business on its way to being a dynasty. The Dukes had already begun using the first automated cigarette-rolling machine and cornered about 40 percent of the cigarette market. In 1890, they talked four major competitors into a merger, forming the American Tobacco Company. Within two decades, it had acquired 250 more companies and controlled about 80 percent of U.S. production of cigarettes, chewing and smoking tobacco, and snuff. The family's wealth endowed what in 1924 became Duke University.

Vol. I. No. 1.

THE

NATIONAL GEOGRAPHIC

MAGAZINE.

PUBLISHED BY THE

NATIONAL GEOGRAPHIC SOCIETY.

WASHINGTON, D. C.

Price 50 Cents.

The scientists and scholars who founded the National Geographic Society in 1888 wanted its flagship magazine to cover "the world and all that is in it."

411. JANUARY 13, 1888

EXPLORERS AND SCIENTISTS ESTABLISH THE NATIONAL GEOGRAPHIC SOCIETY

At the upper-crust Cosmos Club in Washington, D.C., 33 explorers, scientists, and scholars gathered on this day to organize "a society for the increase and diffusion of geographic knowledge." They named it the National Geographic Society and, later that year, began publishing a magazine that went on to become known for its yellow-bordered cover, groundbreaking photography, and wide-ranging journalism. Alexander Graham Bell—the society's second president and son-in-law of co-founder Gardiner Greene Hubbard—famously said of the enterprise, "The world and all that is in it is our theme—and if we can't find anything to interest ordinary people in that subject, we better shut up shop."

412. MARCH 12, 1888

GREAT BLIZZARD OF '88 CLAIMS LIVES, BURIES CITIES

Starting just after midnight on this day, one of the most punishing blizzards in the nation's recorded history lashed the Atlantic coast from Maine to Maryland. Called the Great White Hurricane and the Great Blizzard of '88, the storm dropped more than 50 inches of snow in spots; extreme gusting winds produced drifts towering 50-plus feet, and downed lines left cities without electricity and telephone service for days. The three-day storm claimed more than 400 lives, caused at least $25 million (about $850 million today) in damage, prompted the relocation of utility lines underground, and encouraged the construction of subway systems in both Boston and New York City.

413. OCTOBER 21, 1888

LEADING SPIRITUALIST MAGGIE FOX COMES CLEAN

For 40 years, the famous Fox sisters claimed they could communicate with the dead: Maggie and Kate first made claims as children before involving their adult sister, Leah.

The Fox sisters convinced audiences they were spiritualists who could contact the dead—until 1888, when one of them came clean about the true nature of their séances.

★ ★ ★

IT'S A FRAUD. SPIRITUALISM IS A FRAUD FROM BEGINNING TO END! IT'S ALL A TRICK! THERE'S NO TRUTH IN IT!

Maggie Fox, *confession as reported in the* New York Herald *(1888)*

They demonstrated this feat in public performances that captured the popular imagination, sparking a widespread fascination with spiritualism. But in her *New York World* interview on this day, Maggie explained the rapping heard in their séances was a ruse. Despite her confessions, spiritualism, in one form or another, continued to thrive.

414. JANUARY 1, 1889

NATIVE AMERICAN GHOST DANCE CULT REEMERGES

When a solar eclipse shadowed western Nevada on this day, a Northern Paiute man named Wovoka told tribe members he'd had a vision. In it, he went to heaven, where God anointed him to teach dances and songs that would hasten the eviction of white people and reclamation of their tribal land and customs. A movement called the Ghost Dance had formed around such visions decades before; through Wovoka's evangelism, it again gained followers among tribes, including the Sioux. Though some Army leaders dismissed the "Messiah craze," others feared the Ghost Dance would spur violence. That fear would color future encounters with Sitting Bull and at Wounded Knee, South Dakota.

415. MARCH 30, 1889

ANDREW CARNEGIE OPENS HIS FIRST U.S. LIBRARY IN BRADDOCK, PENNSYLVANIA

Andrew Carnegie was 12 when his impoverished family moved from Scotland to Allegheny, Pennsylvania. He educated himself thanks to a local citizen who let workers borrow books from his library—a kindness Carnegie vowed he'd repay "if ever wealth came to me." That it did: Through hard work, connections, and investments in railroad, steel, and oil industries, Carnegie became one of the world's richest men by his 30s and devoted his later years to philanthropy. On this day, he dedicated the first of 1,681 U.S. public libraries built with more than $40 million he'd donated. He managed to give away about 90 percent of his fortune before his death in 1919.

416. APRIL 22, 1889

SETTLERS RACE TO PARTAKE IN OKLAHOMA LAND RUSH

"Land rush" was no exaggeration. At noon on this day, when a cannon sounded, more than 50,000 would-be landholders ran their fastest to marked-off 160-acre plots of Oklahoma District land. The rushers laid base logs for a cabin or started digging a well to reinforce their claims, but by federal law, they were required to live on and develop the land for five years to receive its title. Some two million acres were up for grabs after land was set aside for the area's Native American tribes. A U.S. Census head count of the area 14 months later reckoned more than 250,000 residents.

417. MAY 31, 1889

DAM COLLAPSE SPURS THE DEADLY JOHNSTOWN FLOOD

Fourteen miles from Johnstown, Pennsylvania, 450 feet up a mountainside, the earthen South Fork Dam was built to contain the Lake Conemaugh reservoir. When a state canal system no longer needed the reservoir, the monied South Fork Fishing and Hunting Club acquired the property. As the dam aged, the club made some repairs and—what proved to be damaging—modifications. At 3:15 p.m. on this day, the dam burst, releasing 20 million tons of water that formed a wall 35 to 40 feet high. When the flood hit Johnstown, it destroyed some 1,600 homes; 2,209 people were listed as dead and more than 900 missing; a third of the bodies found were never identified.

418. SEPTEMBER 18, 1889

HULL-HOUSE OFFERS EXTENSIVE AID TO POOR

Inspired by London social settlement houses where middle- and upper-middle-class people lived among and sought to assist the poor, Jane Addams and Ellen Gates Starr set out to open such a facility in America. On this day, in a working-class immigrant neighborhood in Chicago, the reformers moved into Hull-House (named for a former owner). It would offer area residents a communal kitchen and gymnasium, help with child care and education, job skill training, and more. Addams and other Hull-House staff also advocated on issues such as workplace rights and juvenile court and tenant law reform. For her efforts, Addams was a co-awardee of the 1931 Nobel Peace Prize—only the second woman to receive the prize.

419. DECEMBER 9, 1889

CHICAGO CELEBRATES DAZZLING AUDITORIUM BUILDING

Chicago civic leaders envisioned a theater where people of all economic strata could enjoy

In 1889, the failure of an earthen dam uphill from Johnstown, Pennsylvania, loosed 20 million tons of reservoir water that devastated the town.

the arts—and on this day, they opened its doors: the Auditorium Building on Michigan Avenue in the Loop district. Believed to be the tallest, costliest, and heaviest structure of its time, the combination theater, hotel, and office building was designed by innovative architects Dankmar Adler and Louis Sullivan. Their work helped inspire the Prairie School, an architectural style characterized by horizontal lines, open floor plans, and natural materials. An Adler & Sullivan draftsman named Frank Lloyd Wright went on to become one of the style's foremost proponents.

420. JANUARY 25, 1890

NELLIE BLY FINISHES CIRCLING THE GLOBE

Muckraking journalist Nellie Bly was known for going great lengths to report stories for the *New York World* newspaper, including famously going undercover in a New York City mental hospital to expose its shocking treatment of patients. On this day, Bly completed a feat that literally took her great lengths: around the globe by train, ship, horse, rickshaw, and donkey. After reading the popular Jules Verne novel *Around the World in Eighty Days,* Bly set out to break that record for circumnavigation; *New York World* published her daily accounts from the trip, which she completed in 72 days, a world record.

In 1889, journalist Nellie Bly set out to best the circumnavigation record described in Jules Verne's popular novel *Around the World in Eighty Days.*

421. JUNE 5, 1890

CITY SLUMS ARE EXPOSED IN *HOW THE OTHER HALF LIVES*

Growing up in mid-1800s Denmark, Jacob Riis wanted to be a carpenter, not a writer like his father had hoped. But on this day, at age 21, Riis emigrated to New York City, where he struggled to survive in slums packed with other impoverished immigrants. He found work as a night police reporter, writing about people most New Yorkers never saw in crime-ridden streets and tenements. To tell stories more vividly, Riis began taking photos, deploying flash photography in the city's darkest corners. His reformist photojournalism, lectures, and books, including his most famous work, *How the Other Half Lives,* spurred city officials to clean up neighborhood conditions.

422. AUGUST 1, 1890

JOHN MUIR'S ODE HELPS MAKE YOSEMITE A NATIONAL PARK

"No temple made with hands can compare with Yosemite. Every rock in its walls seems to glow with life." To naturalist and writer John Muir, the sights of Yosemite Valley were as breathtaking "as if into this one mountain mansion Nature had gathered her choicest treasures." So Muir wrote an article titled "The Treasures of the Yosemite"—and its publication on this day in *The Century* magazine was part of his strategy to obtain federal protection for the area. Two months later, Congress created Yosemite National Park, which helped build momentum for the establishment of the National Park System.

423. OCTOBER 1, 1890

U.S. WEATHER BUREAU IS FOUNDED

Two decades before, President Ulysses S. Grant signed a congressional resolution putting the military in charge of observing weather. Specifically, a division of the U.S. Army Signal Service Corps was to "provide for taking meteorological observations at the military stations in the interior of the continent, and at other points in the States and Territories ... and for giving notice on the northern [Great] Lakes and on the seacoast, by magnetic telegraph and marine signals, of the approach and force of storms," the resolution said. On this day, Congress created the U.S. Weather Bureau as a civilian agency; since then, the scope and complexity of meteorological observation has only grown.

424. DECEMBER 15, 1890

SIOUX CHIEF SITTING BULL DIES IN A SHOOT-OUT

Though Sitting Bull initially defied orders to resettle his people on reservation land, he moved them onto the Standing Rock Reservation in 1883. He remained an influential

Depictions of Yosemite's wonders—by writer John Muir and painter Albert Bierstadt, among others—hastened its formal protection as a national park in 1890.

The music room was just one of the opulent spaces in the Newport, Rhode Island, "summer cottage" William Vanderbilt gave his wife, Alva, in 1892.

leader there, to the alarm of U.S. officials, who mistakenly associated him with the Ghost Dance, an apocalyptic spiritual movement they feared would eventually cause an uprising. On this day, when Indian police attempted to arrest Sitting Bull, tribesmen came to his defense, and shots were exchanged. Sitting Bull died instantly from bullets to his head and chest; his son, six tribesmen, and seven Indian police were also killed. Two weeks later, U.S. troops tried to disarm a Lakota Sioux camp at Wounded Knee Creek and slaughtered between 150 and 300 people—around half of them women, children, and elders.

425. FEBRUARY 10, 1891

PATENT IS GRANTED FOR "OUIJA OR EGYPTIAN LUCK-BOARD"

The applicant, Baltimore attorney Elijah J. Bond, explained that with the board, "two or more persons can amuse themselves by asking questions of any kind and having them answered by the device used and operated by the touch of the hand, so that the answers are designated by letters on a board." Bond was one of five investors in the Kennard Novelty Company, whose "wonderful talking board" soon captivated a public eager for any form of spiritualism.

426. MAY 5, 1891

CARNEGIE HALL OPENS IN MANHATTAN

Philanthropist and steel baron Andrew Carnegie was on his honeymoon in the spring of 1887 when his new wife, Louise, a member of the Oratorio Society of New York, encouraged him to underwrite creation of a great music venue in New York City. Four years later, what one critic would call "the most beautiful Music Hall in the world" opened on this day. Boasting superb acoustics, Carnegie Hall launched with a sold-out concert that featured the American debut of Pyotr Ilyich Tchaikovsky conducting his composition *Marche Solennelle*. Over the years, the venue—which was renovated in the 1960s after a period of disrepair—has hosted musical luminaries from Béla Bartók and George Gershwin to Billie Holiday and the Beatles.

NO MAN CAN DERIVE MORE PLEASURE FROM MONEY OR POWER THAN I DO FROM SEEING A PAIR OF BASKETBALL GOALS IN SOME OUT OF THE WAY PLACE.

James Naismith *(1892)*

427. DECEMBER 21, 1891

JAMES NAISMITH ENTERTAINS STUDENTS WITH THE FIRST BASKETBALL GAME

On this day in Springfield, Massachusetts, when winter weather precluded outdoor sports, physical education teacher James Naismith needed a way to occupy his bored students at the International YMCA Training School (later renamed Springfield College). Charged with inventing a game that would be active but not too injury-prone, Naismith nailed up peach baskets to be goals at either end of the gymnasium and wrote rules directing students to aim at the goals with a soccer ball. Naismith's students played the first game of "basket ball," a new sport that quickly became popular around the world.

428. JANUARY 17, 1892

VANDERBILTS INAUGURATE MARBLE HOUSE

For Alva Vanderbilt's 39th birthday, her husband, William—the eldest son of Cornelius "Commodore" Vanderbilt and heir to his railroad fortune—gave her a transformative gift: a spectacular coastal "cottage" in Newport, Rhode Island, then known as a quiet summer retreat. Their new Marble House transformed the town into the seasonal watering hole of the Gilded Age, where other Northeast elite flocked to build their own opulent mansions. In 1895, the Vanderbilts divorced, but Alva retained the estate and continued

continued on page 222

SPOTLIGHT

COMMUNICATION

IN APRIL 1860, sending an urgent message from Sacramento, California, to St. Joseph, Missouri, took 12 days, requiring 75 horses carrying a relay of Pony Express riders more than 1,800 miles. But 18 months later, that same message could travel almost instantaneously from Sacramento to New York City on the country's newly connected transcontinental telegraph lines. That dynamic characterized 19th-century communications, as technological leaps made information sharing faster, easier, and more affordable.

In the 1840s in New York, Richard March Hoe invented the first rotary printing press, a steam-powered machine with a rolling cylinder that applied ink to thousands of sheets of paper an hour. Hoe's printer upgrades, paired with Ottmar Mergenthaler's 1886 invention of the Linotype typesetting machine, helped meet the demand for newspapers in growing urban, literate populations. Telegram communication advanced from Samuel Morse's 1840 patent for his electrical telegraph to the first commercial telegraph line (between Washington, D.C., and Baltimore, Maryland) in 1845, with thousands more miles of lines soon crisscrossing the country.

The early 1870s brought dramatic growth of the railroad system, which author and journalist James Meigs likens to "the internet of the 19th century," enabling communication and commerce over vast distances. In 1876, Alexander Graham Bell secured a patent for his telephone—a device so popular that by 1900, 600,000 were on Bell's phone system. As the century ended, America's Nikola Tesla, Italy's Guglielmo Marconi, and others were laying groundwork for the next communication breakthrough: radio.

In 1876, America's first world's fair featured demonstrations of the steam-powered rotary printing press invented by Richard March Hoe.

WHAT GUNPOWDER DID FOR WAR, THE PRINTING-PRESS HAS DONE FOR THE MIND.

Wendell Phillips, *abolitionist (1864)*

continued from page 219

to cut a wide swath, becoming a women's suffragist and holding two movement conferences at the mansion.

429. AUGUST 11, 1892

INVESTIGATORS ACCUSE LIZZIE BORDEN OF MURDER

On this day, 32-year-old Lizzie Borden was arrested on charges she used a hatchet to kill her father, Andrew, and stepmother, Abby, on August 4 in the family's Fall River, Massachusetts, home. Police and investigators found Borden's alibis inconsistent, and at trial, a witness testified that on August 7 Borden had burned a dress in the kitchen stove. But the jury acquitted her, whether due to her innocence or her timid demeanor, upper-class status, and prestigious defense lawyers, depending on one's perspective. Though Borden moved to a new, posh neighborhood, she couldn't escape the suspicion that she'd committed the unsolved murders immortalized in the morbid rhyme that begins "Lizzie Borden took an axe ..."

In 1893, a jury acquitted Lizzie Borden of murdering her father and stepmother. But suspicions about her role in the crimes lingered as the murders remained unsolved.

430. SEPTEMBER 8, 1892

PLEDGE OF ALLEGIANCE DEBUTS

Published for the first time in the *Youth's Companion,* a popular family periodical, the simple pledge was written by Francis Bellamy, a former minister turned writer for the magazine. He successfully lobbied Congress to endorse patriotic school ceremonies on the 400th anniversary of Columbus's arrival to the New World, and among those ceremonies would be his one-line salute to the flag: "I pledge allegiance to my Flag and the Republic for which it stands: one Nation indivisible, with Liberty and Justice for all." In the decades to follow, the various phrases and lines that are recited today were gradually added.

431. NOVEMBER 12, 1892

WILLIAM HEFFELFINGER BECOMES FIRST PRO FOOTBALL PLAYER

William Walter Heffelfinger—a six-foot-three, 200-pound Minnesotan nicknamed "Pudge"—was a natural at gridiron football. He was a high schooler who played at college level, a Yale varsity player from his freshman year, and an all-American for the first three years the honor was bestowed. Small wonder that after college, Heffelfinger became football's first documented pro player. On this day, he received $500 (plus travel expenses) from the Allegheny Athletic Association, which he led to victory over the Pittsburgh Athletic Club. After a coaching career, Heffelfinger played football in exhibition games, retiring at age 65.

432. JANUARY 17, 1893

U.S. INTERESTS OVERPOWER THE HAWAIIAN QUEEN

In the late 1800s, U.S. business interests, especially sugar planters, challenged Hawaii's

Native rulers for control of the island kingdom. In 1887, a militia affiliated with the business faction forced King Kalākaua to sign a constitution that greatly lessened his powers and stripped the rights of Native Hawaiians. When the king died four years later, he was succeeded by his sister, Queen Lili'uokalani, who vowed to restore the monarchy and Hawaiian rights. To stop her, on this day, the business bloc, with support from the U.S. minister to Hawaii and a group of Marines, orchestrated a coup that deposed the queen, abolished the monarchy, and imposed an American-led provisional government. Though Lili'uokalani and supporters appealed her overthrow, she was never reinstated; in 1898, the United States annexed Hawaii.

433. MARCH 13, 1893

ORIGINAL WALDORF HOTEL OPENS IN NEW YORK CITY

William Waldorf Astor, motivated in part by a dispute with his aunt, built the grand hotel next door to her house in midtown Manhattan at Fifth Avenue and 33rd Street. It revolutionized how New York socialized, bringing the social elite out of their private homes

New York City's Waldorf-Astoria hotel, 1898

The Ferris wheel debuted at the 1893 Chicago World's Fair, which celebrated the 400th anniversary of Christopher Columbus's arrival in the Americas.

and clubs into a public space. It also revolutionized stays away from home, offering guests electricity and private bathrooms. In 1897, William's cousin John Jacob Astor IV opened the equally opulent Astoria Hotel beside the Waldorf. Eventually, the two merged to form the renowned Waldorf-Astoria, once called "the unofficial Palace of New York" by the *New York Times*.

434. MAY 1, 1893

CHICAGO WORLD'S FAIR MAKES ITS MARK

For six months starting on this day, Chicago celebrated the 400th anniversary of Christopher Columbus's landing in the Americas with the World's Columbian Exposition, otherwise known as the Chicago World's Fair. More than 200 buildings—an entire "White

City" of beaux arts structures—were built on some 686 acres of fairgrounds at the riverfront Jackson Park. The star attraction of the Midway Plaisance amusement ground was the Ferris wheel ride invented for the event. More than 65,000 exhibits showcased new wonders, from technologies (the zipper, elevator, automatic dishwasher) to delicacies (Juicy Fruit gum, Cracker Jack, Aunt Jemima pancake mix).

435. MAY 4, 1893

PANIC OF 1893 THUMPS AMERICAN MARKETS

It seemed a modest start for an economic catastrophe: On this day, a New Jersey twine and rope manufacturer called the National Cordage Company failed to secure a large loan and went bankrupt. That news soon reached Wall Street, sparking a huge stock sell-off. As stock prices kept falling, businesses defaulted on loans; major railroads went bankrupt, as did banks that couldn't get loans repaid; and bank insolvencies frightened depositors, causing bank runs that deepened the crisis. Following what became known as the Panic of 1893, more than 15,000 businesses failed by year's end, national unemployment approached 20 percent, and America's worst depression yet lingered for four years.

SELL THE COOK THE STOVE IF NECESSARY AND COME. YOU MUST SEE THIS FAIR.

Hamlin Garland, *author, to his parents about the Chicago World's Fair (1893)*

436. DECEMBER 15, 1893

***NEW WORLD SYMPHONY* SERENADES IN ITS AMERICAN DEBUT**

While working in the United States as a conservatory director, Czech composer Antonín Leopold Dvořák shared a wish: that U.S. composers would draw inspiration from the spirit of Native American and African American music. Dvořák did just that in his *New World Symphony* (Symphony No. 9), which premiered at Carnegie Hall on this day; "Largo," the symphony's second movement, was inspired by Black spirituals. "In the negro melodies of America I discover all that is needed for a great and noble school of music," Dvořák famously said. One of history's most popular symphonies, it was carried to the moon by astronaut Neil Armstrong during the 1969 Apollo 11 mission.

437. FEBRUARY 11, 1894

HENRY FLAGLER OPENS HIS ROYAL POINCIANA HOTEL—AND DEVELOPS MUCH OF SOUTH FLORIDA

The frame hotel overlooking Lake Worth in Palm Beach would, in the next decade, become the world's largest, with almost 1,100 guest rooms and three miles of corridors. A founder of Standard Oil, Gilded Age tycoon Henry Flagler was intent on promoting and developing the Florida wilds. He did so by building grand hotels (including The Breakers, still operating in Palm Beach) and creating a railroad system that ran from Jacksonville to Key West. He was also the driving force behind the development of Palm Beach, St. Augustine, and Miami.

In 1895, before a predominantly white audience, Black educator Booker T. Washington called for efforts to "make the interests of both races one."

438. FEBRUARY 5, 1895

J. P. MORGAN CUTS A DEAL

In the depression following the Panic of 1893, "large dollar-holders ... scrambled to convert their paper [currency] to gold," historian H. W. Brands observed. The depletion of Treasury gold "resembled runs that had brought down thousands of commercial banks ... But now the imperiled institution was the federal government." Enter banker J. P. Morgan, who met with President Grover Cleveland on this day and proposed a remedy. Using a statutory loophole that let the Treasury issue bonds without consulting Congress, a group Morgan organized would provide $65 million in gold in exchange for bonds payable (with interest) 30 years hence. The clandestine deal stabilized the Treasury but, once public, cost Cleveland his party's nomination in 1896.

439. SEPTEMBER 18, 1895

BOOKER T. WASHINGTON URGES RACIAL COMPROMISE

On this day at an Atlanta exposition showcasing southern states' postwar progress, Black educator and orator Booker T. Washington delivered what came to be known as his "Atlanta Compromise" address. Speaking to a predominantly white audience, Washington called for "a blotting out of sectional differences and racial animosities and suspicions, in a determination to administer absolute justice." But he also asserted that "the wisest among my race understand that the agitation of questions of social equality is the extremest folly." And he suggested Black Americans "interlac[e] our industrial, commercial, civil, and religious life with yours in a way that shall make the interests of both races one."

440. MAY 18, 1896

***PLESSY* V. *FERGUSON* RULING MAKES "SEPARATE BUT EQUAL" THE LAW OF THE LAND**

Although federal law was supposed to protect Black Americans from discrimination and segregation, many states circumvented the protections by passing so-called Jim Crow laws, named for a character in a demeaning blackface performance. In 1892, to challenge the constitutionality of regulations that separated facilities by race, Homer Plessy, who was seven-eighths white and one-eighth African American, sat in a "whites-only" train car in Louisiana and was arrested. After Judge John Ferguson ruled against Plessy, the case wound up in the Supreme Court, where the constitutionality of separate facilities was upheld on this day. The "separate but equal" doctrine of *Plessy* v. *Ferguson* would not be overturned for nearly six decades.

441. OCTOBER 1, 1896

U.S. POST OFFICE DEPARTMENT ADOPTS FREE RURAL MAIL DELIVERY

The U.S. Post Office Department had delivered mail free to city dwellers for more than three decades by the time that service was extended to rural residents, who had been traveling to sometimes distant post offices to collect their mail or paying private companies to deliver it. On this day, riders began rural free delivery (RFD) along the first five routes in West Virginia. After 1898 farmers could obtain mail delivery simply by petitioning their congressmen, and by 1905 some 32,000 RFD routes were in service, meaning less isolation for rural Americans and a boom in business for mail-order houses.

442. DECEMBER 25, 1896

JOHN PHILIP SOUSA COMPOSES AMERICA'S NATIONAL MARCH

Young John Philip Sousa grew up at rehearsals of the U.S. Marine Band, in which his father, John Antonio Sousa, played trombone; by the age of 26, John Philip was directing the band. Touring with it and later with his own band, Sousa became "the greatest

The U.S. Post Office Department established systems to deliver soldiers' mail in 1861, cities' mail in 1863, and rural mail in 1896.

Within two months of hearing that gold had been found in the Yukon Territory's Klondike River, 9,000 people left Seattle for Canada to join the 1897 gold rush.

musical star of his era, combining the charisma and popularity of Leonard Bernstein and the Beatles," according to the Library of Congress. On this day, to memorialize a good friend who had died, Sousa composed what would become his best known work: "The Stars and Stripes Forever." A 1987 act of Congress designated it America's national march.

443. JANUARY 2, 1897

NOVELIST STEPHEN CRANE ESCAPES DEATH IN AN OCEAN ORDEAL

The Civil War novel *The Red Badge of Courage* had earned Stephen Crane notoriety as a fiction writer. But the next story he'd tell would be all too real: On this day, Crane was aboard the S.S. *Commodore,* heading for Cuba on a newspaper assignment, when the boat sank 16 miles out from Florida. Though eight men from the *Commodore* died, Crane and two others made it back to shore after more than 30 hours fighting treacherous waves in a 10-foot dinghy. He described the ordeal in a newspaper account and then in one of his most famous short stories, "The Open Boat."

444. JULY 17, 1897

GREAT KLONDIKE GOLD RUSH STRIKES A FEVER PITCH

"GOLD! GOLD! GOLD! GOLD!" The *Seattle Post-Intelligencer's* front-page headline on this day left no doubt what was arriving on the steamship *Portland,* along with 68 miners. Though gold was first found nearly a year before in a tributary of the Yukon Territory's Klondike River, the big news reached Seattle when the *Portland* did—with more than a ton of gold in its hold. So began the exodus from Seattle as hopeful prospectors, dubbed "stampeders," joined the fortune hunt. Within two months, an estimated 9,000 people, with 3,600 tons of supplies, had departed via Seattle for the Great Klondike gold rush.

NOT ONE IN TEN, OR A HUNDRED, KNEW WHAT THE JOURNEY MEANT NOR HEEDED THE VOICE OF WARNING.

Tappan Adney, The Klondike Stampede *(1899)*

445. OCTOBER 19, 1897

GEORGE PULLMAN OF RAILROAD FAME DIES

When George Pullman's railroad car manufacturing company slashed employees' wages but not what they paid to live in the company town, workers rebelled, and American Railway Union members took up their cause. In the summer of 1894, at the height of a 10-week strike and boycott, up to 250,000 workers in 27 states took part, snarling travel, mail, and commerce; after some strikers turned violent, public sympathy for them waned and federal troops were called in. The animus against Pullman remained so great that after his death on this day, he was buried in a steel-reinforced, concrete-filled vault so enemies couldn't dig up and deface his body.

446. FEBRUARY 15, 1898

DESTRUCTION OF U.S.S. *MAINE* SPURS THE SPANISH-AMERICAN WAR

Concerned for American interests in Cuba as rebels there fought Spain for independence, the U.S. government sent the U.S.S. *Maine* to Havana Harbor. The battleship was anchored there on this day when a massive explosion destroyed it, killing 266 crew members. A naval inquiry blamed the explosion on an external mine (though later investigations suggested the cause was an accidental fire inside the ship); U.S. public opinion turned against Spain, fanned by inflammatory "yellow journalism" in William Randolph Hearst's *New York Journal,* among others. Amid public rallying cries of "Remember the *Maine,* to hell with Spain," Congress declared war against Spain on April 25, instigating the Spanish-American War.

447. MARCH 22, 1898

SEEKING CHANGE, AN ANTI-LYNCHING ACTIVIST VISITS THE WHITE HOUSE

Born into slavery in Mississippi during the Civil War, Ida B. Wells-Barnett became a journalist, educator, and leading crusader against the lynchings that killed and terrorized Blacks and their defenders, especially in the American South. When Black postmaster Frazier Baker and his two-year-old daughter Julia were murdered in South Carolina, Wells-Barnett sought President William McKinley's help to find and punish those responsible. After she visited McKinley in the White House on this day, he ordered an investigation, which led to 13 white men being charged in the Bakers' deaths. But the case ended in a mistrial.

The saga of the Wild Bunch began in 1899 near Wilcox, Wyoming, when the robbers held up a train and made off with tens of thousands of dollars.

448. APRIL 25, 1898

SUPREME COURT UPHOLDS MISSISSIPPI VOTER REQUIREMENTS

Under the Mississippi Constitution of 1890, residents were required to meet several conditions before they could register to vote, including paying a tax at the polls and passing a literacy test, unless they could satisfy the "grandfather clause" by proving that their father's father had voted. Moreover, only registered voters were put on juries, which essentially prevented African Americans from serving. After Henry Williams, a Black man, was indicted by an all-white jury, he challenged the indictment as a violation of federal civil rights protections. But in *Williams* v. *Mississippi,* the Supreme Court ruled against Williams on this day, concluding that Mississippi's constitution and statutes "do not, on their face, discriminate between the white and negro races," even if they might be applied at times with discriminatory effect.

449. DECEMBER 10, 1898

TREATY OF PARIS SETTLES THE SPANISH-AMERICAN WAR

The Spanish-American War officially ended on this day when Spain and the United States signed the Treaty of Paris, concluding what U.S. diplomat John Hay once called a "splendid little war." During the nearly eight months of the conflict, U.S. forces had overwhelmed Spain's naval defense of its colonies in the Philippines and destroyed the Spanish Caribbean squadron. With France as a go-between to negotiate peace terms, the adversaries agreed to a ceasefire on August 12. In addition to guaranteeing Cuba's independence, the treaty forced Spain to relinquish Guam and Puerto Rico, and to sell the Philippines to the United States for $20 million.

450. MAY 31, 1899

HARRIMAN EXPEDITION SHINES A LIGHT ON BRITISH COLUMBIA AND ALASKA

For the two-month expedition that left Seattle on this day, railroad magnate Edward

Harriman had outfitted a steamship with luxury staterooms, a 500-book library, an organ and piano—and a laboratory workspace. Though his family entourage was along for the adventure, Harriman had recruited a cadre of eminent scientists, naturalists, writers, and artists who used the 9,000-mile cruise along British Columbia and Alaska to survey the coastal wilderness and record what they discovered. Their output included descriptions of 13 new genera and almost 600 new species; 12 volumes of data and 100 trunks of specimens; and more than 5,000 photographs and paintings of natural wonders, flora and fauna, and Native peoples.

451. JUNE 2, 1899

BUTCH CASSIDY AND THE WILD BUNCH BECOME AMERICA'S MOST NOTORIOUS OUTLAWS

On this day near Wilcox, Wyoming, a robber band known as the Wild Bunch held up a Union Pacific Railroad train, dynamited a safe, and took tens of thousands of dollars. The

The signing of the Treaty of Paris in 1898 marked the end of the Spanish-American War, and of Spain's colonies in the Pacific and the Americas.

The final assembly line at the Ford Motor Company factory in Highland Park, Michigan

next year, the gang used the same approach on another train in Wyoming, possibly making off with an even larger haul, though the exact amount is not known. Thus was born the legend of the Wild Bunch, with its bowler-hatted ringleader Butch Cassidy (real name, Robert Parker) and his sharpshooting collaborator, Sundance Kid (real name, Harry Longabaugh). The two are widely believed to have fled to South America and died there in 1908, but inconclusive identifications have allowed the legend to live on.

452. AUGUST 5, 1899

HENRY FORD PIONEERS AUTOMOBILE MANUFACTURING

Young Henry Ford had learned about steam engines on the farm west of Detroit where he grew up, studied electrical engineering while working at the Edison Illuminating Company of Detroit, and built his first gasoline-engine vehicle in a Detroit woodshed. After Ford demonstrated a gas-powered vehicle to lumber merchant William H. Murphy on a 3.5-hour test drive in southeastern Michigan, Murphy became one of the first 12 investors (along with Detroit's mayor) in the Detroit Automobile Company, founded on this day. Though that company struggled and dissolved in early 1901, Ford and his investors reorganized by year's end into the Henry Ford Company.

453. AUGUST 10, 1899

MARSHALL "MAJOR" TAYLOR SETS A CYCLING RECORD

Gilbert Taylor, a Black Civil War veteran, moved with his family from Kentucky to Indiana, where he found work as a coachman for a wealthy Indianapolis family. Gilbert's employers gave his son Marshall, later known as Major, an education—and a bicycle, on which he excelled from childhood. By age 18, Major dominated bicycle races, to the chagrin of some white racing officials; by age 20, he held seven world records. On this day, Taylor won the world one-mile track cycling championship, becoming the first African American athlete to reach the world champion level in any sport.

THE PUBLIC WAS MORE INTERESTED IN BEING CARRIED THAN IN BEING PULLED.

Henry Ford *(1923)*

454. SEPTEMBER 18, 1899

SCOTT JOPLIN COPYRIGHTS "MAPLE LEAF RAG"

On this day at the U.S. Copyright Office, as journalist Neely Tucker recounts it, "a little-known pianist and composer named Scott Joplin" registered a copyright on an early composition. It was "a highly syncopated, upbeat piano piece with intense flurries of notes—more than 2,000 in a song that took less than three minutes to perform." The piece was called "Maple Leaf Rag," and, Tucker continues, it "blew the doors off everything." The composition would become the exemplar for other ragtime composers and a landmark in American popular music. Royalties for its sheet music would give Joplin a modest income for the rest of his life (he died in 1917).

455. OCTOBER 20, 1899

THE 10TH AMERICA'S CUP PROPELS TECH REVOLUTION

Off Sandy Hook, New Jersey, the American sailing team, backed by J. P. Morgan, won the international yacht-racing competition against the British, sponsored by Sir Thomas Lipton. But the contest had implications far beyond sailing. Newly arrived in the U.S., Italian inventor Guglielmo Marconi had outfitted two American boats with his wireless telegraph to convey news of the race to New York newspapers. This sparked enthusiasm for communication via radio waves; a year later, Marconi filed for a now infamous patent: No. 7777, for Improvements in Apparatus for Wireless Telegraphy. (In 1943, the Supreme Court overturned Marconi's patent, evidence to some that Nikola Tesla had invented the radio, not Marconi.)

★ ★ ★ The ★ ★ ★
20th CENTURY

ERA OF ADVANCEMENTS

ASK NOT WHAT YOUR COUNTRY CAN DO FOR YOU—ASK WHAT YOU CAN DO FOR YOUR COUNTRY.

John F. Kennedy, *inaugural address (1961)*

THE UNITED STATES' ROLE in the 20th century, Henry Luce wrote, should be to spread "especially American" ideals around the globe: "a love of freedom, a feeling for the equality of opportunity, a tradition of self-reliance and independence." But his 1941 *Life* magazine essay declared that, so far, America had "miserably failed to solve the problems of our epoch."

Throughout the 1900s, currents of events and ideals collided repeatedly, as optimism and achievement overlapped with conflict and tragedy. Americans were behind the first powered airplane flight and the first moon landing, the first successful organ transplant and the precursor network to the internet. U.S. troops contributed to Allied victories in World Wars I and II—and dropped the first atomic bombs in wartime on Japan. America withdrew combat forces from Vietnam after eight years of escalating protests, including those at Kent State University, where armed forces killed students during a campus protest. Court rulings and legal reforms established a woman's right to abortion, increased civil rights for African Americans, and in many realms outlawed discrimination based on race, national origin, gender, religion, sexual orientation, and disability.

At the century's end, when Luce's *Time* magazine named its 1999 Person of the Year, it chose digital commerce pioneer Jeff Bezos of Amazon.

By the turn of the century, Republican William McKinley was in the White House; he won two terms using campaign souvenirs like this kerchief. An anarchist shot McKinley, who died September 14, 1901, becoming the third president assassinated (after Abraham Lincoln and James Garfield). ***OPPOSITE TOP:*** Steelworkers share lunch on a beam 800 feet in the air during construction of the RCA Building at Manhattan's Rockefeller Center. ***OPPOSITE BOTTOM:*** The New York City subway's first trip departed in 1904 from the City Hall station, an architectural gem with vaulted tile ceilings.

DECEMBER 17, 1903
Wright brothers take flight
On the sand flats of North Carolina, the celebrated entrepreneurs achieved the first powered, sustained flight of a heavier-than-air craft.

JUNE 28, 1919
Treaty of Versailles ends World War I
Its terms made Germany pay reparations for starting the war that redrew the map of Europe.

AUGUST 26, 1920
Women win the right to vote
Already granted in 15 states, women's right to vote became the law of the land.

JUNE 2, 1924
Indigenous people gain citizenship
The Indian Citizenship Act assured the vote to Native Americans in the Alaska Territory and the United States.

MAY 21, 1927
Charles Lindbergh completes solo transatlantic flight
Flying from New York to Paris in 33.5 hours brought the intrepid pilot fame and a cash prize.

OCTOBER 28, 1929
Stock market begins to crash on "Black Monday"
Sell-offs caused the stock market to lose almost 13 percent in a single day.

DECEMBER 7, 1941
Japanese forces bomb Pearl Harbor
The bombing of the Hawaii base destroyed ships and aircraft and killed 2,300 people.

AUGUST 6, 1945
***Enola Gay* drops the first atomic bomb on the Japanese city of Hiroshima**
When Japan didn't surrender, a larger bomb was dropped on the city of Nagasaki three days later.

MAY 17, 1954
Supreme Court strikes down segregated schools
The unanimous decision overturned a previous ruling allowing "separate but equal" schools.

A photograph of the Apollo 11 lunar module *Eagle* departing from the moon on July 21, 1969

TIMELINE

1900-1999

A CENTURY OF PIONEERING TECHNOLOGICAL AND CULTURAL ACHIEVEMENTS UNFOLDS.

ON JULY 20, 1969, as the Apollo 11 lunar module *Eagle* descended toward the moon's surface, its onboard Apollo Guidance Computer (AGC) had to manage numerous tasks at once. By today's standards, the AGC seems primitive: Its storage capacity was 72 kilobytes (KB)—compared to a modern smartphone's roughly six million KB—and its processing speed was just over one megahertz (MHz), roughly 3,000 times slower than that of smartphones. How could that computer safely land the first men on the moon?

It was, in part, thanks to Margaret Hamilton's foresight. Hamilton headed the Massachusetts Institute of Technology (MIT) laboratory that NASA chose to program Apollo computer software—and at a time when programming was often regarded as menial, she took what she called "software engineering" seriously. Knowing that too many simultaneous tasks could overload AGC's processor, Hamilton's team programmed it to detect and recover from such overloads by dropping lower-priority tasks. With less than seven minutes to *Eagle's* touchdown, alarms went off, requiring the NASA flight controllers to quickly make a "go/no-go" decision. As Hamilton recounted, a NASA computer specialist realized what the alarms meant: that the processor was nearing overloaded (later blamed on power drain from a mis-set switch) "but that the software was compensating for it" by focusing on critical landing functions. "Some things one never forgets," Hamilton later said of that moment. With seconds of fuel to spare, the *Eagle* had landed.

MARCH 9, 1959
Barbie makes her debut
The 11-inch-high doll, designed by Mattel co-founder Ruth Handler, first appeared at the American International Toy Fair.

MAY 9, 1960
FDA approves first birth control pill
Two years after "the pill" became available, more than two million women were using it.

NOVEMBER 22, 1963
An assassin kills President John F. Kennedy
As Kennedy rode in a convertible in a Dallas motorcade, he was struck by two bullets, one to the head.

MARCH 8, 1965
First U.S. combat troops reach Vietnam
On this day, 3,500 U.S. troops arrived in South Vietnam; by year's end, 180,000 more had arrived.

APRIL 4, 1968
Martin Luther King, Jr., is assassinated
The civil rights leader died after being shot by escaped fugitive James Earl Ray in Memphis.

JULY 20, 1969
Apollo 11 lands on the moon
Astronaut Neil Armstrong called his first step onto the lunar surface "one giant leap for mankind."

JANUARY 22, 1973
Supreme Court decides *Roe* v. *Wade*
The court ruled that a constitutionally protected right to privacy allowed abortion until a fetus was viable.

AUGUST 9, 1974
President Richard Nixon leaves office
Dogged by accusations of wrongdoing, he was the first sitting U.S. president to resign.

APRIL 29, 1992
Riots break out in Los Angeles
After a jury failed to convict police officers seen on videotape beating Black motorist Rodney King, violence engulfed the city.

The "Ballad of Casey Jones" tells how a railroad engineer died trying to prevent his speeding train from a collision.

456. APRIL 30, 1900

CASEY JONES DIES IN A TRAIN COLLISION

"Come, all you rounders, if you want to hear / The story told of a brave engineer." Wallace Saunders's "Ballad of Casey Jones" immortalized the courage and sudden death of railroad engineer John Luther "Casey" Jones. In the wee hours of April 30, Jones was driving the steam locomotive *Cannonball Express* on its run from Memphis to Canton, Mississippi, when he saw a stalled train on the tracks ahead. With one hand on the brake and the other on the whistle, Jones told his fireman, Sim Webb, to jump while he stayed at the helm. Webb jumped and the train slowed, but not enough to save Jones's life. All the passengers survived. Soon afterward, railroad worker Saunders wrote the celebrated ballad (and inspired a Grateful Dead hit) that made Jones a folk hero.

457. SEPTEMBER 8, 1900

A HURRICANE WIPES OUT GALVESTON, TEXAS

The deadliest hurricane in American history hit Galveston, Texas, with little warning as darkness fell. With winds estimated at 140 miles an hour, the storm propelled a "great gray wall" of seawater over the low-lying city. The waters and wind tore apart buildings, streetcar tracks, and ships at anchor until two-thirds of the city was destroyed. At least 8,000 people died. Galveston rebuilt, incorporating seawalls and raising street levels, but the city lost much of its business as a port to nearby Houston.

458. OCTOBER 4, 1900

MARGARET ABBOTT BECOMES THE FIRST U.S. FEMALE OLYMPIC CHAMPION

In 1900, the Paris Olympic Games were spread out over several months and multiple venues. Only five events, including golf, allowed women to participate. Chicagoan Margaret Ives Abbot (along with her mother) entered the nine-hole golf tournament held during the Paris Exposition (a world's fair). Margaret won it with a score of 47, for which she was awarded a ceramic bowl. She never knew that she had in fact won Olympic gold rather than an exposition medal. She was the first American woman in history to win an Olympic event.

459. OCTOBER 23, 1900

WALTER REED ANNOUNCES THE MECHANISM FOR YELLOW FEVER

From the 17th through the 19th centuries, outbreaks of yellow fever devastated port cities in the Americas. Physicians of the era wrongly believed it spread directly from patient to patient. In 1900, U.S. Army surgeon Maj. Walter Reed used human volunteers to prove a theory first proposed and suggested to him by Cuban physician Carlos Finlay: Biting mosquitoes transmitted the disease. Reed presented his findings in a paper for the American Public Health Association meeting in Indianapolis. As a result of his work, public

Condemned at publication as too racy, the novel *Sister Carrie* tells the story of the libertine chorus girl depicted on its cover.

health officials were able to rein in yellow fever outbreaks by setting up mosquito screens and draining breeding grounds. Today, a vaccine exists for the disease.

460. NOVEMBER 8, 1900

SISTER CARRIE IS PUBLISHED

Theodore Dreiser's gritty novel of a chorus girl on the rise shocked some readers when it was published late in 1900. Caroline Meeber, the main character, unashamedly lives with one man and then another, while leaving factory work to pursue success on the stage. Under pressure, Dreiser edited out some of the racier passages before Doubleday issued the book. It sold just 456 copies for its unenthusiastic publisher. The author eventually bought the book's plates and reissued the novel in 1907 with a different company. It went on to be considered a masterpiece of American naturalism and a clear-eyed portrait of the inhabitants of a new century: urban, working-class, and upwardly striving.

461. FEBRUARY 25, 1901

U.S. STEEL HAS A BILLION-DOLLAR BIRTH

At the beginning of the 20th century, the United States dominated the world steel industry—and Andrew Carnegie's company, Carnegie Steel, was that industry's biggest player. In early 1901, Carnegie agreed to a plan put forth by financier J. P. Morgan to merge his company with nine others. The resulting United States Steel Corporation, incorporated on this day, controlled the steel business from start to finish, owning mines, manufacturing, and finished products. With a capitalization of $1.4 billion, it became the largest company in the world. In the 21st century, it remains a major player among the world's steel producers, though outpaced by many Asian companies.

An employee tests molten metal at Chicago's South Works of U.S. Steel, a behemoth formed by merging 10 steel companies in 1901.

462. MAY 21, 1901

CONNECTICUT ESTABLISHES THE FIRST STATE SPEED LIMIT

Motor vehicles had been trundling down American roads for just a handful of years when Connecticut enacted the first statewide speed limit. At the time, U.S. automobiles consisted of a few thousand steam-powered, electric, and gas-powered cars. They weren't remotely speedy by modern standards, but lawmakers were concerned about their potential for accidents, particularly because the cars shared the road with easily spooked animals. Connecticut's law set a speed limit of 12 miles an hour in the city and 15 miles an hour on other roads. Drivers were required to slow down or stop when approaching horse-drawn vehicles. Today, all 50 states have established speed limits, with top highway speeds ranging from 60 miles an hour in Hawaii to 85 miles an hour in some parts of hard-charging Texas.

463. SEPTEMBER 6, 1901

ANARCHIST SHOOTS PRESIDENT MCKINLEY

President William McKinley was a popular chief executive half a year into his second term when he visited the Pan-American Exposition in Buffalo, New York. Just after 4 p.m. on September 6, McKinley was greeting the public in a reception line at the exposition's Temple of Music when he was approached by a young, dark-haired man with a handkerchief wrapped around one hand. McKinley bowed and extended his hand. The man, laborer and anarchist Leon Czolgosz, shot him in the chest and abdomen with a revolver. "There was an instant of almost complete silence," according to a newspaper account. "The President stood stock still, a look of hesitancy, almost of bewilderment, on his face." Czolgosz was immediately captured. McKinley died eight days later. Czolgosz was executed that October; he reportedly said, "I didn't believe one man should have so much service, and another man have none."

464. OCTOBER 16, 1901

BOOKER T. WASHINGTON DINES WITH PRESIDENT THEODORE ROOSEVELT

Former vice president Theodore Roosevelt, elevated to the country's highest office after the assassination of President William McKinley, did not let the official mourning period stop him from hosting near-nightly dinners at the White House. On October 16, his dinner guests included the prominent educator Booker T. Washington. It was the first time an African American guest had been invited to a White House dinner, and not for the last time a furor ensued that was largely divided along North/South lines. The Memphis *Commercial Appeal* wrote: "President Roosevelt has committed a blunder that is worse than a crime." The African American paper *Washington Bee* declared that the dinner ended any notion "that President Roosevelt was opposed to the negro."

465. OCTOBER 24, 1901

ANNIE EDSON TAYLOR BARRELS OVER NIAGARA FALLS

According to schoolteacher Annie Edson Taylor's own account, the 62-year-old widow was casting about for ways to make money when it came to her "like a flash of light, 'Go over Niagara Falls in a barrel.'" Taylor designed her own four-and-a-half-foot barrel, hired

I WOULD RATHER FACE A CANNON KNOWING THAT I WOULD BE BLOWN TO PIECES THAN GO OVER THE FALLS AGAIN.

Annie Edson Taylor

Being the first person to survive going over Niagara Falls in a barrel wasn't the moneymaking stunt Annie Edson Taylor had hoped it would be.

President Theodore Roosevelt refused to make an unsportsmanlike kill during a bear hunt, inspiring the creation of "Teddy" bear toys.

a promotion manager, and literally took the plunge on October 24, her 63rd birthday. "I did not think it wrong," she wrote later, "as there was nothing immodest in the act, nor did it involve the life of anyone but myself." Taylor emerged from the river with just a few scrapes to show for her adventure. She was the first person to ride a barrel over the falls and survive.

466. NOVEMBER 14, 1902

TEDDY ROOSEVELT REFUSES TO KILL A BEAR

Theodore Roosevelt, known to be an enthusiastic hunter, had not bagged a single black bear during a hunting trip in Mississippi. So his companions caught one and presented it to him for the kill—accounts vary that it was old, injured, or just young. Roosevelt refused to shoot the helpless beast. Newspapers and their cartoonists picked up the tale of Roosevelt's gallant act and the story spread quickly. In Brooklyn, a candy store owner and his wife began to craft and sell stuffed toy bears, which they called "Teddy's bears," and in Germany, the Steiff company did the same. Although Roosevelt disliked the nickname "Teddy," his campaign knew a good thing when they saw one and adopted the teddy bear as a mascot; the toy went on to worldwide popularity.

467. DECEMBER 29, 1902

SCOTT JOPLIN PUBLISHES "THE ENTERTAINER"

Classically trained pianist Scott Joplin was in the early stages of a successful career when he wrote the "The Entertainer." Described as a "Rag Time Two Step," the piece features the upbeat syncopations and intricate variations that came to be associated with Joplin's music. As sheet music and as a player piano roll, "The Entertainer" became quickly popular. "It is a jingling work of a very original character," the *St. Louis Globe-Democrat* noted approvingly. After Joplin's death, the tune faded from public notice but was revived—and then some —after it became the immensely popular signature tune of the 1973 movie *The Sting.*

468. MARCH 14, 1903

PELICAN ISLAND BECOMES THE NATION'S FIRST NATIONAL WILDLIFE REFUGE

The millinery of the late 19th century had a devastating effect on the waterbirds of the Florida coast. Their beautiful plumage, which adorned women's hats, was in high demand and fetched high prices. Hunters and unofficial bird wardens fought to the death near nesting grounds. In 1903, bird advocates visited Theodore Roosevelt at his home and laid out their case for creating protected habitats. Roosevelt agreed. He signed an executive order establishing Pelican Island, on Florida's east coast, as a federal bird reservation. It was the first time the U.S. government set aside land as a wildlife refuge.

A foundational work on the role of race in America, W. E. B. Du Bois's essay collection *The Souls of Black Folk* was published in 1903.

469. APRIL 18, 1903

W. E. B. DU BOIS PUBLISHES *THE SOULS OF BLACK FOLK*

W. E. B. Du Bois was a sociologist, writer, and activist who laid out the role of race in American life as few others could. In the introduction to his essay collection, *The Souls of Black Folk,* he announced, "The problem of the twentieth century is the problem of the color line." The essays went on to highlight an essential duality in African American existence. "One ever feels his twoness," he noted, "an American, a Negro; two souls, two thoughts, two unreconciled strivings." Du Bois went on to become one of the founders of the National Association for the Advancement of Colored People (NAACP) and a leader in the civil rights movement.

470. JULY 26, 1903

TWO MEN AND A DOG SET A CROSS-COUNTRY RECORD

In the spring of 1903, Vermont doctor Horatio Nelson Jackson made a $50 bet with his drinking companions: He would drive a car from San Francisco to New York in 90 days or fewer. Jackson embarked on May 23 in a two-cylinder Winton automobile, accompanied by a mechanic named Sewall Crocker and a stockpile of tools, gas, and food. Along the way, the motorists picked up a pit bull named Bud and fitted him with motoring goggles. Many of the roads were unpaved; gas stations were nonexistent and maps and signs scarce. Nevertheless, after breakdowns and detours, the dusty trio arrived in New York City, completing the country's first cross-country drive 63 and a half days after they set out.

471. DECEMBER 1, 1903

THE GREAT TRAIN ROBBERY SPURS THE BIRTH OF THE MOTION PICTURE INDUSTRY

Directed by Edwin S. Porter, a former cameraman for Thomas Edison, *The Great Train Robbery* was an instant hit when it was released at the end of 1903. The 12-minute silent film follows four bandits as they rob a moving train, escape on horseback, and are pursued and killed by a posse. Porter's movie was the first to combine multiple scenes into one coherent narrative and to employ sophisticated crosscutting techniques to show simultaneous action. Its success paved the way for longer, more complex movies and the growth of the motion picture industry.

Orville Wright (right) piloted the first powered flight—12 seconds aloft, covering 120 feet—of the *Wright Flyer* he and brother Wilbur built.

472. DECEMBER 17, 1903

WRIGHT BROTHERS TAKE FLIGHT

Orville and Wilbur Wright, brothers from Dayton, Ohio, worked as printers and as bicycle mechanics before turning to a risky new venture: powered flight. For four years, they worked tirelessly in a shed on the lonely beaches of North Carolina's Outer Banks, shaping and reshaping the wings, rudders, engines, and propellers of a series of prototypical flying machines. On December 17, 1903, a freezing, windy day, they tested their latest creation: the *Wright Flyer.* A coin flip had determined the pilot, so Orville took the controls as the engine warmed up. At 10:35 a.m., the *Flyer* took off and flew 120 erratic feet for 12 seconds before plowing into the sand: the first powered, sustained flight of a heavier-than-air craft. The brothers made two more flights that day, the final one covering 852 feet in about one minute. Then the wind caught the grounded *Flyer* and tossed it across the sand, wrecking it. It didn't matter. "SUCCESS" wrote Orville in a cable to his family that evening, ending "HOME FOR CHRISTMAS."

WE WERE LUCKY ENOUGH TO GROW UP IN AN ENVIRONMENT WHERE THERE WAS ALWAYS MUCH ENCOURAGEMENT TO CHILDREN TO PURSUE INTELLECTUAL INTERESTS.

Orville Wright *(1943)*

473. APRIL 30, 1904

ST. LOUIS WORLD'S FAIR OPENS

The Louisiana Purchase Exposition, better known as the St. Louis World's Fair, opened to a crowd of 200,000 and went on to dazzle 20 million visitors for the next seven months. It wasn't the first or last such fair held in the United States, but it was one of the grandest of the new century and a showcase for the Missouri metropolis. Spanning 1,200 acres, it was a city within a city, with classically styled buildings, avenues, waterways, a Ferris wheel, and displays from around the world. Some exhibited technological wonders, such as automobiles, typewriters, and an x-ray machine. Fairgoers marveled at contortionists, Spanish dancers, and Beautiful Jim Key, the "Educated Horse." The fair's president, David R. Francis, closed the exhibition on December 1 with the words, "Farewell, a long farewell to all thy splendor!" before cutting off its electric lights.

474. OCTOBER 3, 1904

MARY MCLEOD BETHUNE OPENS A SCHOOL FOR BLACK GIRLS

On this day, Mary McLeod Bethune opened the Daytona Literary and Industrial Training Institute for Negro Girls in Daytona Beach, Florida. Desks were made out of crates and pencils from charred wood. By 1923 the rapidly expanding school had become Bethune-Cookman College, the first historically Black college to be headed by a woman. It was just one of the tireless educator's many achievements in a long career dedicated to advancing civil rights, educational access for all, and women's rights. Bethune went on to work under President Franklin D. Roosevelt and became the only female member of the unofficial advisory group known as the "Black Cabinet." "I believe," she wrote, "… in doing well whatever task is assigned to me."

475. OCTOBER 27, 1904

NEW YORKERS BEGIN TO RIDE THE SUBWAY

A middle-age woman from Brooklyn paid five cents, received a paper ticket, and became the first person to ride the New York City subway on that October evening. With construction beginning in 1900, the IRT (Interborough Rapid Transit) lines ran for just over nine miles from City Hall to Grand Central Terminal, through Times Square, and up to 145th Street in Harlem. While it wasn't the first subway in the United States (that was Boston's), it soon became (and remains) the largest in the country, incorporating 472 stations along more than 600 miles of track.

476. NOVEMBER 7, 1904

"GIVE MY REGARDS TO BROADWAY" BECOMES A HIT

George M. Cohan's patriotic musical *Little Johnny Jones* opened at New York's Liberty Theatre and ran for a healthy 221 performances over the next three years. The tale of a scrappy American jockey who triumphs over British snobs, the musical was not a record-breaker and is little known today, but two of its songs have become legendary: "I'm a Yankee Doodle Dandy" and "Give My Regards to Broadway." Both were written and performed by Cohan, who was the play's director, writer of the book and lyrics, and lead actor. "Give My Regards to Broadway" appears twice in the musical. The first time, the homesick jockey sings it slowly and sadly; the second time, at the end, the tune has the triumphant tempo that is currently associated with the song—now a canonical tune for theater lovers everywhere.

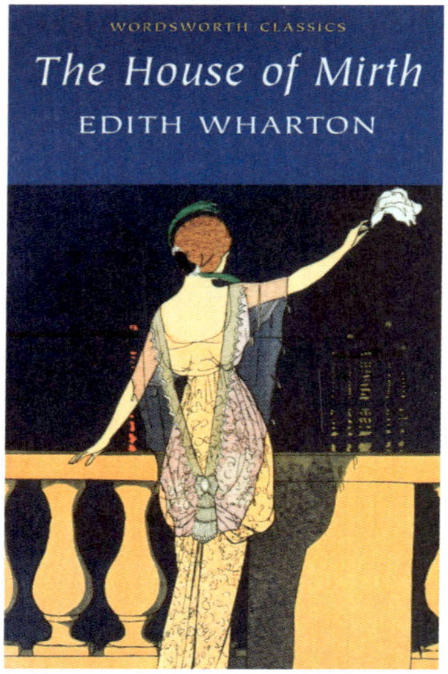

The House of Mirth, a Gilded Age saga blending romance and commentary, launched novelist Edith Wharton into a distinguished career.

477. OCTOBER 14, 1905

EDITH WHARTON PUBLISHES *THE HOUSE OF MIRTH*

Wharton's novel traces the social descent of upper-class, penniless Lily Bart. The 29-year-old Bart needs a husband to secure her place in snobbish Gilded Age drawing rooms, but she is unable to decide between two suitors. She falls into debt, eventually dying of a drug overdose. On the surface a story of romantic disappointment, the novel weaves together many of the era's social issues, including women's roles, bigotry, and the huge divide between the wealthy and everyone else. Published by Charles Scribner's Sons, *The House of Mirth* was the first big success for the 43-year-old Wharton, reaching the top of bestseller lists within months. The author became known as a keen chronicler of American aristocracy, going on to win the Pulitzer Prize for *The Age of Innocence* (1920).

478. DECEMBER 30, 1905

BOMBING STOKES FEARS OF UNION VIOLENCE

During his time as Idaho governor, Frank Steunenberg took a harsh line against labor unions. In 1905, almost five years after he left office, Steunenberg was returning from a walk when he opened his gate, triggering a bomb, and was killed. Detectives arrested an

The Great San Francisco Earthquake set off a three-day conflagration that caused hundreds of deaths and $400 million in damages.

itinerant former union member, Harry Orchard, who was found with bombmaking materials. Under pressure, Orchard claimed that three leaders of the Western Federation of Miners union, including the famous organizer "Big Bill" Haywood, had instructed him to carry out the assassination. Officials arrested the leaders, and their trial became a national sensation. Celebrated defense lawyer Clarence Darrow, known for his advocacy for workers, made the case a referendum on the righteousness of labor unions generally. No hard evidence connected the labor leaders to the killing, and the three men were acquitted.

479. APRIL 18, 1906

EARTHQUAKE AND FIRES DEVASTATE SAN FRANCISCO

At 5:12 a.m., a massive earthquake began to shake San Francisco and its surroundings, tearing apart the northernmost 296 miles of the San Andreas Fault. Buildings all over the city collapsed, particularly in areas built on soft or reclaimed land. With gas lines ruptured and lanterns toppled, fires broke out, destroying almost 500 city blocks over three days. More than 3,000 citizens were killed, and more than half the city was made homeless.

Subsequent studies led to significant advances in understanding earthquakes and their effects—particularly important in California, which is still the country's riskiest state for major earthquakes.

480. JUNE 25, 1906

HARRY THAW MURDERS ARCHITECT STANFORD WHITE

Beautiful young actress Evelyn Nesbit had the misfortune to be pursued by not one but two rich and obsessive older men. When she was just 16 and working as a chorus girl in New York, she was swept up in an abusive affair with the famous architect Stanford White, known for designing New York City landmarks like Madison Square Garden. At the age of 20, she married unstable Pittsburgh millionaire Harry Thaw. On this night, Thaw sought out White as they all attended a performance of the musical *Mam'zelle Champagne* on the rooftop of Madison Square Garden. As the chorus sang "I Could Love a Thousand Girls," Thaw approached White and shot him three times, killing him. A sensational trial ended in a hung jury for Thaw. A subsequent trial found the millionaire not guilty by reason of insanity; he was released after seven years.

Seeking freedom and prosperity in America, millions of émigrés passed through the facility synonymous with U.S. immigration: Ellis Island.

481. AUGUST 4, 1906

MARY MALLON STARTS AN OUTBREAK

In the early 1900s, Mary Mallon, an Irish immigrant, worked as a cook for wealthy families in New York City and on Long Island. Unbeknownst to any of them, she was an asymptomatic carrier of typhoid fever, a dangerous bacterial disease spread in contaminated food and water. Mallon seems to have infected people in households for years, but when the first cases showed up in an Oyster Bay house soon after she began work there on this day, the home's owner hired sanitary engineer George Soper to investigate. He eventually tied Mallon to multiple cases of the disease. In all, "Typhoid" Mary, as the newspapers dubbed her, probably infected at least 50 people (three of whom died), possibly many more. Her widely publicized case alerted the public to the role of asymptomatic carriers and sanitation in disease outbreaks.

THERE WAS NEVER ANY EFFORT BY THE BOARD AUTHORITY TO DO ANYTHING FOR ME EXCEPTING TO CAST ME ON THE ISLAND AND KEEP ME A PRISONER.

Mary Mallon *(1909)*

482. APRIL 17, 1907

ELLIS ISLAND SEES A RECORD NUMBER OF IMMIGRANTS

On this day, 11,747 immigrants—the largest such group in the New York island's history—were processed through Ellis Island's Registry Room. Drawn by America's booming economy, the immigrants were primarily Catholics from southern, central, and eastern Europe, as well as Jews fleeing pogroms in tsarist territories. Before being admitted to the United States, each new arrival was given a six-second physical by Ellis Island physicians and asked a series of questions by inspectors (translators were on hand, as only about half of the immigrants spoke English). Over a million immigrants passed through the island in 1907, as the country became known as a beacon for those responding to the Statue of Liberty's promise to give refuge to "your tired, your poor, your huddled masses."

483. OCTOBER 16, 1907

COLLAPSING BANKS START THE PANIC OF 1907

When two financial speculators, F. Augustus Heinze and Charles W. Morse, tried and failed to corner the market on United Copper stock, the institutions with which they were associated suffered enormous losses. Within days, a widespread panic had driven the stock market close to collapse. Bankers begged for help from the famous financier J. P. Morgan, who called in other tycoons and bank presidents, and organized loans to the endangered banks and trusts. By November, the crisis was over. Realizing that they could not rely on the intervention of millionaires to regulate financial markets, U.S. politicians went on to establish the Federal Reserve System in 1913.

484. JANUARY 27, 1908

HOUDINI ESCAPES FROM A MILK CAN IN ST. LOUIS

Escape artist Harry Houdini (born Erik Weisz) was already famous for extricating himself from handcuffs when he decided to inaugurate a bigger, more dangerous stunt in his first theatrical appearance. In front of a tense crowd at the Columbia Theater in St. Louis, Missouri, Houdini climbed into a waist-high, water-filled, metal milk can. Helpers lowered and padlocked the lid before concealing the can from the audience with a cloth cabinet. The magician "made his audience thoroughly uncomfortable for the space of two or three minutes," wrote the *St. Louis Globe-Democrat,* before he emerged, dripping but alive, a living testament to America's growing appetite for mass entertainment.

A 1912 poster depicts Harry Houdini's Chinese Water Torture Cell, one of the hallmarks of his 35-year career as an escape artist.

485. MAY 2, 1908

"TAKE ME OUT TO THE BALL GAME" IS COPYRIGHTED

"On a Saturday, her young beau / Called to see if she'd like to go, / To see a show but Miss Kate said 'No, / I'll tell you what you can do.'" These words, among the opening lines to "Take Me Out to the Ball Game," are rarely sung by baseball fans today. They flesh out the song's backstory, which tells of Katie Casey's wish to see a baseball game rather than a theatrical performance. Lyricist Jack Norworth and composer Albert Von Tilzer wrote the song and made it a hit despite never having seen a game. The jaunty tune, fun to sing if not a masterpiece, became one of the most recognizable songs in the country. It also accelerated the sales of Cracker Jack, introduced in 1893.

486. JULY 26, 1908

FBI AGENTS REPORT FOR DUTY

Although the U.S. Department of Justice had been in existence since 1870, before 1908 it had no investigators of its own. To look into federal crimes—for example those that crossed state lines—the department had to hire private detectives or lease investigators from other agencies. In May 1908, Congress banned even those agents from working for other departments. So Attorney General Charles Bonaparte (grand-nephew of the emperor) created his own force of 34 federal agents. They reported to his chief examiner, Stanley Finch, on July 26. Within a year, the Office of the Chief Examiner was renamed the Bureau of Investigation. In 1935, it became the Federal Bureau of Investigation.

487. SEPTEMBER 27, 1908

MODEL T'S REACH THE MASSES

On this day, "Model 2090, car #1" received its finishing touches at the Piquette plant in Detroit: the first Ford Model T automobile to enter the marketplace. Ford had not yet begun to use an assembly line, but since Model T's were standardized, with interchangeable parts, they were affordable to typical middle-class buyers at a price of $825. Boasting a top speed of 42 miles an hour, the four-cylinder Model T's were immediately popular. By the time they were discontinued, Ford had sold 15 million and autos had gone from toys for the rich to everyday transportation for the masses. And no, they didn't come only in black: The earliest Model T's were gray, green, blue, and red. The all-black line appeared in 1914.

488. FEBRUARY 12, 1909

NAACP IS FOUNDED

In August 1908, a brutal scene unfolded in Springfield, Illinois, when thousands of white residents attacked their Black neighbors following accusations of rape. Shocked by the riots, an interracial group that included Ida B. Wells and W. E. B. Du Bois met in 1909 and formed the National Association for the Advancement of Colored People (NAACP). Du Bois served as one of the group's first officers. The organization grew rapidly and gained hundreds of thousands of members and more African American leaders in the next decades, remaining vigorous into the 21st century.

489. JULY 12, 1909

16TH AMENDMENT PROPOSES INCOME TAXES

The United States had briefly instituted income taxes during the Civil War and again in 1894, but both times they were repealed or struck down by the courts. In the early 20th century, progressives again campaigned for such a tax. Conservatives countered by proposing it as a constitutional amendment, sure that it would not be ratified by three-fourths of the states. They were wrong. The amendment, allowing congress to "lay and collect taxes on incomes, from whatever source derived," did in fact pass and went into effect on February 3, 1913. Less than one percent of the population was affected, at a rate of one

The Ford Model T's sticker price of $825—equivalent to some $29,500 in 2026 dollars—made the vehicle affordable to the middle class.

Less than three hours after hitting an iceberg on a moonless night, the *Titanic* sank in the icy waters of the North Atlantic.

percent of net income. (By the 2020s, well over half the population paid federal income taxes at an average rate of about 15 percent.)

490. DECEMBER 21, 1909

PLAYGOERS ARE DELIGHTFULLY DISMAYED BY FITCH'S *THE CITY*

Clyde Fitch's play *The City,* with its themes of murder, drug addiction, and incest, was a hit with both critics and the public when it opened at New York's Lyric Theatre. As drama moved away from 19th-century attitudes, audiences seemed to enjoy the play's racy approach: Among other things, it pioneered the use of swear words on the American stage ("you're a goddam liar!"). According to some accounts, the deceased playwright's ghost (or an actor who looked very much like him) took a bow at the end. Some audience members are said to have fainted.

491. JULY 4, 1910

JACK JOHNSON DEFEATS JIM JEFFRIES IN THE "FIGHT OF THE CENTURY"

On this day, Black heavyweight boxing champion Jack Johnson fought white former heavyweight champion Jim Jeffries in what was touted as the "Fight of the Century." Taking place in a hastily constructed amphitheater in Reno, Nevada, the event was widely viewed as a contest between Black and white: Jeffries became known as the "white men's hope." Johnson won decisively in 15 rounds. His victory triggered violence against Black citizens around the country. Johnson's detractors tried to quash a film made of the match; in 1912, Congress banned the interstate transportation of all boxing films, a restriction that was not lifted until 1940. Meanwhile, Johnson opened a nightclub with his winnings and went on to fight more matches, though none as consequential.

492. OCTOBER 11, 1910

THEODORE ROOSEVELT TAKES TO THE AIR

Not one to turn down an adventure, former president Theodore Roosevelt took to the skies in a Wright Model B, becoming the first president to fly in an airplane. The craft, flown by Wright demonstration team pilot Arch Hoxsey, took off from Kinloch Field in St. Louis and circled the field twice. Roosevelt frightened his pilot by waving vigorously to the crowd, wiggling the two-seat, single-engine flier. Upon landing, Roosevelt exclaimed, "It was great! First class!" Thirty-three years passed before an airplane carried a sitting president: Teddy's distant cousin, Franklin D. Roosevelt.

OF COURSE, THERE HAVE BEEN WINTER GALES AND STORMS AND FOG AND THE LIKE. BUT IN ALL MY EXPERIENCE I HAVE NEVER BEEN IN AN ACCIDENT OF ANY SORT WORTH SPEAKING ABOUT.

E. J. Smith, Titanic *captain (1907)*

493. MARCH 25, 1911

TRIANGLE FACTORY FIRE LEADS TO DEATH AND REFORM

When a fire broke out on the eighth floor of a building partly occupied by the Triangle Shirtwaist Company, hundreds of garment workers—almost all of them women and immigrants—were trapped by locked doors. One hundred forty-six workers died in the fire, many by leaping to their deaths onto nets that could not hold them. Among the horrified onlookers was 30-year-old Frances Perkins, who would become the U.S. secretary of labor in 1933. "It was a horrifying spectacle," she said later. "We ... felt as though we had been part of it all." The fire eventually led to reforms in worker safety and working conditions. Perkins said that this was "the day the New Deal was born."

494. APRIL 14, 1912

TITANIC SINKS

The White Star luxury liner *Titanic* was on her maiden voyage from Southampton, England, to New York City when it struck an iceberg at 11:40 p.m. Scraping down its side, the iceberg opened up portions of the starboard hull to seawater. Approximately 2,200 passengers were aboard, ranging from immigrants traveling in third-class quarters to millionaires, including the American magnate John Jacob Astor IV. *Titanic*'s 20 lifeboats could not carry all of them, and many were launched only partially filled. When the massive liner sank bow down into the freezing Atlantic at 2:20 a.m., the waters were filled with passengers wearing life vests but unable to withstand the freezing temperatures. More than 1,500 died. A nearby ship, the *Carpathia,* picked up the survivors. Among the dead were more than 100 Americans, including Astor. The tragedy made headlines in the United States and around the world, and remained a source of fascination in books and movies.

In 1985, deep-sea explorer Robert Ballard and his team discovered the remains of the great ship in the North Atlantic Ocean.

495. JULY 7, 1912

JIM THORPE BECOMES THE FIRST NATIVE AMERICAN TO WIN OLYMPIC GOLD

When Swedish king Gustav V presented American athlete Jim Thorpe with gold medals for both the pentathlon and decathlon during a midsummer ceremony, he told Thorpe, "You, sir, are the greatest athlete in the world." Thorpe, with Sac and Fox ancestry, was a fantastically talented athlete. He excelled at track, baseball, and football. In 1913, Thorpe was stripped of his gold medals because he had briefly played minor league baseball, which violated the Olympics' strict rules against professionalism. He went on to play professional baseball and football. His gold medals and first-place finishes were restored in 2022.

The first Native American athlete to win Olympic gold, track star Jim Thorpe later played professional football and baseball.

496. OCTOBER 14, 1912

WOULD-BE ASSASSIN SHOOTS THEODORE ROOSEVELT

Two-time president Theodore Roosevelt had been out of office for four years and was seeking an unprecedented third term with the National Progressive, or "Bull Moose," Party when he left his hotel in Milwaukee that evening. As he stood to wave at the crowd from the back seat of his open car, an unemployed saloonkeeper named John Schrank shot him in the chest with a Colt revolver. The bullet ended up lodging in Roosevelt's rib but was slowed by the candidate's glasses case and a 50-page speech, folded in half, both of which he carried in his breast pocket. Onlookers tackled the assailant, and Roosevelt continued on to the auditorium, where he made his speech. "It takes more than that to kill a Bull Moose," he said. He did not, however, win the election, conceding his defeat to Woodrow Wilson.

497. MARCH 3, 1913

GREAT SUFFRAGE PARADE MEETS HECKLERS IN D.C.

Organizers Alice Paul and Lucy Burns orchestrated their parade demanding women's suffrage for maximum effect. In addition to 5,000 marchers, the procession included 24 floats, nine bands, and a photogenic herald on a white horse. Held on the day before Woodrow Wilson's inauguration, the march along Pennsylvania Avenue drew a crowd of about 250,000. As the women proceeded, the crowds grew increasingly unruly. Men who marched were derided with cries of "Henpecko!" and "Where are your skirts?" Though the grand final spectacle was delayed, the mob scene, attendant publicity, and sympathy helped amplify the suffrage movement in the long run.

498. JUNE 7, 1913

FOUR CLIMBERS MAKE THE FIRST ASCENT OF MOUNT MCKINLEY

Alaska was not yet a state and Denali was known to most outsiders as Mount McKinley when four climbers first reached the mountain's summit. The tallest mountain in North America at 20,310 feet, it was famous for its steep slopes and ferocious weather. In 1913, a Native Alaskan, 21-year-old Walter Harper, became the first to reach the south peak. He was followed closely by Episcopal archdeacon Hudson Stuck; Robert Tatum, a theology student; and Harry Karstens, co-leader of the expedition with Stuck. "I remember no day in my life so full of toil, distress, and exhaustion, and yet so full of happiness and keen gratification," Stuck wrote later.

499. FEBRUARY 8, 1915

THE BIRTH OF A NATION PREMIERES IN LOS ANGELES

D. W. Griffith's feature-length film premiered at L.A.'s Clune's Auditorium under its original name, *The Clansman.* (The title was changed before the film's New York opening in March.) It was both a triumph of filmmaking and an unrepentantly racist tribute to the Ku Klux Klan. Griffith was a seasoned director of shorter films, and *The Birth of a Nation* showed off his innovations in cinematography, editing, and sheer spectacle. The story, which extols the role of the Klan in protecting the "Aryan birthright" during

continued on page 258

Though the 1913 women's suffrage parade drew a big crowd and attention to the cause, women didn't get the vote for nearly seven and a half more years.

SPOTLIGHT

THE VISUAL ARTS

"ART IS ANYTHING you can get away with," Canadian theorist Marshall McLuhan posited. His words would inspire a generation of American visual artists. Shaped by the 20th century's transformational conflicts and cultural revolutions, these men—and, increasingly, women—pioneered new artistic movements. Pop artist Andy Warhol changed the visual landscape with his unorthodox creations featuring Campbell's soup cans and celebrities including Marilyn Monroe and Elizabeth Taylor. Romare Bearden embraced the geometric shapes and fragmentation of cubism, championed in Europe by Pablo Picasso and Georges Braque. Louise Bourgeois and Alexander Calder employed the organic shapes and unexpected juxtapositions of surrealism, favored by Salvador Dalí in Spain and André Breton in France. Jackson Pollock, Willem de Kooning, and Mark Rothko experimented with the spatters, drips, and muscular brushwork of abstract expressionism.

Other artists made their marks in expressly American movements. During the 1930s and '40s, regionalist artists Thomas Hart Benton and Grant Wood depicted small-town and rural life after the Great Depression; painter Edward Hopper brought urban landscapes vividly to life. In a career spanning more than six decades, Georgia O'Keeffe became known as the "mother of American modernism" for her paintings of New Mexico desert landscapes and close-focus flowers. Meanwhile, photography grew in stature: American innovators included experimental surrealist Man Ray, still life virtuoso Edward Weston, landscape legend Ansel Adams, portraitist Richard Avedon, war photographers Margaret Bourke-White and Robert Capa, and documentarians Walker Evans, Diane Arbus, and Dorothea Lange.

Edward Hopper's "Nighthawks" (1942) was completed during World War II and was inspired by his home in New York City's Greenwich Village. An iconic American painting, it's now housed at the Art Institute of Chicago.

IN GENERAL IT CAN BE SAID THAT A NATION'S ART IS GREATEST WHEN IT MOST REFLECTS THE CHARACTER OF ITS PEOPLE.

Edward Hopper *(1933)*

A 1916 act of Congress placed the Old Faithful geyser and other natural wonders under the authority of the new National Park Service.

continued from page 255

Reconstruction, re-created Civil War battle scenes and Abraham Lincoln's assassination over its three-hour length. Crowds in many cities protested the film's offensive message, and in some places it was censored. But *The Birth of a Nation* went on to great success, becoming the highest-grossing film until *Gone With the Wind*. It continued to be a recruiting film for the KKK into the late 20th century.

500. NOVEMBER 19, 1915

UTAH FIRING SQUAD EXECUTES JOE HILL

Joe Hill (born Joel Hägglund) was a Swedish immigrant who became famous as a labor organizer and songwriter. (His song "The Preacher and the Slave" coined the phrase "pie in the sky.") In 1914, he was arrested for the murder of a Utah grocery store owner. Hill had reported to a doctor with a bullet wound, which he said he'd received in a fight over a woman. The trial seemed to be as much about his labor activism as the evidence, and Hill was sentenced to death. Despite appeals for clemency, a Utah firing squad executed Hill at Utah's Sugar House Park, which housed the state prison. As a martyr for the cause of labor, Hill became far more famous in death than he was in life.

501. AUGUST 25, 1916

WOODROW WILSON ESTABLISHES THE NATIONAL PARK SERVICE

After Yellowstone became the country's (and the world's) first national park in 1872, the U.S. government brought dozens of other parks and monuments under its protection, including Yosemite, Crater Lake, and Mesa Verde. These were administered by various U.S. agencies, including the Department of the Interior, the War Department, and the Department of Agriculture. The National Park Service Organic Act of 1916 created an agency within Interior that pledged to "conserve the scenery and the natural and historic objects and the wild life therein and ... leave them unimpaired for the enjoyment of future generations." By the 2020s, the country's national parks welcomed more than 300 million visits a year, almost one visit for every U.S. citizen.

Margaret Sanger was jailed for opening her first birth control clinic. Sanger's efforts ultimately led to legal contraception access.

502. OCTOBER 16, 1916

MARGARET SANGER OPENS A BIRTH CONTROL CLINIC

Margaret Sanger knew that the birth control clinic she opened at 46 Amboy Street in Brooklyn would not last long; in New York, contraception and information about it was banned. The clinic Sanger started in the poor, immigrant-dominated neighborhood drew long lines of women and their baby carriages for nine days before police shut it down. Sanger and her sister, who had aided her efforts, were sentenced to 30 days in jail. The publicity from the trial and sentences helped raise awareness of contraception as a health issue, and laws began to change so that doctors could prescribe birth control as a medical measure.

503. JANUARY 25, 1917

SAN FRANCISCO SEX WORKERS MARCH TO CHURCH

Approximately 300 sex workers from San Francisco's Tenderloin district marched to the Central Methodist Church to confront its pastor, Reverend Paul Smith, who had been leading an anti-prostitution reform movement. The working women put on their finest apparel and, with Reverend Smith's permission, filled his church that Thursday in a demonstration of solidarity. "Nearly all these women before you are mothers, are supporting children. Do you know that?" asked madam Reggie Gamble from the pulpit. The women drew sympathetic onlookers but did not win the hearts of local lawmakers. In the coming weeks, officials closed every brothel and shut down more than 200 cafés and "parlor houses" in the Tenderloin neighborhood.

504. APRIL 2, 1917

JEANNETTE RANKIN IS SWORN IN TO CONGRESS

Congress had not given women the vote on a national basis, but Montana and other states had already done so when Jeannette Pickering Rankin was elected to an at-large U.S. House seat from Montana in 1916. She became the first woman to hold office in the U.S. Congress. Rankin was a longtime advocate for women's suffrage as well as a staunch pacifist. In her first week in office, she joined 49 others in voting against entry into World War I. After her congressional seat was redistricted, she left the assembly for more than 20 years. She was reelected just as the country was entering World War II. This time, Rankin's was the only vote against entering the war.

505. APRIL 6, 1917

U.S. JOINS THE FIRST WORLD WAR

President Woodrow Wilson won reelection in 1916 with the slogan "He kept us out of war." Many Americans had favored neutrality in the almost three-year-old European conflict, but sympathies and supplies generally went to the Allies. The sinking of *Lusitania* renewed submarine attacks on American ships in 1917, and the revelation that Germany was trying to win Mexico to its side pushed U.S. lawmakers into a more aggressive stance.

Despite protection efforts like these U.S. Army medics' masks, a global flu pandemic killed at least 21 million in 1918 and 1919.

On April 2, Wilson addressed Congress and asked for a declaration of war, saying, "the world must be made safe for democracy." On April 6, the U.S. House adopted the war resolution, and America joined what was not yet known as World War I.

506. MARCH 4, 1918

FIRST U.S. SOLDIER REPORTS SICK WITH THE "SPANISH" FLU

On this day, a soldier at Kansas's Camp Funston (now Fort Riley) missed roll call due to influenza. Within three weeks, more than 1,000 of the camp's 56,000-plus soldiers were sick. Soon, other bases as well as Navy ships began reporting illnesses, followed by outbreaks among Allied troops when those ships reached Europe. The severe influenza, which could kill within a day, spread via train and ship through military and civilian populations. It became a worldwide pandemic, killing in three devastating waves during 1918 and early 1919. The illness became known as the "Spanish" flu only because early cases were widely reported in Spanish newspapers and suppressed in other countries. At least 21 million people eventually died; some estimates put the total closer to 100 million.

AS A WOMAN I CAN'T GO TO WAR, AND I REFUSE TO SEND ANYONE ELSE.

Jeannette Rankin *(1941)*

507. MARCH 19, 1918

DAYLIGHT SAVING TIME BECOMES OFFICIAL

Following the example of many European countries during World War I, President Woodrow Wilson signed into law the Standard Time Act of 1918 and instituted daylight saving time (DST) across the United States. The bill recognized the five time zones that railroads across the country had already adopted. Congresses over the years have had mixed feelings about DST, as constituents complained about the dark mornings or evenings. It was repealed in 1919, reinstituted in 1942, repealed again in 1945, and brought back in 1966.

508. OCTOBER 26, 1918

CHOCTAW TELEPHONE SQUADS BAFFLE THE ENEMY IN FRANCE

Though they were not yet acknowledged as U.S. citizens, thousands of Native American soldiers fought in World War I. There, they played a vital role in transmitting messages in their own languages on Allied telephones, which German intelligence had often compromised. On this day during the Meuse-Argonne offensive, Choctaw soldiers on each end of a telephone line coordinated the retreat of Allied troops from Chuffilly-Roche; an attack the next day caught the Germans by surprise. The success of Choctaw and other Indigenous troops as communicators led to their increased role as code talkers in World War II.

509. JANUARY 15, 1919

GREAT MOLASSES FLOOD SWEEPS THROUGH BOSTON'S NORTH END

An industrial disaster near the Boston waterfront gave rise to the phrase "as slow as molasses in January." Around 12:30 p.m., a 50-foot-high, shoddily constructed tank holding more than two million gallons of molasses ruptured and sent a tsunami of the sticky fluid rumbling through the city's streets. The wave was initially up to 40 feet high and traveled as fast as 35 miles an hour, knocking down people, horses, and houses. As it cooled and slowed, it became even more dangerous, trapping injured people in a dense, viscous shroud and filling their noses and mouths. Rescuers, covered from head to foot in molasses, pulled victims out of collapsed buildings. Twenty-one people were killed and 150 injured. The tank's owner, United States Industrial Alcohol Company, was eventually found liable for the accident, paying out more than $600,000 to the victims and their families.

510. JANUARY 16, 1919

STATES RATIFY THE 18TH AMENDMENT

"The last nail was driven into the coffin of King Alcohol yesterday," wrote the *Carbondale Leader* on January 17, after the state of Nebraska ratified the Eighteenth Amendment to the Constitution. The amendment, which prohibited the "manufacture, sale, or transportation of intoxicating liquors," had been long in the making. Movements to ban alcohol had begun in the 19th century and gained ground in the 20th, with motives ranging from the religious to the nativist. In October, Congress passed the Volstead Act over Woodrow Wilson's veto, providing for the enforcement of the amendment. Prohibition went into effect in 1920, but enforcement had limited success. The 21st Amendment repealed the 18th Amendment in 1933, and King Alcohol crawled back out of his coffin.

COOKE'S ARMY STORES FOR CLOTHING and BOOTS. 9, Cheapside, Derby.

Daily Derby Express

HoulstoN DIAMOND, SAPPHIRE, EMERALD, RUBY, PEARL, OPAL RINGS DERBY

JUNE 28, 1919.

STORY OF THE GREATEST WAR IN HISTORY.

PEACE SIGNED.

GERMAN REPRESENTATIVES PUT PEN TO PAPER TO-DAY.

LONG-DRAWN NEGOTIATIONS COME TO AN END AT LAST.

Let the joy bells ring, for Peace, at any rate so far as the arch enemy is concerned, has been signed, and the German dream of world dominion lies humbled in the dust. That is the meaning of the brief telegram just received at the "Express" Office as follows:—

German Envoys have signed the peace terms to-day.

The nightmare which had held the world in thrall for nearly five long years has at last been lifted, for though the killing and maiming of men ceased when the armistice was signed on the never-to-be-forgotten 11th of November last, yet there remained the lurking fear that the obstinacy of the defeated Huns would entail a resumption of fighting and the calling up of men who had been demobilised—men who had never expected they would be soldiers, yet who had offered their all in the good cause. Now, at long last, when the travail and the turmoil are over, we can sing songs of triumph, of victory of the right over wrong. To-day is a day of history—a day which will stand out as an epoch day in the annals of time. What England has done is immeasurably greater than anything she has ever done before. She risked all her glory, all her wealth, all her pride of leadership for the cause of justice, and right amply has her ideals been justified—been proved. Yet in these days of triumph—in days when it feels good to be alive, let not mere triumph reign in our hearts, but let us recall the memories of those who alas will never return, and with one accord let us render thanks to Him in whose hands destiny is hid. Let us humbly accord to Him the glory, and pray that the ideals for which we have fought may never forsake this island, this gem in the Western Seas.

LATEST NEWS

"Victory of the right over wrong": That's how a Derby, England, newspaper hailed the signing of the Treaty of Versailles that ended World War I.

511. FEBRUARY 26, 1919

CONGRESS ESTABLISHES GRAND CANYON NATIONAL PARK

One of the world's great natural wonders, Arizona's Grand Canyon runs 277 miles east to west; it drops one mile from its rim to the Colorado River. Native American peoples such as the Havasupai, Navajo, Southern Paiute, Hopi, and more, have long lived within or next to the canyon, but the remote area first came to outside notice when European explorers began to venture in during the 1500s. By the 19th century, writers and photographers publicized its beauty, and the canyon underwent a long process of government protection, designated a forest reserve in 1893 and a national monument in 1908. On this day, Congress under President Woodrow Wilson passed an act naming the Grand Canyon as a national park. Today, it is the third most visited national park in the United States.

512. MAY 27, 1919

ALBERT C. READ FLIES ACROSS THE ATLANTIC

Eight years before Charles Lindbergh made the first solo, nonstop flight across the Atlantic, Lt. Cmdr. Albert C. Read of the U.S. Navy and a five-man crew completed the first world's first transatlantic flight in their Curtiss NC-4 flying boat. The four-engine seaplane took off from Newfoundland on May 16, navigating by following a line of naval ships stationed at 50-mile intervals on the sea below. The crew stopped at the Azores while waiting for the weather to clear and reached Lisbon, Portugal, on May 27.

Native American peoples had explored and inhabited the Grand Canyon for thousands of years before it was named a national park in 1919.

513. JUNE 28, 1919

TREATY OF VERSAILLES ENDS WORLD WAR I

In the glittering Hall of Mirrors of France's Palace of Versailles, world leaders including U.S. president Woodrow Wilson, British prime minister David Lloyd George, French prime minister Georges Clemenceau, and Italian prime minister Vittorio Orlando signed a treaty with Germany, formally ending the Great War. More than 100,000 Americans died in battle or from disease during the conflict. The treaty began to refashion the map of Europe, redrawing borders for such countries as Germany, France, and Poland. It also required heavy reparation payments from Germany, while calling for the establishment of a League of Nations. Despite Wilson's advocacy for the league, that provision met serious opposition in the U.S. Senate upon the president's return home. In March 1920, the Senate rejected the entire treaty, opting instead to execute the Knox-Porter Resolution the following year.

514. OCTOBER 9, 1919

"BLACK SOX" LOSE THE WORLD SERIES

By a score of 10 to 5, the Cincinnati Reds beat the Chicago White Sox to win the 1919 World Series. The White Sox losses had been marked by bouts of inexplicably poor

Bill Wambsganss (left, with teammate Elmer Smith) made baseball history with the only unassisted triple play in a World Series game.

pitching, hitting, and fielding. The press immediately began to question the outcome, with some speculating—correctly as it turned out—that players had thrown the series in exchange for payments from gambling interests. In the end, eight White Sox players were indicted for being in on the fix, including star slugger "Shoeless" Joe Jackson and the usually unhittable pitcher Eddie Cicotte. Baseball commissioner Kenesaw Mountain Landis threw the eight players out of the game permanently, and the 1919 team became known in history as the Black Sox.

515. AUGUST 26, 1920

WOMEN WIN THE RIGHT TO VOTE

More than 70 years had passed since women at the Seneca Falls Convention had called for the right to vote. But on August 18, 1920, they gained that agency when the state of Tennessee ratified the 19th Amendment. The amendment, certified eight days later, stated, "The right of citizens of the United States to vote shall not be denied or abridged by the United States or any State on account of sex." Fifteen states had already granted voting rights to women, but the amendment promised the vote across the country. Barriers to voting still remained in the form of poll taxes, literacy tests, and other restrictions that disproportionately affected women of color—barriers that were not addressed until the Voting Rights Act of 1965.

516. OCTOBER 10, 1920

BILL WAMBSGANSS MAKES AN UNASSISTED TRIPLE PLAY

Runners were on first and second with no outs in the fifth inning of World Series Game 5 between the Brooklyn Robins and the Cleveland Indians. Robins pitcher Clarence Mitchell stepped up to bat and hit a line drive to Indians second baseman Bill Wambsganss. Wambsganss caught the line drive, stepped on second base as that runner was dashing toward third, and tagged the runner from first, completing the only unassisted triple play in World Series history.

517. NOVEMBER 2, 1920

RADIO REACHES OUT

The Westinghouse Electric and Manufacturing Company launched the mass media age when it sponsored the first commercial radio broadcast from newly formed station KDKA in Pittsburgh, Pennsylvania. On the station's first night, announcer Leo Rosenberg relayed the live results of the presidential race between Warren G. Harding and James Cox. Westinghouse was hoping that the new medium would help them sell their home radio receivers, but broadcast radio quickly became much more than a sales tool. Within four years, the country had 600 commercial radio stations.

THAT WAS THE SADDEST DAY OF MY LIFE. THAT RIOT CHEATED US OUT OF CHILDHOOD INNOCENCE.

Beulah Lane Keenan Smith, *survivor of the Tulsa race massacre (1921)*

518. MAY 31, 1921

WHITE MOBS DESTROY A TULSA NEIGHBORHOOD

Tulsa, Oklahoma's prosperous Greenwood neighborhood was known as "Black Wall Street." Enraged by a false report that a young African American man had attacked a white female elevator operator, white mobs rioted, fought Black defenders, and destroyed the area in what would become known as the Tulsa race massacre. White authorities and National Guard troops moved thousands of African American residents to detention centers and held them there while looters robbed their homes before setting the buildings on fire. Witnesses reported that airplanes dropped flaming turpentine bombs on rooftops. As many as 300 residents may have been killed, and at least 1,250 homes were lost. No one ever served prison time for the riots, and Black residents were unable to recover money from their insurance companies. The entire incident was buried in historical records until a commission began to investigate it in the 1990s.

519. AUGUST 16, 1921

FIRST POP-UP BREAD TOASTER IS PATENTED

Minnesota inventor Charles Strite was tired of burned toast. At the factory where he ate breakfast, the commercial toasting machines were cumbersome contraptions that toasted bread on only one side and had to be turned off manually. So Strite devised and patented the "Bread-toaster," the first pop-up, two-sided toaster. "An object," he wrote in his application, "is to provide a device of this character which may be set to toast bread for different lengths of time according to the degree of crispness desired and in which the heat will be automatically cut off after the expiration of a period of time ... Another object is to provide a device in which the toasted bread is lifted partly out of the casing when the operation is completed." The Bread-toaster was renamed the Toastmaster and went on to huge success in restaurants and home kitchens; Toastmaster toasters continue to be sold today.

520. AUGUST 30, 1921

BATTLE OF BLAIR MOUNTAIN BEGINS

Ten thousand coal miners, protesting dangerous working conditions and low wages, began to march through southwestern West Virginia into a face-off with local sheriffs and civilian recruits near Logan County's Blair Mountain. The two sides battled for five days, using World War I–era machine guns, rifles, and other firearms. On September 2, President Warren G. Harding ordered federal troops and airplanes into the fight against the miners. The union workers, whose fight was directed toward mine owners and not the government, laid down their arms on September 4. An estimated 16 miners died in the battle, one of the largest labor uprisings in history.

Robert Frost claimed his poem "Stopping by Woods on a Snowy Evening" took only "a few minutes" to write one morning in June 1922.

521. APRIL 14, 1922

NEWS BREAKS ABOUT THE TEAPOT DOME SCANDAL

While the *Wall Street Journal* did not use the word "corrupt" when it broke the news that a U.S. Cabinet member had secretly leased valuable federal land to a patron, the implications were clear. The newspaper revealed that Secretary of the Interior Albert Fall had granted exclusive rights to oil-rich land near Wyoming's Teapot Dome outcropping to oil baron Harry Sinclair. He granted similar rights to other oil lands to another oilman, Edward Doheny. Subsequent investigations showed that Sinclair and Doheny then passed on $200,000 in bonds and $100,000 in cash, respectively, to Fall. Investigations dragged on, but in 1929, Fall was sentenced to one year in prison. The scandal stained President Warren G. Harding's reputation, though he was not directly involved; "Teapot Dome" became a watchword for government corruption, much as "Watergate" did in the 1970s.

522. MAY 30, 1922

LINCOLN MEMORIAL IS DEDICATED

On this day, President Warren G. Harding, Chief Justice William Howard Taft, and Tuskegee Institute president Robert Moton dedicated the Lincoln Memorial on the National Mall. Flanking the 19-foot-tall seated sculpture of Lincoln were the carved words of his Gettysburg Address and his Second Inaugural Address. Although 57 years had passed since Lincoln's assassination, reminders of the Civil War era lived on in the segregation of the audience into white and Black sections and in the presence of Lincoln's eldest son, 78-year-old Robert Todd Lincoln—a living reminder of the martyred president—at the ceremony.

523. SEPTEMBER 13, 1922

STRAW HAT RIOTS ERUPT IN NEW YORK

In an era when virtually all men, from dockworkers to stockbrokers, wore hats on the street, an unwritten rule dictated that summer's straw hats be exchanged for felt hats on September 15. For years, obstreperous youths had marked the day by snatching and smashing the straw hats of anyone who wore them on the street. In 1922, they jumped the gun and began grabbing and destroying straw hats on the 13th. Outraged hat wearers fought back, and the clashes erupted into larger riots. Many rioters were arrested, and the brawls died down within two days. A New York magistrate, aptly named Hatting, imposed

Modeled after the Parthenon in Athens, the Lincoln Memorial was dedicated before a crowd of some 50,000 on Washington's National Mall.

Enslaved African men, women, and children introduced the dance known as the juba to South Carolina; from the dance's roots grew the global dance craze the Charleston.

fines on the hat squashers and declared that a man "has a right to wear [a straw hat] in a January snowstorm if he wishes."

524. MARCH 7, 1923

ROBERT FROST PUBLISHES "STOPPING BY WOODS ON A SNOWY EVENING"

The New England poet wrote his most famous poem in a single burst on a June morning in 1922, after staying up all night finishing his long poem "New Hampshire." It appeared in the *New Republic* in 1923 before being published in his volume *New Hampshire,* which won the Pulitzer Prize in 1924. Deceptively simple, with allusions to the alluring darkness at the end of life, the poem became a classroom and eulogy staple.

525. OCTOBER 29, 1923

***RUNNIN' WILD* INTRODUCES THE CHARLESTON**

"Charleston! Charleston! Made in Carolina / Some dance, some prance, I'll say there's nothing finer / Than the Charleston, Charleston." The origins of the wildly popular Charleston dance of the 1920s are obscure, but African Americans had been performing the arm-waving, forward-and-back gambol for years when composer James P. Johnson captured it on the stage in his Broadway musical *Runnin' Wild.* That show, now largely forgotten, featured a large cast of singers and dancers and made the Charleston music and dance a staple for flappers everywhere, as well as an enduring symbol of the upbeat energy of the jazz age.

526. FEBRUARY 18, 1924

NEW YORK BECOMES THE BIG APPLE

For decades, the term "big apple" had meant a big deal, an object of desire. In the 1920s, it came to mean New York City. The nickname was popularized by horse racing columnist John J. Fitz Gerald, whose column in New York's *Morning Telegraph* debuted under the title "Around the Big Apple." Under the title were the lines: "The Big Apple. The dream of every lad that ever threw a leg over a thoroughbred and the goal of all horsemen. There's only one Big Apple. That's New York." The nickname was widespread through the 1930s, faded for a few decades, and was revived in the 1970s as part of a tourism campaign that would make the moniker both ubiquitous and universally recognized.

A NOVEL SIGHT, THAT DINNER—WHITE CRITICS, WHOM "EVERYBODY" KNOWS, NEGRO WRITERS, WHOM "NOBODY" KNEW—MEETING ON COMMON GROUND.

New York Herald*, reporting on the noted Harlem dinner (1925)*

527. MARCH 21, 1924

A DINNER SPARKS THE HARLEM RENAISSANCE

By the early 1920s, as African Americans moved north during the Great Migration, New York's Harlem neighborhood had become home to established and unknown artists. Recognizing the influx of talent, Alain Locke, a professor at Howard University, and Charles Johnson, the editor of *Opportunity* magazine, turned a book launch dinner for author Jessie Fauset at Manhattan's Civic Club into an intellectual brainstorming session. Among the guests were W. E. B. Du Bois, Countee Cullen, Eugene O'Neill, Gwendolyn Bennett, and Carl Van Doren. The dinner's organizers committed themselves to attracting and supporting the writers and other artists who would go on to become the heart of the Harlem Renaissance, an artistic and literary movement that would celebrate and promote African American identity and culture.

528. JUNE 2, 1924

INDIGENOUS PEOPLE GAIN CITIZENSHIP

Although more than 12,000 Native Americans served in World War I, not all Native Americans in the United States and Alaska were acknowledged as American citizens until Calvin Coolidge signed into law 1924's Indian Citizenship Act. Prior to this decree, only some Indigenous people had been granted citizenship—primarily those who had accepted plots carved out from tribal lands as part of the government's attempts to assimilate Native Americans into white culture. The Indian Citizenship Act granted "all non-citizen Indians born within the territorial limits of the United States" full citizenship, without impairing their right to tribal property.

529. OCTOBER 16, 1924

MA RAINEY RECORDS "SEE SEE RIDER BLUES"

Blues singer Gertrude "Ma" Rainey performed her iconic song "See See Rider Blues" for years to both Black and white audiences in traveling tent shows. The languorous tune begins in sadness and ends in retribution: "See, see, rider, see what you done done, Lawd, Lawd, Lawd / Made me love you, now your gal done come … I'm gonna buy me a pistol just as long as I am tall, Lawd, Lawd, Lawd / Gonna kill my man and catch the Cannonball." In October 1924, Rainey recorded the song at Paramount Records with a crack team of musicians including Louis Armstrong on cornet and Fletcher Henderson on piano. It became one of the most iconic and enduring blues songs: More than 100 versions of "See See Rider" have been performed since 1924. Opinions still vary on just who or what the "rider" was.

It has come to be known as the "great American novel," but when first published, *The Great Gatsby* sold poorly and got mixed reviews.

530. FEBRUARY 2, 1925

FIRST SEARS RETAIL STORE OPENS

Already a successful mail-order company, Sears, Roebuck & Co. opened its first retail store in the company's enormous Merchandise Mart in Chicago's West Side on this day. The comprehensive department store included an optical shop and a soda fountain. Within two years Sears had expanded to 27 stores that appealed to America's rapidly growing population of car owners, who didn't mind driving to a city's outskirts for shopping. At its height, the retailer—with close to 3,500 outposts across the country—was hailed as the epitome of old-fashioned American values. It filed for bankruptcy in 2018.

531. APRIL 10, 1925

F. SCOTT FITZGERALD PUBLISHES *THE GREAT GATSBY*

The Great Gatsby, F. Scott Fitzgerald's classic jazz age novel of American ambition and deception, was published on this day to middling reviews and poor sales. H. L. Mencken called it "no more than a glorified anecdote," though he did praise the "charm and beauty of the writing." The book did not become a bestseller until it was handed out for free to American troops during World War II, several years after the author's death. It then garnered renewed attention from the literary establishment and has since been called the Great American Novel. Today, it is a foundational part of the American literary canon, commonly taught in high schools across the country.

532. MAY 7, 1925

JOHN SCOPES IS ARRESTED FOR TEACHING EVOLUTION

In March 1925, the state of Tennessee passed the Butler Act, which made it illegal for any public schoolteacher to impart "any theory that denies the story of the Divine Creation of man as taught in the Bible, and to teach instead that man has descended from a lower order of animals." The American Civil Liberties Union (ACLU) believed the law violated the First Amendment and sought a teacher who would serve as a test case in court. John Scopes,

Blues singer Gertrude "Ma" Rainey and her instrumentalists toured the United States performing "See See Rider Blues" and other hits.

a popular young science teacher in Dayton, Tennessee, volunteered; the ensuing trial riveted the nation. More than 100 correspondents reported on the "Monkey Trial" as famed defense attorney Clarence Darrow squared off against equally famous politician and Christian speaker William Jennings Bryan. In the end, Scopes was convicted of violating the law, but his conviction was overturned on a technicality by the state supreme court. The Butler Act remained on the books until 1967, though it was never again enforced; teaching evolution in public schools continued to be contested in the courts into the 21st century.

533. AUGUST 8, 1925

KKK MARCHES IN WASHINGTON

In the mid-1920s, the Ku Klux Klan was at the peak of a second wave of popularity. Millions of Americans belonged to the white supremacist group, including well-known business owners, church leaders, and politicians. To demonstrate its strength and apparent respectability, the Klan organized a vast march down Pennsylvania Avenue in Washington, D.C. Some 30,000 white-robed members, wearing pointed hats but with their faces uncovered, walked in formation 22 abreast from the Capitol to the Washington Monument. There, a thunderstorm struck and the marchers hastily dispersed. Despite the show

Crowds greeted Charles Lindbergh at an airport outside Paris after his 33.5-hour nonstop flight across the Atlantic from New York.

of strength, the KKK gradually diminished in numbers after the march, though it did not disappear. In the 21st century, some chapters remained in the Midwest and Southeast, with Klan members mingling online among other right-wing extremists.

534. JUNE 23, 1926

FIRST SAT TEST IS ADMINISTERED

"A steel cylinder, 20 inches in diameter, is being turned on a lathe at a speed of 1,000 revolutions per minute. To what speed must the lathe be changed in order to retain the same surface speed on the cylinder when it is turned down from 20 inches to 10 inches?" This and 314 other questions appeared on the first Scholastic Aptitude Test in 1926. The standardized test replaced an earlier, essay-based exam from the College Board that favored the kinds of students who could translate passages into Latin and Greek. Just over 8,000 students, mostly male, took the first SAT in an era when less than 5 percent of Americans graduated from college. More than three million students currently take the SAT or the similar American College Test (ACT) each year.

535. APRIL 21, 1927

LEVEES BEGIN TO BURST DURING THE GREAT MISSISSIPPI FLOOD

After months of heavy rains, the Mississippi River broke through its bounds throughout the South in the spring of 1927, covering more than 27,000 square miles to depths up to 30 feet. Muddy, debris-filled floodwaters drowned parts of Illinois, Indiana, Missouri, Kentucky, Texas, Oklahoma, Kansas, Tennessee, Arkansas, Mississippi, and Louisiana. More than 700,000 people were displaced in this, the largest flood in American history. In its wake, the U.S. government put in place a new system of levees and floodways. Herbert Hoover's adept handling of the crisis as commerce secretary led to his election as president (a role in which he was not as adept, losing the goodwill of the American people as he failed to contain the Great Depression).

536. MAY 21, 1927

CHARLES LINDBERGH COMPLETES SOLO TRANSATLANTIC FLIGHT

At 10:22 p.m., the formerly obscure young airmail pilot Charles Lindbergh touched down amid frenzied crowds at Le Bourget Aerodrome in Paris, completing the world's first solo, nonstop flight across the Atlantic. It took Lindbergh 33.5 sleepless hours to fly his single-engine aircraft, *The Spirit of St. Louis,* from Roosevelt Field on Long Island across waters without navigational markers. Lindbergh's success won him the $25,000 Orteig Prize and also made him immensely famous: An estimated four million people flocked to a ticker-tape parade in his honor when he returned to New York.

WHY SHOULDN'T I FLY FROM NEW YORK TO PARIS? I'M ALMOST TWENTY-FIVE.

Charles Lindbergh, The Spirit of St. Louis *(1953)*

537. SEPTEMBER 7, 1927

PHILO FARNSWORTH INVENTS TELEVISION

By the time he was 15, Utah farm boy Philo Farnsworth had already thought up the mechanism for electronic television and sketched it out for his high school chemistry teacher. By the time he was 21, he had gathered investors who backed him as he turned the sketch into reality. On September 7, 1927, Farnsworth's "image dissector" vacuum tube camera captured the image of a single straight line and transmitted it electronically to a receiver in another room in his San Francisco lab. "We've done it," he announced to onlookers. "There you have electronic television." Farnsworth patented his device and eventually formed his own company, Farnsworth Television, which struggled and was taken over by International Telephone & Telegraph in 1949. Farnsworth earned millions from this invention and many others but managed to spend almost all of it before his death in 1971.

538. DECEMBER 25, 1928

NOUN AND VERB RODEO BEGINS IN NEW YORK

Endurance contests of all kinds were immensely popular in the 1920s. Few were as odd and off-putting, though, as the Noun and Verb Rodeo, which began on this day in

Manhattan's 71st Regiment Armory. The 36 contestants, each with his or her own tent, were required to speak without stopping for as long as possible (except for a few scheduled breaks). Speakers included actors, a steeplejack, and an orator billing himself as "Sirfessor F. W. Wilkesbarr, Lord of Interpretations, Master of Mentoidology, the Demigod of the Demi-Damned." Despite the colorful monikers, the spectacle proved to be just as dreary and unwatchable as it sounded. After four days and nights, the contest ended in a tie; it is unclear whether the two winners—lifeguard Betty Wilson and steeplejack Howard Williams—ever received their portions of the $1,000 prize.

539. FEBRUARY 14, 1929

SEVEN ARE SHOT IN THE ST. VALENTINE'S DAY MASSACRE

On this morning, four men—two of them dressed as police officers—lined up seven men associated with George "Bugs" Moran's bootlegging gang and machine-gunned them against the wall of a garage in Chicago. No one was ever charged in the killings, but the assailants were widely believed to belong to rival gangster Al Capone's gang. Capone himself was in Florida at the time of the murders; Bugs Moran was supposed to be at the garage but had been running late. The shocking murders cemented Capone's control over Chicago gangs, but they also made him a focus of federal attention. In 1931, a tax evasion charge ended his career. Public horror at the killings led to the nation's first federal gun control law, the National Firearms Act of 1934, which curtailed the sales of the kind of machine guns used in the killings.

540. MARCH 15, 1929

EDWIN HUBBLE'S DISCOVERIES PROVE THE UNIVERSE IS EXPANDING

Astronomer Edwin Hubble and the newly built Mount Wilson telescope, with its huge, 100-inch lens, were an ideal match. Working at Mount Wilson in 1925, Hubble showed that distant clouds of gas, called nebulae, were actually galaxies like our own in a vast universe. In 1929, he topped that discovery with a paper published in the *Proceedings of the National Academy of Sciences.* In it, he showed that the farther a galaxy was from our own, the faster it was moving away. In other words, the universe was expanding. This discovery naturally led astronomers to the next conclusion: If we track the expansion backward in time, the universe once must have been unimaginably small before it blew outward in what we now call the big bang.

541. OCTOBER 7, 1929

WILLIAM FAULKNER PUBLISHES *THE SOUND AND THE FURY*

Mississippi writer William Faulkner had published several books by 1929, but *The Sound and the Fury* was the novel that established him as a major American writer. The ambitious work traces the downfall of an old southern family from the perspective of four narrators, one of them an intellectually disabled man. Some sections unfold in a stream-of-

The recording artists in Kansas City's thriving African American music scene included jazz pianist Bennie Moten and his orchestra.

consciousness style. Faulkner himself struggled with the writing and considered the book a "splendid failure." But over time it was recognized as a great American novel; *The Sound and the Fury* was among the works that earned Faulkner the Nobel Prize in 1949.

542. OCTOBER 17, 1929

KANSAS CITY JAZZ GAINS A HEADQUARTERS

Excluded from white workers' unions in the thriving Kansas City music scene, African American musicians formed their own union in 1917. By the 1920s, they were so successful that, on this day, they purchased their own headquarters, remodeling it to include studios and a dance hall. The building and union members formed the heart of the influential Kansas City style of music and drew musicians from around the country; the membership came to include such artists as Lester Young, Charlie Parker, and Count Basie. The building remains one of the oldest continually operating jazz venues in the U.S. and is a central factor in making Kansas City the country's only UNESCO City of Music.

Once the world's tallest building at 1,250 feet, the Empire State Building also became famous as a giant ape's perch in the 1933 film *King Kong*.

543. OCTOBER 28, 1929

STOCK MARKET BEGINS TO CRASH ON "BLACK MONDAY"

In the wake of World War I, the U.S. economy boomed. The stock market boomed along with it, rising 600 percent from 1921 to 1929. Many individual investors put their money into stocks for the first time, often using borrowed funds. A slowing economy and the feverish market began to spook some investors, and on Thursday, October 24, Wall Street saw its first big sell-off. The market recovered by Friday, but on what came to be called Black Monday, the big crash began. The stock market fell by close to 13 percent that day, followed by a further 12 percent the next day. The crash did not in itself cause the Great Depression, but it was a sizable warning sign. By 1930, the market had recovered somewhat before plunging to the lowest levels of the 20th century two years later in the Depression.

544. FEBRUARY 18, 1930

CLYDE TOMBAUGH DISCOVERS PLUTO

Kansas farm boy Clyde Tombaugh could not afford to attend college, but in his spare time he pursued his passion for astronomy using a telescope he made from old farm machinery and car parts. In 1929, he sent some of his astronomical drawings to the director of Arizona's Lowell Observatory, who hired the 22-year-old to look for the hypothetical Planet X, a body past the orbit of Neptune whose existence had been inferred from gravitational effects. On this day, Tombaugh compared two photographic plates of the stars taken six days apart and saw that a small, fuzzy dot had moved in the foreground from one plate to the next. It was Planet X, later named Pluto, after the Roman god of the underworld. In 2006, it was reclassified as a dwarf planet.

545. OCTOBER 15, 1930

DUKE ELLINGTON RECORDS "MOOD INDIGO"

Edward "Duke" Ellington claimed that he wrote his bluesy, innovative jazz masterpiece in 15 minutes while waiting for his mother to cook dinner. In truth, he built it around a melody known as "Dreamy Blues," a tune that became the clarinet solo in the expanded work. What set Ellington's composition apart from other jazz of the time was his use of instrumental voicing. The muted trombone was used at the top of its range, while the clarinet was employed at the lower end. The upside-down arrangement gave the piece a distinctive timbre. Although Ellington had been on the music scene for years, the song is recognized as his first major composition. With the later addition of lyrics, "Mood Indigo" went on to become a jazz standard for both bands and vocalists.

TAGGING BASHFULLY BEHIND ITS BROTHERS, THE NEW PLANET'S EXACT WHEREABOUTS, SIZE AND AGE ARE STILL UNKNOWN.

New York Times, *in an article announcing Pluto's discovery (1930)*

546. DECEMBER 11, 1930

BANK RUN DEEPENS THE DEPRESSION

In November, a series of bank failures in the South was followed by a bigger blow. The fourth largest bank in New York City, the Bank of the United States, had failed in its attempts to merge with three other financial institutions: the Manufacturers Trust, the Public National Bank and Trust, and the International Trust. The failure started a run on the bank, which closed on this day after depositors rushed to withdraw their money before it failed altogether. (Federal deposit insurance did not become a reality until later in the 1930s.) This bank run caused a wider panic and further runs on other banks. Within months, the panic subsided. But the remaining anxiety cast a pall on business and helped push the country deeper into the Depression.

547. APRIL 11, 1931

EMPIRE STATE BUILDING LIGHTS UP

President Herbert Hoover flicked a symbolic switch in Washington, D.C., and the lights went on in New York's brand-new Empire State Building. It was the tallest building in the world at 1,250 feet (to the top of the lightning rod) and 102 stories. Financed by investors including former New York governor Al Smith and members of the du Pont family, the skyscraper went up in just one year and 45 days at a rate of up to four and a half stories a week. It immediately became one of the most recognizable buildings in the world, a status reinforced by its starring role in 1933's blockbuster movie *King Kong*.

SPOTLIGHT

A NATION OF IMMIGRANTS

B

BETWEEN THE LATE 1800s and early 1920s, 25 million immigrants arrived in the United States in what 20th-century historians called the great wave of immigration. This new migration would shape the United States socially, economically, and culturally as the century unfolded.

Immigration would become a contentious issue as certain groups were excluded for entering the country illegally. Quotas that Congress set in the 1920s favored northern and western Europeans, and after World Wars I and II, some two million immigrants arrived, bringing skills and customs from home. After reforms in 1965 eliminated the pro-Europe predilection and prioritized family reunification, people from more diverse nations could immigrate, making the United States more multilingual and multicultural.

In the two decades after the Vietnam War, some 1.2 million Southeast Asian refugees arrived, resettling in California, the Gulf Coast, and the Midwest. After Fidel Castro rose to power, roughly 1.2 million Cubans left for the United States. From 1965 to 2000, more than nine million Mexicans, two million Central Americans, and 1.9 million South Americans immigrated, hoping to get jobs, join relatives, or seek asylum.

In time, the country would enact stronger limits on immigration. The Refugee Act of 1980 instituted a system for asylum claims; a 1986 measure beefed up patrols at borders and set penalties for employers that knowingly hired unauthorized migrants. In the last third of the century, the foreign-born fraction of the U.S. population rose from 5 to 15 percent.

The early 1900s great wave of immigration included families from Europe fleeing poverty or persecution and seeking better lives.

OUR STREETS ... ARE PAVED WITH THE PROMISE THAT MEN AND WOMEN WHO LIVE HERE ... CAN RISE AS FAST, AS FAR AS THEIR SKILLS WILL ALLOW.

Edward Kennedy *(1965)*

Eight days after President Franklin D. Roosevelt's inauguration, he delivered the first of many "fireside chats" to U.S. radio listeners.

548. DECEMBER 10, 1931

JANE ADDAMS IS AWARDED THE NOBEL PEACE PRIZE

For her work "to revive the ideal of peace," social reformer Jane Addams became the first American woman to receive the Nobel Peace Prize. Addams was known as the founder of Hull-House, a settlement house in Chicago that brought women of all social classes together and provided job training, day care, and education to thousands. Addams opposed the U.S. entry into World War I and went on to play a leading role in international peace organizations, including the Women's International League for Peace and Freedom.

549. JANUARY 12, 1932

HATTIE CARAWAY BECOMES FIRST WOMAN ELECTED TO THE SENATE

Although an earlier woman, Rebecca Felton, had been appointed to the Senate to fill a one-day vacancy in 1922, Arkansas politician Hattie Caraway became the first to be elected and then reelected to the legislative body. The governor of Arkansas appointed her to the seat on November 13, 1931, after the death of her husband, Senator Thaddeus Caraway, but she surprised him and most observers by deciding to run for reelection in both 1932 and 1938—facing off that year against a congressman whose slogan was "We need another man in the Senate." She finished out her term in 1945.

550. OCTOBER 1, 1932

BABE RUTH DOES (OR DOES NOT) CALL A HOME RUN SHOT

One of the most famous, and famously disputed, moments in baseball history came when Yankees slugger Babe Ruth stepped up to the plate at Wrigley Field in Game 3 of the 1932 World Series. The score was 4–4, and members of the opposing team, the Cubs, were heckling Ruth from their dugout. Ruth was down by two strikes when he pointed with two fingers at center field. On the next pitch, he smacked a home run over the center field wall. The Yankees went on to win the game, and the legend was born that the Babe had called his home run shot. Some observers later disputed this, saying that Ruth was just gesturing to the Cubs dugout or indicating that he had two strikes, but his teammate Lou Gehrig backed up the story: "He called his shot and then made it. I ask you: What can you do with a guy like that?"

551. MARCH 12, 1933

FDR BROADCASTS HIS FIRST FIRESIDE CHAT

"My friends, I want to talk for a few minutes with the people of the United States about banking." Surrounded by bulky microphones in the White House Diplomatic Reception Room, President Franklin D. Roosevelt made canny use of the mass medium of radio when he began his first fireside chat address to the American public just eight days after his inauguration. The country had been undergoing a banking crisis, and in his talk, Roosevelt reassured listeners that he had the situation under control. The president continued to deliver regular, reassuring addresses to millions of American listeners until 1944, calming the nation's jittery nerves through the Depression and into World War II.

552. MAY 22, 1933

HARRY HOPKINS SPEARHEADS THE NEW DEAL

In 1933, 15 million Americans—a quarter of the workforce—were unemployed. President Franklin D. Roosevelt embarked on an aggressive series of programs that came to be known as the New Deal—and to lead these programs, he chose a onetime social worker named Harry Hopkins. In May 1933, he put Hopkins in charge of the Federal Emergency Relief Administration, followed later by the Civil Works Administration and the Works Progress Administration. The programs employed millions of people in building and repairing highways, schools, bridges, and other public spaces, allowing formerly unemployed workers to dig their way out of poverty without going on the public dole. Many of the New Deal initiatives were reshaped over time into permanent government programs, including the Social Security Administration.

553. FEBRUARY 23, 1934

HUEY LONG MAKES A PIVOTAL SPEECH

Louisiana senator Huey "Kingfish" Long tapped into Depression-era discontent with his "Share Our Wealth" radio address. The flamboyant politician—formerly governor of Louisiana and still effectively in charge of the state—used the speech to launch the Share Our Wealth movement with the stirring phrase "Every man a king." In an address that referenced the Founding Fathers, the Scriptures, Socrates, and more, he vowed to enact a wealth tax on multimillionaires, with the proceeds redistributed to the poor. Long was considered a contender in the next presidential race until he was assassinated at the Louisiana State Capitol in 1935. The assassin was most likely Carl Weiss, the son-in-law of a judge who opposed Long; some historians believe Long was killed accidentally by his own bodyguards while they were shooting at and killing Weiss, who had approached Long in a hallway.

Flash Gordon leaped from comic books onto the airwaves in 1935, when his interplanetary adventures were turned into radio episodes.

554. JULY 22, 1934

FBI AGENTS SHOOT JOHN DILLINGER

Bank robber John Dillinger's crime spree lasted only 11 months, from September 1933 to July 1934. But in that short time, he became an outlaw hero and the FBI's first public enemy number one. Working with a gang that included "Baby Face" Nelson, Dillinger robbed at least 11 banks and broke out of jail three times, once using a wooden gun. Acting on a tip from a Chicago-area madam, the FBI caught the outlaw as he emerged from Chicago's Biograph Theater, a woman on each arm; the bright dress worn by one of them was a secret signal that her companion was Dillinger. As the agents approached, Dillinger reached for his pistol, and three agents shot and killed him. Crowds posed for pictures around his spilled blood.

555. APRIL 14, 1935

BLACK SUNDAY DUST STORM BURIES THE PLAINS

As if the Depression wasn't taxing enough, America's prairie states suffered through the worst drought in decades in the early 1930s. Years of overfarming, which wiped out the area's drought-resistant grasses, had depleted and dried the soil. Windstorms began to toss dust across the farmlands, but the Black Sunday storm was the worst. After a clear, sunny morning, cold winds started to blow from the northwest. A towering wall of black dirt and sand swept across Oklahoma and the Texas Panhandle, moving at up to 60 miles an hour. People trapped in the darkness could not see for more than a few inches. Dispossessed by this and other dust storms, more than two million people left the Dust Bowl states for what they hoped were greener pastures farther west. In California, the incoming "Okies" took low-paying farm jobs and struggled for years before beginning to blend in during the 1940s.

556. APRIL 27, 1935

FLASH GORDON RADIO SHOW DEBUTS

Against a backdrop of stormy violins, the first radio broadcast of *The Amazing Interplanetary Adventures of Flash Gordon* took listeners to the planet Mongo, where the athletic hero and his girlfriend would battle archvillain Ming the Merciless for 26 15-minute episodes. A classic example of the golden age of radio, the popular show allowed listeners to escape from the reality of the Depression into the thrilling events taken from the Flash Gordon comic strip; the equally popular Flash Gordon movies and television shows followed into the 1990s.

557. OCTOBER 10, 1935

***PORGY AND BESS* OPENS ON BROADWAY**

George Gershwin's pioneering opera *Porgy and Bess* opened at New York City's Alvin Theater before a star-studded audience that included Katharine Hepburn and Joan Crawford. The work was based on the novel and play *Porgy* by Charleston author DuBose

I SAW AND APPROACHED THE HUNGRY AND DESPERATE MOTHER AS IF DRAWN BY A MAGNET.

Dorothea Lange, *speaking of Florence Owens Thompson (1960)*

Florence Owens Thompson, the migrant worker mother in Dorothea Lange's photo, epitomizes the despair of farmers wiped out by the Depression and dust storms.

Heyward, featuring a disabled African American beggar who struggles to rescue his lover, Bess, from predatory men. Gershwin's opera, with lyrics by his brother Ira and a libretto by Heyward, called for an all-Black cast, a requirement that stands to this day. It met mixed reviews upon its opening. Over time, its reputation improved; in the 1950s, *Porgy and Bess* became the first American opera performed at Milan's La Scala opera house. Today, it is considered a staple of American musical theater.

558. NOVEMBER 7, 1935

U.S. MANDATES RED, YELLOW, AND GREEN TRAFFIC SIGNALS

By 1935, more than 26 million motor vehicles were registered in the United States, and navigating intersections could be confusing and dangerous. Traffic signals in earlier years had sometimes used red (stop) and green (go) lights, with no interval between them, or lighted arms that lifted and lowered to indicate stop, go, or stop in all directions. In 1935, the American Association of State Highway Officials' *Manual on Uniform Traffic Control Devices* for the first time mandated the three vertical lights that control intersections today, stating:

A colorized postcard captures Hoover Dam, built at the Arizona-Nevada border to direct water and draw energy from the Colorado River.

> The three prescribed lenses shall be of the following colors only and shall be arranged vertically in the signal face in the following positions:
> Red—At the top
> Yellow—Below the red
> Green—Below the yellow.

Simple and effective, the system remains in use today.

559. MARCH 1, 1936

HOOVER DAM IS COMPLETED

Though it was named for his predecessor, Herbert Hoover, President Franklin D. Roosevelt pressed a golden telegraph key and officially began operations at a massive arch-gravity dam on the Colorado River between Arizona and Nevada on this day. The dam was designed to provide a stable source of water for western fields and supply power to cities such as Los Angeles. Built between 1931 and 1935, it employed 21,000 workers and killed at least 96 in the hot, difficult conditions. At 726 feet high and 1,244 feet long, the structure contains enough concrete to pave a highway from San Francisco to New York.

Jesse Owens's four gold medals and record times at the Berlin Olympics stood as a rebuke to the host country's racist Nazi regime.

560. MARCH 11, 1936

***SAN FRANCISCO NEWS* PUBLISHES "MIGRANT MOTHER"**

In early 1936, Resettlement Administration photographer Dorothea Lange was driving home with a seat full of undeveloped film when she saw a sign for a pea-pickers camp on the side of the highway in Nipomo, California. After some deliberation, she pulled off and found a migrant worker and her children resting, exhausted, in a lean-to tent. Lange's photo of 32-year-old Florence Thompson and three of her children was published on this day in the *San Francisco News*. It soon became emblematic of the physical and mental toll of the Great Depression. Thompson was not named in the story, nor was she ever compensated.

561. AUGUST 9, 1936

JESSE OWENS WINS HIS FOURTH OLYMPIC GOLD MEDAL

James Cleveland "Jesse" Owens had already won three gold medals when he led the U.S. 4×100-meter relay team to victory at the 1936 Olympics in Berlin. He and teammate Ralph Metcalfe were last-minute replacements for two other runners, both Jewish; it was rumored, but never confirmed, that coaches had removed the men under pressure from the Nazi organizers. After winning gold in the 100-meter, long jump, and 200-meter races, the African American athlete helped his team achieve a world-record time of 39.8 seconds in the relay. Owens was the most successful athlete at the Olympics that year. Accounts that say Hitler refused to shake his hand are not entirely true: Hitler refused to shake anyone's hand after the first day of the games.

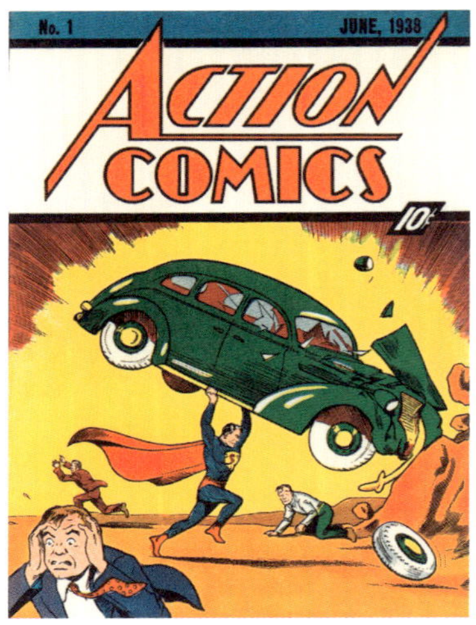

In the debut of the superhero, Superman appears in his origin story in 1938.

562. DECEMBER 1, 1936

AN OFFICIAL RECORDS THE FIRST SOCIAL SECURITY NUMBER

The vast job of assigning the first Social Security numbers to American workers reached a key stage in 1936, when an official began processing records in Baltimore and pulled number 055-09-0001 for John David Sweeney, Jr., the first to officially receive such a number. The 23-year-old Princeton graduate, described by *Time* magazine as "blue-eyed, sturdy, unmarried," noted that his retirement was a long way off. (He did not in fact live long enough to collect Social Security, dying of a heart attack at the age of 61, but his widow was able to receive survivor benefits.)

563. JANUARY 25, 1937

***HOW TO WIN FRIENDS AND INFLUENCE PEOPLE* HITS NUMBER ONE**

Before he was a best-selling author, Dale Carnegie taught popular public-speaking and human relations courses at a YMCA in New York. An editor from Simon & Schuster encouraged him to put his rules in writing, and the self-help tome that resulted became one of the best-selling American books of the 20th century. *How to Win Friends and Influence People,* essentially, encourages people to be nice. Carnegie's primary principles include "Don't criticize, condemn or complain," "Give honest and sincere appreciation," and "Smile." The book has sold more than 30 million copies around the world.

564. MAY 6, 1937

***HINDENBURG* EXPLODES**

The huge, luxurious German airship *Hindenburg*—a dirigible craft that used gas to fly under its own power—was completing a routine three-day trip from Frankfurt to the Naval Air Station at Lakehurst, New Jersey, on the evening of May 6. The weather had been stormy, but docking seemed to be proceeding normally until flames burst out of the rear of the aircraft. Within seconds, the hydrogen-fueled ship was engulfed. Passengers and crew nearest the windows jumped out; those deeper inside could not escape. The flaming airship crumpled to the ground in front of observers, including distraught reporter Herb Morrison, whose exclamation "Oh, the humanity!" became forever associated with the accident. Remarkably, 62 of the 97 people aboard survived, though some were injured. Later investigations suggested that atmospheric electricity had sparked escaping gas to start the conflagration. The well-publicized accident effectively put an end to dirigible travel in an age when airplanes were becoming roomier and more efficient.

565. JULY 2, 1937

AMELIA EARHART DISAPPEARS

Amelia Earhart had already made her mark as the first woman to fly solo and nonstop across the Atlantic, the first woman to fly solo and nonstop across America, and the first person to fly solo from the Hawaiian Islands to the mainland. In 1937, she undertook her most difficult feat yet: flying around the world. Earhart and her navigator, Fred Noonan, set out on one of the final legs of the trip on July 2, traveling 2,556 miles from New Guinea to tiny Howland Island in the Pacific. They never made it. After several radio messages to a U.S. Coast Guard cutter near Howland that morning, nothing more was heard from her Lockheed Electra. Theories about her fate include speculation that she was wrecked on another island or captured by the Japanese, but the most widely accepted explanation is that the aviator simply ran out of fuel and crashed into the depths of the Pacific.

566. APRIL 18, 1938

FIRST SUPERMAN COMIC IS PUBLISHED

After numerous rejections, comic book creators Jerry Siegel and Joe Shuster sold their burly superhero creation Superman to Detective Comics, Inc. The refugee from Krypton first appeared on the cover of Action Comics #1, lifting a green automobile over his head while terrified villains ran for cover. The original comic book hero, Superman became a hugely successful character who went on to star in television shows and movies. As was customary at the time, Siegel and Shuster had sold all rights to their character and for the most part did not share in the super income that Superman later brought in.

GAS IS RUNNING LOW. BEEN UNABLE TO REACH YOU.

Amelia Earhart, *in one of her final radio transmissions (1937)*

567. JUNE 22, 1938

JOE LOUIS DEFEATS MAX SCHMELING

Before a sold-out crowd at Yankee Stadium and 70 million radio listeners, American boxer Joe Louis defeated German boxer Max Schmeling in a highly touted rematch. Schmeling

Amelia Earhart's bid to fly around the world ended in tragedy when the plane carrying her and her navigator vanished over the Pacific.

What cheered Americans during grim days early in World War II? Big band tunes like "In the Mood" by Glenn Miller and His Orchestra.

had KO'd the American star in their first encounter in 1936; by 1938, their next fight had taken on mythic proportions. Americans saw Schmeling as an avatar of the bigoted Nazi regime (although he was not a Nazi supporter), while Louis represented American pluralism and freedom (though Louis had met with plenty of racism in his career). This time, Louis triumphed easily, smashing Schmeling to the ground three times in just two minutes and four seconds. "The whole damn country was depending on me," he said.

568. OCTOBER 30, 1938

"WAR OF THE WORLDS" BROADCAST FRIGHTENS LISTENERS

At 8 p.m. on the night before Halloween, Orson Welles's *Mercury Theatre on the Air* broadcast an hour-long radio program containing increasingly frightening news bulletins. Apparently, Martians were invading New Jersey. The program began and ended with announcements that it was a theatrical production, but many listeners seemingly did not notice or understand these. Instead, they were terrified to hear that a "humped shape is rising out of the pit. I can make out a small beam of light against a mirror. What's that? There's a jet of flame springing from the mirror, and it leaps right at the advancing men!"

Reports that people panicked in the streets were exaggerated, but many listeners did call in to CBS and to local police stations in alarm. Despite criticism of his lack of journalistic ethics, the 23-year-old Welles—the director and actor later known for his masterpiece film *Citizen Kane*—launched his career with this effective drama.

569. AUGUST 2, 1939

ALBERT EINSTEIN WEIGHS IN ON NUCLEAR POWER

In 1939, fearing that Germany would develop an atomic bomb, physicist Leo Szilard persuaded the world's most esteemed scientist, Albert Einstein, to write to President Franklin D. Roosevelt. The letter, drafted by both men and signed by Einstein, reads in part:

> In the course of the last four months it has been made probable—through the work of Joliot in France as well as Fermi and Szilard in America—that it may become possible to set up a nuclear chain reaction in a large mass of uranium, by which vast amounts of power and large quantities of new radium-like elements would be generated. Now it appears almost certain that this could be achieved in the immediate future.
>
> This new phenomenon would also lead to the construction of bombs, and it is conceivable—though much less certain—that extremely powerful bombs of a new type may thus be constructed.

The letter convinced Roosevelt to move forward with the Manhattan Project, America's top secret government program that developed the atomic bomb. After the war, the pacifist Einstein said, "Had I known that the Germans would not succeed in producing an atomic bomb, I would never have lifted a finger."

570. SEPTEMBER 1, 1939

PHONE CALL ALERTS FDR TO THE START OF WORLD WAR II

President Franklin D. Roosevelt was asleep in his White House bedroom when, at 2:50 a.m., his phone rang. On the other end was the American ambassador in Paris, William C. Bullitt, who informed FDR that German planes were bombing cities in Poland. The president knew this meant the start of a larger war in Europe—one that might well come to include the United States. American sympathies lay with the nations under attack, but it would be more than two years before U.S. forces officially joined the fight.

571. FEBRUARY 10, 1940

GLENN MILLER'S "IN THE MOOD" HITS NUMBER ONE

The dark days of early World War II called for bright music to keep up the nation's spirits, and Glenn Miller's big band version of "In the Mood," recorded for RCA, fit the bill. The jazz standard, which became a number one hit on the pop charts in 1940, had its origins in an earlier composition, "Tar Paper Stomp," by Wingy Manone. But in 1939, bandleader

Miller cut and arranged it into the upbeat jitterbug number familiar today. After joining up in 1942, Miller led bands in that tune and others across the U.S. and Europe. He died in a plane crash flying to Paris in 1944.

572. FEBRUARY 29, 1940

GONE WITH THE WIND WINS EIGHT ACADEMY AWARDS

David O. Selznick's blockbuster film *Gone With the Wind* was immediately popular when it was released in 1939. Based on Margaret Mitchell's best-selling novel, the movie follows its headstrong heroine, Scarlett O'Hara, through the Civil War and afterward. In 1940, the movie won a record eight Academy Awards: Best Picture, Best Director, Best Screenplay, Best Art Direction, Best Cinematography, Best Editing, Best Actress, and of particular note, Best Supporting Actress. That award went to Hattie McDaniel, the first African American actor to win an Oscar.

Scarlett and Rhett and Ashley and Melly: These and other characters helped the film *Gone With the Wind* win a then record eight Academy Awards.

573. MAY 15, 1940

MCDONALD'S FAMOUS BARBECUE RESTAURANT OPENS

On this day, juice stand operators Dick and Mac McDonald opened a small, octagonal restaurant in downtown San Bernardino, California. Carhops at McDonald's Famous Barbecue delivered quick meals, which came to include hamburgers, fries, and shakes, directly to car windows. Later in the 1940s, the entrepreneurial brothers devised an efficient, assembly-line operation, simplified their menu, and put up the golden arches that came to symbolize their growing fast-food business—an enterprise that salesman Ray Kroc bought out in 1961 and turned into an empire, with 38,000 locations worldwide feeding 68 million people a day in the 2020s.

574. OCTOBER 21, 1940

ERNEST HEMINGWAY PUBLISHES _FOR WHOM THE BELL TOLLS_

The *New York Times* called Ernest Hemingway's fourth full-length work of fiction "the first major novel of the Second World War." Set during the Spanish Civil War, it follows the protagonist Robert Jordan over the course of a few days in which he befriends Spanish guerrillas, falls in love, blows up a bridge, and, gravely wounded, prepares to die. "He has all his life in those days," wrote Hemingway to his editor, Maxwell Perkins, "and, at the end there is only death there for him [and] he truly isn't afraid of it at all because he has the chance to finish his mission." Considered one of the writer's best books, it was an immediate bestseller and a finalist for the Pulitzer Prize.

575. MAY 1, 1941

CITIZEN KANE IS RELEASED

Originally titled *American,* Orson Welles's film *Citizen Kane* had its premiere this day at the RKO Palace Theatre in New York City. Welles, just 25 years old, produced, directed, co-wrote, and starred in the film, the story of the rise and fall of a newspaper magnate based on William Randolph Hearst. The movie's suspenseful narrative and striking camerawork earned it strong praise from reviewers. But Hearst's threats hampered both its advertising and wide release, and it was, at first, a financial failure. In the long run, *Citizen Kane* became acknowledged as one of the best films ever made, reaching number one on the American Film Institute's list of all-time greatest American movies.

576. JULY 1, 1941

WNBT AIRS FIRST TV COMMERCIAL

Television executives had been experimenting with commercials for a few years, but only in 1941 did the Federal Communications Commission issue the first commercial licenses, beginning with 10 stations across the United States. On July 1, the first approved commercial aired during a Brooklyn Dodgers–Philadelphia Phillies baseball game on New York's WNBT. Nine seconds long, it consisted of a shaky picture of a Bulova watch face and the narration, "America runs on Bulova time." It cost the company just $9 in an era when New Yorkers possessed only 4,000 television sets. Today, about 15 minutes of every hour of television is devoted to commercials.

The McDonald's Famous Barbecue restaurant in San Bernardino, California, begot a fast-food chain that grew into a global burger empire.

Rescue boats move in on the battleships U.S.S. *West Virginia* (foreground) and U.S.S. *Tennessee* after the Japanese surprise attack on Pearl Harbor, Hawaii.

577. DECEMBER 7, 1941

JAPANESE FORCES BOMB PEARL HARBOR

By the autumn of 1941, as war ravaged Europe, relations between Japan and the United States were at a low point. Japan was marching through Indochina and had established an alliance with Germany and Italy. The U.S. had cut off Japan's supplies of petroleum. In late November, a fleet of Japanese ships convened at sea 275 miles north of the U.S. Pacific Fleet's base at Pearl Harbor on the Hawaiian island of Oahu. At 7:55 a.m., the first Japanese dive-bombers took the American fleet by surprise. Just a few American planes were able to take to the skies in defense as Japanese bombers in two waves sank or severely damaged 16 ships, including eight battleships, and some 300 aircraft. More than 2,300 Americans were killed, with more than 1,000 others injured. The United States was on the brink of war.

578. DECEMBER 8, 1941

FDR ASKS TO DECLARE WAR

Just hours after President Franklin D. Roosevelt received word of the Japanese attack on Pearl Harbor, he drafted a speech asking Congress for a declaration of war on Japan. The next day, in front of a joint session of Congress and behind a row of radio microphones, FDR made his request to the representatives and the American public. His six-minute speech began: "Yesterday, December 7, 1941—a date which will live in infamy—the United States of America was suddenly and deliberately attacked by naval and air forces of the Empire of Japan." Congress sent him the declaration the same day. Three days later, on December 11, the war widened when Germany and Italy declared war on the U.S., which responded with its own declaration in turn.

579. FEBRUARY 19, 1942

ROOSEVELT ORDERS JAPANESE AMERICANS INTO CAMPS

Wartime fears and racism combined to ugly effect in early 1942, when President Franklin D. Roosevelt was persuaded to evict people of Japanese descent from their homes on the West Coast. His Executive Order No. 9066 moved and confined 122,000 men, women, and children, most of them American citizens, to 10 fenced-in internment camps in California, Washington, Oregon, Arizona, Utah, Wyoming, Colorado, Idaho, and Arkansas. In the process, many lost their homes and businesses. The camps were not shut down until late 1945 and early 1946. Few people were fully reimbursed for their confiscated property.

PENICILLIN WILL SAVE MORE LIVES THAN WAR SPENDS.

***Time* magazine** *cover story (1944)*

580. MARCH 14, 1942

PENICILLIN SAVES A DYING WOMAN

Penicillin's antibiotic effects had been known since 1928, but not until the early 1940s were scientists able to make a viable medicine from the *Penicillium* mold. In 1942, a 33-year-old patient at New Haven Hospital (now Yale New Haven Hospital) named Anne Miller was dying from an infection following a miscarriage. Fortuitously, a physician at the Yale School of Medicine knew a British researcher who had access to England's newly created but still rare penicillin medicine. The New Haven doctors were able to obtain a 5.5-gram dose to treat the feverish, dying woman. The next day, her fever had disappeared, and she recovered completely. Miller was the first American to be successfully treated with the new drug, which soon went into large-scale production due to wartime demand. Today, it is widely used to treat a range of bacterial infections, from strep throat to pneumonia.

581. JUNE 13, 1942

HAUDENOSAUNEE CONFEDERACY DECLARES WAR ON GERMANY

Asserting their status as sovereign peoples, the six Haudenosaunee (Iroquois) Nations issued a separate declaration of war on Germany and its allies. Leaders representing the Mohawk, Oneida, Onondaga, Cayuga, Seneca, and Tuscarora Nations read a statement on the steps of the U.S. Capitol. "We represent the oldest, though smallest, democracy in the world today ... Now we do resolve that it is the sentiment of this council that the Six Nations of Indians declare that a state of war exists between our Confederacy of Six

Nations on the one part and Germany, Italy, Japan and their allies against whom the United States has declared war, on the other part." (The peace treaty at war's end did not include the Haudenosaunee, so in theory the nations are still at war.)

The last confirmed sighting of the ultrarare ivory-billed woodpecker—a black-crested female, not a male with a red crest—occurred in 1944.

582. APRIL 5, 1944

ARTIST IS LAST TO SEE THE IVORY-BILLED WOODPECKER

The flamboyant black, white, and red markings of the big ivory-billed woodpecker were hard to miss, but it was unclear by 1944 if any of the species had survived; their only known remaining habitat, Louisiana's forested Singer Tract, was shrinking as lumber companies cut into it. In 1944, the president of the Audubon Society sent young artist Don Eckelberry to the tract to see if he could spot and sketch the elusive bird. After two weeks, success: A female ivory-bill landed nearby with "one magnificent upward swoop." Eckelberry frantically started sketching but never saw her again. Despite occasional claims over the years, his remains the last accepted, verified sighting of the ivory-billed woodpecker, though the bird has not been officially declared extinct. The spectacular bird became a symbol of the disappearance of endangered species and the loss of habitat across the country as the century went on.

583. JUNE 6, 1944

TROOPS STORM NORMANDY BEACHES ON D-DAY

The long-awaited Allied invasion of western Europe began around midnight as thousands of paratroopers dropped in the dark onto the Normandy coast. Just after dawn, 54,000 U.S. infantry troops, joined by 54,000 from Britain and 21,400 from Canada, waded through rough surf onto five beaches code-named Omaha, Utah, Gold, Sword, and Juno. The soldiers took heavy fire as they came ashore; more than 9,000 were killed or wounded. The invasion was the beginning of a nearly year-long offensive that led to the German surrender in 1945.

584. OCTOBER 30, 1944

***APPALACHIAN SPRING* PREMIERES AT THE LIBRARY OF CONGRESS**

Commissioned by Elizabeth Sprague Coolidge and presented at the auditorium named after her at the Library of Congress, *Appalachian Spring* was the first collaboration between choreographer Martha Graham and composer Aaron Copland. For a fee of $500, the composer created a chamber work with joyful folk and hymnlike melodies, including the Shaker tune "Simple Gifts." Graham envisioned her accompanying ballet as "a legend of American living. This has to do with living in a new town, someplace where the first fence has just gone up." The premiere, with the role of a bride danced by Graham, was a great success and became a standard part of the American ballet repertoire. Copland later adapted the piece into larger orchestrations.

585. FEBRUARY 16, 1945

ALASKA PASSES THE FIRST EQUAL RIGHTS ACT

The first antidiscrimination law passed by any U.S. state or territory was the brainchild of Tlingit activist Elizabeth Peratrovich. Working with Alaska's governor, she pushed for years to pass an antidiscrimination bill. At a hearing in 1945, territorial senator Allen Shattuck asked, "Who are these people, barely out of savagery, who want to associate with us whites with 5,000 years of recorded civilization behind us?" In the public gallery, Peratrovich put down her knitting and stood to reply, saying, "I would not have expected that I, who am barely out of savagery, would have to remind the gentlemen with 5,000 years of recorded civilization behind them of our Bill of Rights." The bill, allowing all Alaskans full and equal enjoyment of public establishments, passed and was signed by the governor on February 16.

586. MAY 8, 1945

U.S. AND ITS ALLIES CELEBRATE V-E DAY

Partyers filled New York's Times Square the day after German general Alfred Jodl signed surrender documents in Reims, France, on May 7, 1945. The signing occurred

Allied troops' arrival in northern France in June 1944 began the rout of enemy forces that culminated in Germany's May 1945 surrender.

The first electronic computer was 1,400 times faster than hand calculators of the time—but weighed 30 tons and filled 1,500 square feet of space.

just 11 months after Allied forces landed on the beaches of Normandy. (Soviet leader Joseph Stalin insisted on a second ceremony the next day, May 8.) With the end of fighting in Europe, celebrations broke out around the world on May 8, which became known as Victory in Europe, or V-E, Day. For the first time since wartime brownouts darkened the city, lights shone on the Statue of Liberty.

587. JULY 16, 1945

ATOMIC AGE BEGINS IN THE DESERT

Seconds before 5:30 a.m., an atomic bomb exploded in the New Mexico desert. Its searing light, shock wave, heat, and mushroom cloud ushered in the nuclear age. A product of the five-year-long Manhattan Project, the weapon was a plutonium device with a novel implosion mechanism, and the gathered scientists were not at all sure it would work as designed. Observers stationed at three corners of the Trinity test site at the Alamogordo Bombing and Gunnery Range south of Los Alamos were simultaneously relieved, overjoyed, and appalled by the successful test. The invention would end a war and begin a new and frightening era of nuclear threat.

588. AUGUST 6, 1945

ENOLA GAY DROPS THE FIRST ATOMIC BOMB ON HIROSHIMA

At 8:15 a.m. local time, the U.S. bomber *Enola Gay* dropped a 9,700-pound atomic bomb, nicknamed "Little Boy," on the Japanese city of Hiroshima. It detonated with the force of 15,000 tons of TNT 1,900 feet over a parade field filled with soldiers. "A bright light filled the plane," wrote the pilot, Col. Paul Tibbets, later. "The first shock wave hit us ... We turned back to look at Hiroshima. The city was hidden by that awful cloud ... boiling up, mushrooming, terrible and incredibly tall." The explosion killed approximately 70,000 people in the initial blast and more than 100,000 later from injuries and radiation sickness. Because the Japanese would not surrender unconditionally, the Americans dropped a second bomb on Nagasaki three days later. Japan formally surrendered on September 2 to end the war.

589. FEBRUARY 14, 1946

ENIAC COMPUTER IS DEDICATED AT THE UNIVERSITY OF PENNSYLVANIA

Until the 1940s, the word "computer" usually referred to mathematically employed people who solved complex equations by hand. In 1946, engineers at the University of Pennsylvania unveiled the first electronic, general-purpose computer, ENIAC (Electronic Numerical Integrator and Computer). Weighing 30 tons, the U-shaped machine filled a 30- by 50-foot room and was powered by 18,000 vacuum tubes. Operators had to program each set of calculations manually; programs could not be stored. Even so, the big machine was 1,400 times faster than the hand calculators used at the time. Until it was decommissioned in 1955 as stored-program and transistor computers took over, ENIAC calculated ballistics, predicted the weather, and studied cosmic rays, among other areas of research.

With the first test explosion of an atomic bomb in the New Mexico desert, the mushroom cloud became an iconic image of the nuclear age.

590. APRIL 1, 1946

TSUNAMI STRIKES ALASKA AND HAWAII

On this day, an earthquake near the Aleutian Islands triggered one of the worst tsunamis of the 20th century. The quake's epicenter was south of Unimak Island; the earthquake may have triggered an underwater landslide. Waves 115 feet high destroyed the sturdy Scotch Cap Light on Unimak, killing five men, and tore into the Pacific, reaching shores from California to Chile. Worst hit was the Big Island of Hawaii. There, multiple waves at least 30 feet high killed 159 people, many of them children. In all, some 165 people died. The devastation led to the creation of the Pacific Tsunami Warning Center, still operating today.

591. JULY 14, 1946

THE COMMON SENSE BOOK OF BABY AND CHILD CARE IS PUBLISHED

"Trust yourself," the book begins. "You know more than you think you do." This kind of reassuring advice for anxious parents made Benjamin Spock's *The Common Sense Book of*

continued on page 300

SPOTLIGHT

COOKING IN THE 20TH CENTURY

COOKING FROM SCRATCH made food preparation a full-time job in the late 1800s. But during the 20th century, cooking in America would change significantly, from what dishes were made to how long they took and what tools were used. Home cooks began to take inspiration from trailblazing, high-profile chefs; average food preparation time decreased from six hours a day in 1910 to less than two hours a day in the 1960s, thanks in part to canned foods developed during wartime.

As the years unfolded and cooking became a more unisex pursuit, women reduced and men increased the time they spent on food preparation. Kitchens began to be stocked with more time-savers: prepared foods and laborsaving devices such as microwave ovens and food processors. James Beard, the first U.S. chef with a TV cooking show, was followed by Julia Child and Jacques Pépin, who demystified French cuisine; Galloping Gourmet Graham Kerr, who popularized more refined dishes; Frugal Gourmet Jeff Smith, who made them affordable; and Emeril Lagasse, who pioneered the chef as entertainer format, hosting one of the first cooking shows on TV's Food Network, launched in 1993.

Star chefs and their fans became part of a "foodie" culture (celebrated dining critic Gael Greene coined the name in 1980). It flourished from then on, promoting cooking and eating well as a creative outlet. But as Americans also ate more processed and fast foods, some 65 percent of U.S. adults would become overweight or obese by the end of the century and the beginning of the next.

Julia Child demystified wine pairings in addition to cooking skills on her television cooking series *The French Chef* (1962-1973).

EVERYTHING CAN HAVE DRAMA IF IT'S DONE RIGHT. EVEN A PANCAKE.

Julia Child, Esquire *magazine (2000)*

Jackie Robinson was honored as Rookie of the Year in 1947, the same year his entry into Major League Baseball broke the league's color barrier.

continued from page 297

Baby and Child Care one of the best-selling books of the 20th century. In contrast to the schedule-driven, discipline-oriented child care books of earlier years, *Baby and Child Care* emphasized understanding and flexibility. Published just in time for the start of the baby boom, the book went through numerous revisions over the years, with new sections on fighting gender stereotypes and increasing the role of fathers. In its various editions, it has sold more than 50 million copies.

592. DECEMBER 20, 1946

IT'S A WONDERFUL LIFE OPENS IN NEW YORK

Director Frank Capra's film about a man (played by Jimmy Stewart) reassessing his disappointing life opened at New York City's Globe Theatre shortly before Christmas. Reviews were mixed—the *New York Times'* Bosley Crowther described it as engaging but sentimental—and the movie underwhelmed at the box office. In 1974, its copyright was not renewed, which led to a surprising second life for the film. Television studios began to play it at Christmastime as a cheap fill-in, and the movie gained widespread recognition and popularity. Today, it is recognized as an American classic.

593. FEBRUARY 10, 1947

WILLIE SUTTON ESCAPES AGAIN

Bank robber Willie Sutton, sometimes known as "Slick Willie" or Willie "the Actor," became as famous for his prison escapes as he was for his robberies. Over his decades-long career, the polite and dapper thief stole from banks and jewelry stores wearing a variety of disguises, and was caught and imprisoned multiple times. His most daring escape came in 1947 when he and four other inmates walked across the yard of Holmesburg Prison in Philadelphia wearing stolen guards' uniforms and scaled two ladders lashed together to climb over the facility's 35-foot walls. Tower guards spotted them but were apparently reassured when Sutton called out "It's okay," or "It's all right." He was recognized and caught five years later, returned to prison, and paroled in 1969.

594. FEBRUARY 21, 1947

EDWIN LAND DEMONSTRATES AN INSTANT CAMERA

Edwin Land was a prolific inventor whose company, Polaroid, specialized in polarizing films and optical devices. In the 1940s, after his young daughter asked him why they couldn't instantly see the photos from their camera, he applied his knowledge of film and optics to create the world's first instant camera. He demonstrated the Polaroid Land camera in front of the Optical Society of America in New York in 1947, showing how the four-pound instrument could produce a sepia-toned print in exactly 60 seconds. When the Model 95 camera went on sale the next year, it sold out on the first day. Black-and-white

Polaroid cameras soon followed in 1950, then the instantly popular color versions in 1963. Sales declined later in the century with the advent of smaller conventional and then digital cameras, only to rise again in the 21st century on a wave of nostalgia.

595. APRIL 15, 1947

JACKIE ROBINSON INTEGRATES MAJOR LEAGUE BASEBALL

Jackie Robinson, playing first base for the Brooklyn Dodgers against the Boston Braves, took a throw from third base to put out Braves' shortstop Dick Culler. In so doing, he became the first African American to play in the major leagues in the modern era. Dodgers general manager Branch Rickey had signed Robinson to his big-league contract just five days earlier, having recruited him not only for his athletic prowess but also for his even temperament. The first baseman went on to be Rookie of the Year, 1949's Most Valuable Player, a member of the Baseball Hall of Fame, a civil rights leader, and an American hero.

596. JULY 8, 1947

***ROSWELL DAILY RECORD* REPORTS A FLYING SAUCER CRASH**

The *Roswell Daily Record*'s headline "RAAF Captures Flying Saucer on Ranch in Roswell Region" started a long, inexhaustible national fascination with aliens from outer space—

Though it premiered to middling reviews and ticket sales, Frank Capra's *It's a Wonderful Life* is now regarded as a U.S. film classic.

More than 17,000 homes were built in regimented rows in the suburb of Levittown on Long Island in New York.

from flying saucers and government cover-ups to little green men. The excitable headline did not reflect the facts of the story: A New Mexico rancher had found shredded metallic fabric, sticks, and rubber scattered on his land. Officers from the nearby Roswell Army Airfield investigated and were told by higher-ups that it was the wreck of a UFO. They retracted the claim the next day and stated it was a weather balloon, but the damage was done. Flying saucer mania began to sweep the country. Experts now definitively believe the wreckage came from a downed U.S. surveillance balloon, launched to track Soviet nuclear tests.

597. JULY 14, 1947

LEVITT & SONS ADVERTISE THEIR FIRST HOUSE

An ad for Levitt & Sons' new housing venture on Long Island, New York, announced "$52 a Month, for Veterans Only!" The community that would come to be known as Levittown began as a few thousand inexpensive, mass-produced houses on winding streets. For just $7,500, returning veterans facing housing shortages could buy a modern house complete with a full kitchen and a television set. Not mentioned in the ads: a covenant that in early years barred Black buyers. The Long Island town became so successful that the company built two others in Pennsylvania and New Jersey, even though the conformity and segregation of these new suburbs inspired criticism and satire. The towns still exist, with most of the houses modified for 21st-century needs.

598. APRIL 3, 1948

TRUMAN SIGNS THE MARSHALL PLAN INTO LAW

In the wake of World War II, much of Europe lay in ruins. In the opinion of American Secretary of State George Marshall, that destruction left the countries open to the rapidly growing influence of the Soviet Union. Beginning in 1947, Marshall campaigned to persuade American lawmakers that they should extend massive amounts of financial aid to Europe. In April 1948, President Harry S. Truman signed into law the Economic Recovery Act of 1948, which came to be known as the Marshall Plan. The $13.3 billion extended to 17 western and southern European nations over four years did in fact help the countries rebuild and regain political stability. Today, the plan is seen as a force for peace in the postwar world; it earned George Marshall a Nobel Peace Prize in 1953.

HEY! THE WATER'S FINE ... AND SO IS LIFE IN LEVITTOWN! ... THE PRICE WE SAY IS THE PRICE YOU PAY!

Advertisement for Levittown *(1950s)*

599. MAY 3, 1948

SUPREME COURT RULES AGAINST RACIAL COVENANTS

In 1945, an African American couple, J. D. and Ethel Lee Shelley, bought a two-story brick house in St. Louis. The evening they moved in, they were served with court papers ordering them to leave. A neighbor, Louis Kraemer, had filed suit because neighborhood covenants forbade "people of the Negro or Mongolian Race" from living there. In 1948, the case made its way to the Supreme Court, where the justices ruled in *Shelley* v. *Kraemer* that racial covenants, though legal as private agreements, violated the Fourteenth Amendment of the Constitution when the state enforced them. (Three of the justices had to recuse themselves because their own houses were covered by race-based covenants.) The Shelleys were able to stay in their house, and the ruling began the demise of the widespread practice of housing discrimination—though it would not be explicitly banned until 1968's Fair Housing Act.

600. JULY 26, 1948

TRUMAN DESEGREGATES THE MILITARY

Executive Order No. 9981, which President Harry S. Truman signed on this day, ordered "equality of treatment and opportunity for all persons in the armed services without regard to race, color, religion or national origin." Although more than a million African Americans had served in the military throughout U.S. history, they had been confined to segregated units and typically held back from promotion. Following the executive order, the armed forces integrated at varying speeds and degrees of enthusiasm. But when the Korean War began and all the services needed fighters, barriers began to break down for good. Today, all areas of the military are integrated, with African American members accounting for between 8 and 21 percent of the forces, depending upon the branch.

A Broadway hit and Pulitzer Prize winner, *Death of a Salesman* showed the human toll of a failed quest for the American dream.

601. DECEMBER 10, 1948

UN ADOPTS ELEANOR ROOSEVELT'S UNIVERSAL DECLARATION OF HUMAN RIGHTS

Former first lady Eleanor Roosevelt was a lifelong progressive activist—but perhaps her proudest moment was the passage of the Universal Declaration of Human Rights by the United Nations on this day. Roosevelt, who had been widowed since 1945, became a delegate to the UN in 1946 and chaired the United Nations Commission on Human Rights, where she helped to draft the declaration. The nonbinding document recognizes, among other things, that all human beings are born free and equal and are entitled to life, liberty, freedom of thought and religion, and an adequate standard of living. Eleanor Roosevelt died in 1962; a memorial to her work stands in front of the UN headquarters in Geneva, Switzerland.

602. FEBRUARY 10, 1949

DEATH OF A SALESMAN OPENS IN NEW YORK

Arthur Miller's play *Death of a Salesman,* directed by Elia Kazan and starring Lee J. Cobb as the tragic salesman Willy Loman, opened at Broadway's Morosco Theatre to strong reviews. It went on to rack up 742 performances in its first run and win a Pulitzer Prize and six Tony Awards. Premiering in an era that touted hard work and family values, the play cast a harsh light on the American dream as it followed the failure, disillusionment, and suicide of a traveling salesman. "By common consent, this is one of the finest dramas in the whole range of the American theatre," wrote *New York Times* theater critic Brooks Atkinson.

603. APRIL 4, 1949

DEAN ACHESON SIGNS THE NORTH ATLANTIC TREATY

With World War II a recent memory and the Cold War warming up, 12 countries signed on to the newly created North Atlantic Treaty. Secretary of State Dean Acheson signed for the United States and was joined by leaders from Canada, Belgium, Denmark, France, Great Britain, Iceland, Italy, Luxembourg, the Netherlands, Norway, and Portugal. The nations pledged to settle international disputes by peaceful means and to come to the aid of any member nation under attack. "It is a simple document," said President Harry S. Truman that day, "but if it had existed in 1914 and in 1939, supported by the nations who are represented here today, I believe it would have prevented the acts of aggression which led to two world wars."

604. FEBRUARY 8, 1950

DINERS USE THE FIRST CREDIT CARD

Created and first used by Frank X. McNamara and Ralph Schneider at a restaurant in New York, the Diners Club card initially encompassed 14 restaurants and 200 members. The cardboard rectangle allowed the holder to charge dinner and pay up at the end of the month. Technically a charge card (the balance could not be carried over to the next month), the Diners Club card was quickly adopted by businesses outside the restaurant trade and by hundreds of thousands of consumers who were willing to trade an annual fee of a few dollars for the convenience of leaving cash behind. In time, more modern credit cards overtook Diners Club, and Discover Financial Services bought the company in 2008.

605. JUNE 17, 1950

RICHARD LAWLER PERFORMS THE FIRST KIDNEY TRANSPLANT

Dr. Richard Lawler had performed experimental organ transplants in dogs, but in 1950 he took the risk of transplanting a kidney from one human to another. The patient was 44-year-old Ruth Tucker, who was dying of polycystic kidney disease; the donor was an unrelated woman with the same blood type. The operation at Little Company of Mary Hospital in suburban Chicago was a qualified success. Because immunotherapy was relatively new, Tucker's body rejected the organ within 10 months, but the patient survived for five more years. Performed in an era before immunosuppressive drugs or tissue typing, the operation was risky and controversial, and Lawler never performed another one.

606. JULY 1, 1950

FIRST U.S. TROOPS ARRIVE IN KOREA

Once a single country, though for decades under Japanese rule, South Korea and North Korea were divided at the end of World War II at the 38th parallel. In June 1950, North Korea, backed by the Soviet Union, invaded South Korea. In response, the United States asked the United Nations to support military assistance to South Korea. Although the U.S. never formally declared war on North Korea, the United Nations authorized its members, including the United States, to enter the conflict on June 27. On July 1, the first American troops arrived from Japan and began fighting. Outnumbered and overpowered, they were pushed south for weeks before reinforcements arrived.

"Terrific" was the verdict woven in spider silk—and echoed by critics and readers of *Charlotte's Web*, a classic of children's literature.

607. APRIL 11, 1951

TRUMAN FIRES GENERAL MACARTHUR

"I deeply regret that it becomes my duty as President and Commander in Chief of the United States military forces to replace you as Supreme Commander, Allied Powers." With this order, President Harry S. Truman fired one of the most lauded military commanders of the 20th century, Gen. Douglas MacArthur. Truman and MacArthur disagreed about the course of the Korean War: When MacArthur defied Truman's direct orders and invaded North Korea across the 38th parallel, Truman felt he had no choice but to fire him. The decision was unpopular with the American public, which revered the hard-charging general. "Old soldiers never die," MacArthur told Congress afterward, "they just fade away." MacArthur's reputation as a controversial, complicated, and talented general has not faded.

608. JUNE 9, 1951

"ROCKET 88" HITS THE TOP OF THE R & B CHARTS

With its electric guitar and fuzzy, distorted sound, "Rocket 88" is considered by many music historians to be the first rock and roll song. The bluesy tribute to the Rocket 88 Oldsmobile was credited to Jackie Brenston and His Delta Cats, but the primary force behind its novel arrangement and emphatic piano was musician Ike Turner. (Brenston played saxophone in Turner's band but was the lead vocalist on this number.) Chess Records released the influential song, which went to the top of the Billboard R & B charts in the summer of '51.

609. SEPTEMBER 23, 1952

RICHARD NIXON MAKES HIS "CHECKERS" SPEECH

California senator Richard Nixon was running for vice president alongside Dwight D. Eisenhower when news broke that the VP candidate was using money from a secret political fund for personal expenses. While it was true that Nixon drew funds from an account his backers supplied, the practice was not strictly illegal. Nevertheless, the story became a scandal. In a widely watched television address, Nixon pleaded his innocence against the charges. He denied any wrongdoing, noting that his wife, Pat, "doesn't have a mink coat. But she does have a respectable Republican cloth coat." Most famously, he did admit receiving a special gift from a supporter: a black-and-white cocker spaniel, Checkers. Nixon's address convinced enough listeners of his innocence that he and Eisenhower were elected to office in November.

610. OCTOBER 15, 1952

E. B. WHITE PUBLISHES *CHARLOTTE'S WEB*

"Where's Papa going with that ax?" could have been the opening of a horror novel, but in 1952 it introduced the story of Wilbur the pig and Charlotte the spider in E. B. White's soon-to-be-classic children's book *Charlotte's Web.* "A farm is a peculiar problem for a man who likes animals," wrote White to his editor, "because the fate of most livestock is that they are murdered by their benefactors ... Anyway, the theme of 'Charlotte's Web' is that a pig shall be saved." The book became a bestseller and, with its quiet messages about mortality and friendship, is now considered one of the great works of children's literature.

OLD SOLDIERS NEVER DIE. THEY JUST FADE AWAY.

Douglas MacArthur, *quoting a West Point ballad (1951)*

Despite Gen. Douglas MacArthur's stature and popularity, President Harry S. Truman fired him for invading North Korea against orders.

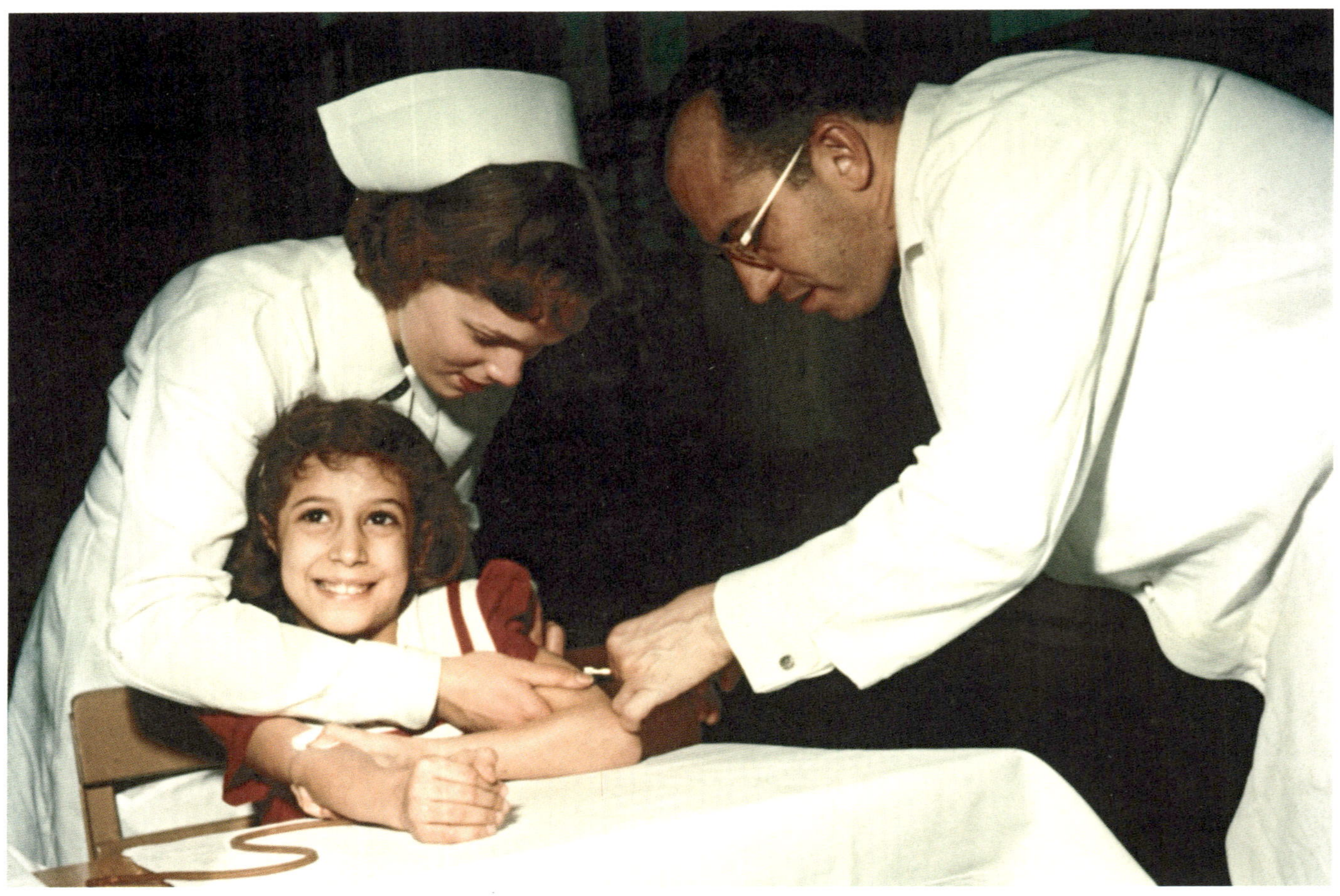

Though shots seldom bring smiles, Jonas Salk's polio vaccine discovery did: In a few years, it virtually wiped out polio in America.

611. MARCH 26, 1953

JONAS SALK INTRODUCES THE POLIO VACCINE

By mid-century, the infectious viral disease polio had become a dreaded annual visitor, erupting in regular summertime epidemics. In 1952 alone, tens of thousands of cases appeared in the U.S. Young children were among the worst affected, and parents kept their children home from swimming pools and summer camps in hopes of protecting them. Good news finally arrived in March 1953, when virologist Jonas Salk announced on CBS Radio that he had developed an experimental vaccine against the disease. Two days later, he reported his successful trials in the *Journal of the American Medical Association*. Although widespread use of the vaccine was still two years away, the announcement marked a turning point; the vaccine virtually eradicated the disease in the United States within a few years.

612. JULY 27, 1953

ARMISTICE ENDS THE KOREAN WAR

Talks to end the Korean War began just one year after the conflict started and dragged on for 158 meetings and two more years. A primary sticking point was the fate of prisoners of war in South Korea: North Korea wanted them all returned, while South Korea believed that many would rather remain in South Korea. The issue was finally settled in favor of voluntary repatriation only; representatives from the UN Command, the North Korean army, and the Chinese People's Volunteer Army signed the official armistice agreement in Panmunjom, near the border between the two states. The armistice established the demilitarized zone that exists between North and South Korea to this day. More than 28,000 U.S. troops remain on bases in South Korea.

613. APRIL 25, 1954

BELL LABS DEMONSTRATES THE FIRST PRACTICAL SOLAR CELL

Scientists had been pursuing the goal of turning sunlight into electricity for decades, but early solar cells produced only a smidgen of energy. It took three disparate researchers at New Jersey's Bell Labs—an engineer, a chemist, and a physicist—combining their specialties to create the first practical solar cell. By mixing silicon with other elements, the scientists produced a variation that converted 6 percent of the sunlight received into electricity—a huge improvement on earlier efforts. In April, they demonstrated their success by hooking their solar panel to a toy Ferris wheel and set the toy spinning. By the 21st century, solar technology had become a widespread and inexpensive source of energy in the United States.

614. MAY 17, 1954

SUPREME COURT STRIKES DOWN SEGREGATED SCHOOLS

Attorney Thurgood Marshall represented five plaintiffs, including Oliver Brown of Topeka, Kansas, in arguing before the Supreme Court that segregated public schooling violated the 14th Amendment guaranteeing equal protection under the law to all citizens. On this day, the court's Chief Justice Earl Warren delivered a ruling that upheld Marshall's case. The unanimous decision in *Brown* v. *Board of Education of Topeka, Kansas* overturned the 60-year-old legacy of *Plessy* v. *Ferguson* asserting that public schools could be "separate but equal." Warren concluded that "in the field of public education, the doctrine of 'separate but equal' has no place. Separate educational facilities are inherently unequal." The decision officially ended segregation in public schools, but in practice desegregation remains an issue in some parts of the country today.

615. JUNE 9, 1954

JOSEPH WELCH CONFRONTS JOSEPH MCCARTHY

Joseph R. McCarthy, Republican senator from Wisconsin, made his name in the early '50s by accusing government agencies of harboring communists. In 1954, as head of the Senate Permanent Subcommittee on Investigations, he turned his attention to the Army, who had hired attorney Joseph Welch to represent it. On the 30th day of the contentious, nationally televised hearings, McCarthy accused a young member of Welch's law firm of being a communist. Welch had reached the end of his rope. "Until this moment, Senator, I think I never really gauged your cruelty, or your recklessness," Welch said. "Have you no sense of decency, sir, at long last? Have you left no sense of decency?" Welch's impassioned question echoed the feelings of many Americans watching the hearings; McCarthy's reputation never recovered after the hearings ended in June. In December, the Senate voted to censure the senator, who died in 1957.

616. SEPTEMBER 3, 1955

EMMETT TILL'S FUNERAL DRAWS THOUSANDS

Fourteen-year-old Emmett Till might have remained just another victim of racist violence were it not for the activism of his mother, Mamie Till-Mobley. While visiting relatives in Money, Mississippi, Till was beaten and murdered by two white men who believed he had whistled at a white woman in town. His body was found in the Tallahatchie River three days later. Mobley asked to have her son sent back to Chicago, where she arranged for an open-casket funeral and allowed the press to photograph his mutilated body. Tens of thousands attended the funeral, and the photographs were published nationally, bringing increased anger and urgency to the civil rights movement. The men who killed Till were found not guilty by an all-white jury but later confessed in magazine interviews. (They could not be tried again due to double jeopardy rules.) In 2022, Congress made lynching a federal hate crime in the Emmett Till Antilynching Act.

Civil rights protests followed the arrest of Black seamstress Rosa Parks for sitting in a "whites-only" bus zone.

617. DECEMBER 1, 1955

ROSA PARKS IS ARRESTED

The police report that day stated: "We received a call upon arrival the bus driver said he had a colored female sitting in the white section of the bus and would not move back." The "colored woman" was department store seamstress and NAACP stalwart Rosa Parks. Her deliberate defiance of Alabama's segregation laws spurred a nationally publicized bus boycott in the city, led by 26-year-old minister Martin Luther King, Jr. Parks lost her job as the 381-day boycott continued, but a legal case challenging the discrimination made its way to the Supreme Court. On November 13, 1956, that court ruled that bus segregation violated the 14th Amendment. The boycott ended in December, while the fight for civil rights gained new ground.

618. APRIL 26, 1956

SHIPPING CONTAINERS SPEED UP WORLD TRADE

Unsexy but vital to the world economy, intermodal shipping containers were first loaded onto the tanker *Ideal-X* in Newark, New Jersey, bound for Houston. Invented by trucking and shipping entrepreneur Malcom McLean, all-purpose containers that could go from truck to ship and back again revolutionized world trade. They replaced an expensive, laborious system that involved loading hundreds of thousands of odd-shaped barrels, bags,

Expanding her repertoire, jazz singer Ella Fitzgerald recorded a double album of Cole Porter tunes. They remain popular classics.

IT ISN'T WHERE YOU CAME FROM ... IT'S WHERE YOU'RE GOING THAT COUNTS.

Ella Fitzgerald

and crates into warehouses and onto ships by hand and reversing the process at the other end. Standardized containers—essentially, truck bodies—that could be lifted by crane directly from trailers and stacked high on ships' decks were far more efficient. Today, 20 million containers travel the seas every year, holding 90 percent of all purchased goods.

619. MAY 15, 1956

ELLA FITZGERALD RELEASES THE *COLE PORTER SONG BOOK*

By 1956, jazz singer Ella Fitzgerald was already a legend for her impeccable style and three-octave range. But she wanted to break free from the novelty and scat tunes that had come to define her. That year, she joined forces with manager Norman Granz and his newly formed Verve Records to issue a double album of Cole Porter songs. The first in what became the Great American Songbook series, *Ella Fitzgerald Sings the Cole Porter Song Book* included such classics as "Anything Goes," "Begin the Beguine," and "Night and Day." It and subsequent albums in the series are considered to be among the best recordings ever made of American jazz classics.

620. OCTOBER 8, 1956

DON LARSEN PITCHES A PERFECT WORLD SERIES GAME

In the history of Major League Baseball, only one man has pitched a perfect game in the World Series, and that man was the workmanlike Yankees right-hander Don Larsen. In Game 5 of the series between the Yankees and Dodgers, Larsen and his efficient, no-windup

A gritty take on *Romeo and Juliet*, Leonard Bernstein's *West Side Story* took the American musical in new directions, to great acclaim.

delivery faced only 27 batters. The Dodgers hit some close calls, but all were fielded efficiently by the Yankees for outs. At game's end, no Dodger had a hit or a walk; no Dodger had reached base. As the *Washington Post* sports reporter Shirley Povich wrote: "The million-to-one shot came in. Hell froze over. A month of Sundays hit the calendar." Larsen never came close to matching this feat again; he finished his career with a win-loss record of 81–91.

621. SEPTEMBER 25, 1957

LITTLE ROCK NINE BEGIN CLASSES

Pressured by a court order in the wake of *Brown* v. *Board of Education,* Arkansas's formerly segregated Central High School prepared to admit its first African American students on September 4. There, the 10 students were blocked by Arkansas National Guard troops brought in by the state's governor, Orval Faubus. The students tried again two days later, but rioting broke out. On September 24, President Dwight D. Eisenhower federalized the Arkansas National Guard and sent in units of the U.S. Army's 101st Airborne Division to protect the nine teenagers. (One dropped out of the group after her father was told he would lose his job if she attended.) On September 25, escorted by soldiers and under the gaze of television cameras, the students began their first full day of classes. The students continued to be harassed throughout the year, and for the entire following school year, Little Rock public high schools were closed in an attempt to prevent desegregation. All of the Little Rock Nine went on to get college degrees, with two receiving their Ph.D.

622. SEPTEMBER 26, 1957

***WEST SIDE STORY* OPENS ON BROADWAY**

Leonard Bernstein's musical *West Side Story,* a contemporary take on *Romeo and Juliet,* opened this day at Broadway's Winter Garden Theatre. It had an all-star pedigree: Arthur Laurents wrote the book, Jerome Robbins choreographed the innovative dances, and the young songwriter Stephen Sondheim wrote the lyrics to Bernstein's music. With a plot featuring gang warfare, racism, and general urban grittiness, Bernstein's creation pushed the American musical into new territory. *West Side Story* ran for 732 performances and won Tony Awards for Best Choreographer and Best Scenic Design. Now considered an American classic, the musical was made into two films: Robert Wise's 1961 version won 10 Academy Awards, and Steven Spielberg's 2021 movie was nominated for seven.

623. JUNE 16, 1958

WHAM-O INTRODUCES THE HULA-HOOP

"The whole family gets into the act with the Hula-Hoop by Wham-O," claimed the advertisement for the new toy, featuring a svelte woman in capri pants. Introduced to Wham-O toy executives by a visitor from Australia, the hip-twirling plastic toy was featured on *The Dinah Shore Chevy Show* and became an instant craze. Wham-O and its competitors sold tens of millions of Hula-Hoops in 1958 alone. Adults and children alike took to the hoops, bringing them to parties, joining in endurance contests, and learning trick moves such as spinning more than a dozen at one time. Hula-Hoops have seen repeated ups and downs in popularity, with hoop-spinning contests persisting around the world into the 21st century.

624. OCTOBER 5, 1958

FIRST REPORTS OF BIGFOOT COME TO LIGHT

"Giant footprints puzzle residents along Trinity River," read the report in the *Humboldt* (California) *Times*. Accompanying the story was a photo of construction worker Jerry Crew holding a plaster cast of a huge footprint more than 16 inches long. Crew claimed to have made the cast from a set of prints he found along a local creek. The creature that left them, he said, had a 50-inch stride. A columnist at the paper dubbed it "Big Foot"—and a legend was born. In 1967, a film showing an apparent Bigfoot walking along the creek boosted interest in the creature. The fact that the footprints were later revealed to be a hoax and that the film is widely believed to be a sham has not dimmed public interest in the fabled biped.

In 1967, Bob Gimlin and Roger Patterson compare detailed plaster casts taken of the alleged footprints of Bigfoot.

625. OCTOBER 18, 1958

SCIENTISTS CREATE THE FIRST VIDEO GAME

The analog computer at the Brookhaven National Laboratory could calculate trajectories for bullets and missiles—why not a tennis ball? Physicist William Higinbotham thought "it might liven up the place to have a game that people could play." So he tweaked the computer's programming to create an interactive two-person tennis game, visible on a small oscilloscope screen as a bouncing ball of light over a line (the net). Players used controllers with buttons to bat the ball back and forth. In a sign of things to come, people eagerly lined up at the lab's annual visitors' days to play "Tennis for Two," considered by many to be the first true video game in what would become a major industry.

Often called the best jazz album ever made, *Kind of Blue* teamed Miles Davis with stars including John Coltrane and Cannonball Adderley.

626. DECEMBER 28, 1958

JOHNNY UNITAS LEADS COLTS TO VICTORY

It wasn't the smoothest game of football ever played, but the back-and-forth thrills of the Colts-Giants NFL championship bout have earned it the title of "greatest game ever played." Multiple fumbles and a goal-line stand kept the game swinging from one team to the other. Down 17 to 14 with under two minutes left, 25-year-old Colts quarterback Johnny Unitas moved the ball downfield and set up a tying field goal with seven seconds left. The game entered the first overtime ever played in pro football. Unitas took his team to the goal line with an 80-yard drive, where the Colts scored a touchdown to win the game 23–17. Following disappointing seasons in the 1970s, the Colts, then of Baltimore, Maryland, made a surprise move to Indianapolis, Indiana, in the middle of the night in 1984.

627. FEBRUARY 3, 1959

ROCK AND ROLL STARS DIE IN PLANE CRASH

The Winter Dance Party tour across the upper Midwest was a miserable experience for the musicians involved. Buddy Holly, Ritchie Valens, J. P. Richardson ("The Big Bopper"), and several other rock and roll stars and their bands were shuttling from one town to another in subzero temperatures on an unheated bus. Fed up with the terrible traveling conditions, Buddy Holly chartered an airplane in Clear Lake, Iowa, to take him to the next gig. The two other empty seats were filled by Richardson and by Valens, who won the seat in a coin toss with Holly's tourmate Tommy Allsup. In snowy weather five miles from the airport, the plane crashed, killing the three musicians and the pilot. The crash later became known as "the day the music died" from the lyrics of Don McLean's song "American Pie."

628. MARCH 2, 1959

MILES DAVIS RECORDS *KIND OF BLUE*

On this day, a jazz supergroup consisting of Miles Davis, John Coltrane, Cannonball Adderley, Wynton Kelly, Bill Evans, Paul Chambers, and Jimmy Cobb recorded the first three tracks of Miles Davis's masterpiece album, *Kind of Blue*. After recording "So What,"

"Freddie Freeloader," and "Blue in Green" at Columbia's 30th Street Studio in New York on March 2, the group finished with "All Blues" and "Flamenco Sketches" on April 22. The cool, moody, bluesy pieces were mostly improvised around scales and captured in single takes. Most critics consider *Kind of Blue* the best jazz album ever produced. It is also the most successful, selling more than five million copies as of 2019.

629. MARCH 9, 1959

BARBIE MAKES HER DEBUT

Ponytailed Barbie Millicent Roberts from fictional Willows, Wisconsin, made her first appearance at the American International Toy Fair wearing a black-and-white striped swimsuit. The 11-inch-high doll was designed by Mattel co-founder Ruth Handler, who based the toy on a German doll named Lilli and named it after her own daughter, Barbara. "Little girls dream of being curvaceous, dreamy, exciting," she said. "They want—someday—to have gorgeous clothes, be chic and look like movie stars." Barbie prompted controversy at first because of her adult figure, but in her many varieties and with an ever expanding wardrobe, she was a hit with kids. Mattel sold 300,000 Barbies in her first year;

EVERY LITTLE GIRL NEEDED A DOLL THROUGH WHICH TO PROJECT HERSELF INTO HER DREAM OF HER FUTURE.

Ruth Handler, *creator of Barbie (1977)*

A Barbie doll poses atop a camera in a photograph used in an advertising campaign in 1959.

Playwright Lorraine Hansberry's childhood experiences of racial discrimination shaped the plot of her classic drama *A Raisin in the Sun.*

the doll became a sales powerhouse, with a sister, best friend, boyfriend, house, car, endless clothes, and a 2023 hit movie filling Mattel's coffers.

630. MARCH 11, 1959

A RAISIN IN THE SUN OPENS IN NEW YORK

Lorraine Hansberry's play, the first by an African American woman to reach Broadway, starred Sidney Poitier, Ruby Dee, and Claudia McNeil. The story follows the struggles of a Chicago family as they try to claim their own piece of the American dream by buying a house in an affordable, but hostile, white neighborhood. The plot stemmed in part from the 29-year-old playwright's own childhood, in which her parents had fought a legal battle to hold on to their house in the face of white opposition. Hansberry's play won the New York Drama Critics' Circle Award for Best American Play. Hansberry died of cancer in 1965 and did not live to see her work regularly revived and taught in schools as part of the American literary canon.

631. FEBRUARY 1, 1960

GREENSBORO SIT-INS ARE INITIATED

Four young Black men—freshmen at North Carolina Agricultural and Technical State University—sat at a whites-only Woolworth's lunch counter in Greensboro, North Carolina, on this day and politely asked for service. Later dubbed the "Greensboro Four," Franklin McCain, Joseph McNeil, Ezell Blair, Jr. (later Jibreel Khazan), and David Richmond had carefully planned their lunch counter request to draw attention to widespread segregation throughout the South. When they were refused service, they calmly remained in their seats until the store closed. Over the next days and weeks, other supporters joined in with well-publicized sit-ins and protests at that same counter and in dozens of southern cities. The Greensboro store integrated by July 1960, followed by many, though not all, similar venues across the South. The sit-ins were among the most successful actions of the civil rights era.

632. MAY 9, 1960

FDA APPROVES FIRST BIRTH CONTROL PILL

The culmination of years of feminist campaigning and medical research, the first oral contraceptive, Enovid, was approved by the Food and Drug Administration (FDA) on this day. The birth control pill—which soon became known simply as "the pill"—had been authorized in 1957, but only for menstrual disorders. In 1960, the pharmaceutical company G. D. Searle managed to get the high-dose pill approved for birth control as well. Within three years, 2.3 million American women were using the pill, leading over the coming decades to, among other things, a large decrease in unwanted births and an increase in the number of married women in the labor force. Today, amid a greater range of contraceptive options, more than 10 million American women of childbearing age use one of the dozens of brands of contraceptive pills.

Author Harper Lee saw "something universal" in the small-town southern life of her youth: the setting for her book *To Kill a Mockingbird.*

633. JULY 11, 1960

HARPER LEE PUBLISHES *TO KILL A MOCKINGBIRD*

Harper Lee was an unknown, previously unpublished southern writer when J. B. Lippincott brought out her first novel, *To Kill a Mockingbird.* Based in part on her childhood in Monroeville, Alabama, the story went on to win readers worldwide with its depiction of a young girl's awakening to injustice, racism, and heroism among everyday people. "I would like to be the chronicler of something that I think is going down the drain very swiftly," said Lee in a rare interview. "And that is small town middle-class southern life. There is something universal in it. There's something decent to be said for it, and there's something to lament when it goes." The book won the Pulitzer Prize in 1961 and is now considered one of the great American novels, taught in high schools across the country and dramatized on stage and screen.

634. SEPTEMBER 8, 1960

WILMA RUDOLPH WINS THIRD GOLD MEDAL

On this day, track-and-field star Wilma Rudolph anchored the U.S. women's 4×100-meter relay team at the Rome Olympics to win her third gold medal: the most collected by any American woman at a single Olympic Games. Her victory was even more significant because of the obstacles Rudolph had overcome. The 20th of 22 children, she suffered from polio as a child and wore a leg brace until the age of nine. On her triumphant return to the United States, Rudolph refused to attend a segregated welcome-home celebration, instead choosing to appear at the first ever integrated event in her hometown of Clarksville, Tennessee.

635. JANUARY 24, 1961

H-BOMBS DROP ON NORTH CAROLINA

The 1960s Air Force mission Operation Chrome Dome kept nuclear-armed B-52s in the air 24 hours a day. Some of them flew out of Seymour Johnson Air Force Base near Goldsboro, North Carolina. On this day, a B-52 with eight crew members developed a fuel leak and then tore apart over a field as it returned to base. Five crew members were able to successfully parachute to the ground and survive. Also dropping to the ground were the plane's two 3.8-megaton hydrogen bombs; one floated down under a chute and landed safely, upright, in a stand of trees, while the other plowed into the ground and broke into pieces. The Air Force moved in quickly to clean up, and accounts vary about whether one of the bombs was close to detonating. Still buried deep in that cotton field is the plutonium core that the Air Force could not retrieve.

Author Rachel Carson's *Silent Spring* dramatically raised public awareness of how DDT and other pesticides were poisoning life on Earth.

636. MAY 5, 1961

ALAN SHEPARD LEAVES EARTH'S ATMOSPHERE

At 9:34 a.m., astronaut Alan Shepard rocketed into suborbital space to become the first American to leave Earth's atmosphere. Shepard, a World War II veteran and test pilot, was the chosen representative of NASA's group of astronaut trainees, known as the Mercury 7. A Redstone rocket carried his Freedom 7 spacecraft 116 miles high, giving Shepard five minutes of weightlessness inside the cramped capsule before it plummeted, parachuting into the ocean. It was not quite the triumph that NASA had hoped it would be, given that the U.S.S.R. had launched cosmonaut Yuri Gagarin into orbit just 25 days earlier. Even so, Shepard's successful flight gave the green light for the Apollo missions to the moon.

637. MARCH 2, 1962

WILT CHAMBERLAIN SCORES 100 POINTS

Wilt ("Wilt the Stilt," "the Big Dipper") Chamberlain was a fearsome seven-foot-one-inch, 275-pound juggernaut on the basketball court. His team, the Philadelphia Warriors, was playing the New York Knicks at an out-of-the-way arena in Hershey, Pennsylvania. By the beginning of the fourth quarter, Chamberlain had scored 69 points and his teammates began to pass him the ball at every opportunity. As the fans chanted—"Give it to Wilt! Give it to Wilt!"—he amassed exactly 31 more points with 46 seconds left to go. His 100-point single-game scoring record still stands.

638. SEPTEMBER 27, 1962

RACHEL CARSON PUBLISHES *SILENT SPRING*

Silent Spring opens with a fable: "There was once a town in the heart of America where all life seemed to live in harmony with its surroundings." But all is not well: "There was a strange stillness. The birds, for example—where had they gone?" Carson was already a best-selling author when *Silent Spring* was published in 1962. She had written three books about the sea and had won the National Book Award for one of them. But *Silent Spring* was harder-hitting. It made the case that many chemicals—notably pesticides, including DDT—were poisoning the web of life, human life included. First published as a three-part series in the *New Yorker, Silent Spring* roused considerable opposition from chemical companies, but in the long run the book was acclaimed as a seminal work in the modern environmental movement. Today, it is considered a classic with a still relevant message.

639. OCTOBER 24, 1962

U.S. REACHES DEFCON 2 DURING THE CUBAN MISSILE CRISIS

The United States came as close as it ever has to nuclear war during a standoff with the Soviet Union after the U.S.S.R. installed nuclear missiles in Cuba. After a U.S. spy plane photographed launch sites on the island, President John F. Kennedy instituted a naval

continued on page 324

I REALIZED UP THERE THAT OUR PLANET IS NOT INFINITE. IT'S FRAGILE.

Alan Shepard, Los Angeles Times *(1994)*

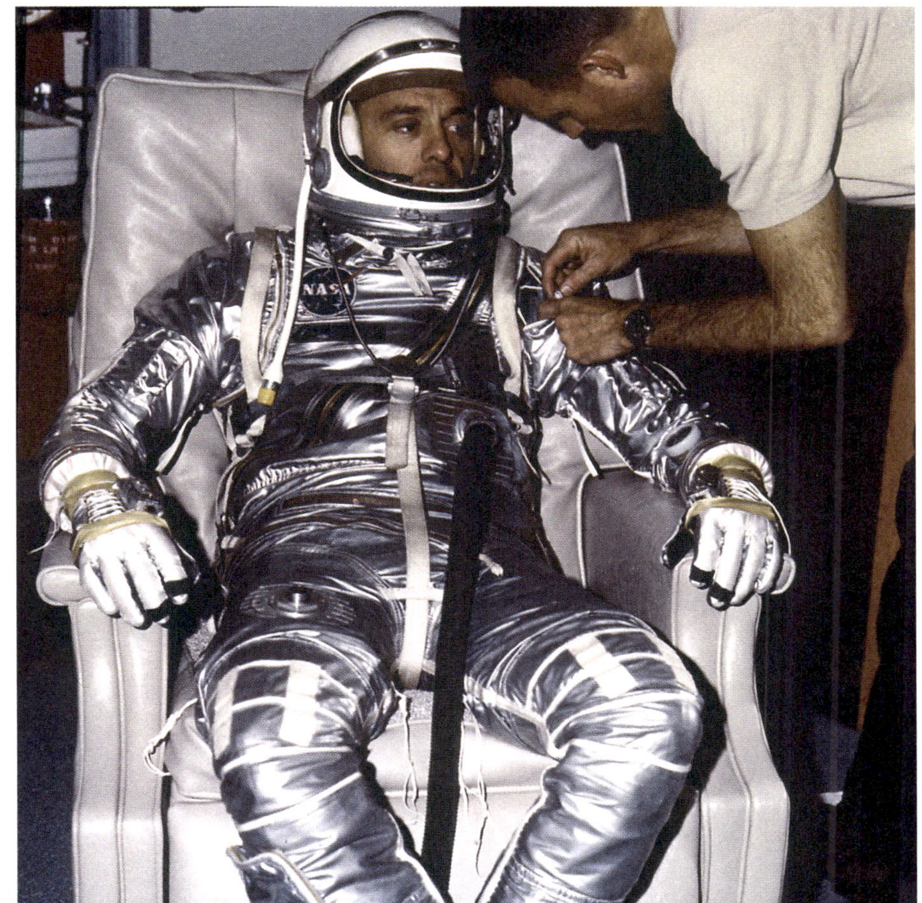

Alan Shepard rocketed 116 miles high to become the first U.S. astronaut in suborbital space 23 days after a Soviet cosmonaut went into orbit.

MICHAEL BESCHLOSS

MICHAEL BESCHLOSS IS AN AWARD-WINNING HISTORIAN AND BEST-SELLING AUTHOR OF 10 BOOKS. NBC'S PRESIDENTIAL HISTORIAN AND A CONTRIBUTOR TO *PBS NEWSHOUR*, HE HAS ALSO BEEN A CONTRIBUTING COLUMNIST TO THE *NEW YORK TIMES*.

DAVID M. RUBENSTEIN: Which person had the most impact on the 20th century, and why?

MICHAEL BESCHLOSS: Franklin Roosevelt. Had he not been elected in 1932, we might have had Al Smith or John Nance Garner as president in the late 1930s, or other figures who were not of Roosevelt's caliber. The only way America helped [the Allies] prevail in World War II was that Roosevelt had the courage to rearm beginning before 1940. I don't think those other leaders would have had that kind of foresight or ability.

DMR: Theodore Roosevelt was president from 1901 to 1909. Did he essentially change what the presidency is all about?

MB: For much of the first century of American history, presidents did some pretty important things, but they were not the center of our political universe. After Roosevelt, that changed.

Roosevelt felt that a president shouldn't send an annual message to Congress explaining how the country *was,* but instead call on Congress to *do* certain things. As a result, since his time, people expect presidents to be activists in a way we didn't at first.

DMR: What forces led to the 19th Amendment's ratification in 1920, allowing women the right to vote? How did that change America's politics and democracy?

MB: For well over a century after the signing of the Constitution, half the United States—women—could not vote. When Woodrow Wilson became president in 1913, he wasn't particularly interested in the issue. But having gone through World War I and witnessing the enormous contribution of women to the workforce and armed forces, he felt it would be challenging to end the war and refuse women the vote.

DMR: Did the Treaty of Versailles lead to World War II?

MB: In retrospect, it's impossible to imagine any treaty at the end of World War I that would have prevented some form of World War II. The Treaty of Versailles was flawed in all sorts of ways—including the enormous penalties for Germany, which caused Germans to be resentful and almost urged them to become a major power again. But another issue—the fact that the U.S. wouldn't join the League of Nations—originated at home.

DMR: Could World War I have been prevented with better diplomacy?

MB: Given the issues involved and potential for conflict, Europe was a hotbed for world war. However, you can make the case that it didn't need to grow into as large a conflict as it did. [Historian and two-time Pulitzer Prize–winning author] Barbara Tuchman argues that one reason World

War I was so bad was because of a failure to communicate. If you're president of the United States facing the dangers of a major war, the most important thing you can do is make sure that there are no miscommunications.

DMR: Did Wilson's wife really run the presidency for the year or so following his stroke?
MB: It makes a nice story to think of Edith Wilson as the first female president who was operating in the absence of her husband. A better description would be that her husband was in bed, intellectually damaged and physically weak, so she ran interference among Wilson, his Cabinet, and the public.

DMR: What was the cause of the stock market crash in October 1929? Could the crash and Great Depression have been avoided with better leadership from the president, Congress, or business community?
MB: In 1929 there was rampant speculation, very loose regulation, and a tightening of credit. We were as close to "free capitalism" as we've ever had in America. But experiments in that space often don't work quickly.

DMR: How did Franklin D. Roosevelt overcome polio to become president in 1932?
MB: Roosevelt was a person of sheer will and ambition. Before he got polio in 1921, he had the ambition, but he hadn't faced personal crisis. The fact that he was trying to teach himself to walk again and function, *and* one day run for president—all that changed him in a way almost nothing else could have. The Roosevelt of those three terms was born of the fact that he had encountered the abyss and was able to surmount it.

DMR: Why was Europe so unwilling to confront Hitler before World War II began in earnest in September 1939?
MB: Europe had been through World War I; they knew how crushing it had been. Many had hoped they could negotiate with Hitler. That turned out not to be true.

DMR: Why was the U.S. reluctant to get involved in the war in a meaningful way until Pearl Harbor?
MB: The U.S. had been promised, by Wilson, that if they succeeded in World War I, they wouldn't have to fight another war for a long time. When they saw it happening again, Congress put enormous obstacles in front of Roosevelt, essentially saying, We don't want you to make the mistake of once again dragging us into an unnecessary world war.

DMR: Why did Japan attack Pearl Harbor on December 7, 1941?
MB: Japan wanted to establish a sphere of influence that conflicted with what the United States was trying to do in the Pacific. It was also trying to get negotiations going to get more resources and improve its economy, which wasn't happening in December 1941. That's why the attack began. Despite present-day conspiracy theories, the attack didn't begin because Roosevelt encouraged it or wanted it.

DMR: How did FDR develop into a wartime leader? What was the nature of his relationship with Churchill?
MB: Roosevelt was an almost instantly effective wartime leader. During World War I, he was close to Wilson, so he had experience. His relationship with Churchill was awful; he was suspicious of Churchill and his motives. He recognized, though, that unless America and Britain fought the Axis powers side by side, it was going to be hard to prevail.

DMR: Was the Cold War—which stretched from 1949 to 1991—inevitable? Or could Americans have taken steps after World War II to prevent Russia from controlling Eastern Europe and seeking to impose communism around the world?
MB: Some form of a Cold War was inevitable, because the Soviets got to Berlin before the Allied powers did. America was exhausted after winning World War II. They weren't primed to instantly turn against what had been our Russian ally.

DMR: How did the assassination of John F. Kennedy on November 22, 1963, affect the U.S. and alter the Cold War?
MB: Kennedy's assassination was not only a shock but

changed history. For the first time, America had an enormous blow to its self-confidence, even beyond Pearl Harbor. Americans began to suspect their government's actions behind the scenes. To some extent, this led to later conspiracy theories about Kennedy's assassination.

The other effects were twofold. Kennedy was very determined by the end of 1963 to reach some kind of détente with the Soviet Union. This ended, because Lyndon B. Johnson became president and wasn't as interested. The evidence also shows that Kennedy would have resisted demands to escalate the Vietnam War in a way that Johnson did not.

DMR: Why did Johnson feel the need to escalate the war?
MB: Johnson had an ambitious domestic program called the Great Society, which favored aid to education, voting rights, and civil rights. He wasn't going to jeopardize these goals with criticism from Republicans or hard-line Americans saying he was soft on Vietnam. So his priority in his first two years, tragically, was toward making sure he wouldn't encounter the criticism that might bring down his domestic program. As a result, he escalated the war almost beyond the point of no return, with catastrophic consequences for America.

DMR: What prompted Richard Nixon's effort to open relations with China?
MB: Two reasons: He thought it was dangerous to let a country as large and populous as China to be, as Nixon said, nurtured in its grievances. So he thought it was important to begin an open negotiating track. He also felt that if America had a relationship with China, it would put pressure on the Soviet Union to end the Vietnam War.

DMR: With the Watergate scandal, Nixon took steps to prevent resigning the presidency. Was Ford's pardon of him a political blunder, an act of courage, or both?
MB: If Nixon, in late 1972 or early '73, had genuinely told the truth about Watergate—even with the resulting embarrassment—it might have allowed him to survive it. But Nixon's instincts were to contain the political crisis.

Ford's pardon of Nixon a month after Nixon resigned was an act of political courage, because it brought down his poll ratings in advance of the 1976 election. Ford was a religious person. He believed in mercy, along with justice, and he felt that if he hadn't pardoned Nixon, the next two years would've been overwhelmed with trials and talk of the former president, which might have further clouded Ford's chance for reelection.

You can argue that by pardoning Nixon and not requiring him to sign an ironclad statement of guilt before the pardon was accepted, Ford opened the door for later presidents to think they could get away with violating the law as well.

DMR: What was the impact of Jimmy Carter's support of human rights around the world and in the future?
MB: When Carter supported global human rights, he did so in a long historical tradition going back to Thomas Jefferson: the hope that the contagion of democracy and freedom would spread around the world. Soviet dissidents of the 1970s and '80s say that Carter's words gave them hope to resist.

DMR: How did the U.S. government not see the looming Iranian revolution and prevent its 52 embassy employees from being held hostage for 444 days starting in 1979?
MB: Carter felt that to admit the shah to the United States would be an act of mercy. He didn't anticipate it would lead to hostages being taken, putting their lives in jeopardy, and doing a lot to crush his reelection.

On that note, Harry Truman once said that any high school student with 20/20 hindsight can make better decisions than a president can, since he's operating with fragmentary evidence and doesn't know everything a historian will later.

DMR: How did Ronald Reagan, as president, reshape the U.S. government and its relationship with the Soviet Union?
MB: Reagan often said in 1980 when he was running for president, "I want to show that the West isn't devoid of the will to defeat the Soviet Union. Once that's demonstrated, I'll sit down for as long as it takes to see if we can reduce the Cold War." Reagan hated nuclear weapons. It had a lot to do with his strong private religious views.

Lunar module pilot Edwin "Buzz" Aldrin stands beside the American flag, planted on the moon during the Apollo 11 mission and held aloft by a pole across the top.

DMR: Who was most responsible for the collapse of the Soviet Union in 1991?

MB: Reagan, Bush Sr., Gorbachev, and other leaders were responsible for the collapse of the Soviet Union. So were the people inside the Soviet Union. So were people of the West who kept the pressure on the Soviets for decades or more.

Reagan really did want to end the Cold War, and he gave Gorbachev and earlier Soviet leaders the sense that they couldn't just "tough out" the West. As a result, Gorbachev was brought to power and essentially sued for peace. Bush gave Gorbachev the respect of not boasting about Western successes, such as the opening of the Berlin Wall. Another, more triumphalist president might not have done that.

DMR: How did Vladimir Putin, a little-known bureaucrat, come to be Russia's leader at the end of the century?

MB: If you have not had the chaos of Boris Yeltsin, you would not have had a desire for more order and a leader like Putin, who was more in the old tradition of Russia.

DMR: At the end of the 20th century, was the U.S. the undisputed world leader in economic, financial, military, and technological matters?

MB: Yes, the United States was the world's dominant power, which happened because of the collapse of the Soviet Union—and the fact that China hadn't grown as much as it would later.

DMR: What do you feel is the most significant occurrence of the 20th century?

MB: There are two. First, World War II: Had America and our allies lost, we would have been a country dominated by authoritarian Germans and Japanese, and the rest of the century would have been different. Another occurrence that looms large in this century is the moon landing in 1969. Presuming that human beings travel to other planets in the future, the moment when we landed on the moon and how it happened may seem much more important to people than it does today.

A quarter million people joined the March on Washington, ending at the Lincoln Memorial with Martin Luther King, Jr.'s "I Have a Dream" speech.

continued from page 319

blockade. The two superpowers hovered on the brink of war for days, and the U.S. military went to DEFCON (Defense Condition) 2, the last stage before DEFCON 1 and nuclear war. Kennedy and Soviet premier Nikita Khrushchev began an intense correspondence. "You wish to ensure the security of your country, and this is understandable," wrote Khrushchev. "But how are we, the Soviet Union, our Government, to assess your actions which are expressed in the fact that you have surrounded the Soviet Union with military bases?" In late October, the Soviets began to dismantle their Cuban missile installations. The following year, the U.S. removed its own missiles from Turkey as its part of the agreement, although that aspect of the negotiations was kept secret for decades. Historians today still debate whether Kennedy saved the world through skilled negotiation or recklessly brought it to the brink of disaster.

640. JULY 7, 1963

THE FIRE NEXT TIME HITS NUMBER ONE ON THE NONFICTION BESTSELLER LIST

The two essays that make up James Baldwin's *The Fire Next Time* were a thoughtful and timely examination of what it meant to be Black in 20th-century America. Baldwin reflected on his upbringing in Harlem, his experiences with religion, and the possible paths forward for both white and Black Americans. "A bill is coming in that I fear America is not prepared to pay," Baldwin wrote. "The price … is the unconditional freedom of the Negro; it is not too much to say that he, who has been so long rejected, must now be embraced, and at no matter what psychic or social risk. He is *the* key figure in his country, and the American future is precisely as bright or as dark as his." Published just before the March on Washington, the book had a special resonance in the heart of the civil rights movement.

641. AUGUST 28, 1963

CIVIL RIGHTS DEMONSTRATORS MARCH ON WASHINGTON

Approximately 250,000 demonstrators took part in the March on Washington for Jobs and Freedom, including civil rights activists Martin Luther King, Jr., John Lewis, Bayard Rustin, and celebrity singers Mahalia Jackson, Bob Dylan, and Joan Baez. The march had been organized by a coalition of civil rights and labor groups. King was the final speaker of the day. Standing on the steps of the Lincoln Memorial, he gave the 16-minute oration that has come to be known as his "I Have a Dream" speech. Echoing the Bible, he said, "We will not be satisfied until justice rolls down like waters, and righteousness like a mighty stream." After the march, King and other leaders met with President John F. Kennedy and Vice President Lyndon B. Johnson in the White House to press for civil rights legislation, which would pass the following year.

WE CANNOT WALK ALONE. AND AS WE WALK, WE MUST MAKE THE PLEDGE THAT WE SHALL ALWAYS MARCH AHEAD. WE CANNOT TURN BACK.

Martin Luther King, Jr., *"I Have a Dream" speech (1963)*

642. SEPTEMBER 15, 1963

BOMBING KILLS FOUR GIRLS IN BIRMINGHAM, ALABAMA

As church services began that Sunday morning in Birmingham's 16th Street Baptist Church, a powerful bomb exploded on the building's east side. Killed in the explosion were four girls in the Sunday School classroom: 14-year-olds Addie Mae Collins, Denise McNair, and Carole Robertson and 11-year-old Cynthia Wesley. Addie's sister Sarah lost an eye. The bombing was clearly a racist attack on a well-known civil rights meeting place; Reverend Martin Luther King, Jr., sent a telegram to Alabama's segregationist governor, George Wallace, informing him that "the blood of our little children is on your hands." Although the FBI quickly identified four KKK members as suspects, Director J. Edgar Hoover stalled the investigation, and it was many years before three of them were convicted of the crime and sentenced to life in prison. (One bomber died before charges were brought.)

643. NOVEMBER 22, 1963

AN ASSASSIN KILLS PRESIDENT KENNEDY

President John F. Kennedy was looking toward his reelection campaign in 1964 when he embarked on a motorcade through downtown Dallas, Texas. Riding with Kennedy in the open convertible were his wife, Jacqueline, Texas governor John Connally, and Connally's wife, Nellie; the Connallys were sitting in jump seats in front of the Kennedys. As the

This photo of President John F. Kennedy in a Dallas motorcade is among the last images taken before he was felled by an assassin's bullets.

motorcade traveled through Dallas's Dealey Plaza, bystanders heard gunfire. Two bullets struck Kennedy, and the one that hit him in the head probably killed him instantly. The first bullet that passed through his body struck John Connally, injuring him. Kennedy was rushed to Parkland Memorial Hospital, where doctors worked frantically but pronounced him dead at 1 p.m.

Meanwhile, investigators found a rifle belonging to ex-Marine Lee Harvey Oswald inside the Texas School Book Depository, which overlooked the motorcade route; within hours, police caught Oswald hiding in a movie theater after he had also gunned down a Dallas police officer. At 2:38 p.m., Lyndon B. Johnson was sworn in as the 36th president of the United States aboard Air Force One, with Jacqueline Kennedy standing next to him in her blood-stained suit.

644. JANUARY 11, 1964

SURGEON GENERAL'S REPORT LINKS SMOKING TO PREMATURE DEATH

Surgeon General Luther Terry didn't want to disturb the stock market, so he held his landmark press conference on smoking and health on a Saturday morning. In front of hundreds of reporters, Terry (himself a smoker) presented his committee's findings that smoking caused both lung and laryngeal cancer and was probably linked to other serious respiratory diseases such as emphysema. As a result of the findings, within several years cigarette advertising was banned in broadcast media and cigarette packages had to carry a health warning. In 1964, more than 40 percent of Americans smoked; by the 2020s, the percentage had dropped to under 12 percent.

645. FEBRUARY 9, 1964

THE BEATLES PERFORM ON *THE ED SULLIVAN SHOW*

The Beatles' first visit to the United States in 1964 injected a welcome dose of upbeat energy into a country still mourning John F. Kennedy's death. The British lads were already wildly popular after the release of their first album, *Introducing the Beatles,* when they landed in the United States and appeared on *The Ed Sullivan Show* two days later. In front of 700 screaming audience members, mostly young women (including Richard Nixon's daughter Julie), the group played "All My Loving," "I Want to Hold Your Hand," and other hits. Watching at home were an estimated 73 million TV viewers—approximately 60 percent of the television-watching audience that night. Today, the Beatles have sold approximately 500 million albums worldwide.

After the U.S. surgeon general linked smoking to cancer and other diseases, cigarette ads were curbed and health warnings required.

646. JULY 2, 1964

PRESIDENT JOHNSON SIGNS THE CIVIL RIGHTS ACT

With Martin Luther King, Jr., standing behind him in the East Room of the White House, President Lyndon B. Johnson signed into law the Civil Rights Act of 1964, which banned discrimination on the basis of race, color, religion, sex, or national origin. The legislation, which encompassed voting, employment, education, and public accommodations, had been one of John F. Kennedy's key initiatives. After JFK's assassination, Johnson and leaders in the House and Senate, including Hubert Humphrey and Everett Dirksen, were able to rally enough votes to overcome the opposition of southern Democrats and pass the bill.

647. FEBRUARY 21, 1965

ASSASSINS KILL MALCOLM X

Civil rights leader Malcolm X had just taken the stage at Manhattan's Audubon Ballroom when a commotion broke out in the audience. A man ran onto the stage and shot Malcolm in the chest with a sawed-off shotgun; two other men reached the edge of the stage and shot him as well. Malcolm was pronounced dead at a local hospital soon afterward. The activist had recently broken his ties to the Nation of Islam (NOI) in favor of Sunni Islam, and three men connected to the NOI were arrested, charged with his murder, and imprisoned. Only one confessed to the killing, and the guilt of the other two, based on disputed eyewitness accounts, was long in question. In 2021, New York's supreme court vacated their convictions. The identity of the other assassins remains unclear.

648. MARCH 7, 1965

SELMA MARCHES BEGIN ON "BLOODY SUNDAY"

A march from Selma, Alabama, to the state capital in Montgomery—intended to protest barriers to Black voting—turned into a bloody assault and three marches in total. The first, on Sunday, March 7, was led by John Lewis of the Student Nonviolent Coordinating Committee (SNCC) and Hosea Williams of the Southern Christian Leadership Conference (SCLC). On the Edmund Pettus Bridge leading out of Selma, troopers and others attacked the marchers with clubs, bullwhips, and tear gas, leaving many, including Lewis, badly injured. Civil rights leader Martin Luther King, Jr., led a second demonstration just to the bridge on March 9; that night, members of the Ku Klux Klan attacked and killed a white clergyman who had joined the protests. A third, massive demonstration reached Montgomery on March 25. The televised protests and violence outraged much of the American public and prompted a formerly indecisive Lyndon B. Johnson to push for the Voting Rights Act of 1965.

649. MARCH 8, 1965

FIRST U.S. COMBAT TROOPS REACH VIETNAM

Amid heavy surf, 3,500 Marines from the 9th Marine Expeditionary Brigade waded ashore at Da Nang in South Vietnam—the first, but certainly not the last American troops to set foot in the embattled country as combatants. Although they had been deployed there to protect a U.S. air base from attack, the Marines were greeted not by enemy fire but by schoolgirls who placed flowered wreaths around their necks. They joined more than 20,000 American advisers who had been training the South Vietnamese army to fight North Vietnamese forces. By the end of the year, more than 180,000 American troops had been added to the first Marine contingent as the war escalated.

Hollywood took Americans' interest in space, added one genie in a bottle from folklore, and created a TV hit, *I Dream of Jeannie.*

650. AUGUST 6, 1965

PRESIDENT JOHNSON SIGNS THE VOTING RIGHTS ACT INTO LAW

The 15th Amendment to the Constitution, adopted in 1870, recognized the voting rights of African American men. But obstacles such as poll taxes and literacy tests effectively stalled the exercise of those rights afterward, especially in the South. In 1965, civil rights demonstrations, particularly the Selma marches, led President Lyndon B. Johnson and Congress to pass the Voting Rights Act. "We have already waited a hundred years and more, and the time for waiting is gone," said Johnson after two of the marches. The legislation banned the discriminatory taxes and tests and allowed the government to step in if voting rights were being withheld. It led to a dramatic rise in Black voter registration throughout the South.

651. SEPTEMBER 18, 1965

I DREAM OF JEANNIE PREMIERES

I Dream of Jeannie, whose first episode aired this day, answered the burning question: What would happen if an astronaut lived with a genie? In the pilot episode of the television series, "The Lady in the Bottle," Captain Tony Nelson (Larry Hagman) crash-lands on a desert island, where he finds an old bottle containing an adoring blonde genie, named Jeannie (Barbara Eden). Jeannie hides in the bottle in his duffel bag as he returns home and, over the next five seasons, lives with him and causes mischief in Florida; the two characters eventually marry. Running until 1970, the show reached approximately 12 million viewers at its peak.

652. JANUARY 17, 1966

TRUMAN CAPOTE PUBLISHES *IN COLD BLOOD*

Already famed as a novelist, Truman Capote broke new ground as a writer when he published his "nonfiction novel" *In Cold Blood.* "One morning in November, 1959," said Capote in a later interview, "while flicking through the *New York Times,* I encountered on a deep-inside page, this headline: 'Wealthy Farmer, 3 of Family Slain.'" With the assistance of his close friend, the writer Harper Lee, Capote spent the next six years researching the murders of four members of the Clutter family in Holcomb, Kansas, and the eventual capture of their two killers. He published the tale in four installments in the *New Yorker* in 1965 before issuing it in book form. Widely acclaimed, *In Cold Blood* became an instant hit, selling millions of copies over the course of its lifetime, and is considered a forerunner of the unconventional techniques of New Journalism.

The first 3,500 U.S. combat troops arrived in Vietnam in March 1965. By year's end, as the war escalated, another 180,000 had joined them.

An early 1967 "be-in" in San Francisco set the stage for the Summer of Love that drew 100,000 hippies and counterculture activists.

653. SEPTEMBER 8, 1966

MARLO THOMAS BECOMES "THAT GIRL"

Independent, single workingwomen were a rarity on television until the debut of *That Girl* in 1966. Starring Marlo Thomas as an aspiring actress also working temp jobs, the show was a comedy with a feminist edge that ran for five seasons. "I remember saying to the network, 'I don't want to be the wife of somebody, I don't want to be the daughter of somebody, I don't want to be the secretary of somebody, I want to be the somebody,'' Thomas said.

654. JANUARY 14, 1967

"HUMAN BE-IN" HERALDS THE SUMMER OF LOVE

Luminaries of 1960s counterculture, including Allen Ginsberg, Dick Gregory, and Jerry Rubin, joined at least 20,000 young Americans in San Francisco's Golden Gate Park for a "Human Be-In" on this day. Advertised in the *San Francisco Oracle,* the event was intended to bring together apolitical lifestyle hippies and Berkeley's more politically oriented counterculture movement. Psychologist Timothy Leary, whose experiments with

LSD would make the drug famous, took the stage to encourage the crowd to "tune in, turn on, drop out," and bands including the Grateful Dead and Jefferson Airplane performed. The rally marked the beginning of the Summer of Love that attracted up to 100,000 people to the Haight-Ashbury neighborhood.

655. JANUARY 27, 1967

APOLLO 1 ASTRONAUTS DIE IN FIRE

To conduct a routine countdown simulation, astronauts Virgil "Gus" Grissom, Ed White, and Roger Chaffee suited up and climbed inside the Apollo 1 capsule on the Cape Kennedy launchpad. The astronauts and ground crews sealed the spacecraft's heavy hatches and waited as the capsule filled with pure oxygen. At 6:31 p.m., Roger Chaffee sent a message: "Fire!" A conflagration had broken out in the capsule. The astronauts struggled to open a hatch but couldn't manage it with the increased pressure. All three died within minutes from asphyxiation. The investigation determined that loose wires had sparked the fire, which was fed by pure oxygen and flammable materials. The three astronauts' deaths led to greatly improved safety measures for the remaining Apollo flights.

THINK FOR YOURSELF. QUESTION AUTHORITY.

Timothy Leary, How to Operate Your Brain *(1993)*

656. JUNE 12, 1967

SUPREME COURT SUPPORTS INTERRACIAL MARRIAGE

A few weeks after Richard and Mildred Loving—a white man and a Black/Native American woman—were married in the District of Columbia in 1958, they were awakened in their Virginia bedroom by policemen with flashlights. "They asked Richard who was that woman he was sleeping with?" reported Mildred Loving later. "I say, 'I'm his wife,' and the sheriff said, 'Not here, you're not.'" Virginia was one of 18 states that prohibited interracial marriage. The Lovings were convicted of violating that law and moved to Washington, D.C., but in the 1960s they asked the American Civil Liberties Union to help them overturn their conviction. On this day, the Supreme Court ruled unanimously in favor of the Lovings, stating that laws banning interracial marriage violated the 14th Amendment's Equal Protection Clause. After that ruling, intermarriages increased fivefold in the United States between 1967 and 2015.

657. AUGUST 17, 1967

FIRST PRACTICAL COUNTERTOP MICROWAVE GOES ON SALE

Big commercial microwave ovens had been around since the 1940s, but in 1967 the Amana Corporation introduced the first true countertop version. The Radarange had the steep (for then) price of $495 (equivalent to $4,600 today) and weighed 80 pounds, but Amana assured nervous consumers that the company would send a trained technician to the home of every purchaser to help them understand the newfangled machine. Amana's ads that winter touted the benefits for at least some owners: "Give it to your wife for Christmas," they promised, "and you'll never have to wait for a meal again."

658. AUGUST 30, 1967

NATIONAL ORGANIZATION FOR WOMEN PICKETS THE *NEW YORK TIMES*

Wearing suffrage-era clothing, members of the recently formed National Organization for Women (NOW) picketed the *New York Times,* protesting the newspaper's gender-segregated help wanted ads. That day's paper, for instance, grouped ads for secretaries, receptionists, and typists under the heading "Help Wanted—Female" while ads for accountants, engineers, and management trainees appeared under the heading "Help Wanted—Male." In an article the next day, the *Times* quoted a vice president who said the ads were segregated "for the convenience of readers." NOW took its grievance to the Equal Employment Opportunity Commission, which ruled in 1968 that the ad headings violated the Civil Rights Act. That December, the *Times* changed its headings to "Help Wanted—Male-Female."

659. DECEMBER 31, 1967

PACKERS PLAY COWBOYS IN THE "ICE BOWL"

The temperature at Lambeau Field in Green Bay, Wisconsin, was minus 13 degrees Fahrenheit and dropping when the NFL championship game began between Vince Lombardi's Green Bay Packers and the Dallas Cowboys. The breath of the players hung in the air, and the 50,000 fans wore thick parkas. A crust of ice on the field made the athletes feel as though they were running on asphalt. Nevertheless, the two teams gave the fans a thrilling game that ended when Green Bay quarterback Bart Starr charged across the goal line to win what became known as the Ice Bowl, 21 to 17.

660. JANUARY 1, 1968

FEDERAL LAW REQUIRES CARS TO HAVE SEAT BELTS

In 1967, motor vehicle accidents were the leading cause of non-illness-related death. Car safety reformers, including Ralph Nader, had argued that the country needed legislation to protect drivers from themselves. In 1968, for the first time, federal safety regulations required car manufacturers to install seat belts in every car. These rules did not mandate that people actually wear the belts—that was up to individual states, and those laws appeared slowly over the years. (New Hampshire remains the only state that does not require adults, only children under 18, to wear seat belts.) Seat belt standards and local laws eventually saved hundreds of thousands of lives.

661. MARCH 31, 1968

LBJ ANNOUNCES HE WILL NOT RUN AGAIN

President Lyndon B. Johnson shocked most of his close advisers, the news media, and the nation generally when he concluded a televised speech about the Vietnam War with these words: "I do not believe that I should devote an hour or a day of my time to any personal partisan causes or to any duties other than the awesome duties of this office—the Presi-

The day after Martin Luther King, Jr., told supporters, "I may not get [to the Promised Land] with you," he was assassinated in Memphis.

dency of your country. Accordingly, I shall not seek, and I will not accept, the nomination of my party for another term as your President." Johnson had long been an eager political operator, but the growing unpopularity of the war and his own poor health had taken a toll on the 36th president. He became the sixth chief executive to decline a second term. Later that year, Richard Nixon was elected president; Johnson died of a heart attack in 1973.

662. APRIL 4, 1968

MARTIN LUTHER KING, JR., IS ASSASSINATED

Martin Luther King, Jr., had traveled to Memphis, Tennessee, to support striking sanitation workers. As he stood on his balcony at the Lorraine Motel in the evening, talking to colleagues from the Southern Christian Leadership Conference who had gathered in the parking lot, he was shot and killed by a rifle bullet fired from a nearby boardinghouse. Investigators traced the rifle to escaped fugitive James Earl Ray and tracked down the killer in England on June 8. Grief and anger consumed the country in the wake of the assassination. In a speech the night before his death, King had said, "I've seen the Promised Land. I may not get there with you. But I want you to know tonight, that we, as a people, will get to the Promised Land." James Earl Ray was sentenced to 99 years in prison, where he died in 1998.

663. JUNE 5, 1968

ASSASSIN FATALLY SHOOTS ROBERT F. KENNEDY

It was just after midnight when presidential candidate Senator Robert F. Kennedy finished a speech in a ballroom of the Ambassador Hotel in Los Angeles and decided to exit through the hotel kitchen. As he shook hands with 17-year-old busboy Juan Romero, an assassin, Sirhan Sirhan, stepped out and fired multiple shots with a .22 revolver. Kennedy was fatally wounded, and five others were also hit. Kennedy's friends wrestled the gunman to the ground while Romero knelt beside him, cradling his head. Kennedy died the next day—a little under five years after the assassination of his brother President John F. Kennedy. Sirhan, a Jordanian citizen who reportedly hated Kennedy for his support of Israel, was convicted of murder and sentenced to life in prison.

Apollo 8 mission astronauts (from left) James Lovell, Jr., William Anders, and Frank Borman were the first humans to orbit the moon.

664. DECEMBER 24, 1968

APOLLO 8 GOES INTO ORBIT AROUND THE MOON

Crewed by two Gemini veterans, Frank Borman and James Lovell, Jr., and one rookie, William Anders, the Apollo 8 spacecraft became the first piloted spacecraft to leave Earth's gravitational influence and orbit the moon. As a result, the astronauts were also the first humans to see the far side of the moon with their own eyes. Reaching their destination on Christmas Eve, the crew made an impression on listeners back home by reading from Genesis. On the same day, Anders grabbed the craft's Hasselblad camera and color film and snapped the iconic "Earthrise" photo that captured a sunlit planet rising over the lunar surface. The image helped to jump-start the environmental movement back home.

665. MARCH 29, 1969

RON RIDENHOUR EXPOSES THE MY LAI MASSACRE

In March 1968, American soldiers in the Army's Charlie Company, 11th Infantry Brigade, killed hundreds of unarmed Vietnamese civilians, including women and children, in the village of My Lai. The soldiers' immediate superiors either ignored or encouraged the killings, but a few horrified American soldiers eventually managed to expose the massacre. Among them was Ron Ridenhour, who wrote to President Richard Nixon and members of Congress. "If [my sources] could be believed," he wrote, "then not only had Charlie Company received orders to slaughter all the inhabitants of the village—but those orders had come from the commanding officer." The Department of Defense investigated and confirmed the murders, and newspapers published stories exposing them. Though 25 men were initially charged with war crimes or cover-ups, only one person, Lt. William Calley, was ever convicted.

666. JUNE 28, 1969

STONEWALL UPRISING BEGINS

Raids on gay bars were nothing new in 1969, nor were acts of resistance. But when police stormed Greenwich Village's Stonewall Inn shortly after midnight, the movement for

After a speaking event in Los Angeles, Senator Robert F. Kennedy was assassinated—the same fate his brother, the president, met in 1963.

ONLY THOSE WHO DARE TO FAIL GREATLY, CAN EVER ACHIEVE GREATLY.

Robert F. Kennedy *(1966)*

LGBTQIA+ rights took on new life. As the police arrested employees for illegally selling alcohol and patrons for not wearing at least three "gender-appropriate" items of clothing (per current law), the gay, lesbian, and transgender people inside and on the street began to fight back, struggling and throwing bottles. Fighting in the streets waxed and waned for five more days and inspired communities across the country. In 2019, NYPD commissioner James O'Neill apologized for the department's oppressive response. The inn and its surroundings are now a national monument.

667. JULY 18, 1969

TED KENNEDY DRIVES OFF A BRIDGE AT CHAPPAQUIDDICK

Massachusetts senator Ted Kennedy hosted a party on tiny Chappaquiddick Island, off the coast of Martha's Vineyard, joined by a few friends and staffers from his late brother Robert's presidential campaign. Sometime close to midnight, Kennedy left the party in a black Oldsmobile with 28-year-old Mary Jo Kopechne, one of RFK's former staffers, in the passenger seat. Shortly afterward, he drove off a small bridge and into the water; his car overturned. Kennedy was able to climb out, but Kopechne was trapped and drowned. The senator did not report the accident for 10 hours. After an inconclusive inquest, Kennedy received a two-month suspended sentence for leaving the scene of an accident. The scandal and mystery around the details of the crash overshadowed Kennedy the rest of his life.

668. JULY 20, 1969

APOLLO 11 LANDS ON THE MOON

Just over eight years after President John F. Kennedy vowed to land an astronaut on the moon before the decade was out, Neil Armstrong set foot on the lunar surface. The Apollo 11 mission had taken off on July 16, carrying astronauts Armstrong, Edwin "Buzz" Aldrin, and Michael Collins into lunar orbit. On July 20, Armstrong and Aldrin went into lunar module *Eagle,* leaving Collins to pilot the command module *Columbia.* On automatic pilot as they neared the surface, the astronauts saw that their proposed landing site was covered with boulders. Armstrong took manual control of the lander and put it down safely with just a few seconds of fuel in the tank. "Houston, Tranquility Base here," he announced at 4:18 p.m. "The *Eagle* has landed." At 10:39 that night, watched on television by an estimated 650 million people around the world, Armstrong descended the *Eagle's* ladder to become the first person to stand on another world. "That's one small step for a man," he said, "one giant leap for mankind." Armstrong would later confirm that he did say "a man" in the famous line, though the audio muffled the vowel.

Fans at Woodstock partook of sex, drugs, and rock and roll; performers included Graham Nash and David Crosby of Crosby, Stills & Nash.

669. AUGUST 9, 1969

MANSON FOLLOWERS COMMIT MURDERS IN LOS ANGELES

California cult leader Charles Manson did not personally commit any of the murders that are now forever linked to his name, but he was the driving force behind all the brutal killings, which he may have believed would trigger a race war. On his orders, soon after midnight on August 9, Manson's followers Charles Watson, Susan Atkins, Patricia Krenwinkel, and Linda Kasabian drove to the Los Angeles house where actress Sharon Tate and three others were staying. They killed all four as well as a teenager who was visiting a caretaker on the property. The next night, the four killers and two others—Leslie Van Houten and Steven "Clem" Grogan—killed grocery store executive Leno LaBianca and his wife, Rosemary, at their house. In October, Susan Atkins was arrested for another crime and boasted to a cellmate that she had been involved in the killings. All, including Manson, were arrested and eventually convicted (Kasabian was given immunity in exchange for her testimony).

Apollo 11 astronaut Neil Armstrong's boot print, preserved in lunar dust, represents the first time a human set foot on another world.

670. AUGUST 15, 1969

WOODSTOCK FESTIVAL BEGINS

The Woodstock Music & Art Fair did not take place in Woodstock, New York, but in a farmer's field in Bethel, some 60 miles away. (The town of Woodstock had denied permission to the organizers.) The sprawling, rainy, muddy, drug-infused four-day "Aquarian Exposition" boasted a long list of rock and roll legends and legends in the making, including The Who, Janis Joplin, the Grateful Dead, Santana, Jimi Hendrix, and Crosby, Stills & Nash. More than 400,000 concertgoers, most of whom had entered for free, danced, dropped acid, and left feeling connected by the music and the quintessential '60s vibe.

671. NOVEMBER 10, 1969

FIRST EPISODE OF *SESAME STREET* AIRS

The brainchild of public television producer Joan Ganz Cooney, *Sesame Street* made its debut with a show sponsored by the letter *W* and the number 2 and featuring such soon-to-be-famous Muppets as Kermit the Frog, Bert and Ernie, and Big Bird. The show for preschoolers aired on the National Educational Television network, which soon afterward became the Public Broadcasting Service; it broke new ground with its creative educational approach, urban set, and diverse characters, human and otherwise. *Sesame Street* received excellent reviews and went on to become the longest-running children's television show in history, with more than 4,500 episodes aired by the 2020s and the show still going strong.

672. NOVEMBER 20, 1969

INDIGENOUS ACTIVISTS OCCUPY ALCATRAZ

Led by Mohawk ironworker Richard Oakes and Shoshone-Bannock organizer LaNada War Jack, dozens of Native American activists landed on San Francisco's deserted Alcatraz Island and claimed it for their own. "We will purchase said Alcatraz Island for twenty-four

Some 20 million people participated in the first Earth Day to raise awareness and plan actions aimed at safeguarding the environment.

dollars in glass beads and red cloth," read the group's proclamation, "a precedent set by the white man's purchase of a similar island about 300 years ago." Then they settled in for the long haul. They set up a school and a radio station and subsisted in part on donations from supporters. However, negotiations with authorities went nowhere, and federal officers evicted the final occupiers in June 1971.

673. DECEMBER 4, 1969

POLICE KILL BLACK PANTHER FRED HAMPTON

Fred Hampton was a charismatic young leader in Illinois's Black Panther Party and a target of FBI paranoia, when he was shot and killed by Chicago police during a nighttime raid on his apartment. Acting on information from an FBI informant, 14 officers opened fire on the sleeping Hampton, his pregnant fiancée, and others in the apartment, killing Hampton and another Black Panther, Mark Clark. The officers claimed that they were returning fire during a search for illegal weapons, but investigations later showed that all but one of the bullets fired came from police guns. Hampton and Clark's families later received a settlement from the federal government, the city of Chicago, and Cook County. Twelve police officers, as well as the state's attorney who ordered the raid and his assistant, were tried and acquitted. The killings remain a touchpoint in Chicago's turbulent political history.

674. APRIL 22, 1970

FIRST EARTH DAY IS HELD IN THE U.S.

Wisconsin senator Gaylord Nelson was horrified by the oil-covered animals he saw when he toured the site of a California oil spill in 1969. Inspired by students conducting antiwar teach-ins on college campuses, he reached out to allies in Congress and at universities to organize a national environmental teach-in day. The idea tapped into growing public concern about pollution, extinctions, and loss of habitat. The observance caught on and spread not only across colleges but also into a wide range of schools and communities. Some 20 million people participated in the first Earth Day activities on April 22. By the 2020s, more than one billion people around the world observed the day.

675. MAY 4, 1970

FOUR STUDENTS ARE KILLED AT KENT STATE

Demonstrations against the Vietnam War escalated when Americans learned that U.S. forces were moving into Cambodia after secretly bombing the country for months. Students at Kent State University, near Cleveland, Ohio, began to collect in protest on May 1. Ohio governor James Rhodes ordered Ohio National Guard troops to the campus, where they confronted students with loaded rifles, bayonets, and tear gas. On the afternoon of May 4, a group of Guardsmen on the grassy university Commons inexplicably fired on the students, killing four and wounding nine (one of whom became paralyzed). Two of the dead were not protesters, but simply students walking to class. Eleven days later, another shooting

A blue-collar bigot who called relatives Dingbat and Meathead, Archie Bunker was the lead character in the TV hit *All in the Family*.

would take the lives of two and injure dozens more at Mississippi's Jackson State College. The pair of killings shocked the country and galvanized the anti-war movement.

I HAD A FATHER WHO WAS A BIT OF AN ARCHIE BUNKER.

Norman Lear, *creator of* All in the Family *(2021)*

676. DECEMBER 31, 1970

NIXON SIGNS THE CLEAN AIR ACT

With American city dwellers regularly suffering under a dirty pall of air pollution, a bipartisan group of legislators pushed through the Clean Air Act, which President Richard Nixon signed on this day. The act was designed "to protect and enhance the quality of the Nation's air resources so as to promote the public health and welfare"; it gave the newly established Environmental Protection Agency the authority to regulate polluting industries. The act has been credited with reducing air pollution by at least 70 percent by the 2020s.

677. JANUARY 12, 1971

FIRST EPISODE OF *ALL IN THE FAMILY* AIRS

Norman Lear's provocative show, inspired by the British sitcom *Till Death Do Us Part,* featured a bigoted, working-class New Yorker, Archie Bunker, his sweet but spacey wife, and their liberal daughter and son-in-law, all living in the same household. There they argued about race, feminism, religion, homosexuality, and other hot-button topics. The show's network, CBS, was nervous about these controversial aspects, and the first reviews were mixed: *The Hollywood Reporter* wrote that "the majority of television viewers will find this show tasteless, crude, and very unfunny." Nevertheless, by its second season *All in the Family* had reached the top of the Nielsen ratings and stayed there for five years.

678. MARCH 30, 1971

FIRST STARBUCKS OPENS

On this day, the first Starbucks store opened just outside Seattle's Pike Place Market. Located near the waterfront, the company took its name from the first mate in *Moby-Dick*. Three young friends, Jerry Baldwin, Gordon Bowker, and Zev Siegl, chipped in $1,350 apiece to start the business. The small shop had just one employee (Siegl) and sold whole-bean coffee, spices, and tea but not brewed coffee. That innovation did not take place until the 1980s. Today, Starbucks has more than 32,000 outlets around the world.

679. NOVEMBER 15, 1971

INTEL ANNOUNCES THE FIRST MICROPROCESSOR

The Intel Corporation was just a few years old when it took on the task of creating a general-purpose microprocessor to be used in Japanese calculators. The result was the Intel 4004, a central processing unit on a chip about the size of a fingernail. The chip contained 2,300 transistors, which allowed it to perform about 1,200 calculations per

When the first Starbucks opened, it sold coffee beans but not brewed coffee—now sold at 32,000 Starbucks outlets worldwide.

second. (Today's chips can hold billions of transistors.) Intel built on the success of the 4004 to produce faster and faster chips, including the 8088, which would become the heart of IBM's personal computers.

680. NOVEMBER 24, 1971

DAN COOPER PARACHUTES INTO THE NIGHT

Aboard a Northwest Orient flight from Portland to Seattle, a man in a business suit gave a flight attendant a note saying he had a bomb in his briefcase; he opened the case to show her a mass of wires and red dynamite-like sticks. So began the strange saga of Dan Cooper (the fake name he used to buy his one-way ticket, later misheard by a reporter as "D. B. Cooper"). After the plane landed in Seattle, Cooper allowed the passengers to leave in exchange for four parachutes and $200,000 in $20 bills. He then forced the 727's crew to take off again to the south. Somewhere over Washington State, Cooper took off his clip-on tie, lowered the aft stairs, and jumped into the night, never to be seen again. Cash from the hijacking was later found near the Columbia River, but the true identity and fate of the hijacker remain a mystery.

681. JUNE 17, 1972

BURGLARS BREAK INTO WATERGATE OFFICES

On this day, five burglars carrying cash and bugging equipment broke into the offices of the Democratic National Committee in Washington, D.C.'s Watergate office complex. Security guard Frank Wills first spotted tape holding open a door latch shortly after midnight. He removed the tape but noticed later that the door had been mysteriously retaped, so he called the police. When the police entered the DNC's sixth-floor offices, a man jumped up from behind a desk and cried out, "Don't shoot!" One of the burglars, James McCord, Jr., turned out to be the security chief of the Richard Nixon–supporting Committee to Re-elect the President. The relatively petty burglary grew into a massive scandal over corruption and cover-ups during President Nixon's reelection campaign, leading to his resignation two years later.

682. JUNE 27, 1972

VIDEO GAMES HIT THE BIG TIME WITH ATARI

Video games existed before the 1970s, but the first company to take them to the public in a big way was Atari, founded by electrical engineers Ted Dabney and Nolan Bushnell. Their breakout game was the two-person game Pong, in which players compete to knock a lighted dot back and forth across a dashed-line net, like table tennis. The game was soon adopted on video arcade consoles around the country and gained even greater success when Atari released it on home consoles in 1975. Home Pong became the precursor to a home video game industry that by the 21st century had become a multibillion-dollar business.

SPOTLIGHT

FASHION

THE 20TH CENTURY was a period of dramatic and rapid reinvention in Americans' attire: a fashion epoch that began with tight-laced corsets and ended with loose-fitting athleisure wear.

The looks that evolved were both innovative and diverse. In the early 1900s, women used corsets for a shape labeled the S-curve or pigeon breast: back arched, stomach flattened, breasts pushed forward. In the 1920s, a boyish silhouette reigned: unfitted shifts with hemlines at the knee. In the 1940s, women filling the jobs of men at war wore one-piece denim coveralls and mannish business suits. The postwar '50s swung back to ultrafeminine dresses, while Coco Chanel created a comfortably boxy jacket for her women's suit: a classic dubbed "one of the most recognizable high-fashion looks of the 20th century" by the Museum at the Fashion Institute of Technology.

By mid-century, new cultural standards prevailed. The 1960s featured more skin and fewer undergarments, hemlines reaching new heights with the miniskirt, and a counterculture hippie aesthetic. Denim went designer in the 1970s, with status versions of blue jeans by Calvin Klein and other fashion leaders. Dueling forces shaped the 1980s: avant-garde looks influenced by Japanese brands, dress-for-success power suits, easy separates from Donna Karan, high-priced sneakers from Michael Jordan/Nike. And by the 1990s, fashion encompassed athletic attire as streetwear, music-inspired grunge looks, and logomania, featuring conspicuously placed design branding on every creation, transforming apparel into "status symbols of luxury consumerism," according to the Museum at the Fashion Institute of Technology.

Designers Pam, Craig, Marsha, and Jim model their "punk fashion" creations, one of many new styles born in this anything-goes century.

CREATE YOUR OWN INDIVIDUAL STYLE … I'M INTERESTED IN A GIRL WHO PUTS HERSELF TOGETHER IN AN ORIGINAL, INDEPENDENT WAY.

Anna Wintour, *global editorial director,* Vogue

683. OCTOBER 21, 1972

MARINE MAMMAL PROTECTION ACT IS SIGNED INTO LAW

The American public in the 1960s and '70s was increasingly concerned with ecology and the environment, and marine mammals such as dolphins and whales came to represent threatened species generally. In 1972, responding to these worries, President Richard Nixon signed into law the Marine Mammal Protection Act. The broadly defined law prohibited not just hunting and killing any marine mammal in U.S. waters but also capturing, harassing, or feeding the animals. It also protected their habitats. The act's safeguards led to the recovery of many threatened species, including humpback whales, gray seals, and California sea lions.

684. NOVEMBER 27, 1972

MARLO THOMAS RELEASES *FREE TO BE … YOU AND ME*

Fresh off her success as the star of *That Girl,* Marlo Thomas turned to producing an innovative album of children's songs titled *Free to Be … You and Me*. Disappointed by the gender stereotypes she saw in books she read to her young niece, Thomas and other actors and celebrities recorded such songs as "William's Doll" and "It's All Right to Cry," the latter of which was sung by football star Rosey Grier. The album—which would help to define childhood for a generation of children—was a hit and led to an equally successful book, television special, and foundation.

Marlo Thomas's breakout role was in TV's *That Girl,* for which she won a Golden Globe in 1967.

685. DECEMBER 23, 1972

FRANCO HARRIS MAKES AN IMMACULATE RECEPTION

The Pittsburgh Steelers trailed the Oakland Raiders 7–6 with 22 seconds left in a divisional playoff game. Steelers quarterback Terry Bradshaw threw a pass toward running back John "Frenchy" Fuqua, but the ball bounced off a collision between Fuqua and a defender. As it dropped toward the field, running back Franco Harris scooped it up just inches above the ground and ran for a touchdown to win the game. What became known as "the immaculate reception" remains one of football's most famous plays.

686. JANUARY 22, 1973

SUPREME COURT DECIDES *ROE* V. *WADE*

In 1969, 21-year-old, pregnant Texan Norma McCorvey contacted a pair of attorneys who were looking to challenge the state's ban on abortions. The two lawyers, Sarah Weddington and Linda Coffee, took her case and filed suit against the local district attorney, Henry Wade. The lawsuit made its way to the Supreme Court in 1971. (By then, McCorvey had given birth and placed the baby with adoptive parents.) To protect McCorvey's identity, the case was filed using the pseudonym Jane Roe. On this day, the Court ruled (7–2) that abortion until a fetus becomes viable was protected by the 14th Amendment's due process clause, which includes the right to privacy.

American Indian Movement activists prepare a purification ceremony at the site of the 1890 Wounded Knee Massacre, with Sacred Heart Church in the background.

687. FEBRUARY 27, 1973

ACTIVISTS OCCUPY WOUNDED KNEE

Led by Russell Means and Dennis Banks, members of the American Indian Movement (AIM) occupied the Oglala Lakota Reservation site of Wounded Knee, where the U.S. Cavalry killed hundreds of Lakota in 1890. Among other things, the activists demanded that the U.S. government honor its earlier treaties with Indigenous peoples. In response, U.S. Marshals surrounded the area. Thus began a 71-day standoff marked by bouts of gunfire between the two sides. Two of the protesters were killed and a marshal was seriously injured. After officials agreed to investigate their complaints, the activists ended the siege. Though the standoff did not persuade the federal government to reverse its stand on earlier treaties, it did result in increased public attention to the rights and plight of Native Americans generally.

688. APRIL 3, 1973

MARTIN COOPER USES A CELL PHONE

Standing on Sixth Avenue in New York, Motorola engineer Martin Cooper made the world's first cell phone call to a competitor at Bell Labs: "I'm calling you on a cell phone, but a real cell phone, a personal, handheld, portable cell phone," he gloated. The mobile

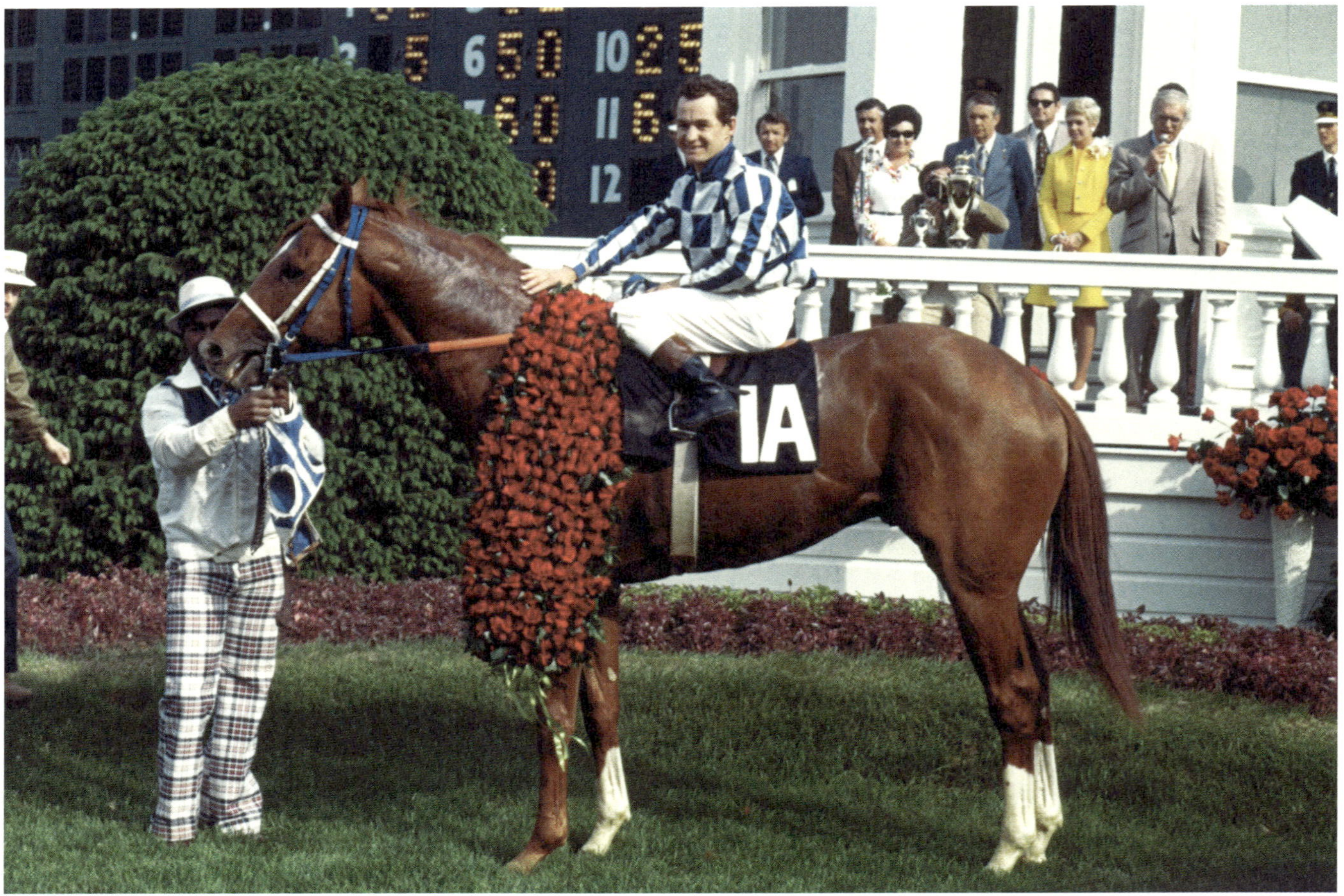

Ron Turcotte and Secretariat pause for photos after winning the Belmont Stakes.

phone that Cooper had designed and was about to demonstrate at a press conference was a bricklike device almost 10 inches high and weighing about two and half pounds. It would be about 10 more years before Motorola marketed its first commercial cell phone, a hefty device that cost almost $4,000. Today, 98 percent of Americans own a cell phone.

689. JUNE 9, 1973

SECRETARIAT RACES TO A WORLD RECORD

Thoroughbred racehorse Secretariat had already won two of the three Triple Crown horse races when he entered the starting gate at Belmont Park on this day. Under jockey Ron Turcotte, the handsome three-year-old chestnut had conquered the Kentucky Derby with a time of 1:59.4, a world record. Two weeks later, he dominated the Preakness Stakes with an unofficial world record of 1:53 (racecourse timers were unreliable for that race). But at the Belmont Stakes, "Big Red" entered racing history. Ridden by Turcotte, the stallion dominated the race, galloping to a record 31-length victory over his nearest competitor in a time of 2:24—again, a world record. Secretariat retired to stud duties later that year. His Triple Crown record times still stand.

690. SEPTEMBER 20, 1973

BILLIE JEAN KING DEFEATS BOBBY RIGGS

Bobby Riggs's best tennis days were behind him—he had been a top player in the 1940s—but that did not stop him from claiming that, as a man, he was inherently better than even the best female players. In 1973, tennis champion Billie Jean King took him on in the highly publicized "Battle of the Sexes" tennis match. Playing in the Houston Astrodome and followed by an estimated 90 million television viewers, 29-year-old King beat Riggs in straight sets, 6–4, 6–3, 6–3, to win the $100,000 prize. "I thought it would set us back 50 years if I didn't win that match," said King later. "To beat a 55-year-old guy was no thrill for me."

691. SEPTEMBER 26, 1973

U.S. PASSES ITS FIRST MAJOR DISABILITY RIGHTS ACT

Before this year, people with disabilities were regularly excluded from jobs and education, sometimes for purported safety reasons. Drawing on the expertise of civil rights activists, protesters began to stage demonstrations to urge the passage of a disability rights act that President Richard Nixon had twice vetoed as being too expensive. Under pressure, Nixon finally signed the Rehabilitation Act of 1973. Among other things, it prohibited discrimination against people with disabilities in federal employment, by federal contractors, or in any program receiving federal assistance. The act paved the way for the broader Americans with Disabilities Act of 1990.

PRESSURE IS A PRIVILEGE, AND CHAMPIONS ADJUST.

Billie Jean King *(2000)*

692. APRIL 8, 1974

HANK AARON SETS HOME RUN RECORD

It was early in the baseball season, but a sellout crowd packed Atlanta stadium in the cold to find out if Braves slugger Hank Aaron would break Babe Ruth's home run record of 714. After walking his first time up, at 9:07 p.m. Aaron hit a fastball over the left field fence for home run 715 and the all-time record. What was going through the 40-year-old player's mind after he hit the homer? "All I thought about was that I wanted to touch all the bases," Aaron said.

693. APRIL 15, 1974

PATTY HEARST ROBS A BANK

In February 1974, newspaper heiress Patty Hearst was at home with her boyfriend in Berkeley, California, when she was kidnapped by armed intruders, members of a small, violent extremist group calling itself the Symbionese Liberation Army (SLA). The ensuing search for the missing heiress riveted the public. Two months later, Hearst shocked the nation by joining her kidnappers in robbing San Francisco's Hibernia Bank, where she was caught on camera. The Los Angeles police eventually found and killed most of the SLA members; Hearst remained at large until 1975. At her trial, she described being held

"You're gonna need a bigger boat" became a widely quoted catchphrase after the movie *Jaws* turned out to be a summer box office smash.

in a closet, abused, and brainwashed by her captors. Nevertheless, she was sentenced to seven years in prison, a sentence that President Jimmy Carter commuted after 22 months.

694. AUGUST 9, 1974

NIXON LEAVES OFFICE

"I have never been a quitter," said President Richard Nixon in a televised address on August 8, 1974. "To leave office before my term is completed is abhorrent to every instinct in my body." Nevertheless, he went on, "I shall resign the Presidency effective at noon tomorrow." With these words, Nixon became the first sitting American president to relinquish his office. Although he had been reelected in 1972, his second term was dominated by hearings into the Watergate break-in and other instances of corruption by his administration. In July, the House Judiciary Committee passed articles of impeachment. After tendering his resignation on August 9, Nixon departed the White House by helicopter. His successor, President Gerald Ford, issued him a full pardon the next month.

695. APRIL 4, 1975

GATES AND ALLEN FOUND MICROSOFT

In early 1975, the Micro Instrumentation and Telemetry Systems (MITS) Altair 8800 microcomputer appeared on the cover of *Popular Electronics.* Childhood friends Bill Gates and Paul Allen, both computer aficionados, decided to join forces to write BASIC software for this innovative personal computing device. Gates, 19, dropped out of Harvard to join Allen, 22, in Albuquerque. By March, they had drafted the software, and in April they formed a company they would later market as Micro-soft. Sales their first year totaled $16,005. Today, the company is valued at more than $3 trillion.

696. APRIL 30, 1975

SAIGON FALLS

U.S. involvement in the Vietnam War had officially ended with the Paris Peace Accords in 1973, but for most Americans, the true end to the war came on the day that the U.S. Embassy in Saigon fell to the North Vietnamese. With the local air base destroyed, American and South Vietnamese Embassy employees could leave only by helicopter from the embassy grounds. Thousands frantically scrambled over embassy walls and crowded aboard the last helicopters out of the city. In all, some 7,000 people were evacuated, including more than 5,000 Vietnamese citizens.

697. JUNE 20, 1975

***JAWS* OPENS WIDE**

The *Jaws* poster, featuring a giant shark targeting a lone swimmer, captured the seminal movie's terrifying appeal. Directed by 27-year-old Steven Spielberg, the story of the fish that terrorized Long Island is considered to be the first summer blockbuster of modern times. Opening in more than 400 theaters, it quickly became the highest-grossing film to date. At 1976's Academy Awards, *Jaws* won Oscars for Film Editing and Sound, as well as for the score that incorporated John Williams's soon-to-be-iconic two-note motif.

698. APRIL 1, 1976

JOBS AND WOZNIAK FOUND APPLE COMPUTER COMPANY

Steve Jobs and Steve Wozniak, both college dropouts, attended the same high school and worked for Atari and Hewlett-Packard, respectively, in the early 1970s. Tinkering in the Jobs family's garage, they joined forces to build what became the first computer with a typewriter-style keyboard and the ability to connect to inexpensive monitors such as television screens. On this day, Jobs, Wozniak, and investor Ronald Wayne formed the Apple Computer Company to market the new device. Wayne soon had doubts about the enterprise and dropped out of the company for a payment of $800, sacrificing what would become billions of dollars in eventual wealth.

699. JULY 4, 1976

BICENTENNIAL CELEBRATIONS LIGHT UP THE COUNTRY

America was ready for a big party in 1976 after the dark years of Watergate and the fall of Saigon; celebrations in honor of the country's 200th birthday sprang up everywhere. But among the most notable were the American Freedom Train, which steamed through

Steve Jobs (left) provided the garage space where he and "gadget guy" Steve Wozniak developed technology that revolutionized computing.

all 48 contiguous states for 21 months, as well as a floating parade of tall ships from around the world that convened in New York Harbor. Queen Elizabeth II and Prince Philip showed there were no hard feelings from 1776 by touring the country during the ceremonies and dining with President Gerald Ford and his wife, Betty.

700. AUGUST 17, 1976

ALEX HALEY PUBLISHES *ROOTS*

Journalist Alex Haley described his novel *Roots* as "faction": a combination of fact and fiction. The book, which viscerally confronts the brutalities and agony of slavery, traces the history of Haley's family from Kunta Kinte, an enslaved ancestor from the Gambia, to the author himself. In a time when many African Americans knew little of their origins, the book was a sensation, reaching the bestseller list and inspiring many to research their own genealogy. A *Roots* television series aired in 1977 and was also a major success.

After opening in just 32 theaters, *Star Wars* exploded in popularity. Almost a half century later, it's a multibillion-dollar phenomenon.

701. MAY 25, 1977

***STAR WARS* PREMIERES**

Director George Lucas had gained some recognition with his 1973 film *American Graffiti.* But even so, his *Star Wars* (now known as *Star Wars: Episode IV—A New Hope)* opened midweek in May 1977 in just 32 theaters. It was a sensation. Lines formed on sidewalks before each showing, and fans returned time and time again to the science fiction adventure. Reviews were positive, granting that the movie was good fun if not an artistic masterpiece. Showings quickly expanded to many more theaters, and the box office was stellar, making *A New Hope* the highest-grossing film since *Jaws.* In time, it became a multibillion-dollar franchise including multiple film sequels, television series, books, comics, video games, and a wide range of merchandise.

702. FEBRUARY 22, 1978

DEPARTMENT OF DEFENSE LAUNCHES THE FIRST GPS SATELLITE

On this day, an Atlas F booster rocket sent the first NAVSTAR (Navigation Satellite Timing and Ranging) satellite into orbit from Vandenberg Air Force Base. Commissioned by the U.S. Department of Defense, it was the first of 11 experimental satellites that the military launched to test a new technology, allowing users on the ground to navigate with special receivers. High-quality, accurate global positioning technology was available only to military until the turn of the 21st century. Today, the U.S. flies 31 operational GPS satellites in equally spaced orbits around Earth.

703. JULY 15, 1978

"THE LONGEST WALK" ENDS IN WASHINGTON, D.C.

A walk that began with a couple dozen Native American participants on Alcatraz Island in California ended some 3,000 miles away in Washington, D.C., with thousands of

Alex Haley's novel *Roots* drew on his family history, starting with an ancestor from the Gambia who was enslaved in the United States.

IN ALL OF US THERE IS A HUNGER, MARROW-DEEP, TO KNOW OUR HERITAGE—TO KNOW WHO WE ARE AND WHERE WE HAVE COME FROM.

Alex Haley *(1977)*

marchers who had joined along the way. American Indian activists had undertaken "The Longest Walk" to call attention to 11 bills before Congress that would deprive Indian nations of treaty rights and curtail programs that supported hospitals, schools, and housing. The demonstrators camped and held rallies and religious ceremonies on the National Mall, with celebrity supporters including comedian Dick Gregory and actor Marlon Brando joining the protests. In the wake of the demonstrations, all 11 bills in question were defeated.

704. MARCH 1, 1979

SWEENEY TODD OPENS ON BROADWAY

"Attend the tale of Sweeney Todd / He served a dark and a vengeful god / What happened then, well that's the play," sing citizens of London as *Sweeney Todd* begins. Stephen Sondheim's 10th Broadway musical opened at New York's Uris Theatre with Len Cariou as the killer barber and Angela Lansbury as his pie-making accomplice, Mrs. Lovett. The tale of murder and revenge was almost entirely sung, with a complex score and a mix of black humor and horror. *Sweeney Todd* received strong reviews—the *New York Times* called it "an extraordinary, fascinating, and often ravishingly lovely effort"—and went on to win eight Tony Awards. It set the stage for other complex Broadway musicals in the years to come, including Sondheim's own *Sunday in the Park with George,* 1987's *Les Misérables,* and 2015's *Hamilton.*

705. MARCH 28, 1979

THREE MILE ISLAND SUFFERS A PARTIAL MELTDOWN

In the predawn hours of March 28, a combination of equipment and human errors damaged a nuclear plant and panicked residents around Harrisburg, Pennsylvania, and across the nation. After a relief valve got stuck on one of the stations' two nuclear reactors, located on an island in the Susquehanna River, the reactor's core suffered a partial meltdown, releasing radioactivity into the air. Within days, schools and businesses in the area had closed and tens of thousands of people had fled. Meanwhile, employees managed to shut down the malfunctioning reactor; it was later determined that the radioactivity it had released was negligible. Three Mile Island Unit 2 was closed permanently; the other reactor remained in service until 2019.

706. JULY 22, 1979

SOPHIE'S CHOICE REACHES NUMBER ONE ON BESTSELLER LISTS

William Styron's fifth and final novel tells the story of a young, Styron-like writer named Stingo, who meets the beautiful Auschwitz survivor Sophie Zawistowska at their Brooklyn boardinghouse. Over time, Sophie tells him her story, which includes the terrible choice she was forced to make regarding the lives of her two children at the concentration camp. Despite, or perhaps because of, its dark themes, Styron's novel became a bestseller and won the National Book Award for fiction in 1980. The phrase "Sophie's choice" entered the general vocabulary to mean a no-win, difficult decision.

707. NOVEMBER 4, 1979

IRANIANS TAKE AMERICANS HOSTAGE IN TEHRAN

After the U.S. took in Mohammad Reza Shah Pahlavi, the deposed shah of Iran, fundamentalist Iranian students attacked the U.S. Embassy in Tehran, taking 66 people there and at the Iranian foreign ministry hostage. In 1980, Canadian diplomats managed to rescue six American diplomats who had avoided capture; 14 others were eventually released on the orders of Iranian religious leader Ayatollah Ruhollah Khomeini. Despite intensive efforts by U.S. president Jimmy Carter, the remaining hostages were not freed until 1981, the day of the inauguration of Carter's successor, Ronald Reagan. The hostage crisis is considered a key element in Carter's failure to win a second term.

708. MARCH 21, 1980

"WHO SHOT J.R.?" EPISODE DEBUTS

The wildly popular and soapy prime-time drama *Dallas* set up one of the all-time television cliff-hangers when, on this day, an unseen assailant shot archvillain J.R. Ewing (played by Larry Hagman) at the end of the show's third season. Viewers had to wait until November to learn if the would-be killer was J.R.'s wife or perhaps one of his business rivals. During the suspenseful summer, the mystery of "Who shot J.R.?" became a major, if not entirely serious, story in the media. Approximately 90 million viewers tuned in to the November premiere to find out: The shooter was J.R.'s sister-in-law/mistress, Kristin.

709. MAY 18, 1980

MOUNT ST. HELENS ERUPTS

The most active volcano in western North America's Cascade Range rumbled with thousands of earthquakes through the spring of 1980. By May 17, a large bulge had grown out of its north-facing flank. At 8:32 a.m. on May 18, the volcano's summit and bulge disintegrated and slid away in what became the largest landslide in recorded history. The volcano erupted with a blast upward and to the north traveling at 300 miles an hour; eruptions and avalanches continued for hours as ash clouds darkened the skies. Smaller outbursts occurred the next day and over the next several months. The eruptions devastated more than 230 square miles and killed more than 50 people, including volcanologist David Johnston, who was monitoring the volcano from six miles away.

A 5.1-magnitude earthquake set off the May 18, 1980, eruption of Mount St. Helens, which produced the largest landslide in history.

710. JUNE 1, 1980

VERA RUBIN FINDS EVIDENCE OF DARK MATTER

On this day, American astronomer Vera Rubin published a paper in *The Astrophysical Journal* that upended scientific understanding of the visible universe. Rubin and her co-author, Kent Ford, had been observing the Andromeda galaxy and realized that the stars in its outer arms were traveling as fast as those near its center. This could only happen if that galaxy had a tremendous but unseen amount of mass. Other galaxies, she found, behaved the same way. "The conclusion is inescapable that non-luminous matter exists beyond the optical galaxy," she wrote. This "non-luminous matter"—its composition still unknown—is now called "dark matter" and is believed to make up approximately 85 percent of all matter in the universe.

711. DECEMBER 8, 1980

JOHN LENNON IS ASSASSINATED

As the songwriter and ex-Beatle John Lennon and his wife, Yoko Ono, walked toward their New York City apartment building on this night, a man waiting on the street shot Lennon four times in the back and shoulder, killing him. The killer, 25-year-old Mark David Chapman, dropped his gun and stood reading *The Catcher in the Rye* while he waited for police to arrive. Chapman was apparently devoted to Salinger's book and had decided that Lennon was a "phony," a catchword in the book, who deserved to die. Lennon's death was met by an outpouring of grief worldwide; Chapman was sentenced to 20 years to life in prison, where he has been repeatedly denied parole and remains incarcerated.

A disenchanted onetime fan fatally shot John Lennon as the former Beatle and his wife, Yoko Ono, approached their Manhattan apartment.

712. MARCH 30, 1981

RONALD REAGAN AND THREE OTHERS ARE SHOT

As President Ronald Reagan was leaving Washington, D.C.'s Connecticut Avenue Hilton following a speech to union leaders, 25-year-old John Hinckley, Jr., fired a .22-caliber revolver. One of his shots ricocheted off a car and struck Reagan under the armpit, though the president did not feel it in the moment. Other shots struck a policeman, a Secret Service agent, and Reagan's press secretary James Brady, who was seriously injured. Reagan underwent surgery and recovered. Hinckley, who had shot the president in an effort to impress actress Jodie Foster, was found not guilty by reason of insanity and confined to a mental hospital.

713. APRIL 12, 1981

SPACE SHUTTLE *COLUMBIA* LAUNCHES

More than five years had passed since the U.S. had sent an astronaut into space. During that time, NASA developed a new, reusable craft that could make the outbound trek on the back of two booster rockets and a fuel tank. On this day, the first Space Transportation System (STS-1), better known as the space shuttle *Columbia,* took off from the Kennedy Space Center carrying astronauts John Young and Robert Crippen. This first test flight carried no payload; it was devoted mainly to testing out the shuttle's many components. After two days and 36 orbits, *Columbia* landed safely at Edwards Air Force Base. NASA went on to fly 135 space shuttle missions before the program ended in 2011.

714. JUNE 5, 1981

FIRST REPORT DESCRIBES AIDS

A short article in the Centers for Disease Control and Prevention's (CDC) *Morbidity and Mortality Weekly Report* described a puzzling illness in five gay men in Los Angeles. All were young and previously healthy, but they had developed pneumocystis pneumonia—rare in healthy adults. "All the above observations suggest the possibility of a cellular-immune dysfunction related to a common exposure," the report concluded. It was the first public notice of the devastating illness that in 1982 would come to be known as AIDS: acquired immunodeficiency syndrome. Within days of the report, the CDC set up a task force to investigate. By 1992, the disease was the leading cause of death in young American men. But highly effective antiretroviral treatments in the late 1990s and beyond dramatically increased lifespans and began to curb the disease's spread.

AS YOU HURTLE FROM EARTH IN A CRAFT UNLIKE ANY OTHER EVER CONSTRUCTED, YOU WILL DO SO IN A FEAT OF AMERICAN TECHNOLOGY AND AMERICAN WILL.

President Ronald Reagan, *addressing the* Columbia *astronauts (1981)*

The space shuttle *Columbia* was built to be reusable: It could be carried aloft by booster rockets and return for an airplane-like landing.

Sandra Day O'Connor testified before the Senate Judiciary Committee before being sworn in as a judge on the Supreme Court.

715. AUGUST 1, 1981

MTV GOES LIVE

The cable television network known as Music Television began its innovative programming with the words, "Ladies and gentlemen, rock and roll." Promising "the best of TV combined with the best of radio," the network then premiered its first music video, "Video Killed the Radio Star" by the new wave band the Buggles. By the mid-1980s, MTV had become a major force in the music business, helping propel the star-studded careers of video-savvy performers such as Madonna and Michael Jackson. The Buggles broke up in 1981; MTV moved away from music videos and into animation and reality television programming in the 1990s. In the new millennium, it reached more than 12 million viewers with its Video Music Awards show.

716. AUGUST 12, 1981

IBM UNVEILS ITS FIRST PC

The IBM Corporation built its first viable personal computer in a relatively short time and unveiled it at press conferences on this day. The IBM Model 5150, which used Microsoft's MS-DOS operating system, came with up to 64 kilobytes of memory and one or two floppy disk drives. Including the optional monochrome monitor, the first units sold for $2,880. Although the computer's common components made it easily cloned by other companies, IBM's overall market dominance made their PC the office standard for years. Today, the average cost of a personal computer is between $500 and $1,000.

717. SEPTEMBER 25, 1981

SANDRA DAY O'CONNOR IS SWORN IN

On this day, Chief Justice Warren Burger swore in Sandra Day O'Connor as the first female Supreme Court justice in front of President Ronald Reagan, eight other—male—justices, and 400 spectators. Reagan nominated O'Connor to replace retiring justice Potter Stewart and to fulfill a campaign pledge to appoint the first female Supreme Court judge; the Senate unanimously approved her nomination. The 51-year-old Arizona native had previously served as a state senator and a Court of Appeals judge. Reagan described her as a "person for all seasons," and she proved to be a moderate voice on the Court for 25 years.

718. JUNE 11, 1982

STEVEN SPIELBERG RELEASES *E.T. THE EXTRA-TERRESTRIAL*

Director Steven Spielberg said that he drew on his own memories of loneliness and longing to craft his hit film *E.T.,* released on this day. Scripted by Melissa Mathison, the heart-warming story of a 10-year-old boy who befriends a marooned alien became an instant hit for both its emotional content and stirring visuals. The movie went on to win four Academy Awards and remains one of the highest-grossing films (adjusted for inflation) in history. It also spurred healthy sales in E.T. merchandise and Reese's Pieces, the candy that the protagonist Elliott uses to lure E.T. into his house. The film is considered one of the best of all time and was added to the U.S. National Film Registry in 1994.

719. JULY 2, 1982

LARRY WALTERS TAKES FLIGHT

On this day, Los Angeles truck driver Larry Walters lifted off from a San Pedro, California, backyard in a Sears aluminum-framed lawn chair. Attached to the chair were 42 helium-filled weather balloons, as well as plastic jugs holding water as ballast. Walters rapidly soared to approximately 16,000 feet, where airline pilots spotted him. "This is TWA 231, level at 16,000 feet," one reported. "We have a man in a chair attached to balloons in our ten-o'clock position, range five miles." Walters shot out some of his balloons and descended, only to become entangled in power lines. Los Angeles police rescued him, and the Federal Aviation Administration charged him with, among other things, operating a non-airworthy craft.

720. DECEMBER 13, 1982

MARTHA STEWART PUBLISHES *ENTERTAINING*

In 1977, Martha Stewart met Crown Publishing chief Alan Mirken at a party she catered, and he asked her to write a cookbook. The lavishly illustrated guide to big parties that resulted—*Entertaining*—launched her into a far-reaching career in publishing and television that at its height would be valued at a billion dollars. Though the book did not always seem aimed at the average host, featuring as it did such meals as a midnight omelet dinner for 30, it became widely popular and led Stewart to write other cookbooks, start her own magazine, star in a television show, and eventually become the influential head of a media empire, Martha Stewart Living Omnimedia. Although she would become notorious for her 2004 conviction and five-month prison sentence on grounds of insider trading, she recovered to publish many more books and sold her company for more than $350 million.

Martha Stewart's book *Entertaining* launched her rise to business and multimedia success as an authority on all things tasteful.

721. JANUARY 2, 1983

MICHAEL JACKSON RELEASES "BILLIE JEAN"

Singer/songwriter Michael Jackson released a hit album, *Off the Wall,* in 1979. But 1983 brought him new levels of fame with his *Thriller* album and its funky pop song "Billie Jean." Jackson recorded the main vocals to "Billie Jean" in a single take and the overdubs through a cardboard tube. The accompanying video showed off Jackson's dancing skills and his signature toe-stand move. "Billie Jean" became a number one hit around the world; *Thriller* became the best-selling album of all time, moving more than 60 million copies.

722. JUNE 18, 1983

SALLY RIDE BECOMES THE FIRST AMERICAN WOMAN IN SPACE

Astronaut Sally Ride had a Ph.D. in physics and years of experience in NASA's shuttle program. But as she prepared to become the first American woman in space, reporters still asked her about her makeup. Ride had entered NASA in 1978 in the first group of astronaut trainees to admit women. In 1982, the agency announced that she would join the crew of the space shuttle *Challenger* as a mission specialist. Twenty years almost to the day since the first woman cosmonaut (Valentina Tereshkova) reached orbit, Ride worked with four male crewmates on a successful mission devoted to deploying satellites, returning to Earth on June 24. Ride went on to crew another shuttle mission in 1984. She left NASA in 1987 to become a physics professor at the University of California San Diego in 1989, then founded her own company to encourage girls and women to pursue science and technology careers.

723. SEPTEMBER 17, 1983

VANESSA WILLIAMS IS CROWNED MISS AMERICA

Underneath the seemingly frivolous surface of the 20th-century Miss America beauty pageant lay a history of racial discrimination. In the 1930s, the pageant's rule book explicitly stated that the contestants must be "of the white race." Not until 1970 did the first Black contestant reach the Atlantic City finals. And only in 1983 did the first Black contestant win the crown when Vanessa Williams, Miss New York, became Miss America. She did not hold the title for the full year, being forced to resign in July 1984 after nude photos taken earlier in her career surfaced. The scandal, which some saw as racially motivated, did not prevent Williams from going on to a long and successful career as a singer and actress.

724. JANUARY 24, 1984

APPLE INTRODUCES THE MACINTOSH

On this day, Apple co-founder Steve Jobs unveiled the Macintosh, an all-in-one personal computer, in front of an enthusiastic audience in Cupertino, California's Flint Center. The computer was a small, square, beige box accompanied by a small beige mouse, but its graphical user interface was an innovation. As the Apple press release touted, "Users tell Macintosh what to do simply by moving a 'mouse'—a small pointing device—to select among functions listed in menus and represented by pictorial symbols on the screen." The computer was the first to popularize a screen ("desktop") with icons, the ability to run multiple programs simultaneously in various windows, drop-down menus, and copy-and-paste functionality. Apple went on to diversify into music players, smartphones, and other areas in the 21st century and became one of the largest publicly traded companies in the world.

SUCCESS IS THE BEST REVENGE.

Vanessa Williams *(1990)*

725. SEPTEMBER 10, 1984

ALEX TREBEK HOSTS *JEOPARDY!*

"And now, here is the host of *Jeopardy!*, Alex Trebek!" announced Johnny Gilbert for the first time. The answer-and-question television show had aired previously with host Art Fleming, but Canadian American Trebek brought with him an air of erudition that made it into a decades-long hit. Trebek had previously hosted game shows such as *High Rollers*

The Miss America pageant ran for 63 years before crowning its first African American winner, Vanessa Williams, who was Miss New York.

and *The Wizard of Odds,* but on *Jeopardy!* he emphasized the educational content. "It's a quiz show, not a game show, and people take those intellectual-type pursuits more seriously," he said. Under Trebek's guidance, *Jeopardy!* won multiple Emmys and a Peabody Award. Trebek passed away in 2020; the show has aired more than 9,000 episodes to date.

726. MAY 13, 1985

PHILADELPHIA BOMBS ITS OWN CITIZENS

The city of Philadelphia and the Black liberation group MOVE had been in conflict for years before Mayor Wilson Goode gave the order to evict the group from its building at 6221 Osage Avenue. MOVE refused, and on this day almost 500 police officers in SWAT gear surrounded the city block, fired into the house, flooded the basement with water, and shot tear-gas canisters into the home. Finally, the city dropped a bomb containing C-4 explosives on the roof. Flames spread through the neighborhood, destroying more than 61 homes and displacing more than 250 residents. Eleven MOVE members died, including five children. At the time, the city ruled that the deaths were accidental; in 2022, the death certificates were amended to state that the dead were victims of homicide. Ultimately, the city paid millions of dollars to survivors and homeowners whose properties had been damaged.

727. OCTOBER 19, 1985

FIRST BLOCKBUSTER VIDEO STORE OPENS IN DALLAS, TEXAS

Video rental stores existed in the early 1980s, but software entrepreneur David Cook may have been the first to see the potential in starting a big, efficient video-rental franchise. In the fall of 1985, he launched the first Blockbuster in Dallas, Texas, with 10,000 VHS and Beta videotapes. The store's sizable inventory and computerized checkout made it a success, and Cook rapidly opened others, as well as a large centralized warehouse. With a no-porn policy, the chain quickly became the family video store of choice across the country. It remained a dominant force in home entertainment until the early 2000s, with the advent of Netflix and streaming video.

728. JANUARY 28, 1986

FREEZING TEMPERATURES DOOM THE *CHALLENGER*

Space shuttle launches had become almost routine by 1986, but the *Challenger* mission on this chilly Florida morning had drawn more public attention than usual. Among the seven-person crew was the first civilian to go into space, teacher Christa McAuliffe. Schoolchildren around the country were watching the launch on television when, at 73 seconds into its flight, the shuttle blew apart in a spiraling, flaming explosion, killing its entire crew. Investigations later revealed that an O-ring—a rubber seal in the right solid rocket booster—had stiffened in the unusually cold temperatures and failed, allowing flames to leak through and ignite the liquid fuel in the shuttle's tank. NASA redesigned its program and did not launch another shuttle until 1988; the last of these reusable vehicles flew in 2011.

Oprah Winfrey's success in journalism, films, books, magazines, television, and more earned her the nickname "queen of all media."

729. SEPTEMBER 8, 1986

OPRAH WINFREY LAUNCHES AN INFLUENTIAL TALK SHOW

The first episode of *The Oprah Winfrey Show* was the old-fashioned but heartfelt "How to Marry the Man or Woman of Your Choice." Winfrey had been hosting a successful half-hour morning talk show in Chicago when her friend, movie critic Roger Ebert, persuaded her to go national and challenge the reigning talk show king, Phil Donahue. Winfrey's empathetic style appealed to viewers and propelled her show into long-lasting success. Her spin-off book club, monthly magazine, and food and multimedia businesses would make her one of the first female African American billionaires.

730. OCTOBER 5, 1986

IRAN-CONTRA AFFAIR BEGINS TO COME TO LIGHT

President Ronald Reagan and his administration worried that the leftist Sandinista government of Nicaragua would spread communism through the region, posing a threat to U.S. security. Congress had passed a law in 1984 banning aid to the Contra rebels fighting the Sandinistas, but somehow weapons were secretly reaching them from the United

continued on page 364

SPOTLIGHT

THE AMERICAN WORKER

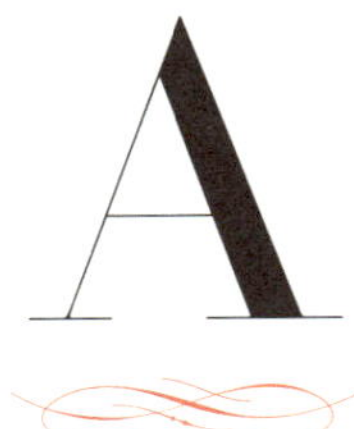

AS WAVES OF changes impacted 20th-century employees and employers, labor unions championed worker rights.

Rapid industrialization in the early 1900s exposed many workers to long hours, low wages, and poor conditions such as unsafe and toxic workplaces. Unions arose to represent them: the American Federation of Labor (AFL), which organized workers by skill and trade, and the Industrial Workers of the World (IWW), which organized across skills by industry. Both attempted strikes and other actions with mixed success.

During the 1930s, President Franklin D. Roosevelt's administration backed the National Labor Relations Act, which guaranteed workers the right to unionize and bargain collectively. It passed in 1935—the same year the Congress of Industrial Organizations (CIO) formed to organize mass-production workers, broadening the movement's reach by winning wage hikes and employer-sponsored pensions and health coverage.

Union power was curbed by the 1947 Taft-Hartley Act, which placed limits on strikes and political contributions; it also allowed states to enact "right-to-work" laws that prohibited workplaces from requiring union membership. In the 1950s and '60s—despite a Red Scare that spurred purges of alleged communists within labor ranks—unions and a merged AFL-CIO helped secure gains for workers. In the latter half of the century, private-sector union strength waned, but public-sector unions grew. At labor's peak in the 1940s and '50s, about 33 percent of the U.S. workforce belonged to unions; at the end of the 20th century, about 15 percent did.

With the Chrysler Building's spire in the background (at right), an ironworker toils on the Empire State Building construction site.

THERE IS NO SUBSTITUTE FOR HARD WORK.

Thomas Edison *(1930)*

continued from page 361

States. That became clear when, on this day, Sandinistas shot down an American plane carrying supplies to the Contras. The plane's lone survivor, American Eugene Hasenfus, later confessed to the operation. An American commission found that the supply missions were financed through illegal arms sales from the U.S. to Iran. American officials, including National Security Council member Oliver North, were subsequently convicted on various charges, but most escaped consequences when they were pardoned or their convictions were overturned.

731. JANUARY 3, 1987

ARETHA FRANKLIN IS INDUCTED INTO THE ROCK & ROLL HALL OF FAME

Aretha Franklin had been an outstanding recording artist since she was a teenager; in 1967 her signature soaring vocals turned Otis Redding's song "Respect" into one of the great R & B recordings of all time. At the age of 44, Franklin became the first woman inducted into the Rock & Roll Hall of Fame on this day. Her membership in the Rock Hall was notable not only because it recognized her as a major musical figure but also because the foundation had a reputation for ignoring women in rock and roll; Franklin was the only woman among 26 men or all-male groups inducted in its first two years. In later years,

Poisoned wildlife was only part of the toll when the tanker *Exxon Valdez* ran aground, spilling 11 million gallons of oil into the sea.

Franklin went on to win a Kennedy Center Honor, receive the Presidential Medal of Freedom, and sing at President Barack Obama's inauguration.

732. OCTOBER 16, 1987

RESCUERS PULL "BABY JESSICA" FROM A WELL

On October 14, 18-month-old Jessica McClure fell into an eight-inch well pipe in her aunt's backyard in Midland, Texas. The toddler got stuck 22 feet down with one leg lodged next to her head. Over the next two days, the entire country tuned in to follow the "Baby Jessica" drama as rescuers drilled a parallel shaft to reach her; the girl could be heard singing inside the well. After 58 hours, she was safely pulled out and survived without serious injury.

733. JUNE 23, 1988

JAMES HANSEN TESTIFIES ABOUT GLOBAL WARMING

"Global Warming Has Begun, Expert Tells Senate" read the headline the next day in the *New York Times*. It was 100°F in Washington, D.C., when NASA climate scientist James Hansen testified to the reality of human-caused climate change before a Senate Committee on Energy and Natural Resources. "The greenhouse effect has been detected, and it is changing our climate now," he said. Hansen's testimony was the first widely publicized national alert to the existence and dangers of ongoing climate change.

734. MARCH 24, 1989

***EXXON VALDEZ* RUNS AGROUND**

Just after midnight, the Exxon Corporation oil tanker *Exxon Valdez,* bound for California, veered out of normal shipping lanes and ran aground on Bligh Reef in Alaska's Prince William Sound. The ruptured vessel leaked 11 million gallons of crude oil into the seawater, where it spread across more than 1,300 miles of shoreline. Professional and volunteer cleanup crews attempted to corral the spilled oil and cleanse the shores, but it quickly coated animals and beaches. The spill killed approximately 250,000 seabirds, 2,800 sea otters, and billions of salmon and herring eggs, as well as harbor seals, bald eagles, and orcas in one of the largest environmental disasters in U.S. history.

735. APRIL 24, 1990

HUBBLE TELESCOPE REACHES SPACE

Watching the stars through Earth's thick atmosphere, space scientist James Odom once observed, is like "birdwatching from the bottom of a lake." In 1990, after more than a decade of development, NASA engineers overcame this problem by launching the first large, sophisticated space observatory: the Hubble Space Telescope. Carried into high orbit by the space shuttle *Discovery,* the telescope ushered in a new era not just of astronomical discovery but also of public interest in the cosmos and its visual wonders. Other

R-E-S-P-E-C-T: Aretha Franklin's quarter-century singing career earned her place as the first woman in the Rock & Roll Hall of Fame.

Songs keyed to an alienated generation gave the grunge band Nirvana hit singles and a chart-topping, best-selling album in 1992's *Nevermind.*

space telescopes would be launched in the years to come, but Hubble remains in orbit as a major contributor to astronomical knowledge.

736. SEPTEMBER 14, 1990

FIRST SUCCESSFUL GENE THERAPY TREATS A FOUR-YEAR-OLD GIRL

Ashanti DeSilva was born without a gene that builds the immune system, leaving her at the mercy of multiple infections. At the age of four, she became the first patient to undergo gene therapy. Doctors at the National Institutes of Health injected her with one billion of her own white blood cells, which had been removed and altered to contain the lifesaving gene. The treatment was a success; although not completely cured, DeSilva did well and grew up to become a genetic counselor.

737. FEBRUARY 24, 1991

U.S. BEGINS OPERATION DESERT SABRE

In August 1990, Iraqi forces invaded the neighboring country of Kuwait, intent on seizing its oil fields, among other goals. Three months later, the U.N. Security Council authorized the use of force against Iraq if their troops failed to withdraw by January 15, 1991; on January 16, the United States and other allied countries began a counterattack dubbed Operation Desert Storm. It began with a devastating air offensive and finished, beginning on this day, with an overwhelming ground offensive: Operation Desert Sabre. The entire operation wrapped up in just 100 hours, with Iraqi troops surrendering and retreating—but not before they set fire to more than 700 Kuwaiti oil fields, filling the skies with black smoke. The conflict marked a new approach to international cooperation in the era after the Cold War.

738. SEPTEMBER 24, 1991

NIRVANA RELEASES *NEVERMIND*

Seattle grunge band Nirvana—a three-man group fronted by singer and songwriter Kurt Cobain—tapped into a generational sense of cultural alienation with its best-selling second album, *Nevermind.* The band's label, DGC, had modest hopes for the release, but the album soon sold out, thanks in part to its nihilistic lead single, "Smells Like Teen Spirit." "Load up on guns, bring your friends," the song begins, "It's fun to lose and to pretend." The album also grabbed attention with its striking cover image of a swimming baby chasing a dollar bill. *Nevermind* hit number one on the Billboard 200 chart in 1992; the group was inducted into the Rock & Roll Hall of Fame in 2014.

739. DECEMBER 12, 1991

FIRST U.S. WEBSITE GOES ONLINE

Physicist Paul Kunz and his colleagues at the Stanford Linear Accelerator Center (SLAC) launched the nation's first website on this day. Inspired by British web pioneer Tim

The 1992 acquittal of four Los Angeles police officers who beat Black motorist Rodney King sparked six days of riots in which 63 people died.

CAN WE ALL GET ALONG?

Rodney King *(1992)*

Berners-Lee, who created the world's first website at the nuclear research organization CERN in Switzerland, Kunz and others set up their own web server and created a browser to provide access to SLAC files. Their first website contained three lines of text and two links: to email addresses and a preprint database. Today, more than 133 million websites are registered in the United States.

740. APRIL 29, 1992

RIOTS BREAK OUT IN LOS ANGELES

On March 3, 1991, African American motorist Rodney King was pulled over and severely beaten by a large group of police officers, most from the Los Angeles Police Department. A local resident videotaped the beatings, and the recordings became public to widespread outrage. Four of the officers, all white, were brought to trial in nearby Simi Valley, where on this day a jury that contained no Black members found them not guilty (with one count deadlocked for one officer). News of the verdict sparked riots in Los Angeles. Fires, looting, and gunfire kept much of the city on lockdown for six days; more than 50 people were killed. Two of the four officers originally tried were later sentenced in civil court for violating King's civil rights.

741. APRIL 19, 1993

BRANCH DAVIDIAN COMPLEX IN WACO BURNS AFTER STANDOFF

In February 1993, the Bureau of Alcohol, Tobacco, and Firearms (ATF) raided a Waco, Texas complex housing members of the cultlike Branch Davidian religious community, led by David Koresh. The ATF raid, in search of illegal weapons, ended in a gun battle with four ATF agents and five or six Branch Davidians dead. A 51-day siege of the Waco compound by hundreds of FBI agents and other personnel, armed with tanks and tear gas, followed. On this day, law enforcement pumped tear gas into the compound in an attempt to get the Davidians to leave, igniting a battle. Fires broke out in the complex, possibly set by the Davidians, and possibly fueled by inflammable tear gas. Seventy-six of the 85 Branch Davidians, including more than 20 children, died in the flames. For many, the deadly event would become an example of government overreach.

742. MAY 4, 1993

ANGELS IN AMERICA: MILLENNIUM APPROACHES PREMIERES ON BROADWAY

Tony Kushner's play—the first of a two-part work—takes place in the mid-1980s, but looks back to the '50s and forward toward the turn of the century. The play encompasses gay life, AIDS, religion, politics, angels, ghosts, love, and treachery, but centers on the character of Prior Walter, who learns that he has AIDS and is abandoned by his lover. It opened at Broadway's Walter Kerr Theatre to strong reviews and went on to win a Pulitzer Prize and a New York Drama Critics' Circle Award for Kushner, as well as four Tony awards. The play and its successor, *Perestroika,* captured a country's reckoning with its troubled past and its worries and hopes about the coming century.

Facing sexism during her early career gave Justice Ruth Bader Ginsburg a keen interest in women's rights issues before she joined the Supreme Court.

743. AUGUST 10, 1993

RUTH BADER GINSBURG IS SWORN IN TO THE SUPREME COURT

On this day, Ruth Bader Ginsburg became the second woman, and the first Jewish woman, to become a justice on the Supreme Court. Ginsburg was known as an advocate for women's rights; as well as working for the Southern District of New York, she also co-founded the ACLU's Women's Rights Project and served as the ACLU's General Counsel. At the time that President Bill Clinton nominated her to the Court, she was a judge on the U.S. Court of Appeals in the District of Columbia. Ginsburg became an energetic and well-respected presence on the Court, where she authored more than 200 majority opinions, at the same time becoming a cultural icon affectionately portrayed on TV skits, T-shirts, and more. Some believe her controversial decision to stay on the Court following a diagnosis of pancreatic cancer contributed to a solidly conservative majority upon her death in 2020.

744. OCTOBER 7, 1993

TONI MORRISON WINS THE NOBEL PRIZE

Writer Toni Morrison was not expecting to win the Nobel Prize in Literature: She learned it was hers when a colleague at Princeton heard the announcement on television and called her. With the award, she became the second American woman and the first African American woman to win the literature prize. The Nobel Committee noted that "in novels characterized by visionary force and poetic import, [she] gives life to an essential aspect of American reality." Morrison's books, which include *The Bluest Eye, Song of Solomon,* and *Beloved,* tell the stories of African American men and women and their communities in different eras of history.

745. DECEMBER 8, 1993

PRESIDENT CLINTON SIGNS BROAD-REACHING NAFTA AGREEMENT

On this day, President Bill Clinton signed into law the North American Free Trade Agreement, creating the largest free trade zone in the world. The trade pact eliminated most tariffs and trade barriers among the United States, Canada, and Mexico. In the years to follow, the agreement did increase trade among the three nations, though its overall effects were hard to quantify in a complex world economy. In 2020, NAFTA was replaced by the United States-Mexico-Canada Agreement (USMCA) advocated by President Trump.

746. JANUARY 6, 1994

CHAMPION SKATER NANCY KERRIGAN IS ATTACKED

Figure skater Nancy Kerrigan, a favorite to win the 1994 U.S. Figure Skating Championship, was attacked by a man wielding a baton, who struck her twice above the knee as she walked down a hall in Detroit's Cobo Arena on this day. The attack left her unable to

Through the lens of the 1980s AIDS crisis, the play *Angels in America* explored topics including human connection, politics, and religion.

O. J. Simpson forced a police chase before his arrest for the murders of his ex-wife Nicole Brown Simpson and her friend Ronald Goldman.

compete in the finals, which her competitor Tonya Harding won. Within days, two men connected to Harding were arrested for the attack, which Harding's ex-husband, Jeff Gillooly, turned out to have planned. Eventually, Gillooly and three other men were convicted of planning and executing the crime; Harding, who was apparently aware of the plans, was banned from U.S. figure skating. Kerrigan went on to win a silver medal at that year's Winter Olympics.

747. JUNE 17, 1994

O. J. SIMPSON LEADS POLICE ON A CHASE

Car chases in dramas are usually high-speed affairs, but in 1994 the nation was riveted by a slow, almost plodding 60-mile chase involving a white Bronco and a convoy of police cars. The Bronco was driven by Al Cowlings, a friend of football and movie star O. J. Simpson, who was in the back seat. Simpson was a suspect in the murder of his ex-wife Nicole Brown Simpson and her friend Ronald Goldman. Instead of turning himself in to police that morning as planned, he persuaded Cowlings to drive him through Los

Angeles to his mansion in Brentwood, where he was then arrested. An estimated 95 million enthralled people watched the slow-speed chase on television. Simpson was acquitted of the crime in 1995, but was found liable for the deaths in a civil suit in 1997.

748. JULY 5, 1994

JEFF BEZOS LAUNCHES THE WORLD'S FIRST BIG ONLINE STORE

Continuing an early internet tradition of working from a garage, Jeff Bezos quit his hedge fund manager job and launched an online bookstore out of his carport in Bellevue, Washington. Bezos originally named the store Cadabra but reputedly changed it to Amazon after realizing it sounded like "cadaver." Amazon's first sale was appropriately wonkish: Douglas Hofstadter's *Fluid Concepts and Creative Analogies,* bought by a computer scientist. The company lost money at first but grew rapidly and boomed as the new millennium arrived. Today, the company, known colloquially as "The Everything Store," is worth more than two trillion dollars.

NICOLE BROWN SIMPSON TOLD EVERY FRIEND SHE HAD THAT O. J. SIMPSON WAS GOING TO KILL HER AND GET AWAY WITH IT.

Dominick Dunne, Vanity Fair *(2014)*

749. JANUARY 12, 1995

WOLVES ARE REINTRODUCED TO YELLOWSTONE

Roughly 70 years after gray wolves had been hunted to eradication in Yellowstone National Park, biologists trucked in the first eight of the endangered animals to rebuild the park's wolf population. The move was controversial, as local ranchers feared the animals would leave the park's boundaries and kill their livestock. Scientists pointed out that in the absence of these natural predators, the park's ecosystem was out of balance—for instance, the elk population had boomed and was wiping out native plants. In the end, the wolves became established and by the 2020s numbered about 100 individuals in multiple packs. Though the animals do occasionally prey upon local livestock, they are also credited with helping to restore a healthy balance of plants and animals within the park.

750. APRIL 19, 1995

BOMB KILLS 168 IN OKLAHOMA CITY

At 9:02 in the morning, a Ryder truck holding an explosive mixture of ammonium nitrate fertilizer and diesel fuel blew up in front of the Alfred P. Murrah Federal Building in Oklahoma City, Oklahoma. The massive blast blew off the front of the building, killed 168 people (including 19 children in a day care center), and injured more than 500. FBI agents traced the rental truck to 26-year-old Timothy McVeigh and were surprised to learn he was already in jail, having been picked up for driving without a license plate and carrying a concealed weapon. An associate of McVeigh's, Terry Nichols, was also implicated in the plot. Both men shared beliefs with far-right groups who denied the legitimacy of the federal government and were outraged by the deaths at Waco in 1993; they targeted the Oklahoma building as a government symbol. McVeigh and Nichols were convicted on multiple counts in 1997. McVeigh was executed in 2001, and Nichols was sentenced to life without parole. The Oklahoma City bombing was the largest domestic terrorism incident in American history.

751. SEPTEMBER 19, 1995

NEWSPAPERS PUBLISH THE UNABOMBER MANIFESTO

"The Industrial Revolution and its consequences have been a disaster for the human race," wrote the man known only as the Unabomber. They "have destabilized society, have made life unfulfilling, have subjected human beings to indignities … We therefore advocate a revolution against the industrial system." After much debate, the *New York Times* and the *Washington Post* published the Unabomber's 35,000-word manifesto, which he had sent them that June under the pseudonym "FC." Since 1978, the mysterious author had become infamous for mailing homemade bombs to academics and others, killing three and injuring 23 others. The manifesto's publication led to the identification and capture of Theodore Kaczynski, a former mathematician living in a Montana cabin. In 1998, he was sentenced to life without parole; he died in a prison medical center in 2023.

752. OCTOBER 7, 1996

RUPERT MURDOCH STARTS FOX NEWS CHANNEL

Intending to compete with cable news channels such as CNN, Australian-born media mogul Rupert Murdoch launched his Fox News Channel by paying cable companies to

Tiger Woods was presented with the iconic Masters green jacket by Nick Faldo (left) at the winner's ceremony for the 61st Masters Tournament.

carry his shows, rather than requiring them to pay him. Murdoch hired former Republican political consultant Roger Ailes as the channel's CEO. From the start, Fox News was associated with conservative politics and had some of its greatest success with opinion programming that featured personalities like Bill O'Reilly and Sean Hannity. By 2002, the new channel had passed CNN in total viewership and today is the most successful cable news channel, gaining notoriety for its opposition to President Barack Obama and its overwhelming support of Donald Trump and his political MAGA (Make America Great Again) movement.

753. JANUARY 1, 1997

SIX DEGREES SOCIAL NETWORK HITS THE WEB

Entrepreneur Andrew Weinreich launched the country's first social networking site, Six Degrees, to connect friends and families via the internet. The site took its name from the theory that everyone on Earth is connected to one another by no more than six people. Six Degrees encouraged users to create profiles, set up friends lists, and send messages. Although it reached millions of people in the next few years, the site never truly took off, probably because only a minority of Americans were online in the late '90s. The business shut down after Weinreich sold it to YouthStream Media Networks in 2000.

754. APRIL 13, 1997

TIGER WOODS WINS THE MASTERS

At 21, golfer Eldrick "Tiger" Woods set a host of records when he won the Masters Tournament in Augusta, Georgia. He was the youngest player and the first of African or Asian descent to win the title. His score of 18 under par 270 broke a record shared by Jack Nicklaus. His 12-stroke margin of victory was the largest in the 20th century. By June of that year, Woods was ranked number one in the world—a title he held 11 different times, including for a record-breaking 281 consecutive weeks from 2005 to 2010.

755. APRIL 30, 1997

ELLEN DEGENERES GOES PUBLIC

In an era when many celebrities hid their sexual identities and no television show had a gay lead character, popular actress and comedian Ellen DeGeneres came out as gay on her successful television sitcom, *Ellen.* Although the show's character was fictional, she was clearly a stand-in for the actress. The script was titled "The Puppy Episode" to keep its contents secret. In the weeks before it aired, word began to spread about the episode's revolutionary nature; more than 40 million viewers would watch its premiere. "The Puppy Episode" went on to win a Peabody and an Emmy Award. After *Ellen* ended in 1998, DeGeneres followed up with an award-winning daytime talk show, *The Ellen DeGeneres Show,* from 2003 to 2022.

756. DECEMBER 19, 1997

TITANIC (THE MOVIE) MAKES ITS MAIDEN VOYAGE

Running more than three hours long and with a budget of roughly $200 million, James Cameron's film *Titanic* was a financial risk but a huge success. The tale of the doomed romance between plucky working-class Jack (Leonardo DiCaprio) and unhappy upper-class Rose (Kate Winslet) aboard the ill-fated ship became famous for its lavish and scrupulously accurate production values. *Titanic* went on to win 11 Oscars and set box office records, grossing more than two billion dollars by the 2020s. The movie's theme song, Celine Dion's "My Heart Will Go On," was also a major hit, quickly reaching number one on Billboard charts.

James Cameron bet a $200 million movie budget that *Titanic* would be a hit, and it was, setting box office records and winning 11 Academy Awards.

757. MAY 14, 1998

SEINFELD ENDS ITS RUN

"I do not know how, or under what circumstances, the four of you found each other," states the judge in the final episode of *Seinfeld,* "but your callous indifference and utter disregard for everything that is good and decent has rocked the very foundation upon which our society is built." The two-part finale of comedian Jerry Seinfeld's long-running, immensely popular television comedy "about nothing"—aka the trials and tribulations of daily life in New York City's Upper West Side—concluded with its four self-centered main characters sentenced to jail for violating a Good Samaritan law. More than 76 million viewers watched the finale, but reactions to the show's sardonic conclusion were mixed. *USA Today* called it "dismal"; the *New York Times,* "hilarious." By its last episode, the show had turned its four lead actors, particularly Julia Louis-Dreyfus, into household names.

758. JUNE 14, 1998

MICHAEL JORDAN SINKS A CHAMPIONSHIP SHOT

The Utah Jazz were leading the Chicago Bulls 86–85 in the final 19 seconds of Game 6 of the NBA Finals when legendary Bulls shooting guard Michael Jordan stole the ball from Karl Malone, drove down court, and sank a 20-foot jumper to win the game and the tournament. It was the capper to a stellar career in basketball as well as the end of a Bulls dynasty. Jordan retired after that season, although he returned briefly from 2001 to 2003 to play with the Washington Wizards before retiring again.

759. SEPTEMBER 4, 1998

SERGEY BRIN AND LARRY PAGE FOUND GOOGLE

Sergey Brin, a graduate student, and Larry Page, a prospective graduate student, met while Brin showed Page around the campus of Stanford University. Working out of their dorm rooms first and then a garage in Menlo Park, California, they devised a creative new search engine, initially called BackRub, that ranked web pages based on the number of other pages linked to them, as well as the importance of those linked pages. With a $100,000 investment from Sun Microsystems co-founder Andy Bechtolsheim, Brin and Page incorporated their

Sergey Brin (left) and business partner Larry Page met while college students and went on to found the internet search giant Google.

new company and renamed it Google, after the mathematical expression googol, a 1 followed by 100 zeros. By 2002, the generic term "google," meaning to search the web, had entered the public vocabulary. Today, the company is worth more than two trillion dollars.

760. NOVEMBER 6, 1998

BIOLOGIST CULTIVATES HUMAN STEM CELLS

Led by University of Wisconsin biologist James Thomson, a team of scientists announced in the journal *Science* that they had successfully cultivated and sustained human embryonic stem cells. The cells were taken from fertilized human eggs and, because they had not yet specialized into specific tissues, could potentially be used to cure a host of illnesses and injuries. "These cell lines," the paper's authors stated, "should be useful in human developmental biology, drug discovery, and transplantation medicine." A long-sought but controversial element of biological research, stem cells have been used in each of those fields—in testing new drugs, growing new tissues for transplantation, and treating spinal cord injuries, blood cancers, hearing disorders, and more—since Thomson first cultivated them.

761. DECEMBER 19, 1998

PRESIDENT CLINTON IS IMPEACHED

The House of Representatives voted on this day in favor of two articles of impeachment against President Bill Clinton—the second president, after Andrew Johnson, ever to be impeached. Following an investigation by counsel Kenneth Starr, the second-term president was charged with the "high crimes and misdemeanors" of perjury and obstruction of justice. The charges stemmed primarily from claims of sexual harassment by a previous associate of Clinton's, Paula Jones, and from Clinton's attempted cover-up of his affair with White House intern Monica Lewinsky. After debate in a divided Senate, Clinton was acquitted of both charges in February 1999, but the proceedings highlighted the increasingly adversarial nature of modern politics going into the 21st century.

762. JANUARY 10, 1999

THE SOPRANOS CHANGES TELEVISION

"What line of work are you in?" asks psychiatrist Jennifer Melfi. "Waste management consultant," answers Mafia boss Tony Soprano (James Gandolfini). The first episode of

The U.S. Women's National Team—including (left to right) Cindy Parlow, Lorrie Fair, Tiffany Roberts, Mia Hamm, and Briana Scurry—clinched a penalty-kick nail-biter to win the 1999 World Cup.

the groundbreaking television series *The Sopranos,* created by David Chase, introduced the world to the mobster's conflicted life, torn between his own family and his mob family and between his need to keep his life secret and his need to open up in Melfi's office. The saga of murder and psychotherapy ran for six seasons and won 21 Emmy Awards; it is credited with introducing a new age of high-end television.

763. APRIL 20, 1999

STUDENTS KILL 13 AT COLUMBINE HIGH SCHOOL

In one of the nation's worst mass shootings to date, Columbine High School students Eric Harris and Dylan Klebold killed 12 fellow students, one teacher, and then themselves on this day. Twenty-three others were injured. The trench-coated seniors used semi-automatic weapons in their attacks and planted bombs inside and outside the school as well, though the most destructive did not detonate. The shootings shocked the country and set off a debate about gun violence, teen alienation, and the role of the Second Amendment in public life. They were not the last mass shootings that year, nor in the years to come.

THE THINGS WE DO IN THE COURSE OF COMPETITION OFTEN TRANSCEND THE MOMENT AND REFLECT WHO WE ARE.

Brandi Chastain, *U.S. soccer champion (2004)*

764. JULY 10, 1999

U.S. WOMEN'S SOCCER TEAM WINS WORLD CUP

The championship game of the FIFA Women's World Cup came down to a cliff-hanger: a penalty kick shoot-out between the U.S. and China. As defender Brandi Chastain prepared to take her shot, coach Tony DiCicco told her to kick with her left, nondominant foot. She did, the ball flew into the goal, and the U.S. won the game. Chastain ripped off her shirt and dropped to her knees in triumph. Played in front of more than 90,000 fans in California's Rose Bowl, the game drew the largest crowd in U.S. women's sports history. It was a major milestone on the road to bringing women's sports to the world's attention.

765. DECEMBER 31, 1999

CROWDS CELEBRATE THE NEW MILLENNIUM AMID Y2K FEARS

Fireworks bloomed across the country, crowds in Times Square watched a Waterford crystal ball drop, and celebrities joined President Bill and First Lady Hillary Clinton on the Capitol Mall as the 20th century and the millennium ended. Adding to the excitement was relief that computer software around the world did not, in fact, crash due to the Y2K bug. In the years before the century ended, programmers realized that some programs had abbreviated years using just the last two digits, leading to fears that the year 2000 would ring in widespread shutdowns in transportation, banking, and other crucial systems. However, programmers managed to fix the bugs in time, and the new millennium arrived without a hitch as clocks ticked over to 12:00 and into 2000.

★ ★ ★ *The* ★ ★ ★
21st CENTURY

TOWARD A MORE PERFECT UNION

THE TIME HAS COME TO REAFFIRM OUR ENDURING SPIRIT; TO CHOOSE OUR BETTER HISTORY.

Barack Obama, *first inaugural address (2009)*

AT THE START OF the new millennium, a White House council convened by the George W. Bush administration outlined goals for America in the 21st century. They included preserving historic sites and celebrating founding principles; leading a new age of discovery in science and technology; and investing in education, service, and building community to reinforce democracy.

Then, in the fall of 2001, terrorists in hijacked jets shattered the nation's sense of security. U.S. troops went on to fight in Afghanistan and Iraq—and were still there when the COVID-19 pandemic descended 19 years later.

Like their forebears in the last quarter of the 18th century, Americans in the first quarter of the 21st century faced lethal threats and shocking loss. Still, they pressed on.

In the 21st century, digital technologies advanced and proliferated, with U.S. companies in the vanguard and consumers buying ever more devices. NASA planned a return to the moon, as mechanized explorers roamed Mars and space telescopes peered into deep space.

Breakthroughs in genetics and personalized medicine enabled more potent therapies for diseases. While U.S. officials joined or left global climate change efforts depending on the party in power, U.S. consumers increasingly invested in electric and hybrid vehicles, solar panels, and other renewable technologies. Drives for equality also produced gains, including the 2008 election of Barack Obama as the nation's first Black president, though political polarization fanned later conflicts such as the January 6, 2021, siege of the Capitol.

The official portrait of First Lady Michelle Obama was unveiled in 2018. **OPPOSITE TOP:** In the years since terrorists destroyed the World Trade Center, blue beams representing the former twin towers shine skyward every September 11—an art installation titled "Tribute in Light." **OPPOSITE BOTTOM:** *Curiosity* was one of four NASA rovers that explored Mars in the first quarter of the 21st century, returning groundbreaking data and images from the red planet.

DECEMBER 12, 2000
Supreme Court settles the presidential election
A high court order ending Florida's vote recount after an almost evenly split election gave George Bush the win over Al Gore.

SEPTEMBER 11, 2001
Hijackers use jets as weapons of destruction
Terrorists forced planes to crash into the World Trade Center, Pentagon, and a Pennsylvania field.

FEBRUARY 1, 2003
Space shuttle *Columbia* crew perishes
Damage from a debris strike to its left wing caused the shuttle to break apart on reentry.

FEBRUARY 4, 2004
TheFacebook makes its debut
A website launched by Harvard University students became a social networking phenomenon.

JANUARY 4, 2007
U.S. House welcomes its first female speaker
The historic choice is a veteran California congresswoman, Democrat Nancy Pelosi.

DECEMBER 19, 2008
Government bailout saves failing U.S. automakers
The funding preserves jobs despite automakers' slumping sales against foreign competition.

JANUARY 20, 2009
Barack Obama is inaugurated as America's first Black president
His "Yes We Can" campaign swept the junior senator past seasoned competitors.

MARCH 23, 2010
Affordable Care Act overhauls U.S. health care system
Its dramatic reforms aimed to give more Americans better insurance coverage at lower cost.

DECEMBER 22, 2010
U.S. allows gay, lesbian, and bisexual Americans to serve in the military
President Barack Obama repealed the policy that let services bar or discharge personnel who identify as gay, lesbian, or bisexual.

Two golds earned at the 2023 World Artistic Gymnastics Championships in Belgium brought Simone Biles's medal total to 37, making her history's most decorated gymnast.

TIMELINE

2000-2025

THE BREAKTHROUGH OF THE CENTURY TAKES HUMANITY TOWARD "REWRITING THE CODE OF LIFE."

ONE OF VICTORIA GRAY'S first memories—from the year she was four—is a harrowing hospitalization for sickle cell disease (SCD). The genetic disorder, which deforms blood cells, can be painful and destructive. During the next 30 years, SCD episodes kept the Mississippi native out of school and sports and stifled her career dreams.

Then, in 2019, Gray became the first patient in a clinical trial that employed a DNA-editing system called CRISPR-Cas9 to treat SCD. Doctors extracted stem cells from her bloodstream, modified them to produce healthy blood, and returned them to her body. Gray has been symptom free since 2020—the same year the Nobel Prize in Chemistry was awarded to CRISPR-Cas9 co-developers Emmanuelle Charpentier of France and Jennifer Doudna of the United States.

In Gray's case, the cell edits were made outside the patient's body *(ex vivo)*. But in 2024, a Pennsylvania infant named KJ was diagnosed with a life-threatening genetic disorder that caused a buildup of toxic ammonia; to address it, in vivo edits were required. Within six months, scientists developed a custom drug infusion that could reach and modify KJ's faulty gene; after three doses, the child was recovering well.

Awarding the chemistry prize to two women for the first time in history, the Nobel Committee declared that Doudna and Charpentier's achievements had "taken the life sciences into a new epoch."

MAY 1, 2011
Al Qaeda leader Osama bin Laden is slain
U.S. Navy SEALs shot the mastermind of the 9/11 attacks in his Pakistan hideout.

MAY 13, 2013
Researchers clone human embryonic stem cells
Patient-specific, the cells could be used to cure individuals of disease.

JUNE 26, 2015
Same-sex couples' right to marry is affirmed by high court
The Supreme Court ruled that marriage is a constitutionally assured privilege.

JUNE 1, 2017
President Donald Trump announces U.S. withdrawal from international climate accord
Two years after nations signed the Paris Agreement to fight climate change, Trump announced America's intention to withdraw from the pact.

OCTOBER 5, 2017
Movie impresario Harvey Weinstein faces sexual assault charges
Reports from Weinstein accusers energized the #MeToo movement of women revealing similar abuse.

MARCH 13, 2020
COVID-19 becomes a deadly global contagion
After the World Health Organization confirmed the pandemic, President Donald Trump declared COVID-19 a national emergency in America.

JANUARY 6, 2021
Protesting presidential vote certification, a crowd overruns the Capitol
Claiming fraud cost President Donald Trump the 2020 election, his supporters stormed the Capitol Building; the rampage resulted in five deaths.

JUNE 24, 2022
Abortion rights decision *Roe* v. *Wade* is overturned
The Supreme Court ruled that the Constitution does not confer a right to abortion.

766. JANUARY 1, 2000

Y2K COMPUTER CATASTROPHE FAILS TO LAUNCH

After months of dire warnings that the turn of the millennium would trigger massive computer malfunctions, the dreaded Y2K "apocalypse" did not materialize on this day. The issue stemmed from the computer coding practice of using two digits to denote the current year; as 2000 approached, people had widespread concern that software might misinterpret "00" as 1900, with grave consequences (planes falling from the sky, security and 911 systems failing). Fear of a civilization-ending crash spurred some to stockpile supplies in bunkers or take measures such as duplicating important documents and pulling cash out of banks. But thanks to tech experts around the world replacing date-sensitive components before the stroke of midnight on January 1, the year 2000 bug's bite was negligible.

767. FEBRUARY 12, 2000

"PEANUTS" LEGEND CHARLES M. SCHULZ PASSES AWAY

On this day, world-famous cartoonist Charles M. Schulz died at 77; a day later, the final original "Peanuts" Sunday strip appeared in many newspapers. Raised in St. Paul, Minnesota, near his father's barbershop, Schulz honed his cartooning skills at an art correspondence school and in an Army stint during World War II. In 1950, he landed his first syndication deal for the comic strip he called "Li'l Folks," renamed "Peanuts" by the publisher. Schulz never liked that name for his creation, but Americans embraced its characters: dejected hero Charlie Brown, his imaginative dog Snoopy, and assorted playmates—who live on today in comic reruns, as well as in TV and films, a Broadway musical, towering parade balloons, and an expansive array of merchandise.

768. MARCH 10, 2000

DOT-COM BUBBLE HITS ITS HIGH MARK

Driven by rampant speculation and overvaluation of new internet-based businesses, the "dot-com bubble" in the U.S. stock market reached its apex on this day. As the technology-heavy Nasdaq index hit 5,048.62—nearly twice its high a year before—tech titans including Cisco and Dell ordered big stock sales. This triggered other investors to panic sell amid a growing realization that most tech start-ups wouldn't turn a profit soon, if ever. In the space of a few weeks, the stock market lost a tenth of its value; some 18 months after the Nasdaq had peaked, it would fall to below 1,139. The slow recovery after the crash would be dubbed the "Lost Decade," as the market took more than a dozen years to regain its precrash highs.

769. APRIL 22, 2000

ELIÁN GONZÁLEZ GOES HOME

On this day, federal agents seized six-year-old Elián González from his relatives' home in Miami, Florida, and returned him to his Cuban father, ending one of the most publicized custody battles in U.S. history. The boy came to personify the decades-long clash between Cubans who remained on the island under pro-Soviet leader Fidel Castro and those who had fled Castro's regime to live in exile in the United States. In a November 1999 escape attempt, Elián's mother and 11 others drowned when their small boat capsized; fishermen found the boy floating in an inner tube. Raised by his father after his return to Cuba, he would become an engineer there and a member of the nation's congressional assembly.

770. MAY 31, 2000

SURVIVOR DEBUTS

CBS aired the first episode of the television show *Survivor* on this day. The show became an instant hit, launching the 21st-century phenomenon of reality TV. Inspired by the Swedish TV show *Robinson* (whose name alludes to *The Swiss Family Robinson* castaway film), the show drops small groups of contestants on an isolated island, where they're

In the first season of television's juggernaut reality series *Survivor*, victor Richard Hatch used shifting alliances to eliminate opponents, including (from left) Sean Kenniff, Susan Hawk, and Kelly Wiglesworth.

pitted against one another in survival trials. As fellow players vote losers off the island, tribes shrink to a few individuals, and finally one "sole survivor" receives a prize of a million dollars. Richard Hatch, the first season's victor, was jailed for not paying taxes on his winnings—but the show's popularity continued, airing two seasons a year for a quarter century.

771. AUGUST 14, 2000

DORA BECOMES AN EXPLORER

On this day, the cartoon character Dora the Explorer made her first appearance on the Nickelodeon network. An adventurous seven-year-old befriended by a cast of human and animal sidekicks, Dora Márquez chats with children in Spanish and English, sharing lessons about Hispanic culture and computer literacy. The cartoon was the network's first to feature a Latino character as a protagonist—a breakthrough in multicultural programming that premiered in 22 Latin American countries as well as the United States. Dora would grow up and into other shows: She was an animated 10-year-old in a 2014 TV spin-off and a teenager in a 2019 live-action film. For the character's 25th anniversary, young Dora was back in cartoon form, rebooted in a computer-animated series on networks, streaming services, and YouTube.

Producers initially balked at the *Cats* premise—but in 1997 it became Broadway's longest-running show, a feat celebrated with fireworks.

772. SEPTEMBER 10, 2000

FINAL CURTAIN FOR *CATS*

After 7,485 shows—a record at the time for the longest Broadway run—the musical *Cats* closed on Broadway on this evening. A spectacle as popular with tourist audiences as it was ridiculed by theater highbrows, the show was based on *Old Possum's Book of Practical Cats,* a 1939 poetry collection by T. S. Eliot. Music composed by Andrew Lloyd Webber included the cult song "Memory," which the *Evening Standard* called "perhaps the most famous musical theatre song ever written." Some 30 singers and dancers performed the show in elaborate cat costumes. As of this writing, the *Cats* record for longest Broadway run had been surpassed by four other shows: *The Phantom of the Opera* (13,981), *Chicago* (1996 revival; 11,401; still running), *The Lion King* (11,025; still running), and *Wicked* (8,562; still running).

IF ALL GOES WELL IN COMING YEARS, THIS COULD MARK THE START FOR AMERICANS OF CONTINUOUS OPERATIONS IN SPACE.

***New York Times* editorial board,** *on the opening of the International Space Station (2001)*

773. OCTOBER 12, 2000

AL QAEDA ATTACKS THE U.S.S. *COLE*

On this day, the U.S.S. *Cole,* a U.S. Navy guided-missile destroyer bound for the Arabian Gulf, anchored for routine refueling at the Port of Aden, Yemen. As crew members lined up for lunch in the galley, two al Qaeda suicide bombers guided a small boat near the ship's port side and detonated explosives. The blast tore a 40-foot-wide hole in the *Cole*'s hull; 17 sailors were killed and more than three dozen were injured. Two years after the militant Islamist group bombed two U.S. embassies in East Africa, the *Cole* attack added urgency to U.S. government efforts to capture al Qaeda leader Osama bin Laden.

774. NOVEMBER 2, 2000

INTERNATIONAL SPACE STATION BECOMES A HOME

On this day, NASA astronaut Bill Shepherd and cosmonauts Yuri Gidzenko and Sergei Krikalev became the first crew to reside on board the International Space Station (ISS). Building on what visiting crews did during ISS construction, the first residents performed tasks that NASA described as "bringing the station to life"—turning on lights, engaging oxygen and pressurization equipment, and activating the hot water system and toilet. By the time the space shuttle *Discovery* picked up the Expedition 1 crew and returned to the Kennedy Space Center on March 21, 2001, the trio had lived on the ISS for 141 days and inaugurated what's now nearly a quarter century of continuous human presence in space.

775. DECEMBER 12, 2000

SUPREME COURT SETTLES THE PRESIDENTIAL ELECTION

On this day, a controversial 5–4 decision by the Supreme Court ended a Florida vote recount in the November 7 presidential contest between Republican George W. Bush and

Democrat Al Gore, handing Bush the victory. After close votes in other states, a win hinged on the Florida results, where misread and incompletely punched ballots triggered legal challenges and recounts. As the December 18 deadline for certifying Florida's electors neared, the high court concluded a statewide recount couldn't be conducted in time and reversed the Florida Supreme Court's order for one. That gave Bush Florida's electoral college votes and the presidency with 271 to Gore's 266. In the popular vote, Gore bested Bush by more than 500,000.

776. JANUARY 15, 2001

WIKIPEDIA IS LAUNCHED

The 1990s brought the wiki—an internet publication whose content management system allows users to collaboratively write and edit articles via web browser. Then came Wikipedia, which posted its first edited content on this day. Creators christened it the "free encyclopedia" because the operating software, as well as the articles published, were free to use and adapt. Since Wikipedia's founding, editions have been created in more than 300 languages; the original English language version has grown to some 6.9 million articles as of this writing. Today, it is run by the Wikimedia Foundation, a nonprofit group funded largely by reader donations.

Called "the Intimidator" for his aggressive driving style, Dale Earnhardt, Sr., won seven NASCAR Cup championships before a fatal crash in 2001.

777. JANUARY 20, 2001

GEN. COLIN POWELL MAKES HISTORY

On this day, Colin Powell became the first African American secretary of state in U.S. history. Raised in New York's gritty South Bronx by Jamaican parents, Powell received numerous awards for heroism during two tours of Army duty in Vietnam. When his 35-year military career ended, Powell was, according to the *New York Times,* "the most popular public figure in America, owing to his straightforwardness, his leadership qualities and his ability to speak in blunt tones that Americans appreciated." He would distinguish himself again as the first African American to be national security adviser and Joint Chiefs of Staff chair, as well as secretary of state. Based on what he'd later say was bad intelligence, Powell told a UN audience in 2003 that Iraq possessed weapons of mass destruction—a claim that was proved false and tarnished his reputation. He would be remembered as an illustrious but controversial figure.

778. FEBRUARY 18, 2001

AUTO RACING LOSES A STAR

The National Association for Stock Car Auto Racing (NASCAR), which hosts one of America's most popular spectator sports, lost a legend when driver Dale Earnhardt, Sr., was killed in a three-car crash in the final lap of the Daytona 500 on this day. In the wake of Earnhardt's death, NASCAR instituted rigorous safety upgrades in car, driver, and track equipment—and since then, no driver has perished in the sport's top Cup Series. In July

As content on the internet has grown, so has Wikipedia, its "free encyclopedia" run by a non-profit and edited by users.

2001—in the first race at the Daytona International Speedway since Earnhardt's death—the winning driver was his son Dale Earnhardt, Jr.

779. APRIL 28, 2001

FIRST PRIVATE PASSENGER EXPLORES SPACE

"Space tourist" was a misnomer, Dennis Tito insisted. The American businessman was the first private individual to buy a trip on a space flight, paying $20 million to join two cosmonauts on a supply mission launched on this day to the International Space Station (ISS). But no mere tourist would have been so prepared, Tito contended. In the 1960s, he was a NASA aerospace engineer working on Mars missions, among other projects. A career switch into investing had given him the wealth to afford passage; in 2000, he trained at Star City, the Russian space program base. After six days on the ISS, Tito and the crew would ride a Soyuz craft back to Earth and parachute into a field in Kazakhstan.

780. JULY 2, 2001

INTERNET PIONEER NAPSTER SHUTS DOWN

On this day, the digital music-sharing application Napster began closing its doors after the Recording Industry Association of America took legal action to stop the free acquisition of copyrighted MP3 music files made possible by its software. For decades, the industry had controlled distribution and cost of recorded music, but once Napster provided an alternative, consumers weren't willing to give it up. As a result, a Pew Research Center study reported, "the music ecology radically changed." Not only would streaming music become the norm, but consumers would also come "to expect that a digitized version of a product—such as news, movies or television shows—should be available online for free."

781. SEPTEMBER 11, 2001

HIJACKERS RAIN DESTRUCTION ON U.S. TARGETS

In the deadliest terrorism attack ever to occur on U.S. soil, al Qaeda hijackers turned American passenger jets into weapons aimed at U.S. capitals of power. They flew two

This homemade memorial, situated on a New Jersey rooftop with a view of Manhattan, was one of countless tributes to victims of the 9/11 attacks.

commercial airplanes into the twin towers of New York City's World Trade Center—a site that became known as ground zero for its utter devastation—and a third into the Pentagon in Arlington, Virginia. The fourth plane appeared to be headed for the U.S. Capitol or White House until a band of crew and passengers stormed the cockpit; that plane crashed in a field near Shanksville, Pennsylvania. The death toll from the attacks: 2,977.

782. OCTOBER 4, 2001

LETHAL ANTHRAX ARRIVES BY MAIL

Weeks after the 9/11 attacks, a new threat terrified Americans: poisoned postal mail. Health officials in Florida announced that Robert Stevens, a tabloid photo editor at American Media, Inc. (AMI), had been diagnosed with pulmonary anthrax—the first such case in the United States in almost 25 years. By November, 22 people would be infected and five would die after coming into contact with anthrax through letters mailed to journalists, celebrities, and politicians. After nearly seven years investigating the attacks, the Federal Bureau of Investigation was poised to charge microbiologist and biodefense researcher Bruce Ivins in the attacks, but Ivins committed suicide before he could be charged.

TERRORIST ACTS CAN SHAKE THE FOUNDATION OF OUR BIGGEST BUILDINGS, BUT THEY CANNOT TOUCH THE FOUNDATION OF AMERICA.

George W. Bush *(2001)*

783. OCTOBER 7, 2001

U.S. AND ITS ALLIES LAUNCH ATTACKS ON AFGHANISTAN

The U.S. combat response to the 9/11 attacks—code name, Operation Enduring Freedom—commenced on this day with air strikes against al Qaeda and its Taliban protectors in Afghanistan. The same day, President George W. Bush told Americans the operation's prime objectives: to capture al Qaeda leaders, destroy training camps, and rout terrorists from Afghanistan. Other nations committed troops to Afghanistan—which in time adopted a constitution and held democratic elections—and to task forces sent to contain terrorist movements in the Philippines and East Africa. The combat operation would last more than a dozen years, and the conflict far beyond that.

784. OCTOBER 23, 2001

IPOD HITS SHELVES

Revealing Apple's newest product, founder Steve Jobs declared it "a quantum leap"—and "huge," in part because it's so small. The iPod MP3 player was about the size of a deck of cards (roughly 4 by 2.5 inches and 0.4 inch thick), yet its five-gigabyte drive stored up to 1,000 songs. In Jobs's words, "Your entire music library fits in your pocket" and could be downloaded to the device in less than 10 minutes—30 times faster than rival MP3 players. At a retail price of $399, it became the first of six generations of iPod Classic, followed by other models (Mini, Nano, Shuffle, Touch). But much as the iPod overtook the Walkman audiocassette player, the rise of iPhones and music streaming service apps would eventually make iPods obsolete.

785. NOVEMBER 15, 2001

XBOX ENTERS THE GAMING RACE

In the multibillion-dollar market for gaming systems, Nintendo was the U.S. leader, with 15 years of Nintendo Entertainment System (NES) and Game Boy momentum. PlayStation was the contender, with six buzzy years of PS1 and PS2. But where was Microsoft, the multinational tech behemoth? Nowhere—until the debut on this day of the Xbox, the company's first foray into the game console market. A few features made the newcomer competitive: improved processing power, added storage, and a port to connect to Xbox Live, an early entry in fee-based online gaming. Some of Xbox's first games, such as Halo and Halo 2, would become long-lived classics.

786. DECEMBER 2, 2001

ENERGY GIANT ENRON GOES BUST

Created from a 1985 merger of two Texas natural gas transport companies, Enron Corporation became a hugely successful energy and commodities trading business—and then, on this day, the largest bankruptcy in U.S. history. The company was sunk by discoveries that it had fabricated financial records and overstated its successes. The fraud and scandal would ultimately send top Enron executives to prison and spell the downfall of the company's auditing firm, Arthur Andersen, which had urged the shredding of incriminating Enron documents. The Enron scandal put a deep and enduring dent in the American public's trust of stock market investing.

787. JANUARY 11, 2002

CUBAN NAVAL BASE BECOMES A PRISON

To hold suspects detained in the Bush administration's "Global War on Terror," the U.S. government opened a detention camp at the Guantanamo Bay Naval Base in Cuba on this day. Located on 45 square miles at the southeastern tip of the island, the prison wasn't subject to all U.S. or Geneva Conventions provisions on detainee rights, administration officials said. Therefore, alleged "illegal enemy combatants"—Muslim militants and suspected terrorists—were held indefinitely without charges, many subjected to what human rights groups said was inhumane treatment and torture. Although later presidents tried unsuccessfully to close the prison, some 780 men from 48 countries would be held there over the years; most eventually were repatriated, but in early 2025, 15 inmates remained.

788. MARCH 14, 2002

SPACEX IS FOUNDED

On this day, Elon Musk—a South African–born tech entrepreneur who made fortunes in the United States by developing and selling businesses—founded the interplanetary transportation company SpaceX. To further his dream of helping establish a colony on Mars, Musk aimed to make space travel more cost-effective, in part by creating rockets that could carry payloads into space and return to Earth for reuse. In its first two decades, SpaceX would become the first private business to transport U.S. astronauts on missions and would partner with NASA to run resupply trips to the International Space Station.

789. JUNE 11, 2002

AMERICA GETS A TV *IDOL*

The concept was simple: a cast of undiscovered singers compete to win a recording contract. It started off in 1999 as a TV show in New Zealand called *Popstars* and inspired a TV show in Britain called *Pop Idol* two years later. That became the beloved American TV franchise *American Idol: The Search for a Superstar.* The program debuted on this day with a trio of music industry judges praising or panning auditions by variably talented vocalists. Once competition began, contestants were either sent home or kept for the next performance round, based on viewers' voting. Within two years, *Idol* became the most watched show on U.S. television. Several seasons' contestants—Kelly Clarkson, Carrie Underwood, Jennifer Hudson, Adam Lambert—would go on to global stardom.

After Kelly Clarkson won the first season of *American Idol,* both she and the television show that made her a star went on to monumental popularity and success.

790. JULY 21, 2002

WORLDCOM FRAUD ENDS IN BANKRUPTCY

Six months after fraudulent accounting landed Enron Corporation in the biggest bankruptcy in U.S. history, it lost that dubious distinction to the telecommunications giant WorldCom. Once a small Mississippi-based long-distance phone company, the organization prospered through mergers and acquisitions to become a corporate behemoth. After a proposed 1999 merger with Sprint was blocked, WorldCom's growth slowed. In response, executives falsified financial statements, dramatically overstating profits to keep up both appearances and the stock price. The company's own auditors blew the whistle, WorldCom declared bankruptcy, and top executives went to prison.

791. JULY 28, 2002

"MIRACLE RESCUE" SAVES MINE WORKERS

In the coal country of southwest Pennsylvania, a 77-hour nightmare had a happy ending: Nine workers trapped in a flooding mine 240 feet underground were brought out alive. The ordeal began when laborers in the Quecreek Mine accidentally broke through to an abandoned, flooded shaft not on their maps; 75 million gallons of water gushed in.

Yusef Salaam (in suit, around the time of his trial) was one of the notorious "Central Park Five," a group of teenagers convicted and later exonerated for the sexual assault of a jogger in Central Park.

As the miners huddled in a spot that still had air, emergency crews fought against equipment setbacks to drill a rescue tunnel. Early on the ordeal's fourth day, a steel mesh escape capsule was lowered into the mine. One by one, the men were rescued, none with major injuries.

792. OCTOBER 10, 2002

DOT-COM BUBBLE BURSTS

How buoyant the dot-com bubble seemed: In this heady era, investors were lavishly funding legions of internet start-ups, even if the businesses weren't yet turning a profit, or expected to anytime soon. Between 1995 and 2000, the tech stock–heavy Nasdaq index had risen by more than 580 percent to a high of 5,048 on March 10, 2000. Analysts had warned that the bubble would eventually burst—and on Wall Street, this was the day: the Nasdaq sank to 1,108, a drop of nearly 77 percent from its peak.

ALONG CAME THE DOT-COM BUBBLE AND SUDDENLY THE ENTIRE STOCK MARKET MADE NO SENSE AT ALL.

Michael Lewis, The Big Short *(2010)*

793. OCTOBER 24, 2002

"BELTWAY SNIPERS" ARE ARRESTED

On this day, police apprehended the so-called Beltway snipers after a 23-day killing spree that terrorized the Washington, D.C., region, leaving 10 people dead and three more injured. John Allen Muhammad and Lee Boyd Malvo randomly chose victims while concealed in what the FBI called "a rolling sniper's nest": a Chevrolet sedan with a hole in the trunk through which they fired a semiautomatic rifle. Trial testimony revealed that Muhammad, 41, had convinced his surrogate son Malvo, 17, that the shootings would start a race revolution (while also providing cover to kill Muhammad's ex-wife, who had custody of their children). For their crimes, Muhammad would be executed in 2009. Malvo was sentenced to life in prison.

794. NOVEMBER 25, 2002

CONGRESS CREATES THE HOMELAND SECURITY DEPARTMENT

On this day, an act of the U.S. Congress established the Department of Homeland Security (DHS) to better coordinate national anti-terrorism efforts in the wake of the 9/11 attacks. The new DHS was formed by combining all or part of 22 federal departments and agencies into a unified enterprise, with responsibilities including immigration and customs enforcement, border protection, transportation security, federal emergency management, cybersecurity, infrastructure protection, and more. Its first secretary was Thomas Ridge, formerly governor of Pennsylvania and a U.S. Congress member from the state.

795. DECEMBER 19, 2002

JUDGE EXONERATES CENTRAL PARK FIVE

In 1989, a white woman jogging in Manhattan's Central Park was brutally raped. A year later, five boys aged 14 to 16, who would become known as the Central Park Five, were convicted on varying charges after confessions they later said were coerced. What became known as the Central Park jogger case transfixed the country. Thirteen years later, in 2002, a convicted rapist named Matias Reyes confessed to attacking the jogger; his DNA matched evidence at the crime scene. On this day, the victim's supposed assailants—Antron McCray, Kevin Richardson, Yusef Salaam, Raymond Santana, Jr., and Korey Wise—were exonerated and had their convictions vacated. The five sued for damages and were awarded multimillion-dollar settlements for their time in prison.

796. DECEMBER 20, 2002

U.S. CONGRESS WELCOMES LISA MURKOWSKI AS THE FIRST WOMAN TO REPRESENT ALASKA

On this day, Republican Lisa Murkowski became the first woman to represent Alaska in the U.S. Congress. Her ascension to the job was not without controversy: She was appointed by her father, Frank Murkowski, to fill the vacant U.S. Senate seat that he resigned after being elected Alaska's governor. Then a 45-year-old who'd served only a few years in the state legislature, she weathered nepotism accusations to win re-election to the Senate in 2004—and three more times, including in 2010 when she won as a write-in candidate. An advocate for her state's interests on issues including energy, fisheries, public lands, natural resources, and tourism, Murkowski is now the Senate's second most senior Republican woman.

Lisa Murkowski was the first Alaska-born member of the U.S. Congress, as well as the first woman to represent the state.

797. DECEMBER 25, 2002

U.S. BUSINESS BANKRUPTCIES MOUNT

The year drew to a close with a record-setting sum of American corporations' assets in bankruptcy: more than $368 billion. BankruptcyData.com, an organization that tracked U.S. business failures, reported that although fewer publicly traded companies filed for bankruptcy in this year than the last—191 compared to 257—the size of the bankruptcies was far larger. Major companies filing included the retailer Kmart, communications corporation Adelphia, United Airlines' parent UAL, insurance carrier Conseco, and air carrier U.S. Airways. That's in addition to telecommunications giant WorldCom, whose collapse ranked as the largest bankruptcy in U.S. history.

798. JANUARY 22, 2003

HISPANICS BECOME THE LARGEST U.S. MINORITY

According to new data released by the U.S. Census bureau on this day, Hispanic Americans surpassed African Americans to become the largest minority group in the U.S. The nation's Hispanic population had grown to 38.8 million, due in part to immigration and higher birth rates, while its Black population totaled about 36.2 million. On the 2000 Census questionnaire, respondents for the first time could indicate that their heritage included more than one race, an option the previous forms lacked. Using that selection, people could identify themselves as white and Hispanic or as Black and Hispanic.

799. FEBRUARY 1, 2003

SPACE SHUTTLE *COLUMBIA* CREW PERISHES

After 16 days in space performing science experiments, the seven crew members of space shuttle *Columbia* were killed when the craft broke into pieces on reentry. During launch, pieces of insulating foam had split off *Columbia*'s external fuel tank and one struck the craft's left wing. NASA concluded that the *Columbia* was safe to fly, despite the debris strike. That was wrong: Gases entering a hole in the wing led to "loss of control, failure of the wing, and breakup of the orbiter" shortly before it was to have landed at Florida's Kennedy Space Center, the disaster investigation report concluded. The loss of *Columbia* led to harsh criticism regarding NASA's organizational and safety culture, and grounding of the shuttle program for two years.

Before their untimely demise, the seven crew members of the space shuttle *Columbia* had collectively served NASA for more than 50 years.

SPOTLIGHT

TECHNOLOGY

FROM THE INSTANT the 21st century dawned—without the Y2K computer catastrophes that had been predicted—technological advances have touched virtually every corner of American life. Among the innovations with the greatest cultural impact: social media platforms, smart devices, biotechnology, and artificial intelligence (AI). Conversation and social networking came online in 2002 with Friendster, succeeded in 2003 by Myspace and in 2004 by Facebook. The platforms kept proliferating through YouTube (2005), Twitter (2006), Tumblr (2007), and on to Instagram (2010), Snapchat (2011), Vine (2013), and TikTok (2016), among others.

To digest all this new information, users turned to the BlackBerry and Palm—handheld devices that were progenitors to generations of sophisticated smartphones, including at least 47 models of the iPhone since its introduction in 2007. The same phenomenon of relentless upgrading has occurred with smartwatches and fitness trackers, e-readers and tablets, VR headsets and personal assistants. Today, homes are bursting with smart devices: doorbells, security cameras, thermostats, lights, appliances, and entertainment systems. In the fields of science and commerce, 21st-century advances include quantum computing and biotechnology breakthroughs, from gene editing and personalized medicine to blockchain and cryptocurrency systems. Applications of AI—ranging from facial recognition to self-driving vehicles—are growing exponentially. World Economic Forum founder Klaus Schwab calls this era the Fourth Industrial Revolution; humanity's challenge, he observes, is "to ensure that it is empowering and human-centered, rather than divisive and dehumanizing."

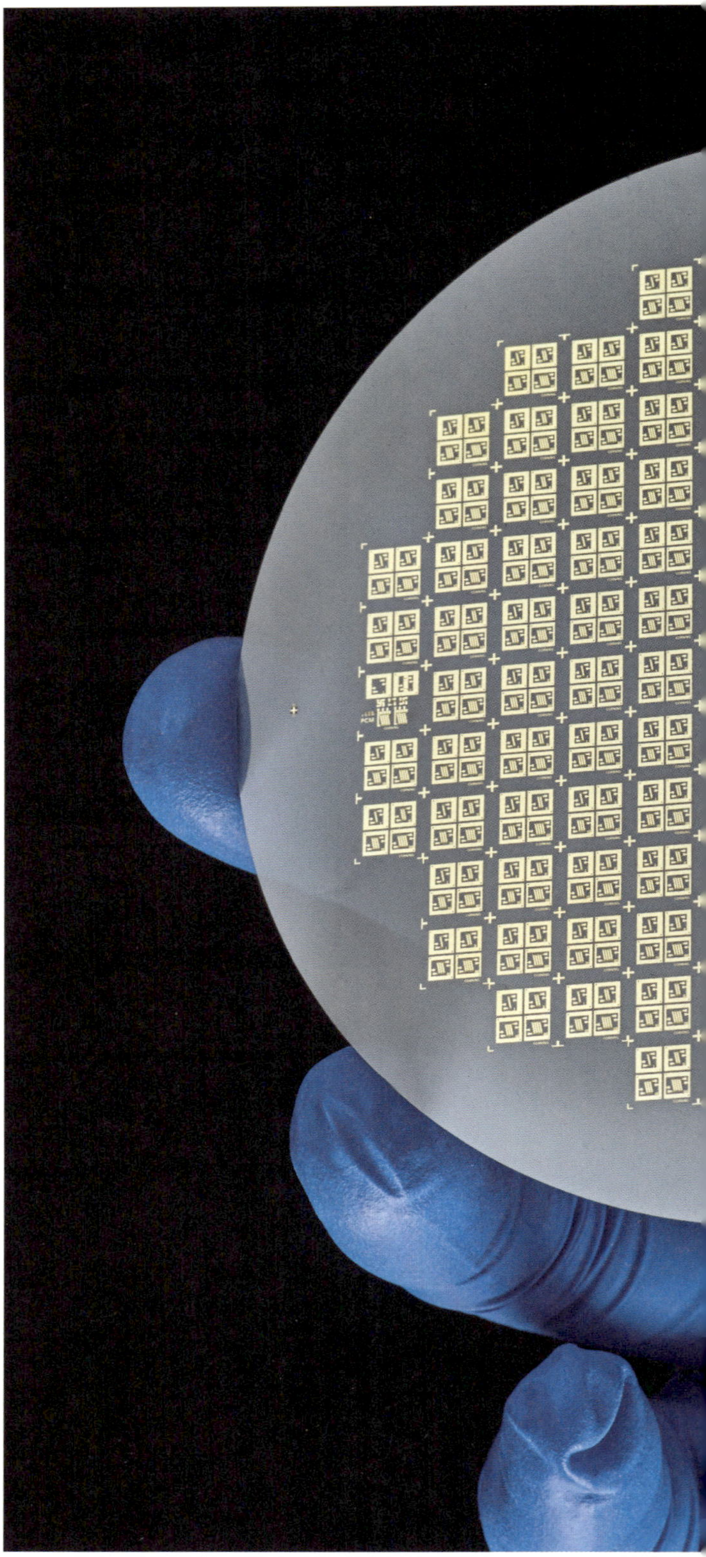

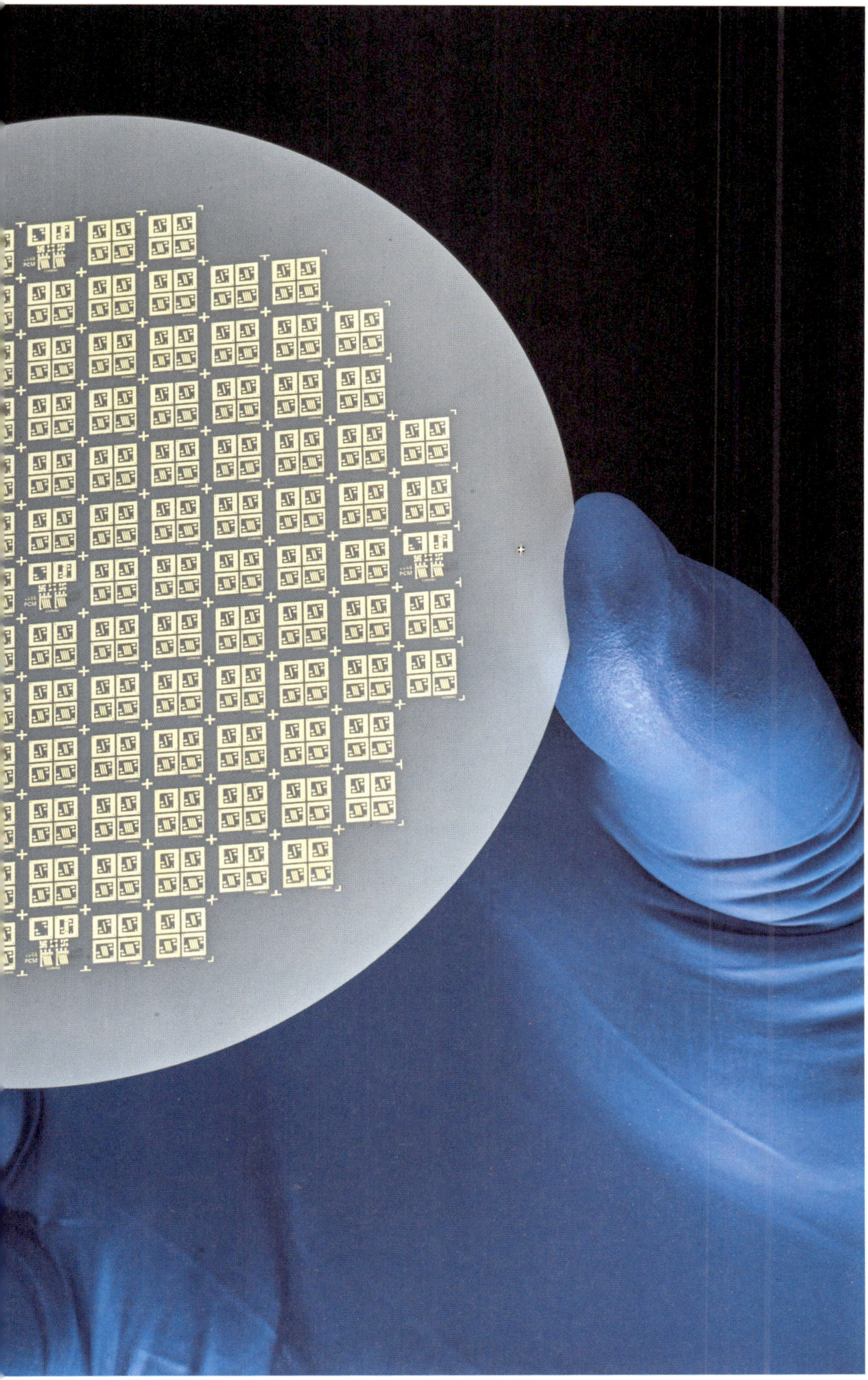

The semiconductor wafer is key to the technology revolution, enabling modern computing, connectivity, consumer electronics, and more.

THE FUNDAMENTAL AND GLOBAL NATURE OF THIS REVOLUTION MEANS IT WILL AFFECT AND BE INFLUENCED BY ALL COUNTRIES, ECONOMIES, SECTORS, AND PEOPLE.

Klaus Schwab, *World Economic Forum founder (2016)*

800. MARCH 11, 2003

"DO NOT CALL" BECOMES A LAW

To the relief of consumers fed up with nuisance telephone calls, the U.S. Congress passed the Do-Not-Call Implementation Act on this day, creating a registry where Americans could submit their phone numbers to opt out of being called by most telemarketers. The law didn't shield consumers from calls placed by political or charity groups and survey takers, or companies with whom they've recently done business. But it did require most telemarketers to check the list quarterly and remove the numbers of consumers who opted out—or risk fines of up to $11,000 per call. (In the list's first two decades, roughly a quarter of a billion numbers would be registered.)

A museum visitor studies a digital representation of the human genome, which took more than 30 years to sequence in its entirety.

801. MARCH 19, 2003

IRAQ WAR BEGINS

The George W. Bush administration had implicated Iraq in training the perpetrators of the 9/11 attacks, accused Iraqi president Saddam Hussein of collecting weapons of mass destruction, and given him a 48-hour ultimatum to leave Iraq. When that time expired in the evening on this day (the morning of March 20 in Iraq), U.S. and allied forces launched the first air strikes of the Iraq War. With weeks of ground and air assaults, troops would take control of Baghdad and its airport, then other key cities. Though Hussein would elude capture until mid-December, President Bush announced on May 1 that major combat was over. But guerrilla warfare and sectarian violence would keep U.S. occupying forces in Iraq until December 2011.

802. APRIL 14, 2003

HUMAN GENOME IS SEQUENCED

An international consortium of thousands of researchers began work in 1990 to decode the hereditary information that determines the individual characteristics a parent can pass to offspring. On this day, the consortium announced that the task had been achieved with an essentially complete version of the sequence: one that accounted for 92 percent of the human genome, with fewer than 400 information gaps. The Human Genome Project provided an unprecedented resource for biomedical research, as well as for the diagnosis and treatment of hereditary diseases. (Not until 2022 were the final gaps filled in to produce a complete human genome sequence.)

803. JUNE 10, 2003

NASA ROVERS HEAD TO MARS

A spacecraft carrying Spirit, the first of twin NASA rovers bound for Mars, launched on this day from Cape Canaveral, Florida. It reached the red planet on January 3, 2004. In a lander package equipped with massive airbags, retro-rockets, and a parachute, Spirit descended the last four to five miles, hit the Martian surface traveling about 46 feet a second, and bounced

28 times before rolling to a stop roughly eight miles from NASA's intended target. Within two hours, it had deployed solar panels and was relaying images back to Earth via the 2001 Mars Odyssey robotic spacecraft orbiting the planet. In more than six years of operations, Spirit found strong evidence of a much wetter Mars that might once have hosted life.

804. JUNE 21, 2003

POTTER-MANIA REIGNS AS ADULTS SWELL THE READERSHIP OF YOUTH-ORIENTED FICTION

Waiting throngs surged into bookstores at 12:01 a.m. on this day to buy J. K. Rowling's latest entry in the *Harry Potter* series—and in its first 24 hours on sale, *Harry Potter and the Order of the Phoenix* would rack up some five million copies sold worldwide. Contributing to the growing trend of adults embracing what was once deemed children's or YA (young adult) literature, grown-ups joined in on Potter-mania, from costumed book-release parties and film openings to fan fiction and theme park attractions. The phenomenon broadened

Popular young adult fiction like the *Harry Potter* series drew fans of all ages to bookstores—sometimes in costume.

audiences for publishers, marketers, and creators, setting the stage for the success of franchises such as *The Hunger Games* and *Twilight.*

805. JULY 1, 2003

TESLA MOTORS JOINS THE LUXE ELECTRIC VEHICLE MOVEMENT

On this day, Marc Tarpenning and Martin Eberhard founded the luxury electric car company Tesla Motors. Engineers and entrepreneurs, the two shared a fondness for sporty cars and a desire to reduce fossil fuel use; they had become well-versed in lithium batteries after developing an e-reader together. Eberhard says the first car Tesla Motors produced was inspired by what he saw in driveways in prosperous California neighborhoods: plain but eco-friendly Toyota Priuses parked next to luxury cars. He concluded that consumers wanted environmentally conscious vehicles that were still upscale and fun to drive. Tech magnate Elon Musk invested in the company in 2004 and later took it over from its founders.

806. JULY 14, 2003

"PLAME AFFAIR" REVEALED

On this day, newspaper columnist Robert Novak named a veteran diplomat's wife, Valerie Plame, as a CIA covert operative—and ignited a firestorm about the motives of George W. Bush administration officials. In early 2002, the CIA asked Plame's husband, former ambassador Joseph Wilson, to explore claims that Niger had sold Iraq potential nuclear weapons material; Wilson concluded the sale was "highly doubtful." After Bush used his 2003 State of the Union speech to claim Iraq was developing weapons of mass destruction and seeking African uranium, Wilson countered in an op-ed that facts were being manipulated to "justify an invasion." Eight days later, Novak's column revealed Plame as a CIA operative—an act Plame and Wilson said was retaliation by government officials, who purposefully leaked her name to Novak as retribution for Wilson's criticism. It would end Plame's career and put her covert contacts at risk.

807. AUGUST 1, 2003

MYSPACE MAKES ITS DEBUT

Posting your Top 8 friends list. Choosing your profile song. Getting views by trading *f4f* and *pc4pc,* reciprocating all the follows and photo comments you receive. If this sounds familiar, you spent time on Myspace, the first social media website, launched on this day. "Digital camera in hand, everyone had their mirror selfies as their Myspace profile photos," journalist James Barrett recalled. "It was a place to establish your social presence." Rupert Murdoch's News Corp would pay $580 million for Myspace in 2005; the next year it would become America's most visited website, surpassing Google. But unable to compete with rival Facebook—launched in 2004 as TheFacebook—it would sell in 2011 for $35 million.

Since pumpkin spice was introduced as a latte flavor at Starbucks, the flavor has become a seasonal craze used in myriad products.

808. OCTOBER 10, 2003

IT'S A DRINK FLAVOR, A SEASON, A PHENOMENON: PUMPKIN SPICE LATTE

A seasonal taste craze was born on this day when Starbucks locations in Washington, D.C., and Vancouver, Canada, taste-tested a new beverage: the Pumpkin Spice Latte (or PSL, an acronym the company later trademarked). The flavor "pumpkin spice" soon splashed across other merchandise—cereals, candles, deodorants, even cottage cheese—and was added to Merriam-Webster's dictionary in 2022 as "a mixture of usually cinnamon, nutmeg, ginger, cloves, and often allspice." Two decades after PSL's launch, it is Starbucks' most popular seasonal beverage of all time and makes the company an estimated $500 million a year.

809. DECEMBER 16, 2003

REGULATORS CAN UNWANTED SPAM

On this day, spam became more than a canned, processed meat product, transforming into the subject of America's first national standards for unsolicited commercial email. Giving the nickname "spam" to irritating junk mail was inspired by the annoying, repetitive use of the word in a 1970 sketch by comedy troupe Monty Python. The congressional measure to regulate spam—the Controlling the Assault of Non-Solicited Pornography and Marketing (or CAN-SPAM) Act—forbade misleading or deceptive wording in headers or subject lines and required that emails of this type be labeled as advertising, with a way for recipients to opt out.

810. JANUARY 3, 2004

AMERICAN TOP 40 HOST SIGNS OFF

"This is Casey Kasem in Hollywood, and in the next three hours, we'll count down the 40 most popular hits in the United States this week, hot off the record charts of *Billboard* magazine ..." So began many classic broadcasts of *American Top 40,* the hit-music radio show that disc jockey Kasem helped create in 1970. Kasem retired from the show this weekend, handing the reins to television personality Ryan Seacrest on January 10. During his career, the Detroit-born Kasem hosted two iterations of *American Top 40,* as well as countdown shows for other radio formats.

811. FEBRUARY 4, 2004

THEFACEBOOK GOES LIVE

Reigning social media market leader Myspace boasted a million members—but on this day, a web developer named Mark Zuckerberg and three fellow Harvard University students launched a new social networking website called TheFacebook.com. Initially, only Harvard students could post and see information and photographs; soon, students at other big-name universities were allowed to join in. Popularity would grow as TheFacebook

Along with two others, Harvard University students Mark Zuckerberg (left) and Chris Hughes co-founded the social networking site TheFacebook.com, now shortened to Facebook.

added a bulletin board–like Wall where users could leave posts for each other, and a "tagging" tool for adding people's names to photographs. In 2005, the name would be shortened to Facebook; in 2009, the site would overtake Myspace in unique visitors worldwide. Today, it has 3.07 billion users worldwide.

812. MARCH 4, 2004

MCDONALD'S SUPER SIZING ELIMINATED

On this day, America's reigning fast-food enterprise scrapped one of its menu's big ideas: Super Size portions. The extra-large servings of McDonald's french fries and soft drinks, introduced in 1987, were phased out as a matter of "menu simplification," according to a company spokesperson. But the year before, McDonald's had begun selling entrée salads and other healthier options, partly in response to criticism that it was contributing to America's rising obesity rate. The Super Size portions were removed from the menu not long after the Sundance Film Festival premiere of the documentary *Super Size Me,* about filmmaker Morgan Spurlock's experiment with eating only McDonald's meals for one month.

THERE IS A SAYING THAT IF YOU GET SOMETHING FOR FREE, YOU SHOULD KNOW THAT YOU'RE THE PRODUCT. IT WAS NEVER MORE TRUE THAN IN THE CASE OF FACEBOOK AND GMAIL AND YOUTUBE.

Yuval Noah Harari, *historian, in* Time *magazine (2017)*

813. MARCH 29, 2004

NATO EXPANDS

In the largest expansion since its founding in 1949, the North Atlantic Treaty Organization (NATO) accepted seven new members on this day. All former Soviet republics—Bulgaria, Estonia, Latvia, Lithuania, Romania, Slovakia, and Slovenia—they brought NATO membership to a total of 26 nations. The alliance, founded to preserve stability and peace in the North Atlantic, was organized around mutual self-defense. As outlined in its key passage, Article 5, it agreed "that an armed attack against one or more of [any member nation] in Europe or North America shall be considered an attack against them all."

814. APRIL 1, 2004

GMAIL IS BORN

On this day, tech behemoth Google LLC announced the release of Gmail, billed as a new and improved program for the nearly one billion users who sent electronic messages via computer networks. Engineer Paul Buchheit designed the program to fix what he found wanting in his own email use. Specifically, Gmail offered abundant storage—1,000 megabytes (MB), compared to 4 MB in other email programs; a more robust search function, to find that one message in a brimming inbox; and a web browser interface to let users access their account from anywhere online.

815. APRIL 28, 2004

ABU GHRAIB PRISON ABUSES ARE EXPOSED

Outrage and revulsion followed images of American soldiers physically abusing and humiliating Iraqi prisoners in the Abu Ghraib prison facility near Baghdad, which aired on CBS's

60 Minutes II on this day. Photos and other evidence documented "numerous incidents of sadistic, blatant, and wanton criminal abuses," according to the report of an Army major general who investigated the mistreatment. Smiling U.S. soldiers appeared in some of the photos with detainees who were beaten, naked, or in degrading poses. Though the Bush administration would disavow the abuses, some humanitarian organizations called the acts consistent with brutal tactics at other U.S. overseas detention centers like Guantanamo Bay. Ultimately, 11 U.S. soldiers were convicted of prisoner maltreatment, and a civil suit awarded $42 million in damages to three Iraqi detainees abused by military contractors.

816. MAY 1, 2004

LANCE ARMSTRONG LAUNCHES THE LIVESTRONG BRACELET

Lance Armstrong's yellow Livestrong bracelet ushered in a rainbow of silicone wristbands that would raise money and awareness for multiple causes.

Livestrong bracelets introduced this month by pro cyclist Lance Armstrong's cancer charity became a hugely popular fashion and advocacy statement. The success of the $1 silicone gel wristbands sparked other charities and groups to sell similar bracelets to raise funds and awareness for their causes. After Armstrong was barred for life from his sport in 2013 for using banned performance-enhancing substances, critics would shed the bracelets (or edit them so they read "LIE STRONG" or "LIVEWRONG"). But two decades after the band was introduced, almost 100 million had been sold.

817. MAY 6, 2004

LAST *FRIENDS* EPISODE AIRS

From the release of its debut episode in 1994, NBC's juggernaut sitcom *Friends* drew TV viewers into a fictional New York City coffeehouse called Central Perk—and the lives of six 20-somethings who frequented it. When the show's finale aired on this day, *Friends* had entered the cultural zeitgeist, setting television ratings and revenue records and earning six Emmy Awards. Ten successful seasons made stars of the actors playing the core characters—Ross, Monica, Rachel, Phoebe, Joey, and Chandler—and brought pop culture acclaim to Rachel's haircut, Phoebe's song "Smelly Cat," and Joey's pickup line, "Hey, how *you* doin'?" The finale found Joey contentedly single, the rest paired off in happy endings—and all headed to Central Perk for one more cup.

818. JUNE 5, 2004

"GREAT COMMUNICATOR" REAGAN PASSES AWAY

After suffering more than a decade from Alzheimer's disease, former U.S. president Ronald Reagan died on this day at the age of 93. A conservative Republican and former Hollywood movie actor, Reagan was nearly 78 years old when he completed his second White House term in 1989, and observers had noted he was sometimes forgetful and fumbled for words. Still, his nickname was the Great Communicator, and in late 1994 Reagan released a statement telling the world about his illness with the hope that disclosing his diagnosis "might promote greater awareness of this condition." He added, "at the moment I feel just fine."

The hit TV series *Friends* made stars of (from left) David Schwimmer, Jennifer Aniston, Courteney Cox, Matthew Perry, Lisa Kudrow, and Matt LeBlanc.

819. JUNE 30, 2004

BLACK HOMEOWNERSHIP PEAKS

On this day, U.S. Census data showed that in the year's second quarter, Black homeownership had reached its highest point in U.S. history, with 49 percent of Black households owning their dwellings (though still a far cry from the homeownership rate for white households, at 76 percent). The gap had implications for generations of Black families, because homeownership is a significant way of building and transferring wealth to heirs. Over the next two decades, that record-high rate of Black homeownership would decline steadily to 43 percent, while white homeownership dipped to 73 percent.

820. JULY 16, 2004

DOMESTIC DOYENNE MARTHA STEWART GETS PRISON TIME

On this day, lifestyle and publishing magnate Martha Stewart was sentenced to five months in prison. Though Stewart maintained she'd done nothing wrong, a jury found her guilty of obstructing justice and lying to investigators about why she sold about 4,000 shares of ImClone Systems' stock the day before one of its drugs failed to secure

Food and Drug Administration approval and the stock's price dropped. ImClone CEO Samuel Waksal had tipped friends and relatives to sell their stock before the FDA action; in 2003, he was sentenced to seven years in prison. Prosecutors contended that Stewart sold her ImClone shares after getting a message from the stockbroker she and Waksal shared. The scandal tanked the value of Stewart's media company, worth a billion dollars at its height.

821. JANUARY 5, 2005

A DWARF PLANET IS DISCOVERED

If Earth were the size of a nickel, the dwarf planet Eris would be the size of a popcorn kernel—about one-fifth Earth's size, making it one of the largest dwarf planets in our solar system. Also known as 2003 UB313, Eris was discovered on this day, billions of miles beyond Neptune's orbit in a zone of icy debris called the Kuiper belt. The discovery prompted a debate within the International Astronomical Union as to what constitutes a planet. In time, the debate would have consequences for another object in the Kuiper belt: Pluto. Named in 1930 as our solar system's ninth planet, it would be demoted to the classification "dwarf planet" in 2006 when the International Astronomical Union revised its planetary definitions.

822. JANUARY 26, 2005

CONDOLEEZZA RICE IS NAMED SECRETARY OF STATE

On this day, as President George W. Bush began his second term, Condoleezza Rice became his secretary of state: the first African American woman to hold that position. An Alabama native and gifted young pianist who entered university at age 15, Rice had planned to major in music but switched her focus to international relations. In the 1980s and 1990s, she was a faculty member and provost at Stanford University, as well as an adviser to the Ronald Reagan and George H. W. Bush administrations on nuclear strategy and the Soviet Union. Serving as George W. Bush's national security adviser (also the first woman in that post) and then secretary of state, she helped shape the response to the 9/11 terrorist attacks.

823. FEBRUARY 8, 2005

GOOGLE MAPS IS BORN

"Happy trails." With that post on the official Google blog, a project manager introduced a new product on this day: Google Maps. Though online maps were already available via MapQuest and Yahoo! Maps, among others, Google Maps changed the game. Using innovative mapping and geospatial visualization technologies from start-ups the company acquired, Google developed a tool to scroll, search, and manipulate maps dynamically in a web browser. Google Maps would go on to become the world's most visited map website; today, it has more than two billion monthly users.

824. JUNE 28, 2005

PERCY JACKSON SERIES DEBUTS

A second grader who loved Greek mythology, Haley Riordan asked his dad to tell him bedtime stories drawn from Greek myths. Soon, Rick Riordan was spinning new tales where figures from legend crossed paths with a contemporary 12-year-old named Percy Jackson. As the saga begins, the boy learns he's a demigod fathered by Poseidon, finds others like himself in training at Camp Half-Blood, and must clear his name when accused of stealing Zeus's lightning bolt. Published on this day, *The Lightning Thief* would be the first in a seven-book series of young adult fantasy novels that rivaled the *Harry Potter* series in popularity. Today, Rick Riordan's books have sold more than 190 million copies worldwide.

825. JULY 9, 2005

GIANT PANDA IS BORN IN CAPTIVITY

Giant panda procreation isn't a cinch. Even in the native habitat of China's mountains, panda females ovulate only once a year, and their time to conceive is brief. In captivity, births are rare; a gift from China's government, the first panda pair housed at Washington, D.C.'s National Zoo produced five cubs in 20 years, but none survived. That made the

Captive giant pandas retain some wild behaviors, such as eating bamboo. But since breeding them in captivity is difficult, births are rare.

arrival at the capital city's zoo on this day exceptional: a male born to mother Mei Xiang, who'd been artificially inseminated with sperm from father Tian Tian after the pair failed to mate naturally. The cub, named Tai Shan ("peaceful mountain"), would be the zoo's first to survive; in 2010, he was returned to China to father cubs himself.

826. JULY 26, 2005

POST-DISASTER, THE SPACE SHUTTLE FLIES AGAIN

Before launching the space shuttle *Discovery* on this day, NASA had spent more than two years on research and safety upgrades designed to head off the kind of problem that destroyed the space shuttle *Columbia* on reentry in February 2003. That meant scrutinizing and photographing the thermal protective tiles on shuttle surfaces during launch and throughout the mission, as well as staging a spacewalk specifically to remove material protruding from gaps between tiles. The mission lasted nearly 14 days, with bad weather at Florida's Kennedy Space Center delaying landing four times before the shuttle successfully touched down at Edwards Air Force Base in California.

827. AUGUST 29, 2005

HURRICANE KATRINA WREAKS HAVOC ON GULF COAST STATES

After intensifying over the Gulf of Mexico into one of the most powerful Atlantic storms

Images from the U.S. Coast Guard show the flooding from Hurricane Katrina in New Orleans.

on record, Hurricane Katrina made landfall in Louisiana on this day. A powerful Category 4, it then scoured coastal Mississippi, producing a storm surge more than 26 feet high. Some 1.2 million New Orleans residents evacuated ahead of the event, but tens of thousands were still there when the levee system was overwhelmed, and fouled floodwaters covered more than 80 percent of the city. By the time military and relief personnel moved in, the world had seen images of devastation, looting, and primitive conditions for evacuees crowding the damaged Superdome. Katrina's toll: more than 1,800 deaths, millions displaced, and more than $201 billion in damages (accounting for inflation).

828. OCTOBER 5, 2005

TWILIGHT IS PUBLISHED, LAUNCHING BELOVED FICTION FRANCHISE

The romance between brooding teen Bella Swan and 104-year-old vampire Edward Cullen began on this day with the publication of *Twilight.* The first book in the Twilight Saga—Stephenie Meyer's fantasy fiction series about vampires, werewolves, clan clashes, and young love—it was followed by *New Moon* (2006), *Eclipse* (2007), and *Breaking Dawn* (2008), as well as later companion and spin-off volumes that have sold more than 160 million copies worldwide. The books spawned five successful (though not often critically acclaimed) movies between 2008 and 2012 that collectively grossed more than $3.36 billion. In the following decade, stories blending paranormal and fantasy elements with breathless romance would grow into a subgenre with its own name: "romantasy."

IT'S ALL RIGHT TO BE THE FIRST TO DO SOMETHING, BUT I DIDN'T WANT TO BE THE LAST WOMAN ON THE SUPREME COURT.

Sandra Day O'Connor *(2012)*

829. DECEMBER 15, 2005

YOUTUBE MAKES ITS DEBUT

A 19-second clip of elephants at a zoo: This was the first submission to YouTube, uploaded by software engineer Jawed Karim on April 23, 2005, to the video-sharing website he conceived with fellow techies Steve Chen and Chad Hurley. The three developed the YouTube website and social media platform on a hunch that amateur videographers would be eager to share their work—an idea that proved wildly successful. During its test phase in spring of 2005, the site was drawing about 30,000 visitors a day. By the time YouTube formally launched on this day, its daily video views exceeded two million.

830. JANUARY 31, 2006

SUPREME COURT'S FIRST FEMALE JUSTICE RETIRES

After 24 years on the Supreme Court, where she was the first woman justice, Sandra Day O'Connor retired from the bench to care for her husband after his diagnosis with Alzheimer's disease. Appointed by President Ronald Reagan and widely thought to be a conservative jurist, O'Connor confounded expectations with some of her opinions; still, she came to be thought of as a "majority builder" over her term. O'Connor also provided the swing vote in a number of notable decisions, including a 1992 ruling that reaffirmed the *Roe* v. *Wade* decision legalizing abortion.

Playing guitar took young Riley B. King from poverty in Mississippi to musical stardom, where he was known as B. B. (for "Blues Boy") King.

831. MARCH 21, 2006

TWITTER TAKES OFF

Fittingly, the announcement was only two dozen characters long: "just setting up my twttr," engineer Jack Dorsey posted, thereby launching the Twitter short message system on this day. The social media platform would revolutionize online communication with brief, blog-style updates called tweets—first limited to 140 characters and then 280. It became a networking phenomenon, as well as a tool for newsgathering, politics, emergency alerts, and much more. In 2013, Twitter became a publicly held company, valued at some $31 billion—but it wouldn't turn a profit in six of the next eight years. In 2022, billionaire entrepreneur Elon Musk bought the company, renaming it X the following year.

832. APRIL 18, 2006

BLUESMAN B. B. KING HITS A MILESTONE

Guitarist B. B. King, a legend of American blues music, performed his 10,000th concert in New York City on this day. A sharecropper's son, Riley B. King rose from poverty in Mississippi's cotton fields after learning his first guitar chords from a local preacher. He performed with gospel groups and worked as a disc jockey nicknamed Blues Boy—B. B. for short—before recording his first record at age 25. So began a life of touring with his cherished guitar, Lucille, playing 300 or more dates a year. His signature song—"The Thrill Is Gone," recorded in 1969—won him the first of 15 Grammy Awards in a career that lasted until a few months before his death at the age of 89 in 2015.

833. JUNE 8, 2006

HPV VACCINE IS AUTHORIZED

On this day, the FDA approved the first vaccine shown to eradicate the forms of human papillomavirus (HPV) most likely to lead to cervical cancer, the second most common cancer affecting women. In the next two decades, the U.S. National Cancer Institute reported, the HPV vaccination would prove "extremely effective at reducing infections with the types of the virus that can lead to cancer"—not just cervical, but head, neck, and genital-area cancers in both men and women. Within two decades after the vaccine's approval, the forms of HPV infection that cause most cancers have decreased 81 percent among teenage girls and 88 percent among young women.

834. JUNE 15, 2006

LARGEST U.S. MARINE PRESERVE IS ESTABLISHED

Known for its profusion of coral reefs and rare bird and animal species, Papahānaumokuākea Marine National Monument near the Hawaiian Islands was created on this day in a presidential proclamation by George W. Bush. It's one of the largest marine conservation areas in the world, with almost 583,000 square miles of ocean waters, including 10 islands and atolls of the Northwestern Hawaiian Islands. It's also the largest contiguous fully protected conservation area under the U.S. flag—an area larger than all the country's national parks combined. Its reefs are home to more than 7,000 marine species, a quarter of which are found only in this archipelago.

835. AUGUST 22, 2006

U.S. IMPORT OF E-CIGARETTE DEVICES IS AUTHORIZED

Three years after their invention in China, the first electronic cigarette devices were approved for import into the United States on this day. A 5.5-inch-long metal tube with a plastic mouthpiece, the initial e-cigarettes were basically battery-powered inhalers that used atomizers to dispense a "smoke" of nicotine-laced vapor. With tobacco use increasingly indicted for its health effects, the vaping devices would be promoted as tools in smoking cessation and a less harmful mode of delivering nicotine. But in 2020, a report from the U.S. surgeon general would declare that "there is presently inadequate evidence to conclude that e-cigarettes, in general, increase smoking cessation."

SPOTLIGHT

MEDICAL BREAKTHROUGHS

D

DESPITE DECADES OF progress, Americans' life expectancy fell for the first time in more than a century. In 2020 and 2021, the rate dipped from 78.8 to 76.1 years—chiefly due to the respiratory virus COVID-19, which caused nearly 1.2 million deaths in the United States. But the early 21st century brought remarkable health breakthroughs as well.

First and foremost was the devastating COVID-19 pandemic, curbed in record time thanks to the first major global deployment of mRNA vaccines. Employing bits of genetic material as "messengers" to summon an immune response, mRNA technology's safe and effective use against COVID-19 demonstrated its impressive potential. Other breakthroughs included the 2007 discovery that stem cells can be reverted to an embryonic-like state, allowing them to develop into many other cell types crucial to curing disease; the 2012 discovery of CRISPR-Cas9, a revolutionary technique for precise gene editing; and the advent of personalized immunotherapy, a cutting-edge remedy that uses genetically engineered cells to attack cancer cells. The FDA approved the treatment for leukemia in 2017.

Artificial intelligence also drove impressive medical breakthroughs. Its pioneering use in health care yielded greater accuracy and speed in research, drug discovery, and disease diagnosis, plus AI-powered tools that can detect illness via the human eye, voice, and breath. High-tech healing solutions ranged from bionic prosthetics controlled by brain signals to xenotransplantation—transplanting pig hearts and kidneys into humans, a potential solution to organ shortages.

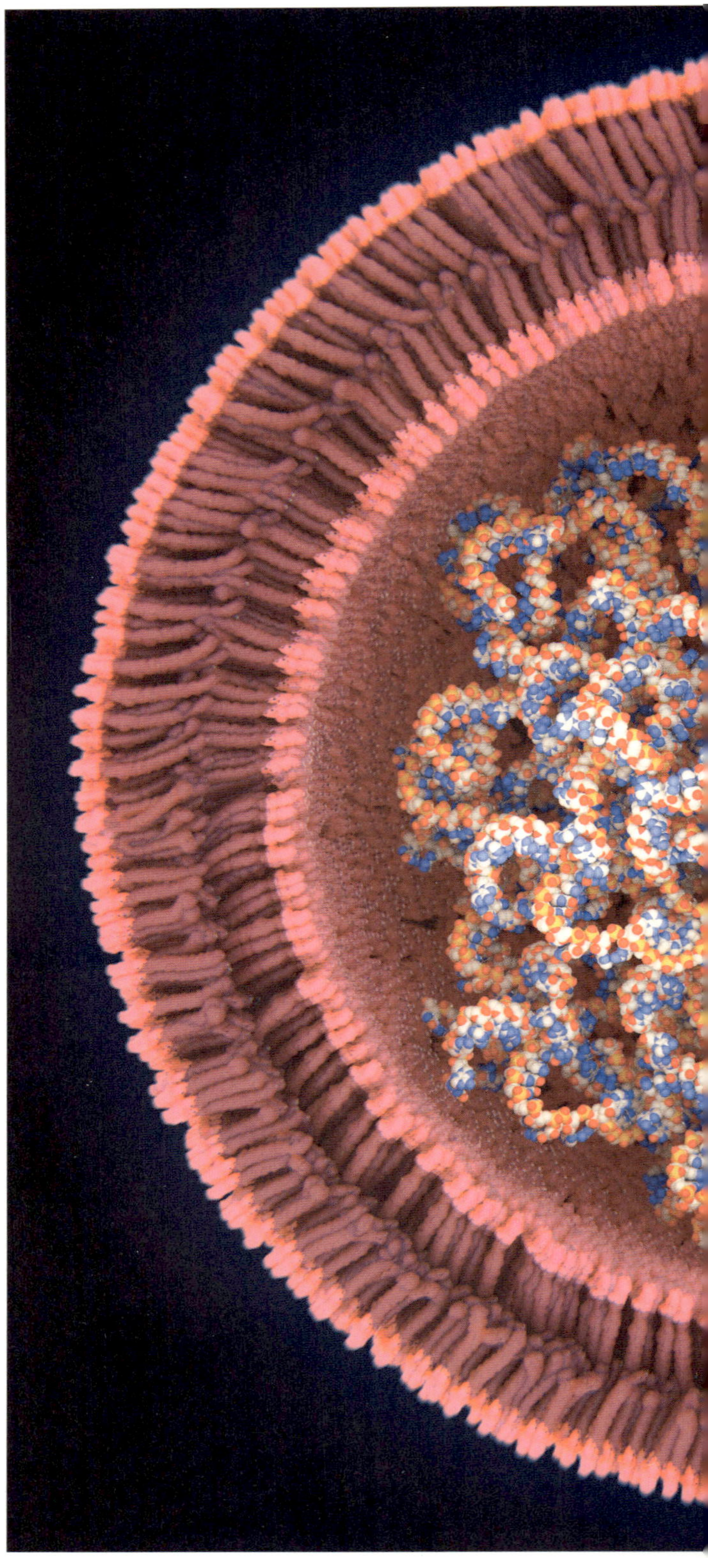

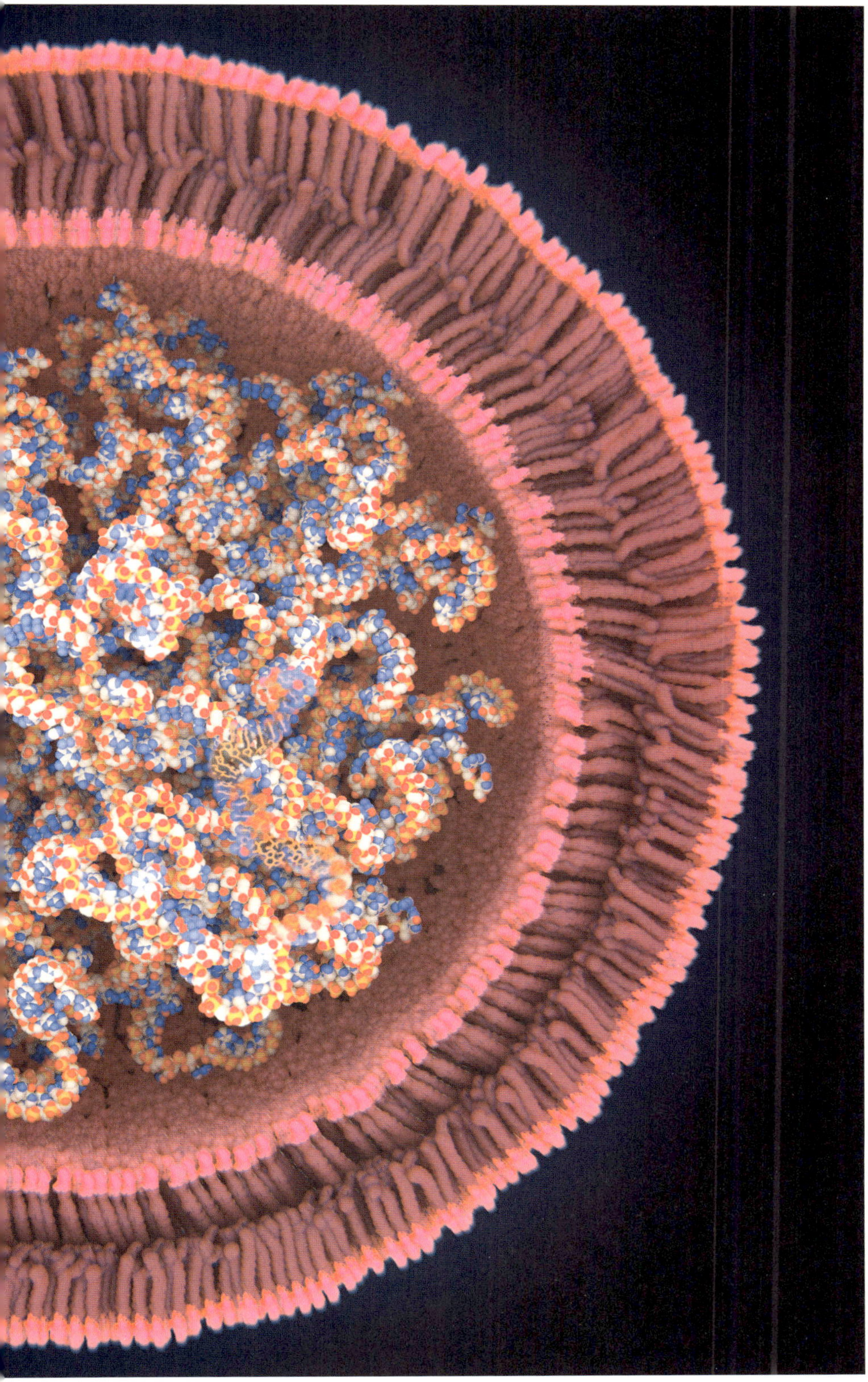

The COVID-19 vaccine, shown in microscopic detail, was the first major deployment of mRNA (messenger ribonucleic acid) vaccine technology.

CRISPR IS NOT MERELY A TOOL FOR RESEARCH. IT'S BECOMING A DISCIPLINE, A DRIVING FORCE, AND A PROMISE THAT SOLVES LONG-STANDING CHALLENGES.

Stanley Qi, Stanford Report *(2024)*

836. AUGUST 24, 2006

PLUTO IS DEMOTED AND DUBBED A DWARF PLANET

In 1930, when astronomers first identified a ninth planet in Earth's solar system, they named the dark, distant world Pluto after the Roman god of the underworld. Pluto soon became lodged in the public consciousness; Mickey Mouse's cartoon dog was named for it, and schoolchildren counted the planets on nine fingers. But on this day, Pluto was revised out of the planetary lineup after a Prague meeting of the International Astronomical Union approved new definitions for what constitutes a planet. Pluto was reclassified as a dwarf planet because it didn't meet one criterion for a true one: It didn't have gravity sufficient to "clear the neighborhood" around its orbit of same-size objects other than its moons.

837. AUGUST 25, 2006

CALIFORNIA REDWOOD IS DECLARED EARTH'S TALLEST TREE

Forest ecologist Stephen Sillett had admitted to "an obsession with the tallest trees." So it was only fitting that he was called in to verify and measure—by personally climbing—the

A forest expert climbed this 379-foot old-growth redwood in a California park to certify it as the tallest tree on Earth.

379-foot old-growth redwood that, on this day, was officially labeled the world's tallest living tree. In a remote area of California's Redwood National and State Parks, naturalists Chris Atkins and Michael Taylor had found the tree and estimated it to be taller than Stratosphere Giant, the 370.5-foot-tall redwood that had held the record since 2004. After an initial height check with a laser range finder, Sillett climbed and took a precise measurement from the top of the tree, named Hyperion after a titan in Greek mythology whose name means "watcher from above."

838. OCTOBER 13, 2006

#METOO MOVEMENT IGNITES

On this day in Selma, Alabama, social activist and sexual assault survivor Tarana Burke filed incorporation papers for Just Be, Inc., a group founded to "work with young women of color to advance their self-esteem." In many cases, that meant helping girls escape or recover from sexual harassment and violence that too many had endured. Convinced that the exchange of empathy among sexual violence survivors would help heal and empower them, Burke coined a two-word catchphrase for the group's brand of solidarity: "me too." The term would go viral and spark worldwide conversations in 2017.

This image of Pluto was captured in 2015, about a decade after it was reclassified from the ninth planet in Earth's solar system to a dwarf planet.

839. DECEMBER 25, 2006

***TIME*'S PERSON OF THE YEAR: YOU**

Time magazine's tradition of annually selecting a Man of the Year (later, a Person of the Year) began in 1927. It favored singular individuals: a head of state, a war hero, a science pioneer, a spiritual leader. But on this day, *Time* editors announced a choice of unprecedented scope: Its 2006 Person of the Year was You—all the people using Web 2.0 tools to create "community and collaboration on a scale never seen before." The magazine praised "You" for "wresting power from the few and helping one another for nothing"—and glowingly foresaw efforts that would produce "an opportunity to build a new kind of international understanding."

840. JANUARY 4, 2007

FIRST MUSLIM AND BUDDHIST REPRESENTATIVES JOIN THE U.S. CONGRESS

Since 1789, when the Constitution established the U.S. House of Representatives, the legislative body's membership has been reshuffled biennially by popular elections. So it's often called "the People's House," as if representative of the nation's diversity—though historically its members have been mostly white, male, and Christian. On this day, the 110th U.S. Congress began its session amid signs of growing religious breadth. Members starting their terms included Democrat Keith Ellison of Minnesota, the House's first Muslim member, and Democrats Mazie Hirono of Hawaii and Hank Johnson of Georgia, the body's first two Buddhist members.

841. JANUARY 4, 2007

PELOSI BECOMES THE FIRST FEMALE SPEAKER OF THE HOUSE

On this day, as a new session of the U.S. Congress convened with a record 88 women members and Democrats in the majority, California's Nancy Pelosi was elected Speaker of the House: the first woman to hold that position in the body's history. Born into a prominent Maryland Democratic family, Pelosi began volunteering for the party in the 1970s in Northern California while raising five children with her husband, Paul. She rose through state party ranks, was elected in 1987 to fill a vacant House seat, and repeatedly won reelection. Known as a shrewd political liberal who built alliances with moderates and conservatives, Pelosi would be the House Democrats' leader from 2003 to 2023—the first woman to lead any party in Congress. She would serve as speaker from 2007 to 2011 and again from 2019 to 2023.

842. JANUARY 9, 2007

STEVE JOBS INTRODUCES THE IPHONE, APPLE'S FIRST SMARTPHONE

"Every once in a while, a revolutionary product comes along that changes everything," Apple CEO Steve Jobs told the Macworld Expo audience in San Francisco on this day. He then presented Apple's long-awaited entry into the smartphone market: the iPhone. In a body

CEO Steve Jobs reveals Apple's new iPhone in 2007—the first of 51 models released as of 2025.

about 4.5 by 2.5 inches and 0.5 inch thick, it combined the media-play features of the popular iPod, internet browsing and email capacity, a camera—and control via a touch screen nearly the size of the device. Jobs proclaimed the iPhone "literally five years ahead of any other mobile phone," and one million of them sold in the first 74 days after release. Today, some 150 million iPhones are in circulation in the United States.

843. JUNE 1, 2007

ASSISTED SUICIDE PIONEER IS RELEASED FROM PRISON

On this day, "right to die" activist Jack Kevorkian was released from prison after serving eight years of a 10- to 25-year sentence. His crime? Administering a lethal injection in 1998 to a 52-year-old man with Lou Gehrig's disease (ALS). Kevorkian, who said he had helped some 130 ailing patients terminate their lives, was freed after agreeing not to participate in any more assisted suicides—which by 2025 would be legal in 10 states and Washington, D.C. After Kevorkian's death in June 2011, an *American Medical News* article noted, "Some think his aggressive push for physician-assisted suicide forced the medical profession to take a closer look at care of the terminally ill. But others say ... his actions were motivated more by a desire to advance his agenda than compassion for patients."

THIS GREAT CONSERVATION ACHIEVEMENT MEANS MORE AND MORE AMERICANS ACROSS THE NATION WILL ENJOY THE THRILL OF SEEING BALD EAGLES SOAR.

George W. Bush *(2007)*

844. JUNE 10, 2007

AMBIGUOUS FINALE AIRS FOR TV HIT *THE SOPRANOS*

With the airing this Sunday night of the series finale of *The Sopranos,* one of the most acclaimed and influential shows in TV history left its fans in the dark—literally. During six seasons on HBO, the series' episodes set cable audience records, drawing up to 12 million viewers. That many tuned in for the last scene in the Soprano family saga: patriarch and mob boss Tony Soprano in a diner booth, glancing at the door every time someone enters. Hearing the door's bell again, Tony looks up ... and the camera cuts to black. Through the years, as *The Sopranos* caught on with new generations, critics and fans would argue about the ending—but never about the impact of the series, which won fistfuls of awards and ushered in a whole new era of gritty, sophisticated television drama.

845. JUNE 28, 2007

BALD EAGLE REMOVED FROM ENDANGERED SPECIES LIST

After decades classified as an endangered or threatened species, America's national bird shed that label on this day. In the 20th century, the bald eagle's numbers had declined sharply: Human encroachment shrank its habitat, and reproduction plummeted when exposure to the pesticide DDT weakened its eggshells. The raptor's recovery began in 1967 with its listing as a federal endangered species; recovery continued after DDT was banned in 1972, and federal acts in 1973 and 1978 broadened protections of eagles and their habitats. Thanks to captive breeding and other efforts, eagle populations rose to more than 11,000 nesting pairs by 2007—and to more than 71,400 occupied nests in 2020.

846. AUGUST 7, 2007

BARRY BONDS BREAKS THE HOME RUN RECORD

"Bonds stands alone!" This was the broadcast announcer's call after slugger Barry Bonds of the San Francisco Giants hit his 756th career home run, breaking the record held for 33 years by the legendary Hank Aaron. Baseball journalists never voted Bonds into the sport's Hall of Fame, likely because of questions about performance-enhancing drug use. But during 22 years with the Pittsburgh Pirates and the Giants, Bonds became Major League Baseball's only player to hit 500 home runs and steal 500 bases. He set the single-season record for home runs (73 in 2001). And before he retired after the 2007 season, Bonds would raise his home run total to 762—a record that still stands.

A sci-fi saga of postapocalyptic survival contests, the *Hunger Games* books have sold more than 100 million copies and were made into hit movies.

847. OCTOBER 14, 2007

KARDASHIAN FAMILY TAKES TO TV

On this day, a new era in reality television was launched with the premiere of *Keeping Up With the Kardashians,* starring the blended family of celebrities headed by wealthy socialite Kris Kardashian Jenner. Married to Olympic great Bruce Jenner, Kris led the cast as "momager" of the glamorous careers and lives of her children, notably five daughters: Kourtney, Kim, and Khloé Kardashian and Kylie and Kendall Jenner. In its 14-year run, the show would air 20 seasons of episodes and spawn several spin-offs, drawing more than 130 million global viewers. Over the years, it documented the women's multimillion-dollar business ventures; the high-profile romances, marriages, and divorces; the births of at least a dozen children; and the transition to womanhood of Kris's former husband, Caitlyn Jenner.

848. AUGUST 17, 2008

MICHAEL PHELPS BREAKS THE OLYMPIC GOLD MEDAL RECORD

At the summer Olympic Games in Beijing, U.S. swimmer Michael Phelps won his eighth gold medal, setting a new record for most golds in a single Olympics. The haul gave the 23-year-old Baltimore native what he'd come to Beijing to achieve: one more gold medal than the seven won by swimmer Mark Spitz in the 1972 Munich Games. U.K. sportswriter Robert Kitson said the feat "confirms Phelps as the Neptune of the Olympic pool and sets a high-water mark which future generations will struggle to eclipse."

849. AUGUST 19, 2008

LADY GAGA'S DEBUT ALBUM SPURS STARDOM

The 22-year-old singer-songwriter was flamboyant, talented, and largely unknown. But after the release on this day of her debut album, *The Fame,* its first single "Just Dance" topped music charts worldwide, the single "Poker Face" followed, and Lady Gaga was launched into the pop pantheon. The former Stefani Germanotta would become famous for outrageous feats—simulating a hanging during a performance, wearing a dress made of meat—and for trying on new guises: singing jazz with crooner Tony Bennett, acting in television shows and movies, and performing at the 2024 Paris Summer Olympics. Thanks to fans known as Little Monsters (and she's their Mother Monster), Lady Gaga has sold an estimated 170 million records to date and has won 14 Grammy Awards.

850. SEPTEMBER 14, 2008

FIRST BOOK IN THE *HUNGER GAMES* SERIES IS RELEASED, SPARKING A POP CULTURE PHENOMENON

In Panem, a fictional nation conjured by author Suzanne Collins—part war zone, part mythic realm, part reality TV contest—adolescents compete in a fight to the death to win housing and food for their families. That postapocalyptic tale was published on this day as *The Hunger Games,* the first book in a trilogy aimed at young adult and science fiction readers. The books would go on to sell more than 100 million copies worldwide and be translated into more than 50 languages. Movies based on the trilogy would make more than three billion dollars at the box office and boost the careers of actors including Jennifer Lawrence, Josh Hutcherson, and Liam Hemsworth.

Catapulted to fame by her first album's hit singles, the outrageous singer Lady Gaga has sold some 170 million records and won 14 Grammy Awards.

851. SEPTEMBER 15, 2008

LEHMAN BROTHERS GOES DOWN

Once a leading global investment bank, Lehman Brothers filed for bankruptcy on this day with $613 billion in debt: the largest bankruptcy in U.S. history. From the mid-1980s into 2007, the U.S. economy had enjoyed what Federal Reserve bankers dubbed the Great Moderation, a period of low inflation and relative economic stability. Then recession hit in late 2007 and deepened as corporations floundered. Lehman would become a symbol of the Great Recession as its bankruptcy triggered other business failures, rocked the stock market, and cost tens of thousands of jobs. Because the federal government intervened to save others, Lehman would be the only "big five" investment bank to go under.

852. SEPTEMBER 28, 2008

SPACEX PUTS ITS FIRST ROCKET INTO ORBIT

Rising from a palm-fringed Marshall Islands test site into the azure sky above Micronesia, the Falcon 1 rocket successfully lifted off on this day, becoming the first privately developed liquid-fuel rocket to orbit Earth. For commercial spaceflight company SpaceX and its CEO Elon Musk, the achievement came after three failed attempts to launch the rocket, designed to lift a half-ton payload into low Earth orbit. As Musk would later tell an

Los Angeles chef Roy Choi's Kogi BBQ mobile kitchen ignited the food truck craze, populated by fleets of rolling restaurants that served gourmet fare across the nation.

aeronautics conference, the effort "was the last money that we had for Falcon 1. The fourth launch worked, or that would have been it for SpaceX."

853. NOVEMBER 19, 2008

CHEF SERVES CULINARY DELIGHTS FROM A FOOD TRUCK—AND IGNITES A CRAZE

Kimchi quesadillas? Korean-barbecue tacos? Los Angeles chef Roy Choi not only produced tasty fusion cuisine—but starting on this day, he served it from his rolling kitchen, adding haute cuisine cachet to street food and igniting a gourmet food truck craze that swept the nation. Before Choi, food trucks often had been branded low-end "roach coaches" serving undistinguished food at best. But from his Kogi BBQ restaurant on wheels, Choi created inventive fare that won him a Best New Chefs award from *Food & Wine* magazine. He also pioneered the use of social media to publicize the truck's stops, drawing crowds of urban diners to what became "viral eatery" events.

ALWAYS [BE] OPEN TO WHATEVER IS COMING YOUR WAY. IF IT'S A PHONE CALL THAT SAYS, "LET'S GO SELL TACOS ON THE STREET," THEN IT'S A PHONE CALL THAT MIGHT SHIFT EVERYTHING IN YOUR LIFE.

Roy Choi, *chef (2019)*

854. DECEMBER 11, 2008

FBI ARRESTS BERNIE MADOFF FOR A $65 MILLION INVESTOR SCAM

When Federal Bureau of Investigation agents visited financier Bernard Madoff at his Manhattan apartment on this morning, he told them what he'd told his sons a day earlier: that the investment advisory business he'd operated since the early 1990s was "one big lie." The fraud Madoff had masterminded would turn out to be the largest Ponzi scheme in history, bilking thousands of individuals, pension funds, and charities out of some $65 billion they had entrusted to him. In a stunning fall for a man who'd once been chairman of the Nasdaq stock exchange, Madoff would be sentenced to 150 years in prison; he died there in 2021.

855. DECEMBER 19, 2008

GOVERNMENT BAILOUT SAVES FAILING U.S. AUTOMAKERS

Largely due to poor fuel efficiency, competition from foreign models, and the lingering economic crisis, a sharp drop in sales of American-made cars had left U.S. automakers on the brink of bankruptcy. In one of the last major acts of his presidency, George W. Bush diverted money on this day from a fund meant to save failing banks and gave $17.4 billion of it to General Motors and Chrysler, with Ford eligible for future assistance. Asked later why he approved a bailout after Congress had refused to, Bush explained: "I didn't want there to be 21 percent unemployment."

856. JANUARY 3, 2009

GENESIS BLOCK IS MINED, MARKING CREATION OF BITCOIN

It was the dawn of cryptocurrency with the first trade in Bitcoin, which took place on this day. A digital facsimile of gold or legal tender, Bitcoin was devised by the pseudonymous individual or group called Satoshi Nakamoto to be mined, earned, and traded via computer transactions. It made its debut, as Bankrate.com noted, "in the months after the global financial crisis obliterated economies ... [when] moving monetary policy out of the hands of governments and central banks" seemed particularly appealing. The Bitcoin supply was limited to 21 million coins; that affected the demand and thus the market value. In the first 15 years, the value of a single Bitcoin would range from about a tenth of a cent to more than $93,000. In 2025, more than $75 billion in Bitcoin is traded every day.

857. JANUARY 15, 2009

PILOT MAKES "MIRACLE" LANDING ON HUDSON RIVER

US Airways flight 1549 began routinely: a departure around 3:25 p.m. on this day from New York's LaGuardia Airport, bound for Charlotte, North Carolina. About 3,000 feet up, the Airbus A320 hit a flock of Canada geese, disabling both engines—and with no airport in range, Captain Chesley "Sully" Sullenberger had to attempt an extraordinarily risky emergency landing on the Hudson River. Sullenberger set down the plane safely, and all 155 people aboard were rescued in 24 minutes as the plane filled with icy water. Sullenberger's feat would become one of modern aviation's most famous emergency landings—and earn the universal sobriquet "Miracle on the Hudson."

858. JANUARY 20, 2009

BARACK OBAMA BECOMES AMERICA'S FIRST BLACK PRESIDENT

Before a jubilant Inauguration Day crowd, 1.8 million strong despite the bitter cold, Barack Obama was sworn in as the United States' first African American president on this day. His winning campaign slogan—"Yes We Can"—seemed fitting for his determined ascent, which swept up the nation at large in a tide of hope. The son of an absent father, he became an Ivy League honors graduate, and as a junior senator, he triumphed over political veteran Hillary Clinton in the Democratic presidential primary. On November 4, 2008, Obama was elected America's 44th president by a comfortable margin over war hero Senator John McCain, whose running mate, Alaska Governor Sarah Palin, was the nation's first Republican female vice presidential nominee.

859. APRIL 17, 2009

H1N1 FLU SPARKS A GLOBAL PANDEMIC

For decades, seasonal outbreaks of influenza around the world had caused fever, body aches, coughing, and sore throat that generally passed within a week. But a novel flu strain first detected in North America brought unprecedented patterns of severe illness and death. On this day, the Centers for Disease Control (CDC) would determine that this virus, labeled H1N1pdm09, contained "a unique combination of influenza genes not previously identified in animals or people," so fewer people had immunity from prior exposure. In the first year of what would be called the 2009 H1N1 pandemic, the virus

caused some 61 million cases and 12,500 deaths in the United States, and as many as 575,000 deaths worldwide, according to the CDC.

Barack and Michelle Obama greet the audience at a concert before his inauguration in 2009 as the nation's first African American president.

860. JUNE 22, 2009

NEW LAW DISCOURAGES SMOKING, RESTRICTS SALES

With tobacco smoking a current habit for roughly one in five Americans ages 18 and older—and a factor in an estimated 420,000 deaths in the U.S. annually—President Barack Obama signed the Family Smoking Prevention and Tobacco Control Act into law on this day. Passed easily in both houses of Congress, the measure gave the U.S. Food and Drug Administration broad authority to regulate tobacco products, with particular focus on discouraging young people from using them. The new measure prohibited sales to people under 21; limited vending machines to 21-and-over establishments; restricted tobacco brand sponsorships of entertainment, sports, and cultural events; and banned promotional giveaways of sample tobacco products or items with tobacco brand logos.

861. SEPTEMBER 18, 2009

GUIDING LIGHT DEPARTS THE SOAP OPERA FIRMAMENT

Remy and Christina got married, Fletcher and Alexandra left to travel the world, and Reva and Josh reconciled as the sun set on *Guiding Light,* the longest-running soap opera in U.S. history. The serial aired its last episode on this day after 72 years on radio and TV, during which generations of viewers came to know generations of characters almost like family. *Guiding Light*'s cancellation marked the beginning of the decline of daytime dramas: With more women in the workforce, cheaper genres like reality TV growing, and the rise of the internet and streaming media, three more major soaps would be canceled in the next three years.

862. SEPTEMBER 29, 2009

A NEW AMERICAN AGE OF WEARABLE HEALTH TRACKERS STARTS WITH A SMALL BLACK CLIP

Americans have long associated fitness with footsteps: think runners, hikers, marathoners, mall walkers. But on this day, counting those steps entered the computer-assisted realm with the U.S. release of the Fitbit Classic, a digital tracker that *Wired* magazine said "looked like a clothespin had mated with a stapler." Clipped onto clothes, the device measured steps, distance, calories burned, and sleep patterns—then wirelessly downloaded the data through a base to the wearer's computer. As Fitbit devices were upgraded and built into wristbands, the company reached a 67 percent share of the tracker market—but gradually was overtaken after 2015 by Apple and other smartwatch makers. More than a third of Americans now use wellness-tracking wearables—and users worldwide are expected to exceed 462 million in 2026.

As more Americans sought to log the steps they walked and calories they burned, wearable fitness trackers evolved from simple clip-ons to high-tech watches.

863. DECEMBER 24, 2009

JOE ROGAN'S PODCAST DEBUTS

A martial arts champ in his teens, a stand-up comedian in his 20s, an actor and TV reality show host in his 30s, multi-hyphenate Joe Rogan funneled those experiences into his everyman persona as host of the podcast he debuted on this day. During two or three unscripted hours, Rogan interviewed athletes and entertainers, scientists and politicians. A self-described libertarian with socially liberal leanings, he addressed controversial issues from across the political spectrum. Critics observed that Rogan spread bigotry and disinformation, while fans said he defended free speech and blasted hypocrisy. By 2025, *The Joe Rogan Experience* consistently ranked as America's top podcast by listenership, reaching an estimated 8.9 million unique listeners.

864. JANUARY 1, 2010

GEN ALPHA BEGINS

So long, Gen Z—the diverse population raised on smartphones and social media, whose

Generation Alpha, the first population group born entirely in the 21st century, is expected to be the most tech-savvy cohort yet.

birth years straddled the turn of the century (1997–2012). On this day, a new population era commenced: Generation Alpha, the first group born entirely in this century, between 2010 and 2024. Demographer Mark McCrindle—who named the cohort Alpha to mark it as the "start of something new"—projected that it would become the "largest generation the world has ever seen, numbering more than 2 billion," and members would be "the most materially endowed generation ever, the most technologically savvy generation ever, and [would] enjoy a longer life span than any previous generation."

865. JANUARY 21, 2010

CITIZENS UNITED CASE LOOSENS NATIONAL ELECTION SPENDING RULES

Issuing an opinion that overturned century-old limits on election spending, the Supreme Court ruled on this day that restricting groups' and corporations' "independent political spending" would violate their First Amendment free speech rights. The high court decided the case by a 5–4 margin in favor of Citizens United, a conservative organization that challenged campaign finance rules governing its expenditures. The decision would prove controversial, with critics asserting that it allowed virtually limitless election spending by special interest groups, super PACs, and wealthy donors—actors already wielding disproportionate influence in politics.

866. MARCH 23, 2010

AFFORDABLE CARE ACT OVERHAULS U.S. HEALTH CARE SYSTEM

In the most consequential change to U.S. health care policy since the launch of Medicare and Medicaid, President Barack Obama signed into law the Affordable Care Act (ACA), also known as Obamacare, on this day. The act mandated a system of state marketplaces where health insurance would cost less for Americans with lower incomes, and required a host of changes in how the U.S. insurance industry would treat consumers. The ACA eliminated lifetime or annual caps on expenses insurance companies would cover; required the companies to extend parents' coverage to dependent children up to age 26; forbade companies to deny coverage because of patients' preexisting conditions; and banned cancellation of coverage if patients developed costly illnesses. Obama said he signed the law "on behalf of my mother, who argued with insurance companies even as she battled cancer in her final days."

867. APRIL 20, 2010

DEEPWATER HORIZON OIL SPILL IGNITES AN ENVIRONMENTAL CRISIS

On this night at the Deepwater Horizon offshore oil drilling rig in the Gulf of Mexico, a burst of natural gas broke the concrete seal of a wellhead in the seabed 5,000 feet below.

A new communication era dawned as the FaceTime app allowed smartphone and tablet users to make video calls over internet provider networks.

The gas surged up a pipeline to the rig platform and ignited; the resulting fire killed 11 workers and injured 17 more. A day and a half later, the rig sank and oil gushed from the ruptured pipeline in what would become history's largest marine oil spill. Rig leaseholder BP and government officials would try controlled burns and air-dropped dispersants to manage the oil; BP admitted 1,000 barrels a day were spilling into the Gulf, but the U.S. government estimated up to 60 times that amount. The disaster spurred a drilling moratorium, proposals for more regulation (though little was passed), and orders that BP pay $8.8 billion in restoration of natural resources as part of a $20.8 billion settlement.

868. JUNE 7, 2010

FACETIME DEBUTS

Inventors first began experimenting with two-way audio and video communication devices in the late 19th century. A 1936 German prototype, whose name translated to "visual telephone system," sent calls by coaxial cable. A 1959 Picturephone from Bell Laboratories transmitted clear video—one frame every two seconds. Some early 2000s mobile phones supported video calls, with network limitations. But on this day, videotelephony turned a corner when Apple announced the FaceTime app for its new iPhone 4. The handset's front-facing camera made initiating calls more natural, and FaceTime ran on internet provider networks, rather than requiring a special video call carrier. "Video calling" and "FaceTiming" have become interchangeable terms, as the FaceTime app is now preinstalled on all Apple devices. As of 2021, Android users were enabled to connect to FaceTime calls.

THE IPHONE 4 IS THE BIGGEST LEAP SINCE THE ORIGINAL IPHONE. FACETIME VIDEO CALLING SETS A NEW STANDARD FOR MOBILE COMMUNICATION.

Steve Jobs, *Apple CEO (2010)*

869. JULY 5, 2010

FIRST PASSENGER HAILS AN UBER RIDE

After entrepreneurs Garrett Camp and Travis Kalanick couldn't find a ride on a wintry night in Paris, they hatched a revolutionary idea: What if a hired car could be summoned using a smartphone app? The pair developed a prototype app that let a passenger request a ride with one click, located the passenger using GPS, dispatched a vehicle, and then automatically billed the fare to a passenger's credit card. On this day, the first ride via Uber—then known as UberCab—was requested for a trip across San Francisco. Within five years, Uber would raise enough venture capital funding to be ranked as the world's most valuable start-up, worth $51 billion. Today, it operates in some 70 countries and 15,000 cities.

870. AUGUST 4, 2010

THE GIVING PLEDGE IS INAUGURATED

On this day, billionaires Warren Buffett, Bill Gates, and Melinda French Gates launched an endeavor in which ultrarich people—themselves included—commit to giving away

continued on page 430

SPOTLIGHT

CONSERVATION

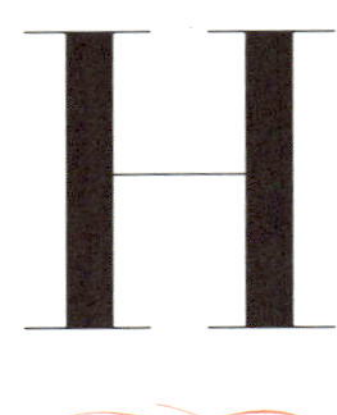

HISTORICALLY, STEWARDSHIP OF America's natural resources consists of two competing approaches: conservation and preservation. Early environmentalists described the balancing act this way: Conservation seeks "the proper use of nature"—that is, exploiting it responsibly—while preservation seeks "the protection of nature from use" to prevent any human impact.

In the 21st century thus far, U.S. conservation and preservation policies have shifted depending on the politicians in power. A high-profile example: the 19.6-million-acre Arctic National Wildlife Refuge (ANWR) in northeastern Alaska, subject of a decades-long debate about opening areas for oil and gas drilling. President George W. Bush (in office 2001–09) supported the sale of drilling leases, but Congress did not approve it. In 2017, President Donald Trump authorized lease sales; the first occurred in 2021, just before he left office. His successor, President Joe Biden, later canceled the leases, saying the environmental impact hadn't been adequately studied.

The National Park Service—which celebrated its hundredth anniversary in 2016—plays an outsize role in safeguarding wild places. It oversees some 85.1 million acres of protected lands: more than 60 national parks and 420 national monuments, preserves, and memorials. President Barack Obama (in office 2009–2017) authorized the protection of several sites, including Utah's Bears Ears National Monument, the first established at Native American tribes' request. In his first term, Trump reduced the size of Bears Ears and other monuments, opening the lands to commercial use; in 2021, Biden reversed the Trump actions. And in early 2025, the second Trump administration moved to reverse Biden's reversals.

Successive administrations have changed plans for Grand Staircase-Escalante National Monument, known for its sandstone formations.

THESE PLACES—THE ROCKS, THE WIND, THE LAND—THEY ARE LIVING, BREATHING THINGS THAT DESERVE TIMELY AND LASTING PROTECTION.

Russell Begaye, *eighth president of the Navajo Nation (2016)*

Instagram's winning formula—where users post images and videos, comment on posts, and "like" their favorites—has yielded three billion monthly active users and counting.

continued from page 427

their fortunes. The effort, known as the Giving Pledge, asked America's 404 recorded billionaires (at the time) to vow to give away 50 percent or more of their wealth while living or via their estates. In 2010, 57 of those 404 (14 percent) signed the pledge. As of 2025, 11 of them were no longer billionaires; 14 were deceased, most with their pledges unmet; and the combined net worth of the rest had grown dramatically since 2010. Topping that list: pledgers Priscilla Chan and her husband, Facebook founder Mark Zuckerberg, whose wealth had increased by more than 4,000 percent.

871. AUGUST 31, 2010

IRAQ WAR ENDS

After more than seven years of U.S. combat operations in Iraq, the mission known as Operation Iraqi Freedom officially ended, President Barack Obama announced in a televised address on this day. The operation by the numbers: more than 4,400 U.S. casualties, 110,000 Iraqis killed, $800 billion spent, and some 50,000 Americans still in Iraq, slated to depart by the end of 2011. The U.S. entered a new phase of involvement aimed at training Iraqi forces, partnering with them in counterterrorism efforts, and protecting U.S. government projects as their personnel were drawn down. But Operation Iraqi Freedom ended under harsh criticism for spending lives and dollars without meeting objectives such as rooting out the Taliban and al Qaeda.

872. OCTOBER 6, 2010

INSTAGRAM IS BORN

The app for Instagram—a new photo-sharing, social media, and networking platform—acquired 25,000 users on this first day of public release. The auspicious launch followed a modest beginning: Stanford University graduate Kevin Systrom designed his platform for posting mobile-device photos, along with the location-based check-ins popular on sites such as Foursquare. A spirits aficionado, Systrom called his creation Burbn—but once he acquired venture capital funding and a partner, fellow Stanford grad Mike Krieger, they changed the name. What didn't change was Instagram's stripped-down approach: a focus on posting photos, comments, and "likes." Some 18 months later, Facebook bought the platform for a billion dollars; today, its estimated worth is more than $200 billion.

873. DECEMBER 22, 2010

U.S. ALLOWS GAY, LESBIAN, AND BISEXUAL AMERICANS TO SERVE IN THE MILITARY

"We are not a nation that says, 'Don't ask, don't tell.' We are a nation that says, 'Out of many, we are one.'" With that assertion, President Barack Obama signed the repeal of the military policy that barred gay Americans from openly serving and permitted their discharge if their sexual orientation became known. More than 13,000 personnel were forced from service by the policy. When the repeal took effect in September 2011, Obama declared: "As of today, patriotic Americans in uniform will no longer have to lie about who they are in order to serve the country they love." Another longstanding policy was changed about two years later, opening all combat roles to women service members in late 2015.

874. MARCH 9, 2011

NASA RETIRES SPACE SHUTTLE *DISCOVERY*

What NASA calls "the champion of the shuttle fleet," the space shuttle *Discovery,* was formally retired on this day after a record 27 years in service. *Discovery* flew 39 missions,

Retired after a record 27 years, the space shuttle *Discovery* had flown more missions and miles than any other shuttle in the fleet.

the most of any shuttle in the fleet; covered some 150,000,000 miles, more than any of the other orbiters; and spent 365 days in space, carrying a total of 184 men and women. Among its history-making missions were the deployment and servicing of the Hubble Space Telescope and 13 flights to the International Space Station, including the first docking of a shuttle at the station in 1999.

875. MARCH 25, 2011

FDA APPROVES KEY BUILDING BLOCK OF IMMUNOTHERAPY, SUPERCHARGING THE FIGHT AGAINST CANCER

On this day, immunotherapy—a game-changing treatment that uses the body's own immune system to ward off cancer—entered a promising new era, when the U.S. Food and Drug Administration approved the first immune checkpoint inhibitor (ICI) drug, ipilimumab. ICIs work by preventing inhibition of the body's immune response, so that the full force of cancer-killing cells reaches tumors. Ipilimumab's use against the deadly skin cancer melanoma significantly improved survival rates, leaving patients disease free long-term. As more ICIs were developed and approved, checkpoint inhibitors "dramatically transformed the treatment landscape for various malignancies," according to a review in the journal *Molecular Cancer*. Today, immunotherapy has been foundational in treating blood, bladder, kidney, skin, and non–small cell lung cancer, among others.

876. APRIL 17, 2011

FANTASY SAGA *GAME OF THRONES* PREMIERES

The continents of Essos and Westeros. Targaryens and Lannisters, Baratheons and Starks, feuding medieval families vying for the Iron Throne. Icy villains called White Walkers, and a heroine called the Mother of Dragons (she commands three of them). These and many more fictional creations burst onto the screen in the television series *Game of Thrones,* which debuted on this day on HBO. Based on the mega-best-selling fantasy novel series *A Song of Ice and Fire* by George R. R. Martin, the saga would gather an impassioned cultlike following around the world, winning numerous awards during the eight seasons it aired.

877. MAY 1, 2011

U.S. NAVY SEALS KILL AL QAEDA LEADER OSAMA BIN LADEN

In an elaborate secret operation, U.S. Navy SEALs raided the hideout of Osama bin Laden and fatally shot the al Qaeda network leader on this day. The death ended a nearly decade-long manhunt for the mastermind of the September 11, 2001, terrorist attacks. Based on intelligence that bin Laden was hiding in a compound in Abbottabad, Pakistan, the SEALs helicoptered there from a base in Afghanistan, exchanged fire with bin Laden relatives and aides in the compound, then found and killed bin Laden in his bedroom. The forces then flew out with confiscated documents and electronics, as well as bin Laden's body, which was buried at sea.

Medieval fantasy plots (and a few dragon eggs) were hatched on the hit TV series *Game of Thrones* during the eight seasons it aired beginning in 2011.

878. MAY 13, 2011

USDA APPROVES A DRUG TO TREAT HEPATITIS C

On this day, the U.S. Food and Drug Administration approved the first direct-acting antiviral agent to treat the hepatitis C virus (HCV): a drug called boceprevir. Since the 1970s, an unknown virus had been blamed for transfusion-related hepatitis infections and was considered a chief cause of liver cancer, cirrhosis, and transplants. In 1989, the infectious agent was identified as HCV—and this approval of a new class of drugs transformed the fight against it, making HCV the first curable chronic viral infection. Within roughly two decades, the use of direct antiviral agents would make it possible to eradicate HCV in more than 98 percent of cases.

879. MAY 25, 2011

OPRAH ENDS GROUNDBREAKING TV SHOW

The last original episode of television's *Oprah Winfrey Show* aired on this day after 25 seasons that made its eponymous host a global celebrity and multimedia titan, with more than

5,000 episodes taped across its run. Overcoming an impoverished Mississippi childhood, Winfrey started in broadcasting as a reporter, then hosted a syndicated program that became America's number one daytime talk show, thanks to her penetrating interviews, engaging style, and provocative topics. Recognized as one of the world's wealthiest and most influential African American women, she earned the title "Queen of All Media" by producing and starring in TV projects and films, including *The Color Purple;* establishing the Oprah Winfrey Network cable channel; and publishing books and a magazine.

880. SEPTEMBER 17, 2011

OCCUPY WALL STREET MOVEMENT HITS THE STREETS

Decrying the social and economic inequality between them and the wealthiest one percent of Americans, demonstrators chanting "We are the 99 percent" launched the Occupy Wall Street movement on this day. A march, rally, and tent city in New York City's Zuccotti

The wealth gap between America's richest one percent and the rest of the population inspired the country's Occupy Wall Street demonstrations.

Park kicked off what would become months of demonstrations at some 900 U.S. and international locations. Among the movement's triggers: the 2007–08 financial crisis and the Great Recession that followed; the lack of criminal charges for financiers involved in the crisis; and the economic downturn's toll on many Americans' standard of living.

881. NOVEMBER 18, 2011

MINECRAFT LAUNCHES

A new blocky, buildable world opened on this day with the official release of the video game Minecraft. Unlike games with a single theme such as warfare or sports, Minecraft gave players a largely unformed realm where improvising and creating were the only objectives. As players move their avatars through angular territories called biomes, they fashion structures, tools, and landscapes from materials they mine and encounter "mobs" of creatures from pigs and chickens to skeletons and zombies. In 2021, *Forbes* gaming reviewer Erik Kain ranked Minecraft among the past decade's "most important games"—and in 2025, Guinness World Records declared it the best-selling video game of all time.

882. FEBRUARY 26, 2012

UNARMED YOUTH TRAYVON MARTIN'S DEATH SPARKS NATIONWIDE OUTRAGE

In a Sanford, Florida, gated community where 17-year-old Trayvon Martin was visiting, the Black teen stepped out to a convenience store to buy snacks. As Martin walked back, he was spotted by George Zimmerman, 28, a neighborhood watch volunteer who called 911 to report a "suspicious guy." After Zimmerman approached Martin, a separate 911 recording captured sounds of confrontation and cries for help; Zimmerman then shot Martin at close range, killing him. Criminally charged with second-degree murder in April 2012, Zimmerman would be found not guilty under Florida's broad self-defense law in July 2013. The verdict sparked outrage; after activists Alicia Garza, Patrisse Cullors, and Opal Tometi (now known as Ayọ Tometi) called for recognition that "Black lives matter," the phrase gave rise to a movement.

A poster for the millennial hit HBO television series *Girls* features its four stars, (from left) Jemima Kirke, Allison Williams, Lena Dunham, and Zosia Mamet.

883. APRIL 15, 2012

MILLENNIALS USHER IN THE AGE OF THE "GIRL"

Debuting on this day: *Girls,* the ironically named, groundbreaking HBO series created by 20-something writer/actor/director Lena Dunham. Her characters weren't *Sex and the City*'s accomplished fashionistas; they were cash-short, impulsive young women grappling with big life issues. Both loved and reviled during its 2012–17 run, *Girls* launched Dunham's career. Meanwhile, 20-something entrepreneur Sophia Amoruso parlayed online vintage clothes sales into the multimillion-dollar retail empire Nasty Gal—then recounted how she built the business in the 2014 book *#GIRLBOSS* (later a Netflix series). Amoruso defined a #GIRLBOSS as an ambitious woman "who's in charge of her own life [and] gets what she wants because she works for it."

884. AUGUST 21, 2012

AN ENGINEER'S ONE-WORD ANSWER TO THE VIDEOCONFERENCING NEEDS OF VIRTUAL TEAMS: ZOOM

Working as an engineer at WebEx and Cisco, Eric Yuan heard what customers wanted but weren't getting: cloud-based conference room and desktop sharing with good audio and video quality for far-flung participants. Yuan founded a start-up with those goals—and on this day, it launched a beta version of Zoom, a videoconferencing system that let up to 15 people join with a click. Tech leaders gave Zoom glowing reviews as its features and capacity grew; within 11 months of launch, the platform reported hosting 5,500 meetings a day. Zoom soon morphed into a verb—"Let's Zoom instead of texting"—and became a default for meetings during COVID-19 shutdowns starting in 2020.

885. SEPTEMBER 25, 2012

VOYAGER SPACE PROBE ENTERS UNCHARTED TERRITORY

On this day, the space probe Voyager 1 gave unique meaning to its name: It became the first spacecraft to travel beyond Earth's solar system and cross into interstellar space. Launched 35 years previously from Cape Canaveral, Florida, on a mission to send back data from flybys of Jupiter and Saturn, the probe performed those tasks memorably, capturing views of the planets' atmospheres, rings, and moons, as well as discovering new moons. Voyager then bypassed Uranus and Neptune, continued through the heliosphere—a bubble of electrically charged gas blown by the solar wind outward from the sun—and across the boundary where the solar wind wanes and interstellar winds dominate. Several of Voyager 1's instruments continue to send back data to Earth as of this writing.

886. OCTOBER 8, 2012

CÉSAR E. CHÁVEZ NATIONAL MONUMENT IS INAUGURATED

On 116 acres near Bakersfield, California, a national monument was established on this day to honor United Farm Workers (UFW) founder César Chávez (1927–1993), one of the key U.S. labor and human rights leaders of the 20th century. An Arizona native whose family turned to migrant farmwork after losing its small homestead, Chavez left school after eighth grade to work in the fields full time. In 1962, he launched the UFW, the first successful farmworkers union in American history; it used boycotts and other nonviolent tactics to secure better work contracts and conditions and was an early force for immigration reform.

887. OCTOBER 29, 2012

HURRICANE SANDY RAKES THE U.S. EAST COAST

A week after it began as a tropical depression in warm Caribbean waters, a monstrous cyclone dubbed Superstorm Sandy made landfall on this night in New Jersey. At its peak, the storm measured approximately 1,000 miles in diameter. After tearing a path across

Jamaica, Cuba, Haiti, the Dominican Republic, and the Bahamas, it wreaked its greatest harm in the mid-Atlantic and northeastern United States, flooding tunnels in New York City and destroying part of Atlantic City's boardwalk. Sandy's winds and flooding would ultimately result in 147 deaths and more than $70 billion in damages, making it one of America's costliest natural disasters.

888. NOVEMBER 6, 2012

TWO WESTERN STATES LEGALIZE RECREATIONAL MARIJUANA USE

In elections that took place on this day in the states of Colorado and Washington, voters approved the use of marijuana for recreational purposes—the first states to do so. The initiative in Washington made small amounts of marijuana-related products legal for individuals 21 and older, and mandated that most revenue from taxing marijuana sales be spent on substance abuse prevention and public health programs. In Colorado, an amendment to the state constitution allowed people 21 and over to cultivate and possess small amounts of marijuana for recreation, and earmarked part of tax revenues for education programs, including school construction and bullying prevention.

The first two states to legalize recreational use of marijuana were Washington—the location of this Seattle grow room—and Colorado.

889. DECEMBER 14, 2012

NATION IS ROCKED BY SHOOTINGS AT SANDY HOOK ELEMENTARY

In Newtown, Connecticut, on this day, a heavily armed 20-year-old named Adam Lanza entered Sandy Hook Elementary School and fired more than 150 rounds in less than five minutes, killing 20 children and six adults before fatally shooting himself. A little more than five years later in Parkland, Florida, Nikolas Cruz, a 19-year-old former student at Marjory Stoneman Douglas High School, entered that school with a semi-automatic rifle and fatally shot 14 students and three employees before slipping out with evacuating students. Cruz was sentenced to 34 consecutive life sentences. Since the tragedies, the names Sandy Hook and Parkland are immutably identified with mass school shootings.

The "Netflix era," in which studios created TV series for the DVD and streaming-media business, launched with the release of the juggernaut *House of Cards.*

890. FEBRUARY 1, 2013

NETFLIX INITIATES A NEW ERA IN TELEVISION

This day marked the release of the first 13 episodes of *House of Cards,* a political thriller that was the first television series produced by a studio for the streaming service Netflix. It was part of a revolution in viewing: the growth of streaming television services as they overtook older transmission forms such as over-the-air, cable, and satellite television. Launched as a DVD-delivery business in the late 1990s, Netflix became the first dominant company in the streaming market, delivering other studios' content and then producing its own. The success of Netflix would inspire the creation of other streaming services including Hulu, YouTube Premium, Amazon Prime Video, and Disney+.

891. MARCH 4, 2013

RESEARCHERS CURE THE FIRST BABY BORN WITH THE AIDS VIRUS

On this day, medical researchers announced a hopeful finding: A baby born infected with HIV in 2010 was now a thriving tot, functionally cured of the AIDS virus by the use of antiretroviral drugs (ARVs). In the first well-documented case of its kind, the infant was started on ARVs 30 hours after birth to a mother with HIV infection; the regimen was continued for 18 months as less and less virus was found in blood samples. After months off the drugs, the child showed undetectable levels of HIV in blood tests starting in fall 2012. The case provided "a promising lead for additional research toward curing other children," said National Institute of Allergy and Infectious Diseases director Anthony Fauci.

892. MAY 10, 2013

CRONUT BECOMES A VIRAL SENSATION

If the doughnut beloved in America were crossed with the croissant adored in France, what would be the result? The Cronut, introduced on this day by veteran pastry chef Dominique Ansel. Hailed as the "Willy Wonka of pastries and dessert" by *Condé Nast Traveler* magazine, Ansel spent three months developing the hybrid treat at the New York City bakery that

bears his name. An instant hit, his Cronut takes three days to prepare—from mixing, resting, and fermenting the dough to frying, filling, and glazing the finished product. Fans lined up outside the bakery before it opened in a delicious example of how social media and online influencers can help products—or phrases, brands, and events—explode in popularity.

By crossing an all-American doughnut with a French croissant, New York City pastry chef Dominique Ansel created the toothsome Cronut.

893. MAY 15, 2013

RESEARCHERS CLONE HUMAN EMBRYONIC STEM CELLS

After years of failed attempts, scientists cloned human embryonic stem cells (ESCs), the journal *Nature* reported on this day. Patient-specific, the cells could be used to cure individuals of disease. The breakthrough, by a team at the Oregon Health and Science University in Beaverton, began when a patient's tissue cell was fused with an unfertilized ovum with its nucleus removed. The ovum "reprogrammed" the donated cell's DNA to an embryonic state; after sufficient cell division, cells could be harvested and cultured to yield genetically matched ESCs that could grow as virtually any type of cell in the patient's body. Though some criticized the breakthrough on ethical grounds as a step toward creating cloned human babies, the Oregon researchers stressed that their goal was simply to develop replacement tissue for use in treating diseases.

894. MAY 31, 2013

STORM CHASERS PERISH IN AMERICA'S LARGEST RECORDED TORNADO

Tim Samaras once linked his fascination with intense storms to his childhood viewing of *The Wizard of Oz:* "When the tornado appeared, I was hooked." On this day, his storm-chasing career ended tragically. Samaras, his son, Paul, and his chase partner Carl Young were killed near El Reno, Oklahoma, in a subvortex of a 2.6-mile-wide tornado that was the largest recorded in U.S. history. An engineer and National Geographic Explorer, Samaras, 55, invented the first probes that could survive inside tornadoes. The field data he collected made valuable contributions to the understanding and prediction of storm behaviors.

895. JUNE 9, 2013

WHISTLEBLOWER LEAKS REVEAL U.S. SURVEILLANCE OF CITIZENS

On this day, federal contractor Edward Snowden revealed himself to news outlets as the source of an explosive intelligence leak: documents showing the National Security Agency (NSA) had been conducting top secret mass surveillance of the U.S. population, including

The heartwarming tale of ice queen Elsa and her sister, Anna, made the Disney movie *Frozen* the top-grossing animated film to date.

collecting phone records from telecommunications companies. Working for the NSA since 2009, Snowden secretly gathered information on data-mining programs he deemed intrusive. After leaving the U.S. and leaking documents to newspapers who reported on them, he identified himself as the whistleblower. Within days, the U.S. would file espionage charges against Snowden, who took refuge in Russia, which declined to extradite him. A decade after the leaks, Snowden still lived in Russia with his wife and two young sons.

896. NOVEMBER 10, 2013

FROZEN CASTS ITS MAGIC AT THE BOX OFFICE

After its world premiere on this day, the Disney movie *Frozen* snowballed in popularity and became the top-grossing animated film to date with $1.3 billion in sales worldwide. The saga of royal sisters Elsa and Anna sparked what was called the "Let It Go effect": an extraordinary global embrace of its characters, costumes, merchandise, and especially its self-acceptance theme song. "Let It Go"—translated into 41 languages besides English—was belted by children the world over, adopted by causes as an empowerment anthem, and honored as Best Original Song at the 2014 Academy Awards. Six years later, the sequel *Frozen II* performed even better than the original, grossing more than $1.45 billion worldwide.

EVERYONE COULD IDENTIFY WITH ELSA. SHE WASN'T YOUR TYPICAL PRINCESS ... EVERYONE COULD INTERPRET HER IN A UNIQUE WAY AND FIND THAT THE ARC OF HER STORY APPLIED DIRECTLY TO THEM.

The *New Yorker*, on *Frozen* (2014)

897. APRIL 25, 2014

UNHEALTHY WATER SOURCE TRIGGERS THE FLINT WATER CRISIS

On this day, the city of Flint in Michigan switched over to the Flint River for its municipal water source, triggering what would become known as the Flint water crisis. The state's Department of Environmental Quality insisted the water was safe, even as customers complained of rashes and other reactions from using the discolored, smelly, and foul-tasting water. Despite months of mounting evidence, including increased blood lead levels in children, it would take more than a year before switching to another water source—and three more months before officials declared a state of emergency, urging residents to use filtered or bottled water. Ultimately, an extensive project replaced the lead pipes, and crisis victims were awarded settlements totaling more than $640 million.

898. JULY 15, 2014

ICE BUCKET CHALLENGE HELPS SEEK CURE FOR ALS

In a social media post on this day, pro golfer Chris Kennedy challenged his network to either donate to help find a cure for ALS—the terminal neurodegenerative disease afflicting a cousin of his—or get a bucket of ice water poured over their heads. Kennedy's video of his own dousing created a viral sensation, as people around the world—including celebrities, pro athletes, and political leaders—posted their imaginative variations on what would become known as the Ice Bucket Challenge. A decade after the challenge began, it had sparked more than 17 million video posts that got some 10 billion views, raising awareness and more than $220 million for ALS care, research, and advocacy.

899. JULY 17, 2014

ERIC GARNER'S DEATH UNDERSCORES BLACK SUFFERING AT POLICE HANDS

"I can't breathe." Video showed Eric Garner, a Black father of six, repeating that phrase on this day as a New York Police Department officer pinned him in an illegal choke hold until he lost consciousness. When Garner's death was ruled a homicide but the officer was not indicted, demonstrations spread across the nation. The next month in Ferguson, Missouri, a police officer fatally shot Michael Brown, an unarmed Black 18-year-old. And less than four months after that, Tamir Rice—a Black 12-year-old playing with a pellet gun—was shot and killed by Cleveland police. The Garner case ended with a $5.9 million settlement and the officer fired five years later; the Brown case with no charges against police and a $1.5 million settlement; and the Rice case with a $6 million settlement and the officer fired three years later for unrelated reasons.

900. DECEMBER 17, 2014

U.S. REOPENS DIPLOMATIC RELATIONS WITH CUBA

More than a quarter century after the Cold War closure of the U.S. Embassy in Havana, President Barack Obama announced that the United States and Cuba would begin normalizing relations. Though scarcely 100 miles of ocean separated them, the nations' once close bonds were broken by the 1959 revolution that installed a leftist government. When Premier Fidel Castro sought closer ties with the Soviet Union, the U.S. government responded with overthrow attempts; in 1962, the Soviets' plan to site missiles in Cuba brought the superpowers to the brink of nuclear crisis. Because 50 years of isolation "hasn't worked," Obama declared, "we will find new ways to cooperate."

901. MAY 20, 2015

JUSTICE DEPARTMENT FINES BANKS FIVE BILLION DOLLARS

On this day, the world's largest banks faced the music as the Justice Department, Federal Reserve, and other agencies settled charges of exchange rate manipulation with more than five billion dollars in fines. In what Attorney General Loretta E. Lynch called "brazenly illegal behavior," six banks were caught rigging both foreign exchange and interest rates for years via an online chat room, which netted them billions in profit. The banks included Barclays, J. P. Morgan, UBS—and Citicorp, which was hit with a $925 million fine (the largest of its kind) for violating the Sherman Antitrust Act, as well as a private class action settlement of $394 million.

902. MAY 20, 2015

***LATE SHOW*'S RECORD-SETTING DAVID LETTERMAN SIGNS OFF**

After 33 years of broadcasts filled with top 10 lists, hilarious interviews, and wacky stunts, David Letterman bid adieu to late-night television on this evening. With Tom Hanks and Bill Murray in the wings as guests and the Foo Fighters playing "Everlong," the longtime talk show host wrapped his final *Late Show*—and cemented his record as the longest-tenured late-night talk show host in American history. But it was not the end of celebrity interviews for the Indiana-bred comedian: A few years later, he would return to TV with *My Next Guest Needs No Introduction With David Letterman* on Netflix.

903. JUNE 22, 2015

OBESITY IN AMERICA REACHES EPIDEMIC PROPORTIONS

Scientific findings released on this day confirmed a global stereotype: that more than two-thirds of American adults were overweight or obese. Tracking a group of more than 15,000 men and women over the age of 25, researchers analyzed five years of data to reach the conclusion published in *The Journal of the American Medical Association*. They determined that disease screening and prevention would no longer be enough and urged the health care system to begin targeting those at risk of unhealthy weight with better diets, exercise, and treatment strategies. Changing American diets, however, proved challenging.

After 33 years of shows, all with Paul Shaffer as his bandleader, David Letterman ended his late-night television run on May 20, 2015.

WALTER ISAACSON

WALTER ISAACSON IS A JOURNALIST AND BIOGRAPHER OF BENJAMIN FRANKLIN, HENRY KISSINGER, ALBERT EINSTEIN, STEVE JOBS, JENNIFER DOUDNA, AND ELON MUSK. HE IS A PROFESSOR OF HISTORY AT TULANE UNIVERSITY.

DAVID M. RUBENSTEIN: What do you think is the most significant occurrence of the 21st century so far?

WALTER ISAACSON: The 20th century began as a century of physics, with everybody from Einstein to Marie Curie to Niels Bohr exploring how the atom works. That led us to invent everything from nuclear power to space travel to semiconductors. The second half of the 20th century was one of information technology: a digital revolution that came from the invention of computers, the microchip, the internet.

The first quarter of the 21st century has been a century of the life sciences, and especially of the genetic revolution. The century began in the year 2000, when the Human Genome Project mapped human DNA. And then, more important, when the discoverers of the gene-editing technology CRISPR—namely Jennifer Doudna, Jillian Banfield, and Emmanuelle Charpentier—figured out how we can edit our genes.

There are a lot of scientific revolutions going on [today]. But the first part of this century has set the groundwork for what will be our ability to rewrite our own genetic code. That's historic.

DMR: When you were the editor of *Time* magazine, there was an effort to name the most important person of the 20th century—I remember Mahatma Gandhi, FDR, and Albert Einstein. Ultimately, *Time* selected Einstein. If you were to be the editor of *Time* today, who would you select as the most important person of the 21st century?

WI: When we considered the Person of the Year for the 20th century, we decided that applying all the amazing advances in science to technology had been the most important achievement, and that they all stemmed from Einstein's papers from 1905 to 1919. So far, I think this has been a century of the life sciences, but there's been no great political or artistic leader. Sometimes in the arts, it takes a little while to figure out who this will be.

The other contenders for the field of science and tech are developing artificial intelligence. [Google DeepMind CEO] Demis Hassabis, who has done the most to bring us into the era of artificial intelligence, along with [Open AI CEO] Sam Altman and a few others, would so far be contenders for Person of the 21st Century.

DMR: Do you think any of the presidents in this century will be remembered 75 or 100 years from now for having done something transformative?

WI: Yes. I think Barack Obama is the historic figure who will be remembered—and not simply for whatever policies he did as president. When you take in the history of our nation for 250 years, all of it is grappling with race and the legacies of racial discrimination and enslavement. It was a historic step when Barack Obama became president. There was a coalescing then that [showed] we could be a future-looking country, a hopeful country.

Since then, the presidents haven't exactly been avatars of the future. A century from now, I don't think that there will be a lot of other presidents remembered in the first 25 years of this century.

DMR: Are there any books that have been written in the 21st century that you think will be remembered 20, 30, 40 years from now, because they've been so significant?
WI: I think Kazuo Ishiguro's books, such as *Klara and the Sun* and *Remains of the Day,* will be remembered as great literature.

DMR: The 20th century is often known as the American Century, because America became the largest economic, military, social, and cultural power in the world. Do you think the 21st century will be known 75 years from now as the Chinese Century, the Indian Century, or some other century?
WI: I believe our times are more defined by science and technology and the breakthroughs of innovation than they are by politics or political leaders. The question of the U.S. versus China—the main rival for who will control the century—is therefore much more dependent upon China's ability to develop both artificial intelligence and life sciences, as well as combining computational biology with the life sciences.

China has some advantages. They certainly have more data and can focus their investments better. But they also have a problem: the open system in the United States and Europe, where people can take risks and try things. That tends to lead to more innovation.

If the United States can keep its innovative edge, [I believe] it's America's century to lose, because we can out-innovate and out-discover other countries.

DMR: In 1776, the Declaration of Independence was signed. It contains a sentence that may be the most famous in the English language: "We hold these truths to be self-evident, that all men are created equal, that they are endowed by their Creator with certain unalienable Rights, that among these are Life, Liberty and the pursuit of Happiness." Do you think by the end of the 21st century, we might actually be in a position where we have equal opportunities and rights for everybody in the United States? Or will that still be another century away?
WI: The arc of progress doesn't always go smoothly. And we've gone through a period in the first 25 years of this century where things, I think, went in a problematic direction: Wealth disparities got bigger. The notion that "I subscribe to a free trade, free minds, free markets, free movement of people" all being wonderful for the economy—it didn't turn out to be great for a lot of people. They got left behind.

So, if we're going to fulfill the promise of our mission statement from the Declaration of Independence, we're going to have to figure out how to create more equal opportunity and bring more people in. That's been the course of American history as more and more people were embraced into the right to vote and to succeed.

DMR: Under the Constitution, the American president was considered to be the leader of the executive branch. But that was conceived as one part of three equal branches of the government. Do you think that by the end of the 21st century, the U.S. president will be as powerful as he is now? Do you see an evolution in which there's more or less power accruing to the presidency?
WI: For better and for worse, I see the American president as retaining more power. Because at a time when everything moves very fast—when technology and foreign policy and wars are happening at breakneck speed—it's hard for a legislative system to be the driving force, and even harder for a judicial system. Technology and the pace of history tend to favor a powerful executive branch.

DMR: You wrote a book about Elon Musk, who has said that people will be living on Mars at some point in the future. Do you think people will actually be living on Mars by the end of this century?

WI: Yes, I think by the end of this century, there will be human missions to Mars. I don't know about self-sustaining colonies. That's the hard part. It takes two or three years to get to Mars; it's not like going from Washington to New York. But I do think that by the end of the first half of the 21st century, we will have had a human mission to Mars.

DMR: Based on normal life expectancy, you and I may not be around to see that mission. Do you think by the end of the 21st century it will be possible for humans to regularly live to 100 years old and have the body and mental capabilities of somebody aged 40, 50, or 60?

WI: I think it's realistic. The advances in both genetic engineering and the ability to use RNA and DNA technology as messengers to tell our bodies what proteins to build with will solve a whole lot of issues that come with age, and regenerative biology will be able to do that.

I suspect, too, that we will see some breakthroughs in treating cancer, which has proved insidiously difficult. That doesn't mean we'll live to be 140 or 150. But living to age 100 in pretty good health could become something that's not exceptional but commonplace.

DMR: The human brain has an incredible memory for negative events. For example, I remember exactly where I was when 9/11 occurred. Would you say that's the event that, in the United States, is most likely for people to remember 50 or 75 years from now?

WI: Definitely. I think 9/11 is something we'll all remember. We thought we were at the end of history—that liberal democratic capitalism had triumphed over communism and, before that, Nazism. Suddenly we weren't having wars. And now, we realize that because of 9/11, major conflicts are still going to happen. It not only affected history—it's seared into our minds.

DMR: Most American cities today have a lot of things in common: a McDonald's, a Starbucks, the same supermarkets, and so forth. But there is one city that tries to be different than all others: New Orleans. Seventy-five years from now, will New Orleans still be different than other cities? Or will Creole culture have evaporated?

WI: It depends on the Corps of Engineers keeping the levees strong, because we know what happens when the levees break.

I think American culture, and to some extent global culture, went through a period of homogenization. You could call it the McDonald's-ing of various cities. In the 1940s after WWII and into the '50s, everything from urban renewal to interstate highways turned a lot of beautiful parts of cities into expressways and strip malls. Cities began to lose their identity. They didn't have the local department store and the haberdasher, like we have in New Orleans.

As I travel around the world now, there's this notion of people wanting distinctiveness, whether it be a craft beer or cocktail or an urban environment. That hunger has risen, and we're seeing the revitalization of old parts of downtowns, such as in Chattanooga or St. Louis. That's really important. Cities that keep their diversity, uniqueness, and heritage will benefit in the 21st century.

DMR: One of the great phenomena of the 21st century has been the concern around the world for climate change. By the end of the 21st century, the average temperature is estimated to be about four degrees Celsius above where it was at the beginning of the century. The goal is to get it back down to about 1.4 degrees Celsius. Do you think that's realistic?

WI: One way to get there is for all sides to embrace technology and innovation more. One of my frustrations with people who worry—correctly—about climate change is they flinch at finding new ways to do nuclear power.

Here in Louisiana, we're doing a lot of carbon capture. There are ways to reduce methane, which is probably one of the worst offenders, in the same way we can use technology to try to decarbonize our energy system. For too long, there were parts of the climate change movement that resisted technological fixes. Maybe I'm a technology

Science and technology breakthroughs, like this quantum computer, are a defining aspect of 21st-century America, says historian Isaacson.

optimist, but we have to rally behind technology as opposed to considering it a threat.

DMR: At the end of this century, which of your books do you think will be the one that people are still reading?
WI: [My biography of] Leonardo da Vinci. He was able to know everything about what was knowable at the time, and that made him one of the greatest engineers and artists in history.

DMR: What are your hopes for the future of America?
WI: I hope that the American democracy will still be following what you referenced at the beginning of this conversation: our mission statement that "we hold these truths to be self-evident, that all men created equal, that they are endowed by their Creator with certain unalienable Rights." That was written by three people: Thomas Jefferson, Benjamin Franklin, and John Adams.

If we're still following that mission, then Benjamin Franklin is the patron saint of a middle-class democracy that believes in the wisdom of the common person and the ingenuity of creating things, from lightning rods to clean-burning stoves to scientific discovery.

I hope he remains, at the end of this century, the patron saint he was at the birth of America.

904. JUNE 26, 2015

HIGH COURT AFFIRMS SAME-SEX COUPLES' RIGHT TO MARRY

On this day, same-sex couples from Ohio, Michigan, Kentucky, and Tennessee took their fight for marriage equality to the Supreme Court—and won. In a 5–4 ruling on the case *Obergefell* v. *Hodges*, state agencies that either banned or refused to recognize same-sex marriage were found to violate participants' constitutional rights. The high court declared that the 14th Amendment guarantees marriage as a fundamental liberty for all, and same-sex couples in all 50 states were granted full recognition and rights. James Obergefell, the plaintiff, originally filed the lawsuit against the state of Ohio to recognize his marriage, which was legally performed in Maryland, on his partner's death certificate.

905. AUGUST 6, 2015

MUSICAL *HAMILTON* TAKES THEATER WORLD BY STORM

As intent on success as its lead character—who vows, "I am not throwin' away my shot!"—the musical *Hamilton* opened on Broadway and skyrocketed to legend status. Playwright Lin-Manuel Miranda read Ron Chernow's prizewinning biography of American revolutionary Alexander Hamilton in 2007 and began to envision it rendered in rap and hip-hop. After selling out its months-long opening off-Broadway run, *Hamilton* found mass appeal and rave reviews on Broadway: "Yes, it really is that good," the *New York Times* observed.

American history set to hip-hop and rap, the musical *Hamilton* became a stage phenomenon, winning Tony and Grammy Awards and a Pulitzer Prize.

The show would go on to win the Pulitzer Prize for Drama and 11 Tony Awards; the cast album would top the Billboard rap music charts and snag a Grammy.

906. SEPTEMBER 14, 2015

SCIENTISTS DOCUMENT GRAVITATIONAL WAVES, WRINKLES IN SPACE-TIME

After nearly a century scanning the cosmos, scientists directly observed gravitational waves—wrinkles in the fabric of space-time itself—for the first time on this day. The waves were emitted as two black holes, one with 36 times the mass of the sun and the other with 29, and "spiraled into one another and eventually collided," space science expert Nadia Drake reported for *National Geographic*. "From roughly 1.3 billion light-years away, these waves spread like ripples in the cosmic pond and washed over Earth [today]." And though the waves aren't normally perceptible, these were measured in U.S. detectors in Louisiana and in Washington State.

THIS IS A STORY ABOUT AMERICA THEN, TOLD BY AMERICA NOW, AND WE WANT TO ELIMINATE ANY DISTANCE BETWEEN A CONTEMPORARY AUDIENCE AND THIS STORY.

Lin-Manuel Miranda, *on* Hamilton *(2015)*

907. SEPTEMBER 28, 2015

NASA DISCOVERS WATER ON MARS

Those looking for signs of life in the cosmos rejoiced when NASA indicated on this day that it had found evidence of water on Mars. A spacecraft known as the Mars Reconnaissance Orbiter, which launched in 2005, had captured images of streaks that scientists believed to have been formed by flowing water. Two years later, a new report would offer another possibility: that the dark lines, known as recurring slope lineae, may have been formed by sand. However, the report couldn't explain how the sand flows began and suggested that the process might have involved a small amount of water.

908. APRIL 1, 2016

NATIVE AMERICANS PROTEST AGAINST A PROPOSED OIL PIPELINE

Today marked a watershed moment in Native American history: the start of a protest movement that would inspire support throughout North America. Residents of the Standing Rock Sioux Tribe, along with hundreds of Native and non-Native allies, established a 50-acre camp on federal land to protest a proposed oil pipeline in North Dakota. The Dakota Access Pipeline would move 450,000 barrels daily 1,172 miles to Illinois, crossing an aquifer and the Missouri River; protesters asserted that the pipeline violated a treaty that guarantees the Standing Rock Sioux "undisturbed use and occupation" of the land. After seven months of protests, President Donald Trump issued an order expediting the pipeline's construction. Though tribes and environmental groups continue to object, the pipeline has been allowed to operate while an environmental impact statement is underway.

909. JUNE 28, 2016

JD VANCE BEGINS POLITICAL RISE WITH BLOCKBUSTER MEMOIR *HILLBILLY ELEGY*

Published on this day, JD Vance's book *Hillbilly Elegy* is "what a Horatio Alger story reads like in 21st century America," a *Washington Post* editor observed. Vance's memoir described his Ohio upbringing by his grandparents in America's Rust Belt, his father absent and his mother grappling with addiction. He escaped that life by joining the Marines, getting a Yale Law School degree, then working as a lawyer, venture capitalist, and commentator on the cultural and political phenomena that fueled Donald Trump's ascendance. Notoriety from the best-selling book (and its 2020 film adaptation) helped fuel Vance's rise to U.S. senator from Ohio in 2022 and subsequent selection as Trump's second-term vice president.

910. JULY 6, 2016

POKÉMON GO SOARS INTO HISTORY

The augmented reality game Pokémon Go released in America on this day, luring thousands outdoors. Originally conceived as an April Fools' Day prank, the mobile game lets players capture virtual Pokémon characters they see superimposed upon the real world. The app was downloaded more times in its first week than any in Apple history, roping in one in 10 Americans and raking in more than six million dollars a day from in-app purchases. Before long, Hillary Clinton would talk about Pokémon Go on the campaign trail and Justin Bieber would be spotted playing it in Central Park—firmly establishing the game in the country's zeitgeist.

911. AUGUST 2, 2016

"MILLENNIAL PINK" BECOMES A THING

The latest omnipresent, on-trend color is "ironic pink, pink without the sugary prettiness," fashion writer Véronique Hyland explained in a blog essay published on this day. It expresses the "ambivalent girliness" among the era's 20- to 35-year-olds who were "raised to distrust pink," Hyland wrote—so she labeled the color "millennial pink." A muted, salmon tone that was a far cry from the bubblegum-and-Barbie pinks of the past, it was subsequently splashed across clothes and cosmetics, interiors and electronics, publications and packaging. The color arbiters at Pantone named a version of millennial pink, Rose Quartz, as the 2016 Color of the Year—and though the trend cooled, the shade lingered as a flattering option for home goods and clothing.

912. AUGUST 25, 2016

U.S. NATIONAL PARK SERVICE TURNS 100

One hundred years ago on this day, President Woodrow Wilson signed an act creating the National Park Service, charging the agency with protecting 35 national parks and monuments "by such means as will leave them unimpaired for the enjoyment of future generations." As the system celebrated its centennial, American parks stretched across 84 million acres; during the anniversary year, a record 331 million visitors stretched their legs and snapped their photographs in protected nature. The concept of a national park, which began with the conservation of Yellowstone in 1872, sparked a movement to preserve land and wildlife that would take root across America and the world.

A speech by President Barack Obama at Yosemite National Park was among events marking the 100th anniversary of the U.S. National Park Service.

913. AUGUST 26, 2016

FOOTBALL STAR COLIN KAEPERNICK TAKES A KNEE

Sparking a divisive period in National Football League history, San Francisco 49ers quarterback Colin Kaepernick stayed seated during the national anthem in protest of police brutality and racial injustice. At subsequent games, he knelt on the sidelines during the anthem, and other players joined him in taking a knee. The protests drew both positive and negative responses from players, owners, and fans, until the NFL eliminated the issue by having players enter the stadium after the anthem played. After his season of protests, Kaepernick became a free agent but wasn't acquired by another NFL team.

914. OCTOBER 13, 2016

BOB DYLAN WINS THE NOBEL PRIZE IN LITERATURE

On this day, the exalted list of Americans who have won the Nobel Prize in Literature—Ernest Hemingway, John Steinbeck, Toni Morrison, William Faulkner, Saul Bellow, and Pearl S. Buck—added its first musician. The Nobel Foundation announced that its 2016 prize was awarded to singer-songwriter Bob Dylan "for having created new poetic expressions within the great American song tradition." During more than a half century as a recording artist, Dylan became known as "the Bard" for his poetic, socially conscious

Land occupied by humans for 13,000 years in what is now Utah was designated for preservation as Bears Ears National Monument.

lyrics. Among the hundreds of songs he wrote, classics such as "Blowin' in the Wind" and "The Times They Are a-Changin'" made him the voice of a generation.

915. NOVEMBER 3, 2016

CUBS TRIUMPH AFTER MORE THAN A CENTURY WITHOUT A WORLD SERIES WIN

Each year, the World Series trophy goes to one baseball team—and in the wee morning hours on this day (the game began on November 2 at 8:02 p.m.), it went to a ball club that had spent 108 years without it. Often ridiculed for the longest drought in World Series history, the Chicago Cubs beat the Cleveland Indians in the deciding seventh game of the series. Excitement built when the game was delayed by rain after the ninth inning ended in a 6–6 tie. But the Cubbies gave fans their long-awaited championship in dramatic fashion: with an 8–7 victory in the 10th inning. The win broke the curse that had gripped the Cubs since their series win in 1908 against the Detroit Tigers.

916. DECEMBER 14, 2016

RECORD DATA HACK AFFECTS THREE BILLION YAHOO ACCOUNTS

It would be known as the worst data breach in U.S. history: Yahoo! Inc. revealed on this day that the private information of a billion-some users had been stolen by a team of Russian hackers. Though Yahoo! Inc. was only now disclosing the cyberattacks, it had discovered them more than two years prior to the announcement—a revelation that landed the company in hot water. And a few months later, investigations would reveal that, in fact, all three billion Yahoo accounts had been compromised. The hack resulted in dozens of class action lawsuits and a $35 million fine from the Securities and Exchange Commission.

917. DECEMBER 28, 2016

BEARS EARS NATIONAL MONUMENT PROTECTS HALLOWED TRIBAL LAND

On this day, President Barack Obama announced the establishment of a 1.35-million-acre protected area in southeastern Utah, to be known as Bears Ears National Monument. For more than a century, tribal nations, led by the Hopi, Navajo, Ute, and Zuni peoples, had sought protected status for the area to conserve the canyons, desert mesas, mountains, and monoliths along with archaeological evidence of 13,000 years of human occupation. In 2017, President Donald Trump would reduce the designated monument lands by more than 1.1 million acres; President Joe Biden would reverse that action in 2021, only to have second-term President Trump vow in 2025 to reimpose his original cuts.

918. MAY 21, 2017

CELEBRATED CIRCUS FOLDS ... FOR A WHILE

The lions took their final bow on this evening as the Ringling Bros. and Barnum & Bailey Circus ended its high-flying run. In 1871, the father of American entertainment launched the show as P. T. Barnum's Grand Traveling Museum, Menagerie, Caravan & Hippodrome. But 146 years later, in an era of TV and video games, plummeting ticket sales made it difficult to maintain a traveling circus, which moved with 500 crew and 100 animals on trains a mile long. At the final show, in Uniondale, New York, fans told reporters they dreamed of a future comeback. They would get their wish in 2023, when an animal-free version of the circus relaunched.

919. JUNE 1, 2017

PRESIDENT DONALD TRUMP ANNOUNCES U.S. WITHDRAWAL FROM INTERNATIONAL CLIMATE ACCORD

Two years after the groundbreaking Paris Agreement tied together nations in a pledge to combat climate change, President Trump announced that the U.S. would withdraw from the deal. The agreement sought to limit the global temperature rise by having countries pledge reductions in greenhouse gas emissions. Adopted by 195 parties in 2015, it went into force after 55 nations representing at least 55 percent of global emissions ratified it. Under accord rules, Trump's announced withdrawal wouldn't take effect for three years; in 2020, the U.S. became the first nation to pull out of the agreement.

Climber Alex Honnold made a dramatic free solo—an ascent without ropes or safety gear—of Yosemite National Park's El Capitan formation.

920. JUNE 3, 2017

ALEX HONNOLD MAKES UNPRECEDENTED YOSEMITE CLIMB

As a shy youth in California, Alex Honnold often went free soloing—climbing rock faces without the aid of ropes, belays, or safety equipment—because it was easier than finding a climbing buddy. He became a top competitive climber, received sponsorships and set records in the sport, traveling among climb sites to repeatedly practice the most challenging routes. On this day, at age 31, Honnold achieved what *National Geographic* deemed "may be the greatest feat of pure rock climbing in the history of the sport": In just under four hours, he free soloed the 3,000-foot Freerider route on the El Capitan formation in Yosemite National Park.

921. JULY 27, 2017

JOHN MCCAIN DEFIES PARTY ON OBAMACARE VOTE

On this day, Arizona Republican Senator John McCain cemented his national image as a maverick by casting a deciding vote against his party's effort to repeal the Affordable Care Act, otherwise known as Obamacare. McCain said he voted against the measure because he doubted it would "actually reform our health care system and deliver affordable, quality health care." A 30-year Senate veteran and his party's 2008 presidential nominee, McCain was a Navy pilot who was shot down over Vietnam and tortured while a prisoner of war. To cast the Obamacare vote, he returned to work shortly after undergoing surgery for a brain tumor; he died from complications of brain cancer on August 25, 2018.

922. AUGUST 12, 2017

NEO-NAZI KILLS ONE, INJURES DOZENS AS WHITE NATIONALISTS PROTEST

Ku Klux Klansmen, neo-Nazis, and other white supremacists—under the banner of "Unite the Right"—staged protests in Charlottesville, Virginia, on this day after the city voted to remove a statue of Confederate general Robert E. Lee. As they marched through the University of Virginia campus wielding torches and shouting racist chants, they were met by anti-racist counterprotesters; a neo-Nazi drove his car into a group of them, killing one and injuring dozens more. President Donald Trump's response would be questioned after he said of the instigators, "You had some very bad people in that group. But you also had people that were very fine people on both sides."

THERE'S A CONSTANT TENSION IN CLIMBING—AND REALLY ALL EXPLORATION—BETWEEN PUSHING YOURSELF INTO THE UNKNOWN BUT TRYING NOT TO PUSH TOO FAR.

Alex Honnold *(2015)*

923. SEPTEMBER 20, 2017

MONSTER HURRICANE PLUNGES PUERTO RICO INTO RECORD POWER OUTAGE

An African wave moving across the Atlantic Ocean became a tropical storm and then a hurricane, making landfall in Puerto Rico early on this morning. At Category 5, Hurricane Maria battered the island nation with winds, rain, and flooding that produced catastrophic damage. Nearly all residents lost electricity, and some wouldn't regain power for nearly a year: the longest blackout in U.S. history. An estimated 4,645 people were killed, eclipsing the death toll from Hurricane Katrina 12 years earlier. By the end of 2017, a total $306 billion in damages and 4.7 million victims requiring aid would make this the costliest year yet for weather disasters.

924. OCTOBER 5, 2017

SEXUAL ASSAULT CHARGES SINK MOVIE IMPRESARIO HARVEY WEINSTEIN, FUEL #METOO

The explosive *New York Times* story headlined "Harvey Weinstein Paid Off Sexual Harassment Accusers for Decades" reported on this day that powerful Hollywood producer Weinstein had reached at least eight settlements with women who accused him of sexual misconduct. The story would spark Weinstein's own company to fire him within a few days, as scores of women came forward with similar accounts. Five days after the *Times* report, the *New Yorker* published Ronan Farrow's article "From Aggressive Overtures to Sexual Assault: Harvey Weinstein's Accusers Tell Their Stories"—and the #MeToo movement shifted into overdrive.

925. OCTOBER 19, 2017

SOLAR SYSTEM RECEIVES FIRST VISITOR FROM ANOTHER STAR

'Oumuamua, the first confirmed object to visit Earth's solar system, was discovered on this day by Hawaii's Pan-STARRS1 telescope, which observed it approaching from the direction of the northern constellation Lyra. NASA described it as "a rocky, cigar-shaped object with a somewhat reddish hue," about a quarter mile long. The name chosen by its discoverers—pronounced oh MOO-uh MOO-uh—means "a messenger from afar arriving first" in Hawaiian. The object had been traveling through the Milky Way for hundreds of millions of years before entering our solar system, and astronomers noted that no other known asteroid or comet varied so dramatically in brightness. NASA hoped 'Oumuamua could offer clues into how other solar systems formed.

926. OCTOBER 26, 2017

U.S. PRONOUNCES OPIOID USE AND OVERDOSES A PUBLIC HEALTH CRISIS

On this day, President Donald Trump declared the opioid crisis a nationwide public health emergency. For 2017, the opioid-related overdose death rate for the U.S. population was 14.9 per 100,000 people—a quadruple increase from the 1999 rate of 2.9 deaths per 100,000. For Americans under 50, drug overdoses became the leading cause of death. And opioid addiction had become "an escalating public health crisis ... made more deadly by an influx of illicitly manufactured fentanyl and similar drugs," the *New York Times* reported. Under a national emergency declaration, federal funds could be allocated to combat opioid abuse, though critics said that the need outweighed the commitment.

927. JANUARY 24, 2018

COURT SENTENCES U.S. GYMNASTICS TEAM DOCTOR FOR MULTIPLE SEXUAL ASSAULTS

Two years after a former gymnast accused USA Gymnastics team doctor Larry Nassar of sexual assault—and more than 265 women and girls echoed her claims—Nassar was sentenced to 40 to 175 years in federal prison on this day. In court, victim after victim detailed the abuse, which Judge Rosemarie Aquilina described as "calculated" and "manipulative." Nassar refused to admit guilt, but more than $138 million in damages was paid to his victims. Three months later, comedian Bill Cosby was found guilty of aggravated indecent assault of Andrea Constand, one of dozens of women who'd come forward since 2014 claiming Cosby sexually assaulted them. His three- to ten-year prison sentence was later overturned on due process violations.

928. MARCH 17, 2018

ANALYTICS FIRM UTILIZES DATA FROM LARGEST EVER FACEBOOK LEAK

Facebook user data was harvested and profiled by a firm called Cambridge Analytica and used by U.S. and U.K. political operations, according to an investigation revealed by the

Guardian, the *Observer,* and the *New York Times* on this day. Then GOP candidate Donald Trump's election team exploited the data, as did the Brexit campaign in Britain, which resulted in the U.K. separating from the European Union. Christopher Wylie, a whistle-blower inside Cambridge Analytica, revealed how the system was built to target users with customized political ads. Tens of millions of Facebook profiles were subject to the collection—the largest data leak in Facebook history—but some candidates promoted in political ads lost while some won, meaning the firm's data use had mixed impact at best.

929. APRIL 16, 2018

KENDRICK LAMAR BECOMES FIRST RAP ARTIST TO WIN THE PULITZER PRIZE

On this day, the Pulitzer Prize for Music was bestowed upon an artist outside of jazz and classical music for the first time, as rapper Kendrick Lamar received the award for his 2017 album *DAMN.* The Pulitzer announcement praised the album—featuring tracks like "Humble" and "Loyalty"—as "a virtuosic song collection unified by its vernacular authenticity and rhythmic dynamism that … [captures] the complexity of modern African-American life." Lamar, who has been called the poet laureate of hip-hop, said in a *Vanity Fair* interview that receiving "the recognition that it deserves as a true art form" is something that "should have happened with hip-hop a long time ago."

Receiving the Pulitzer Prize for Music made rapper Kendrick Lamar the first artist outside the jazz and classical genres to claim this honor.

930. MAY 8, 2018

PRESIDENT TRUMP WITHDRAWS U.S. FROM IRAN NUCLEAR ARMS PACT

Calling it a deal "that should have never, ever been made," President Donald Trump pulled the United States out of a breakthrough nuclear agreement with Iran on this day. In 2015, President Barack Obama had committed to the agreement alongside the United Kingdom, France, and Germany; the deal waived oil and banking sanctions in exchange for Iran limiting its nuclear program. After Trump announced the withdrawal, politicians on both sides of the aisle criticized the action; Iranian president Hassan Rouhani warned that his country would "start enriching uranium more than before" if the deal collapsed globally. The Biden administration tried unsuccessfully to revive the treaty during its single term before Trump was voted back to the White House in 2024.

931. JUNE 18, 2018

GORILLA WHO PROVED INTERSPECIES COMMUNICATION POSSIBLE PASSES AWAY

After revolutionizing human understanding of great ape communication, emotions, and thoughts, Koko the lowland gorilla died in her sleep on this day at age 46. One of the

The rise of social media app TikTok has allowed millions of influencers to get their messages to the masses by posting short videos.

most famous animals in the world for decades, Koko was a year old when a Ph.D. student named Francine Patterson taught her sign language. Thus began a crucial study of inter-species communication: Over her lifetime, Koko learned 1,000 signs and understood 2,000 words in English. She appeared twice on the cover of *National Geographic* magazine; in 1985, when reporter Cynthia Gorney asked Koko where gorillas go when they die, Koko signed: "Comfortable hole bye."

932. SEPTEMBER 29, 2018

TIKTOK TAKES OFF

The international social media phenomenon began on this day when a Chinese company called ByteDance merged its video app TikTok with a new acquisition: Musical.ly, a social media start-up that helped users create short videos. Scarcely two months later, the new and improved TikTok overtook Facebook, Instagram, YouTube, and Snapchat as the most downloaded app in America. Released to the international market in 2017 and the U.S. market earlier this year, TikTok quickly became the place for millions of people to get their news. Its influence in American politics sparked widespread debate about its power to manipulate, along with threats to ban it. Though President Donald Trump once had favored the ban, upon his 2024 reelection he sought ways to keep TikTok operating in the U.S.

WE SHARED SOMETHING EXTRAORDINARY: LAUGHTER.

Robin Williams, *comedian, on his interaction with Koko (2001)*

933. OCTOBER 2, 2018

SAUDI ARABIA ADMITS GUILT IN MURDER OF U.S. JOURNALIST

On this day, *Washington Post* columnist Jamal Khashoggi, an outspoken critic of Saudi Crown Prince Mohammed bin Salman, entered the Saudi Arabian consulate in Istanbul to obtain a marriage document and never emerged. The Saudi government claimed Khashoggi left the building through a back door, but the *Post* obtained intelligence showing that Saudi officials planned to abduct the journalist, who had moved to the U.S. to be able to write freely. Ultimately, Saudi Arabia confirmed Khashoggi was murdered and dismembered in the consulate, and prosecuted 11 agents it deemed responsible. In 2021, a U.S. intelligence report would conclude the prince approved plans to "capture or kill" Khashoggi.

934. OCTOBER 27, 2018

SYNAGOGUE SHOOTING BECOMES DEADLIEST ANTI-SEMITIC ATTACK IN THE U.S.

On this day, a gunman opened fire on worshippers at a Pittsburgh synagogue, killing 11 people and injuring seven in the deadliest anti-Semitic attack in American history. The gunman, Robert Bowers, a 50-year-old truck driver who posted white supremacist diatribes online, only stopped shooting after he ran out of ammunition. His victims, gathered at the Tree of Life synagogue for Shabbat prayers, included a 97-year-old woman and developmentally disabled brothers. The gunman would be found guilty of 63 federal charges and sentenced to death in 2023.

935. JANUARY 25, 2019

LONGEST GOVERNMENT SHUTDOWN TO DATE COMES TO AN END

Furloughed federal employees rejoiced with the American public as the longest government shutdown in history lifted after 35 days. The duration exceeded all 21 previous government shutdowns, including the former record holder of 21 days in the mid-1990s under President Bill Clinton. The first government shutdown occurred in 1977 over disagreements on whether Medicaid could be used to pay for abortion services. Shutdowns became more frequent and severe, starting in the 1980s with a ruling from the U.S. attorney general that barred agencies from spending unless they had appropriations passed by Congress, which couldn't happen while the government was closed.

936. MARCH 5, 2019

REALITY TV STAR KYLIE JENNER STRIKES IT RICH

Soon after rolling out a new line of lipsticks at malls across America, 21-year-old Kylie Jenner, daughter of reality maven Kris Kardashian and Caitlyn Jenner (formerly the Olympic gold medalist Bruce Jenner), became the world's youngest self-made billionaire on this day, beating out Facebook creator Mark Zuckerberg by two years (he hit the milestone at age 23). Kylie skyrocketed past her reality television family members—many of them already moguls, based on the success of their hit show *Keeping Up With the Kardashians*—when her company, Kylie Cosmetics, became worth at least $900 million with the launch of her signature lip kits. But later reporting by *Forbes* would question whether Kylie Jenner, like other fortune seekers, had inflated her worth to claim the title.

Thanks to sales of her Kylie Cosmetics makeup line, reality TV star Kylie Jenner claimed the title of world's youngest self-made billionaire at age 21.

937. MARCH 12, 2019

OPERATION VARSITY BLUES REVEALS ADMISSIONS BRIBERY AT TOP UNIVERSITIES

Money talks at elite education institutions: That's the lesson Americans learned when on this day the Justice Department unsealed an investigation, known as "Operation Varsity Blues," into bribes given by wealthy parents to help their children win spots at top schools. The case revolved around William Singer, president of Edge College and Career Network, who paid off standardized test administrators, athletics officials, and coaches to gain entry for privileged students at schools including Yale University, Georgetown University, Stanford University, and the University of California, Los Angeles. Fifty people, including such celebrities as actor Felicity Huffman, were charged in what would become the largest ever college admissions case.

938. MARCH 19, 2019

RARE "SUPERBLOOM" PAINTS THE CALIFORNIA DESERT

In a mass event that local officials dubbed Poppypalooza, hordes of tourists flocked to a usually barren California desert on this day to see hills blanketed with poppies in a once-

in-a-lifetime "superbloom." Desert flowers often spring to life after wet winters, but not in recent memory had such a spectacularly colorful sight consumed Walker Canyon. So many visitors poured into the region that weekend—as many as 150,000—that the nearby city tried to close the freeway exit ramp to prevent overcrowding. It didn't work. Everyone wanted a view, and even satellites hovering 480 miles above Earth's surface captured images of the orange-speckled desert.

A profusion of poppies—a rare "superbloom" in the California desert in 2019 after an extra-wet winter—was visible to orbiting satellites.

939. MARCH 31, 2019

IN BEND, OREGON, RETAIL OUTLET BECOMES THE WORLD'S LAST BLOCKBUSTER STORE

When a Blockbuster video rental store in Australia closed its doors at the end of this day, it left just one remaining outlet in the world: a location in Bend, Oregon. The iconic blue-and-yellow chain was once the world's largest video rental outlet, but it fell victim to the era of streaming services. It filed for bankruptcy in 2010, and before long only a few franchises remained. In Bend, a snowy vacation town in eastern Oregon, the family-operated store continues to offer video rentals to its loyal and nostalgic customer base and also indulges tourists stopping in for a novelty photo or souvenir.

SPOTLIGHT

ACTIVISM

ON ISSUES FROM climate change to LGBTQ rights, in movements from #BlackLivesMatter to #OccupyWallStreet, 21st-century activists used social media for much more than posting personal updates. Increasingly, social media platforms became delivery channels for mass protest messages and forums for strategizing and organizing. The approach has been called "hashtag activism" or, more pejoratively, "slacktivism."

Skeptics questioned whether online actions could promote social change as effectively as in-person, frontline actions; a 2010 essay by the *New Yorker*'s Malcolm Gladwell described the connections made on social media as "weak ties" that "seldom lead to high-risk activism." Challenging that view, historians have argued that social media has played a vital role in some of the 21st century's most consequential activism events. In other nations, these included the Arab Spring (2010–13) uprisings throughout the Middle East and North Africa, and the Umbrella Revolution—79 days of pro-democracy protests that drew 100,000 supporters to Hong Kong's streets (2014). In the United States, social media contributed significantly to the #BlackLivesMatter movement, sparked by the 2013 acquittal of a neighborhood watch volunteer in the shooting death of Black teen Trayvon Martin; the #OccupyWallStreet movement (two months of demonstrations in Manhattan and elsewhere protesting economic inequality and corporate influence in politics in 2011); and the Women's March for social change (2017), which exploded from one Facebook suggestion into more than 670 demonstrations worldwide, drawing an estimated five million participants.

LGBTQ pride, embodied in this huge flag at a San Francisco parade, was among rights movements that proliferated in the early 21st century.

GOD MAY BE IN THE DETAILS, BUT THE GODDESS IS IN CONNECTIONS.

Gloria Steinem, *during her Women's March speech (2017)*

940. APRIL 10, 2019

TELESCOPE NETWORK CAPTURES FIRST IMAGE OF A BLACK HOLE

It was as fiery and forbidding as you'd imagine: The first image of a black hole appeared on this day as a glowing orange doughnut surrounded by darkness in galaxy M87, 55 million light-years from Earth. The orange glow is derived from hot gas swirling around the black hole, which has such a strong gravitational pull that everything around it, including light, is sucked in. Black holes remain a mystery to scientists, who believe they're formed when a massive star is finished evolving. The picture was captured by the Event Horizon Telescope, an international collaboration that links existing telescopes and radio dishes around the globe.

The first image of a black hole, captured by the Event Horizon Telescope, shows a ring of glowing, hot gas—the only nearby light not consumed by its gravitational pull.

941. APRIL 28, 2019

NEW DIVE TO OCEAN'S DEEPEST POINT BREAKS RECORD

At the bottom of the Pacific Ocean—deeper than humans had ventured alone before—something caught Victor Vescovo's eye: a plastic bag. Over two dives, one on this day and the next on May 1, Vescovo returned to the surface in a submersible craft and reported his findings from the Mariana Trench: four new species, but also man-made trash, including the bag and candy wrappers. His first dive reached depths of 35,856 feet, and the second, 35,826. As deep as Mount Everest is tall, the Mariana Trench is a tantalizing target for underwater explorers; Vescovo's visit broke the record for deepest solo dive previously held by *Titanic* director James Cameron. It was part of a mission to conduct detailed sonar mapping at the five deepest spots in Earth's oceans.

942. MAY 22, 2019

SLAVE WRECKS PROJECT UNEARTHS SHIP THAT CARRIED ENSLAVED AFRICANS TO THE U.S.

In 1860, a wooden schooner called the *Clotilda* brought 110 enslaved Africans to Mobile Bay, Alabama, where they'd be smuggled onto land and the ship would be burned and sunk. For 52 years, it had been illegal to bring enslaved people into the United States, and this would be the last known transport of its kind. Descendants of the *Clotilda*'s captives—many still living in the Alabama community called Africatown—had long dreamed of finding the evidence of their origin story. On this day, the discovery of the ship's remains was announced by a network of researchers and institutions known as the Slave Wrecks Project.

943. JUNE 20, 2019

COLLEGE-EDUCATED U.S. WOMEN MAKE NOTABLE GAINS IN THE WORKFORCE

On this day, it was reported that women had become the majority of America's college-educated workforce for the first time, representing 50.2 percent—an increase from 45.1 percent in 2000. (They would go on to surpass men overall by 2022.) For nearly 30 years, women had been the majority of college-educated adults but didn't enter the workforce

A cutaway depiction of the schooner *Clotilda* shows where enslaved Africans were held en route to Alabama, the last known transport of its kind.

at the same rate as men. As this shifted, earnings rose significantly for women with a college education. Despite these strides, and with a dip during the COVID-19 pandemic, the U.S. Bureau of Labor Statistics projected women would make up slightly less than half the overall workforce through 2032.

944. JULY 17, 2019

DRUG KINGPIN "EL CHAPO" IS BROUGHT TO JUSTICE IN U.S. COURT

On this day in a Brooklyn courtroom, a life-plus-30-years prison sentence ended the bloody career of an infamous Mexican drug kingpin. Joaquín Guzmán Loera, also known as "El Chapo"—head of a cartel reputed to have brought more than a million kilograms of illegal drugs into the United States—was found guilty on 10 firearms, money laundering, and drug trafficking charges. On the lam from Mexican and American authorities for nearly 15 years, he was apprehended in a blaze of gunfire in 2016. A sensational trial, in which 56 witnesses described him as a brutal killer, lifted the veil on the inner workings of Mexico's Sinaloa cartel and earned Guzmán incarceration in a Colorado supermaximum security prison.

945. SEPTEMBER 20, 2019

MORE THAN SEVEN MILLION GLOBAL CITIZENS DEMAND CLIMATE CHANGE MITIGATION

Beginning on this day, the largest climate mobilization in history brought an estimated 7.6 million people into the streets for a week in nations around the world, demanding change to slow the planet's warming. The march was organized by the youth organization Fridays for Future, founded by 15-year-old Greta Thunberg, who gained global recognition for her climate protests outside the Swedish Parliament. Strikes hit companies across the world, and websites went dark to support the protesters, who demanded a transition to 100 percent renewable energy by 2030 and a halt to all fossil fuel extractions.

946. NOVEMBER 17, 2019

FIRST SIGNS OF A PERNICIOUS VIRUS APPEAR

In China's Hubei Province, local newspapers began carrying reports on this day of a mysterious new virus. It took another month for the first cases of SARS-CoV-2, or COVID-19, to be identified in hospitalized patients in the city of Wuhan. Years later, when researchers at the University of California San Diego mapped out early cases, they determined that those first documented cases in early November did not originate at a seafood market as originally believed. The researchers suggested instead that COVID-19 became a global epidemic due to its wide dispersal into urban areas where transmission was easier.

947. DECEMBER 18, 2019

CONGRESS VOTES AGAINST IMPEACHING TRUMP FOR ABUSE OF POWER

During a tense session of Congress on this day, the U.S. House of Representatives issued two articles of impeachment against President Donald Trump for abuse of power and obstruction of Congress. Specifically, Trump was accused of conspiring with foreign governments to help his 2020 reelection campaign and then obstructing lawmakers' investigations into his actions by ignoring subpoenas for testimony and documents. The impeachment trial the following year would begin on January 16 and end on February 5 with Trump's acquittal in the Senate. Trump was only the third U.S. president to be impeached—and in 2021, he'd make history again as the only U.S. president to be impeached twice—this time, for fomenting the January 6 siege of the U.S. Capitol.

948. JANUARY 26, 2020

BASKETBALL GREAT KOBE BRYANT AND HIS DAUGHTER DIE IN CRASH

National Basketball Association superstar Kobe Bryant and his 13-year-old daughter, Gianna, were among nine people killed on this day when the helicopter carrying them crashed into a Southern California hillside in dense fog. Bryant was 41. Before retiring in 2016, he had played his whole NBA career with the Los Angeles Lakers and was the team's all-time leading scorer and the third leading scorer in NBA history. A charismatic and competitive figure, he racked up All-Star and Most Valuable Player honors and helped the Lakers win five NBA championships in the 2000s. In retirement, he promoted women's sports, mentored athletes, and ran a basketball academy about 20 minutes from where the helicopter crashed.

949. MARCH 13, 2020

COVID-19 SPURS A DEADLY GLOBAL PANDEMIC

Two days after the World Health Organization (WHO) declared COVID-19 a pandemic, President Donald Trump declared the virus outbreak a national emergency on this day. Within a week, COVID-19 cases were confirmed in all 50 states, and governors of 27 states activated the National Guard to assist with response. Citing risks of COVID's spread, Trump invoked a U.S. Code provision that stopped asylum-seeking migrants at the U.S.-Mexico border. It would be eight months before the FDA would authorize the use of a COVID-19 vaccine by Americans aged 16 and older. By then, WHO reported more than 61 million cases and more than 1.4 million deaths from the virus. Over the course of the pandemic, WHO reported, some 7.1 million people worldwide would succumb.

A composite of 30 hours of photos shows some 670,000 flags displayed on the National Mall—each representing a U.S. death from COVID-19.

950. MARCH 15, 2020

HYBRID AND REMOTE OFFICE SCHEDULES USHER IN A NEW WAY OF WORKING

Starting on this day, 42 U.S. states and territories issued stay-at-home orders aimed at curbing the spread of COVID-19. Those whose jobs could be done remotely abruptly shifted to telework—an occupational sea change that has persisted. A Pew Research Center survey found that before the coronavirus outbreak, only 14 percent of people with "teleworkable" jobs worked from home all the time—but by October 2020, 55 percent were doing just that. By October 2024, though COVID-19 was largely controlled, 32 percent still were teleworking full-time, while 43 percent had hybrid schedules, working partly at home and partly in reopened workplaces. But by 2025, 75 percent of workers reported that their employers required them to work on-site more often (compared to 63 percent in 2023).

951. MAY 25, 2020

GEORGE FLOYD'S DEATH AT POLICE HANDS IGNITES NATIONWIDE PROTESTS

On this day, police were called to a Minneapolis convenience store, where the clerk claimed that customer George Floyd, 46, had passed a counterfeit $20. When Floyd resisted

After George Floyd died with a police officer kneeling on his neck, protests erupted worldwide, further empowering the Black Lives Matter movement.

entering the police car, officers tackled him to the ground. One of the group, Derek Chauvin, pressed his knee on Floyd's neck as the prone man repeated, "I can't breathe." Bystander and body cam videos recorded Chauvin kneeling on Floyd's neck for almost nine and a half minutes as Floyd fell still. Chauvin would be convicted on murder charges and imprisoned with a projected 2037 release date. Floyd's death threw light on other recent police-involved killings of Black people—Ahmaud Arbery in Georgia, Breonna Taylor in Kentucky—and sparked protests worldwide, powering the growth of the Black Lives Matter (BLM) movement.

952. AUGUST 21, 2020

DNA TRACKING LEADS TO APPREHENSION AND SENTENCING OF A FUGITIVE MASS KILLER

On this day, the murderer and rapist known as the Golden State Killer was sentenced to 26 life prison sentences, brought to justice using DNA evidence after he had evaded capture for four decades. In a plea deal to avoid the death penalty, former California police officer Joseph James DeAngelo pleaded guilty to 13 murders and more than 50 charges related to rapes; prosecutors maintained that this was only part of the toll of DeAngelo's "simply staggering" violent crime spree, involving 87 victims across 11 California counties between 1975 and 1986. The long-cold case was cracked with an approach called genetic genealogy: using crime-scene DNA to create a profile on public genealogy databases, where family tree matches might lead to potential suspects.

WHAT BEGAN AS A CURIOSITY-DRIVEN INVESTIGATION MORPHED INTO A PROJECT THAT HAD MUCH BROADER IMPLICATIONS.

Jennifer Doudna, *on CRISPR technology (2020)*

953. OCTOBER 7, 2020

JENNIFER DOUDNA SHARES NOBEL PRIZE FOR GENE-EDITING METHOD

American biochemistry professor Jennifer Doudna and French biochemist Emmanuelle Charpentier were announced as the winners of the 2020 Nobel Prize in Chemistry for their revolutionary work in genome editing. Doudna had extensively studied a molecular sequence known as clustered regularly interspaced short palindromic repeats—CRISPR—when she and Charpentier partnered on research. In 2012, they reported that combining CRISPR with an enzyme, Cas9, created a precision system for manipulating DNA strands—essentially rewriting the genetic code within the cells of animals and plants. The gene-editing technique would be widely hailed as the most significant scientific breakthrough in a century.

954. OCTOBER 8, 2020

EXTREMISTS AIM TO KIDNAP MICHIGAN GOVERNOR

On this day, Michigan's attorney general disclosed that a group of right-wing extremists had conspired to kidnap Governor Gretchen Whitmer and stage violent acts aimed at sparking "civil war." As Michigan's COVID-19 rates rose in early 2020, Whitmer ordered a lockdown and called for more federal help; President Donald Trump rebuked her publicly, and the extremists stepped up plans to attack her. Some joined armed protesters that stormed Michigan's capitol in April, but Whitmer wasn't there. By fall, the would-be kidnappers were casing Whitmer's vacation home—but the FBI uncovered the plot and arrested more than a dozen conspirators.

955. NOVEMBER 7, 2020

INCUMBENT DONALD TRUMP IS OUSTED BY JOE BIDEN IN A CLOSE VOTE

The 2020 presidential contest was so close that it took until today—four days after the election—for the Democratic ticket of Senators Joe Biden and Kamala Harris to secure the 270 electoral votes needed for victory over the incumbent Republicans, President Donald Trump and Vice President Mike Pence. During the campaign, political analysts questioned Biden's age (77) and fitness for the job, as well as Trump's White House record, including his handling of the economy and the pandemic. The election of Harris—whose heritage is Indian and Jamaican—would give the United States its first female, first Black, and first Asian American vice president.

956. JANUARY 3, 2021

DAY OF NATIONWIDE EMANCIPATION BECOMES JUNETEENTH HOLIDAY

When the Emancipation Proclamation took effect on the first day of 1863, it officially freed all enslaved people in states that seceded to form the Confederacy. But as the Civil War raged on, there was no freedom—no way to enforce the proclamation—in areas that Confederate forces still controlled. Among the last of those areas was Galveston Bay, Texas, where Union troops delivered the emancipation order for the state's 250,000 enslaved people on June 19, 1865. Newly freed people celebrated by naming the day Juneteenth—and on this day, the U.S. Congress declared Juneteenth a federal holiday.

957. JANUARY 6, 2021

PROTESTING PRESIDENTIAL VOTE CERTIFICATION, CROWD OVERRUNS CAPITOL

Through weeks of claiming (without evidence) that voter fraud stole the presidency from him, President Donald Trump exhorted supporters to gather in Washington, D.C., on this day, when Congress was to certify states' electoral votes. When thousands came to a rally, Trump urged them to "demand that Congress do the right thing" and not confirm Joe Biden's victory. A crowd marched to the Capitol, overwhelmed its police force, and surged through the building vandalizing property and hunting lawmakers. Hours later, with the building secured, Congress certified the electoral college vote. The siege resulted in at least five deaths and an estimated $2.7 billion in damages and spurred a second impeachment trial of Trump—but only 57 senators would vote to impeach him for inciting the violence, far short of the 67 votes needed to move forward.

President Joe Biden signs the act that made Juneteenth (June 19) a federal holiday. On that day in 1865, two years after the passage of the Emancipation Proclamation, the last enslaved people were liberated.

958. JANUARY 12, 2021

CONGRESSWOMAN LIZ CHENEY TAKES A STAND

Powerful conservative congresswoman Liz Cheney of Wyoming announced on this day that she would vote to impeach President Donald Trump for his role in the January 6, 2021, attack on the Capitol that aimed to prevent the counting of 2020 electoral votes. The daughter of former vice president Dick Cheney and the third ranking House Republican, Cheney declared that "the president of the United States summoned this mob, assembled the mob, and lit the flame of this attack." Republicans responded by revoking Cheney's leadership post and supporting Trump-endorsed Harriet Hageman, who would go on to win Cheney's seat in 2022.

959. FEBRUARY 18, 2021

MARS ROVER PERSEVERANCE EXPLORES THE RED PLANET

On this day, Perseverance—the fifth rover that NASA has sent to Mars—set down on the red planet after a more than six-month journey from Earth. A $2.7 million instrument about the size of a small car, Perseverance landed in an ancient Martian river delta in the hopes of finding fossils of what space scientist Kristen Miller called "microorganisms in Mars' wet past." The rover was also equipped to perform several firsts: recording sounds on Mars and sending them back to Earth, deriving oxygen from Mars's carbon dioxide atmosphere, and flying drones to capture aerial views of the landscape.

960. JUNE 30, 2021

NCAA ALLOWS COLLEGE ATHLETES TO PROFIT FROM THEIR OWN NAMES

In a change from its longtime policy on amateur athletic status, the National Collegiate Athletic Association (NCAA) today agreed to allow college athletes to be paid for the use of their names, images, and likenesses—for example, with product endorsement deals, paid appearances, merchandise sales, and social media activities. The action came after California and several other states passed laws prohibiting NCAA or university rules that would keep student athletes from monetizing their fame and retaining agents.

961. AUGUST 30, 2021

U.S. MILITARY EXITS AFGHANISTAN

On this day, the last U.S. forces departed Afghanistan after a prolonged military presence, leaving the capital Kabul under Taliban control and making good on President Joe Biden's recent statement that "It's time to end America's longest war." The last two weeks of the U.S. withdrawal were chaotic: More than 120,000 people were evacuated, many via the

The Netflix series *Squid Game*, a dystopian thriller about a deadly contest for a fortune, inspired fans to don costumes and mimic show events.

Kabul airport, where an attack on a checkpoint left at least 95 dead (including 13 U.S. service members) and 150 injured. As Taliban forces seized Afghanistan's provincial capitals and took control of border crossings, the Afghan government collapsed and President Ashraf Ghani escaped from Kabul by helicopter.

962. SEPTEMBER 17, 2021

TELEVISION SERIES *SQUID GAME* HAS A GRIP ON AMERICAN AUDIENCES

After its Netflix release on this day, the dystopian thriller TV series *Squid Game* became the most watched streaming program in the United States, as well as 93 other nations. The saga of a life-or-death contest in which debt-saddled players compete for a fortune, the South Korean–made series remained America's most watched series by a wide margin in its third and final season, and inspired viewers to stage their own games and themed parties. Though the series was "explicitly sending up the depravities of capitalism," according to GQ.com, fans involved in cosplay—or just looking for a topical Halloween costume—sparked a boom in sales of the fictional contestants' teal green track suits and white slip-on sneakers. The series' global popularity ushered in a new audience standard for streaming content.

963. SEPTEMBER 23, 2021

NEW FINDINGS ILLUMINATE EARLY HUMAN PRESENCE IN NORTH AMERICA

Judging from fossilized footprints found in New Mexico's White Sands National Park, humans inhabited the continent about 10,000 years earlier than previously thought, according to a study published on this day. At a site where an Ice Age lake grew and shrank depending on droughts, the lakeshore retained thousands of footprints—of animals as well as human adults and children. Using sophisticated dating techniques on pollen, plant seeds, and gypsum grains from the same rock strata as the prints, geologists concluded they were roughly 21,000 to 23,000 years old. Archaeologists had long believed that humans arrived some 13,000 years ago across a land bridge between Alaska and Siberia.

Tens of millions of fans regularly play Wordle, invented by a Welsh software engineer and now published by the *New York Times.*

964. JANUARY 31, 2022

NEW YORK TIMES ACQUIRES WORDLE

To amuse his partner Palak Shah during the pandemic, Welsh software engineer Josh Wardle created a web-based word-guessing game and named it (sort of) after himself: Wordle. In a matter of weeks, the game's number of players zoomed from 90 into the millions. On this day, the *New York Times* announced it had paid "in the low seven figures" to add Wordle to its games portfolio. A viral sensation, the game gives players six tries to arrange letters in five-character rows guided by colored feedback: green for a correct letter in a correct space; yellow for a correct letter in a wrong space; gray for a letter not in the word. By 2022, the game had been played more than four billion times. Today, it has tens of millions of regular participants.

In 2019, the U.S. women's soccer team won the Women's World Cup—along with equal pay and treatment via a lawsuit settled by the U.S. Soccer Federation.

965. FEBRUARY 22, 2022

U.S. WOMEN'S NATIONAL SOCCER TEAM PREVAILS IN EQUAL PAY CASE

It was the long-awaited answer to fans' chant of "Equal pay!" as the U.S. team won the Women's World Cup soccer final in 2019. On this day, players from the U.S. women's national team settled their class action lawsuit for equal pay against the U.S. Soccer Federation (USSF) for $24 million. Also part of the settlement: The federation committed to equal pay for men's and women's national teams in the future as part of a new collective bargaining agreement that the women's team players ratified. In the past, men had earned significantly more than women for almost every activity, including games, appearances, and bonuses.

966. JUNE 24, 2022

***ROE* V. *WADE* RULING ON ABORTION RIGHTS IS OVERTURNED BY A HIGH COURT ACT**

Nearly 50 years after the Supreme Court ruled in *Roe* v. *Wade* that the U.S. Constitution protected abortion as a basic right, the Court today announced a decision overturning that ruling. In its 6–3 ruling in *Dobbs* v. *Jackson Women's Health Organization,* the Court upheld the constitutionality of a Mississippi law banning most abortions after the 15th week of pregnancy—and held that the Constitution does not confer a right to abortion. Under the decision, state legislatures regained the power to regulate aspects of abortion not covered by federal law. Half of the justices in the majority were nominees of President Donald Trump, who campaigned on a promise to reverse *Roe.*

967. JUNE 30, 2022

FIRST BLACK WOMAN IS APPOINTED TO THE SUPREME COURT

The swearing-in of Ketanji Brown Jackson as the 116th Supreme Court justice on this day broke ground for the high court. She was the first justice who previously served as a federal public defender and the first since Thurgood Marshall to have represented indigent criminal defendants. She became the first Black woman to sit on the Court, fulfilling one of Joe Biden's campaign promises in his 2020 presidential campaign. And with her arrival, for the first time, four of the Court's nine members were women. Once a clerk for Supreme Court Justice Stephen Breyer, Jackson filled the vacancy left by Breyer's retirement.

THIS IS A WIN FOR EVERYONE. THIS SETTLEMENT IS A MAJOR STEP FORWARD FOR U.S. SOCCER, FOR THE WOMEN'S TEAM, AND WOMEN'S SPORTS AND WOMEN IN GENERAL.

Cindy Parlow Cone, *U.S. Soccer president (2022)*

968. JULY 11, 2022

NASA RELEASES FIRST IMAGE FROM JAMES WEBB SPACE TELESCOPE

Since April 1990, when the Hubble Space telescope was placed into orbit around Earth, the instrument had sent back data and images that have "changed humanity's understanding of the universe," according to NASA. But with Hubble aging, a new observatory was needed. And so on Christmas Day 2021, the James Webb Space Telescope (JWST) was launched into solar orbit, some 930,000 miles from Earth. On this day, the first full-color image from the JWST was released: a view of thousands of galaxies that NASA called "the deepest and sharpest infrared image of the distant universe so far."

969. NOVEMBER 30, 2022

HIGH-TECH AI CHATBOT IS LAUNCHED

It's the art of conversation with a high-tech transformation: On this day, the AI research company OpenAI launched an artificial intelligence chatbot called ChatGPT. The GPT stands for generative pre-trained transformer—the kind of computerese the chatbot would not favor: Rather, it is trained to generate natural-sounding, relevant answers to questions and requests by drawing on massive stores of data (using an algorithm called a large language model). The fluency of the chatbot concerns scholars, authors, and journalists, among others, who worry about the ability to distinguish between writing developed by ChatGPT and its counterparts versus humans.

970. JANUARY 3, 2023

SENATOR MITCH MCCONNELL SETS TENURE RECORD

As the 118th Congress convened on this day, Republican senator Mitch McConnell, Jr., of Kentucky officially became the U.S. Senate's longest-serving party leader when he surpassed the previous record of 16 years held by Senator Mike Mansfield, a Democrat from Montana (1961–1977). A senator since 1985, McConnell used his positions and influence to significantly shape the judicial system. He forestalled hearings to fill a vacant Supreme Court seat until after the 2016 presidential election, allowing President Donald Trump to appoint three high court justices in four years. McConnell also had a hand in 234 lifetime appointments to the federal bench and confirmation of nearly a third of circuit court judges nationwide, according to his official biography. He announced in 2025 that he would not run for re-election in 2026.

971. FEBRUARY 5, 2023

SUPERSTAR SINGER BEYONCÉ WINS RECORD NUMBER OF GRAMMYS

Her 2011 girl-power anthem asks, "Who run the world?" And on this night at the Grammy Awards, the answer was: Beyoncé. The pop superstar brought home four Grammys (out of nine total nominations) from the star-studded ceremony honoring the year's winners. That brought her career total to 32—more of the coveted gramophone statuettes than any artist, male or female, in history. The feat fueled the running debate about whether the music industry has snubbed Beyoncé: Among all her wins and nominations, she had not won Album of the Year, widely considered the most prestigious Grammy category. But in early 2025 she'd capture that award, too, for her country-inflected album *Cowboy Carter*.

972. MARCH 11, 2023

U.S. ATHLETE BECOMES RECORD-SETTING ALPINE SKIER

Two days before her 28th birthday, Mikaela Shiffrin became the winningest alpine skier of all time with her 87th World Cup victory. The child of two former ski racers, she excelled in the sport from a young age: She notched her first successes in major competitions at age 14 and made it to a World Cup awards podium at age 16. A two-time Olympic gold medalist, she became the youngest athlete (male or female) in history to win an Olympic slalom gold medal, which she procured in Sochi, Russia. When *Time* magazine chose its "100 Most Influential People" at year's end, it listed Shiffrin under the heading "Pioneer."

973. MARCH 29, 2023

EMERGENCY OVERDOSE DRUG IS SOLD DIRECTLY TO CONSUMERS

The U.S. Food and Drug Administration (FDA) approved the first over-the-counter access to the drug naloxone—which it called "a front-line defense in the nation's overdose crisis"—as the nasal spray Narcan. Of the nearly 102,000 drug overdose deaths in the previous year, almost 70 percent involved illicit fentanyl and other synthetic opioids. Naloxone rapidly reverses the effects of opioid overdose, and this FDA action cleared the way for the drug to be sold directly to consumers in places like drugstores, convenience stores, grocery stores, and gas stations, as well as online. By fall 2023, Narcan would be widely available at about $45 for two doses.

974. JULY 26, 2023

AMERICAN CREDIT CARD DEBT REACHES A TRILLION DOLLARS

At this point in time, the average U.S. consumer carried a credit card balance of more than $6,000—and for the first time on record, Americans' collective credit card debt reached a trillion dollars, according to Federal Reserve Bank data released on this day. That staggering sum included both balances paid off every month and revolving balances. Roughly half of cardholders carried balances from month to month, even though interest rates on credit cards were running above 20 percent by February 2025—the highest level in almost 40 years. Not surprisingly, credit card payment delinquencies also rose, especially among younger cardholders.

975. AUGUST 8, 2023

MASSIVE WILDFIRES CLAIM HISTORIC TOWN ON MAUI, HAWAII

On the Hawaiian island of Maui, fires that started in dry, unmanaged brush were driven by hurricane-force winds, and before the spreading blazes could be extinguished, they ravaged beloved areas, including historic Lahaina. The losses devastated the close-knit communities and tourist economy: In Lahaina alone, more than 100 people perished, some 2,200 structures were destroyed, thousands of people were displaced, and the financial toll topped $5.5 billion. An investigation would conclude that the Lahaina fire was

continued on page 480

In 2023, the historic town of Lahaina, Maui, was reduced to ashes by wildfires that caused more than 100 deaths and $5.5 billion in damages.

SPOTLIGHT

WOMEN RISING

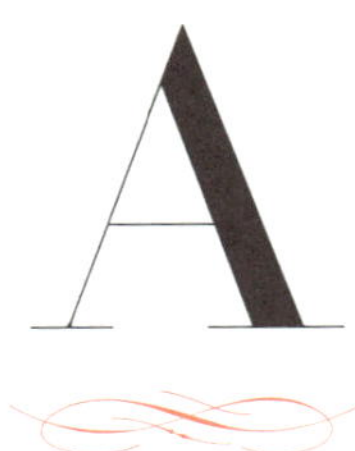

AT A 2016 conference on the state of women, First Lady Michelle Obama asserted that "there is no limit to what we, as women, can accomplish." In the 21st century, women's historic accomplishments crossed virtually all fields of endeavor. Serena Williams won 23 Grand Slam singles titles, the most in the modern tennis era; Simone Biles became the most decorated gymnast in history, with 37 Olympic and world medals. Congresswoman Nancy Pelosi became the first female Speaker of the House (2007). Former secretary of state Hillary Clinton became the first woman presidential candidate of a major party (2016). Senator Kamala Harris became the first female elected vice president (2020); she was sworn in by Justice Sonia Sotomayor, who was the first Latina on the Supreme Court (2009). After Justice Ketanji Brown Jackson joined the high court as its first African American woman (2022), four of the nine justices were women—the highest number in history.

Between 2000 and 2025, however, only 15 of 346 Nobel Prizes in science categories were awarded to women. Six of them were American: in physiology or medicine, Linda Buck (2004) and Carol Greider (2009); in chemistry, Frances Arnold (2018), Jennifer Doudna (2020), and Carolyn Bertozzi (2022); and in physics, Andrea Ghez (2020). Rosa Parks, whose 1955 refusal to give up her bus seat galvanized the civil rights movement, made history once more in death: In 2005, she became the first woman to lie in state in the U.S. Capitol Rotunda.

Serena Williams won 23 Grand Slam singles titles in her career—a record in the modern tennis era—in addition to four Olympic gold medals.

THE SUCCESS OF EVERY WOMAN SHOULD BE THE INSPIRATION TO ANOTHER. WE SHOULD RAISE EACH OTHER UP.

Serena Williams *(2015)*

When he celebrated his gold-medal victory at the 2024 Paris Olympics, U.S. track star Noah Lyles already was known as the world's fastest man.

continued from page 477

started by a downed power line; evacuation and firefighting were complicated by factors like overburdened roads and insufficient resources.

976. AUGUST 20, 2023

NOAH LYLES CLAIMS TITLE OF WORLD'S FASTEST MAN

The label "fastest man in the world" traditionally goes to the gold medal winner in the 100-meter race at the World Athletics Championship—and on this day, in Budapest, Hungary, that person was U.S. runner Noah Lyles. The 26-year-old Florida native also achieved the rare trifecta known as the "sprint treble": He captured gold medals in the 200-meter race and the 4 × 100-meter relay as well as the 100-meter, becoming the first male runner to achieve that feat since track legend Usain Bolt in 2015. A year later he added another gold medal, winning the 100-meter race at the Paris Olympics.

977. SEPTEMBER 6, 2023

GOVERNMENT SUSPENDS FOSSIL FUEL DRILLING IN ARCTIC NATIONAL WILDLIFE REFUGE

After decades of battles over drilling for oil and gas in the Arctic National Wildlife Refuge (ANWR), the Biden administration on this day canceled the last remaining drilling leases permitted by the Trump administration. A 1980 federal law made most of ANWR protected wilderness but allowed 2,300 square miles to be studied for possible fossil fuel development. Though research found that drilling would harm the area's Indigenous people and caribou, a Trump-era law change allowed it, and some leases were sold in 2021. The Biden administration canceled them, pending a new environmental impact study of the area. Trump resumed drilling leases in 2025, continuing the tug-of-war over one of the country's most divisive issues.

978. OCTOBER 7, 2023

HOSTAGES TAKEN IN HAMAS ATTACKS INCLUDE SEVEN U.S. CITIZENS

The Islamist militant group Hamas launched surprise incursions into Israel on this day, killing some 1,200 people and taking more than 240 hostages, including seven U.S. citizens. In the deadliest day for Jews since the Holocaust during World War II, some 2,200 rockets targeted Israel's antimissile defense system, and hundreds of militants breached its borders by land and sea assault, overwhelming military posts and attacking neighborhoods. In response, Israel declared a state of war, vowed to wipe out Hamas, and ordered a siege that cut off food, water, electricity, and fuel to the Gaza Strip, the Hamas power base. About 18 months after the initial Hamas attack, some 34,500 Palestinians and 1,700 Israelis had died in the conflict according to a UN estimate.

AMERICA, I TOLD YOU, I GOT THIS!

Noah Lyles, *on winning Olympic gold in the 100-meter race (2024)*

979. OCTOBER 9, 2023

WORKFORCE SCHOLAR CLAUDIA GOLDIN WINS NOBEL PRIZE IN ECONOMIC SCIENCES

In the 54-year history of the Nobel Prize in Economic Sciences, Claudia Goldin was only the third woman recipient, and on this day, the 77-year-old Harvard University economist received the honor for her research on women in the workforce. Her analysis of more than two centuries of U.S. labor force data showed that despite modernization, a notable gender disparity still persists in the global workforce and the earnings gap between men and women remains persistent. In awarding Goldin the prize, the Royal Swedish Academy of Sciences called her work groundbreaking and "important for society."

980. OCTOBER 25, 2023

MADONNA BECOMES TOP-SELLING FEMALE RECORDING ARTIST

As if there was any doubt that she was still the Material Girl: Singer Madonna retained her status as the top-selling female recording artist of all time, announced by Guinness World Records on this day. The Queen of Pop had reigned since 2009 as the music world's top-selling woman; only men—The Beatles, Elvis Presley, and Michael Jackson—sold more records worldwide. Madonna's record sales were at more than 400 million, a figure that rose as she gave concerts around the world on her Celebration Tour that year. She also accumulated numerous entertainment industry honors, including 20 MTV Video

Music Awards, seven Grammy Awards, two Golden Globe Awards, and induction into the Rock and Roll Hall of Fame.

981. NOVEMBER 17, 2023

THE PLANET WARMS TWO DEGREES CELSIUS ABOVE PREINDUSTRIAL AVERAGE

Earth's warming trend briefly reached a critical threshold on this day. The goal of the 2015 Paris Agreement on climate change was to limit global temperature increases to "well below 2 degrees Celsius above preindustrial levels"—a benchmark based on an average temperature from 1850 to 1900 before the use of fossil fuels produced greenhouse gases that trap heat. For the first time, the global surface air temperature briefly exceeded this level on this day. If nothing is done to slow the warming, the Intergovernmental Panel on Climate Change reported, the planet could persistently experience temperatures 2°C (3.6°F) higher by the 2050s.

982. DECEMBER 12, 2023

TAYLOR SWIFT'S ERAS TOUR BECOMES HIGHEST-GROSSING CONCERT SERIES

As superstar Taylor Swift sang in "Fearless": "I don't know how it gets better than this." Talk about a prescient line. As of this day, Swift's Eras Tour became the highest-grossing concert

The first concert series ever to exceed a billion dollars in revenue, Taylor Swift's Eras Tour drew more than 10 million audience members.

tour of all time. The 152-date, five-continent tour wasn't without crises: In Vienna, Austria, three shows were canceled after a terrorist plan to attack one of them was foiled. Still, the concert tour was the first ever to surpass a billion dollars in revenue. By the time it concluded in late 2024, the tour had entertained 10.1 million audience members, taken in $2.1 billion in ticket sales, and, by some estimates, boosted the U.S. economy by $10 billion.

983. JANUARY 5, 2024

SIDE PANEL BLOWS OFF BOEING-MADE JETLINER IN FLIGHT

About 20 minutes after Alaska Airlines Flight 1282 took off from Portland on this day with 171 passengers and crew on board, a fuselage panel blew out at 16,000 feet, leaving a gaping hole in the side of the Boeing 737 MAX 9. Though the plane landed safely, it was one more disturbing episode for the Boeing Company. For years, the aerospace behemoth had been plagued by problems with this plane series, including fatal crashes, charges that Boeing's officials criminally misled regulators, and reports of quality and safety deficiencies in its plants. An investigation would later conclude that faulty installation caused the Alaska Airlines panel blowout.

984. MARCH 3, 2024

CAITLIN CLARK BREAKS A COLLEGE BASKETBALL RECORD

On this day, University of Iowa superstar guard Caitlin Clark broke the record for most points scored in NCAA Division 1 college basketball, surpassing the one held since 1970 by "Pistol" Pete Maravich (3,667 points) by one point. In her fourth and final season at Iowa, Clark averaged 8.9 assists per game—the best mark in women's college basketball. She also surpassed the point total of Association for Intercollegiate Athletics for Women (AIAW) Large College record holder Lynette Woodard (3,649) but not the point total of AIAW Small College record holder Pearl Moore (4,061). The next month in the NCAA women's championship, Clark's Hawkeyes would fall to the South Carolina Gamecocks 87–75, ending her collegiate career with 3,951 points.

985. APRIL 11, 2024

MORE MEASLES OUTBREAKS RAISE FEARS OF DISEASE COMEBACK

As of this day, the number of measles cases in the United States was already double the number it had been in all of 2023. The disease was officially declared eliminated from the U.S. in 2000, meaning there were new cases only when infected people brought them in from abroad. But that elimination status was threatened by recent increases in measles outbreaks, defined as three or more related cases, as fewer U.S. kindergartners were vaccinated and measles activity around the world increased. As 2024 ended, the U.S. Centers for Disease Control and Prevention reported 16 outbreaks, quadruple the number reported in 2023. In the first months of 2025, 378 cases were confirmed in 17 states—and an unvaccinated Texas child became the first U.S. death from measles since 2015.

986. MAY 6, 2024

COLUMBIA UNIVERSITY GRADUATION CEREMONY IS CANCELED IN THE WAKE OF POLITICAL PROTESTS

After weeks of pro-Palestinian demonstrations spurred by the escalating Israeli-Palestine conflict had roiled New York City's Columbia University campus, officials announced on this day that the university's main graduation ceremony on May 15 would be canceled. Over the previous few weeks, more than 2,650 protesters had been arrested on college campuses across the country, according to CNN research. By late May, protests had occurred at higher education institutions in 45 states as well as in Europe, the Middle East, Australia, Asia, Canada, and Mexico. College student bodies were polarized by conflicting passions about the Israel-Hamas War, and Jewish college students on many U.S. campuses said they were disturbed by anti-Semitic attitudes, as well as anti-Israel encampments and events.

987. JULY 21, 2024

JOE BIDEN DROPS PRESIDENTIAL BID

In the wake of a stumbling debate performance that heightened concerns about his fitness to serve a second term, 81-year-old President Joe Biden announced he would be dropping his reelection bid. He revealed his decision to exit the race after mounting pressure from party mates, only weeks before the Republican and Democratic nominating conventions—and less than four months before Election Day. Biden swiftly endorsed his vice president, Kamala Harris, as the Democratic Party's best hope to beat former president Donald Trump, the presumptive Republican Party nominee who survived a July 13 assassination attempt at a campaign rally.

988. JULY 22, 2024

EARTH SUFFERS HOTTEST DAYS ON RECORD

After 13 straight months of rising temperature readings on Earth, July 21 was the hottest day in the history of human measurement—until this day, when the temperature went even higher. The global record-breaking heat—measured in surface air temperature averaged over the entire planet—was reported by the European climate service Copernicus. Its director and other international scientists attributed the escalating warming to human-caused climate change. Unless the nations of the world take steps to reduce heat-trapping carbon dioxide gas, UN negotiator Christiana Figueres warned, "we all scorch and fry."

989. AUGUST 2, 2024

"VERY DEMURE" CATCHPHRASE BLOWS UP ON TIKTOK

It was a very tongue-in-cheek trend among TikTok devotees: applying the tagline "very demure" to a little bit of everything. The expression took off after influencer Jools Lebron, a trans woman of color who works as a makeup artist, used it to describe a deft cosmetic touch-up in a video she uploaded on this day. Lebron went on to post about the "very demure, very mindful" ways she did other things, from dressing for the workplace to boarding an airplane. Throngs of TikTokers followed with both serious and spoof videos including demure and mindful ways to, say, eat watermelon or block phone calls from an ex.

990. OCTOBER 4, 2024

AI-GENERATED FAKE IMAGES DAMAGE PUBLIC TRUST

Hurricane Helene's destructive path through the U.S. South and Southeast was captured in grim disaster photos—and the mayhem was compounded by fake images generated by AI, an emerging problem on digital media. Writing on this day for Forbes.com, digital forensics expert Lars Daniel flagged two "highly edited or outright fake" images that circulated widely, purporting to show a tearful child holding a puppy in a boat surrounded by Helene's floodwaters. Photorealistic deepfakes proliferated as AI image generators improved, and Daniel observed that they take a toll: "Repeated exposure to fake content can erode public trust in legitimate news and information sources."

991. NOVEMBER 5, 2024

DONALD TRUMP WINS A SECOND PRESIDENTIAL TERM

After an unprecedented 107-day contest that effectively began when incumbent president Joe Biden dropped out of the race in July 2024, former president Donald Trump beat

Donald Trump was only the second U.S. president to win two nonconsecutive terms. (The first was Grover Cleveland, who won in 1884 and 1892.)

Biden's replacement, Vice President Kamala Harris. Trump won his second term in the White House with 49.8 percent of the popular vote, or 77,302,580 votes, and received 312 electoral votes—well above the 270 needed to win. Harris received 48.3 percent of the popular vote, or 75,017,613 votes, and 226 electoral votes. The nonpartisan organization PolitiFact called Trump's victory "clear, but not a landslide by historical standards." Trump called it "an unprecedented and powerful mandate."

992. NOVEMBER 12, 2024

DEPARTMENT OF GOVERNMENT EFFICIENCY IS ESTABLISHED

A week after winning a second term, President-elect Donald Trump announced plans to create a new entity called the Department of Government Efficiency (DOGE). To lead it, he named Elon Musk—the world's wealthiest individual, head of companies including SpaceX and Tesla—and Vivek Ramaswamy, a biotechnology entrepreneur and ex-presidential candidate. Ramaswamy left the team before DOGE launched; Musk said DOGE should be able to eliminate "at least $2 trillion" in federal spending by cutting employees and bureaucracy, but budget experts noted the discretionary budget was only $1.7 billion total. One of Trump's first acts on Inauguration Day was to issue the executive order creating DOGE and linking it with government digital agency, giving Musk's team broad access to federal technology and information.

993. JANUARY 7, 2025

"PERFECT STORM" OF FACTORS DRIVES SOUTHERN CALIFORNIA FIRES

On this day, exceptionally intense Santa Ana winds fanned fires that would ravage the Los Angeles area and spread destruction over six Southern California counties. Dry vegetation and extreme drought conditions fed a series of wildfires; attempts to fight the flames were hamstrung by water shortages and hurricane-force winds. More than 200,000 people were forced to evacuate as at least 18,000 homes and structures burned on more than 57,000 acres. At least 30 people perished. Most of the damage and loss of life occurred in the two largest fires, in the Eaton Fire in Altadena and Pasadena and the Palisades Fire in the Pacific Palisades area; they would not be extinguished until January 31.

994. JANUARY 20, 2025

TRUMP IS SWORN IN AS 47TH U.S. PRESIDENT

Donald Trump took the oath of office for his second presidential term on this day, in ceremonies moved from the Capitol steps to its rotunda because of cold, windy weather. This was only the second nonconsecutive re-inauguration of a president in U.S. history (after Grover Cleveland's in 1893). In his inaugural address, President Trump declared that "during every single day of the Trump administration, I will very simply put America first." And he promised that his administration would "move with purpose and speed to bring back hope, prosperity, safety, and peace for citizens of every race, religion, color, and creed." On this first day back in office, Trump signed some 200 proclamations, memos, and executive orders.

995. FEBRUARY 28, 2025

PICKLEBALL BECOMES THE FASTEST-GROWING SPORT IN THE U.S.

Summer 1965: To amuse a bored teen on a vacation, three Seattle families rounded up scattered sports equipment—Ping-Pong paddles, a Wiffle ball, a badminton net—and improvised a new racket sport. They named it pickleball after the rowing term "pickle boat," for a crew composed of nonstarter athletes from various teams. Because the hybridized sport could be played by people of many ages and skill levels, it grew in popularity, with 19.8 million players in 2024. On this day, data from the Sports & Fitness Industry Association confirmed pickleball as America's fastest-growing sport for the fourth year in a row.

Players of many ages and skill levels made pickleball—a mash-up of Ping-Pong, tennis, and badminton—America's fastest-growing sport.

Robert Francis Prevost, a Chicago native who had been a missionary in Peru and an official at the Vatican, became the first pope from the United States.

996. MAY 8, 2025

ROBERT FRANCIS PREVOST BECOMES FIRST AMERICAN-BORN POPE, LEO XIV

The death of Pope Francis on April 21 ended the 12-year reign of the first pontiff from Latin America—a humble leader who lived simply, reformed Vatican governance, and spoke out on issues such as the environment, immigration, and the death penalty. At the conclave to elect Francis's successor, the world's cardinals chose Chicago-born Robert Francis Prevost, a longtime missionary in Peru and an experienced Vatican official who became the first American-born pope on this day. The new pope took the name Leo XIV, associating himself with the reformist vision and social justice teachings of Pope Leo XIII, who'd led the church 1878–1903.

997. MAY 27, 2025

COUNTRY ROCKER KENNY CHESNEY IS ANOINTED BY *BILLBOARD*

"No Shoes, No Shirt, No Problems"—the song's title sums up the laid-back outlook of country-rock star Kenny Chesney and his fans, collectively known as No Shoes Nation. On this day, the Nation cheered the news that Chesney was named Top Country Artist of the 21st Century by *Billboard,* which tracks music industry rankings and sales. Seventeen of the 20 albums Chesney released in this century have reached number one on country album charts, *Billboard* noted—and he's had 33 songs ranked number one for airplay, more than any other artist in the charts' history. It was Chesney's year: He was also a 2025 inductee to the Country Music Hall of Fame.

998. JULY 9, 2025

NVIDIA BECOMES THE WORLD'S MOST VALUABLE COMPANY

Since its founding in 1993, the California-based NVIDIA Corporation grew into a titan among technology companies, first becoming the dominant supplier of GPUs (graphics processing units) for video gaming, desktop and laptop computers, and then for high-performance and scientific computing. With the rise of artificial intelligence, the company's business exploded, since its GPUs were integral to such AI technologies as OpenAI's ChatGPT. On this day, NVIDIA became the first public company in the world to reach and surpass a market valuation of $4 trillion, making it the most valuable company on the planet. Less than four months later, it would reach a valuation of $5 trillion.

999. AUGUST 26, 2025

YOUTUBE AND OTHER STREAMERS COMMAND LION'S SHARE OF TV VIEWING

In a prime example of how the streaming revolution shuffled the media landscape, Nielsen Media Research reported on this day that, for the sixth month in a row, YouTube led all other media companies for share of U.S. TV viewing. According to Nielsen's data, streamers took a record-high 47.3 percent share of all TV use in July 2025. Just two of them—YouTube and Netflix—accounted for more than a fifth of all TV viewing, drawing as many viewers as all cable networks combined.

HELP EACH OTHER TO BUILD BRIDGES, WITH DIALOGUE, WITH MEETINGS, UNITING US ALL TO BE ONE PEOPLE, ALWAYS IN PEACE.

Pope Leo XIV, *during his first public address (2025)*

1000. JULY 4, 2026

CONGRATULATIONS ON 250 YEARS OF INDEPENDENCE, AMERICA! YOU'VE COME A LONG WAY.

By the 250th anniversary of the nation's independence, the United States and its population had changed dramatically from its founding era. The first U.S. census was conducted in 1790 in the original 13 states, as well as three districts that would later become states (Kentucky, Maine, and Vermont) and the so-called Southwest Territory (the future Tennessee). The 1790 census reported a population of 3,929,214 living at an average density of 4.5 persons per square mile. The young nation's largest urban area was New York City, with 33,131 people, followed by Philadelphia, Boston, Charleston, and Baltimore. U.S. Census Bureau data projected that the nation's population in its 50 states and five territories would reach 342,598,000 by July 2026, with an average density more than 20 times higher than in 1790. Only one of the five largest cities in the first census still holds that title today: New York City, whose projected population of some 8.4 million is more than 250 times larger than the 1790 headcount. Today's next four most populous cities are, in order: Los Angeles, Chicago, Houston, and Phoenix. The American experiment continues.

ACKNOWLEDGMENTS

Many thanks to the creative team at National Geographic Books: executive editor Hilary Black; editorial project manager Ashley Leath; designers Sanáa Akkach, Nicole Roberts, and TJ Tucker; photo editor Matt Propert; senior production editor Michael O'Connor; copy editor Heather McElwain; proofreader Mary Stephanos; and indexer Connie Binder. And a special shout-out to writers Patricia Daniels, Patricia Edmonds, and Karen Kostyal; fact-checkers Adrienne Izaguirre, Pamela Juarez, and Alice Milliken; and historical adviser David Trowbridge.

CONTRIBUTORS

DAVID M. RUBENSTEIN (introduction and interviews) is an investor, philanthropist, interviewer, and historian. The author of several best-selling books, he is co-founder and co-chairman of the Carlyle Group, one of the world's largest and most successful private investment firms.

DAVID TREUER (prologue), a professor of English at the University of Southern California, is the author of the *New York Times* bestseller *The Heartbeat of Wounded Knee: Native America From 1890 to the Present.* An Ojibwe from Minnesota's Leech Lake Reservation, he has written four novels and two works of nonfiction and was a finalist for the National Book Award.

MICHAEL BESCHLOSS is an award-winning historian, scholar of leadership, and best-selling author of 10 books. NBC's presidential historian and a contributor to PBS *NewsHour,* he has also been a contributing columnist to the *New York Times.*

DOUGLAS BRINKLEY is the Katherine Tsanoff Brown Professor in Humanities and professor of history at Rice University, CNN's Presidential Historian, and a contributing editor at *Vanity Fair.* A best-selling author, he works in many capacities in the world of public history, including on boards and at museums, colleges, and historical societies.

ANNETTE GORDON-REED is the Carl M. Loeb University Professor at Harvard University. She has won 16 book prizes, including the Pulitzer Prize for History in 2009 and the National Book Award in 2008.

WALTER ISAACSON is a best-selling historian and biographer and a professor of history at Tulane University. He has been the CEO of the Aspen Institute, the CEO of CNN, and the editor of *Time* magazine.

ILLUSTRATIONS CREDITS

2–3, smartstock/iStock/Getty Images; 4 (LE), B Christopher/Alamy Stock Photo; 4 (CTR LE), IanDagnall Computing/Alamy Stock Photo; 4 (CTR RT), Buyenlarge/SuperStock; 4 (RT), Bettmann/Getty Images; 6, Kline, Hibberd Van Buren (b.1885) (after)/American/© Hagley Museum and Library, Wilmington, Delaware/Bridgeman Images; 7, Sarin Images/GRANGER; 8, Jack R Perry Photography/Shutterstock; 10, Prisma Archivo/Alamy Stock Photo; 11, North Wind Pictures/Bridgeman Images; 14, Ira Block/National Geographic Image Collection; 18, Mark Thiessen, National Geographic; 20 (UP), ICP/incamerastock/Alamy Stock Photo; 20 (LO), Artokoloro/Penta Springs Limited/Alamy Stock Photo; 21, Chronicle/Alamy Stock Photo; 22, IanDagnall Computing/Alamy Stock Photo; 24, Charles Phelps Cushing/ClassicStock/Alamy Stock Photo; 25, Classic Image/Alamy Stock Photo; 26, ICP/incamerastock/Alamy Stock Photo; 27, John Singleton Copley, 1773, Metropolitan Museum of Art, Morris K. Jesup Fund, 1931; 28, Backyard/Ingram Publishing/SuperStock; 30, Pictures Now/Alamy Stock Photo; 31, Huntington Library/SuperStock; 32, North Wind Picture Archives/Alamy Stock Photo; 33, Private Collection/Peter Newark American Pictures/Bridgeman Images; 34, tokar/Shutterstock; 37, John Trumbull (American, 1756–1843), Yale University Art Gallery, Trumbull Collection; 38–9, Superstock/Bridgeman Images; 40, © Courtesy, American Antiquarian Society, Worcester, Massachusetts/Bridgeman Images; 41, Chappel, Alonzo (1828–87)/American/© Chicago History Museum/Bridgeman Images; 42, Chappel, Alonzo (1828–87)/American/© Heckscher Museum of Art/August Heckscher Collection/Bridgeman Images; 44, Science History Images/Alamy Stock Photo; 45, Photo Researchers/Science History Images/Alamy Stock Photo; 46, Everett Collection/Bridgeman Images; 49, Chronicle/Alamy Stock Photo; 50, Photo Researchers/Science History Images/Alamy Stock Photo; 51, North Wind Picture Archives/Alamy Stock Photo; 52, Ralph Earl (American, 1751–1801), Yale University Art Gallery, Gift of Mrs. Paul Moore in memory of her nephew Howard Melville Hanna, Jr., B.S. 1931; 54–5, © The New York Historical/Bridgeman Images; 57, Dunsmore, John Ward (1856–1945)/American/Private Collection/SuperStock/Bridgeman Images; 58, Gardner, Daniel (1750–1805)/English/Philadelphia History Museum at the Atwater Kent/Bridgeman Images; 60, North Wind Picture Archives/Alamy Stock Photo; 61, IanDagnall Computing/Alamy Stock Photo; 62, John Trumbull (American, 1756–1843), Yale University Art Gallery, Trumbull Collection; 64, © Courtesy, American Antiquarian Society, Worcester, Massachusetts/Bridgeman Images; 65, The Reading Room/Alamy Stock Photo; 66, IanDagnall Computing/Alamy Stock Photo; 68, Everett Collection/Bridgeman Images; 70, courtesy Annette Gordon-Reed; 73, Historical Images Archive/Alamy Stock Photo; 74, Ian Dagnall/Alamy Stock Photo; 76, The History Collection/Alamy Stock Photo; 79, ICP/incamerastock/Alamy Stock Photo; 80, IanDagnall Computing/Alamy Stock Photo; 81, © NPL — DeA Picture Library/M. Seemuller/Bridgeman Images; 82, Sarin Images/GRANGER; 85, Special Collections, J. Willard Marriott Library, University of Utah; 86, Kean Collection/Archive Photos/Getty Images; 88–9, Bettmann/

Getty Images; 90, piemags/Alamy Stock Photo; 91, Castellini, G. (19th century)/Italian/Private Collection/The Stapleton Collection/Bridgeman Images; 92, © Chicago History Museum/Bridgeman Images; 93, © Courtesy, American Antiquarian Society, Worcester, Massachusetts/Bridgeman Images; 94, IanDagnall Computing/Alamy Stock Photo; 95, ICP/incamerastock/Alamy Stock Photo; 96 (UP), © Chicago History Museum/Bridgeman Images; 96 (LO), American Photo Archive/Alamy Stock Photo; 97, Chronicle/Alamy Stock Photo; 98, photo-fox/Alamy Stock Photo; 101, North Wind Picture Archives/Alamy Stock Photo; 102, Adam, V. (19th century) (after)/French/Bibliothèque nationale, Paris, France/© Archives Charmet/Bridgeman Images; 105, Wyeth, Newell Convers (1882–1945)/American/Private Collection/Peter Newark American Pictures/Bridgeman Images; 106, Stuart, Gilbert (1755–1828)/American/White House, Washington D.C., USA/Bridgeman Images; 107, © The New York Historical/Bridgeman Images; 109, North Wind Picture Archives/Alamy Stock Photo; 110, Gilbert Stuart, ca. 1820–22, Metropolitan Museum of Art, Bequest of Seth Low, 1916; 112, John Quidor, 1858, Smithsonian American Art Museum, Museum purchase made possible in part by the Catherine Walden Myer Endowment, the Julia D. Strong Endowment, and the Director's Discretionary Fund, 1994.120; 113, Artokoloro/Alamy Stock Photo; 114, GL Archive/Alamy Stock Photo; 115, Everett Collection/Bridgeman Images; 116, Photo © North Wind Pictures/Bridgeman Images; 118–9, The Artchives/Alamy Stock Photo; 120, Sarin Images/GRANGER; 122, North Wind Picture Archives/Alamy Stock Photo; 123, © The New York Historical/Bridgeman Images; 124, Sarin Images/GRANGER; 126, 3LH-Fine Art/SuperStock; 128, Photo Researchers/Alamy Stock Photo; 129, Bierstadt, Albert (1830–1902)/American/© Butler Institute of American Art, Youngstown, Ohio/Gift of Joseph G. Butler III, 1946/Bridgeman Images; 130, Currier, N. (1813–88) and Ives, J.M. (1824–95)/American/Universal History Archive/UIG/Bridgeman Images; 132, Private Collection/© Look and Learn/Bridgeman Images; 133, North Wind Picture Archives/Alamy Stock Photo; 134, akg-images; 135, Cornwell, Dean (1892–1960)/American/Private Collection/Peter Newark American Pictures/Bridgeman Images; 137, Sarin Images/GRANGER; 138–9, North Wind Picture Archives/Alamy Stock Photo; 140, Picturenow/UIG/Getty Images; 141, Bettmann/Getty Images; 142, Heritage Images/Hulton Archive/Getty Images; 143, PAINTING/Alamy Stock Photo; 144, Niday Picture Library/Alamy Stock Photo; 145, Private Collection/© Look and Learn/Bridgeman Images; 146, Buyenlarge/SuperStock; 148, VCG Wilson/Corbis via Getty Images; 149, Pictorial Press Ltd/Alamy Stock Photo; 150, Smith Archive/Alamy Stock Photo; 152, Photo12/Ann Ronan Picture Library/Alamy Stock Photo; 153, McClure, Louis Charles (1867–1957)/American/Private Collection/Peter Newark American Pictures/Bridgeman Images; 154, Sarin Images/GRANGER; 157, Fosten, Bryan (b.1928)/English/Private Collection/Peter Newark American Pictures/© Bryan Fosten. All rights reserved 2025/Bridgeman Images; 158–9, © Chicago History Museum/Bridgeman Images; 160, Stocktrek Images/Alamy Stock Photo; 161, Photo

Researchers/Science History Images/Alamy Stock Photo; 162, GRANGER; 164, Dappled-History/Alamy Stock Photo; 165, CSU Archives/Everett Collection/Bridgeman Images; 166, Painters/Alamy Stock Photo; 169, Classic Image/Alamy Stock Photo; 170, Private Collection/Peter Newark American Pictures/Bridgeman Images; 171, The Print Collector/Heritage Images/Alamy Stock Photo; 172, North Wind Picture Archives/Alamy Stock Photo; 173, Alexander Gardner/National Portrait Gallery, Smithsonian Institution, Frederick Hill Meserve Collection; 175, North Wind Picture Archives/Alamy Stock Photo; 176, Sangorski, Alberto (1862–1932)/British/Private Collection/Christie's Images/Bridgeman Images; 178, Matt Winkelmeyer/Getty Images for Amazon Studios; 181, incamerastock/Alamy Stock Photo; 182, Archive Photos/Getty Images; 183, Charles Rascher/Alamy Stock Photo; 184, Universal History Archive/Universal Images Group via Getty Images; 186, Private Collection/Peter Newark American Pictures/Bridgeman Images; 187, © Newberry Library, Chicago, Illinois/Bridgeman Images; 188, Corbis Historical/Getty Images; 191, GL Archive/Alamy Stock Photo; 192, Artefact/Alamy Stock Photo; 195, Sarin Images/GRANGER; 196, Currier, N. (1813–88) and Ives, J.M. (1824–95)/American/Yale University Art Gallery, New Haven, CT/Bridgeman Images; 199, Remington, Frederic (1861–1909)/American/Museum of Fine Arts, Houston/The Hogg Brothers Collection, Gift of Miss Ima Hogg/Bridgeman Images; 200–1, Barfoot, James Richard (1794–1863)/American/Private Collection/The Stapleton Collection/Bridgeman Images; 202, Chronicle/Alamy Stock Photo; 203, Corbis Historical/Getty Images; 204, Fototeca Gilardi/Bridgeman Images; 205, Stocktrek Images, Inc./Alamy Stock Photo; 206, Private Collection/© Look and Learn/Bridgeman Images; 208, U.S. Naval History and Heritage Command Photograph, Collection of Mr. Ray Spear, 1933; 210, North Wind Picture Archives/Alamy Stock Photo; 211, Paul Popper/Popperfoto via Getty Images; 212, National Geographic Archives; 213, Fototeca Gilardi/Bridgeman Images; 215, Niday Picture Library/Alamy Stock Photo; 216, Private Collection/© Aunaies/Bridgeman Images; 217, Bierstadt, Albert (1830–1902)/American/The Putnam Foundation/© Timken Museum of Art, San Diego/Bridgeman Images; 218, © Boltin Picture Library/Bridgeman Images; 220–1, Sarin Images/GRANGER; 222, IanDagnall Computing/Alamy Stock Photo; 223, Geo. P. Hall & Son/The New York Historical/Getty Images; 224, Private Collection/© Look and Learn/Bridgeman Images; 226, Harris & Ewing/Library of Congress Prints and Photographs Division, LC-H25-14111-B; 227, Buyenlarge/Archive Photos/Getty Images; 228, History and Art Collection/Alamy Stock Photo; 230, Green, Harry (b.1920)/British/Private Collection/© Look and Learn/Bridgeman Images; 231, Buyenlarge Archive/UIG/Bridgeman Images; 232, Bettmann/Getty Images; 234 (UP), Bettmann/Getty Images; 234 (LO), The Miriam and Ira D. Wallach Division of Art, Prints and Photographs: Picture Collection, The New York Public Library. (1906). City Hall Subway Station, New York, #836151; 235, The New York Historical Society/Getty Images; 236, NASA/Michael Collins; 238, Pictorial Press/Alamy Stock Photo; 239, Buyenlarge/SuperStock; 240, Bettmann/Getty Images; 241, Private Collection/Prismatic Pictures/Bridgeman Images; 242, Sarin Images/GRANGER; 243, Library of Congress/Corbis/VCG via Getty Images; 244, Bettmann/Getty Images; 246, Stan Pritchard/Alamy Stock Photo; 247, Underwood Photo Archives/SuperStock; 248, Library of Congress Prints and Photographs Division, LC-DIG-ppmsc-00157; 250, Fine Art Images/Heritage Images via Getty Images; 251, National Motor Museum/Motoring Picture Library/Alamy Stock Photo; 252, Raymond Wong/National Geographic Image Collection;

254, Private Collection/Prismatic Pictures/Bridgeman Images; 255, Paul Thompson/Topical Press Agency/Getty Images; 256–7, Hopper, Edward (1882–1967)/American/© Art Institute of Chicago/Friends of American Art Collection/Bridgeman Images; 258, Library of Congress Prints and Photographs Division, LC-DIG-ppmsca-13399; 259, Library of Congress Prints and Photographs Division, LC-DIG-ggbain-20859; 260, The U.S. National Archives and Records Administration; 262, John Frost Newspapers/Alamy Stock Photo; 263, Private Collection/© Look and Learn/Bridgeman Images; 264, George Rinhart/Corbis via Getty Images; 266, KEYSTONE Pictures USA/Alamy Stock Photo; 267, National Archives/Getty Images; 268, Unknown Artist (20th century)/Private Collection/© Giancarlo Costa/Bridgeman Images; 270, Pictorial Press/Alamy Stock Photo; 271, Music-Images/Lebrecht Music & Arts/Alamy Stock Photo; 272, Pictorial Press/Alamy Stock Photo; 275, Bridgeman Images; 276, Bailey, Vernon Howe (1874–1953)/American/Private Collection/The Stapleton Collection/Bridgeman Images; 278–9, PictureLux/The Hollywood Archive/Alamy Stock Photo; 280, Sarin Images/GRANGER; 282, Chronicle/Alamy Stock Photo; 283, Dorothea Lange/Library of Congress Prints and Photographs Division, LC-DIG-fsa-8b29516; 284, GRANGER; 285, IanDagnall Computing/Alamy Stock Photo; 286, Private Collection/Futuras FotosAlamy Stock Photo; 287, Archive Pics/Alamy Stock Photo; 288, Archive PL/Alamy Stock Photo; 290, © Selznick International Pictures/Metro-Goldwin-Mayer Pictures/Diltz/Bridgeman Images; 291, Everett Collection/Bridgeman Images; 292, Bettmann/Getty Images; 294, Catesby, Mark (1679–1749)/English/Royal Collection Trust/© His Majesty King Charles III, 2025/Bridgeman Images; 295, JT Vintage/Glasshouse Images/Alamy Stock Photo; 296, Bettmann/Getty Images; 297, Universal History Archive/Universal Images Group via Getty Images; 298–9, © Sony Pictures Classics/Entertainment Pictures/Alamy Stock Photo; 300, Circa Images/Glasshouse Images/Alamy Stock Photo; 301, © R.K.O. Radio Pictures/Bridgeman Images; 302, Ewing Galloway/Alamy Stock Photo; 304, CBS Photo Archive via Getty Images; 306, Cover to Cover/Alamy Stock Photo; 307, World History Archive/Alamy Stock Photo; 308, Bettmann/Getty Images; 310, Photo12/Universal Images Group via Getty Images; 311, PictureLux/The Hollywood Archive/Alamy Stock Photo; 312, Billy Rose Theatre Division, The New York Public Library. (1957). West Side Story, ps_the_cd67_1042; 313, GRANGER; 314, CBW/Alamy Stock Photo; 315, Dan Moss/Alamy Stock Photo; 316, RGR Collection/Alamy Stock Photo; 317, Pictorial Press/Alamy Stock Photo; 318, JHU Sheridan Libraries/Gado/Getty Images; 319, NASA; 320, Patrick McMullan via Getty Images; 323, NASA; 324, Stocktrek Images/Alamy Stock Photo; 326, Bettmann/Getty Images; 327, adsR/Alamy Stock Photo; 328, SCREEN GEMS/Album/Album Archivo/SuperStock; 329, Bettmann/Getty Images; 330, Steve Schapiro/Corbis via Getty Images; 333, Hulton-Deutsch Collection/Corbis via Getty Images; 334, NASA via Space prime/Alamy Stock Photo; 335, Harry Benson/Express/Getty Images; 336, Henry Diltz/Corbis via Getty Images; 337, NASA/Buzz Aldrin; 338, Hulton Archive/Getty Images; 339, PictureLux/The Hollywood Archive/Alamy Stock Photo; 340, PePoP Images/Stockimo/Alamy Stock Photo; 342–3, Allan Tannenbaum/Getty Images; 344, Bettmann/Getty Images; 345, Bettmann/Getty Images; 346, Jerry Cooke/Corbis via Getty Images; 348, Shawshots/Alamy Stock Photo; 349, Tom Munnecke/Getty Images; 350, Shawshots/Alamy Stock Photo; 351, Bridgeman Images; 353, R. Lamb/ClassicStock/Getty Images; 354, Jack Mitchell/Getty Images; 355, NASA; 356, Science History Images/Alamy Stock Photo; 358, Susan Wood/Getty Images;

359, Associated Press; 361, HBO/Album/Alamy Stock Photo; 362–3, Lewis Hine/Everett Collection/Bridgeman Images; 364, Bob Hallinen/Anchorage Daily News/Tribune News Service via Getty Images; 365, Anthony Barboza/Getty Images; 366, Pictorial Press/Alamy Stock Photo; 367, Lindsay Brice/Getty Images; 368, Mark Reinstein/Alamy Stock Photo; 369, Joan Marcus; 370, Branimir Kvartuc/ZUMA Press/Alamy Stock Photo; 372, David Cannon/Allsport/Getty Images; 374, BFA/Alamy Stock Photo; 375, JOKER/Martin Magunia/ullstein bild via Getty Images; 376, Jon Buckle/EMPICS via Getty Images; 378 (UP), Sean Pavone/Alamy Stock Photo; 378 (LO), NASA/JPL-Caltech/MSSS; 379, Luciano Leon/Alamy Stock Photo; 380, Naomi Baker/Getty Images; 383, CBS Photo Archive via Getty Images; 384, AP Photo/Doug Kanter; 386, Robert Laberge/Hulton Archive/Getty Images; 387, pixinoo/Shutterstock; 388, Joseph Sohm/Shutterstock; 391, Steve Granitz/WireImage/Getty Images; 392, Clarence Davis/NY Daily News Archive via Getty Images; 394, Mark Reinstein/Shutterstock; 395, NASA; 396–7, Christopher Payne/National Geographic Image Collection; 398, Mario Tama/Getty Images; 399, Jayakri/Shutterstock; 401, Beata Zawrzel/NurPhoto via Getty Images; 402, Rick Friedman/Alamy Stock Photo; 404, MediaNews Group/Reading Eagle via Getty Images; 405, Warner Bros. Television/Getty Images; 407, Karen Bleier/AFP via Getty Images; 408, Kyle Niemi/US Coast Guard via Getty Images; 410, AP Photo/Richard Drew; 412–3, Juan Gaertner/Science Photo Library/SuperStock; 414, wildnerdpix/Alamy Stock Photo; 415, Heritage Space/Heritage Images via Getty Images; 416, David Paul Morris/Getty Images; 418, John Wilcox/MediaNews Group/Boston Herald via Getty Images; 419, Karwai Tang/WireImage/Getty Images; 420, Stefanie Keenan/WireImage/Getty Images; 423, Robyn Beck/AFP via Getty Images; 424, Guido Mieth/DigitalVision/Getty Images; 425, DragonImages/Alamy Stock Photo; 426, Luis Alvarez/DigitalVision/Getty Images; 428–9, Scott Wilson/Alamy Stock Photo; 430, Antlii/Shutterstock; 431, James Nielsen/Houston Chronicle via Getty Images; 433, Moviestore Collection/Alamy Stock Photo; 434, Randy Duchaine/Alamy Stock Photo; 435, HBO/Album/Alamy Stock Photo; 437, AP Photo/Ted S. Warren; 438, Rachel Murray/Getty Images for Netflix; 439, martiapunts/iStock/Getty Images; 440, Pictorial Press/Alamy Stock Photo; 443, Jeffrey R. Staab/CBS via Getty Images; 444, Larry Marano/Getty Images; 447, Sven Hoppe/picture alliance via Getty Images; 448, EQRoy/Alamy Stock Photo; 451, Brendan Smialowski/AFP via Getty Images; 452, Aaron Huey/National Geographic Image Collection; 454, Jimmy Chin/National Geographic Image Collection; 457, Theo Wargo/WireImage/Getty Images; 458, Chay_Tee/Shutterstock; 460, Valerie Macon/AFP via Getty Images; 461, Kent Kobersteen/National Geographic Image Collection; 462–3, Justin Sullivan/Getty Images; 464, National Science Foundation via Getty Images; 465, art: Thom Tenery, source: James Delgado, Search, Inc./National Geographic Image Collection; 467, Stephen Wilkes/National Geographic Image Collection; 468, Spencer Platt/Getty Images; 471, Drew Angerer/Getty Images; 472, Siren Pictures/Album/Alamy Stock Photo; 473, Wachiwit/Shutterstock; 474, Maddie Meyer — FIFA/FIFA via Getty Images; 477, Robert Gauthier/Los Angeles Times via Getty Images; 478–9, Victoria Jones/PA Images/Alamy Stock Photo; 480, David Davies/PA Images/Alamy Stock Photo; 482, Allen J. Schaben/Los Angeles Times via Getty Images; 485, Greg Nash-Pool/Getty Images; 487, Sipa USA/Alamy Stock Photo; 488, Francesco Sforza, Vatican Media via Vatican Pool/Getty Images.

INDEX

Boldface indicates illustrations.

C

I

J

K

N

S

T

Since 1888, the National Geographic Society has funded more than 15,000 research, conservation, education, technology, and storytelling projects around the world. National Geographic Partners distributes a portion of the funds it receives from your purchase to National Geographic Society to support their mission to illuminate and protect the wonder of our world.

National Geographic Partners, LLC
1145 17th Street NW
Washington, DC 20036-4688 USA

Get closer to National Geographic Explorers and photographers, and connect with our global community. Join us today at nationalgeographic.org/joinus

For rights or permissions inquiries, please contact National Geographic Books Subsidiary Rights: bookrights@natgeo.com

ISBN: 978-1-4262-2439-3

The authorized representative in the EU for product safety and compliance is Disney Trading B.V., Asterweg 15S, 1031 HL, Amsterdam, The Netherlands
email: DCP.DL-EU.bookscontact@disney.com

Printed in South Korea

26/QPSK/1